T0100620

Handbook of Multimedia for Digital Entertainment and Arts

Borko Furht
Editor

Handbook of Multimedia for Digital Entertainment and Arts

 Springer

Editor
Borko Furht
Department of Computer Science
and Engineering
Florida Atlantic University
777 Glades Road
PO Box 3091
Boca Raton, FL 33431
USA
borko@cse.fau.edu

ISBN 978-0-387-89023-4   e-ISBN 978-0-387-89024-1
DOI 10.1007/978-0-387-89024-1
Springer Dordrecht Heidelberg London New York

Library of Congress Control Number: 2009926305

Printed on acid-free paper

Springer is part of Springer Science+Business Media (www.springer.com)

Preface

The advances in computer entertainment, multi-player and online games, technology-enabled art, culture and performance have created a new form of entertainment and art, which attracts and absorbs their participants. The fantastic success of this new field has influenced the development of the new digital entertainment industry and related products and services, which has impacted every aspect of our lives.

This Handbook is carefully edited book – authors are 88 worldwide experts in the field of the new digital and interactive media and their applications in entertainment and arts. The scope of the book includes leading edge media technologies and latest research applied to digital entertainment and arts with the focus on interactive and online games, edutainment, e-performance, personal broadcasting, innovative technologies for digital arts, digital visual and auditory media, augmented reality, moving media, and other advanced topics. This Handbook is focused on research issues and gives a wide overview of literature.

The Handbook comprises of five parts, which consist of 33 chapters. The first part on Digital Entertainment Technologies includes articles dealing with personalized movie, television related media, and multimedia content recommendations, digital video quality assessments, various technologies for multi-player games, and collaborative movie annotation. The second part on Digital Auditory Media focuses on articles on digita music management and retrieval, music distribution, music search and recommendation, and automated music video generation. The third part on Digital Visual Media consists of articles on live broadcasts, digital theater, video browsing, projector camera systems, creating believable characters, and other aspects of visual media.

The forth part on Digital Art comprises articles that discuss topics such as information technology and art, augmented reality and art, creation process in digital art, graphical user interface in art, and new tools for creating arts. The part V on Culture of New Media consists of several articles dealing with interactive narratives, discussion on combining digital interactive media, natural interaction in intelligent spaces, and social and interactive applications based on using sound-track identification.

With the dramatic growth of interactive digital entertainment and art applications, this Handbook can be the definitive resource for persons working in this field as researchers, scientists, programmers, and engineers. The book is intended for a wide variety of people including academicians, animators, artists, designers, developers, educators, engineers, game designers, media industry professionals, video producers, directors and writers, photographers and videographers, and researchers and graduate students. This book can also be beneficial for business managers, entrepreneurs, and investors. The book can have a great potential to be adopted as a textbook in current and new courses on Media Entertainment.

The main features of this Handbook can be summarized as:

- The Handbook describes and evaluates the current state-of-the-art in multimedia technologies applied in digital entertainment and art.
- It also presents future trends and developments in this explosive field.
- Contributors to the Handbook are the leading researchers from academia and practitioners from industry.

I would like to thank the authors for their contributions. Without their expertise and effort this Handbook would never come to fruition. Springer editors and staff also deserve our sincere recognition for their support throughout the project.

Borko Furht
Editor-in-Chief
Boca Raton, 2009

Contents

Contributors

Jakob Adesser
Fraunhofer Institute, Ilmenau, Germany

Harry Agius
Brunel University, Uxbridge, United Kingdom

Dewan Tanvir Ahmed
University of Ottawa, Ottawa, Canada

Salah Uddin Ahmed
Norwegian University of Science and Technology, Norway

Marios Angelides
Brunel University, Uxbridge, United Kingdom

Lora Aroyo
Eindhoven University of Technology, Eindhoven, The Netherlands

Shumeet Baluja
Google, Mountain View, CA, USA

Pieter Bellekens
Eindhoven University of Technology, Eindhoven, The Netherlands

Oliver Bimber
Bauhaus University Weimar, Germany

Leslie Bishko
Simon Fraser University, Vancouver, Canada

Alan Bovik
University of Texas at Austin, Austin, Texas, USA

Karlheinz Bradenburg
Fraunhofer Institute, Ilmenau, Germany

Pedro Sergio Branco
Computer Graphics Center, Guimaraes, Portugal

Antony Brooks
Aalborg University, Esbjerg, Denmark

Siwoo Byun
Anyang University, Anyang, Korea

Yiwei Cao
Technical University of Aachen, Aachen, Germany

Cristoforo Camerano
University of Catania, Italy

Petros Caravelas
Athens University of Economics and Business, Athens, Greece

Matina Charami
Athens University of Economics and Business, Athens, Greece

Michele Covell
Google, Mountain View, CA, USA

Christian Ditmar
Fraunhofer Institute, Ilmenau, Germany

Peter Dunker
Fraunhofer Institute, Ilmenau, Germany

Magy Seif El-Naser
Simon Fraser University, Vancouver, Canada

Stefano Ferretti
University of Bologna, Bologna, Italy

Michael Fink
The Hebrew University of Jerusalem, Israel

Jennele Fokker
Delft University of Technology, Delft, The Netherlands

Luigi Fortuna
University of Catania, Italy

Mattia Frasca
University of Catania, Italy

Yeung Siu Fung
The Chinese University of Hong Kong, Ma Liu Shui, China

Marco Furini
University of Modena and Reggio Emilia, Italy

Daniel Gartner
Fraunhofer Institute, Ilmenau, Germany

Holger Grossmann
Fraunhofer Institute, Ilmenau, Germany

Matthias Gruhne
Fraunhofer Institute, Ilmenau, Germany

Ian Gwilt
University of Technology, Sydney, Australia

Masaki Hoshino
Sony Corporation, Tokyo, Japan

Geert-Jan Houben
Eindhoven University of Technology, Eindhoven, The Netherlands

Wolfgang Huerst
Utrecht University, Utrecht, The Netherlands

Letizia Jaccheri
Norwegian University of Science and Technology, Norway

Matthias Jarke
Technical University of Aachen, Aachen, Germany

Subng Ho Jin
Information and Communications University, Deajon, Korea

Yohan Jin
University of Texas at Dallas, Texas, USA

Naoki Kamimaeda
Sony Corporation, Tokyo, Japan

Mohan Kankanhalli
National University of Singapore, Singapore

Munchurl Kim
Information and Communication University, Daejeon, Korea

Munjo Kim
Information and Communication University, Daejeon, Korea

Ralf Klamma
Technical University of Aachen, Aachen, Germany

Bumshik Lee
Information and Communication University, Daejeon, Korea

Han-kyu Lee
Electronics and Telecommunications Research Institute, Deajeon, Korea

Heekyung Lee
Electronics and Telecommunications Research Institute, Deajeon, Korea

In-Kwoon Lee
Yonsei University, Seoul, Korea

George Lekakos
Athens University of Economics and Business, Athens, Greece

Hua-Fu Li
Kainan University, Taoyuan, Taiwan

Jeongyeon Lim
Information and Communication University, Daejeon, Korea

John C.S. Lui
The Chinese University of Hong Kong, Ma Liu Shui, China

Rastislav Lukac
Epson Canada Ltd., Toronto, Canada

Hanna Lukashevich
Fraunhofer Institute, Ilmenau, Germany

Aderito Fernnades Marcos
University of Minho, Guimaraes, Portugal

David Milam
Simon Fraser University, Surrey, Canada

Manuela Montangero
University of Modena and Reggio Emilia, Italy

Anush K. Moorthy
University of Texas at Austin, Austin, Texas, USA

Michael Nixon
Simon Fraser University, Vancouver, Canada

Stefanie Nowak
Fraunhofer Institute, Ilmenau, Germany

Johan Pouwelse
Delft University of Technology, Delft, The Netherlands

B. Prabhakaran
University of Texas at Dallas, Texas, USA

Marcel Reinders
Delft University of Technology, Delft, The Netherlands

Yong Man Ro
Information and Communication University, Deajon, Korea

Graham Sellers
Advanced Micro Devices, Orlando, Florida, USA

Kalpana Seshadrinathan
University of Texas at Austin, Austin, Texas, USA

Shervin Shirmohammadi
University of Ottawa, Ottawa, Canada

Anastas Sofokleus
Brunel University, Uxbridge, United Kingdom

Sara Owsley Sood
Pomona College, Claremont, CA, USA

Flavia Sparacino
Sensing Places and MIT, Santa Monica, CA, USA

Myunghoon Suk
University of Texas at Dallas, Texas, USA

Tomohiro Tsunoda
Sony Corporation, Tokyo, Japan

Arthanasios Vasiliakos
University of Peloponnese, Nauplion, Greece

Arjen de Vries
CWI, Amsterdam, The Netherlands

Ron Wakkary
Simon Fraser University, Surrey, Canada

Jun Wang
Delft University of Technology, Delft, The Netherlands

Huaxin Wei
Simon Fraser University, Vancouver, Canada

Kay Wolter
Fraunhofer Institute, Ilmenau, Germany

Linxing Xiao
Tsinghua University, Beijing, China

Wei-Qi Yan
Queen's University of Belfast, Belfast, UK

Xubo Yang
Shanghai Jiao Tong University, Shanghai, China

Jong-Chul Yoon
Yonsei University, Seoul, Korea

Damon Daylamani Zad
Brunel University, Uxbridge, United Kingdom

Nelson Troca Zagalo
University of Minho, Braga, Portugal

Veronica Zammitto
Simon Fraser University, Vancouver, Canada

Jie Zhou
Tsinghua University, Beijing, China

Part I
DIGITAL ENTERTAINMENT TECHNOLOGIES

Chapter 1
Personalized Movie Recommendation

George Lekakos, Matina Charami, and Petros Caravelas

Introduction

The vast amount of information available on the Internet, coupled with the diversity of user information needs, have urged the development of personalized systems that are capable of distinguishing one user from the other in order to provide content, services and information tailored to individual users. Recommender Systems (RS) form a special category of such personalized systems and aim to predict user's preferences based on her previous behavior. Recommender systems emerged in the mid-90's and since they have been used and tested with great success in e-commerce, thus offering a powerful tool to businesses activating in this field by adding extra value to their customers. They have experienced a great success and still continue to efficiently apply on numerous domains such as books, movies, TV program guides, music, news articles and so forth.

Tapestry [1], deployed by Xerox PARC, comprises a pioneer implementation in the field of recommender systems and at the same time, it was the first to embed human judgment in the procedure of producing recommendations. Tapestry was an email system capable to manage and distribute electronic documents utilizing the opinion of users that have already read them. Other popular recommender systems that followed are Ringo [2] for music pieces and artists, Last.fm as a personalized internet radio station, Allmusic.com as a metadata database about music genres, similar artists and albums, biographies, reviews, etc, MovieLens [3] and Bellcore [4] for movies, TV3P [5], pEPG [6] and smart EPG [7] as program guides for digital television (DTV), GroupLens [8, 9] for news articles in Usenet and Eigentaste on Jester database as a joke recommender system. Nowadays, Amazon.com [10] is the most popular and successful example of applying recommender systems in order to provide personalized promotions for a plethora of goods such as books, CDs, DVDs, toys, etc.

G. Lekakos (✉), M. Charami, and P. Caravelas
ELTRUN, the e-Business Center, Department of Management Science and Technology,
Athens University of Economics and Business, Athens, Greece
e-mail: glekakos@aueb.gr; scha@ait.gr; pcaravel@aueb.gr

B. Furht (ed.), *Handbook of Multimedia for Digital Entertainment and Arts*,
DOI 10.1007/978-0-387-89024-1_1, © Springer Science+Business Media, LLC 2009

Now more than ever, the users continuously face the need to find and choose items of interest among many choices. In order to realize such a task, they usually need help to search and explore or even reduce the available options. Today, there are thousands of websites on the Internet collectively offering an enormous amount of information. Hence, even the easiest task of searching a movie, a song or a restaurant may be transformed to a difficult mission. Towards this direction, search engines and other information retrieval systems return all these items that satisfy a query, usually ranked by a degree of relevance. Thus, the semantics of search engines is characterized by the "matching" between the posted query and the respective results. On the contrary, recommender systems are characterized by features such as "personalized" and "interesting" and hence greatly differentiate themselves form information retrieval systems and search engines. Therefore, recommender systems are intelligent systems that aim to personally guide the potential users inside the underlying field.

The most popular recommendation methods are collaborative filtering (CF) and content-based filtering (CBF). Collaborative filtering is based on the assumption that users who with similar taste can serve as recommenders for each other on unobserved items. On the other hand, content-based filtering considers the previous preferences of the user and upon them it predicts her future behavior. Each method has advantages and shortcomings of its own and is best applied in specific situations. Significant research effort has been devoted to hybrid approaches that use elements of both methods to improve performance and overcome weak points.

The recent advances in digital television and set-top technology with increased storage and processing capabilities enable the application of recommendation technologies in the television domain. For example products currently promoted through broadcasted advertisements to unknown recipients may be recommended to specific viewers who are most likely to respond positively to these messages. In this way recommendation technologies provide unprecedented opportunities to marketers and suppliers with the benefit of promoting goods and services more effectively while reducing viewers' advertising clutter caused by the large amount of irrelevant messages [11]. Moreover, the large number of available digital television channels increases the effort required to locate content, such as movies and other programs, that it is most likely to match viewe's interests. The digital TV vendors do recognize this as a serious problem, and they are now offering personalized electronic program guides (EPGs) to help users navigate this digital maze [12].

This article proposes a movie recommender system, named MoRe, which follows a hybrid approach that combines content-based and collaborative filtering. MoR's performance is empirically evaluated upon the predictive accuracy of the algorithms as well as other important indicators such as the percentage of items that the system can actually predict (called prediction coverage) and the time required for generating predictions. The remainder of this article is organized as follows. The next section is devoted to the fundamental background of recommender systems describing the main recommendation techniques along with their advantages and limitations. Right after, we illustrate the MoRe system overview and in the section following, we describe in detail the algorithms implemented. The empirical evaluation results are then presented, while the final section provides a discussion about conclusions and future research.

Background Theory

Recommender Systems

As previously mentioned, the objective of recommender systems is to identify which of the information items available are really interesting or likable to individual users. The original idea underlying these systems is based on the observation that people very often rely upon opinions and recommendations from friends, family or associates to make selections or purchase decisions. Motivated by this "social" approach, recommender systems produce individual recommendations as an output or have the effect of guiding the user in a personalized way to interesting or useful objects in a large space of possible options [13].

Hence, recommender systems aim at predicting a user's future behavior based on her previous choices and by relying on features that implicitly or explicitly imply preferences. As shown in Figure 1, the recommendation process usually takes user ratings on observed items and/or item features as input and produces the same output for unobserved items.

Many approaches have been designed, implemented and tested on how to process the original input data and produce the final outcome. Still, two of them are the most dominant, successful and widely accepted: collaborative filtering and content-based filtering. Collaborative filtering is the technique that maximally utilizes the "social" aspect of recommender systems, as similar users, called neighbors, are used in order to generate recommendations for the target user. On the other hand, content-based filtering analyses the content of the items according to some features depending on the domain in order to profile the users according to their preferences.

These two fundamental approaches are presented in a great detail in the following subsections. Next, we describe some other alternative techniques used in producing personalized recommendations. We continue by realizing comparative observations among all aforementioned techniques, underlying the strengths and the shortcomings of each, thus driving the need of combining them in forming hybrid recommender systems. Hybrids form the last subsection of the recommender systems background theory.

Fig. 1 A high level representation of a recommender system

Collaborative Filtering

Collaborative filtering comprises the most popular and widely used approach for generating recommendations [14]. It filters and evaluates items utilizing other people' tastes and attitudes. It operates upon the assumption that users who have exhibited similar behavior in the past can serve as recommenders for each other on unobserved items. Thus, while the term collaborative filtering has become popular since the last decade, its algorithmic behavior originates from something that people use to do centuries no; exchange views and opinions.

According to collaborative filtering, a user's behavior consists of her preferences to products or services. The idea is to trace relationships or similarities between the target user and the remaining users in the database, aggregate the similar users' preferences and use them as a prediction for the target user. As a result, users that seem to prefer and choose common items are identified to have similar purchasing behavior and belong to a neighborhood. The user of a specific neighborhood may receive recommendations from her neighborhood for items that she has not bought, used or experienced in the past with a great possibility of satisfaction as neighbors are characterized from common taste.

Collaborative filtering consists of four fundamental steps.

1. Data collection – Input space
2. Neighbors similarity measurement
3. Neighbors selection
4. Recommendations generation

The first step is an independent one that relates to different alternative ways of collecting the input data for the algorithm, while the rest three describe the algorithmic approach itself.

Data Collection – Input Space

The input space for collaborative filtering may be summarized in a table, called user × ritem matrix, where users form the rows and items form the columns, while each cell C_{ij} of the matrix is filled by the degree of satisfaction of the ith user for the jth item. The degree of satisfaction is usually depicted in the form of ratings from users to items. Ratings can be continuous or discrete in a specific scale, i.e. ranging from 0 to 100 with real numbers or from 1 to 5 with natural numbers respectively. They can alternatively be provided in a dual representation, i.e. "thumbs up", 1 or $\sqrt{}$ imply that the item was liked and "thumbs down", 0 or X entail that the item was not liked. Rating scale chosen depends on the domain of the application. Nevertheless, the most common rating scale being used is the one that ranges from 1 to 5, with 1 denoting totally unpleasantness and 5 denoting absolute satisfaction. The empty cells in the user × item matrix imply that the user has not yet evaluated the specific item.

Besides the representation, rating also varies according to the way that it is collected. There exist two different ways of collecting users' ratings: explicitly and implicitly. Explicit rating refers to a user consciously expressing her preference usually in a discrete numerical scale. The user evaluates an item and assigns it a rate according to the scale used. On the other hand, implicit rating refers to interpreting user behavior or selections to impute a vote or preference. It can be based on browsing data (for example in Web applications), purchase history (for example in online or traditional stores) or other types of information access patterns.

Explicit rating is much more accurate reflecting more precisely each user's taste (as long as users provide consistent ratings), but at the same time, it is much more difficult to collect from all users and for a large percentage of the offered items. Moreover, most users usually rate items that they liked and avoid to deal with the uninteresting ones. Thus, the user × item matrix is generally filled in with positive votes lacking a sufficient amount of negative ones. On the contrary, implicit rating may not always reflect the reality, since users were not asked directly, and in some cases, it can also be misleading (e.g. the interpretation of time spent in a website in the case that the user is idle or has left her computer). Nevertheless, the biggest advantage of implicit rating is the fact that it relieves the user from examining and evaluating an item, it is usually based on positive preferences (thus avoiding the lack of negative ratings) and it manages to continuously collect input data as users interact with the system. No matter what the nature of the input space is, acquiring users' ratings for previously experienced objects comprises the fundamental initial step for collaborative filtering.

Neighbors Similarity Measurement

Collaborative filtering approaches can be distinguished into two major classes: model-based and memory-based [15]. Model-based methods develop and learn a model, which is applied upon the target user's ratings to make predictions for unobserved items. Two widely used probabilistic models are Bayesian classifier and Bayesian network with decision trees. On the other hand, memory-based methods operate upon the entire database of users to find the closest neighbors of the target and weight their recommendation according to their similarities. The fundamental algorithm of the memory-based class is the nearest neighbor (denoted as *NN*), which is considered as one of the most effective collaborative filtering approaches.

Weighting the neighbors' recommendations implies defining and calculating the distance between the target user and her neighbors. This distance may represent either the correlation or the similarity among all users. A typical measure of correlation is the Pearson correlation coefficient, which indicates the degree of linear correlation between two variables. In collaborative filtering, it is applied on the items rated in common by two users. Other popular correlation measures are the Spearman rank correlation, which is similar to Pearson but calculates the correlation between ranked lists instead of ratings, and the mean-squared difference, which emphasizes the bigger distances among ratings instead of the small ones. For further details about correlation measures and examples of some systems in where they were applied, refer to [16].

On the other hand, the similarity is usually calculated using vectors, the so-called similarity vectors. In the field of information retrieval, the similarity between two documents is often measured by treating each document as a vector of word frequencies and computing the cosine of the angle formed by the two frequency vectors. Adopting this formalism to collaborative filtering, users take the role of the documents, items take the role of words and votes take the role of word frequencies. Note that in this case, observed votes indicate a positive preference, there is no role for negative votes and unobserved items receive a zero vote. [15] provides an extensive description of similarity vectors.

Neighbors Selection

Having assigned weights to users, the next step is to decide which users will be selected and used in the recommendations generation process for the target user. In other words, select the users that will form the target user's neighborhood. Theoretically, we could consider all users as neighbors with the closest ones contributing more and with the more distant ones contributing less in the generation of recommendations. However, real commercial recommender systems deal with thousands to millions of users, and hence the approach of considering all users in the neighborhood is infeasible in terms of real time response. Thus, the system should select a subset of users that best form the neighborhood in order to decrease the computational cost and guarantee acceptable response times.

Two techniques have been employed in recommender systems: the threshold-based selection and the approach of k−nearest neighbors (denoted as k–NNs). The former technique selects as neighbors those users whose correlation or similarity to the target user exceeds a certain threshold value. Therefore, we may select neighbors to be over 70% similar to the target user (a high percentage in real online systems). On the contrary, the latter technique selects a predefined number k of best neighbors to form target user's neighborhood. Thus, for example, we may select the 10-best neighbors of the target user.

The threshold-based approach may form quite reliable neighborhoods, since it can guarantee that the neighbors of the target user will be, for example, over 70% similar to her. However, in real applications, the diversity of the users is very high. In such cases, there exist great possibilities of not even forming neighbors for some users and as a result, not generating recommendations for those users. On the other hand, the k−nearest neighbors technique always guarantees the formation of a neighborhood with the cost of possible decrease of results' quality, since the distance between the target user and her neighbors may be actually very big.

There is no panacea in choosing one of the aforementioned techniques; rather the selection of the proper one depends every time on the underlying application domain. In both cases, evaluating the appropriate values for the threshold or for the size of the neighborhood is of vital importance. These values depend on the nature and the size of the input data and are experimentally calculated.

Recommendations Generation

As soon as we have assigned weights to users and selected the ones that will serve as neighbors, we are ready to create predictions for the target user. The recommendation for a new item for the target user is based on the weighted average of her neighbors' ratings, weighted by their similarity to the target user. The recommendation generated is normalized in order for its rating to fall in the very same range used for all items in the domain.

Content-based Filtering

Content-based filtering makes predictions upon the assumption that a user's previous preferences or interests are reliable indicators for her future behavior. This approach requires that the items are described by features, and is typically applied upon text-based documents with predefined format or in domains with structured data, where the extraction of features that uniformly characterize the data is easy [17].

Text documents are semi-structured data, since they do not consist of specific predefined words. The application of content-based filtering in semi-structured data adopts much work from the text information retrieval and the natural language processing fields, such as representing the documents as vectors and measure the similarity between those vectors, utilizing attributes and characteristics of the natural language [18]. Applying content-based filtering in unstructured raw data, like multimedia, proves to be a very interesting and useful task, though a very challenging one that requires a lot of research [19]. Therefore, the majority of developed content-based recommender systems target on textually described items, like books, articles and TV programs. Even in the case of music and movies, recommendation techniques mostly apply on extracted textual features such as title, genre, etc and not on the multimedia itself. Besides, most on-line music databases today, such as Napster and mp3.com and movie databases, such as IMDb, rely on file names or text labels to do searching and indexing, using traditional text processing techniques.

Summarizing, content-based filtering can be applied in book recommender systems using features such as title, author, theme, or even a short summary or description (if available). In the same sense, it can be applied in a large range of other application domains, such as recommending movies (with features such as title, actors, director, genre, plot description), TV programs (with features such as name, type, presenter, hour), music (with features such as title, artist, album, genre), restaurants (with features such as name, cuisine, service, cost, place), and so forth.

TF-IDF (term-frequency times inverse document-frequency) and Information Gain are two metrics commonly applied in content-based filtering [20, 21]. They are statistical measures used to evaluate how important a word is to a document in a collection or corpus. The importance increases proportionally to the number of times a word appears in the document but is offset by the frequency of the word in the collection. The intuition behind these metrics is that the terms with the highest weight occur more often in the current document than in the other documents of the collection, and therefore are more central to the topic of this document. On the other hand, terms that are very frequent to all documents in the collection provide no particular descriptive power for the current document.

Creating a model of the user's preference from the user history is a form of classification learning. Such algorithms are the key component of content-based recommendation systems, because they learn a function that models each user's interests. Given a new item and the user history, the function makes a prediction on whether the user would be interested in the item. Some of the most popular algorithms are traditional machine learning algorithms designed to work on structured data, while other algorithms are designed to work in high dimensional spaces and do not require a pre-processing step of feature selection. [22] reviews a number of such well-known classification learning algorithms.

Other Approaches

Apart from the two previously mentioned approaches of collaborative filtering and content-based filtering, there exist some more alternative techniques that have been deployed in recommender systems. Some of the most popular ones include the collection of demographic data, the use of a utility function, the creation of a knowledge model, and the utilization of well-known data mining techniques.

Demographic recommender systems aim to categorize the user based on personal attributes and make recommendations based on demographic classes. In most of these systems, demographic data for user categorization are collected through the interaction of the user with the system using questionnaires, short surveys, dialogue prompts, etc. In other systems, machine learning is used to arrive at a classifier based on demographic data. Demographic techniques form 'people-to-people' correlations like collaborative ones, but use different data. The benefit of a demographic approach is that it may not require a history of the type needed by collaborative and content-based techniques.

Utility-based and knowledge-based recommenders match user's need with a set of options available. Utility-based recommenders make suggestions based on a computation of the utility of each object for the user. Of course, the central problem is how to create a utility function for each user. The benefit of utility-based recommendation is that it can factor non-product attributes, such as vendor reliability and product availability into the utility computation.

Knowledge-based recommendation attempts to suggest objects based on inferences about a user's needs and preferences. Knowledge-based approaches have knowledge about how a particular item meets a particular user need and can therefore reason about the relationship between a need and a possible recommendation.

Data mining has been applied with a great success in the field of grocery retailing. It usually refers to the automated extraction of implicit but useful information from large databases. Several data mining techniques, such as classification, clustering and association analysis have been also used in the field of e-commerce aiming to extract critical results in order to support fundamental strategic commercial decisions. These techniques can be additionally used in the recommendation process. Association rules and clusters of similar users or similar items may seem very useful approaches [23].

Comparing Recommendation Approaches

All the aforementioned recommendation techniques have their own strengths and shortcomings. Choosing the appropriate approach depends on the application domain, the nature of the corresponding data and the purpose that the recommender system will serve. In this subsection, we compare the previously presented recommendation approaches underlying their advantages and weaknesses.

The best known problem that recommender systems face is the new entry or the so-called from literature 'ramp-u' problem [24]. This term actually refers to two distinct but related problems.

1. **New User**: Most recommender systems realize a comparison between the target user and other users based on the commonly experienced items. As a result, a user with few ratings becomes difficult to categorize.
2. **New Item**: Similarly, a new item that has not got many ratings also cannot be easily recommended. It is also known as the 'early rater' problem, since the first person to rate an item gets little benefit from doing so.

Collaborative recommender systems depend on overlap in ratings across users and have difficulty when the space of ratings is sparse, since few users have rated the same items. Sparsity is a significant problem in many domains, where there are many items available. In these cases, unless the user base is very large, the chance that another user will share a large number of rated items is small.

These problems suggest that pure collaborative techniques are best suited to problems where the density of user interest is relatively high across a small and static space of items. If the set of items changes too rapidly, old ratings will be of little value to new users. If the set of items is large and user interest thinly spread, then the probability of overlap with other users will be small.

Collaborative recommenders work best for a user who acquires many neighbors of similar taste. The technique does not work well for the so-called 'gray sheep' that falls on a border between existing cliques of users. This is also a problem for demographic systems that attempt to categorize users on personal characteristics. On the other hand, demographic recommenders do not have the 'new user' problem, because they do not require a list of ratings from the user. Instead they have the problem of gathering the requisite demographic information.

In content-based filtering the features used to describe the content are of primary importance. The more descriptive they are the more accurate the prediction is. In computational terms, content-based prediction can be performed even if the user has rated at least one similar item though prediction accuracy increases with the number of similar items. Content-based techniques also have the problem that they are limited by the features that are explicitly associated with the objects that they recommend. For example, content-based movie recommendation can only be based on written materials about a movie: actors' names, plot summaries, etc. because the movie itself is opaque to the system. Of course, multimedia information retrieval tries to analyse the multimedia data itself, thus offering news ways to extract more representative features. Still, this field of science is not yet mature and a lot of research is needed towards this direction.

Collaborative systems rely only on user ratings and can be used to recommend items without any descriptive data. Even in the presence of descriptive data, some experiments have found that collaborative recommender systems can be more accurate than content-based ones [24]. The great power of the collaborative approach relative to content-based ones is its cross-genre recommendation ability.

Both content-based and collaborative techniques suffer from the 'portfolio effect.' An ideal recommender would not suggest a stock that the user already owns or a movie she has already seen. The problem becomes more evident in domains such as news filtering, since stories that look quite similar to those already read will never be recommended to the user.

Utility-based and knowledge-based recommenders do not have 'ramp-up' or sparsity problems, since they do not base their recommendations on accumulated statistical evidence. The major benefit of utility-based techniques is that they let the user express all of the considerations that need to go into a recommendation. However, the burden of this approach is that the user must construct a complete preference function and must therefore weight the significance of each possible feature.

Finally, knowledge-based recommender systems are prone to the drawback of knowledge acquisition. The system should have knowledge about the objects being recommended and their features, knowledge about the users and ability to map between the user's needs and the object that might satisfy those needs. Despite this drawback, knowledge-based recommendation has some beneficial characteristics, such as it demands less effort by the user than utility-based recommendation and it does not involve a start-up period during which its suggestions are low quality.

Hybrids

Hybrid recommender systems attempt to combine the aforementioned pure techniques in order to overcome the individual shortcomings and increase the overall quality of predictions. The tricky part in designing a hybrid system lies behind the fact that the produced system jeopardizes to also inherent the weaknesses of the modular techniques. As already mentioned, collaborative filtering is the most popular and efficient recommender approach. Consequently, most hybrid systems combine collaborative filtering along with another technique that solves the ramp-up problem. In their vast majority hybrids utilize combinations of content-based and collaborative filtering [12, 21, 25, 26]. Some of them further extend the two approaches by demographics-based predictions [27], while few of them utilize knowledge-based techniques where domain functional knowledge is exploited [24]. A significant part of research in hybrid recommender systems concerns the techniques that can be used to combine the approaches since they may significantly affect the prediction outcome.

Burke [24, 28] classifies hybridization techniques into seven classes: *weighted* where each of the recommendation approaches makes predictions which are then combined into a single prediction; *switching* where one of the recommendation techniques is selected to make the prediction when certain criteria are met; *mixed* in which predictions from each of the recommendation techniques are presented to the user; *feature combination* where a single prediction algorithm is provided with features from different recommendation technique; *cascade* where the output from one recommendation technique is refined by another; *feature augmentation* where the output from one recommendation technique is fed to another, and *meta-level* in which the entire model produced by one recommendation technique is utilized by another.

Switching, mixed, and weighted hybrids are differentiated from the remaining techniques in Burke's taxonomy by the fact that each one of the base recommendation methods produce independently from each other a prediction which is then presented to the user either as a single prediction (switching, weighted) or as two independent predictions (mixed). Switching hybrids in particular, are low-complexity hybridization methods based on the examination of the conditions that affect the performance of the base algorithms each time a prediction is requested. When such conditions occur the final prediction is the outcome of the base recommendation approach that is not affected (or is less affected) from these conditions.

MoRe System Overview

It has been empirically shown that collaborative filtering is more accurate than content-based filtering predictions provided that certain criteria are met [29, 30]. As discussed earlier, two criteria with significant effect are the neighborhood size and the number of rated items by the target user. In this paper we present a switching hybrid algorithm whose main prediction approach is based on collaborative filtering switched to content-based filtering when the above criteria are met. The proposed hybrid approach besides predictive accuracy also considers two other factors with practical significance: the prediction coverage as well as the time required to make a real-time prediction.

The MoRe system is a Web-based recommender system that collects user ratings concerning movies on one-to-five scale through its graphical user interface. More specifically as soon as a new user is registered with the system she is asked to provide a number of ratings in order for the system to initiate the prediction process (new user problem). The selection of movies that are presented to the user is based on the measure proposed by [31] computed as log *(popularity)* · *entropy*. The selection of the most popular movies increases the possibility to collect the respective ratings since it is most likely that these movies have been actually seen by the new user.

The collected ratings are organized in a user × item matrix and combined with the movies dataset are loaded into the system. MoRe's architectural design, presented in Figure 2, realizes three recommender techniques; a pure collaborative filtering, a pure content-based filtering and a hybrid approach that has been implemented in two versions, called switching and substitute. The two versions of the hybrid algorithm are differentiated by the parameter that controls the switch from collaborative filtering to content-based filtering as will be analyzed in subsequent sections.

The MoRe system utilizes a version of the well-known MovieLens dataset that contains 1,000,000 user ratings provided by 6040 original MovieLens users for about 4000 movies. Each user has rated at least twenty movies in the one-to-five rating scale. The sparsity of the user ratings matrix is 95.86%. Since the dataset

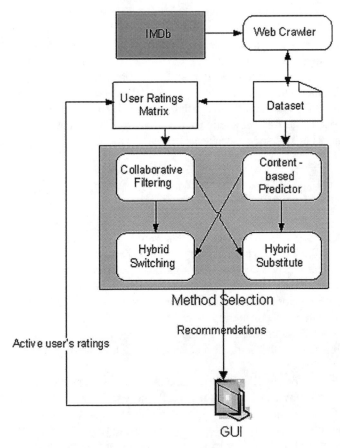

Fig. 2 MoRe system overall design

contains only the name and the production year of each movie, it is necessary to augment the movie description features for the content-based predictor. To accomplish that, we implemented a web crawler that seeks for data in the website of IMDb. The crawler exploits the search tool of IMDb and collects data about the genre, cast, director, writing credits, producers and plot keywords of each movie. The number of plot keywords may exponentially increase the number of features used to describe the movies and therefore the system administrator may remove keywords from the movie description that appear in less than a certain number of movies. In addition, the system creates (at an off-line phase) the set of most similar movies for all available movies in order to speed-up real-time predictions. The size of the set of most similar movies is also determined by the system administrator, as shown in Figure 3.

In order to make recommendations, collaborative filtering uses the ratings matrix while the content-based predictor uses mainly the movie data files. Hybrid techniques use both the content-based and the collaborative engines. Even though the system is able to produce recommendations with more than one technique, only one is applied at any given time. The technique selection, realized in Figure 4, is a task for the administrator of the system.

Figure 5 illustrates that the users receive the recommendations in a ranked list of movies where the prediction appears to the user in a "five-star" scale. The users may additionally provide their feedback directly on the recommended movies.

The system described can also be easily used for parameters tuning and experimental evaluation. The system administrator may select the size of the training and test sets as percentage of the whole dataset and initiate the estimation of the accuracy of the recommendation methods in MoRe.

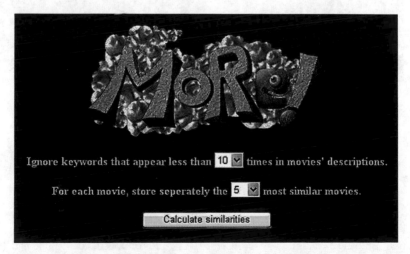

Ignore keywords that appear less than 10 ⌄ times in movies' descriptions.

For each movie, store seperately the 5 ⌄ most similar movies.

Calculate similarities

Fig. 3 Selection of features threshold and pre-computation of similar movies sets

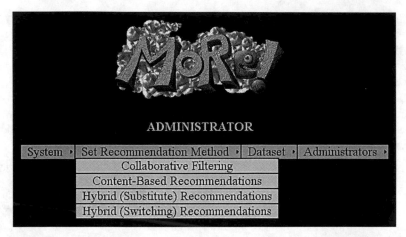

Fig. 4 Method selection in MoRe

Fig. 5 Ranked list of movie recommendations

Recommendation Algorithms

Pure Collaborative Filtering

Our collaborative filtering engine applies the typical neighbourhood-based algorithm [8], divided into three steps: (a) computation of similarities between the target and the remaining of the users, (b) neighborhood development and (c) computation of prediction based on weighted average of the neighbors' ratings on the target item.

For the first step, as formula 1 illustrates, the Pearson correlation coefficient is used.

$$r = \frac{\sum_i (X_i - \overline{X})(Y_i - \overline{Y})}{\sqrt{\sum_i (X_i - \overline{X})^2 \sum_i (Y_i - \overline{Y})^2}} \tag{1}$$

where X_i and Y_i are the ratings of users X and Y for movie I, while $\overline{X}, \overline{Y}$ refer to the mean values of the available ratings for the users X and Y. However, in the MoRe implementation we used formula 2, given below, which is equivalent to formula 1 but it computes similarities faster since it does not need to compute the mean rating values. n represents the number of commonly rated movies by users X and Y.

$$r = \frac{n \sum_i X_i Y_i - \sum_i X_i \sum_i Y_i}{\sqrt{n \sum_i X_i^2 - \left(\sum_i X_i\right)^2} \sqrt{n \sum_i Y_i^2 - \left(\sum_i Y_i\right)^2}} \tag{2}$$

Note that in the above formulas if either user has evaluated all movies with identical ratings the result is a "divide by zero" error and therefore we decided to ignore users with such ratings. In addition, we devaluate the contribution of neighbors with less than 50 commonly rated movies by applying a significance weight of $n/50$, where n is the number of ratings in common [32].

At the neighborhood development step of the collaborative filtering process we select neighbors with positive correlation to the target user. In order to increase the accuracy of the recommendations, prediction for a movie is produced only if the neighbourhood consists of at least 5 neighbors.

To compute an arithmetic prediction for a movie, the weighted average of all neighbors' ratings is computed using formula 3.

$$K_i = \overline{K} + \frac{\sum_{J \in Neighbours}(J_i - \overline{J})r_{KJ}}{\sum_J |r_{KJ}|} \tag{3}$$

where K_i is the prediction for movie i, $\overline{K}$ is the average mean of target user's ratings, J_i is the rating of neighbour J for the movie i, $\overline{J}$ is the average mean of neighbour J's ratings and r_{KJ} is the Pearson correlation measure for the target user and her neighbor J.

Pure Content-Based Filtering

In the content-based prediction we consider as features all movie contributors (cast, directors, writers, and producers), the genre, and the plot words. Features that appear in only one movie are ignored. Each movie is represented by a vector, the length of which is equal to the number of non-unique features of all available movies. The elements of the vector state the existence or non-existence (Boolean) of a specific feature in the description of the movie.

To calculate the similarity of two movies, we use the cosine similarity measure computed in formula 4. a_i and b_i are the values of the i-th elements of vectors $\vec{a}$ and $\vec{b}$.

$$\cos(\vec{a}, \vec{b}) = \frac{\vec{a} \cdot \vec{b}}{\|\vec{a}\| * \|\vec{b}\|} = \frac{\sum_i a_i b_i}{\sqrt{\sum_i a_i^2} \sqrt{\sum_i b_i^2}} \qquad (4)$$

The algorithm we use to produce recommendations is an extension of the top-N item-based algorithm that is described by Karypis in [33]. Since the movie set does not change dynamically when the system is online, the similarities between all pairs of movies in the dataset are pre-computed off-line and for each movie the k-most similar movies are recorded, along with their corresponding similarity values. When a user that has rated positively (i.e four or five) a set U of movies, asks for recommendations, a set C of candidate movies for recommendation is created as the union of the k-most similar movies for each movie j $\in U$, excluding movies already in U. The next step is to compute the similarity of each movie c $\in C$ to the set U as the sum of the similarities between c $\in C$ and all movies j $\in U$. Finally, the movies in C are sorted with respect to that similarity Figure 6 graphically represents the content-based prediction process.

Note that typically content-based recommendation is based upon the similarities between item' features and user's profile consisting of preferences on items' features. Instead, Karypis computes similarities between items upon all users' ratings completely ignoring item features. This approach is also known as item-to-item correlation and is regarded as content-based retrieval. We extend Karypis' algorithm by utilizing the movies' features rather than the user' ratings to find the most similar movies to the ones that the user has rated positively in the past and therefore we preserve the term content-based filtering.

Since we are interested in numerical ratings in order to combine content-based and collaborative filtering predictions, we extend Karypis' algorithm (which is designed for binary ratings) as follows. Let *MaxSim* and *MinSim* be the maximum and minimum similarities for each movie in c $\in C$ to U and Sim_i the similarity of a movie M_i to the set U. The numerical prediction Pr_i for the movie is computed by formula 5.

$$\text{Pr}_i = \frac{(Sim_i - MinSim) \cdot 4}{(MaxSim - MinSim)} + 1 \qquad (5)$$

Formula 5 above normalizes similarities from $[MaxSim, MinSim]$ to $[1, 5]$, which is the rating scale used in collaborative filtering. For example, if $Sim_i = 0.8$, $MinSim = 0.1$, and $MaxSim = 0.9$ then $\text{Pr}_i = 4.5$. Note that the formula applies for any similarity value (above or below one).

Due to the fact that movie similarities are computed offline, we are able to produce content-based recommendations much faster than collaborative filtering

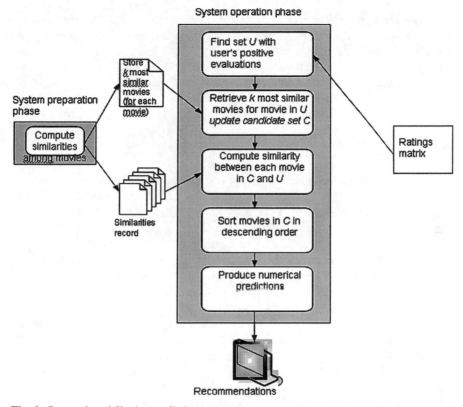

Fig. 6 Content-based filtering prediction process

recommendations. Moreover, in contrast to collaborative filtering, content-based predictions can always be produced for the specific dataset.

In addition, we implemented content-based filtering using the Naïve Bayes algorithm. Each of the five numerical ratings is considered as a class label and prediction u for an item is computed using formula 6:

$$u = \underset{u_j \, e\{1,2,3,4,5\}}{\arg\max} \; P(u_j) \prod_{i=0}^{m} P(a_i | u_j) \tag{6}$$

where u_j is the rating provided by the user $(u_j = 1, 2, 3, 4, 5)$, $P(u_j)$ is the probability that any item can be rated by the user with u_j (computed by the available user ratings), m is the number of terms used in the description of the items and $P(a_i | u_j)$ is the probability to find in the item's description the term a_i when it has been rated with u_j. The probability $P(a_i | u_j)$ is computed by formula 7.

$$P(a_i | u_j) = \frac{n_i + 1}{n + |Vocabulary|} \tag{7}$$

where n is the total number of occurrences of all terms that are used for the description of the items and have been rated with u_j, n_j is the frequency of appearance of the term a_i in the n terms and $|Vocabulary|$ is the number of unique terms appearing in all items that have been rated by the user. The Naïve Bayes algorithm has been successfully used in the book recommendation domain [18].

Hybrid Recommendation Methods

The proposed hybrid recommendation method is implemented in two variations. The first one, called *substitute,* aims to utilize collaborative filtering as the main prediction method and switch to content-based when collaborative filtering predictions cannot be made. The use of collaborative filtering as the primary method is based on the superiority of collaborative filtering in multiple application fields, as well as in the movie domain [29, 30]. Content-based predictions are triggered when the neighborhood size of the target user consists of less than 5 users.

This approach is expected to increase both the prediction accuracy as well as the prediction coverage. Indeed, the collaborative filtering algorithm described above requires at least five neighbors for the target user in order to make a prediction. This requirement increases the accuracy of the collaborative filtering method itself (compared to the typical collaborative filtering algorithm) but leads to a prediction failure when it is not met. For these items (for which prediction cannot be made) content-based prediction is always feasible and therefore the overall accuracy of the substitute hybrid algorithm is expected to improve compared to collaborative filtering as well as content-based filtering. Although this approach is also expected to improve prediction coverage, the time required to make predictions may increase due to the additional steps required by the content-based algorithm. However, this delay may be practically insignificant since the time needed to make content-based recommendations is significantly shorter than the time to produce recommendations with collaborative filtering.

The second variation of the proposed hybrid approach, called *switching*, is based on the number of available ratings for the target user as the switching criterion. Collaborative filtering prediction is negatively affected when few ratings are available for the target user. In contrast, content-based method deal with this problem more effectively since predictions can be produced even upon few ratings. The switching hybrid uses collaborative filtering as the main recommendation method and triggers a content-based prediction when the number of available ratings falls below a fixed threshold. This threshold value can be experimentally determined and for the specific dataset has been set to 40 ratings.

In terms of prediction coverage the switching hybrid is not expected to differ significantly from the collaborative filtering prediction, since content-based filtering may be applied even if a collaborative filtering prediction can be produced, in contrast to the substitute hybrid which triggers content-based prediction upon the "failure" of collaborative filtering to make predictions. Although the two variations above follow the exactly the same approach having collaborative filtering as their main recommendation method, they differ in the switching criterion.

Experimental Evaluation

The objective of the experimental evaluation is to compare the two versions of the hybrid algorithm against each other as well as against the base algorithms (collaborative and content-based filtering). The comparison is performed in terms of predictive accuracy, coverage and actual time required for real-time predictions. Moreover, since pure collaborative filtering, implemented in MoRe, adopts a neighborhood-size threshold (5 neighbors) we will examine its performance against the typical collaborative filtering method without the neighborhood size restriction. We will also demonstrate that the number of features used to describe the movies plays an important role in the prediction accuracy of the content-based algorithm.

The evaluation measures utilized for estimating prediction accuracy is the Mean Absolute Error (MAE). The Mean Absolute Error [2] is a suitable measure of precision for systems that use numerical user ratings and numerical predictions. If $r_1, \ldots, r_n$ are the real values of user in the test, $p_1, \ldots, p_n$ are the predicted values for the same ratings and $E = \varepsilon_1, \ldots, \varepsilon_n = \{p_1 - r_1, \ldots, p_n - r_n\}$ are the errors, then the Mean Absolute Error is computed by formula 8.

$$MAE = |\overline{E}| = \frac{\sum\limits_{i=0}^{n} |\varepsilon_i|}{n} \tag{8}$$

In the experimental process the original dataset is separated in two subsets randomly selected: a training set containing the 80% of ratings of each available user and a test set including the remaining 20% of the ratings. Furthermore, available user ratings have been split in the two subsets. The ratings that belong to the test set are ignored by the system and we try to produce predictions for them using only the remaining ratings of the training set. To compare the MAE values of the different recommendation methods and to verify that the differences are statistically significant we apply non-parametric Wilcoxon rank test, in the 99% confidence space (since normality requirement or parametric test is not met).

The MAE for the pure collaborative filtering method is 0.7597 and the coverage 98.34%. The MAE value for collaborative filtering method (without the neighborhood size restriction) is 0.7654 and the respective coverage 99.2%. The p-value of the Wilcoxon test (p = 0.0002) indicates a statistically significant difference suggesting that the restriction to produce prediction for a movie only if the neighbourhood consists of at least 5 neighbours lead to more accurate predictions, but scarifies a portion of coverage.

Table 1 Number of features
and prediction accuracy

Case	Threshold (movies)	MAE	Number of features
1	2	0.9253	10626
2	3	0.9253	10620
3	5	0.9275	7865
4	10	0.9555	5430
5	15	0.9780	3514

The pure content-based predictor presents MAE value 0.9253, which is significantly different ($p = 0.000$) than collaborative filtering. The coverage is 100%, since content-based predictions ensures that prediction can always be produced for every movie (provided that the target user has rated at least one movie). In the above experiment we used a word as a feature if it appeared in the description of at least two movies. We calculated the accuracy of the predictions when this threshold value is increased to three, five, ten and fifteen movies, as shown in Table 1.

Comparing cases 1 and 2 above we notice no significant differences, while the difference between 2 and 3, 4, 5 ($p = 0.0000$ for all cases) cases are statistically significant.

Thus, we may conclude that the number of features that are used to represent the movies is an important factor of the accuracy of the recommendations and, more specifically, the more features are used, the more accurate the recommendations are. Note that Naïve Bayes algorithm performed poorly in terms of accuracy with $MAE = 1.2434$. We improved its performance when considered ratings above 3 as positive ratings and below 3 as negative ($MAE = 1.118$). However, this error is still significantly higher than the previous implementation and therefore we exclude it from the development of the hybrid approaches.

Substitute hybrid recommendation method was designed to achieve 100% coverage. The MAE of the method was calculated to be 0.7501, which is a statistically important improvement of the accuracy of pure collaborative filtering ($p < 0.00001$).

The coverage of the switching hybrid recommendation method is 98.8%, while the MAE is 0.7702, which is a statistically different in relevance to substitute hybrid and pure collaborative filtering methods ($p = 0.000$). This method produces recommendations of less accuracy than both pure collaborative filtering and substitute hybrid, has greater coverage than the first and lower that the latter method, but it produces recommendations in reduced time than both methods above. Even though recommendation methods are usually evaluated in terms of accuracy and coverage, the reduction of execution time might be considered more important for a recommender system designer, in particular in a system with a large number of users and/or items.

Table 2 depicts the MAE values, coverage and time required for real-time prediction (on a Pentium machine running at 3.2 GHz with 1 GB RAM) for all four recommendation methods.

Note that the most demanding algorithm in terms of resources for real-time prediction is collaborative filtering. If similarities are computed between the target and

Table 2 MAE, coverage, and prediction time for the recommendation methods

	MAE	Coverage	run time prediction
Pure Collaborative Filtering	0.7597	98.34%	14 sec
Pure Content-based Recommendations	0.9253	100%	3 sec
Substitute hybrid recommendation method	0.7501	100%	16 sec
Switching hybrid recommendation method	0.7702	98.8%	10 sec

the remaining users at prediction time then its complexity is $O(nm)$ for n users and m items. This may be reduced at $O(m)$ if similarities for all pairs or users are pre-computed with an off-line cost $O(n^2m)$. However, such a pre-computation step affects one of the most important characteristics of collaborative filtering, which is its ability to incorporate the most up-to-date ratings in the prediction process. In domains where rapid changes in user interests are not likely to occur the off-line computation step may be a worthwhile alternative.

Conclusions and Future Research

The above empirical results provide useful insights concerning collaborative and content-based filtering as well as their combination under the substitute and switching hybridization mechanisms.

Collaborative filtering remains one of the most accurate recommendation methods but for very large datasets the scalability problem may be considerable and a similarities pre-computation phase may reduce the run-time prediction cost. The size of target user's neighbourhood does affect the accuracy of recommendations. Setting the minimum number of neighbors to 5 improves prediction accuracy but at a small cost in coverage.

Content-based recommendations are significantly less accurate than collaborative filtering, but are produced much faster. In the movie recommendation domain, the accuracy depends on the number of features that are used to describe the movies. The more features there are, the more accurate the recommendations.

Substitute hybrid recommendation method improves the performance of collaborative filtering in both terms of accuracy and coverage. Although the difference in coverage with collaborative filtering on the specific dataset and with specific conditions (user rated at least 20 movies, zero weight threshold value) is rather insignificant, it has been reported that this is not always the case, in particular when increasing the weight threshold value [32]. On the other hand, the switching hybrid recommendation method fails to improve the accuracy of collaborative filtering, but significantly reduces execution time.

The MoRe system is specifically designed for movie recommendations but its collaborative filtering engine may be used for any type of content. The evaluation of the algorithms implemented in the MoRe system was based on a specific dataset which limits the above conclusions in the movie domain. It would be very interesting to evaluate the system on alternative datasets in other domains as well in order to examine the generalization ability of our conclusions.

As future research it would also be particularly valuable to perform an experimental evaluation of the system, as well as the proposed recommendations methods, by human users. This would allow for checking whether the small but statistically significant differences on recommendation accuracy are detectable by the users. Moreover, it would be useful to know which performance factor (accuracy, coverage or execution time) is considered to be the most important by the users, since that kind of knowledge could set the priorities of our future research.

Another issue that could be subject for future research is the way of the recommendations presented to the users, the layout of the graphical user interface and how this influences the user ratings. Although there exist some studies on these issues (e.g. [34]), it is a fact that the focus in recommender system research is on the algorithms that are used in the recommendation techniques.

References

1. D. Goldberg, D. Nichols, B.M. Oki, and D. Terry, "Using Collaborative Filtering to Weave an Information Tapestry," Communications of the ACM Vol. 35, No. 12, December, 1992, p.p. 61-70.
2. U. Shardanand, and P. Maes, "Social Information Filtering: Algorithms for Automating "Word of Mouth"," Proceedings of the ACM CH'95 Conference on Human Factors in Computing Systems, Denver, Colorado, 1995, p.p. 210-217.
3. B. N. Miller, I. Albert, S. K. Lam, J. Konstan, and J. Riedl, "MovieLens Unplugged: Experiences with an Occasionally Connected Recommender System," Proceedings of the International Conference on Intelligent User Interfaces, 2003.
4. W. Hill, L. Stead, M. Rosenstein, and G. Furnas, "Recommending and Evaluating Choices in a Virtual Community of Use," Proceedings of the ACM Conference on Human Factors in Computing Systems, 1995, p.p. 174-201.
5. Z. Yu, and X. Zhou, "TV3P: An Adaptive Assistant for Personalized TV," IEEE Transactions on Consumer Electronics, Vol. 50, No. 1, 2004, p.p. 393-399.
6. D. O'Sullivan, B. Smyth, D. C. Wilson, K. McDonald, and A. Smeaton, "Improving the Quality of the Personalized Electronic Program Guide," User Modeling and User Adapted Interaction, Vol. 14, No. 1, 2004, p.p. 5-36.
7. S. Gutta, K. Kuparati, K. Lee, J. Martino, D. Schaffer, and J. Zimmerman, "TV Content Recommender System," Proceedings of the Seventeenth National Conference on Artificial Intelligence, Austin, Texas, 2000, p.p. 1121-1122.
8. P. Resnick, N. Iacovou, M. Suchak, P. Bergstrom, and J. Riedl, "GroupLens: An Open Architecture for Collaborative Filtering of NetNews," Proceedings of the ACM Conference on Computer Supported Cooperative Work, 1994, p.p. 175-186.

9. J. Konstan, B. Miller, D. Maltz, J. Herlocker, L. Gordon, and J. Riedl, "GroupLens: Applying Collaborative Filtering to Usenet News," Communications of the ACM, Vol. 40, No. 3, 1997, p.p. 77-87.

10. G. Linden, B. Smith, and J. York, "Amazon.com Recommendations: Item-to-Item Collaborative Filtering," IEEE Internet Computing, Vol. 7, No. 1, January-February, 2003, p.p. 76-80.

11. G. Lekakos, and G. M. Giaglis, "A Lifestyle-based Approach for Delivering Personalized Advertisements in Digital Interactive Television," Journal Of Computer Mediated Communication, Vol. 9, No. 2, 2004.

12. B. Smyth, and P. Cotter, "A Personalized Television Listings Service," Communications of the ACM, Vol.43, No. 8, 2000, p.p. 107-111.

13. G. Lekakos, and G. Giaglis, "Improving the Prediction Accuracy of Recommendation Algorithms: Approaches Anchored on Human Factors," Interacting with Computers, Vol. 18, No. 3, May, 2006, p.p. 410-431.

14. J. Schafer, D. Frankowski, J. Herlocker, and S. Shilad, "Collaborative Filtering Recommender Systems," The Adaptive Web, 2007, p.p. 291-324.

15. J. S. Breese, D. Heckerman, and D. Kadie, "Empirical Analysis of Predictive Algorithms for Collaborative Filtering," Proceedings of the Fourteenth Annual Conference on Uncertainty in Artificial Intelligence, July, 1998, p.p. 43-52.

16. J. Herlocker, J. Konstan, and J. Riedl, "An Empirical Analysis of Design Choices in Neighborhood-Base Collaborative Filtering Algorithms," Information Retrieval, Vol. 5, No. 4, 2002, p.p. 287-310.

17. K. Goldberg, T. Roeder, D. Guptra, and C. Perkins, "Eigentaste: A Constant-Time Collaborative Filtering Algorithm," Information Retrieval, Vol. 4, No. 2, 2001, p.p. 133-151.

18. R. J. Mooney, and L. Roy, "Content-based Book Recommending Using Learning for Text Categorization," Proceedings of the Fifth ACM Conference in Digital Libraries, San Antonio, Texas, 2000, p.p. 195-204.

19. M. Balabanovic, and Y. Shoham, "Fab: Content-based Collaborative Recommendation," Communications of the ACM, Vol. 40, No. 3, 1997, p.p. 66-72.

20. M. Pazzani, and D. Billsus, "Learning and Revising User Profiles: The identification of interesting Web sites," Machine Learning, Vol. 27, No. 3, 1997, p.p. 313-331.

21. M. Balabanovic, "An Adaptive Web Page Recommendation Service," Proceedings of the ACM First International Conference on Autonomous Agents, Marina del Ray, California, 1997, p.p. 378-385.

22. M. Pazzani, and D. Billsus, "Content-based Recommendation Systems," The Adaptive Web, 2007, p.p. 325-341.

23. B. Sarwar, G. Karypis, J. Konstan, and J. Riedl, "Analysis of Recommendation Algorithms for E-Commerce," Proceedings of ACM E-Commerce, 2000, p.p. 158-167.

24. R. Burke, "Hybrid Recommender Systems: Survey and Experiments," User Modeling and User Adapted Interaction, Vol. 12, No. 4, November, 2002, p.p. 331-370.

25. M. Claypool, A. Gokhale, T. Miranda, P. Murnikov, D. Netes, and M. Sartin, "Combining Content-Based and Collaborative Filters in an Online Newspaper," Proceedings of the ACM SIGIR Workshop on Recommender Systems, Berkeley, CA, 1999, http://www.csee.umbc.edu/ ian/sigir99-rec/.

26. I. Schwab, W. Pohl, and I. Koychev, "Learning to Recommend from Positive Evidence," Proceedings of the Intelligent User Interfaces, New Orleans, LA, 2000, p.p. 241-247.

27. M. Pazzani, "A Framework for Collaborative, Content-Based and Demographic Filtering," Artificial Intelligence Review, Vol. 13, No. 5-6, December, 1999, p.p. 393-408.

28. R. Burke, "Hybrid Web Recommender Systems," The Adaptive Web, 2007, p.p. 377-408.

29. C. Basu, H. Hirsh, and W. Cohen, "Recommendation as Classification: Using Social and Content-based Information in Recommendation," Proceedings of the Fifteenth National Conference on Artificial Intelligence, Madison, WI, 1998, p.p. 714-720.

30. J. Alspector, A. Koicz, and N. Karunanithi, "Feature-based and Clique-based User Models for Movie Selection: A Comparative study," User Modeling and User Adapted Interaction, Vol. 7, no. 4, September, 1997, p.p. 297-304.

31. A. Rashid, I. Albert, D. Cosley, S. Lam, McNee S., J. Konstan, and J. Riedl, "Getting to Know You: Learning New User Preferences in Recommender Systems," Proceedings of International Conference on Intelligent User Interfaces, 2002.

32. J. Herlocker, J. Konstan, A. Borchers, and J. Riedl, "An Algorithmic Framework for Performing Collaborative Filtering," Proceedings of the Twenty-second International Conference on Research and Development in Information Retrieval (SIGIR '99), New York, 1999, p.p. 230-237.

33. G. Karypis, "Evaluation of Item-Based Top-N Recommendation Algorithms," Proceedings the Tenth International Conference on Information and Knowledge Management, 2001, p.p. 247-254.

34. D. Cosle, S. Lam, I. K. Albert, J., and J. Riedl, "Is Seeing Believing? How Recommender Systems Influence Users' Opinions," Proceedings of the SIGCHI Conference on Human Factors in Computing Systems, Fort Lauderdale, FL, 2003, p.p. 585-592.

Chapter 2
Cross-category Recommendation for Multimedia Content

Naoki Kamimaeda, Tomohiro Tsunoda, and Masaaki Hoshino

Introduction

Nowadays, Internet content has increased manifold not only in terms of Web site categories but also other categories such as TV programs and music content. As of 2008, the total number of Web sites in the world exceeded 180 million [1]. Including satellite broadcasting programs, there are thousands of channels in the TV program category. Consequently, in several categories, information overload and the size of database storage are often acknowledged as problems. From the viewpoint of such problems, there is a need for personalization technologies. By using such technologies, we can easily find favorite content and avoid storing unnecessary content, because these technologies can select content that interests the user among a large variety of content.

Recommendation services are one of the most popular applications that are based on personalization technologies. Most of these services provide recommendations for individual categories. By applying recommendation technologies to several different categories, user experience can be improved. By using user preferences involving several categories, the system can figure out more profound nature of user's taste and user's view point to select content. Moreover, it becomes easier to find similar content from other categories. In this article, this kind of recommendation is referred to as "cross-category recommendation."

The purpose of this article is to introduce cross-category recommendation technologies for multimedia content. First, in order to understand how to realize the recommendation function, multimedia content recommendation technologies and cross-category recommendation technologies are outlined. Second, practical applications and services using these technologies are described. Finally, difficulties involving cross-category recommendation for multimedia content and future prospects are mentioned as the conclusion.

N. Kamimaeda (✉), T. Tsunoda, and M. Hoshino
Sec. 5, Intelligence Application Development Dept., Common Technology Division, Technology Development Group, Corporate R&D, Sony Corporation, Tokyo, Japan
e-mail: Naoki.Kamimaeda@jp.sony.com; tsunoda@sue.sony.co.jp; samba@sue.sony.co.jp

B. Furht (ed.), *Handbook of Multimedia for Digital Entertainment and Arts*,
DOI 10.1007/978-0-387-89024-1_2, © Springer Science+Business Media, LLC 2009

Technological Overview

Overview

The technological overview is described in two parts: multimedia content recommendation technologies and cross-category recommendation technologies. The relationship between these technologies is shown in Figure 1.

Multimedia recommendation technologies involve basic technologies that can be used to realize recommendation functions for each category. Cross-category recommendation technologies involve technologies to realize cross-recommendation among categories based on multimedia recommendation technologies. These two technologies have been explained in the following sections.

Multimedia Content Recommendation

In this section, an overview of recommendation technologies for multimedia content is described. There are two types of such technologies: collaborative filtering (CF) and content-based filtering (CBF). First, basic technologies about CF are described. Second, we explain CBF technologies in detail, because in this article, we mainly explain cross-category recommendation technologies using CBF technologies. After that, typical cases of multimedia content recommendation systems are mentioned. Finally, how to realize cross-category recommendation based on CBF technologies is described.

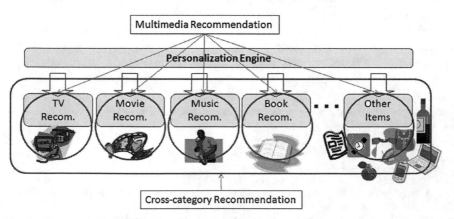

Fig. 1 Two types of recommendation technologies

Basic Technologies Involving CF

Collaborative filtering methods can be categorized into the following two types. One type of CF starts by finding a set of customers whose purchases and rated items overlap the user's purchases and rated items [2]. The algorithm aggregates items from such similar customers, eliminates items the user has already purchased or rated, and recommends the remaining items to the user. This is called user-based CF. Cluster models are also a type of user-based approach.

The other type of CF focuses on finding similar items, and not similar customers. For each of the user's purchased and rated items, the algorithm attempts to find similar items. It then aggregates the similar items and recommends them. This is called item-based CF. Two popular versions of this algorithm are search-based methods and item-to-item collaborative filtering [3].

Both CF methods cannot often work well with completely new items, items with less reusability such as TV programs, high merchandise turnover rate items, and so on. As a simple example of conventional CF, a problem in TV program recommendation can be encountered as follows.

1. Tom watched TV programs named X, Y, and Z.
2. Mike watched TV programs named X and Y but did not watch Z.
3. The system recommends program Z to Mike since Tom and Mike have watched the same programs X and Y, but Mike has never watched program Z before.
4. However, program Z has already been broadcast and Mike cannot watch program Z now.

Although CF methods have this type of problem, CF can be easily applied to cross-category recommendation, because CF is independent of the type of item, but it depends on which items are purchased or rated together. Moreover, technologies using community trends like CF are very important for cross-category recommendation.

Lately, several community-based recommendation services have emerged. Last.fm [4], MusicStrands (Mystrands) [5], and Soundflavor [6] are examples of community-based music recommendation services. These sites obtain the listening logs or playlist data of community members; these song playlists are shared with other community members and are also used to recommend music.

Basic Technologies Involving CBF

Key Elements of a Content Recommendation System Using CBF

A content recommendation system using CBF technologies has four key elements, as shown in Figure 2: content profiling, context learning, user preference learning, and matching.

In content profiling, the machine should understand what the content is in order to recommend it. For example, jazz music has acoustic instrumentation and makes for very relaxed listening. Understanding the content seems like an oversimplifica-

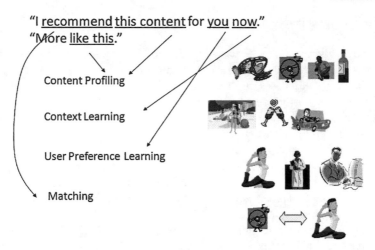

"I recommend this content for you now."
"More like this."

Content Profiling

Context Learning

User Preference Learning

Matching

Fig. 2 Four key elements of a CBF-based content recommendation system

tion, but a machine should manage all the necessary information that represents the content. The next element is context learning. Understanding the user's context is also important for recommending content. The user's interest is influenced by where she/he is, the time of the day, what type of situation she/he is in, or how she/he is feeling. For example, if the user is sitting in a café near a tropical seashore, she/he may prefer to listen to Latin music with a tropical cocktail in his/her hand. Alternatively, the user may prefer to listen to a wide range of music—classic to punk rock music—in the morning. The third element is learning the users' preferences. Learning and understanding the user's taste or preference is important to provide excellent recommendation in order to achieve better user satisfaction. If a user always listens to songs sung by female vocalists, she/he may prefer vocal to instrumental music. The last element is matching. Matching methods are used for recommending or searching relevant content. This key element measures the relevancy between the three abovementioned entities, such as that between user preference and content profile and the similarity between content.

In this chapter, these four key elements are discussed in detail; however, let us briefly introduce other factors such as association discovery, trend discovery (TD), and community-based recommendation. TD is useful from the viewpoint of providing recommendations because users often may wish to check the latest popular trends. For example, the TD system extracts trends from the World Wide Web (WWW) by employing a text mining technique comprising the following steps: (1) identifying frequent phrases, (2) generating histories or phrases, and (3) seeking temporal patterns that match a specific trend [7]. One research group has focused on detecting the sentimental information associated with retail products by employing natural language processing [8].

Content Profiling

Content profiling can be considered as the addition of metadata that represents the content or indexing it for retrieval purposes. It is often referred to as tagging, labeling, or annotation. Essentially, there are two types of tagging methods—manual tagging and automatic tagging. In manual tagging, the metadata is manually fed as the input by professionals or voluntary users. In automatic tagging, the metadata is generated and added automatically by the computer. In the case of textual content, keywords are automatically extracted from the content data by using a text mining approach. In the case of audiovisual (AV) content, various features are extracted from the content itself by employing digital signal processing technologies. However, even in the case of AV content, text mining is often used to assign keywords from the editorial text or a Web site. In both manual and automatic approaches, it is important for the recommendation system to add effective metadata that can help classify the user's taste or perception. For example, with respect to musical content, the song length may not be important metadata to represent the user's taste.

Manual Tagging

Until now, musical content metadata (Figure 3) have been generated by manual tagging. All Media Guide (AMG) [9] offers a musical content metadata by professional music critics. They have over 200 mood keywords for music tracks. They classify each music genre into hundreds of subgenres. For example, rock music has over 180 subgenres. AMG also stores some emotional metadata, which is useful to analyze artist relationships, search similar music, and classify the user's taste in detail. However, the problem with manual tagging is the time and cost involved. Pandora [10] is well known for its personalized radio channel service. This service is based on manually labeled songs from the Music Genome Project; according to their Web site, it took them 6 years to label songs from 10,000 artists, and these songs were listened to and classified by musicians. According to the AMG home page, they have a worldwide network of more than 900 staff and freelance writers specializing in music, movies, and games.

Similarly, Gracenote [11] has also achieved huge commercial success as a music metadata provider. The approach involves the use of voluntary user input and the service—compact disc database (CDDB)—is a de facto standard in the music metadata industry for PCs and mobile music players. According to Gracenote's Web site, the CDDB already contains the metadata for 55 million tracks and 4 million CDs spanning more than 200 countries and territories and 80 languages; interestingly, Gracenote employs less than 200 employees. This type of approach is often referred to as user-generated content tagging.

Fig. 3 Example of a song's metadata

Attribute	Value
Artist	Lisa Girberto
Song	Esperanza
Album	The Best of Lisa Griberto
Relase date	1998
Genre	Latin
Editorial text	She is a wonderfule Brazilian ...
Track No.	5
⟩	⟩
Mood	melancholy
Tempo	83
Related artists	Thomas Jobim, Serdio Nascimento

Automatic Tagging

1) Automatic Tagging from Textual Information

In textual-content-based tagging, key terms are extracted automatically from the textual content. This technique is used for extracting keywords not only from the textual content but also from the editorial text; this explains its usability with respect to tagging the AV content. "TV Kingdom" [12] is a TV content recommendation service in Japan; it extracts specific keywords from the description text provided in the electronic program guide (EPG) data and uses it as additional metadata. This is because the EPG data provided by the supplier are not as effectively structured as metadata and are therefore insufficient for recommendation purposes [13]. TV Kingdom employs the term frequency/inverse document frequency (TF/IDF) method to extract keywords from the EPG. TF/IDF is a text mining technique that identifies individual terms in a collection of documents and uses them as specific keywords. The TF/IDF procedure can be described as follows:

Step 1: Calculate the term frequency (*tf*) of a term in a document.
$freq(i, j) = frequency\ of\ occurenceofterm\ t_i\ indocument\ D_j$
The following formula is practically used to reduce the impact of high-frequency terms.
$tf_j^i = \log(1 + freq(i, j))$

Step 2: Calculate the inverse document frequency (*idf*): idf_i reflects the presumed importance of term t_i for the content representation in document D_j.
$idf_i = \frac{N}{n_i}$

where

n_i = *number of documents in the collection to which term t_j is assigned.*

N = *collection size.*

The following formula is practically used to reduce the impact of large values.

$$idf_i = \log\left(\frac{N}{n_i}\right)$$

Step 3: The product of each factor is applied as the weight of the term in this document.

$$w_i^j = tf_i^j \times idf_i$$

Google [14] is the most popular example of automatic tagging based on textual information. Google's Web robots are software modules that crawl through the Web sites on the Internet, extract keywords from the Web documents, and index them automatically by employing text mining technology. These robots also label the degree of importance of each Web page by employing a link structure analysis; this is referred to as Page Rank [15].

2) Automatic Tagging from Visual Information

Research on content-based visual information retrieval systems has been undertaken since the early 1990s. These systems extract content features from an image or video signal and index them. Two types of visual information retrieval systems exist. One is "query by features"; here, sample images or sketches are used for retrieval purposes. The other is "query by semantics"; here, the user can retrieve visual information by submitting queries like "a red car is running on the road."

Adding tags to image or video content is more complex than adding tags to textual content. Certain researches have suggested that video content is more complex than a text document with respect to six criteria: resolution, production process, ambiguity in interpretation, interpretation effort, data volume, and similarity [16]. For example, the textual description of an image only provides very abstract details. It is well known that a picture is worth a thousand words. Furthermore, video content—a temporal sequence of many images—provides higher-level details that a text document cannot yield. Therefore, query by semantics, which is a content-based semantic-level tagging technique, is still a complex and challenging topic. Nevertheless, query-by-feature approaches such as QBIC and VisualSEEK achieve a certain level of performance with regard to visual content retrieval [17], [18]. This approach extracts various visual features including color distribution, texture, shape, and spatial information, and provides similarity-based image retrieval; this is referred to as "query by example."

In order to search for a similar image, the distance measure between images should be defined in the feature space, and this is also a complex task. A simple example of distance measure using color histograms is shown in Figure 4 in order to provide an understanding of the complexity involved in determining the similarity between images. This figure shows three grayscale images and their color histograms in Panel a, Panel b, and Panel c. It may appear that Image (b) is similar

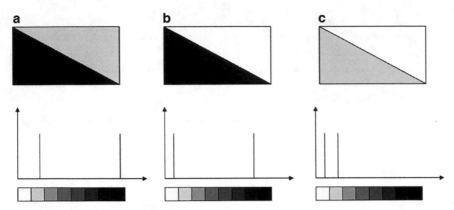

Fig. 4 Typical grayscale image sample

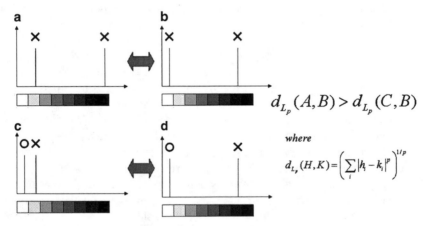

$$d_{L_p}(A,B) > d_{L_p}(C,B)$$

where

$$d_{L_p}(H,K) = \left(\sum_i \left| h_i - k_i \right|^p \right)^{1/p}$$

Fig. 5 Minkowski distance measure

to Image (a) rather than Image (c). However, simple Minkowski distance reveals that Image (b) has greater similarity to Image (c) than Image (a), as shown in Figure 5. There exists a semantic gap between this distance measure and human perception. In order to overcome this type of problem, various distance measures have been proposed, such as earth mover's distance (EMD) [19]. JSEG outlines a technique for spatial analysis using the image segmentation method to determine the typical color distributions of image segments. [20].

In addition to the global-color-based features mentioned above, image recognition technology is also useful for image tagging. A robust recognition algorithm of object recognition from multiple viewpoints has also been proposed [21]. The detection and indexing of objects contained in images enable the query-by-example service with a network-connected camera such as one on a mobile phone. Face recognition and detection technologies also have potential for image tagging. Sony's "Picture Motion Browser" [22] employs various video feature extraction technologies including face-recognition to provide smart video browsing features such as personal highlight search and video summarization. A hybrid method merging both local features from image recognition technology and global-color-based feature will enhance the accuracy of image retrieval.

Many researches pursue the goal of sports video summarization because sports video has a typical and predictable temporal structure and recurring events of similar types such as corner kicks and shots at goal in soccer games. Furthermore, consistent features and fixed number of views allow us to employ less complex content model than those necessary for ordinary movie or TV drama content. Most of the solutions involve the combination of the specific local features such as line mark, global visual features and also employ audio features such as high-energy audio segment.

3) Automatic Tagging from Audio Information

In addition to images, there are various approaches for achieving audio feature extraction by employing digital signal processing. In the MPEG-7 standard, audio features are split into two levels—"low-level descriptor" and "high-level descriptor." However, a "mid-level descriptor" is also required to understand automatic tagging technologies for audio information. Low-level features are signal-parameter-level features such as basic spectral features. Mid-level features are musical-theory-level features, for example, tempo, key, and chord progression, and other features such as musical structure (chorus part, etc.), vocal presence, and musical instrument timbre. High-level features such as mood, genre, and activity are more generic.

The EDS system extracts mid- and high-level features from an audio signal [23]. It involves the generation of high-level features by combining low-level features. The system automatically discovers an optimal feature extractor for the targeted high-level features, such as the musical genre, by employing a machine learning technology. The twelve-tone analysis is an alternative approach for audio feature extraction; it analyzes the audio signal based on the principles of musical theory. The baseband audio signal is transformed into the time–frequency domain and split into 1/12 octave signals. The system can extract mid- and high-level features by analyzing the progression of the twelve-tone signal patterns. Sony's hard-disk-based audio system "Giga Juke" [24] provides smart music browsing capabilities based on features such as mood channel and similar song search by the twelve-tone analysis.

Musical fingerprinting (FP) also extracts audio features, but it is used for accurate music identification rather than for retrieving similar music. Figure 6 shows the framework of the FP process [25]. Similar to the abovementioned feature extraction procedures, FP extracts audio features by digital signal processing, but it generates a more compact signature that summarizes an audio recording. FP is therefore capable of satisfying the requirements of both fast retrieval performance and compact footprint to reduce memory space overhead. Gracenote and Shazam [26] are two well-known FP technologies and music identification service providers.

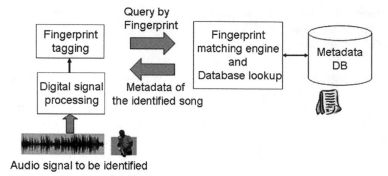

Fig. 6 FP framework

Context Learning

A mobile terminal is a suitable device for detecting the user's context because it is always carried by the user. In the future, user contexts such as time, location, surrounding circumstances, personal mood, and activity can be or will be determined by mobile terminals. Therefore, if the user context can be identified, relevant information or context-suitable content can be provided to the user.

The user's location (physical position) can be easily detected by employing a GPS-based method or cell-network-based positioning technology. The latter encompasses several solutions such as timing advance (CGI+TA), enhanced CGI (E-CGI), cell ID for WCDMA, uplink time difference of arrival (U-TDOA), and any time interrogation (ATI) [27]. The detection of the surrounding circumstances is a challenging issue. One of the approaches has proposed the detection of the surrounding circumstances by using ambient audio and video signals [28]. A 180° wide-angle lens is used for visual pattern learning for different circumstances or events such as walking into a building or walking down a busy street. Personal mood detection is also an interesting and challenging topic. Nowadays, gyrosensor (G-sensor) devices are used in commercial computer gaming systems, wherein user movement can be detected; G-sensors can therefore detect user activity such as whether she/he is running, walking, sitting, or dancing.

User Preference Learning

User preferences can be understood by studying the user's response to the content. A computer system cannot understand user tastes without accessing user listening and watching logs or acquiring certain feedback. For example, people who always listen to classical and ethnic music may prefer such genres and might seem to prefer acoustic music over electronic music. People who read the book "The Fundamentals of Financing" might be interested in career development or might attempt to invest in some venture capitals to avail of a high return for their investments.

To realize this type of user preference learning, the system must judge whether the user's feedback regarding the content is positive or negative. After judging whether the feedback provided is positive or negative, the system can learn the user's preferences based on the content's metadata. There are two types of user feedback—explicit and implicit. "Initial voluntary input of a user's preference regarding the registration process" or "clicking the like/dislike button" are examples of explicit feedback. "Viewing detailed information on the content," "purchasing logs of an e-commerce site," and "operation logs such as play or skip buttons for AV content" are examples of implicit feedback. Generally, the recommendation systems emphasize upon explicit rather than implicit feedback.

After the "like" or "dislike" rating is determined, the system adds or subtracts certain points to or from each attribute, respectively. In a "vector space model" (VSM) (introduced later), the user preference is expressed as an n-dimensional attribute vector based on this process. In the probabilistic algorithm (also introduced in the subsequent section), user preference is expressed in terms of probabilistic parameters in addition to the attribute value. For example, if a user is satisfied with 60 jazz songs per 100 recommended songs, the probabilistic parameter is expressed as $P(\text{like}|\text{genre} = \text{jazz}) = 60/100 = 0.6.$

Matching

There are two types of matching approaches—exact matching and similarity matching. The former seeks contents with the same metadata as that of the search query, such as keywords or tags. The latter seeks contents with metadata similar to that of the search query. In this section, two types of similarity calculation methods—VSM and "naïve Bayesian classifier" (NB)—are introduced; however, there are several other exact matching and similarity matching methods.

1) VSM

One of the simplest approaches for similarity calculation is using the VSM. This model measures the distance between vectors. The most practical distance measure is the cosine distance, as shown in Figure 7. For example, user preference (UP) and

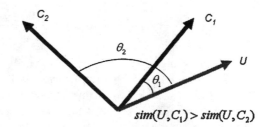

Fig. 7 Example of Similarity in VSM

$$sim(U,C_1) > sim(U,C_2)$$

content profile (CP) are expressed as an n-dimensional feature vector in the VSM. The similarity between UP and CP is usually defined as follows:

$$sim\left(\vec{U},\vec{C}\right) = \cos\theta = \frac{\vec{U}\cdot\vec{C}}{|\vec{U}||\vec{C}|}$$

where

$\vec{U} = (u_1, u_2, , , u_n)$ *user preference vector*
$\vec{C} = (c_1, c_2, , , c_n)$ *contents profile vector*

2) NB Classifier

NB is a probabilistic approach to classify data or infer a hypothesis. It is also practically used in recommendation systems [29]. Let us apply NB to measure the similarity between user preference and content profile. In NB, the initial probabilities of the user's tastes are determined from the training data. For example, if a user is satisfied with 60 jazz songs per 100 recommended songs, the conditional probability P(like|genre = jazz) = 0.6. If she/he is satisfied with 80 acoustic songs per 100 recommended songs, P(like | timbre = acoustic) = 0.8. Therefore, we can hypothesize that the user likes acoustic jazz music. After the learning phase, NB can classify the new songs based on the user's tastes, i.e., whether she/he likes these songs or not. For this, NB calculates which class maximizes $P(c|s)$, as shown in (1); here, s is the content vector expressed in terms of the attribute values (a1, a2, a3,..., an).

$$\hat{c} = \arg\max_c P(c|\vec{s}) = \arg\max_c \frac{P(\vec{s}|c)P(c)}{P(\vec{s})} = \arg\max P(c)P(\vec{s}|c) \quad (1)^*$$

where

$\hat{c}$ = *estimated class (like or dislike)*
c = *class (like or dislike)*
$\vec{s} = (a_1, a_2, , , , a_n)$ *content (song) vector* **expressed by its attribute vector.**
* *Bayes theorem: The posterior probability p(h|D) given D*

$$P(h|D) = \frac{P(D/h)P(h)}{P(D)} \quad (2)$$

In (1), the probability $P(c)$ can be easily estimated by counting the frequency in the training phase. However, it is difficult to calculate $P(s|c) = P(a1, a2, a3, ..., an|c)$. Since there are several possible combinations of attributes, a large number of training sets is required. In order to resolve this problem, NB assumes a very simple rule: the values of the attributes are conditionally independent, as shown in (2). Therefore, by substituting (3) in (1), NB can be simply expressed as (4). It is easy to determine $P(c)$ and $P(a_i|c)$ as the user preference by using explicit and implicit feedback provided by the user.

$$P(\vec{s}|c) = P(a_1, a_2, \ , \ , a_n|c) = \prod_i P(a_i|c) \tag{3}$$

$$\hat{c} = \arg\max_c P(c) \prod_i P(a_i|c) \tag{4}$$

3) Other Approaches

The usage of VSM and NB both poses a problem referred to as "the curse of dimension": as the number of dimensions increases, the discrimination performance deteriorates. Some of the approaches to avoid this problem are dimension reduction (feature selection) and application of weight or bias to the attributes. Feature selection eliminates irrelevant or inappropriate attributes. Principal component analysis (PCA) or probabiliistic latent semantic analysis (pLSA) can be used to this end. The latter models a document as a combination of hidden variables which explain its topics. In addition to dimension reduction, support vector machine (SVM) is an effective and robust tool to classify data into two classes. The application of weight or bias to the attributes based on individual user's viewpoint has also been proposed [30].

Typical Cases of Multimedia Content Recommendation System

There are several matching combinations for content recommendation systems, as shown in Figure 8. Typically, four combinations are often used in recommendation

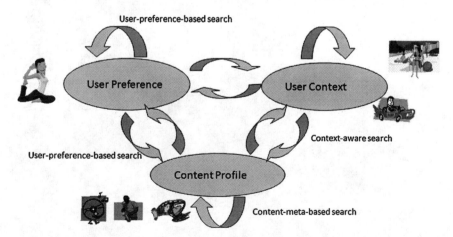

Fig. 8 Matching combinations for a content recommendation system

systems. The first is "content-to-content matching," referred to as "content-meta-based search." The second is "context-to-content matching," also referred to as "context-aware search." The third is "user-preference-to-content matching," also referred to as "user-preference-based search." The last is "user-preference-to-user-preference matching," which is another case of "user-preference-based search." This chapter investigates three types of recommendation systems (shown in Figures 9, 10, and 11).

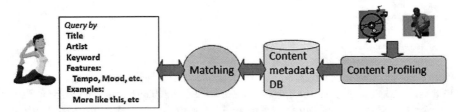

Fig. 9 Content-meta-based search

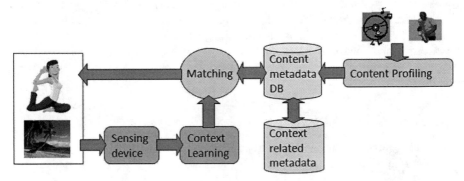

Fig. 10 Context-aware search

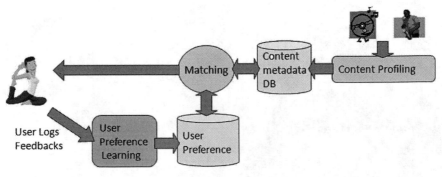

Fig. 11 User-preference-based search

1) Content-meta-based Search

In content-meta-based search, users can acquire relevant content by querying for keywords or features. The content data are initially indexed based on keywords or features by employing a content profiling process. Query by example is a widely used implementation of the content-meta-based search; it is known as the "more like this" function.

2) Context-aware Search

Context-aware search provides relevant content based on "time," "location," "surrounding circumstances," and "personal mood and activity," which are monitored using sensing devices. Context metadata should comprise prior indexed keywords, tags, or features obtained from the sensing devices. Furthermore, this data should also be related to the content metadata in terms of queries such as "which kind of songs are relevant to this context," "when is the last train arriving at this station," and so on. Some of these types of metadata should be automatically tagged based on the user log data rather than by manual tagging by the service provider.

3) User-preference-based Search

User-preference-based search is sometimes narrowly defined as a recommendation system. It is also known as CBF or CF systems [2]. The former employs similarity matching between the user preference and content profile. The latter seeks similar users by conducting user-preference-to-user-preference matching and predicts the user's taste based on the behaviors of similar users. The CF-based content recommendation system of Amazon [31] has achieved some commercial success. Recently, a hybrid solution comprising both CBF and CF was used in commercial TV recommendation systems [13].

Cross-category Recommendation

Key Points of a Cross-category Recommendation

In order to realize the cross-category recommendation using basic CBF technologies, two key points are needed: to prepare common metadata among categories and to generate user preferences separately with respect to each category.

One is the category common metadata. To calculate the content similarity among different categories, this element is necessary. The other is separate user preference generation for each category. Normally, metadata that can be used is different for each category. Moreover, user preference about each metadata such as keyword is likely to be different for each category. For example, the user may like "World Heritage" in the TV category but the user may not like this in the music category. Therefore, it is very important to accurately understand the user preference. In this regard, however, it is necessary to appropriately merge the respective user preferences when the cross-category recommendation list is calculated.

Category Common Metadata

A variety of metadata can be used for each category depending on the category. For example, in the movie and music categories, we can use the metadata extracted from the content signal. However, in the book category, it is impossible to use such kind of metadata. Moreover, even if the same metadata can be used for multiple categories, it is difficult to use this metadata with different master tables. Therefore, it is necessary to prepare the same metadata with the same master table as those among the categories for which cross-category recommendation needs to be realized. In this article, this kind of metadata is called the common metadata. Examples of common metadata are as follows:

1. Specific metadata whose master table is the same among different categories e.g., genre, person, keyword, etc.
2. Abstract metadata that do not depend on the category e.g., mood, impression, user's personality or lifestyle, etc.

After preparing these common metadata, we can realize cross-category recommendation.

Cross-category recommendation can be described as that shown in Figure 12. There are three layers. The first layer is "personalization engine." This is an engine used to calculate the recommendation list. The second layer is "common metadata/preference." When the recommendation engine calculates the cross-category recommendation list among all the categories, the data from this layer is used. For example, when the engine searches books using content metadata in the TV category as content-meta search or using the user preference for TV as a user-preference-

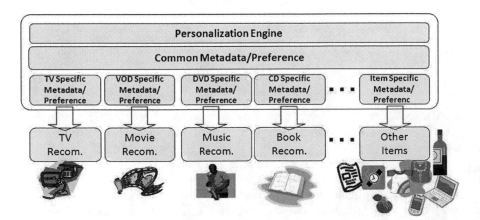

Fig. 12 Cross-category Recommendation

based search, data from this layer is used. "Specific metadata/preference" is the last. When the engine calculates the recommendation list for a specific category, the data from this layer is used. For example, when the engine searches movies using the content metadata in the movie category as the content-meta search or using the user preference for movie as the user-preference-based search, data from this layer is used.

Separate User Preference Generation for Each Category

Useful metadata and user preference are likely to be different for each category. The entire metadata cannot always be treated as common metadata. In addition, a user who likes the keywords such as "World Heritage" and "Travel" in the TV category may not like them in the book category. Therefore, it is better to treat the user preference by each category. In other words, the user preference for each category should be generated from logs for contents in the same category. However by applying this, it is necessary to merge the respective user preference appropriately when the engine calculates the cross-category recommendation list as a user-preference-based search.

The user preference can be merged using several methods. A simple mergence method for user preference is described below.

$$\mathbf{UP}_{merge} = avg(\alpha \mathbf{UP}_1 + \beta \mathbf{UP}_2) \tag{5}$$

In this equation, UP represents one user preference vector for a certain category. α and β are arbitrary variables. By using this equation, three examples can be described below.

(a) Search books using the user preference for TV and for book as the user-preference-based search

$$\mathbf{UP}_{merge} = avg(\alpha \mathbf{UP}_{TV} + \beta \mathbf{UP}_{Book})$$

(b) Search TV content using the user preference for music and for TV as the user-preference-based search

$$\mathbf{UP}_{merge} = avg(\alpha \mathbf{UP}_{Music} + \beta \mathbf{UP}_{TV})$$

(c) Search music content using the user preference for TV and for music as the user-preference-based search

$$\mathbf{UP}_{merge} = avg(\alpha \mathbf{UP}_{TV} + \beta \mathbf{UP}_{Music})$$

Embodiment of Recommendation Engine: Voyager Engine (VE)

In this section, Voyager Engine™ [13] [32] is selected as an example of embodiment of the recommendation engine.

Fig. 13 VE: Hybrid
Personalization Engine

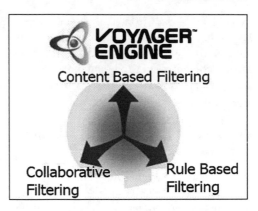

Overview

VE is Sony's original personalization engine. VE can be used for various kinds of applications and is particularly used nowadays to realize recommendation functions. VE is a hybrid personalization engine having three types of filtering: CF, CBF, and rule-based filtering. Figure 13 depicts a hybrid engine.

VE has been implemented to realize not only multimedia content recommendation in a specific category but also for cross-category recommendation. VE adopts a VSM and handles all of the models such as user preference, content profile, and user context with a common vector format. Therefore, it is easy to do cross-matching among all of the models. Consequently, VE can easily realize content-meta-based search, context-aware search, and user-preference-based search.

Moreover, VE has a unique function to show and edit the user preference itself By using this function, users can see their own user preference and change the user preference to adjust the recommendation result.

Explanation of Component

A system overview of VE is shown in Figure 14. VE has four components: recommendation engine (RE), learning engine (LE), mining engine (ME), and database (DB).

The first is the RE. RE has matching functions such as content-meta-based search, context-aware search, or user-preference-based search. By using these functions, RE generates a recommendation list. The second is ME. ME has functions involving content profiling. By using these functions, ME analyzes the content itself to generate the content metadata and generates content profiles from this content metadata. The third is LE. LE has functions involving context learning and user preference learning. By using these functions, LE generates the user preference based on logs. The last is DB. User preferences, content metadata, and user logs are stored into this DB.

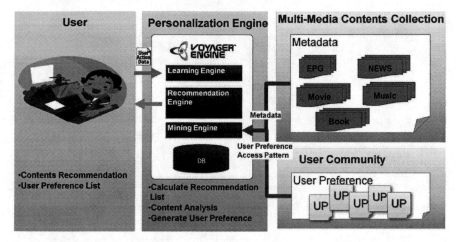

Fig. 14 System Overview of VE

Currently, VE has both client and server libraries. Practical client and server applications using VE are shown in the chapter titled "Example of Practical Applications."

Key Methods to Realize Cross-category Recommendation

In this section, we elaborate upon three methods: automatic metadata expansion (AME), indirect collaborative filtering (ICF), and referred collaborative filtering (RCF). As mentioned earlier, common metadata including specific or abstract metadata from various viewpoints gives us some hints to predict common user's preference in cross category. Moreover, community-based approaches like CF are also important for this purpose, although these approaches have shortcomings for completely new items. For the former one AME is proposed. AME is a method to expand content metadata having rich and abstract information. Regarding the latter one, VE employs ICF and RCF which cover shortcomings of CF. ICF is the method to extract user preference based on other users' preferences. RCF is a method to find relational content based on not only users' logs but also content similarities. These three methods are described in the following section.

AME

AME is a method to create new content metadata from original content metadata in cooperation with the associated concept dictionary (ACD). AME also automatically enhances the ACD if prior associated concept data is given. Figure 15 shows the conceptual diagram of the AME.

First the content metadata is only the original metadata, which is given by a content provider. The original metadata has some information such as cast, genre,

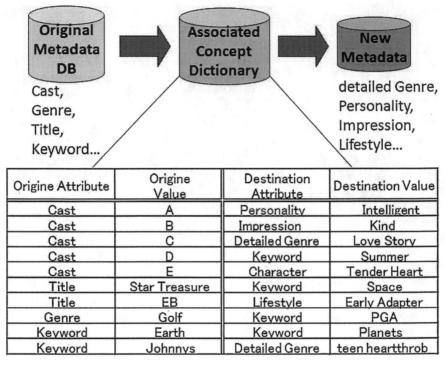

Origine Attribute	Origine Value	Destination Attribute	Destination Value
Cast	A	Personality	Intelligent
Cast	B	Impression	Kind
Cast	C	Detailed Genre	Love Story
Cast	D	Keyword	Summer
Cast	E	Character	Tender Heart
Title	Star Treasure	Keyword	Space
Title	EB	Lifestyle	Early Adapter
Genre	Golf	Keyword	PGA
Keyword	Earth	Keyword	Planets
Keyword	Johnnys	Detailed Genre	teen heartthrob

Fig. 15 Automatic Metadata Expansion

title, keywords, and so on. Content profiles (CP) are created from these data and they consist of some vectors like

CP (i) = (ContentId, Attribute Id, Value Id).

ContentId is a primary key to distinguish between content. Attribute is a class unit such as cast, genre, and so on. Value is an instance of the class. For example, comedy, sports, or drama is a value of an attribute of the genre. We can also find that A, B, C, D, or E is a value of an attribute of cast (Figure 15).

AME creates new content metadata, which are (ContentId, Destination Attribute, Destination Value), from the original content metadata, which are (ContentId, Origin Attribute, Origin Value). Consider the following example with content named 001. It has cast of Mr. A, which becomes vector = (001, Cast, Mr. A). The content gets new metadata (001, Personality, Intelligent) since the ACD declares that the customers think Mr. A is an intelligent person. Therefore, our system can use not only original content metadata but also these expanded metadata for recommendation purposes. These processes are performed in our system as a part of content metadata creation in the mining engine.

If the ACD has knowledge based on the lifestyle, for example a person who likes the title EB is Early Adapter or Follower likes Cast A, it is very efficient to apply this method to cross-category recommendation. Lifestyle is very suitable as common metadata. Moreover, if the content metadata is expanded using lifestyle knowledge, it becomes easier to realize advertisement recommendation.

ICF

The second method is ICF. ICF can recommend items unknown to the user. This has the same advantage as traditional CF methods, but the ICF also works well to recommend completely new items, less reusable items such as TV programs, and high merchandise turnover rate items.

As mentioned earlier, item-based CF selects recommendation items based on groups of similar items and user-based CF selects recommendation items based on groups of similar users. In either case, recommendation items are directly predicted based on these groups (Figure 16).

On the other hand, ICF does not directly select favorable items. ICF predicts the user preferences. These are registered as the expected user preferences as a part of the user preference vector. Then, the recommendation items are selected based on an existing recommendation method like the VSM by using not only the original user preferences but also the expected user preferences. This is why this method is called an "indirect" method (Figure 17).

ICF necessitates the following two steps:

1. The calculation of similarity between the users based on the original user preferences. Similarities between the users are calculated based on the original user preferences such as lifestyle, viewer's age, viewing style, cast, and so on, as mentioned earlier. Formula (2) indicates how to calculate the similarities between user X and user Y.

$$sim_{xy} = \frac{\sum_v (X_v - \overline{X})(Y_{vi} - \overline{Y})}{\sqrt{\sum_v (X_v - \overline{X})^2}\sqrt{\sum_v (Y_v - \overline{Y})^2}} \dots \quad (2)$$

X_v : User X's preference value of V
$\overline{X}$: User X's average preference value.

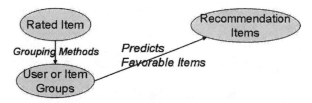

Fig. 16 Traditional (Direct) CF

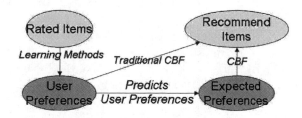

Fig. 17 ICF

When the number of users becomes considerable, we need to decrease the calculation effort to find similar users. In our system, hundreds of typical users can be found by employing some clustering algorithms before performing the similarity calculations.

2. Expectations of user preferences

   User preferences that are not contained with the original user preferences are predicted. They are referred to as the "expected user preferences." Formula (3) indicates how to calculate user X's expected user preference value of V. The expected user preferences are registered in the database for recommendation as a part of the user preference vectors.

$$ ExpectX_v = \overline{X} + \frac{\sum_N (N_v - \overline{N})sim_{XN}}{\sum_N |sim_{XN}|} \cdots \tag{3} $$

N : User who is similar to user X.

Therefore, the user can enjoy the recommendation based on not only the normal user preference vectors but also the expected user preference vectors. The user can find favorable items that she/he has never seen before. Moreover, this method is also beneficial to a system administrator of a recommendation system. This method is easy to apply to an existing recommendation system such as the VSM since the expected user preference vectors have the same style as normal user preference vectors and can be stored in the same table in the database. The system administrator can easily create a multi-algorithm recommendation system with ICF. In VE, ICF is used as a part of the user preference creation in the mining engine.

RCF

As mentioned earlier, CF methods cannot often work well with completely new items. RCF attempts to resolve this problem by using not only traditional CF-based similar items but also CBF-based similar items' CF-based similar items. RCF requires the following two steps:

1. The calculation of similar items based on traditional item-based CF for all of the items
2. The calculation of RCF-based similar items using CBF-based similar items and CF-based similar items
   The following four small steps are involved in this process.

   1) Select several attributes used for the CBF calculation from the metadata.
   2) By using these attributes, CBF-based similar items are calculated based on the cosine measure or inner product.
   3) By using equation (4), calculate the RCF-based similarity based on the CBF-based similarities calculated in step (2) and CF-based similarities calculated in step (1).

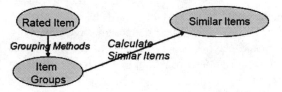

Fig. 18 RCF Step 1:Calculation of Similar Items Based on Traditional Item-based CF

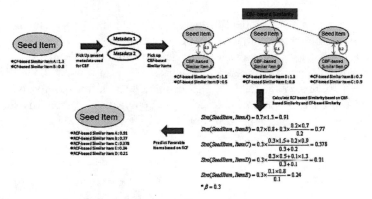

Fig. 19 RCF Step 2: Calculation of RCF-based Similar Items

$$Sim_{RCF}(A, B) = (1 - \beta)Sim_{CF}(A, B) + \beta \frac{\sum_{n \in N} Sim_{CBF}(A, n)Sim_{CF}(n, B)}{\sum_{n \in N} Sim_{CBF}(A, n)}$$

$$(4)$$

In this equation, A, B, and n are items. Here, n represents all of the CBF-based similar items for A. Moreover, Sim represents the calculation of similarity among the two items.

4) Based on step (3), RCF-based similar items are selected as the recommended items.

The images of this algorithm are shown in Figures 18 and 19.

Evidently, this method can work well for almost all of the items even if they are completely new items, unless the CBF-based similar items for the seed item do not exist or all of the CBF-based similar items do not have CF-based similar items. In VE, RCF is used as a part of content profiling in the mining engine.

Example of Practical Applications

Multimedia Content Recommendation

There have already been many systems and studies regarding multimedia recommendation. Here, we introduce two practical systems as examples for multimedia content recommendation: branco [33] and SensMe [34]. branco is an IPTV recommendation service. This recommendation function is realized using the VE. SensMe is an automatic music playlist generator used in mobile phones made by Sony Ericsson [35]. This application is based on the 12 Tone technology [36] developed by Sony Corporation.

branco

branco is an example of content-meta-based search and user-preference-based search. It is an IPTV service that uses IP multicast network and has several channels for broadcast. Therefore, a user can watch content like TV. Moreover, branco adopts an advertising model. Therefore, the users who can connect to the IP multicast network can use branco for free. The recommendation function for this service is realized using VE. As an example, a user-preference-based search is shown in Figure 20. The recommended programs by VE are shown as "anapita" which means just fitting you in Japanese.

SensMe

SensMe is an example of content-meta-based search. It is an automatic playlist generator from the music content of the user. An image of the SensMe application is shown in Figure 21. SensMe analyzes the music automatically and then extracts the music features like speed, tone and mood. After that, SensMe maps the music to an X–Y axis using tempo and mood. On this X–Y dimension, the user can see the music listened to by the user. Moreover, SensMe automatically generates 11 different

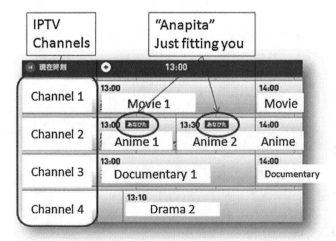

Fig. 20 Recommendation in branco

Fig. 21 SensMe

music channels such as "Morning," "Relax," and "Upbeat." Therefore, by choosing a channel instead of selecting individual tracks, the user can listen to a music playlist generated by SensMe as a recommendation.

Cross-category Recommendation

In this section, we introduce two systems as examples of cross-category recommendation services: VAIO Giga Pocket Digital [37] and TV Kingdom service [12]. Both these systems use the VE to realize recommendation functions. Giga Pocket Digital is a TV content manager for the VAIO system. The TV Kingdom service is an online TV guide service in So-net (So-net Entertainment Corporation). Giga Pocket Digital is an example of crossing categories only for user preference. TV Kingdom is an example of crossing categories not only for user preference but also for recommendation. The explanations for these two systems are described in the following two sections.

VAIO Giga Pocket Digital

Giga Pocket Digital is a TV content manager. Using this system, a user can watch TV programs in real time and record them manually by favorite keyword and user preference. In this system, the VE realizes content-meta-based search and user-preference-based search. For example, Figure 22 shows an image of the user-preference-based search.

VE recommends only TV programs, because this application handles only TV programs. However, VE learns the user preference from not only the user's behavior on this application but also what kind of music the user possesses. This means

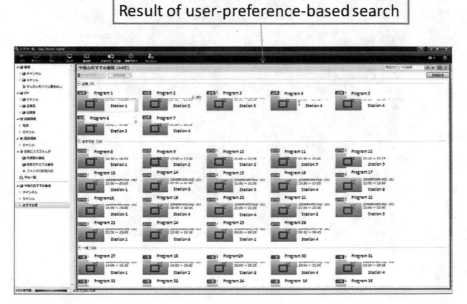

Fig. 22 User-preference-based search

that the user preference is generated from the user's behavior in the TV and music categories. It is very efficient to have cross-categories even if only the user preferences are crossed. By crossing the user preference for the TV and music categories, VE can recommend TV programs in which the user's favorite artist appears.

VE also renders the edit function for user preferences, as shown in Figure 23. This pane is called "My Carte". Here, the user can see his/her own preferences, such as frequently viewed casts, genres, and keywords. These casts include not only the persons watched by the user but also the persons whose music the user possesses. Users can also check their own TV-viewing style e.g., the user's frequently watched sports programs and infrequently watched drama programs. Moreover, users can edit their own preferences to customize the recommendation result.

TV Kingdom Service

TV Kingdom now has 800,000 unique users per month who enjoy not only a conventional TV guide but also a personalized TV guide, which can work together with a consumer electronics appliance or a personal computer. Figure 24 indicates the basic services offered by TV Kingdom.

1. A user can easily find TV programs and enjoy a useful EPG service having interesting functions, such as category-oriented list, recording-ranking list, and cast-oriented list.
2. The user can record and reserve TV programs on her/his local personal video recorder (PVR) through the TV Kingdom EPG by just clicking the iEPG icons.

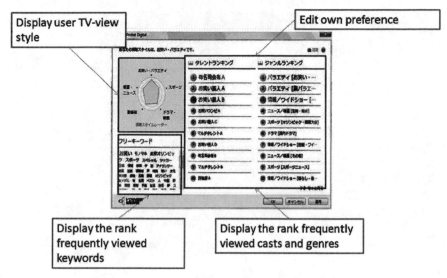

Fig. 23 My Carte

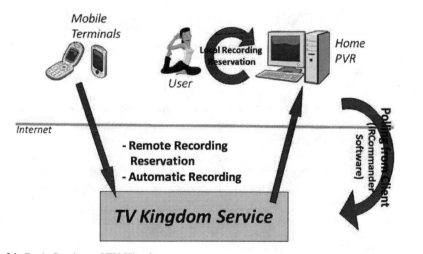

Fig. 24 Basic Services of TV Kingdom

3. The user can record programs on her/his local PVR even when away from home using a mobile PC or cell phones provided by companies such as NTT-DoCoMo, Softbank, and au.
4. The PVR automatically records the programs having the same keywords, such as genre, title, or cast, as registered by the user.

These basic functions are really useful for the PVR user. However, it is somewhat monotonous for the user to find out her/his favorite programs and make a reservation for recording. The automatic recording function resolves this problem on some

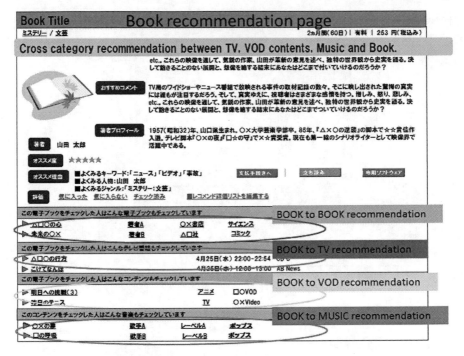

Fig. 25 Example of Cross-category Recommendation

level, but the user has to set her/his favorite keywords manually. We have tried to offer a better solution for this issue by using a VE. Here, content-meta-based search and user-preference-based search are realized by the VE.

Moreover, the TV Kingdom service offers not only TV program recommendations but also video, e-Book, DVD, CD, book, and cross-category recommendation among these categories. An image of the cross-category recommendation service is shown in Figure 25.

VE learns the user preferences from the user's behavior on all the categories. By employing these user preferences, the VE realizes cross-category recommendation among these categories.

Difficulties

There are three difficulties for realizing multimedia content recommendation and cross-category recommendation: how to extract features from content itself for multimedia content recommendation and how to generate common metadata and to merge each category's user preference for cross-category recommendation.

The first problem involves the extraction of features from the content itself. This creates difficulty in realizing multimedia content recommendation. It is necessary to develop feature extraction tools for each category such as music, picture or motion picture. For example, in the motion picture category, scene detection or face recognition tools are necessary to be extracted. However, it is cumbersome to implement these tools for each category. Moreover, sufficient metadata cannot be extracted from some content (e.g., motion picture) for efficient recommendation. Therefore, we need to consider recommendation algorithms using limited metadata when realizing recommendation functions for such content.

The second problem involves the generation of common metadata. This creates difficulty in realizing cross-category recommendation. We can easily employ person and keyword attributes as direct common metadata because almost all of these items have these attributes. However, it is difficult to select other common attributes, because most of these items have different metadata. Therefore, in order to realize a cross-category recommendation system, it is necessary to investigate what kind of metadata the system can actually use. If common metadata do not exist, we should consider an appropriate way to treat such content. For example, VE has personality data for each cast in the ACD and the content metadata are expanded using the AME. Lifestyle segmentation data also can be used as common metadata. Here, a large amount of time is normally required to generate such kinds of data. However, common metadata is a key to successfully realize cross-category recommendation. Therefore, it is very important to consider this issue.

The final problem is how to merge each category's user preference. This creates difficulty in realizing cross-category recommendation. Moreover, this is also essential for successfully realizing cross-category recommendation, because recommended items will be changed based on how to merge the user preference. The best way to merge depends on the system requirements. Therefore we determine how to merge the user preference based on the results of the evaluation experiments for each application and each system. In addition, on the basis of these results, we change the weights of each attribute such as genre and keyword.

Summary and Future Prospects

This article has introduced cross-category recommendation technologies for multimedia content. First, an overview of the recommendation technologies has been outlined. After that, practical applications and services realizing multimedia recommendation and cross-category recommendation have been described. Then, we have mentioned difficulties in cross-category recommendation for multimedia recommendation. These features are imperative to realize a good recommendation system.

Recently, multimedia recommendation technologies have become more important because many products and services that involve multimedia content have been developed. In the near future, cross-category recommendation technologies will be more important. For example these technologies are necessary to realize advertisement recommendations based on TV programs watched by the user or based on the music listened to by the user. Moreover, for enhancing user experience, these technologies will be important, too. This is because these technologies eliminate the differences among categories and support the users to explore the huge information space. In addition, we predict that not only cross-category recommendation but also cross-device recommendation will be important. By realizing cross-device recommendation, user experience can be improved. To turn this into reality, we may need to resolve several issues such as how to translate the user preference among devices. We may need to decide some abstract metadata schema and translation rules. We need to research these kinds of issues.

Acknowledgement We would like to thank our colleagues at the PAO Gp., Intelligent Systems Research Laboratory, System Technologies Laboratories, Corporate R&D, Sony Corporation and Sec.5, Intelligence Application Development Dept., Common Technology Division, Technology Development Group, Corporate R&D, Sony Corporation for their invaluable assistance.

References

1. NetCraft "January 2009 Web Server Survey." http://news.netcraft.com/archives/web_server_survey.html
2. P. Resnick et al. (1994). GroupLens: An Open Architecture for Collaborative Filtering of Netnews. Proc. ACM 1994 Conf. Computer Supported Cooperative Work, ACM Press, pp. 175–186.
3. G. Linden, B. Smith, and J. York (2003). Amazon.com Recommendations: Item-to-Item Collaborative Filtering. IEEE Internet Computing: Industry Report. http://dsonline.computer.org/0301/d/w1lind.htm
4. Last.fm. http://www.last.fm/
5. MusicStrands (MyStrands). http://www.mystrands.com/
6. SoundFlavor. http://www.soundflavor.com/
7. George Chang, Marcus J. Healey, James A.M. McHugh, Jason T.L. Wang, "Mining the World Wide Web", Kluwer Academic Publishers, 2001.
8. Jeongphee Yi, Tetsuya Nasukawa, Razvan Bunescu, Wayne Niblack, "Sentiment Analyzer: Extracting Sentiments about a Given Topic Using Natural Language Processing Techniques", ICDM 2003.
9. All Media Guide. http://www.allmediaguide.com/
10. Pandora Internet Radio. http://www.pandora.com/
11. Gracenote. http://www.gracenote.com/
12. TV Kingdom. (*in Japanese*) http://tv.so-net.ne.jp/
13. T. Tsunoda, M. Hoshino, "Automatic Metadata Expansion and Indirect Collaborative Filtering for TV Program Recommendation System", Euro ITV 2006.
14. Google. http://www.google.com/
15. Google Page Rank technology. http://www.google.com/corporate/tech.html
16. Milan Petkovic, Willem Jonker, "Content-Based Video Retrieval", Kluwer Academic Publishers, 2002.
17. M. Flickner et al., "Query by Image and Video. Content: The QBIC System", IEEE Computer, Vol. 28, No. 9, pp. 23–32, 1995.
18. J. R. Smith, S.-F. Chang, "VisualSEEk: A Fully Automated Content-Based Image Query System", ACM Multimedia, 1996, pp. 87–98.
19. Yossi Rubner, Leonidas J. Guibas, Carlo Tomasi, "The Earth Mover's Distance, Multi-Dimensional Scaling, and Color-Based Image Retrieval", in Proceedings of the ARPA Image Understanding Workshop, New Orleans, LA, May 1997, pp. 661–668.
20. JSEG: Color Image Segmentation. http://vision.ece.ucsb.edu/segmentation/jseg/

21. David G. Lowe, "Distinctive Image Features from Scale Invariant Keypoints", International Journal of Computer Vision, Vol. 60, No. 2, pp. 91–110, 2004.
22. Sony's Picture Motion Browser. http://www.sony.co.uk/product/digital-photography/article/id/ 1224842106509
23. Aymeric Zils, Francois Pachet, "Automatic Extraction of Music Descriptors from Acoustic Signals Using EDS", in Proceedings of the 116th AES Convention, May 2004.
24. Sony's Hard-drive-based Music Systems "Giga Juke." http://www.sony.co.uk/product/hdd-audio
25. P. Cano, E. Battle, T. Kalker, J. Haitsma, "A Review of Algorithm for Audio Fingerprinting", in Workshop on Multimedia Signal Processing, 2002.
26. Shazam. http://www.shazam.com/
27. Ericsson: System Overview Mobile Positioning System (MPS). http://www.ericsson.com/mobilityworld/sub/open/technologies/mobile_positioning/about/mps_system_ overview/
28. Brian Clarkson, Alex Pentland, "Unsupervised Clustering of Ambulation Audio and Video", ICASSP 98.
29. Tom M. Mitchell, "Machine Learning", WCB/McGraw-Hill, 1997, pp. 177–184.
30. N. Yamamoto, M. Saito, M. Miyazaki, H. Koike, "Recommendation Algorithm Focused on Individual Viewpoints", IEEE CCNC 2005 pp. 65–70, 2005.
31. Amazon. http://www.amazon.com/
32. Voyager Engine.[1] (*in Japanese*) from http://www.sony.co.jp/SonyInfo/technology/technology/theme/contents_01.html
33. Sony Marketing (Japan) Inc. (2009). branco home page (*in Japanese*) http://www.branco.tv/
34. SensMe. (*in Japanese*)   http://www.sony.co.jp/SonyInfo/technology/technology/theme/contents_01.html
35. Sony Ericsson Mobile Communications AB. http://www.sonyericsson.com
36. 12 Tone Technology. (*in Japanese*) http://www.sony.co.jp/SonyInfo/technology/technology/theme/12tonealalysis_01.html
37. Sony Corporation (2008). VAIO Giga Pocket Digital homepage (*in Japanese*) http://www.vaio. sony.co.jp/Products/Solution/GigaPocketDigital/

---

[1] "Voyager Engine" is a trademark of Sony Corporation and So-net Entertainment Corporation

Chapter 3
Semantic-Based Framework for Integration and Personalization of Television Related Media

Pieter Bellekens, Lora Aroyo, and Geert-Jan Houben

Introduction

The online information locomotive drives on at an ever increasing pace. Constantly we see expansion of existing methods and systems, while at the same time, new innovations and techniques sprout out of nowhere. These changes bring new possibilities and challenges that affect the whole media chain: from content production, via distribution, to last but not least the end-user (the consumer). Lately however, the consumer himself transformed more and more into a content producer, as shown by Berman [4], making the circle round and the speed of information growth even larger. Subsequently, this breaks the traditional business model where companies and institutions are the sole content providers. We describe in this paper our research focusing on the synergy between available content on various media sources and the consumer at home who wants to experience multimedia content through a connected media centre.

As an effect, the new forms of home media that emerge as digital systems are converging. Different content, e.g., from TV, social networks, music, homemade images and videos, is no longer bound to separate devices or to local storage, and the development of the Internet makes the media boundaries become less limiting. As envisioned by for instance IBM [4], the future media may become more pervasive and offer a more ubiquitous and immersive experience, as increasing technological sophistication brings new media environments. The transfer to digital content along

L. Aroyo (✉)
Department of Computer Science, Free University of Amsterdam, Amsterdam, Netherlands
e-mail: l.m.aroyo@cs.vu.nl

P. Bellekens
Department of Mathematics & Computer Science, Eindhoven University of Technology, Eindhoven, Netherlands
e-mail: p.a.e.bellekens@tue.nl

G.-J. Houben
Department of Software Technology, Delft University of Technology, Delft, Netherlands
e-mail: g.j.p.m.houben@tudelft.nl

B. Furht (ed.), *Handbook of Multimedia for Digital Entertainment and Arts*,
DOI 10.1007/978-0-387-89024-1_3, © Springer Science+Business Media, LLC 2009

with technologies and standards like DVB1[1], HDTV, voice over IP, Blu-ray[2] and TV-Anytime[3] create opportunities to bring new interactivity to the traditional TV concept and change it drastically. The television industry always has been a conservative one. It has not yet experienced a major revolution for the past fifty years, which constitutes a strong contrast to the Internet which has quickly evolved from mere textual information to multimedia content. We believe that using Semantic Web technology in the concept of TV content interaction may provide a change from a traditional one-way communication to a two-way communication where the user changes from a passive viewer to a more active participant and program structures change from fixed to dynamic.

In this paper we try to identify requirements, opportunities and problems in home media centers and we propose an approach to address them by describing an intelligent home media environment. The major issues investigated are coping with the information overflow in the current provision of TV programs and channels and the need for personalization to specific users by adapting to their age, interests, language abilities, and various context characteristics. The research presented in this paper follows from a collaboration between Eindhoven University of Technology, the Philips Applied Technologies group and Stoneroos Interactive Television. The work has been partially carried out within the ITEA-funded European project Passepartout, which also includes partners like Thomson, INRIA and ETRI.

In the following chapter we describe the motivation and research problem in relation to related work, followed by an illustrative use case scenario. Afterwards, we explain our data model which starts with explaining the TV-Anytime structure and its enrichments with semantic knowledge from various ontologies and vocabularies. The data model description then serves as the background for understanding our proposed system architecture SenSee. Afterwards we go deeper into the user modeling part and explain how our personalization approach works. The latter elaborates on a design targeting interoperability and on semantic techniques for enabling intelligent context-aware personalization. In the implementation chapter we describe some practical issues as well as our main interface showcase, iFanzy. Future work and conclusions end this chapter.

Related Work

We investigate the design of a home media architecture of connected devices that can provide access to a wide range of media sources, yet at the same time avoid an overflow of information for the user. In our framework called SenSee, for *sensing* the user and *seeing* the content, and the iFanzy application (a personalized EPG running on top of SenSee), we aim to connect different devices, such as shared

---

[1] http://www.dvb.org

[2] http://www.blu-ray.com

[3] http://www.tv-anytime.org

(large) screens with set-top boxes, personal (small) handheld devices and biosensor-based interfaces, and different media sources like IP, broadcast and local storage. This intentionally goes beyond the traditional limited solution of a single TV screen and simple remote control and thus creates the foundation for an ambient home environment to collect various data about the users and to subsequently use this data for the personalization of his/her interaction with the TV content. Related work on connected homes can be found in the field of ambient intelligence, investigated for instance at the Philips HomeLab [9].

Regarding the information overflow aspect, we assume that the amount of available digital content will increase enormously with the current digital development, as also indicated by Murugesan and Deshpande [18]. Both paper program guides and simple EPGs are thus likely to turn inefficient in terms of helping the user in choosing from an overwhelming amount of content, a situation previously also shown by both Chorianopoulos and O' Sullivan et al. [7, 20]. This creates a need for media systems to support the user by providing intelligent search and recommendations to propose the most relevant and interesting programs. Similar research focused on filtering for interactive TV systems in home environments have previously been done by e.g., Goren-Bar and Glinansky [10]. Here content filtering and user stereotypes were used for capturing and using user preferences.

Various researchers furthermore emphasize that there is a need for personalization in dealing with a vast amount of TV content [1]. We believe that a personalization approach in home media centers is significant in order to handle the user's preferences as basis for the interaction both regarding content and devices. Since users differ in ages, interests, abilities and language preferences, it is important that these preferences can be reflected in the system. For instance, an eight year old person will have very different favorite programs than an adult, and a given user might want the movies to always be displayed on the biggest screen, but private content only on his or her handheld device. By creating a user model, as described by Kobsa [13], for each user of the system, such personal preferences may be stored. This needs to capture both a user profile, with the user's preferences, and a user context, which describes the current situation that the user is in, for example whether the user is alone or with a group, what the available devices are at the moment, what the time is, what the location is etc. [27, 26, 25] argue that not taking contextual information into account for recommendations, seriously limits the relevance of the results, and as in SenSee and iFanzy, they advocate context-awareness as a promising approach to enhance the performance of recommenders. While Yap et al. [27] and Tung et al. [25] illustrate their framework with a restaurant recommender, which takes location, weather and restaurant-related data into account, Woerndl and Groh [26] apply context-aware recommender systems (by using location and acceleration) in the domain of inter-networked cars. The models furthermore constitute a necessary requirement for enabling intelligent filtering of content to make recommendations like explained by van Setten [24]. By this we mean finding and suggesting content that should be interesting for the user, while filtering out unwanted or uninteresting information. Various filtering techniques for recommending movies have previously been explored by Masthoff [15], in which several user models are combined to create group filtering. Other related work is the PTVPlus online recommendation system for the television domain by O'Sullivan et al. [20] and the Adaptive Assistant for Personalized TV by Yu and Zhou [27]. However, in general when new users (with empty profiles) are introduced, recommender systems have a hard time since they miss essential information to provide recommendations. To fill this informational gap, we make use of social networks like Hyves[4] as they often harbor a vast amount of useful preferences and interests. Also in work from Alshabib et al. [1] a social network (LinkedIn) is used to aggregate ratings based on the structure of the network, by calculating the neighborhood of users.

Apart from supplying semantic models of the user, it is also necessary to have sufficient metadata descriptions of the content. This constitutes the basis for content classification, i.e., sorting the content into different types like fiction, non-fiction, news, sports, etc. Intelligent search and filtering of content moreover benefit from metadata descriptions suitable for reasoning, to deduce new information and to enrich content search. Current ongoing research in this area by the W3C Multimedia Annotation on the Semantic Web Task Force has been described by Stamou et al. [23].

Similar research as presented in this paper has furthermore been performed by Hong and Lim [12] who also propose using TV-Anytime for handling content in a personalized way. However, they focus on broadcasted content, whereas we also consider content from IP and removable media like Blu-ray. Furthermore, their solution for content search also uses keywords and user history to recommend content, although the architecture differs in that all processing occurs at a metadata server.

As will be described later, we propose the modeling of TV content with the use of ontologies. Relevant related work in this field can therefore be found in the domain of the Semantic Web. Necib and Freytag [19] have focused on using ontologies in query processing with a similar approach to ours, which aims at refining search queries with synonyms (and yet avoiding homonyms). However, we intend to take this one step further in our process as we also use other semantically related concepts and a measurement for semantic closeness.

Application Scenario

In this section we describe a scenario to illustrate the target functionality of our demonstrator. The setting is in the home of a European, well-off family in the year 2010, which is living in a region outside their original parental background. While they wish for the children to integrate with the local community and live and learn from their neighbors, they also value their heritage (linguistic, cultural and religious), to effectively communicate with distant relatives and friends. The family consists of a mother, a father, a four year old child, a deaf nine year old, and a

---

[4] http://www.hyves.nl

teenager. The parents are determined that the children should be effectively multi-lingual and multi-cultural, and will invest time to adapt the multimedia content in the home. They therefore act as media guides and to some extent teachers for their children, by selecting and adapting the content. Since the parents have immigrated to the region, they will have a different preference of content than the default local selection and they use their home media centre to include also programs from their original home area, e.g., for news, music and movies. They may also choose to alter the language or subtitles of the content.

As the family gathers for a movie night together, the home media centre has suggested a movie that suits each family member's preference and interest. The mother has briefly scanned the story of the movie and discovered that the ending is in her opinion not suitable for the children. She therefore changes to an alternative ending. As they start the movie, they all together use a shared big screen. Although they use subtitles on this shared screen, this evening the deaf child also includes additional sign language on his personal small screen. The teenager on the other hand needs to practice her second language so her parents asked her this time to listen to an alternative language version with her headphones. Although they enjoy the movie together, the father also wants to follow a live soccer game broadcast, and therefore uses his own handheld screen to view this private video stream. The media devices in the home are all connected to the ambient home media environment.

TV-Anytime

A content structure which goes beyond a fixed linear time structure and allows multiple languages, alternative versions, etc. puts high demands on the content model. It needs to have a dynamic structure, rich metadata, and be suitable for various media. We believe that the TV-Anytime[5] standard can serve as the basis for such requirements and therefore we have built our demonstrator upon the TV-Anytime concepts. TV-Anytime is a full and synchronized set of XML specifications established by the TV-Anytime forum built to enable search, selection, acquisition and rightful use of content from both broadcast and online services. It basically consists out of two main parts usually referred to as Phase I and Phase II, each serving their specific goals.

TV-Anytime Phase I

The TV-Anytime Phase I specification is a very extensive metadata schema which describes all content retrieved by the system—a fundamental feature for searching

---

[5] http://www.tv-anytime.org

and filtering. A program description consists out of a set of information tables where each describes a specific aspect of a program P:

- ProgramInformationTable: Overview of metadata fields like title, synopsis, etc.
- GroupInformationTable: Describes the groups P belongs to
- ProgramLocationTable: States where/when P can be found/will be broadcasted
- ServiceInformationTable: States who is the rightful owner/broadcaster of P
- CreditsInformationTable: Contains all the credits of people in P
- ProgramReviewTable: Lists of reviews of P
- SegmentInformationTable: Contains metadata about specific segments of P
- PurchaseInformationTable: Contains the information about how to obtain P

TV-Anytime is built to suit the needs of the future. It contains constructs to model metadata which is currently not widely available yet, e.g. metadata describing specific scenes (segments) within a specific program. This property proves that the TV-Anytime specification is ready when the television market evolves and more metadata will be generated. Among these the tables, the most important one for us is the ProgramInformationTable as it contains all the essential program metadata. In the following example we show an abbreviated example of the metadata in this table for an arbitrary program P:

```
<ProgramInformation programId="crid://bds.tv/13594946">
    <BasicDescription>
        <Title>All Stars</Title>
        <Synopsis>Football, friendship and ...</Synopsis>
        <Genre href="urn:tva:md:cs:ContentCS:2005:3.5.7">
            <Name>Comedy</Name>
        </Genre>
        <Genre href="urn:tva:md:cs:ContentCS:2005:3.2.3.12">
            <Name>Football (soccer)</Name>
        </Genre>
        <Language>EN</Language>
        <ProductionDate>2008-10-11 20:00:00</ProductionDate>
        <ProductionLocation>London</ProductionLocation>
    </BasicDescription>
</ProgramInformation>
```

Every ProgramInformationTable consists of a list of ProgramInformation components, and each has a BasicDescription block which contains P's main description. Apart from technical descriptions such as the screen aspect ratio and the number of audio channels (not shown in the example), we see here for example a title, a synopsis and a list of genres.

In order to keep a grip on what metadata creators use as values in these TV-Anytime fields, the TV-Anytime specification contains a set of controlled term hierarchies which are the only valid values for such properties. A good example is the genre field. The genre description in TV-Anytime is a fine graded taxonomy structure, going from general concepts like fiction/non-fiction down to specific categories in the leaf nodes of the structure (typically well known genres like comedy, drama, daily news, weather forecast, etc.). It should for example be avoided that people can create their own genres considering that one wants to keep interoperability and consistency between various content descriptions intact. The following example shows a part of the genre hierarchy:

```
<Term termID="3.1">
    <Name>NON-FICTION/INFORMATION</Name>
    <Term termID="3.1.1">
            <Name>News</Name>
            <Term termID="3.1.1.9">
                    <Name>Sport News</Name>
                    <Definition>News of sport events</Definition>
            </Term>
    </Term>
</Term>
```

Every genre has an id which exemplifies its depth in the tree and shows which other genre is the parent (e.g. genre 3.1 is the parent of genre 3.1.1). The genre 'sport news' is a specialization of the genre 'news' which in turn belongs to the group of 'non-fiction/information' genres.

To identify a program in TV-Anytime, the notion of a Content Reference Identifier (CRID) is used, following an RFC standard [8]. The program above for example is identified by the CRID "crid://bds.tv/13594946". With such a CRID, which always uniquely identifies a program, we can retrieve the program's metadata. TV-Anytime describes a Metadata Service (MS) which is responsible for the provision of metadata. For every CRID existing, the MS can provide a metadata description, given of course that whoever created the program belonging to this CRID made this description publicly. However, people cannot just start creating CRIDs, as this typically is a process which should be centrally controlled. Therefore, the TV-Anytime specification describes the concept of a CRID Authority (CA) which main purpose is to watch over CRID creation. Everybody who wants to create a new program instance, first needs to ask for a new unique CRID at the CA. In turn, this CRID can then be used to both refer to this program and to obtain its metadata via the MS.

TV-Anytime Phase II

Currently, an important evolution in data retrieval is that different pieces (or sets) of content are being linked together. Whether this is done via similarity properties for recommendations (e.g. Amazon's "Maybe you are also interested in...") or via clustering (e.g. connecting all episodes of Friends), it all serves the need for proper navigation through structured information. Also TV-Anytime accommodates these kinds of data structuring via its packaging concept, described in Phase II of the specification. A package is an interconnected structure where each piece of content is referred to by a CRID, which can here be used for several purposes. Besides identifying program instances, CRIDs are also used to define locators, which give the actual location where the content is stored, or for referring to some other set of CRIDs. The TV-Anytime package is thus a structured collection of related CRIDs.

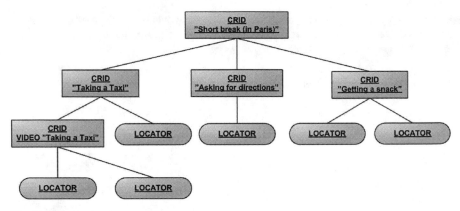

Fig. 1 Package structure

The data model of a package adopts the multi-level structure of the MPEG-21 Digital Item Declaration Language [6], i.e., a container-item-component structure, with some extensions.

For example, a language course structured as a package could be organized and divided into chapters and sections where each chapter or section is identified by a CRID. Figure 1 shows an example "Short break in Paris" language learning package consisting of three exercises, where one of them has additional video clips. Each content element is not stored in the package itself, but is referenced using a locator. Thus some part can be distributed on a disc and another via IP. The main content of the language course could for instance be on a disc that the user has bought, while extra interactive content and trailer for the next course may be distributed via IP. This packaging structure is very dynamic since parts can easily be modified or extended, for example the course could be extended with a new chapter by simply adding a CRID reference. Since packages are complex collections of CRIDs, they need to be resolved to discover which items are contained, as well as to get the locator(s) when viewing the actual content. This resolving process is also performed by the previously described CRID Authority. The response of such resolving request is an XML document containing a list of all CRIDs and locators in which it resolved. Like can be seen in the figure, one object can reside in multiple locations, such that in a certain situation the most appropriate content location in terms of availability, quality, connection speed, etc. can be chosen.

Semantically Enriched Content Model

The content metadata previously described, is fundamental for searching and filtering of content. However, we imagine that due to the potentially vast amount of content, it is not enough to simply describe and classify the content, there must also be more intelligent ways of handling it. We therefore propose adding semantic

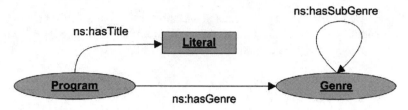

Fig. 2 RDF Graph

knowledge in addition to the TV-Anytime content model, which adds possibilities for reasoning and deducing information about the content. The techniques we have used originate from the research area of the Semantic Web, firstly proposed by Berners-Lee et al. [5], where ontologies are used for modeling semantic relations between concepts. We have used OWL, the Web Ontology Language described by McGuinnes and van Harmelen [16], to make a semantically enriched content model that serves two main purposes—providing us with the ability to:

- Reason and query the TV content
- Add semantic knowledge about the application domain to achieve intelligent behavior of applications

OWL, which is a knowledge representation language, is usually serialized using the RDF syntax. RDF (Resource Description Framework) [14] is a metadata data model specification which follows the XML (tag-based) syntax. Basically, RDF is comprised out of two main building blocks, namely resources and properties. Resources are used to model every possible object like persons, pictures, movies, trees, cars, etc. while properties describe the relations between those concepts. In this way, an RDF model represents a labeled directed graph where every edge in the graph is modeled as a triple consisting of a Subject, Predicate and Object. In Figure 2 we see an example of such a graph where we have two resources (Program and Genre), three properties (hasTitle, hasGenre and hasSubGenre) and one Literal (a String type which contains the value of the property).

Since from origin the TV-Anytime specification is available in regular XML, we needed to translate the specification to RDF/OWL. Moreover, we translated both the TV-Anytime metadata specification as well as the controlled term hierarchies (e.g. the genre classification) in order to incorporate it into the system and enable querying. When having the genre hierarchy as a TV-Anytime genre classification ontology it is possible to exploit the structure and for example deduce that "archery" and "climbing" are both types of a "sports" genre. Otherwise, without being able to use the linkage between the genre classification concepts, applications will not 'know' any semantic difference or connection between them. This facility is important for being able to group content into semantically related collections, which in turn is useful when presenting and navigating available content. In the next example we show the translation of our previous 'Sport news' genre example in RDF/OWL. To exemplify the hierarchy we make use of the "skos:narrower" and "skos:broader" relations which tell us which is a more specific or more general genre respectively. Note that we also introduced new relations (e.g. between the genres 'Sport News' and 'Sport' we have added a "skos:related" relation) by making further use of the SKOS vocabulary. Such relations make the graph more interconnected, and in turn allow us to find more related content.[6]

```
<TVAGenres:genre ID="TVAGenres:3.1.1.9">
    <rdfs:label>Sport News</rdfs:label>
    <skos:broader rdf:resource="TVAGenres:3.1.1"/>
    <skos:related rdf:resource="TVAGenres:3.2"/>
    <skos:definition>News of sport events</skos:definition>
</TVAGenres:genre>

<TVAGenres:genre ID="TVAGenres:3.1.1">
    <rdfs:label>News</rdfs:label>
    <skos:narrower rdf:resource="TVAGenres:3.1.1.9"/>
    <skos:broader rdf:resource="TVAGenres:3.1"/>
</TVAGenres:genre>

<TVAGenres:genre ID="TVAGenres:3.2">
    <rdfs:label>Sport</rdfs:label>
    <skos:related rdf:resource="TVAGenres:3.1.1.9"/>
</TVAGenres:genre>
```

In TV-Anytime there are a number of literal properties which have a meaningless string as value. Even properties which lend themselves perfectly to contain structured information like for example start and end time of a program. Therefore, we have defined mappings from the TV-Anytime annotation elements to other existing ontologies to get as much structured information as possible. Knowledge structures describing time concepts, geography concepts, and lexical concepts improve our possibilities to reason and query enormously. Mapping time concepts to the time ontology devised by Hobbs and Pan [11], e.g., mapping the TV-Anytime annotation <productionDate> to corresponding time ontology concepts of year, month, day, hour, etc. enables temporal reasoning over the data. The following example shows such a mapping from a XML datetime property to an TIME:DateTimeDescription instance:

```
<productionDate>2008-10-11 20:00:00</productionDate>

<TIME:DatetimeDescription ID="TimeDesc1">
    <year>2008</year>
    <month>10</month>
    <day>11</day>
    <hour>20</hour>
    <minute>0</minute>
    <second>0</second>
</TIME:DatetimeDescription>
```

---

[6] http://www.w3.org/2004/02/skos/

If we then, in a similar way, define specific intervals like "noon" or "evening" (which are instances of the class TIME:ProperInterval which has a beginning and an end), a reasoner can deduce for example from a program's startTime property which programs will start today in the evening.

Apart of having mappings from XML tags to ontology concepts, this is also useful when we are searching in text fields e.g., the synopsis. For example, a user might look for movies that take place in the 1970s. A simple search would only find those movies of which metadata explicitly mention some year in this decade (with a number 197*). However, by using concepts from the time ontology we can also find those movies that instead wrote "the seventies" (which is an alternative label to the class). A geographical ontology, like the Geonames geographical repository[7], can likewise be used when searching for programs from "Europe", where we extend the search with all the member countries to improve the results. When searching for programs about the region the user is located in, a geographical ontology gives us the area to use and possibly neighboring cities. As a third ontology, a lexical ontology helps to find synonyms of terms. Therefore we have incorporated the WordNet linguistic ontology by Miller [17] in OWL. To describe people and their interests, we use the FOAF[8] specification.

In Figure 3 we see a small part of the structure of the SenSee content model. The model is divided in three separate layers which we will explain one by one. The top level contains high level classes among which most are coming from

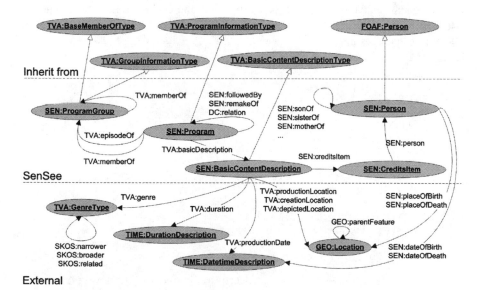

Fig. 3 Part of the SenSee Content Model

---

[7] http://www.geonames.org/

[8] http://www.foaf-project.org/

the TV-Anytime specification. They all describe an object like for example a program (TVA:ProgramInformationType), a group (TVA:GroupInformationType) and a person (FOAF:Person). However, sometimes these classes do not contain all the properties or semantics which are required to support the functionality facilitated by the SenSee framework. Therefore, we introduced a second layer, the SenSee layer (which can be seen in the middle part of the figure), which inherits the semantics from the top layer and extents the semantics. In this middle layer we see SenSee classes (with the namespace 'SEN') which e.g. also describe programs (SEN:Program), groups (SEN:ProgramGroup) and persons (SEN:Person), however they also have extra properties next to the ones they inherit. The SenSee program for example get additional properties like 'SEN:remakeOf' (used mainly for films) or 'DC:relation' (a Dublin Core[9] (DC) property exemplifying that two programs are related) while the person class get extra relation which can exist between different persons (like SEN:sonOf, etc.). The bottom layer in Figure 3 exemplifies all the classes from other domain ontologies which are used in our model. Like previously shown we use classes from the Owl time ontology to describe points in time (TIME:DatetimeDescription) and duration (TIME:DurationDescription), from the geographical ontology (Geonames) to describe a location (GEO:Location) and from the TV-Anytime genre hierarchy. In the figure we can see various properties of SenSee classes exploiting the semantics of these domain ontologies. The Time classes are used for e.g. a program's production date, but also for the date of birth/death of a person. The Geonames location class can be used for various creation/production locations of a program, but also to indicate the place of birth/death of a person.

Coming back to our previous example, the OWL version of the program P described by this data model, which makes use of these ontological enrichments, would then look like:

```
<SEN:Program ID="crid://bds.tv/13594946">
    <TVA:basicDescription rdf:resource="Desc1"/>
</SEN:Program>

<TVA:BasicContentDescription ID="Desc1">
    <TVA:Title>All Stars</TVA:Title>
    <TVA:Synopsis>Football, friendship and...</TVA:Synopsis>
    <TVA:Genre rdf:resource="TVAGenres:3.5.7"/>
    <TVA:Genre rdf:resource="TVAGenres:3.2.3.12"/>
    <TVA:Language>EN</TVA:Language>
    <TVA:ProductionDate rdf:resource="TIME:TimeDesc1"/>
    <TVA:ProductionLocation rdf:resource="GEO:2643743"/>
</TVA:BasicContentDescription>
```

The main difference with the XML description is that we can now refer to the concepts in the respective domain ontologies where the full semantics of the concepts are defined. The genres now refer to the OWL version of the genre hierarchy, the production date is a concept in the TIME ontology like defined above and the

---

[9] http://dublincore.org/

production location now points to a concept in the Geonames geographical ontology where '2643743' is the id for "London". The CRID also is here in place as the global unique identifier, in the Semantic Web referred to as a URI.

Our approach is not limited to use only one ontology per domain. Geographical ontologies sometimes focus on listing countries while others specialize on defining orientations (like "westOf" or "isPartOf"). One time ontology may focus on time zones while another concentrates on hour, day, month, year, etc. By combining the strengths of different ontologies, we can obtain a rich ontological structure. Furthermore, we intend to use specific domain ontologies that model typical topics, with one ontology for each major genre. For example, a "sports" ontology can model knowledge about sports equipment, famous players, and well-known competitions. Such domain ontologies are an additional source of knowledge that when searching for content can be used to semantically enrich the search. Our basic idea in this respect is to go beyond keyword matching, which usually is limited to finding only results which contain the exact keyword.

This flexible semantic structure is the foundation that allows the user to navigate and browse the vast content sets nowadays available. The content we retrieve comes from external data sources like IMDb (a vast dataset listing movies, persons and TV programs) and XMLTV (a format to describe broadcasted program metadata). This integration of TV content and background information both from various heterogeneous sources provides the transparent knowledge structure needed for the desired functionalities.

Personalized Home Media Center

Design of Personalized Home Media Center

We present in this section the architecture of the SenSee system and its components in Figure 4. Like can be seen in the figure, this architecture consists out of four main parts: Content Sources, the main SenSee server, a number of external services and various client applications.

The Content Sources layer represents in our design the input from different content distribution channels, where each has its own specific properties. For example, the "Portable Media" input groups all portable discs which are the system's primary input channel of High Definition content. This is due to its high storage capacity, where we have chosen the Blu-ray disc as technology for this task. The IP channel can offer any type of content and has naturally the advantage of two-way communication, which makes IP well suited for interactive applications and distributing home made content to others. The SenSee demonstrator from the Passepartout project supports the most commonly used IP protocols of HTTP, FTP, streaming media and peer-to-peer technology. Moreover, SenSee is not limited to data described in the TV-Anytime format alone. It allows for retrieval and parsing of content from

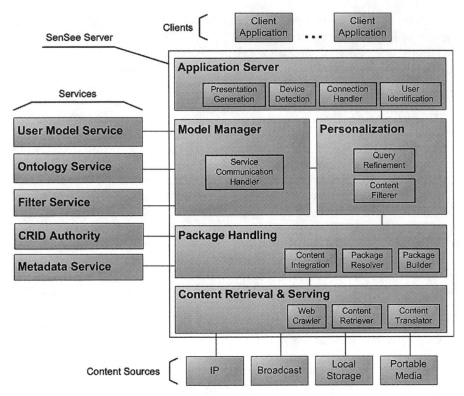

Fig. 4 SenSee Architecture

various heterogeneous sources, which publish their content in different formats and languages.

The SenSee server is the central part of the design which has the responsibility for integrating content from various sources, providing client applications access to the content, keeping track of user data and adaptation functionality. To separate responsibilities in the server design we created four interconnected layers. At the bottom we have the Content Retrieval & Serving layer for retrieval and integration of content, on top of that the Package Handling for transforming content and resolving packages, the Personalization layer which refines queries and filters content, followed by the Application Server providing access to the lower layers and identifying both users and devices.

The main purpose of the Content Retrieval & Serving (CRS) layer is to retrieve content from various sources, as well as publishing content provided by the user. This comprises both the actual audio/video content and the textual information (metadata) describing the content. The content input may be of various formats, such as time-bound sources like broadcast, read-only sources like CD, DVD and Blu-Ray, IP sources, local storage (e.g. personal content, saved content) and peer content (content made available by connected peers). The CRS layer thus contains interfaces for retrieving content from each one of the specific sources that are supported. However, like previously mentioned, not all content is retrieved in the TV-Anytime format, so one of the main responsibilities of this layer is to make all incoming content consistent with our central TV-Anytime based data model. This conversion deals with three issues:

- The format of the data can be diverse (e.g. structured text files, XML, RDF) and is thus converted to RDF/OWL
- The semantics of the data can differ per source (e.g. different sources work with different data schemas like XML-TV) and is translated to TV-Anytime
- All property values which can be describes by specific domain ontologies like time fields, geographical references, etc. are replaced by a URI pointing to the correct instance of the respective vocabulary

By converting incoming metadata, to our central data model we create a consistent transparent set of metadata ready for integration. Furthermore, the added semantics help the system to 'understand' its meaning.

As the CRS layer delivers consistent sets of TV-Anytime compliant metadata descriptions, the Package Handling layer (PH) takes this information and tries to rearrange it into packages. To do so, this layer has connections to the Metadata Service (MS) and the CRID Authority (CA). However, trying to create packages on-the-fly is not trivial. Moreover, it was not even considered by the TV-Anytime forum. They envisioned that content creators would publish the metadata of their content as packages themselves. E.g. Disney could make a "Lion King" package where you can find the three movies, the soundtrack, imagery, character descriptions, etc. Currently however, nobody is creating packages. There is the case of the R&D section of BBC, which is called BBC Backstage, where they publish their channel's metadata in TV-Anytime format, but only Phase I descriptions are made and no packages. Therefore we attempt to create packages automatically and approach this as a clustering problem. Thanks to the conversion of data to RDF/OWL in the CRS layer and the enrichments with extra domain ontologies, creating a package basically becomes nothing more than querying our semantic graph and ordering the results. If we for example search in our structure for "Jennifer Aniston", and find the resource describing her, we can easily find all content which has a relation to this resource. This relation can describe her as an actress in the program, director of a movie, singer of a song, guest in a talk show, etc. After retrieving these programs, the structure of the package can be formed by ordering the results. Ordering by name would put all the "Friends" episodes together, ordering by relation puts all instances together in which she acts, sings, appears, etc. In this way we can simulate packages based on the user's question.

A package normally provides links to the actual content by means of the TV-Anytime locators. However, this proves to be difficult or sometimes even impossible, as it requires agreements with the content owners and is thus only possible in a commercially deployed application. Therefore we currently only use content which is online available for free.

Via the CRS and the PH, we are now able to retrieve, integrate and provide content elements. The next layer shown in the architecture is the Personalization Layer. This layer allows for various access (like searching, getting recommendations, etc.) to the data and presents the personalized results to the user. This reflects a passive role of the user as a receiver of recommendations and/or an active role as searcher. To do so, the system must have some understanding of the user on one hand, and some understanding of relevant domains on the other. For instance, the system must be able to 'know' that the user likes African wildlife programs, or that the user wants to see the weather forecast in the morning but not necessarily at other times. Here, the system must have a way to express and handle the concepts of those statements to be able to utilize them. In other words, there needs to be a user profile for storing user data and domain models for describing the typical concepts that the user preferences refer to. Without a definition of the concept "morning" it is not possible to connect an interest in weather forecast to this time context. Furthermore, if the system has some understanding of TV genres it may know that "African wildlife" programs are documentaries about animals and nature, which makes it possible to recommend other programs with similar topics. Also geographical knowledge is useful, so that e.g. a program entitled "Wild Kenya" can be recognized as being related to Africa and perhaps to be recommended. The Personalization layer is the point where the user data, domain knowledge, filters and the actual content all converge. The layer itself does not hold any of this information, only the functionality to operate on all this data. To get this information into the personalization process, the personalization layer contains a Model Manager which administers all communication and requests to the various models which are maintained in various services (on the left in the figure).

The last layer in the SenSee Server is the Application Server (AS), and functions mainly as administration layer and online access point for facilitating connections from outside. Via an API, clients can make a request to for example search, get recommendations, login, etc. It further keeps track of connected applications, identification of users and devices by sessions containing all relevant information of connected applications. Various devices, such as the TV screen (including a set-top box), PC, handheld mobile or PDA can make a connection to the server. The central SenSee component identifies and keeps track of all connected devices and can direct content streams simultaneously to multiple devices, according to the settings and user requests. Each user is furthermore identified and logged in to the system, in order to personalize the experience. Several users can be logged in and use the system in parallel, where either each user uses one or more devices or multiple users log in via the same device (e.g. a set-top box system). In such case the experience is then personalized for the group comprised of those users. The actual interface and functionality presented to the users are adapted for the devices used, with their own limitations and possibilities. In the figure we show at the top a list of client applications to indicate that multiple different clients can connect simultaneously. In this way also third-parties could make use of the SenSee functionality. Currently there is one application, iFanzy[10], which is developed by a company called Stoneroos Interactive Television and which we will explain in greater detail further down the text, as it is a personalized EPG running on top of the SenSee framework.

At the left in Figure 4, we see the three services which are used by the Personalization layer, namely the User Model Service (UMS), the Ontology Service (OS) and the Filter Service (FS).

The purpose of the User Model Service (UMS) is to provide a general interface giving access to repositories with user related information. The reason for having the user model repositories available as a shared external service is because we want to be able to access it from different places/applications. In this way, different third-party applications would be able to use this UMS as their central user data storage. In such a case all participants would benefit as all of them enrich the storage independently. The UMS is built in such a way that it can keep track off all information which gets stored. In this way we always know who added which information at which time and in which situation. In the future we could even imagine having multiple UMS instances running, keeping each other synchronized and thus providing a richer and more redundant service. Furthermore, since user's preferences are very much depending on situational information (definitely in such a time-sensitive domain as this one), we keep for every fact the context in which this fact was valid. E.g. a user likes to watch a movie in the evening but definitely not in the morning.

Next to the UMS, we have the OS which is basically in charge of maintaining all used ontologies, and thus to 'understand' the semantics of different concepts like time, geographical places, content genres etc. The OS is the main storage for vocabularies and knowledge which is used extensively when searching and filtering content. For example, it can be used to extend search queries with synonyms, e.g. "bike" → "bicycle", and translate keywords to corresponding metadata, e.g. "evening" → "start 18:00:00, end 23:00:00". It can also try to find a conceptualization of a term. When given the string 'sport news', it would respond with the known URI of the TV-Anytime genre 'sport news'.

The third service is the Filter Service (FS) and is intended as the holder of rule-based filters that can be applied for different aspects of content and user data filtering. A rule is a statement which, if a set of preconditions is true, draws a set of conclusions. Since we potentially have to deal with large amounts of rules which may be created by various partners, the rules are accommodated in the FS. Imagine a family with young children where the mother wants to ensure that no unsuited content can reach her children. In such a case a filter could be added where it states that if the age of the current viewer is below 18, then all content should be deleted which is unsuited for this age-group. These filters would be enforced when content is retrieved by the Personalization layer from the Package Handler and can thus not be bypassed.

---

[10] http://www.iFanzy.nl

User Modeling

To enable personalization a good understanding of the user is key. This means that we need to be able to express the user's ideas and reflections on the concepts (e.g. programs, actors, genres, etc.) stored in the data set. To do so, we follow the principle that a rigorous and consistent data model is essential to accomplish this, and that it allows us to express and define the necessary concepts of the user model. Having the user model defined, every action or feedback from the user asserted on any of the different client applications, connecting to the SenSee server, can then be used to populate the user model instance to become the concrete user profile. However, it remains the responsibility of the client applications which kinds of information they elicit from their users and pass on to the UMS. In the case of iFanzy, all user actions are caught and sent to the UMS where it is parsed and used to update the user's profile.

The User Model (UM) has three important parts which are all connected to each other. First we have the User Profile (UP) which allows us to collect and store statements about the current user like age, gender, preferences, liking of a program P, etc. Since content is described with the aid of TV-Anytime metadata, there is enough information to identify the program or movie in order to be precise in remembering the program when storing the liking. Secondly, we have a User Context model (UC) which is able to store the context in which a statement in the UP was valid. E.g. here we find that the 'liking of program P' as described in the UP was valid in context C which says that the user uttered this liking when 'he was watching together with his wife at home in the evening via the set-top box system'. However, when a client application is going to send all generated actions from its users to the UMS, the profile might soon become too large and cumbersome to be used in the personalization process. After all, a compact and well expressed profile is preferred when calculating recommendations or doing intelligent searches. Therefore, we introduced a third part in the UP, which is the User History (UH). The UH basically contains information of the previous behavior of the user. It stores every action that the user has taken in combination with the context in which this action occurred. The purpose of this information is to support attempts to discover patterns in the user's behavior. The valuable patterns found (e.g. a user watches the program 'Friends' every Tuesday evening at 20:00) are then materialized in the UP (e.g. the user likes 'Friends' on Tuesday evening at 20:00) where the information will be taken into account in the personalization process. The User History can become rather extensive after a lot of user interaction with the system. Therefore it is necessary to have a process which can filter the structure periodically and keep only the valuable information. We have for this reason chosen to use two instances of the user history repository: a short term user history which records the information completely, and a more selective long term user history. The latter keeps all information which proved to be valuable after filtering the short term history, which happens at the end of a session when the user logs out. This process also updates the User Profile. The User Model thus develops and grows over time while the user interacts with the system.

Via the User Model Service (UMS) it is possible to set both context-independent values like e.g. 'the user's birthday is 09/05/1975' or 'the user has a hearing disability' as well as context-dependent values like 'the user rates program p with value 5 in the evening'. However, all these statements must adhere to the user model schema (containing the semantics) which is publicly available. In this way, the system 'understands' the given information, and is thus able to exploit it properly. If the system for example needs to filter out all adult content for users whose age is under 18 years old, the filter needs to know which value from the user profile it needs to parse in order to find the user's age. Therefore, all the information added to the profile must fit in the RDF schema of the user model. However, since we are working with public services, it might be that an application wants to add information which does not fit yet in the available schema. In that case, this extra schema information should first be added to the ontology pool maintained by the Ontology Service. Once these extra schema triples are added there, the UMS can accept values for the new properties. Afterwards, the FS can accept rules which make use of these new schema properties.

Context

Like previously mentioned, in order to discern between different situations in which user data was amassed we rely on the concept of context. The context in which a new statement was added to the user profile tells us how to interpret it. In broader sense, context can be seen as a description of the physical environment of the user on a certain fixed point in time. Some contextual aspects are particularly important for describing a user's situation while dealing with television programs:

- Time: When is a statement in the profile valid? It is important to know when a specific statement holds. A user can like a program in the evening but not in the morning
- Platform/Location: Where was the statement elicited? It makes a difference to know the location of the user (on vacation, on a business trip, etc.) as his interests could vary with it. Next to this we can also keep the platform, which tells us whether the information was elicited via a website, the set-top box system or even a mobile phone
- Audience: Which users took part in this action at elicitation time? If a program was rated while multiple users where watching, we can to some extent expect that this rating is valid for all users present

Note that context can be interpreted very widely. Potentially one could for example also take the user's mood, devices, lighting, noise level or even an extended social situation into consideration. Where this in theory indeed could potentially improve the estimation of what the user might appreciate to watch, in our current practice measuring all these states is considered not very practical with current technologies and sensor capabilities.

Working with context is always constrained by the ability to measure it. The UMS allows for client applications to enter a value for these three aspects (time, platform/location, audience) per new user fact added. However, the clients themselves remain responsible to capture this information. Considering the impact of context on personalization in this domain, it would be very beneficial for the client applications to try to catch this information as accurate as possible.

Events

Previously, we made the distinction between context-independent and context-dependent statements. We will refer to the latter from now as 'Events' because they represent feedback from the user on a specific concept which is only valid in a certain context. This means that for every action the user performs on any of the clients, the client can communicate this event to the UMS. We defined a number of events which can occur in the television domain like e.g. adding programs to the user's favorites or to the recording list, setting reminders and/or alerts for certain programs, ranking channels, rating programs, etc. All different events (modeled as the class SEN:Event) are defined in the event model as shown in Figure 5. Each event has a specific type (e.g. 'WatchEvent', 'RateEvent', 'AddToFavoritesEvent', 'Remove-FromFavoritesEvent', etc.), one or more properties, and occurs in a specific context as can be seen in the RDF schema. Each event can have different specific properties. For example, a 'WatchEvent' would have a property saying which program was

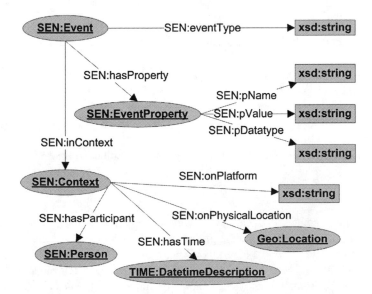

Fig. 5 Event model

watched, when the user started watching and how long he watched it. Since all these event properties are so different from each other, we modeled this in a generic way by the class 'SEN:EventProperty'. This class itself then has a property to model its name, value and data type.

The SEN:Context class has four properties modeling the contextual aspects as explained above. The SEN:onPlatform property contains the platform from which the event was sent, SEN:onPhysicalLocation refers to a concept in the Geonames ontology which will only be filled in once we are able to accurately pinpoint the user's location. The SEN:hasTime property tells us the time of the event by referring to the Time ontology and with the SEN:hasParticipant property we can maintain all the persons which were involved in this event.

All the information we aggregate from the various events, is materialized in the user profile. In the user profile this generates a list of assertions which are filtered from the events generated by the user and act on a certain resource like a program, person, genre, etc. All incoming events are first kept in the short term history. When the session is closed, important events are written to the long term history and the short term is discarded. Sometimes an event is not relevant enough to influence the profile (e.g. a WatchEvent where the user watched a program for 10 seconds and then zapped away). After a certain amount of time, events in the long term history are finally materialized in the user profile. However, it might for example be possible that multiple events are aggregated into one user profile update, like when detecting a certain pattern of events that might be worth drawing conclusions from (e.g. a WatchEvent on the same program every week). Whenever a user starts exhibiting periodic behavior, e.g. watching the same program at the same time of a certain day in the week, the SenSee framework will notice this in the generated event list and can optionally decide to materialize this behavior in the profile. The aggregation of assertions in the user profile can be seen as a filter over the events, and the events as the history of all relevant user actions. For this aggregation we have several different strategies depending on the type of event.

Cold Start

Systems which rely heavily on user information in order to provide their key functionality, usually suffer from the so called cold start problem. It basically describes the situation in which the system cannot perform its main functionality because of the lack of well-filled user profiles. This is not different in the SenSee framework. In order to make a good recommendation the system has to know what the user most likely will be interested in. When a new user subscribes to the system, the UMS requires that besides the user's name also his age, gender and education are given to have a first indication what kind of person it is dealing with. Afterwards, the UMS tries to find, given these values, more user data in an unobtrusive way. Our approach can basically be split in two different methods:

- Via import: importing existing user data, by for example parsing an already existing profile of that user
- Via classification: by classifying the user in a group from which already some
  information is known

Both of these methods can potentially contribute to the retrieval of extra information
describing the current user. In the following two sections we show how exactly we
utilize these two methods to enrich the user profile.

Import of known user profiles

Looking at the evolution and growth of Web 2.0 social networks like Hyves, Facebook[11], LinkedIn[12], Netlog[13], etc. we must conclude that users put a lot of effort
into building an extensive online profile. However, people do not like to repeat this
exercise multiple times. As a consequence, some networks often grow within a single country to become dominant while remaining much less known abroad. Hyves
for example is a huge hit in the Netherlands, while almost not known outside.

Looking at these online profiles, it is truly amazing how much information people
gather on these networks about themselves. Therefore it is no surprise that there has
been a lot of effort in trying to make benefit out of this huge amount of user data.
Facebook started with the introduction of the Facebook platform (a set of APIs)
in May 2007 which made it easy to develop software and new features making
use of this user data. Afterwards, also others saw the benefit of making open API
access to user profiles, Google started (together with MySpace and some other social
networks) the OpenSocial initiative[14] which is basically a set of API's which makes
applications interoperable with all social networks supporting the standard.

In the SenSee framework we have built a proof of concept on top of the Hyves
network. The choice for this particular network was straightforward since it is by
far the biggest network in the Netherlands with over 7.5 million users (which makes
almost 50% of the population). What makes these social networks particularly interesting to consider, is the usually large amount of interests accumulated there by the
users. People utter interest in television programs, movies, their favorite actors, directors, locations and much more. If we can find here that a user loves the Godfather
trilogy, it tells us a lot about the user's general interests.

In Figure 6 we see a part of an average Dutch person's Hyves profile, in which
we specifically zoomed in on his defined interests. Hyves defines a set of categories,
among which we see (translated): movies, music, traveling, media, tv, books, sports,
food, heroes, brands, etc. Most of these are interesting for us to retrieve, as they expose a great deal of information about this person's interests. Given the username

---

[11] http://www.facebook.com/

[12] http://www.linkedin.com/

[13] http://www.netlog.com/

[14] http://code.google.com/apis/opensocial/

Films: 300, American History X, An Inconvenient Truth, Braveheart, Fightclub, Harry Potter, Kaboute Plop, Kill Bill, Lord of the Rings, Pulp Fiction, Scarface, The Matrix, Wedding Crashers, You've got mail

Muziek: 50 Cent, Acda & De Munnik, Air, Akon, Alicia Keys, Aphex Twin, Blof, Bob Marley, Cypress Hill, Don Diablo, Dr Dre, Ella Fitzgerald, Erick E, Faithless, Guus Meeuwis, Mary J Blige, Orbital, The Prodigy

Reizen: Afrika, Amsterdam, Carribbean, Cuba, New York, Parijs, Strand, Wintersport

Overig: Auto's, Technologie

Media: BNN, Computer Totaal, hardware info, MTV, Net 5, RTL 4, RTL 5, RTL 7, SBS 6, The Box, TMF

Gadgets: Creative Zen

Tv: De Lama's

Boeken: Getting Things Done, iets, Lord of the Rings

Sport: Hardlopen, Snowboarden, Tennis

Eten: pizza, Sate

Helden: Roger Federer, Al Pacino

Merken: Asics, Brooks, Calvin Klein, Diesel, EDC, Esprit, G-star, Gilette, Hugo Boss, Jupiler, Lacoste, Le Coq Sportif, Mexx, Nike, Nivea, Oakley, Puma, Replay, Sony, Tommy Hilfiger

Fig. 6 Example Hyves profile interests

and password of a Hyves account our crawler parses and filters the most interesting values of the user's profile page. However, the personalization layer's algorithms work with values and concept defined in the semantic graph. Therefore, in order to be able to exploit interests defined in the Hyves, first a match of those strings in the available categories to concepts in our ontological graph must be made. After all, the string 'Al Pacino' only becomes valuable if we are able to match this string to the ontological concept (an instance of the Person class) representing Al Pacino. Once a match is made, an assertion can be added to the user profile indicating that this user has a positive interest in the concept 'Al Pacino'. Depending on the category of interest a slightly different approach of matching is applied. In the categories 'movies' and 'tv' we try to find matches within our set of TV programs and persons possibly involved in those programs. As Hyves does not enforce any restrictions on what you enter in a certain category, there is no certainty on the percentage we can match correctly. In the 'media' category people can put interests in all kinds of media objects like newspapers, tv channels, magazines, etc. The matching algorithm compares all these strings to all objects representing channels and streams. In this example, 'MTV', 'Net 5', 'RTL 4', etc. are all matched to the respective television channels. The same tactics are applied on the other relevant categories, and thus we match 'traveling' (e.g. 'afrika', 'amsterdam', 'cuba', etc.) to geographical locations, 'sport' (e.g. 'tennis') to our genre hierarchies and 'heroes' (e.g. 'Roger Federer') to our list of persons.

After the matching algorithm is finished, in the best case the user's profile now contains a set of assertions over a number of concepts of different types. These assertions then in turn will help the data retrieval algorithms in determining which other programs might be interesting as well. Furthermore, we also exploit our RDF/OWL graph to deduce even more assertions. Knowing for example, that this user likes the movie 'Scarface' in combination with the fact that our graph tells us that this movie has the genre 'Action' we can deduce that this user has a potential interest in this genre. The same holds for an interest in a location like 'New York'. Here the Geonames ontology tells us exactly which areas are neighboring or situated within 'New York' and that it is a place within the US. All this information can prove useful when guessing whether new programs will be liked too. While making assertions from deductions, we could vary the value (and thus the strength) of the assertion because the certainty decreases the further we follow a path in the graph. It is in such cases that the choice of working with a semantic graph really pays off. Since all concepts are interrelated, propagation of potential user interest can be well controlled and deliver some interesting unexpected results increasing the chance of serendipitous recommendations in the future.

Classification of users in groups

Besides the fact that users themselves accumulate a lot of information in their online profiles, there also has been quite some effort in finding key parameters to predict user interests. Parameter like age, gender, education, social background, monthly income, status, place of residence, etc. all can be used to predict pretty accurately what users might appreciate. However, to be able to benefit in terms of interests in television related concepts, we need large data sets listing, for thousands of persons, what their interests are next to their specific parameters. Having such information allows us to build user groups based on their similarity, to more accurately guess the interests of a new user on a number of concepts. After all, if is very likely that he will share the same opinion on those concepts. This approach is also known as collaborative filtering, introduced in 1995 by Shardanand and Maes [22] and is already widely accepted by commercial systems. However, in order to be able to perform a collaborative filtering algorithm, the system needs at least a reasonable group of users which all gave a reasonable amount of ratings. Secondly, collaborative filtering is truly valuable when dealing with a more or less stable set of items like a list of movies. This is due to the 'first rater' problem. When a new item arrives in the item set, it takes some time before it receives a considerable amount of ratings, and thus it takes some time before it is known exactly how the group thinks about this item. This is in particular a problem in the television world, where new programs (or new episodes of series) emerge constantly, making this a very quickly evolving data set. However, in SenSee the current active user base is still reasonably small for being able to perform just any kind of collaborative filtering strategy. Therefore, until the user base reaches a size that allows us to apply the collaborative filtering that is desired, external groups are used to guess how a person might feel about a certain item. As external data sets we among others use the IMDb ratings classified by demographics.

IMDb keeps besides a general rating over all of its items, also the ratings of all these people spread over their demographics. Besides gender, it also splits the rating data into four age groups. By classifying the SenSee users in these eight specific groups we can project the IMDb data on our users. To show the difference between the groups, let us take a look at the movie 'Scarface', which has a general IMDb rating of 8.1/10. We see that on average, males under 18 years give a rating of 8.7/10 while females over 45 years rate this movie 5.7/10. Like this example clearly shows, it pays off to classify users based on their demographics. Moreover, IMDb does not only have ratings on movies, but also on television series and various other shows. In general we can say that this classification method is very effective in the current situation where our relevant user base selection remains limited (from the perspective of collaborative filtering). Once more and more users rate more and more programs, we can start applying collaborative filtering techniques ourselves exploiting similarities between persons on one side and between groups and television programs on the other side.

Personalized Content Search

This section describes the personalized content search functionality of the SenSee Personalization component. Personalization usually occurs upon request of the user like when navigating through available content, when searching for something specific by entering keywords, or when asking the system to make a recommendation. In all cases, we aim at supporting the user by filtering the information based on the user's own perspective. The process affects the results found in the search in the following aspects:

- A smaller, more narrow result set is produced
- Results contain the items ranked as most interesting for the user
- Results contain the items most semantically related to any given keywords
- Searching goes beyond word matching and considers semantic related concepts
- Results are categorized with links to semantic concepts
- Semantic links can be used to show the path from search query to results

We illustrate this by stepwise going through the content search process as it is depicted in Figure 7. Let us imagine the example that the user via the user application interface enters the keywords "military 1940s" and asks the system to search. This initial query expression of keywords $(k_1, \ldots, k_n)$ is analyzed in a query refinement

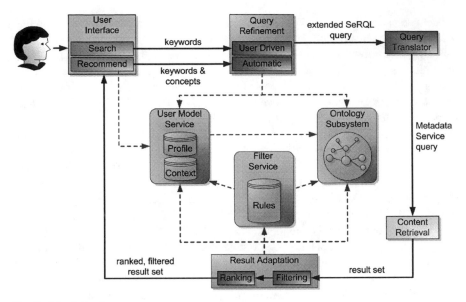

Fig. 7 Adaptation loop

process which aims at adding extra semantic knowledge. By using the set of available ontologies, we first search for modeled concepts with the same name as the keywords. We can in this case get hits in the history and time ontologies, where respectively "military" and "1940s" are found and thereby now are known to belong to a history and time context. Second, since it is not sure that content metadata will use the exact same keywords, we add synonyms from the WordNet ontology, as well as semantically close concepts from the domain ontologies. In this case, apart from direct synonyms, a closely related concept such as "World War II" is found through a semantic link of "military" to "war" and "1940s" to "1945". Furthermore it links it to the geographical concept "Western Europe" which in turn links to "Great Britain", "Germany" etc. However, this leads us to the requirement that the original keyword should be valued higher than related concepts. We solve this by adding a numerical value of semantic closeness, a. In our initial algorithm, the original keywords and synonyms receive an a value of 1.0, related ontology concepts within one node distance receive a value of 0.75 and those two nodes away a value of 0.5, reducing with every step further in the graph. Third, we enrich the search query by adding every occurrence we found together with a link to the corresponding ontology concept. The query is in that process refined to a new query expression of keywords $(k_1, \ldots, k_m)$ $(m \geq n)$, with links from keywords to ontology concepts $(c_1, \ldots, c_m)$, and corresponding semantic closeness values $(a_1, \ldots, a_m)$. Subsequently, the keywords in the query are mapped to TV-Anytime metadata items, in order to make a search request to the Metadata Service. From this content retrieval process the result is a collection of CRID references to packages which has matching metadata.

The next step in the process is result filtering and ranking, which aims at producing rankings of the search result in order to present them in an ordered list with the most interesting one at the top. Furthermore it performs the deletion of items in the list which are unsuitable, for example content with a minimum 18 years age limit for younger users. The deletion is a straightforward task of retrieving data on the user's parental guide limit or unwanted content types. The rules defining this filtering are retrieved from the Filter Service. The ranking consists of a number of techniques which estimate rankings from different perspectives:

- Keyword matching
- Content-based filtering
- Collaborative filtering
- Context-based filtering
- Group filtering

To begin with, packages are sorted based on a keyword matching value i.e., to what extent their metadata matched the keywords in the query. This can be calculated as average sum of matching keywords multiplied with the corresponding a value, in order to adjust for semantic closeness. Content-based filtering like explained by Pazzani [21] is furthermore used to predict the ranking of items that the User Model does not yet have any ranking of. This technique compares the metadata of a particular item and searches for similarities among the contents that already have a ranking, i.e., that the user has already seen. Collaborative filtering is used to predict the ranking based on how other similar users ranked it. Furthermore, context-based filtering can be used to calculate predictions based on the user's context, as previously mentioned. If there is a group of users interacting with the system together, the result needs to be adapted for them as a group. This can be done by for example combining the filtering of each individual person to create a group filtering [15]. Finally, the ranking value from each technique is combined by summarizing the products of each filter's ranking value and a filter weight.

Personalized Presentations

Presentation of content is the responsibility of the client applications working on top of the SenSee framework. However, in order to make the personalization more transparent to the user, the path from original keyword(s) to resulting packages can be requested from the server when the results are presented. The synonyms and other semantically related terms can also be made explicit to the user as feedback aiming to avoid confusion when presenting the recommendation (e.g., why suddenly a movie is recommended without an obvious link to the original keyword(s) given by the user). Since the links from keyword to related ontology concepts are kept, they can be presented in the user interface. Furthermore, they could even be used to group the result set, as well as in an earlier stage in the search process, when used to consult the user to disambiguate and find the appropriate context.

Implementation

SenSee Server

The basic service-based architecture chosen for the system is illustrated in Figure 8. It shows how the different SenSee services and content services connect. A prototype of the system described has been developed and implemented in cooperation with Philips Applied Technologies. The fundamental parts of the IP and system services, content retrieval, packaging and personalization are covered in this implementation. Our initial focus has been on realizing the underlying TV-Anytime packaging concepts and personalization, although not so much on the Blu-ray. Currently, geographical, time, person, content and synonym ontologies have been incorporated in the prototype. Currently, all connections to both the server as to any of the services must be made by either the SOAP or XML-RPC protocols.

Various end-user applications have been developed over time. On the left of the client section in the figure we see the original stand-alone Java 5.0 SenSee application which focused mainly on searching and viewing packages. This application includes not only the client GUI interface but also administration views and pure testing interfaces. Later the need of a Web-based client became clear to enable fast

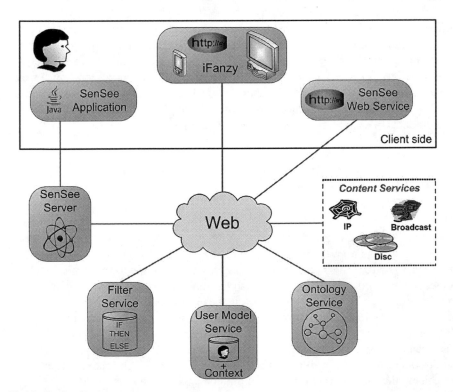

Fig. 8 SenSee Environment

and easy access for external users. The SenSee Web Client (on the right on the client section), was then implemented as an AJAX application. This is enabling us to provide a fluent Web experience without long waiting times. The service was built as first complete proof of concept showing all main functionality of our SenSee server. This version of the client application was nominated as finalist for the Semantic Web Challenge 2007 [3] and ended runner-up. The pages themselves are built with the Google Web Toolkit[15]. Our system currently allows a single user as well as multiple users to log in, where the system adapts to make recommendations for a single and a group of users correspondingly.

The SenSee server is online available as a service, exposing an API to connect to. The User Model Service (USM), the Ontology Service (OS) and the Filter Service (FS) are sometimes referred to as 'external' services although initially they were a part of the SenSee service. However, we realized the benefit of having them as a service because it might help people looking for similar functionality. Moreover, while others make use of these services, the knowledge contained grows which in turn helps us as well. In case of the USM, this enables more varied information being added to the user profiles which helps the collaborative filtering algorithm, improves the performance of the process, and allows for doing an analysis of user behaviors in the large. Furthermore, the use of an external User Model Service gives possibilities for the user to access his profile via other systems or interfaces. However, it may be argued that it can lead to privacy or integrity problems if users are uncomfortable with the thought of having information about their behavior stored somewhere outside their home system, no matter how encrypted or detached from the person's identity it can be done. These issues are currently outside the scope of the reported research.

The devices that currently can be connected are a HDTV screen and set-top box and a LIRC remote control which communicates through a JLIRC interface. Content Services can furthermore handle both local content as well as streaming content via IP. The implementation has mainly been made in Java, where connections of external services are realized by the Tomcat Web Server, Java Web Start, SOAP and XML-RPC. The tools used for the application of semantic models are Sesame[16] and Protégé[17].

iFanzy

One of our major partners at the moment is Stoneroos Interactive Television[18], with whom we are currently developing iFanzy[19], a personalized EPG, which runs on

---

[15] http://code.google.com/webtoolkit

[16] http://www.openrdf.org

[17] http://protege.stanford.edu

[18] http://www.stoneroos.nl

[19] http://www.ifanzy.nl

top of the SenSee framework. iFanzy combines the power of three independent platforms (a Web application, a set-top box + television combination and a mobile phone prototype) which are connected by the SenSee server framework. Every action uttered by the user on any of those three client applications is elicited and passed on to the server, which deals with it like described in previous chapters. Every one of these interfaces is specifically tailored to provide the functionality which is most expected by the user on the respective platform. This makes all three platforms very complementary and gives iFanzy the means of closely monitoring the behavior of the user in most situations. This in turn is very useful since it enhances the contextual understanding of this user, allowing the framework to provide the right content for a specific situation (e.g. available devices, other people around, time of the day, etc.). Every action elicit on any device will have an influence of every other device later on. E.g., rating a program online will have an immediate influence on the generation of recommendations on the set-top box.

iFanzy makes extensive use of the server's context infrastructure because the television domain is context-sensitive. If for example a certain user likes movies from the genre 'action' a lot and a recommendation is done for an action movie at 8 am in the morning, there is a big chance that the user would interpret this as a silly recommendation. Solely based on the facts in the user profile it was a straightforward recommendation; it was just recommended in the wrong context. Therefore, in iFanzy, all contextual information from the user (e.g. time, location, audience) is harnessed and sent to the SenSee server such that it can take the context into account when calculating recommendations. All further information amassed from the user, is accompanied by this user's current context to be able to draw more fine-grained conclusions afterwards.

User feedback such as ratings, but also users setting reminders, alerts, favorites, etc. are all associated with specific content or rather specific data objects: therefore, the user model (that includes the user profile) is closely related to the conceptual model. Every data object in iFanzy is retrieved from the SenSee server and thus contains the unique URI such that the server always knows to which object(s) this user feedback reflects.

The iFanzy Web application became publicly available in the middle of 2008, delivering the first online personalized EPG. Currently, iFanzy is also running on different set-top boxes which are going to be tested extensively in the near future, before being put into family homes. Furthermore, next to the Dutch market there is already also a German version running and more are being planned. Currently we are testing the iFanzy application and SenSee server in a user test involving around 50 participants. The test, will last for about two weeks and tries to test the recommendation quality and the iFanzy interface. Participants are asked to at least use the iFanzy personalized EPG every day for about 5 to 10 minutes. In this time, little assignments are given like 'rate 10 programs', 'mark some programs as favorites', 'set reminders for programs you do not want to miss', etc. By doing so users are generating events, supplying valuable information about their behavior to the system. At this moment in the test on average users generate about 20 useful events per day. At the end of the test a questionnaire will be sent to all participants asking them some concluding questions allowing us to draw conclusions.

Conclusions

In this paper we described an approach for a connected ambient home media management system that exploits data from various heterogeneous data sources, where users can view and interact via multiple rendering devices like TV screens, PDA, mobile telephone or other personal devices. The interaction, especially in content search, is supported by a semantics-aware and context-aware process which aims to provide a personalized user experience. This is important since users have different preferences and capabilities and the goal is to prevent an information overflow. We have presented a component architecture which covers content retrieval, content metadata, user modeling, recommendations, and an end-user environment. Furthermore we have presented a semantically enriched content search process using TV-Anytime content classification and metadata. Our ultimate goal is to propose a foundational platform that can be used further by applications and personalization services. First proof of this feasibility is the current implementation of the iFanzy application which runs on top of SenSee. iFanzy is the general name of three client applications running on different devices and showing a first modest step towards the futuristic scenario sketched in the beginning of this paper.

References

1. H. Alshabib, O. F. Rana, and A. S. Ali. Deriving ratings through social network structures. In ARES '06: Proceedings of the First International Conference on Availability, Reliability and Security, pages 779–787, Washington, DC, USA, 2006. IEEE Computer Society
2. L. Ardissono, A. Kobsa, M. Maybury (ed) (2004) Personalized digital television: targeting programs to individual viewers. Kluwer, Boston
3. P. Bellekens, L. Aroyo, G.J. Houben, A. Kaptein, K. van der Sluijs, "Semantics-Based Framework for Personalized Access to TV Content: The iFanzy Use Case", Proceedings of the 6th International Semantic Web Conference, pp. 887–894, LNCS 4825, Springer, Busan, Korea (2007)
4. S.J. Berman (2004) Media and entertainment 2010. Open on the inside, open on the outside: The open media company of the future. Retrieved November 24, 2005, from http://www-03.ibm.com/industries/media/doc/content/bin/ME2010.pdf
5. T. Berners-Lee, J. Hendler, O. Lassila (2001) The semantic web. Scientific American, New York
6. J. Bormans, K. Hill (2002) MPEG-21 Overview v.5. Retrieved November 24, 2005, from http://www.chiariglione.org/mpeg/standards/mpeg-21/mpeg-21.htm
7. K. Chorianopoulos (2004) What is wrong with the electronic program guide. Retrieved November 24, 2005, from http://uitv.info/articles/2004/04chorianopoulos
8. N. Earnshaw, S. Aoki, A. Ashley, W. Kameyama (2005) The TV-anytime Content Reference Identifier (CRID). Retrieved November 24, 2005, from http://www.rfc-archive.org/getrfc.php?rfc=4078
9. B. de Ruyter, E. Aarts (2004) Ambient intelligence: visualizing the future. In: Proceedings of the working conference on advanced visual interfaces. ACM, New York, pp 203–208
10. D. Goren-Bar, O. Glinansky (2004) FIT-recommending TV programs to family members. Comput Graph 28: 149–156 (Elsevier)

11. J. Hobbs, F. Pan (2004) An ontology of time for the semantic web. In: ACM Transactions on Asian Language Information Processing (TALIP), vol 3, Issue 1. ACM, New York
12. B. Hong, J. Lim (2005) Design and implementation of home media server using TV-anytime for personalized broadcasting service. In: O. Gervasi, M.L. Gavrilova, V. Kumar, A. Laganà, H.P. Lee, Y. Mun, D. Taniar, C.J.K Tan (eds) Computational science and its applications—ICCSA 2005: conference proceedings, part IV, vol 3483. LNCS. Springer, Berlin Heidelberg New York, pp 138–147
13. A. Kobsa (1990) User modeling in dialog systems: potentials and hazards. AI Soc 4(3): 214–231 (Springer-Verlag London Ltd)
14. F. Manola, E. Miller (2004) RDF Resource Description Framework. Retrieved November 24, 2008, http://www.w3.org/TR/rdf-primer/
15. J. Masthoff (2004) Group modeling: selecting a sequence of television items to suit a group of viewers. User Model User-Adapt Interact 14: 37–85 (Kluwer)
16. D.L. McGuinnes, F. van Harmelen (2004) OWL Web Ontology Language. Retrieved November 24, 2008, from http://www.w3.org/TR/owl-features
17. G.A. Miller (1995) WordNet: a lexical database for english. Commun ACM 38(11) (ACM)
18. S. Murugesan, Y. Deshpande (2001) Web engineering, software engineering and web application development. In: S. Murugesan, Y. Deshpande (eds) Web engineering, vol 2016. Lecture notes in computer science. Springer, Berlin Heidelberg New York
19. C.B. Necib, J.-C. Freytag (2005) Query processing using ontologies. In: O. Pastor, J.F. Cunha (eds) Advanced information systems engineering: 17th international conference, CAiSE 2005, vol 3520. Lecture notes in computer science. Springer, Berlin Heidelberg New York, pp 167–186
20. D. O' Sullivan, B. Smith, D. Wilson, K. McDonald, A. Smeaton (2004 Improving the quality of personalized electronic program guide. User Model User-Adapt Interact 14: 5–36 (Kluwer)
21. M.J. Pazzani (1999) A framework for collaborative, content-based and demographic filtering. Artif Intell Rev 13:393–408
22. U. Shardanand, P. Maes (1995) Social information filtering: algorithms for automating "Word of Mouth". In: CHI '95 Proceedings: conference on human factors in computing systems. pp 210–217
23. G. Stamou, J. van Ossenbruggen, J.Z. Pan, G. Schreiber (2006) In: J.R. Smith (ed) Multimedia annotations on the semantic Web. IEEE Multimed 13(1):86–90
24. M. van Setten (2005) Supporting people in finding information: hybrid recommender systems and goalbased structuring. Telematica Instituut fundamental research Series, No. 016 (TI/FRS/016). Universal, The Netherlands
25. H.-W. Tung and V.-W. Soo. A personalized restaurant recommender agent for mobile e-service. In EEE '04: Proceedings of the 2004 IEEE International Conference on e-Technology, e-Commerce and e-Service (EEE'04), pages 259-262, Washington, DC, USA, 2004. IEEE Computer Society
26. W. Woerndl and G. Groh. Utilizing physical and social context to improve recommender systems. In WI-IATW '07: Proceedings of the 2007 IEEE/WIC/ACM International Conferences on Web Intelligence and Intelligent Agent Technology - Workshops, pages 123-128, Washington, DC, USA, 2007. IEEE Computer Society
27. G.-E. Yap, A.-H. Tan, and H.-H. Pang. Dynamically-optimized context in recommender systems. In MDM '05: Proceedings of the 6th international conference on Mobile data management, pages 265-272, New York, NY, USA, 2005. ACM
28. Z. Yu, X. Zhou (2004) TV3P: an adaptive assistant for personalized TV. IEEE Transactions on Consumer Electronics 50 (1):393–399

Chapter 4
Personalization on a Peer-to-Peer Television System

Jun Wang, Johan Pouwelse, Jenneke Fokker, Arjen P. de Vries, and Marcel J.T. Reinders

Introduction

Television signals have been broadcast around the world for many decades. More flexibility was introduced with the arrival of the VCR. PVR (personal video recorder) devices such as the TiVo further enhanced the television experience. A PVR enables people to watch television programs they like without the restrictions of broadcast schedules. However, a PVR has limited recording capacity and can only record programs that are available on the local cable system or satellite receiver.

This paper presents a prototype system that goes beyond the existing VCR, PVR, and VoD (Video on Demand) solutions. We believe that amongst others broadband, P2P, and recommendation technology will drastically change the television broadcasting as it exists today. Our operational prototype system called *Tribler* [Pouwelse et al., 2006] gives people access to all television stations in the world. By exploiting P2P technology, we have created a distribution system for live television as well as sharing of programs recorded days or months ago.

The *Tribler* system is illustrated in Fig. 1 The basic idea is that each user will have a small low-cost set-top box attached to his/her TV to record the local programs from the local tuner. This content is stored on a hard disk and shared with other users (friends) through the *Tribler* P2P software. Each user is then both a program consumer as well as a program provider. *Tribler* implicitly learns the interests of users

J. Wang (✉), J. Pouwelse, and M.J.T. Reinders
Faculty of Electrical Engineering, Mathematics and Computer Science, Delft University of Technology, Delft, The Netherlands
e-mail: {jun.wang; j.a.pouwelse; m.j.t.reinders}@tudelft.nl

J. Fokker
Faculty of Industrial Design Engineering, Delft University of Technology, Delft, The Netherlands
e-mail: j.e.fokker,@tudelft.nl

A.P. de Vries
CWI, Amsterdam, The Netherlands
e-mail: arjen@acm.org

B. Furht (ed.), *Handbook of Multimedia for Digital Entertainment and Arts*,
DOI 10.1007/978-0-387-89024-1_4, © Springer Science+Business Media, LLC 2009

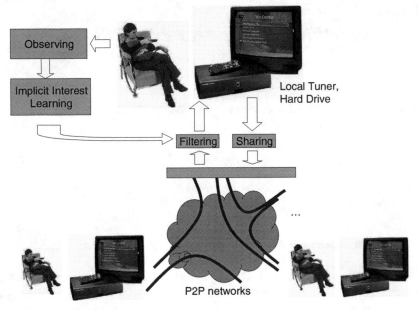

Fig. 1 An illustration of *Tribler*, a personalized P2P television system

in TV programs by analyzing their zapping behavior. The system automatically recommends, records, or even downloads programs based on the learned user interest. Connecting millions of set-top boxes in a P2P network will unbolt a wealth of programs, television channels and their archives to people. We believe this will tremendously change the way people watch TV.

The architecture of the *Tribler* system is shown in Fig. 2 and a detailed description can be found in [Pouwelse et al., 2006]. The key idea behind the *Tribler* system is that it exploits the prime social phenomenon "kinship fosters cooperation" [Pouwelse et al., 2006]. In other words, similar taste for content can form a foundation for an online community with altruistic behavior. This is partly realized by building social groups of users that have similar taste captured in user interest profiles.

The user interest profiles within the social groups can also facilitate the prioritization of content for a user by exploiting recommendation technology. With this information, the available content in the peer-to-peer community can be explored using novel personalized tag-based navigation.

This paper focuses on the personalization aspects of the *Tribler* system. Firstly, we review the related work. Secondly, we describe our system design and the underlying approaches. Finally, we present our experiments to examine the effectiveness of the underlying approaches in the *Tribler* system.

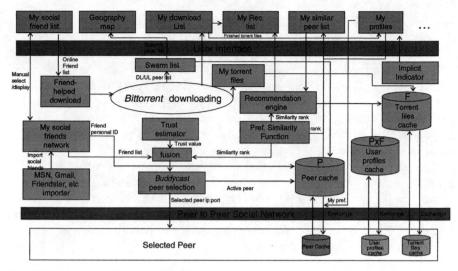

Fig. 2   The system architecture of *Tribler*

Related Work

Recommendation

We adopt recommendations to help users discover available relevant content in a more natural way. Furthermore, it observes and integrates the interests of a user within the discovery process. Recommender systems propose a similarity measure that expresses the relevance between an item (the content) and the profile of a user. Current recommender systems are mostly based on collaborative filtering, which is a filtering technique that analyzes a rating database of user profiles for similarities between users (user-based) or programs (item-based). Others focus on content-based filtering, which, for instance, based on the EPG data [Ardissono et al., 2004].

The profile information about programs can either be based on ratings (explicit interest functions) or on log-archives (implicit interest functions). Correspondingly, their differences lead to two different approaches of collaborative filtering: *rating-based* and *log-based*. The majority of the literature addresses rating-based collaborative filtering, which has been studied in depth [Marlin 2004]. The different rating-based approaches are often classified as memory-based [Breese et al., 1998, Herlocker et al., 1999] or model-based [Hofmann 2004].

In the memory-based approach, all rating examples are stored *as-is* into memory (in contrast to learning an abstraction). In the prediction phase, similar users or items are sorted based on the memorized ratings. Based on the ratings of these similar users or items, a recommendation for the query user can be generated. Examples of memory-based collaborative filtering include item correlation-based methods [Sarwar et al., 2001] and locally weighted regression [Breese et al., 1998]. The advantage of memory-based methods over their model-based alternatives is that they have less parameters to be tuned, while the disadvantage is that the approach cannot deal with data sparsity in a principled manner.

In the model-based approach, training examples are used to generate a model that is able to predict the ratings for items that a query user has not rated before. Examples include decision trees [Breese et al., 1998], latent class models ([Hofmann 2004], and factor models [Canny 1999]). The 'compact' models in these methods could solve the data sparsity problem to a certain extent. However, the requirement of tuning an often significant number of parameters or hidden variables has prevented these methods from practical usage.

Recently, to overcome the drawbacks of these approaches to collaborative filtering, researchers have started to combine both memory-based and model-based approaches [Pennock et al., 2000, Xue et al., 2005, Wang et al., 2006b]. For example, [Xue et al., 2005] clusters the user data and applies intra-cluster smoothing to reduce sparsity. [Wang et al., 2006b] propose a unified model to combine user-based and item-based approaches for the final prediction, and does not require to cluster the data set a priori.

Few log-based collaborative filtering approaches have been developed thus far. Among them are the item-based Top-N collaborative filtering approach [Deshpande & Karypis 2004] and Amazon's item-based collaborative filtering [Linden et al., 2003]. In previous work, we developed a probabilistic framework that gives a probabilistic justification of a log-based collaborative filtering approaches [Wang et al., 2006a] that is also employed in this paper to make TV program recommendation in *Tribler*.

Distributed Recommendation

In P2P TV systems, both the users and the supplied programs are widely distributed and change constantly, which makes it difficult to filter and localize content within the P2P network. Thus, an efficient filtering mechanism is required to be able to find suitable content.

Within the context of P2P networks there is, however, no centralized rating database, thus making it impossible to apply current collaborative filtering approaches. Recently, a few early attempts towards decentralized collaborative filtering have been introduced [Miller et al., 2004, Ali & van Stam 2004]. In [Miller et al., 2004], five architectures are proposed to find and store user rating data to facilitate rating-based recommendation: 1) a central server, 2) random discovery similar to Gnutella, 3) transitive traversal, 4) Distributed Hash Tables (DHT), and 5) secure Blackboard. In [Ali & van Stam 2004], item-to-item recommendation is applied to TiVo (a Personal Video Recorder system) in a client-server architecture. These solutions aggregate the rating data in order to make a recommendation and are independent of any semantic structures of the networks. This inevitably increases the amount of traffic within the network. To avoid this, a novel item-buddy-table scheme is proposed in [Wang et al. 2006c] to efficiently update the calculation of item-to-item similarity.

[Jelasity & van Steen 2002] introduced newscast an epidemic (or gossip) protocol that exploits randomness to disseminate information without keeping any static structures or requiring any sort of administration. Although these protocols successfully operate dynamic networks, their lack of structure restricts them to perform these services in an efficient way.

In this paper, we propose a novel algorithm, called *BuddyCast*, that, in contrast to newscast, generates a semantic overlay on the epidemic protocols by implicitly clustering peers into social networks. Since social networks have small-world network characteristics the user profiles can be disseminated efficiently. Furthermore, the resulting semantic overlays are also important for the membership management and content discovery, especially for highly dynamic environments with nodes joining and leaving frequently.

Learning User Interest

Rating-based collaborative filtering requires users to explicitly indicate what they like or do not like [Breese et al., 1998, Herlocker et al., 1999]. For TV recommendation, the rated items could be preferred channels, favorite genres, and hated actors. Previous research [Nichols 1998, Claypool et al., 2001] has shown that users are unlikely to provide an extensive list of explicit ratings which eventually can seriously degrade the performance of the recommendation. Consequently, the interest of a user should be learned in an implicit way.

This paper learns these interests from TV watching habits such as the zapping behavior. For example, zapping away from a program is a hint that the user is not interested, or, alternatively, watching the whole program is an indication that the user liked that show. This mapping, however, is not straightforward. For example, it is also possible that the user likes this program, but another channel is showing an even more interesting program. In that case zapping away is not an indication that the program is not interesting. In this paper we introduce a simple heuristic scheme to learn the user interest implicitly from the zapping behavior.

System Design

This section describes a heuristic scheme that implicitly learns the interest of a user in TV programs from zapping behavior in that way avoiding the need for explicit ratings. Secondly, we present a distributed profile exchanger, called *BuddyCast*, which enables the formation of social groups as well as distributed content recommendation (ranking of TV programs). We then introduce the user-item relevance model to predict interesting programs for each user. Finally, we demonstrate a user interface incorporating these personalized aspects, i.e., personalized tag-based browsing as well as visualizing your social group.

User Profiling from Zapping Behavior

We use the zapping behavior of a user to learn the user interest in the watched TV programs. The zapping behavior of all users is recorded and coupled with the EPG (Electronic Program Guide) data to generate program IDs. In the *Tribler* system different TV programs have different IDs. TV series that consists of a set of episodes, like "Friends" or a general "news" program, get one ID (all episodes get the same ID) to bring more relevance among programs.

For each user u_k the interest in TV program i_m can be calculated as follows:

$$x_k^m = \frac{WatchedLength\,(m,k)}{OnAirLength\,(m) \cdot freq\,(m)} \tag{1}$$

WatchedLength (m,k) denotes the duration that the user u_k has watched program i_m in seconds. *OnAirLength (m)* denotes the entire duration in seconds of the program i_m on air (cumulative with respect to episodes or reruns). *Freq(m)* denotes the number of times program i_m has been broadcast (episodes are considered to be a rerun), in other words *OnAirLength(m)/freq(m)* is the average duration of a 'single' broadcast, e.g., average duration of an episode. This normalization with respect to the number of times a program has been broadcast is taken into consideration since programs that are frequently broadcast also have more chance that a user gets to watch it.

Experiments (see Fig. 10) showed that, due to the frequent zapping behaviors of users, a large number of x_k^m's have very small values (zapping along channels). It is necessary to filter out those small valued x_k^m's in order to: 1) reduce the amounts of user interest profiles that need to be exchanged, and 2) improve recommendation by excluding these noisy data. Therefore, the user interest values x_k^m are thresholded resulting in binary user interest values:

$$y_k^m = 1 \; if \; x_k^m > T \; and \; y_k^m = 0 \; otherwise \tag{2}$$

Consequently, y_k^m indicates whether user u_k likes program i_m $\left(y_k^m = 1\right)$ or not $\left(y_k^m = 0\right)$.

The optimal threshold T will be obtained through experimentation.

BuddyCast Profile Exchange

BuddyCast generates a semantic overlay on the epidemic protocols by implicitly clustering peers into social networks according to their profiles. It works as follows. Each user maintains a list of top-N most similar users (a.k.a. taste buddies or social network) along with their current profile lists. To be able to discover new users, each user also maintains a *random cache* to record the top-N most fresh "random" IP addresses.

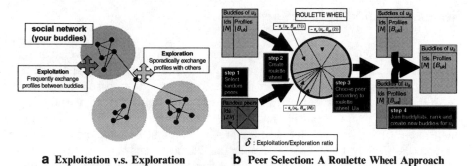

a Exploitation v.s. Exploration   **b** Peer Selection: A Roulette Wheel Approach

Fig. 3 The illustration of the *Buddy Cast* algorithm

Periodically, as illustrated in Fig. 3(a), a user connects either to one of his/her buddies to exchange social networks and current profile list (*exploitation*), or to a new randomly chosen user from the random cache to exchange this information (*exploration*). To prevent reconnecting to a recently visited user in order to maximize the exploration of the social network, every user also maintains a list with the K most recently visited users (excluding the taste buddies).

Different with the gossip-based approaches, which only consider exploration (randomly select a user to connect), *Buddycast* algorithm considers exploration as well as exploitation. Previous study has shown that a set of user profiles is not a random graph and has a certain clustering coefficient [Wang et al., 2006c]. That is the probability that two of user A's buddies (top-N similar users) will be buddies of one another is greater than the probability that two randomly chosen users will be buddies. Based on this observation, we connect users according to their similarity ranks. The more similar a user, the more chance it gets selected to exchange user profiles. Moreover, to discover new users and prevent network divergence, we also add some randomness to allow other users to have a certain chance to be selected.

To find a good balance between exploitation (making use of small-world characteristics of social networks) and exploration (discovering new worlds), as illustrated in Fig. 3(b), the following procedure is adopted. First, δN random users are chosen, where δ denotes the exploration-to-exploitation ratio and $0 \leq \partial N \leq$ number of users in the random cache. Then, these random users are joined with the N buddies, and a ranked list is created based on the similarity of their profile lists with the profile of the user under consideration. Instead of connecting to the random users to get their profile lists, the random users are assigned the lowest ranks. Then, one user is randomly chosen from this ranked list according to a roulette wheel approach (probabilities proportional to the ranks), which gives taste buddies a higher probability to be selected than random users.

Once a user has been selected, the two caches are updated. In random cache, the IP address is updated. In the buddy cache, the buddy list of the selected user is merged. The buddy cache is then ranked (according to the similarity with the own profile), and the top-N best ranked users are kept.

Recommendation by Relevance Models

In the *Tribler* system, after collecting user preferences by using the *BuddyCast* algorithm, we are ready to use the collected user preferences to identify (rank) interesting TV programs for each individual user in order to facilitate taste-based navigation. The following characteristics make our ranking problem more similar to the problem of text retrieval than the existing rating-based collaborative filtering. 1) The implicit interest functions introduced in the previous section generate binary-valued preferences. Usually, one means 'relevance' or 'likeness', and zero indicates 'non-relevance' or 'non-likeness'. Moreover, non-relevance and non-likeness are usually not observed. This is similar to the concept of 'relevance' in text retrieval. 2) The goal for rating-based collaborative filtering is to predict the rating of users, while the goal for the log-based algorithms is to rank the items to the user in order of decreasing relevance. As a result, evaluation is different. In rating-based collaborative filtering, the mean square error (MSE) of the predicted rating is used, while in log-based collaborative filtering, recall and precision are employed.

This paper adopts the probabilistic framework developed for text retrieval [Lafferty & Zhai 2003] and proposes a probabilistic user-item relevance model to measure the relevance between user interests and TV programs, which intends to answer the following basic question:

"*What is the probability that* this *program is relevant to*this*user, given his or her profile?*"

To answer this question, we first define the sample space of relevance: Φ_R. It has two values: 'relevant' r and 'non-relevant' $\bar{r}$. Let R be a random variable over the sample space Φ_R. Likewise, let U be a discrete random variable over the sample space of *user id*'s: $\Phi_U = \{u_1, \ldots, u_K\}$ and let I be a random variable over the sample space of *item id*'s: $\Phi_R = \{i_1, \ldots, i_M\}$, where K is the number of users and M the number of items in the collection. In other words, U refers to the user identifiers and I refers to the item identifiers.

We then denote P as a probability function on the joint sample space $\Phi_U \times \Phi_I \times \Phi_R$. In a probability framework, we can answer the above basic question by estimating the probability of relevance $P(R|U, I)$. The relevance rank of items in the collection Φ_I for a given user $U = u_k$ (i.e., retrieval status value (RSV) of a given target item toward a user) can be formulated as the odds of the relevance:

$$RSV_{u_k}(i_m) = \frac{\log P(r|u_k, i_m)}{\log P(\bar{r}|u_k, i_m)} \tag{3}$$

For simplicity, $R = r$, $R = \bar{r}$, $U = u_k$ and $I = i_m$ are denoted as r, $\bar{r}$, u_k and i_m respectively.

Hence, the evidence for the relevance of an item towards a user is based on both the positive evidence (indicating the relevance) as well as the negative evidence (indicating the non-relevance). Once we know, for a given user, the *RSV* of each item I in the collection (excluding the items that the user has already expressed

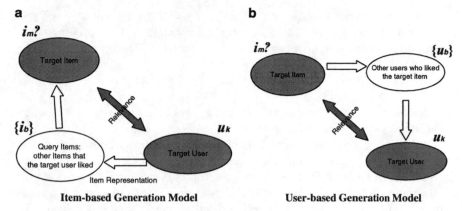

Fig. 4 Two different models in the User-Item Relevance Model

interest in), we sort these items in decreasing order. The highest ranked items are recommended to the user.

In order to estimate the conditional probabilities in Eq. (3), i.e., the relevance and non-relevance between the user and the item, we need to factorize the equation along the item or the user dimension. We propose to consider both *item-based generation*(i.e., using items as features to represent the user) and *user-based generation* (i.e., treating users as features to represent an item). This is illustrated in Fig. 4.

Item-based Generation Model

By factorizing $P\left(\bullet | u_k, i_m\right)$ with

$$\frac{P\left(u_k | i_m, \bullet\right) P\left(\bullet | i_m\right)}{P\left(u_k | i_m\right)},$$

the following log-odds ratio can be obtained from Eq. 3:

$$
\begin{aligned}
RSV_{u_k} & \left(i_m\right) \\
&= \log \frac{P\left(r | i_m, u_k\right)}{P\left(\bar{r} | i_m, u_k\right)} \\
&= \log \frac{P\left(u_k | i_m, r\right)}{P\left(u_k | i_m, \bar{r}\right)} + \log \frac{P\left(i_m | r\right) P\left(r\right)}{P\left(i_m | \bar{r}\right) P\left(\bar{r}\right)}
\end{aligned}
\tag{4}
$$

Eq. (4) provides a general ranking formula by employing the evidences from both relevance and non-relevance cases. When there is no explicit evidence for non-relevance, following the language modeling approach to information retrieval [Lafferty & Zhai 2003], we now assume that: 1) independence between u_k and

i_m in the non-relevance case $(\bar{r})$, i.e., $P\left(u_k|i_m,\bar{r}\right) = P(u_k|\bar{r})$; and, 2) equal priors for both u_k and i_m, given that the item is non-relevant. Then the two terms corresponding to non-relevance can be removed and the *RSV* becomes:

$$RSV_{u_k}\left(i_m\right) = \log P\left(u_k|i_m,r\right) + \log P\left(i_m|r\right) \tag{5}$$

Note that the two negative terms in Eq. (5) can always be added to the model, when the negative evidences are captured.

To estimate the conditional probability $P\left(u_k|i_m,r\right)$ in Eq. (5), consider the following: Instead of placing users in the sample space of *user id*'s, we can also use the set of items that the user likes (denoted L_{u_k} or $\{i_b\}$) to represent the user (u_k) (see the illustration in Fig. 4(a)). This step is similar to using a 'bag-of-words' representation of queries or documents in the text retrieval domain [Salton & McGill 1983]. This implies: $P\left(u_k|i_m,r\right) = P\left(L_{u_k}|i_m,r\right)$. We call these representing items the *query items*. Note that, unlike the target item i_m, the query items do not need to be ranked since the user has already expressed interest in them.

Further, we assume that the items $\{i_b\}$ in the user profile list L_{u_k} (query items) are conditionally independent from each other. Although this naive Bayes assumption does not hold in many real situations, it has been empirically shown to be a competitive approach (e.g., in text classification [Eyheramendy et al., 2003]). Under this assumption, Eq. (5) becomes:

$$
\begin{aligned}
RSV_{u_k}\left(i_m\right) \\
= \log P\left(L_{u_k}|i_m,r\right) + \log P\left(i_m|r\right) \qquad (6) \\
= \left(\sum_{\forall i_b : i_b \in L_{u_k}} \log P\left(i_b|i_m,r\right)\right) + \log P\left(i_m|r\right)
\end{aligned}
$$

where the conditional probability $P\left(i_b|i_m,r\right)$ corresponds to the relevance of an item i_b, given that another item i_m is relevant. This probability can be estimated by counting the number of user profiles that contain both items i_b and i_m, divided by the total number of user profiles in which i_m exists:

$$P_{ml}\left(i_b|i_m,r\right) = \frac{P\left(i_b,i_m|r\right)}{P\left(i_m|r\right)} = \frac{c\left(i_b,i_m\right)}{c\left(i_m\right)} \tag{7}$$

Using the frequency count to estimate the probability corresponds to using its maximum likelihood estimator. However, many item-to-item co-occurrence counts will be zero, due to the sparseness of the user-item matrix. Therefore, we apply a smoothing technique to adjust the maximum likelihood estimation.

A linear interpolation smoothing can be defined as a linear interpolation between the maximum likelihood estimation and background model. To use it, we define:

$$P\left(i_b|i_m,r\right) = (1-\lambda_i)\,P_{ml}\left(i_b|i_m,r\right) + \lambda_i\,P_{ml}\left(i_b|r\right)$$

where P_{ml} denotes the maximum likelihood estimation. The item prior probability $P_{ml}(i_b|r)$ is used as background model. Furthermore, the parameter λ_i in $[0,1]$ is a parameter that balances the maximum likelihood estimation and background model (a larger λ_i means more smoothing). Usually, the best value for λ_i is found from a training data by using a cross-validation method.

Linear interpolation smoothing leads to the following *RSV*:

$$RSV_{u_k}(i_m)$$

$$= \left(\sum_{\forall i_b : i_b \in L_{u_k}} \log \left((1 - \lambda_i) P_{ml}(i_b|i_m, r) + \lambda_i P_{ml}(i_b|r) \right) \right) \tag{8}$$

$$+ \log P_{ml}(i_m|r)$$

where the maximum likelihood estimations of the item prior probability densities are given as follows:

$$P_{ml}(i_b|r) = \frac{c(i_b, r)}{c(r)}, \; P_{ml}(i_m|r) = \frac{c(i_m, r)}{c(r)} \tag{9}$$

User-based Generation Model

Similarly, by factorizing $P(\bullet|u_k, i_m)$ with

$$\frac{P(i_m|u_k, \bullet) \, P(\bullet|u_k)}{P(i_m|u_k)}$$

the following log-odds ratio can be obtained from Eq. (3) :

$$RSV_{u_k}(i_m)$$

$$= \log \frac{P(i_m|u_k, r)}{P(i_m|u_k, \bar{r})} + \log \frac{P(u_k|r) \, P(r)}{P(u_k|\bar{r}) \, P(\bar{r})}$$

$$\propto \log \frac{P(i_m|u_k, r)}{P(i_m|u_k, \bar{r})} \tag{10}$$

When the non-relevance evidence is absent, and following the language model in information retrieval [Lafferty & Zhai 2003], we now assume equal priors for i_m in the non-relevant case. Then, the non-relevance term can be removed and the *RSV* becomes:

$$RSV_{u_k}(i_m) = \log P(i_m|u_k, r) \tag{11}$$

Instead of using the item list to represent the user, we use each user's judgment as a feature to represent an item (see the illustration in Fig. 4(b)). For this, we introduce a list L_{i_m} for each item i_m, where $m = \{1, \ldots, M\}$. This list enumerates the users who have expressed interest in the item i_m. $L_{i_m}(u_k) = 1$ (or $u_k \in L_{i_m}$) denotes that user u_k is in the list, while $L_{i_m}(u_k) = 0$ (or $u_k \notin L_{i_m}$) otherwise. The number of users in the list corresponds to $|L_{i_m}|$.

Replacing i_m with L_{i_m}, after we assume each user's judgment to a particular item is independent, we have:

$$
\begin{aligned}
& RSV_{u_k}(i_m) \\
&= \log P(L_{i_m}|u_k, r) \\
&= \sum_{\forall u_b : u_b \in L_{i_m}} \log P(u_b|u_k, r)
\end{aligned}
\tag{12}
$$

Similar to the item-based generation model, when we use linear interpolation smoothing to estimate $P(u_b|u_k, r)$, we obtain the final ranking formula:

$$
\begin{aligned}
& RSV_{u_k}(i_m) \\
&= \log P(L_{i_m}|u_k, r) \\
&= \sum_{\forall u_b : u_b \in L_{i_m}} \log \left((1 - \lambda_u) P_{ml}(u_b|u_k, r) + \lambda_u P_{ml}(u_b|r) \right)
\end{aligned}
\tag{13}
$$

where $\lambda_u \in [0, 1]$ is the smoothing parameter.

Statistical Ranking Mechanisms

Our models provide a very intuitive understanding of the statistical ranking mechanisms that play a role in log-based collaborative filtering. More formally, from Eq. (8) and (13), we can obtain the following ranking functions for the user-based generation and item-based generation models, respectively (see [Wang et al., 2006a] for the detailed information):

Item-based Generation Model:

$$
\begin{aligned}
Rank_{u_k}(i_m) = & \\
& \left(\sum_{\forall i_b : i_b \in L_{u_k} \cap c(i_b, i_m) > 0} \log \left(1 + \frac{(1 - \lambda_i) P_{ml}(i_b|i_m, r)}{\lambda_i P_{ml}(i_b|r)} \right) \right) \\
& + \log P(i_m|r)
\end{aligned}
\tag{14}
$$

User-based Generation Model:

$$Rank_{u_k}(i_m) =$$

$$\left(\sum_{\forall u_b : u_b \in L_{i_m} \cap c(u_b, u_k) > 0} \log \left(1 + \frac{(1 - \lambda_u) P_{ml}(u_b | u_k, r)}{\lambda_u P_{ml}(u_b | r)} \right) \right) \quad (15)$$

$$+ |L_{i_m}| \log \lambda_u$$

From the item-based generation model (Eq. (14)), we can see that: 1) The relevance rank of a target item i_m is the sum of its popularity (prior probability $P(i_m|r)$) and its co-occurrence (first term in Eq. (14)) with the items i_b in the profile list of the target users. The co-occurrence is higher if more users express interest in target item (i_m) as well as item i_b. However, the co-occurrence should be suppressed more when the popularity of the item in the profile of the target user ($P(i_b|r)$) is higher. 2) When λ_i approaches 0, smoothing from the background model is minimal. It emphasizes the co-occurrence count, and the model reduces to the traditional item-based approach [Deshpande & Karypis 2004]. When the λ_i approaches 1, the model is more smooth, emphasizing the background model. When the parameter equals 1, the ranking becomes equivalent to *coordination level matching*, which is simply counting the number of times for which $c(i_b, i_m) > 0$.

From the user-based generation model (Eq. (15)), we can see that the relevance rank is calculated based on the opinions of other similar users. For a target user and target program, the rank of their relevance is basically the sum of the target user's co-occurrence with other similar users who have liked the target program. The co-occurrence is higher if there are more programs the two users agree upon (express interest in the same program). However, the co-occurrence should be suppressed more when the similar user has liked more programs, since he or she is less discriminative.

Personalized User Interfaces

When designing a user interface for a distributed system like *Tribler*, it is important to reach and maintain a critical mass since the users are the decisive factors of the system's success ([Fokker & De Ridder , 2005]). Therefore, several usability aspects have to be dealt with: 1) the wealth and complexity of content, 2) the lack of trust among users, 3) no guarantee of system or content integrity, and 4) the need for voluntary cooperation among users. Here we only addresses and illustrates the first two aspects.

A user is unable to deal with an unlimited number of programs to choose from. Our distributed recommender system helps to filter according to the implicitly learned interests. Subsequently it becomes important to communicate the results

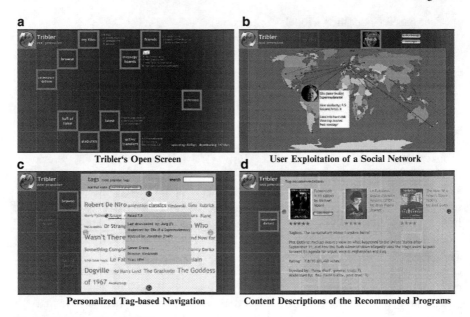

Fig. 5 User interface of Tribler

in a way that makes sense to a user and allows for exploration and exploitation of the available content in spite of the lack of trust amongst users.

In Fig. 5 we illustrate our thoughts on a user interface for a decentralized recommender system, as applied in *Tribler*. Figure 5(a) is *Tribler*'s opening screen. In Fig. 5(b) we show a user's social network in which relations are expressed in social distances: friend, friend-of-a-friend, or taste buddy (which is obtained by running our *Buddycast* algorithm). With this the exploitation of the community is stimulated because users can look into each other's hard disks directly, thus rewarding the risks users take when allowing taste buddies to communicate with them. Figure 5(c) shows the personalized tag-based navigation, which is a popular way of displaying filtered results or recommendations, as in Flickr.com or CiteULike.org. The font size of each tag reflects its relevance towards user. The relevance rank of each tag can be calculated by summing up all the relevance ranks from its attached programs. This feature incorporates a reflection on the origins, and trustworthiness of the recommended content. We believe this will reduce the uncertainty about the quality and integrity of the programs and lack of trust among users. Moreover it stimulates users to explore new content in a natural way. Figure 5(d) demonstrates content descriptions of recommended programs. As with the tag-based navigations, it incorporates a reflection on the origins, quality, and integrity. Furthermore, it provides more background information on items, like in IMDb.com.

Experiments and Results

We have conducted a set of experiments with the *Tribler* system on a real data set containing the TV zapping behavior of users to address the following questions:

1. What zapping behaviors do we observe and what can be learned from these behaviors to implicitly derive the interest of users in TV programs?
2. How sensitive is the recommendation of TV programs as a function of the user interest threshold T and what is the optimal value taking into account the efficiency of exchanging interest between users?
3. How efficient is our proposed *BuddyCast* algorithm compared to the newscast algorithm when we want to exchange user interest profiles?

Data Set

We used a data set that contained the TV zapping behavior of 6000 Dutch users over 19 channels from the SKO foundation[1]. The remote controls actions were recorded from January 1 to January 31, 2003. Some basic characteristics of this data set are shown in Fig. 6. We employed the EPG data set obtained from Omroep.nl (an online TV program guide) to find TV program IDs[2]. This resulted in 8578 unique programs and 27179 broadcasting slots over the 19 Channels in that period (this includes reruns and episodes of the samne TV program). Figure 9 shows statistics about the

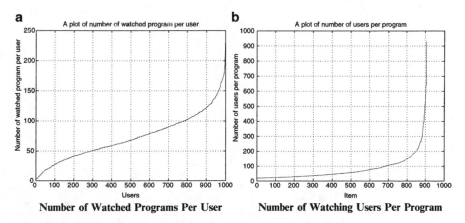

Fig. 6 SKO data set of user actions on remote controls

---

[1] http://www.kijkonderzoek.nl
[2] http://omroep.nl

number of times TV programs are broadcast. For instance, news is broadcast several times a day. Series have different episodes and are broadcast for example weekly.

Another dataset we used to evaluate our recommendation method is called Audioscrobbler dataset. The data set is collected from the music play-lists of the users in the Audioscrobbler community[3] by using a plug-in in the users' media players (for instance, Winamp, iTunes, XMMS etc). Plug-ins send the title (song name and artist name) of every song users play to the Audioscrobbler server, which updates the user's musical profile with the new song. That is, when a user plays a song in a certain time, this transaction is recorded as a form of userID, itemID, t tuple in the database.

Observations of the Data Set

This SKO TV data set can be used to analyze the zapping behavior of users for particular TV programs. In Fig. 7 this is shown for a more popular movie, "Live and Let Die" (1973), and a less popluar movie, "Someone she knows" (1994).

For example, when we look at the beginning of the two programs, it clearly shows the difference of the user attention for the less popular film, i.e., the number of watching users drops significantly for the first 5 minutes or so. Probably, these users first zapped into the channel to check out the movie and realized that it was not interesting movie for them and zapped away. Contrarily, the number of watching users steadily increasing in the first minutes for the more popular.

Another interesting observation in both figures is that during the whole broadcasting time, there were some intervals of about five to ten minutes, in which the

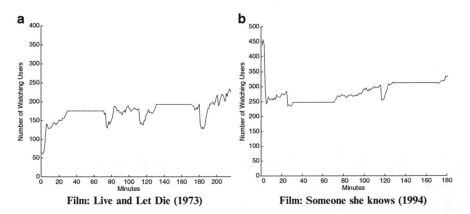

Film: Live and Let Die (1973)   Film: Someone she knows (1994)

Fig. 7 Program attention

---

[3] https://last.fm

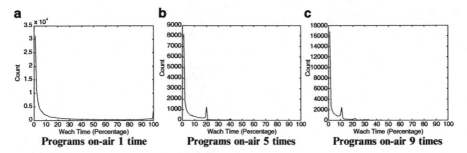

Fig. 8 Percentage of watching time for programs with different on-air times

Fig. 9 Program on-air times
during Jan.1 to Jan 30,2003

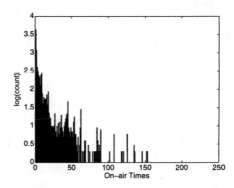

number of watching users dropped. This is because some users left the channel
when commercials began and zapped back again when they had supposedly ended.

Figure 8 shows the number of users with respect to their percentages of watching
times $(WatchLenght(k,m)/OnAirlength(m))$ for programs with different number of
times that they are broadcast (on-air times of 1, 5 and 9).

This shows clearly two peaks: the larger peak on the left indicates a large number
of users who only watched small parts of a program. The second smaller peak on
the right indicates that a large number of users watched the whole programs once
regardless of the number of times that the program was broadcast. That is, the right
peak happens in 20% of the programs that are broadcast five times (one fifth), and
in 11% of the programs that are broadcast nine times (1 ninth), etc. There is a third
peak which happens in 22% in the programs which are broadcast nine times. This
indicates that there are still a few users who watched the entire program twice, for
example to follow a series.

These observations motivated us to normalize the percentage of watching time by
the number of broadcastings of a program as explained in Eq. 2, in order to arrive at
the measure of interest within a TV program. This normalized percentage is shown
in Fig. 10. Now all the second peaks are located at the 100% position.

Fig. 10 Normalized percentage of watching time

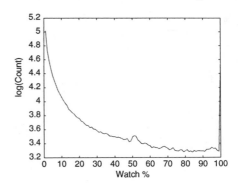

Learning the User Interest Threshold

The threshold level, T, above which the normalized percentage of watching time is considered to express interest in a TV program (Eq. (3)) is determined by evaluating the performance of the recommendation for different setting of this threshold.

The recommendation performance is measured by using *precision* and *recall* of a set of test users. Precision measures the proportion of recommended programs that the user truly likes. Recall measures the proportion of the programs that a user truly likes that are recommended. In case of making recommendations, precision seems more important than recall. However, to analyze the behavior of our method, we report both metrics on our experimental results.

Since we lack information on what the users liked, we considered programs that a user watched more than once $(x_{k,m} > 1)$ to be programs that the user likes and all other programs as shows that the user does not like. Note that, in this way, only a fraction of the programs that the user *truly* liked are caputered. Therefore, the measured precision *underestimates* the true precision [Hull 1993].

For cross-validation, we randomly divided this data set into a training set (80% of the users) and a test set (20% of the users). The training set was used to estimate the model. The test set was used for evaluating the accuracy of the recommendations on the new users, whose user profiles are not in the training set. Results are obtains by averaging 5 different runs of such a random division.

We plotted the performance of recommendations (both precision and recall) against the threshold on the percentage of watching time in Fig. 11. We also varied the number of programs returned by the recommender (top-1, 10, 20, 40, 80 or 100 recommended TV programs). Figure 11(a) shows that in general, the threshold does not affect the precision too much. For the large number of programs recommended, the precision becomes slightly better when there is a larger threshold. For larger number of recommended programs, the recall, however, drops for larger threshold values (shown in Fig. 11(b)). Since the threshold does not affect the precision too much, a higher threshold is chosen in order to reduce the length of the user interest profiles to be exchanged within the network. For that reason we have chosen a threshold value of 0.8.

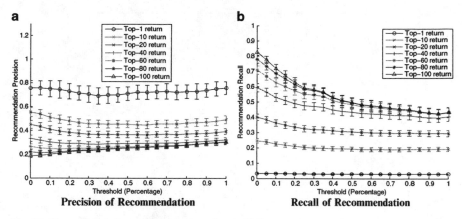

Fig. 11 Recommendation performance *v.s.* threshold *T*

Convergence Behavior of BuddyCast

We have emulated our *BuddyCast* algorithm using a cluster of PCs (the DAS-2[4] system). The simulated network consisted of 480 users distributed uniformly over 32 nodes. We used the user profiles of 480 users. Each user maintained a list of 10 taste buddies ($N = 10$) and the 10 last visited users ($K = 10$). The system was initialized by giving each user a random other user. The exploration-to- exploitation δ was set to 1.

Figure 12 compares the convergence of *BuddyCast* to that of newscast (randomly select connecting users, i.e., $\delta \rightarrow \infty$). After each update we compared the list of top-N taste buddies with a pre-compiled list of top-N taste buddies generated using all data (centralized approach). In Fig. 12, the percentage of overlap is shown as a function of time (represented by the number of updates). The figure shows that the convergence of Buddycast is much faster than that of the Newscast approach.

Recommendation Performance

We first studied the behavior of the linear interpolation smoothing for recommendation. For this, we plotted the average precision and recall rate for the different values of the smoothing parameter λ_i in the Audioscrobbler data set. This is shown in Fig. 13.

Figure 13(a) and (b) show that both precision and recall drop when λ_i reaches its extreme values zero and one. The precision is sensitive to λ_i, especially the early precision (when only a small number of items are recommended). Recall is less

---

[4] http://www.cs.vu.nl/das2

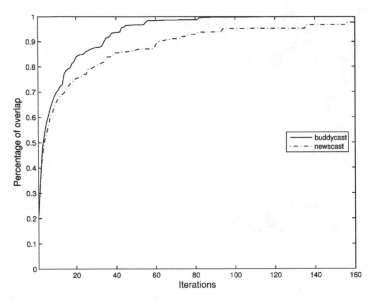

Fig. 12 Convergence of our *buddycast algorithm*

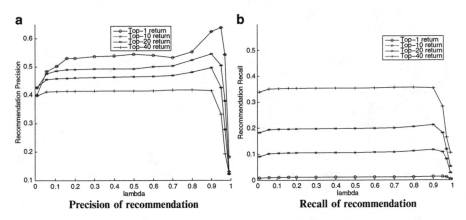

Fig. 13 Recommendation performance of the linear interpolation smoothing

sensitive to the actual value of this parameter, having its optimum at a wide range of values. Effectiveness tends to be higher on both metrics when λ_i is large; when λ_i is approximately 0.9, the precision seems optimal. An optimal range of λ_i near one can be explained by the sparsity of user profiles, causing the prior probability $P_{ml}(i_b|r)$ to be much smaller than the conditional probability $P_{ml}(i_b|i_m, r)$. The background model is therefore only emphasized for values of λ_i closer to one. In combination with the experimental results that we obtained, this suggests that smoothing the co-occurrence probabilities with the background model (prior probability $P_{ml}(i_b|r)^{\cdot}$) improves recommendation performance.

Table 1 Comparison of recommendation performance

	Top-1 Item	Top-10 Item	Top-20 Item	Top-40 Item
(a) Precision				
UIR-Item	0.62	0.52	0.44	0.35
Item-TFIDF	0.55	0.47	0.40	0.31
Item-CosSin	0.56	0.46	0.38	0.31
Item-CorSim	0.50	0.38	0.33	0.27
Item-CorSim	0.55	0.42	0.34	0.27
(b) Recall				
UIR-Item	0.02	0.15	0.25	0.40
Item-TFIDF	0.02	0.15	0.26	0.41
Item-CosSin	0.02	0.13	0.22	0.35
Item-CorSim	0.01	0.11	0.19	0.31
Item-CorSim	0.02	0.15	0.25	0.39

Next, we compared our relevance model to other log-based collaborative filtering approaches. Our goal here is to see, using our user-item relevance model, whether the smoothing and inverse item frequency should improve recommendation performance with respect to the other methods. For this, we focused on the item-based generation (denoted as UIR-Item). We set λ_i to the optimal value 0.9. We compared our results to those obtained with the *Top-N-suggest* recommendation engine, a well-known log-based collaborative filtering implementation[5] [Deshpande & Karypis 2004]. This engine implements a variety of log-based recommendation algorithms. We compared our own results to both the item-based *TF* × *IDF*-like version (denoted as ITEM-TFIDF) as well the user-based cosine similarity method (denoted as User-CosSim), setting the parameters to the optimal ones according to the user manual. Additionally, for item-based approaches, we also used other similarity measures: the commonly used cosine similarity (denoted as Item-CosSim) and Pearson correlation (denoted as Item-CorSim). Results are shown in Table 1.

For the precision, our user-item relevance model with the item-based generation (UIR-Item) outperforms other log-based collaborative filtering approaches for all four different number of returned items. Overall, *TF* × *IDF*-like ranking ranks second. The obtained experimental results demonstrate that smoothing contributes to a better recommendation precision in the two ways also found by [Zhai & Lafferty 2001]. On the one hand, smoothing compensates for missing data in the user-item matrix, and on the other hand, it plays the role of inverse item frequency to emphasize the weight of the items with the best discriminative power. With respect to recall, all four algorithms perform almost identically. This is consistent to our first experiment that recommendation precision is sensitive to the smoothing parameters while the recommendation recall is not.

---

[5] http://www-users.cs.umn.edu/~karypis/suggest/

Conclusions

paper discussed personalization in a personalized peer-to-peer television system called *Tribler*, i.e., 1) the exchange of user interest profiles between users by automatically creating social groups based on the interest of users, 2) learning these user interest profiles from zapping behavior, 3) the relevance model to predict user interest, and 4) a personalized user interface to browse the available content making use of recommendation technology. Experiments on two real data sets show that personalization can increase the effectiveness to exchange content and enables to explore the wealth of available TV programs in a peer-to-peer environment.

References

Ali, K. & van Stam, W., (2004). TiVo: Making Show Recommendations Using a Distributed Collaborative Filtering Architecture. *International ACM SIGKDD Conference on Knowledge Discovery and Data Mining.*

Ardissono, L., Kobsa, A., & Maybury, M. (Ed). (2004). *Personalized Digital Television. Targeting programs to individual users.* Kluwer Academic Publishers.

Breese, J. S., Heckerman, D., & Kadie, C., (1998). Empirical Analysis of Predictive Algorithms for Collaborative Filtering. *Conference on Uncertainty in Artificial Intelligence.*

Claypool, M., Waseda, M., Le, P., & Brow, D. C., (2001). Implicit interest indicators. *International Conference on Intelligent User Interfaces.*

Deshpande, M. & Karypis, G. (2004). Item-based top-n recommendation algorithms. *ACM Transactions on Information Systems.*

Eugster, P.T., Guerraoui, R., Kermarrec, A.M., & Massoulie, L. (2004), From epidemics to distributed computing, *IEEE Computer.* 21(3):341–374.

Eyheramendy, S., Lewis, D., & Madigan. D. (2003). On the naive bayes model for text categorization. In *Proc. of Artificial Intelligence and Statistics.*

Fokker, J.E. & De Ridder, H. (2005). Technical Report on the Human Side of Cooperating in Decentralized Networks. *Internal report I-Share Deliverable 1.2*, Delft University of Technology. http://www.cs.vu.nl/ishare/public/I-Share-D1.2.pdf

Hofmann, T. (2004). Latent Semantic Models for Collaborative Filtering. *ACM Transactions on Information Systems.*

Herlocker, J.L., Konstan, J.A., Borchers, A., & Riedl J. (1999). An algorithmic framework for performing collaborative filtering. *International ACM SIGIR Conference on Research Development on Information Retrieval.*

Hull. D. (1993). Using statistical testing in the evelution of retrieval experiments. *International ACM SIGIR Conference on Research Development on Information Retrieval.*

Jelasity, M & van Steen, M. (2002). Large-Scale Newscast Computing on the Internet. *Internal report IR-503*, Vrije Universiteit, Department of Computer Science.

Lafferty, J., & Zhai, C. (2003). Probabilistic relevance models based on document and query generation. In W. B. Croft and J. Lafferty, editors, *Language Modeling and Information Retrieval.* Kluwer Academic Publishers.

Linden G., Smith, B., & York J. (2003). Amazon. com recommendations: item-to-item collaborative filtering. IEEE *Internet Computing.*

Linden G., Smith, B., & York J. (2003). Amazon. com recommendations: item-to-item collaborative filtering. IEEE *Internet Computing.*

Marlin B. (2004). *Collaborative filtering: a machine learning perspective.* Master's thesis, Department of Computer Science, University of Toronto.

Miller, B.M., Konstan, J.A., & Riedl, J. (2004) PocketLens: Toward a Personal Recommender System. *ACM Transactions on Information Systems.*

Nichols, D. (1998). Implicit rating and filtering. In *Proceedings of 5th DELOS Workshop on Filtering and Collaborative Filtering*, pages 31-36, ERCIM.

Pouwelse, J. A., Garbacki, P., Wang, J., Bakker, A., Yang, J., Iosup, A., Epema, D.H.J, Reinders, M.J.T van Steen, M., & Sips, H.J. (2005). Tribler: A social-based Peer-to-Peer system. *International Workshop on Peer-to-Peer Systems (IPTPS'06).*

Sarwar, B., Karypis, G., Konstan, J., & Riedl, J. (2001). Item-based collaborative filtering recommendation algorithms. *International World Wide Web Conference.*

Wang, J., de Vries, A.P., & Reinders, M.J.T, (2005a). A User-Item Relevance Model for Log-based Collaborative Filtering. *European Conference on Information Retrieval.*

Wang, J., de Vries, A.P., & Reinders, M.J.T, (2006b). Unifying User-based and Item-based Collaborative Filtering by Similarity Fusion. *International ACM SIGIR Conference on Research Development on Information Retrieval.*

Wang, J., Pouwelse, J., Lagendijk, R., & Reinders, M.J.T, (2006c). Distributed Collaborative Filtering for Peer-to-Peer File Sharing Systems, *ACM Symposium on Applied Computing.*

Xue, G, Lin, C., Yang, Q., Xi, W., Zeng, H., Yu, Y., & Chen. Z. (2005). Scalable Collaborative Filtering Using Cluster-based Smoothing. *International ACM SIGIR Conference on Research Development on Information Retrieval.*

Zhai. C., & Lafferty. J. (2001). A Study of Smoothing Methods for Language Models Applied to Ad Hoc Information Retrieval. *International ACM SIGIR Conference on Research Development on Information Retrieval.*

Chapter 5
A Target Advertisement System Based on TV Viewer's Profile Reasoning

Jeongyeon Lim, Munjo Kim, Bumshik Lee, Munchurl Kim, Heekyung Lee, and Han-kyu Lee

Introduction

With the rapidly growing Internet, the Internet broadcasting and web casting service have been one of the well-known services. Specially, it is expected that the IPTV service will be one of the principal services in the broadband network [2]. However, the current broadcasting environment is served for the general public and requires the passive attitude to consume the TV programs. For the advanced broadcasting environments, various research of the personalized broadcasting is needed. For example, the current unidirectional advertisement provides to the TV viewers the advertisement contents, depending on the popularity of TV programs, the viewing rates, the age groups of TV viewers, and the time bands of the TV programs being broadcast. It is not an efficient way to provide the useful information to the TV viewers from customization perspective. If a TV viewer does not need particular advertisement contents, then information may be wasteful to the TV viewer. Therefore, it is expected that the target advertisement service will be one of the important services in the personalized broadcasting environments. The current research in the area of the target advertisement classifies the TV viewers into clustered groups who have similar preference. The digital TV collaborative filtering estimates the user's favourite advertisement contents by using the usage history [1, 4, 5]. In these studies, the TV viewers are required to provide their profile information such as the gender, job, and ages to the service providers via a PC or Set-Top Box (STB) which is connected to digital TV. Based on explicit information, the advertisement contents are provided to the TV viewers in a customized way with tailored advertisement contents. However, the TV viewers may dislike exposing to the service providers their

J. Lim (✉), M. Kim, B. Lee, and M. Kim
Information and Communications University,
119 Munji Street, Yuseong-gu,
Daejeon 305-732, Korea
e-mail: {jylim; kimmj; bslee; mkim}@icu.ac.kr

H. Lee, and H.-K. Lee
Electronics and Telecommunications Research Institute, Daejeon, Korea
e-mail: {lhk95; hkl}@etri.re.kr

B. Furht (ed.), *Handbook of Multimedia for Digital Entertainment and Arts*,
DOI 10.1007/978-0-387-89024-1_5, © Springer Science+Business Media, LLC 2009

private information because of the misuse of it. In this case, it is difficult to provide appropriate target advertisement service.

In this paper, we only utilize implicit information of TV usage history such as the viewing date, viewing time, and genres for TV programs. We design a multi-stage classifier as a profile reasoning algorithm for TV viewers. The proposed multi-stage classifier is trained with real usage history data of 2,522 people for TV programs. We also develop a target advertisement system based on the TV viewers' profile reasoning algorithm. The target advertisement system selects and provides relevant commercials to the targeted groups. This paper is organized as follows: Section 5 presents the architecture of our target advertisement system with possible applications scenarios; Section 5 describes our proposed profile reasoning algorithm for TV viewers, which classifies unknown TV viewers into an appropriate gender–age group; Section 5 addresses a commercial selection method for target advertisement; Plenty of experimental results are provided and analyzed for the profile reasoning performance; and finally we conclude our work in concluding section.

Architecture of Proposed Target Advertisement System

In the proposed target advertisement service system, there are three major entities: a content provider, advertisement companies, and TV viewers. The proposed target advertisement system consists of the following necessary modules; a profile reasoning module to infer a TV viewer's profile by analyzing their TV usage history, a broadcasting transmission module to recommend services based on the inferred result, and a user interface module to protect TV viewers' profile. The terminals at the TV viewers' side send limited information with their TV usage history to the service provider (target advertisement system), and receives the selected commercials which are recommended by the target advertisement service system. Figure 1 shows the architecture of our proposed target advertisement system. The target advertisement system consists of three agents such as an inference agent of TV viewer profiles which has the profile reasoning module for TV viewers, a content provision agent which contains a selection module of appropriate TV commercials to the targeted TV viewers and a transmission module for TV program contents, and a user interface agent which consists of an input interface module and a TV usage history transmission module.

In Fig. 1, the profile inference agent of TV viewers receives the usage history data of TV programs such as TV program titles, genres, channels, viewing times band, and viewing days of the week from the user interface agent. By utilizing this information, the profile inference agent infers the TV viewers' profile in their preferred genres and time bands of TV viewing for the groups of different genders and ages by the profile reasoning module, and the inference results are sent to the content provision agent. Based on the profile inference results, the content provision agent selects appropriate commercial contents to unknown target TV viewers by the advertisement content selection module. The selected commercial contents can be

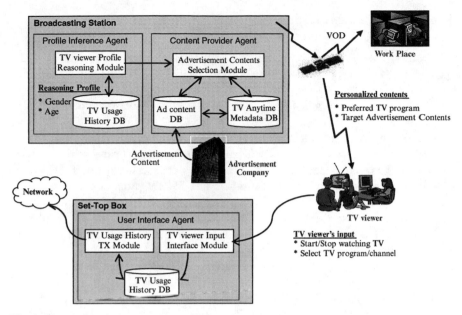

Fig. 1 Target advertisement system architecture

distributed by the broadcasting station with TV program contents or VoD (Video on Demand). The user interface agent provides a GUI which enables TV viewers to consume contents or relative data at the TV terminal. The user interface agent works on the STB (Set-Top Box) which enables the TV viewers to consume the recommended TV commercial contents with TV programs from the content provider agent. While the TV viewers watch TV programs, the user interface agent stores the usage data of the TV programs being watched into the TV usage history DB of STB through the input interface module. By the level of information provision for the TV program consumption, stored information is divided into TV usage information and private information. Only a limited amount of information about TV program consumption is transmitted to the profile inference agent through the TV usage history transmission module, which makes it possible to infer TV viewers' profiles.

Proposed Profile Reasoning Algorithm

In this section, we describe a multi-stage classifier for the proposed profile reasoning algorithm, and explain how to extract feature vectors in order to train the multi-stage classifier.

Analysis of Features Depending on User Profiles

The feature vector for profile reasoning algorithm can be obtained from the TV usage history. In this paper, we use usage history data of TV programs for male and female TV viewers in different ages by AC Nielson Korea. The TV usage history has various fields as shown in Table 1. The TV usage history was recorded by 2,522 people (Male: 1,243 and Female: 1,279) from Dec. 2002 to May, 2003. The TV programs are categorized into eight genres such as *News, Information, Drama&Movie, Entertainments, Sports, Education Child*, and *Miscellaneous*. The usage history data of TV programs were collected via six broadcasting channels. The one TV channel is dedicated for the education and the others provide TV programs in all genres. Figure 2 shows the TV viewing time bands of male and female TV viewers over weekday from the usage history data of TV programs. In Fig. 2, the y-axis indicates the portion of the total TV watching time over different TV watching time bands in the x-axis. As shown in Fig. 2, the watching time bands are different for the TV viewers in different genders and ages. It is observed from Fig. 2 that, in the morning, the portion of TV viewing time by 50s and 60s is relatively higher than those of the other ages. The children (the 0s TV viewers) and teenager groups mainly watch TV programs from 5 to 9 P.M. because the TV programs such as Comics and Drama for the children are usually served after school. The male 20s $\sim$ 40s do not usually have much time to watch TV programs during the day time than others. So, we can guess that they usually watch TV during night. The total TV watching time of male 20s and female 20s is the lowest and that of 60s in both genders is the highest comparatively.

The TV programs are scheduled by the broadcasting stations, and the TV programs have similar schedules except for the specific channel (EBS: Education Broadcasting System). For example, the five broadcasting companies serves *News* program contents during $8 \sim 9$ P.M. The time band of $10 \sim 11$ P.M. is prime time to watch TV drama in Korea. So, we can guess the user's genre preferences can be affected by the TV program schedules by the broadcasting service companies. The longer the TV watching time is, the more various the watched TV program genres are.

Table 1 Fields and description of TV usage history DB

Field Name	Description
id	TV viewer's ID
profile	TV viewer's gender and age group
date	A date of watching TV program
dayofweek	A day of the week for TV program
subscstart_t	Beginning time point of watching TV
subscend_t	Ending time point of watching TV
programstart_t	Scheduled beginning time of TV program
programend_t	Scheduled ending time of TV program
title	Title of TV program
channel	Channel of TV program (six channels)
genre	Genre of TV program (eight genres)

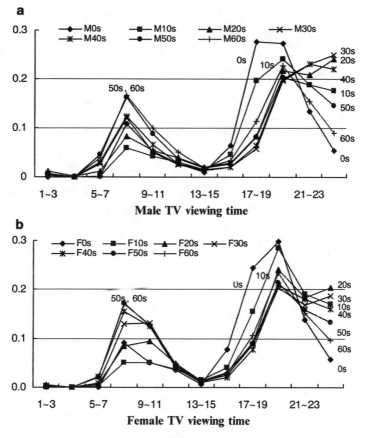

Fig. 2 TV viewing time of each gender and ages

Figure 3 shows the characteristics of TV program consumption patterns by male and female TV viewers. The values in the y-axis are the genre probabilities by counting the number of the watched TV program for each genre. In Fig. 3a and b, both genders show the similar genre preferences. However, the degree of the genre preferences is different. For example, the female TV viewers tend to watch *Drama&Movie* contents in more favour than the *News* contents. On the other hand, the male TV viewers more prefer to the *News* contents than the TV contents in other genres. Therefore, we use genre preference to discriminate TV viewers into different gender-ages groups.

Also, a user's action such as channel hopping exhibits different characteristics, depending on the ages and genders even though the TV viewers in the different ages and genders watch the same TV program contents. Figure 4 shows the genre probabilities of TV program contents which are estimated by the consumed time on each TV program genre compared to the total TV watching time. The whole shapes of the graphs look similar to those in Fig. 3 in which the genre preference

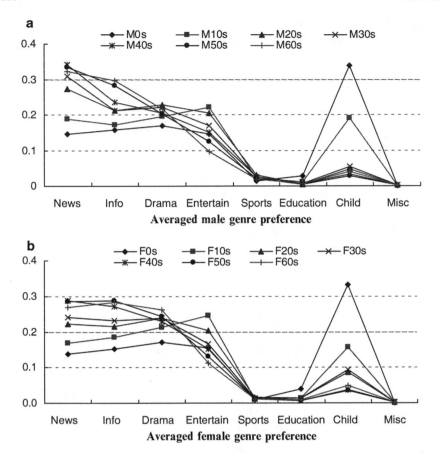

Fig. 3 Genre preferences by the genre probability using the number of watched TV genre

for each gender–ages group was measured as the ratio of the number of watching TV programs in each genre to the total number of watching TV programs in all genres.

As shown in Figs. 3 and 4, we can use as discriminatory features the two genre probabilities of the watching times and watching numbers to distinguish the TV viewers into different gender–ages groups. By analyzing the TV viewer's preference in detail, we can achieve high prediction results on reasoning gender–ages groups for unknown TV viewer by his/her usage history date of TV program consumption.

Finally, specific channel information with education, game, music, stocks and news can be an important key for reasoning the TV viewer's gender–ages groups. As described above, we take into account how many times the TV program contents have consumed in each genre, how long the TV program contents have consumed in each genre, the average TV watching time, and how many times the TV viewers have watched TV program content on each channel.

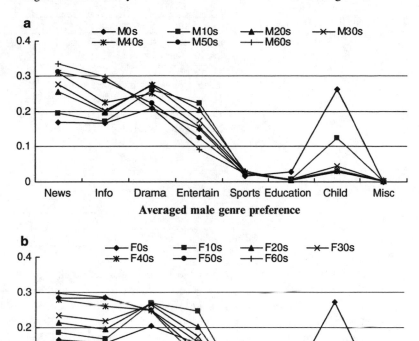

Fig. 4 Genre preferences by the genre probability using the occupied time of watched TV genre

Feature Extraction

For the reasoning of the TV viewer's gender and ages, we consider the number of the watching genre, the watching time of the genre, the averaged watching time and the total occupied time on each channel for the feature vector to distinguish TV viewer's groups.

Before we compute feature vector elements, uncertain history data are removed according to the following conditions:

- $\frac{D_c}{D_p} \geq T_{\mathrm{Th}}$
- $\sum_{m \subset D_o} N_m \geq C_{\mathrm{Th}}$

where D_c and D_c are the total duration and the total watching time of the TV program content, respectively. T_{Th} is a threshold value to compare with the ratio of D_c and D_c. With the first condition, the TV program contents that were consumed during a short period of time are excluded from the training data of the usage history

Table 2 Types and the number of feature values

Types of feature values and equations	Number
Genre Probability based on the number of counts (GPRC) $GPRC_{i,k,a} = GC_{i,k,a}/\sum_{i=1}^{I} GC_{i,k,a}$	8
Genre probability based on the amount of consumption time (GPRT) $GPRT_{i,k,a} = GT_{i,k,a}/\sum_{i=1}^{I} GT_{i,k,a}$	8
Average viewing time (AVT) $AVT_{k,a} = CT_{k,a}/TotTime$	1
Channel probability based on the amount of consumption time (CPR) $CPR_{j,k,a} = C_{j,k,a}/\sum_{j=1}^{J} C_{j,k,a}$	6

Table 3 Feature vector

Index	$1 \sim 8$	$9 \sim 16$	17	$18 \sim 23$
Feature Values	GPRC	GPRT	AVT	CPR

because the amount of consumption time is too short compared to the total time length of the TV program content. The second condition is used to exclude the usage history data for the TV viewers who seldom watched the TV that contains. If the total number $\sum_{m \subset D_o} N_m$ of TV watching during a certain observation period D_o is less that a predefined threshold C_{Th}, then the usage history of the TV viewers are also excluded from the training data. For the usage history data that satisfies the two conditions, we calculate the following feature values described in Table 2.

In Table 2, $GC_{i,k,a}$ is the frequency of watching genre i of a TV viewer k in an gender–ages group a during a pre-determined period, and $GT_{i,k,a}$ is the consumption time of genre i of the TV viewer k in the group a during the period. Also, $CT_{k,a}$ is the consumption time of the TV viewer k in the group a during the period. Lastly, $C_{j,k,a}$ is the consumption time of channel j of the TV viewer k in the group a during the period. I and J are the total numbers of the genres and channels. By utilizing feature values and equations in Table 2, we can generate a feature vector for each TV viewer for each date of every week. The feature vector is expressed as Table 3. The feature vector in Table 3 has 23 feature values. The first eight elements are the genre probability based on the number of counts (GPRC) values and the second eight elements are the genre probability based on the amount of consumption time (GPRT) values for all eight genres. The 17th element is the average viewing time (AVT) and the last six elements indicate the channel probability based on the amount of consumption time (CPR) values for the six channels. We compute the feature vectors for all TV viewers and also calculate the group vectors of the feature vectors for each gender–ages group. Notice that the group vector is the mean vector of the feature vectors for each gender–ages group. Therefore, the group vectors are the representative vectors for their respective gender–ages groups. The profile inference agent in Fig. 1 maintains a look-up table with the group vectors for the gender–ages groups. The multi-stage classifier (MSC) infers a TV viewer's profile from his/her feature vectors by comparing to the group vectors in the look-up table. In usage history data, we compute the feature vectors from Monday to Friday because most gender–ages groups have similar viewing patterns in the weekend.

The First Stage Classifier

The 1st stage classifier is performed by a metric to measure the similarity between a feature vector and all group vectors for a specific day of the week. The similarity measure between two vectors is calculated by the vector correlation (VC) and the normalized Euclidean distance (ED). The VC value to measure the similarity is obtained from (1) [6].

$$VC(x, y) = \cos \theta = \frac{x \cdot y}{\|x\| \cdot \|y\|} = \frac{\sum_{i=1}^{m} x_i y_i}{\sqrt{\sum_{i=1}^{m} x_i^2} \sqrt{\sum_{i=1}^{m} y_i^2}} \tag{1}$$

However, the vector correlation only measures the angle between two vectors. That is, the vector correlation does not take into account the distance between the two vectors.

The normalized Euclidean distance uses the variances as the normalized term of the Euclidean distance. The variances are obtained from feature values in feature vectors for a specific group of gender and ages. Equation (2) shows the normalized Euclidean distance.

$$ED(x, y) = \sqrt{\sum_{i=1}^{m} \frac{(x_i - y_i)^2}{\sigma_{i,g}^2}} \tag{2}$$

In (2), g indicates a specific group of gender and ages. The normalized Euclidean distance only calculates the distance between two vectors. So, we propose a novel method to measure the distance between two vectors. The proposed method considers the distance and the correlation of the feature vector and group vectors at the same time. The VC value between a feature vector as input and each group vector is used as a weight in computing the GVC between the feature vector as input under test and each feature vector in the gender–ages group. The ED value between a feature vector as input and each group vector is used as a weight in computing the GED value between the feature vector as input and each feature vector in the gender–ages group. The novel vector distance metric between two vectors, V_i and V_t, is shown in (3).

$$\begin{aligned}
\text{Dist}(V_i, V_t) &= \text{GVC}(V_i, V_t) + \text{GED}(V_i, V_t) \\
\text{GVC}(V_i, V_t) &= (1 - W_{I,v}) \times (1 - \text{VC}(V_i, V_t)) \\
\text{GED}(V_i, V_t) &= W_{I,E} \times \text{ED}(V_i, V_t)
\end{aligned} \tag{3}$$

In (3), $i \in I$ and I is the index of a specific group. Also, $W_{I,v} = \text{VC}(G_I, V_t)$ and $W_{I,E} = \text{ED}(G_I, V_t)$. G_I is a group feature vector of the group I. That is, $W_{I,v}$ and $W_{I,E}$ are the vector correlation and the normalized Euclidean distance between the group feature vector G_I and V_t. In addition, V_i is the ith feature vector of the group I

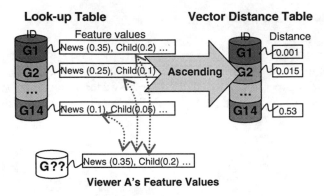

Fig. 5 Example of the first stage classifier

in the look-up table, and V_t is the TV viewer's feature vector to infer his/her profile in terms of gender and ages. Figure 5 shows the first stage classifier to measures the vector distance by (3). In Fig. 5, the feature vector V_t of TV viewer A is arranged in the bottom box. The vector distances between TV viewer A and group I are calculated in the ascending order as shown in Fig. 5.

The Second Stage Classifier

The second stage classifier is constructed by the *k-NN* (*k-Nearest Neighbour*) method. The *k-NN* method uses as input the k smallest vector distances obtained from the 1st stage classifier. However, the traditional *k-NN* method makes a decision, taking only into account the k highest ranked distances in the ascending order. Therefore the *k-NN* method does not utilize information about their distance values in classification. So, the second stage classifier in this paper adopts the weighted-distance *k-NN* that considers the distance values of the k highest ranked distances [7]. The equation for weighted-distance *k-NN* (WDK) of a specific group I is shown in (4).

$$\text{WDK}(I) = \frac{\sum_{i \in I} 1/\text{VDT}(i)}{\sum_{I=1}^{N} \sum_{j=1}^{k} 1/\text{VDT}(j, G_I)} \qquad (4)$$

In (4), $i \in I$, I is the index of a group, and k is k value in *k-NN*. VDT(i) is the ith vector distance value among the k smallest vector distances. N is the total number of gender–ages groups, and VDT(j, G_I) is the vector distance values of G_I group in the k gender–ages groups selected for *k-NN*. Through (4), we can make the weighted distance *k-NN* table for gender–ages groups with the k vector distances. Figure 6 shows an example about how to compute the similarity between the unknown TV viewer and each gender–ages group by the *k-NN* method. In Fig. 6,

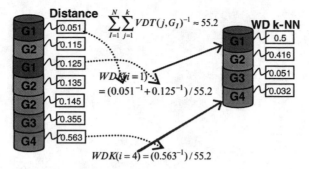

Fig. 6 Example of the second stage classifier

the seven smallest vector distances are selected ($k = 7$). Then the inverse (55.2) of the total vector distances is calculated as a normalization value, which leads to the weighted k-NN. We calculate the normalized inverses (weighted distance k-NN) of the vector distances for all gender–ages groups (G1, G2, G3 and G4). Notice that there are two G1, three G2, one G3 and one G4 groups. The corresponding normalized inverses of the vector distances are 0.5, 0.416, 0.051, and 0.032 for G1, G2, G3 and G4, respectively.

The Third Stage Classifier

After the second stage classifier, we can obtain an inferred TV viewer's profile based on the maximum of the weighted-distance k-NN values in the table for each day of the week day.

The third stage classifier calculates the majority rule table with the maximum weighted distance k-NN values and the gender–ages groups for the weekday. Then the normalized majority rule (NMR) values are calculated by combining the maximum weighted distance k-NN values for the weekday. The normalized majority rule value can be calculated by (5).

$$\text{NMR}(I) = \frac{\max \left\{ \text{WDKT}(d) | d \in D \right\}}{\sum\limits_{d=1}^{D} \max \left\{ \text{WDKT}(d) | d \in D \right\}} \quad (5)$$

In (5), I is the index of the inferred gender–ages group for the weekday, D means the weekday from Monday to Friday, and WDKT(d) is a value of weighted distance k-NN table in d day of the week.

The third stage classifier categorizes the unknown TV viewer to the gender–ages group which has the maximum NMR value as shown in Fig. 7.

The majority rule table in Fig. 7 has the maximum values in the weighted distance k-NN tables and the inference result of the second stage classifier. Since the

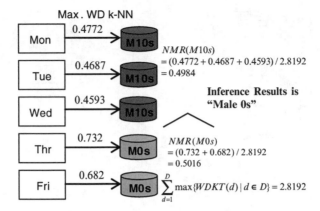

Fig. 7 Example of the third stage classifier

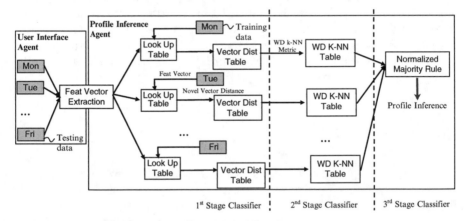

Fig. 8 Architecture of the multistage classifier (MSC)

inference value of 'Male 0s' is lager than that of 'Male 10s', the inference result becomes 'Male 0s'. Figure 8 shows the architecture of multi stage classifier for the user profile inference as describe in this chapter.

Target Advertisement Contents Selection Method

In this section, we explain how to select a target advertisement content based on the TV viewer's profile inference. The target advertisement contents are selected from the target advertisement selection method which utilizes preference values of advertisement contents from the Korea Broadcasting Advertising Corporation (KOBACO).

Target Advertisement Contents Selection Method

In this section, we describe how to select an advertisement content based on the TV viewer's profile (gender and age) inference result. In order to select advertisement contents, it is necessary to know preference information about advertisement contents. In this paper, we utilize a survey result from the KOBACO in order to know the TV viewer's preferences in celebrity endorser, advertising types, and advertising items for gender–ages groups [3]. The survey results of the preference are shown in Tables 4, 5 and 6. In Table 4, the TV viewer's preference of celebrity endorser is presented by the percentage. The preference values for advertising types and advertising items in Tables 5 and 6 are obtained from the pre-classified lists, and the values are up to 6. By using preference information from KOBACO, the celebrity endorser, advertising types, and advertising items are divided by TV viewer's preferring TV viewing as shown in Fig. 9. The numbers in Fig. 9 represent the order of the preferring TV viewing time bands. The time band 1 from 18 to 24 is the most preferred viewing time, and the time band 2 from 6 to 12 is the second preferred viewing time. Three and four and defined in the same way.

Experimental Results

In this section, we show the experimental results of the profile reasoning algorithm with the multistage classifier and the implementation result of a prototype target advertisement system.

Experimental Result of Profile Reasoning

The experiment for the profile reasoning algorithm is conducted with real TV usage history data from the AC Nielson Korea. The TV usage history data was recorded by 2,522 people (Male: 1,243 and Female: 1,279) from Dec. 2002 to May, 2003. In order to perform the experiment, the TV usage history data is divided into two groups such as training data and testing data. The training data is randomly selected from 70% (1,764 people) data of the total TV usage history, and the rest 30% (758 people) is used as the testing data. That is, the training is viewing information about TV program contents of 1,764 people during 6 months, and the testing data is TV usage data of 758 people during 6 months. Also, for more accurate experiment, we created eight different pairs of the training and testing data. The threshold values are set to $C_{Th} = 30$ and $T_{Th} = 0.1$ in order to remove some outliers of the TV usage history data to compute the feature vectors from the training data. Figure 10 shows the experimental results for the gender–ages groups by the proposed multistage classifier (MSC), Euclidian Distance (ED) and Vector Correlation (VC) methods. As shown in Fig. 10, the average accuracy for the performance of the proposed multistage

Table 4 Preference information about celebrity endorser from KOBACO

	M10s	M20s	M30s	M40s	Over M50s	F10s	F20s	F30s	F40s	Over F50s
1	Jeon, JH 22.4	Jeon, JH 24.4	Lee, HL 11.3	Lee, HL 12.5	Lee, YA 9.5	Jeon, JH 16.8	Jeon, JH 15.1	Kwon, SW 11.7	Lee, YA 11.2	Lee, YA 9.7
2	Kwon, SW 12.4	Lee, HL 11.2	Lee, YA 12.2	Lee, YA 8.9	Lee, HL 8.7	Kwon, SW 12.0	Kwon, SW 13.8	Lee, YA 11.6	Kwon, SW 7.7	Kwon, SW 7.1
3	Lee, HL 8.0	Lee, YA 6.6	Jeon, JH 11.4	Jeon, JH 7.7	Ahn, SK 3.2	Kang, DW 9.8	Lee, YA 6.8	Lee, HL 4.8	Ahn, SK 5.3	Lee, HL 4.1
4	Kim C 4.4	Song, HK 4.6	Song, HK 5.2	Song, HK 4.0	Kim, HJ 3.0	Won B 5.9	Lee, HL 4.5	Jeon, JH 4.2	Chae, SL 4.5	Chae, SL 3.7
5	Lee, YA 3.6	Kwon, SW 3.4	Ahn, SK 3.4	Ahn, SK 3.3	Choi, BA 2.8	Rain 5.6	Kang, DW 3.8	Rain 4.0	Song, HK 4.4	Kim, JE 3.4
6	Song, HK 3.6	Kim C 2.5	Kwon, SW 2.9	Kwon, SW 2.9	Kim, JE 2.5	Lee, NY 4.2	Song, HK 3.2	Song, HK 3.9	Kim, JE 4.2	Ahn, SK 3.4
7	Rain 2.6	Kim, JE 2.1	Han, SK 2.6	Kim, JE 2.3	Ko, DS 2.3	Lee, YA 3.1	Jang, DK 3.1	Jang, DK 3.9	Jeon, JH 3.9	Kim, HJ 3.4
8	Han, YS 2.3	Jung, WS 2.1	Kim, JE 2.5	Kim, NJ 2.0	Jeon, JH 2.0	Lee, HL 3.1	Lee, NY 2.9	Kim, JE 3.5	Jang, DK 3.9	Kim, HA 2.6
9	Lee, NY 2.1	Han, YS 1.8	Kim, NJ 2.2	Jeon, IH 1.9	Chae, SL 1.7	Song, HK 2.8	Rain 2.7	Ahn, SK 3.2	Lee, HL 3.8	Song, HK 2.4
10	Boa 2.1	Lee, NY 1.6	Song, YA 1.7	Choi, MS 1.9	Song, HK 1.5	Kim C 2.8	Won B 2.7	Lee, MY 2.6	Jeon, IH 2.9	Ko, DS 2.2

Table 5 Preference information about advertising types from KOBACO

	Humour	Tradition/ humanism	Children entry	Consumer entry	Animal entry	Animation/ comic	Celebrity entry	Entertainer entry	Foreign Star entry	Sexual perception	Comparison ad	Image emphasis ad	Product emphasis ad	Curiosity
M10s	4.8	3.8	3.8	3.6	3.9	4.0	2.9	4.4	3.9	2.8	2.8	2.8	2.8	3.2
M20s	4.8	4.2	3.9	3.8	3.7	3.7	2.9	4.0	3.7	3.3	3.0	3.0	3.0	3.2
M30s	4.6	4.3	4.1	3.9	3.6	3.6	2.9	3.7	3.3	3.0	3.0	3.1	3.1	2.9
M40s	4.3	4.3	4.0	3.9	3.6	3.4	3.1	3.6	3.2	2.9	2.9	3.0	3.1	2.8
M50s	4.3	4.4	3.9	3.8	3.6	3.1	3.2	3.6	3.1	2.6	2.9	3.1	3.1	2.7
F10s	4.8	3.9	4.2	3.7	3.9	4.1	2.9	4.5	3.3	2.5	2.5	2.7	2.7	3.1
F20s	4.8	4.5	4.4	4.0	4.0	3.8	3.0	4.1	3.4	2.6	2.6	2.9	3.0	3.1
F30s	4.7	4.4	4.4	4.0	3.8	3.9	3.1	3.9	3.2	2.5	2.7	3.0	3.1	2.8
F40s	4.5	4.5	4.4	4.1	3.8	3.9	3.2	3.8	3.1	2.3	2.7	3.1	3.3	2.7
F50s	4.3	4.4	4.2	4.0	3.7	3.3	3.2	3.7	3.0	2.3	2.8	3.0	3.1	2.6

Table 6 Preference information about advertising items from KOBACO

	Drink	Cookie	Food	Alcohol	Household	Cosmetic	Car	Medical supplies	Home appliance	Computer	Cell/mobile phone	Department store	Furniture	Clothes	Finance	Study book
M10s	4.0	4.1	3.9	2.8	2.8	2.5	3.4	2.6	3.0	4.3	4.7	3.0	2.4	3.5	2.1	2.3
M20s	3.6	3.4	3.5	3.6	3.1	3.0	4.2	3.0	3.5	4.2	4.5	3.2	2.7	3.6	2.8	2.2
M30s	3.3	3.2	3.3	3.5	3.0	2.7	4.3	3.2	3.4	3.9	4.1	3.0	2.7	3.0	3.1	2.5
M40s	3.3	3.1	3.3	3.5	3.0	2.8	4.0	3.5	3.4	3.6	3.8	3.0	2.7	3.0	3.2	2.6
M50s	3.2	3.0	3.1	3.4	3.0	2.7	3.7	3.5	3.3	3.0	3.4	2.9	2.7	2.9	3.0	2.2
F10s	4.1	4.3	3.9	2.9	3.8	3.9	3.1	2.7	3.2	4.1	5.0	3.5	2.9	4.3	2.4	2.7
F20s	3.8	3.8	3.7	3.4	4.0	4.5	3.6	3.2	3.8	3.7	4.5	3.7	3.3	4.3	3.0	2.6
F30s	3.6	3.5	3.7	3.3	3.9	4.1	3.6	3.6	4.1	3.7	4.0	3.7	3.4	3.9	3.4	3.5
F40s	3.5	3.5	3.6	3.2	3.9	4.0	3.5	3.7	4.0	3.6	3.7	3.6	3.4	3.7	3.4	3.0
F50s	3.2	3.1	3.4	2.9	3.7	3.7	3.1	3.6	3.9	2.9	3.2	3.4	3.1	3.4	3.0	2.0

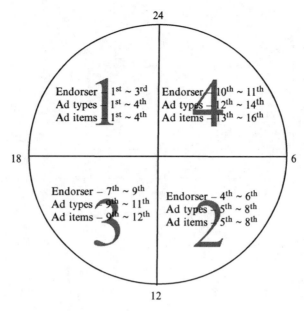

Fig. 9 Example of classification of celebrity endorser, advertising types, and advertising items based on the preferred TV viewing time

classifier is higher than single classifiers only with ED and VC measures, separately. For the male TV viewers, the averaged accuracy in Fig. 10a by the proposed multistage classifier is about 15% higher than other methods, because the male groups have distinct genre or channel preferences in different ages. For better understanding of the experimental results, we model a genre consistency as shown in Fig. 11. For the genre consistency model, we use the feature vectors: GPRC and GPRT. If the location of the preference on *Genre* 1 in Fig. 11 moves to ① or ②, then it can be understood that the preference on *Genre* 1 is increased or decreased. To move the *Genre* 1 to ③means that the TV viewer likes the genre much more than other genres because the ③ TV watching is concentrated on *Genre* 1 by less watching the other TV genre contents. If the *Genre* 1 moves to ④, then the TV viewer frequently watches the TV program contents on *Genre* 1 but the lengths of watching times are very short.

Figure 12 shows the genre consumption consistency (GCC) for all gender-ages groups. In Fig. 12, the male 0s group likes to watch the TV program contents in the *Child* genre. The male 10s group prefers to watch the contents in the *Drama&Movies* genre. The male 20s group likes the *Entertainment* program contents. The male 30s group mostly likes the *News* genre. The male 40s ∼ 50s groups prefer to the similar genres such as *Information, News* and *Drama&Movies*. On the other hand, the male 60s group can be easily distinguished because they stick to a specific channel. In Figs. 10 and 12, it can be noted that the experimental results of the male 0s ∼ 20s groups by the proposed MSC shows similar pattern in average

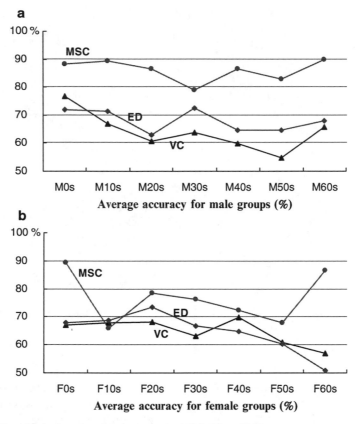

Fig. 10 Experimental results of the accuracy by MSC, ED and VC

accuracy only with ED. Since the genres in the GPRC-GPRT plan are located along the diagonal axis for the male 0s ~ 20s groups, the VC value can no longer be effective instead the ED value becomes an effective discriminatory measure. The average accuracy for the male 30s group by the MSC is relatively low. Even though its average accuracy only with the ED is high, the VC value seems to disturb the discriminatory power in conjunction with the ED for the MSC. The GCC of the male 30s group tends to move along the diagonal axis. For the male 40s ~ 60s groups by the proposed MSC in Fig. 10, the average accuracy curve looks similar to that of the VC. In this case, the VC value becomes an effective measure for discrimination. The locations of different genres are somewhat different for the male 40s ~ 60s groups.

For the female groups in different ages, it is difficult to distinguish the ages groups because the ages groups have similar GCC in the GPRC-GPRT plane. In Fig. 12, the genre distribution of the female 0s group is similar to the male 0s group. These groups can then be distinguished by the channel preference. The GCC of the female 20s ~ 60s groups are similarly distributed. So, the performance for the female groups is not better than that for the male groups as shown in Fig. 10. The

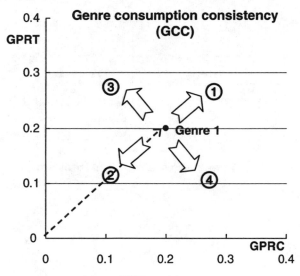

Fig. 11 Genre consumption consistency (GCC) model

genre distribution of the female 10s groups is similar to the male 10s group. Also, the GCC of the female 10s group is distributed to ⑤. So, the accuracy by the proposed MSC is not higher than those by the ED and VC methods in Fig. 10b. The accuracy of the female 30s ∼ 50s groups in the proposed MSC is slightly higher than those by the ED and VC methods. The accuracy curve of the female 30s ∼ 50s is similar to that of the ED methods because the distribution of the genres is similar in the GPRC-GPRT plane. The female 60s group by the proposed MSC shows much better results than by the ED and VC methods as shown in Fig. 10b because the test data is distributed in the direction of ③ and ④ with the low density.

Table 7 shows the experimental results with average accuracy for the multistage classifier (MSC), ED and VC, and the accuracy in Table 7 is the average accuracy of the eight different pairs of the training and testing data.

The Implementation Result of the Prototype Target Advertisement System

We show the implementation result of the prototype target advertisement system based on the profile reasoning algorithm and target advertisement content selection method. For the target advertisement system, we used 28 free advertisement contents from NGTV (http://www.ngtv.net). Figure 13 shows the implementation result of the prototype target advertisement system. In Fig. 13, the feature vectors of a 20-year-old man are extracted from the user interface agent. The extracted feature vector is sent to the profile inference agent. In the profile inference agent, the

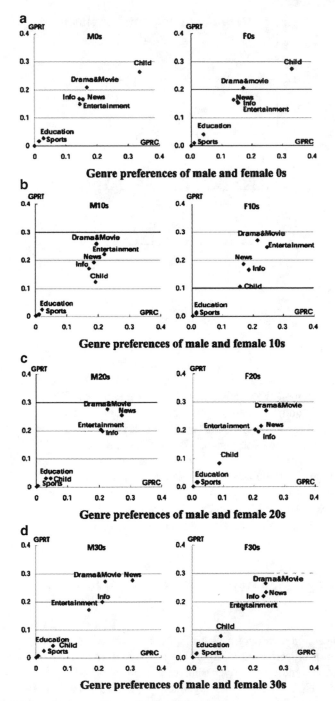

Fig. 12 Distribution of genre preference in all groups

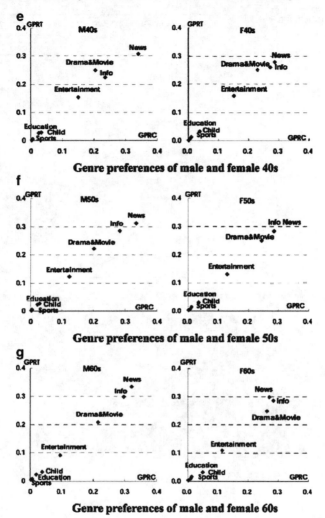

Fig. 12   (continued)

profile (gender and ages) of the TV viewer is inferred by the MSC. The profile inference agent classifies the extracted feature vector into M20s. Next, celebrity endorser,
advertising types and advertising items are obtained from the preference table of advertisement contents based on the profile inference result. The target advertisement
content in Fig. 13 is the advertisement content for a 20-year-old man; that is, the
advertisement content of celebrity endorser is 'Lee, HL', and advertising types is
'Entertainer Entry', and advertising item is 'Cell/Mobile Phone.'

Table 7 Experimental result
of multistage classifier

Gender and Ages Group	Accuracy (%)		
	VC	ED	MSC
Male 0s	76.69	71.96	88.21
Female0s	67.14	67.86	89.28
Male 10s	66.89	71.28	89.29
Female 10s	67.76	68.75	65.79
Male 20s	60.72	62.95	86.50
Female 20s	68.18	73.58	78.49
Male 30s	63.69	72.42	78.80
Female 30s	63.15	66.88	76.17
Male 40s	59.82	64.51	86.59
Female 40s	69.71	64.83	72.25
Male 50s	54.86	64.58	82.86
Female 50s	60.86	60.20	67.91
Male 60s	65.76	67.94	89.77
Female 60s	56.90	50.86	86.61
Avg. Accuracy	64.54	66.81	80.17

Fig. 13 Distribution of genre preference in all groups

Conclusion

In this paper, we address a TV viewer profile reasoning method by utilizing TV
viewers' TV usage history data and introduce a target advertisement system. The
feature vectors are data computed from the TV usage history data and are utilized
to infer TV viewer's profiles by the proposed multistage classifier. The accuracy
of the multistage classifier is about 80% which is higher than other two methods:
Euclidean distance and vector correlation. Also, we proposed the target advertisement system which enables to provide target advertisement contents based on the
inferred TV viewer's profile and preference values about advertisement contents.
Through the proposed target advertisement system, it is expected that TV viewers can watch his/her preferred advertisement contents and advertisement content
providers can see more efficient advertising effects by providing appropriate advertisement contents to their target customers.

References

1. Bozios T, Lekakos G, Skoularidou V, Chorianopoulos K (2001) Advanced techniques for per-sonalised advertising in a digital TV environment: the iMEDIA system. Proceedings of The E-business and E-work conference, pp 1025–1031
2. Katsaros D, Manolopoulos Y (2004) Broadcast program generation for webcasting. Data Knowl Eng 49(1):1–21
3. Korea Broadcasting Advertising Corporation (2005) Media & consumer research 2004—survey on consumer pattern. Retrieved September 03, 2005, from http://www.kobaco.co.kr/kor/infor-mation/study-data/studydata_research_annual.asp
4. Miyahara K, Pazzani MJ (2004) Collaborative filtering with the simple bayesian classifier. Proceedings of the Sixth Pacific Rim international conference on artificial intelligence PRICAI 2000, pp 679–689
5. Shahabi C, Faisal A, Kashani FB, Faruque J (2000) INSITE: a tool for interpreting users inter-action with a web space. Proceeding of 26th international conference on very large databases, pp 635–638
6. Yu Z, Zhou X (2004) TV3P: an adaptive assistant for personalized TV. IEEE Trans Consum Electron 50(1):393–399
7. Yuan W, Liu J, Zhou HB (2004) An improved KNN method and its application to tumor di-agnosis. Proceedings of the 3rd international conference on machine learning and cybernetics, pp 2836–2841

Chapter 6
Digital Video Quality Assessment Algorithms

Anush K. Moorthy, Kalpana Seshadrinathan, and Alan C. Bovik

Introduction

The last decade has witnessed an unprecedented use of visual communication. Improved speeds, increasingly accessible technology and reducing costs, coupled with improved storage means that images and videos are replacing more traditional modes of communication. In this era, when the human being is bombarded with a slew of videos at various resolutions and over various media, the question of what is palatable to the human is an important one. The term 'quality' is one that is used to define the palatability of an image or a video sequence. Researchers have developed algorithms which aim to provide a measure of this quality. Automatic methods to perform image quality assessment (IQA) has made giant leaps over the past few years [1]. These successes suggest that this field is close to attaining saturation [2]. More complex than IQA algorithms are video quality assessment (VQA) algorithms, whose goals are similar to those for IQA but require processing of dynamically changing images. In this chapter, we focus on VQA algorithms for digital video sequences. Digital videos comprise of a set of frames (still images) played at a particular speed (frame-rate). Each frame has the same resolution and the frame is made up of a bunch of picture elements or pixels. These pixels have fixed bit-depth i.e., the number of bits used to represent the value of a pixel is fixed for a video. This definition is valid for *progressive* videos. *Interlaced* videos on the other hand, consist of a pair of 'fields', each containing alternating portions of the equivalent frame. When played out at an appropriate rate, the observer views the videos as a continuous stream. When one defines a digital video sequence as above, one is bound to question the necessity for separate VQA algorithms – Can one not apply an IQA algorithm on a frame-by-frame basis (or on one of the fields) and then average out the score to provide a quality rating? Indeed, many VQA algorithms are derived from IQA algorithms, and some of them do just that; however, the most

A.K. Moorthy, K. Seshadrinathan, and A.C. Bovik (✉)
Department of Electrical and Computer Engineering, The University of Texas at Austin, Austin, Texas, USA
e-mail: anushmoorthy@mail.utexas.edu; kalpsesh@gmail.com; bovik@ece.utexas.edu

B. Furht (ed.), *Handbook of Multimedia for Digital Entertainment and Arts*,
DOI 10.1007/978-0-387-89024-1_6, © Springer Science+Business Media, LLC 2009

important difference between a still-image and a video is the presence of perceived motion, suggesting that modeling of such motion is key to the development of better VQA algorithms. As we shall see, such motion modeling should account for human perception of motion. This is validated by improved performance of VQA algorithms that incorporate some motion modeling.

The performance of any VQA algorithm is evaluated in terms of its correlation with human perception. We will have a lot to say about this towards the end of this chapter. However, note that for the applications we target, the ultimate receiver of a video is the human and hence, when one talks about 'performance', one necessarily means correlation with human perception. This leads to the question – How does one know what the human perceives? The general procedure is to ask a representative sample of the human populace to rate the quality of a given video on some rating bar. The mean score achieved by a video is then said to be representative of the human perception of quality. The International Telecommunications Union (ITU) has provided a set of recommendations on how such quality assessment by humans is to be conducted [3]. Such VQA is generally referred to as *subjective* quality assessment, and as one can imagine, is time-consuming and cumbersome and hence the need for automatic VQA algorithms. Algorithmic assessment of quality is called *objective* quality assessment. Note that the procedure to form a quality score from a subjective study implies that perfect correlation with human perception is almost impossible due to inter-subject variation.

We classify VQA algorithms as: full-reference (FR), reduced-reference (RR) and no-reference (NR). FR VQA algorithms assume that a pristine reference video is available, and the quality of the video under consideration is evaluated with respect to this pristine reference. Note that, by this definition, we are evaluating the *relative* quality of a given video. RR VQA algorithms operate under the assumption that even though the pristine video is unavailable for direct comparison, *some* additional information about the pristine sequence is available. This may include for example partial coefficient information or knowledge about the compression or distortion process [4]-[7]. NR metrics are those that have absolutely no knowledge about the processes involved in the creation of the given video. Simply put, the algorithm is presented with a video and is asked to rate its quality. These algorithms are few, even for image quality assessment [8]. NR VQA algorithms are rare [9]. Our definitions of NR and RR VQA algorithms are not universal though. In some cases, NR algorithms assume a distortion model. The reader will observe that NR VQA algorithms have the potential to be the most useful kind of VQA algorithms, and may question the need for FR VQA algorithms. However, as we shall see through this chapter, our understanding of the process by which humans rate the quality of a video sequence is limited. Indeed, we do not yet have a complete understanding of motion processing in the brain [10, 11]. Given this lack of information, truly blind NR VQA algorithms are still years away. Finally, RR VQA algorithms are a compromise between these two extremes, and are a stepping stone towards a NR VQA algorithm. See [5] and [13] for examples of RR VQA and IQA algorithms. Since most work has been done in the FR domain, and procedures and standards for evaluation of their performance exist, in this chapter we shall discuss only FR VQA algorithms.

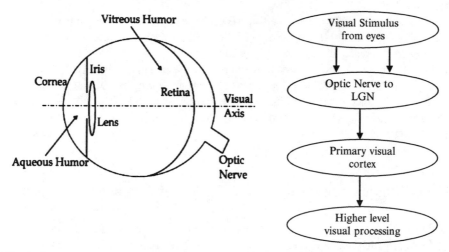

Fig. 1 Schematic model of the human visual system

Let us briefly look at how videos are processed by the human visual system (HVS) in order to better understand some key concepts of algorithms that we shall discuss here. Note that even though there have been significant strides in understanding motion processing in the visual cortex, a complete understanding is still a long way off. What we mention here are some properties which have been confirmed by psycho-visual research. The reader is referred to [10] for a more detailed explanation of these ideas.

Figure 1 shows a schematic model of the HVS. The visual stimulus in the form of light from the environment passes through the optics of the eye and is imaged on the retina. Due to inherent imperfections in the eye, the image formed is blurred, which can be modeled by a point spread function (PSF) [11]. Most of the information encoded in the retina is transmitted via the optic nerve to the lateral geneiculate nucleus (LGN). The neurons in the LGN then relay this information to the primary visual cortex area (V1). From V1, this information is passed on to a variety of visual areas, including the middle-temporal (MT) or V5 region. V1 neurons have receptive fields[1] which demonstrate a substantial degree of selectivity to size (spatial frequency), orientation and direction of motion of retinal stimulation. It is hypothesized that the MT/V5 region plays a significant role in motion processing [12]. Area MT/V5 also plays a role in the guidance of some eye movements, segmentation and 3-D structure computation [14], which are properties of human vision that play an important role in visual perception of videos Unfortunately, as we move from the optics towards V1 and MT/V5, the amount of information we have about the functioning of these regions decreases. The functioning of area MT is an area of active research [15].

---

[1] The receptive field of a neuron is its response to visual stimuli, which may depend on spatial frequency, movement, disparity or other properties. As used here, the receptive field response may be viewed as synonymous with the signal processing term impulse response.

In this chapter we first describe some HVS-based approaches which try to model the visual processing stream described above, since these approaches were originally used to predict visual quality. We then describe recently proposed structural and information-theoretic approaches and feature-based approaches which are commonly used. Further, we describe recent motion-modeling based approaches, and detail performance evaluation and validation techniques for VQA algorithms. Finally, we touch upon some possible future directions for research on VQA and conclude the chapter.

HVS – Based Approaches

Much of the initial development in VQA centered on explicit modeling of the HVS. The visual pathway is modeled using a computational model of the HVS; the original and distorted videos are passed through this model. The visual quality is then defined as an error measure between the outputs produced by the model for the original and distorted videos. Many HVS based VQA models are derived from their IQA counterparts. Some of the popular HVS-based models for IQA include the Visible Differences Predictor (VDP) developed by Daly [16], the Sarnoff JND vision model [17], the Safranek-Johnston Perceptual Image Coder (PIC) [18] and Watson's DCTune [19]. The interested reader is directed to [20] for a detailed description of these models.

A block diagram of a generic HVS based VQA system is shown in Figure 2. The only difference between this VQA system and a HVS-based IQA system is the presence of a 'temporal filter'. This temporal filter is generally used to model the two kinds of temporal mechanisms present in early stages of processing in the visual cortex. Lowpass and bandpass filters have typically been used for this purpose.

The Moving Pictures Quality Metric (MPQM), an early approach to VQA, utilized a Gabor filterbank in the spatial frequency domain, and one lowpass and one bandpass temporal filter [21]. The Perceptual Distortion Metric [22] was a modification of MPQM and used two infinite impulse response (IIR) filters to model the lowpass and bandpass mechanisms. Further, the Gabor filterbank was replaced by a steerable pyramid decomposition [23]. Watson proposed the Digital Video Quality (DVQ) metric in [24], which used the Discrete Cosine Transform (DCT) and utilized a simple IIR filter implementation to represent the temporal mechanism. A scalable wavelet based video distortion metric was proposed in [25]. In this section we describe DVQ and the scalable wavelet-based distortion metric in some detail.

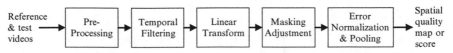

Fig. 2 Block diagram of a generic HVS-based VQA system

Digital Video Quality Metric

Digital Video Quality Metric (DVQ) metric computes the visibility of artifacts expressed in the DCT domain. In order to evaluate human visual thresholds on *dynamic DCT noise* a small study with three subjects was carried out for different DCT (spatial) and temporal frequencies. The data obtained led to a separable model which is a product of a temporal, a spatial and an orientation function coupled with a global threshold.

DVQ metric first transforms the reference and test videos into YOZ color space [26] and undertakes sampling and cropping. The videos are then transformed using an 8×8 DCT, then further transformed to local contrast – expressed as the ratio of DCT amplitude to (filtered) DC amplitude for each block. In the next stage is that of temporal filtering where a second order IIR filter is used. The local contrast terms are converted into units of just-noticeable-differences (JNDs) using spatial thresholds derived from the study followed by contrast masking. Finally, a simple Minkowski formulation is used to pool the local error scores into the final error score (and hence the quality score).

Scalable Wavelet-Based Distortion Metric

The distortion metric proposed in [25] can be used as an FR or RR metric depending upon the application. Further, it differs from other HVS-based metrics in that the parametrization is performed using human responses to natural videos rather than sinusoidal gratings.

The metric uses only the Y channel from the YUV color space for processing. We note that this is true of many of the metrics described in this chapter. Color and its effect on quality is another interesting area of research [27]. The reference and distorted video sequences are temporally filtered using a finite impulse response (FIR) lowpass filter. Then, a spatial frequency decomposition using an integer implementation of a Haar wavelet transform is performed and a subset of coefficients is selected for distortion measurement. Further, a contrast computation and weighting by a contrast sensitivity function (CSF) is performed, followed by a masking computation. Finally, following a summation of the differences in the decompositions for the reference and distorted videos a quality score computation is undertaken. A detailed explanation of the algorithm and parameter selection along with certain applications may be found in [25].

In this section we explained only two of the many HVS models. Several HVS-based models have been implemented in commercial products. The reader is directed to [28] for a short description.

Structural and Information-Theoretic approaches

In this section we describe two recent VQA paradigms that are an alternative to HVS-based approaches – the structural similarity index and the video visual information fidelity. These approaches take into account certain properties of the HVS when approaching the VQA problem. Performance evaluation of these algorithms has shown that they perform well in terms of their correlation with human perception. This coupled with the simplicity of implementation of these algorithms makes them attractive.

Structural Similarity Index

The Structural SIMilarity Index (SSIM) was originally proposed as an IQA algorithm in [29]. In fact, SSIM builds upon the concepts of the Universal Quality Index (UQI) proposed previously [30]. The SSIM index proposed in [29] is a single-scale index i.e., the index is evaluated only at the image resolution (and we shall refer to it as SS-SSIM). In order to better evaluate quality over multiple resolutions, the multi-scale SSIM (MS-SSIM) index was proposed in [31]. SS-SSIM and MS-SSIM are space-domain indices. A related index was developed in the complex wavelet domain in [32] (see also [33]).

Given two image patches x and y drawn from the same location in the reference and distorted images respectively, SS-SSIM evaluates the following three terms: luminance $l(x, y)$, structure $s(x, y)$, and contrast $c(x, y)$ as:

$$l(x, y) = \frac{2\mu_x\mu_y + C_1}{\mu_x^2 + \mu_y^2 + C_1}$$

$$c(x, y) = \frac{2\sigma_x\sigma_y + C_2}{\sigma_x^2 + \sigma_y^2 + C_2}$$

$$s(x, y) = \frac{\sigma_{xy} + C_3}{\sigma_x\sigma_y + C_3}$$

and the final SSIM index is given as the product of the three terms:

$$SSIM(x, y) = \frac{\left(2\mu_x\mu_y + C_1\right)\left(2\sigma_{xy} + C_2\right)}{\left(\mu_x^2 + \mu_y^2 + C_1\right)\left(\sigma_x^2 + \sigma_y^2 + C_2\right)}.$$

where,

μ_x and μ_y are the means of x and y;
σ_x^2, σ_y^2, are the variances of x and y;
σ_{xy} is the covariance between x and y; and
C_1, C_2, and $C_3 = C_2/2$ are constants.

SS-SSIM computation is performed using a window-based approach, where the means, standard deviations and cross-correlation are computed within an 11×11 Gaussian window. Thus SS-SSIM provides a matrix of values of approximately the size of the image representing local quality at each location. The final score for SSIM is typically computed as the mean of the local scores, yielding a single quality score for the test image. However, other pooling strategies have been proposed [34], [35]. Note that SSIM is symmetric, attaining the upper limit of 1 if and only if the two images being compared are exactly the same. Hence, a value of 1 corresponds to perfect quality, and any value lesser than one corresponds to distortion in the test image. MS-SSIM evaluates structure and contrast over multiple-scales, then combines them along with luminance, which is evaluated at the finest scale [31]. Henceforth, the acronym SSIM applies to both SS-SSIM and MS-SSIM, unless it is necessary to differentiate between them.

For VQA, SSIM may be applied on a frame-by-frame basis and the final quality score is computed as the mean value across frames. Again, this pooling does not take into account unequal distribution of fixations across the video or the fact that motion is an integral part of VQA. Hence, in [36], an alternative pooling based on a weighted sum of local SSIM scores was proposed, where the weights depended upon the average luminance of the patch and on the global motion. The hypotheses were - 1) regions of lower luminance do not attract many fixations and hence these regions should be weighted with a lower value; and 2) high global motion reduces the perceivability of distortions and hence SSIM scores from these frames should be assigned lower weights. A block-based motion estimation procedure was used to compute global motion. It was shown that SS-SSIM performs extremely well on the VQEG dataset (see section on performance evaluation).

Video Visual Information Fidelity

Natural scene statistics (NSS) have been an active area of research in the recent past – see [37], [38] for comprehensive reviews. Natural scenes are a small subset of the space of all possible visual stimuli, and NSS deals with a statistical characterization of such scenes. Video visual information fidelity (Video VIF) proposed in [39] is based on the hypothesis that when such natural scenes are passed through a processing system, the system causes a change in the statistical properties of these natural scenes, rendering them *un-natural;* and has evolved from VIF used for IQA [40] (see also [41]). If one could measure this 'un-naturalness' one would be able to predict the quality of the image/video. It has been hypothesized that the visual stimuli from the natural environment drove the HVS and hence modeling NSS and HVS may be viewed as dual problems [40]. As mentioned in the introduction, even though great strides have been made in understanding the HVS, a comprehensive model is lacking, and NSS may offer an opportunity to fill this gap. Previously, NSS has been used successfully for image compression [42], texture analysis and synthesis [43], image denoising [44] and so on.

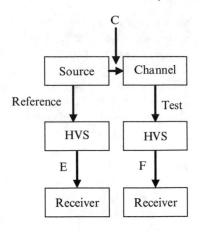

Fig. 3 The model of HVS for Vide VIF. The channel introduces distortions in the video sequence, which along with the references signal is received by cognitive processes in the brain

It has been shown that the distribution of the (marginal) coefficients of a multi-scale, multi-orientation decomposition of a natural image (loosely, a wavelet transform) are heavily peaked at zero, exhibit heavy tails and are well modeled using a first order Laplacian distribution though they are not independent (but may be approximately second-order uncorrelated). These marginals are well-modeled using Gaussian scale mixtures (GSM) [45], [46], though other models have been proposed [37].

An extension of VID to video, video VIF, models the original video as a stochastic source which passes through the HVS, and the distorted video as having additionally passed through a channel which introduces the distortion (blur, blocking etc.) before passing through the HVS (see Figure 3). Derivatives of the video are computed and modeled locally using the GSM model [39].

The output of each spatio-temporal derivative (channel) of the original signal is expressed as a product of two random fields (RF) [45] - a RF of positive scalars and a zero mean Gaussian vector RF. The channels of the distorted signal are modeled as:

$$D = GC + V$$

where, C is the RF from a channel in the original signal, G is a deterministic scalar field and V is a stationary additive zero-mean Gaussian RF with a diagonal covariance matrix. This distortion model expresses noise by the noise RF V and blur by the scalar-attenuation field G. The uncertainties in the HVS are represented using a visual noise term which is modeled as a zero-mean multi-variate Gaussian RF (N and N'), whose covariance matrix is diagonal. Then define:

$$E = C + N$$
$$F = D + N'$$

VIF then computes mutual informations between C and E and between C and F, both conditioned on the underlying scalar field S. Finally, VIF is expressed as a ratio of the two mutual informations summed over all the channels.

$$VIF = \frac{\sum_{j\in channels} I(C^j; F^j | s^j)}{\sum_{j\in channels} I(C^j; E^j | s^j)}$$

where, C^j, F^j, E^j, s^j define coefficients from one channel.

Feature Based Approaches

Feature based approaches extract features and statistics from the reference sequences and compare these features to predict visual quality. This definition applies equally to SSIM and VIF described earlier, however, as we shall see, feature based approaches utilize multiple features, and are generally not based on any particular premise such as structural retention or NSS.

Swisscom/KPN research developed the Perceptual Video Quality Metric (PVQM) [47], which measures three parameters – edginess indicator, temporal indicator and chrominance indicator. Edginess is compared by using local gradients of luminance of the reference and distorted videos. The temporal indicator uses normalized cross-correlation between adjacent frames of reference videos. The chrominance indicator accounts for perceived difference in color information between the reference and distorted videos. These scores are then mapped onto a video quality scores. Perceptual Evaluation of Video Quality (PEVQ) from Opticom was based on the model used in PVQM [48]-[50]. A recent performance evaluation contest was conducted by the ITU-T for standardization of VQA algorithms [51] and the ITU-T approved and standardized four full reference VQA algorithms including PVEQ [52]. Another algorithm that uses a feature based approach to VQA is the Video Quality Metric [53].

Video Quality Metric

Proposed by the National Telecommunications and Information Administration (NTIA) and standardized by the American National Standards Institute (ANSI), Video Quality Metric (VQM) [53] was the top performer in the Video Quality Experts Group (VQEG) Phase-II study [54]. The International Telecommunications Union (ITU) has included VQM as a normative measure for digital cable television systems [55].

VQM applies a series of filtering operations over a spatio-temporal block which spans a certain number of rows, columns and frames of the video sequence to extract seven parameters:

1. a parameter which detects the loss of spatial information, which is essentially an edge detector, applied on the luminance;
2. a parameter which detects the shift of edges from horizontal and vertical orientation to diagonal orientation, applied on the luminance;

3. a parameter which detects the shift of diagonal edges to horizontal and vertical orientation, applied on the luminance;
4. a parameter which computes the changes in the spread of the chrominance components;
5. a quality *improvement* parameter, which accounts for any improvements arising from sharpening operations;
6. a parameter which is the product of a simple motion detection (absolute difference between frames) and contrast and finally,
7. a parameter to detect severe color impairments.

Each of the above mentioned parameters is thresholded in order to specifically account only for those distortions which are perceptible, then pooled using different techniques. The general model for VQM then computes a weighted sum of these parameters to find a final quality index. For VQM, a score of 1 indicates poor quality, while 0 indicates perfect quality. A MATLAB implementation of VQM has been made available for research purposes online [56].

Motion Modeling Based Approaches

Distortions in a video can either be spatial – blocking artifacts, ringing distortions, mosaic patterns, false contouring and so on, or temporal – ghosting, motion blocking, motion compensation mismatches, mosquito effect, jerkiness, smearing and so on [57]. The VQA algorithms discussed so far mainly try to account for loss in quality due to spatial distortion, but fail to model temporal quality-loss accurately. For example, the only temporal component of PVQM is a correlation computation between adjacent frames; VQM uses absolute pixel-by-pixel differences between adjacent frames of a video sequence.

The human eye is very sensitive to motion and can accurately judge the velocity and direction of motion of objects in a scene. The ability to detect motion is essential for survival and for performance of tasks such as navigation, detecting and avoiding danger and so on. It is hence no surprise that spatio-temporal aspects of human vision are affected by motion.

As we discussed earlier, initial processing of visual data in the human brain takes place in the V1 region. Neurons in this front-end (comprising of the retina, LGN and V1) are tuned to specific orientations and spatial frequencies and are well-modeled by separable, linear, spatial and temporal filters. Many HVS-based VQA algorithms use such filters to model this area of visual processing. However, the visual data from area V1 is transported to area MT/V5 which integrates local motion information from V1 into global percepts of motion of complex patterns [58]. Even though responses of neurons in area MT have been studied and some models of motion sensing have been proposed, none of the existing HVS-based systems incorporate these models in VQA. Further, a large number of neurons in area MT are known to be directionally selective and hence movement information in a video sequence may be captured by a linear spatio-temporal decomposition.

Recently a temporal pooling strategy based on motion information was proposed for SSIM [59]. We call this algorithm speed-weighted SSIM and explain some of its features in this section. Note that the original SSIM for VQA [36], used some temporal weighting using motion information as well.

Speed-Weighted SSIM

Speed-weighted SSIM (SW-SSIM) [59] considers three kinds of motion fields -1) absolute motion; which is the absolute pixel motion between two adjacent frames, 2) background/global motion; which is caused by movement of the image acquisition system and 3) relative motion; which is the difference between the absolute and global motion.

It is hypothesized that the HVS is an efficient extractor of information [38]. Visual perception is modeled as an information communication process, where the HVS is the error prone communication channel since the HVS does not perceive all information with the same degree of certainty. A psychophysical study conducted by Stocker and Simoncelli on human visual speed perception suggested that the internal noise of human speed perception is proportional to the true stimulus speed [60]. It was found that for a given stimulus speed, a log-normal distribution provides a good description of the likelihood function (internal noise), which determines the perceptual uncertainty.

SW-SSIM proceeds as follows. First a SS-SSIM map is constructed at each pixel location using SSIM as defined before. Then a motion vector field is computed using Black and Anandan's multi-scale optical flow estimation algorithm [61] - yielding absolute pixel motion. Then, a histogram of the motion vectors in each frame is computed and the vector associated with the peak value is identified as the global vector for that frame. Relative motion computation follows. The weight applied at every pixel is then a function of the relative velocity, the global velocity and the stimulus contrast. The weight is designed such that the importance of a visual event increases with information content and decreases with perceptual uncertainty. Finally, each pixel location is weighted and the scores so obtained for each frame is pooled within and across frames to give a quality index for the video. Note that in this brief explanation, we have skipped over some practical implementation issues; the interested reader is directed to [60] for a thorough description of the algorithm. SW-SSIM was shown to perform well on the VQEG dataset.

Even though SW-SSIM takes into account motion information, only a weighting of spatially-obtained SSIM scores is undertaken based on this information. We believe that computation of temporal quality of a video sequence is as important, if not more, as spatial quality computation. Recently, a new VQA algorithm - motion based video integrity evaluation - that explicitly accounts for temporal quality artifacts was proposed [62], [63].

Motion Based Video Integrity Evaluation

Motion based video integrity evaluation (MOVIE) evaluates the quality of videos sequences not only in space and time, but also in space-time, by evaluating motion quality along motion trajectories.

First, both the reference and the distorted video sequences are spatio-temporally filtered using a family of bandpass Gabor filters. Gabor filters have been used for motion estimation in video [64], [65] and for models of human visual motion sensing [66]-[68]. It has also been shown that Gabor filters can be used to model the receptive field of neurons in the visual cortex [69]. Additionally, Gabor filters attain the theoretical lower bound on uncertainty in the frequency and spatial variables. MOVIE uses three scales of Gabor filters. A Gaussian filter is included at the center of the Gabor structure to capture low frequencies in the signal.

A local quality computation of the band-pass filtered outputs of the reference and test videos is then undertaken by considering a set of coefficients within a window from each of the Gabor sub-bands. The computation involves the use of a mutual masking function [70]. The mutual masking is used to model the contrast making property of the HVS, which refers to a reduction in the visibility of a signal component due to the presence of another spatial component of the same frequency and orientation in a local neighborhood. This masking model is closely related to the MS-SSIM and information theoretic models for IQA [71]. The quality index so obtained is termed as the spatial MOVIE index – even though it captures some temporal distortions.

MOVIE uses the same filter bank to compute motion information i.e., estimate optical flow from the reference video. The algorithm used is a multi-scale extension of the Fleet and Jepson [64] algorithm that uses the phase of the complex Gabor outputs for motion estimation.

Translational motion as an easily accessible interpretation in the frequency domain : spatial frequencies in the video signal are sheared due to translational motion along the temporal frequency dimension without affecting the magnitude of the spatial frequencies and such a translating patch lies entirely within a plane in the frequency domain [72] The optical flow computation provides an estimation of the local orientation of this spectral plane at each pixel. Thus, if the motion of the distorted video matches that of the reference video *exactly*, then the filters that lie along the motion plane orientation defined by the flow from the reference will be activated by the distorted video and outputs of filters that lie far away from this plane will be negligible. In presence of a temporal artifact, however, the motion in the reference and distorted videos do not match and a different set of filter banks may be activated. Thus, motion vectors from the reference are used to construct velocity-tuned responses. This can be accomplished by a weighted sum of the Gabor responses, where positive excitatory weights are assigned to those filters that lie close to the spectral plane and negative inhibitory weights are assigned to those that lie farther away from the spectral plane. This excitatory-inhibitory weighting results in a strong response when the distorted video has motion equal to the reference and a weak response when there is a deviation from the reference motion. Finally, the mean square error is computed between the response vectors from the reference video (tuned to its own motion) and those from the distorted video. The temporal MOVIE index just described essentially captures temporal quality.

Application of MOVIE to videos produces a map of spatial and temporal scores at each pixel location for each frame of the video sequence. In order to pool the scores to create a single quality index for the video sequence, MOVIE uses the coefficient of variation [73]. Although many alternate pooling strategies have been proposed [16], [17], [35], [36], [53] the coefficient of variation serves to capture the distribution of the distortions accurately [74]. The coefficient of variation is computed for the spatial and temporal MOVIE scores for each frame, then the values are averaged across frames to create the spatial and temporal MOVIE indices for the video sequence (temporal MOVIE index uses the square root of the average). The final MOVIE score is a product of the temporal and spatial MOVIE scores. A detailed description of the algorithm can be found in [74].

Performance Evaluation & Validation

Practical deployment of the various VQA algorithms discussed previously requires that a mutually agreed upon testing strategy for evaluation of performance exist. It was in order to create such a test-bed for the VQA algorithms that the VQEG FR-TV phase-I [51] was conducted. A total of 320 distorted video sequences were used in order to test the performance of 10 leading VQA algorithms, along with PSNR. The study found that all of the tested algorithms were statistically indistinguishable from PSNR [51]!.

The test procedure employed by the VQEG was as follows: All of the algorithms were run on the entire database, and then the performance was gauged based on three criterion : prediction monotonicity, prediction accuracy and prediction consistency. The *monotonicity* was measured by computing the Spearman Rank Ordered Correlation Coefficient (SROCC), the *accuracy* was computed using Linear (Pearson's) Correlation Coefficient (CC) and Root Mean Square Error (RMSE). While the SROCC can be computed directly on the scores obtained from the algorithm and subjective testing, the CC and RMSE require a non-linear transformation before their computation. This is due to the fact that the objective scores may be non-linearly related to the subjective scores. This would imply that, although the algorithms predict the quality accurately, in the absence of such a non-linear mapping the CC and RMSE would not be truly representative of algorithm performance. Finally, *consistency* was measured by computing the Outlier Ratio (OR).

The standard procedure to conduct a subjective study in order to obtain the mean opinion scores (MOS) which is representative of the human perception of quality is enlisted in [3]. A similar study to assess the quality of images was conducted soon after [75], where leading IQA algorithms were evaluated in a procedure similar to that followed by the VQEG. The VQEG dataset and the LIVE image dataset are available publicly at [51] and [76].

Table 1 Performance of VQA algorithms on VQEG
phase-I dataset

VQA Algorithm	SROCC	LCC
PSNR	0.786	0.779
Proponent P8 (Swisscom)[47]	0.803	0.827
Frame-SS-SSIM [36]	0.812	0.849
MOVIE [62]	0.833	0.821

In order to obtain a comparison of the results of various VQA algorithms, in Table 1 we detail the performance of PVQM [47], which was the top performer in the VQEG dataset, along with Frame-SS-SSIM and MOVIE. We also include Peak Signal-to-Noise Ratio (PSNR), since it provides the baseline for performance evaluation, as it has been argued the PSNR does not correlate well with human perception of quality [77]. Note that many of the algorithms from the VQEG study have been altered further to enhance performance. Indeed, VQM, whose earlier version was a proponent in the VQEG study, was trained on the VQEG phase-I dataset in order to obtain the parameters of the algorithm. We also note that the VQEG phase-I dataset is the only publicly available dataset for VQA testing.

Although the VQEG dataset has been used in the recent past for performance evaluation of various VQA algorithms, the dataset suffers from severe drawbacks. The VQEG dataset contains some non-natural video sequence – eg., scrolling text on screen – which is not considered 'fair-game' for VQA algorithms which are based on human perception of natural scenes and are not geared towards quality assessment of artificially created environments or text. For example, as demonstrated in [74], MOVIE performs significantly better when such sequences are not considered in the analysis. Further, the dataset is dated - the report was published in 2000, and was made specifically for TV and hence contains interlaced videos. The presence of interlaced videos complicates the prediction of quality, since the de-interlacing algorithm can introduce further distortion before computation of algorithm scores. Further, the VQEG study included distortions only from old generation encoders such as the H.263 [78] and MPEG-2 [79], which exhibit different distortions compared with present generation encoders like the H.264 AVC/MPEG-4 Part 10 [80]. Finally, and most importantly the VQEG phase I database of distorted videos suffers from problems with poor perceptual separation. Both humans and algorithms have difficulty in producing consistent judgments that distinguish many of the videos, lowering the correlations between humans and algorithms and the statistical confidence of the results. We also note that even though the VQEG has conducted other studies [54], oddly, none of the data has been made public.

In order to overcome these limitations the LIVE video quality assessment and the LIVE wireless video quality databases were created. These two databases will alleviate the problems associated with the VQEG dataset and will provide a suitable testing ground for future VQA algorithms. Information regarding these databases may not be ready before this chapter is published, but will soon be provided at [76].

Conclusions & Future Directions

In this chapter we began by motivating the need for VQA algorithms and gave a brief summary of various VQA algorithms. We detailed performance evaluation techniques and validation methods for a number of leading VQA algorithms. Future research may involve further understanding of human motion processing and its incorporation into VQA algorithms. Temporal pooling is another issue that needs to be considered. Gaze attention and region-of-interest remain interesting areas of research, especially in the case of video quality assessment. In this chapter we have detailed only FR VQA algorithms. However, research in the area of RR VQA algorithms is of key interest, considering its practical advantages. The Holy Grail, of course are truly NR VQA algorithms. Further, the statistical techniques used for measuring the performance of algorithms have been questioned [35], [75]. It is of interest to evaluate various possible alternatives to study correlation with human perception.

References

1. Z. Wang and A. C. Bovik, Modern Image Quality Assessment. New York: Morgan and Claypool Publishing Co., 2006.
2. A. K. Moorthy and A. C. Bovik, "Perceptually Significant Spatial Pooling techniques for Image quality assessment ," in *SPIE Conference on Human Vision and Electronic Imaging*, Jan. 2009.
3. "Methodology for the subjective assessment of the quality of television pictures," ITU-R Recommendation BT.500-11.
4. B. Hiremath, Q. Li and Z. Wang "Quality-aware video," *IEEE International Conference on Image Processing*, San Antonio, TX, Sept. 16-19, 2007.
5. H. R. Sheikh, A. C. Bovik, and L. Cormack, "No-reference quality assessment using natural scene statistics: JPEG2000," *Image Processing, IEEE Transactions on*, vol. 14, no. 11, pp. 1918–1927, 2005.
6. C. M. Liu, J. Y. Lin, K. G. Wu and C. N. Wang, "Objective image quality measure for block-based DCT coding," *IEEE Trans. Consum. Electron.*, vol. 43, pp. 511–516, 1997.
7. Z. Wang, A. C. Bovik, and B. L. Evans, "Blind measurement of blocking artifacts in images," in *IEEE Intl. Conf. Image Proc*, 2000.
8. X. Li, "Blind image quality assessment", *IEEE International Conference on Image Processing*, New York, 2002.
9. Patrick Le Callet, Christian Viard-Gaudin, Stéphane Péchard and Emilie Caillault, "No reference and reduced reference video quality metrics for end to end QoS monitoring", *Special Issue on multimedia Qos evaluation and management technologies, E89, (2), Pages: 289-296, February 2006.*
10. W. S. Geisler and M. S. Banks, "Visual performance," in Handbook of Optics, M. Bass, Ed. McGraw-Hill, 1995.
11. B. A. Wandell, Foundations of Vision. Sunderland, MA: Sinauer Associates Inc., 1995.
12. N. C. Rust, V Mante, E. P. Simoncelli, and J. A. Movshon, "How MT cells analyze the motion of visual patterns ", *Nature Neuroscience*, vol.9(11), pp. 1421–1431, Nov 2006.
13. Z. Wang, G. Wu, H. R. Sheikh, E. P. Simoncelli, E.-H. Yang and A. C. Bovik, "Quality -aware images" *IEEE Transactions on Image Processing,* vol. 15, no. 6, pp. 1680-1689, June 2006.
14. R. T. Born and D. C. Bradley, "Structure and function of visual area MT," *Annual Rev Neuroscience*, vol. 28, pp. 157–189, 2005.

15. M. A. Smith, N. J. Majaj, and J. A. Movshon, "Dynamics of motion signaling by neurons in macaque area MT," *Nature Neuroscience*, vol. 8, no. 2, pp. 220–228, Feb. 2005.

16. S. Daly, "The visible differences predictor: an algorithm for the assessment of image fidelity," in Digital Images and Human Vision (A. B. Watson, ed.), pp. 179–206, Cambridge, MA: The MIT Press, 1993.

17. J. Lubin, "The use of psychophysical data and models in the analysis of display system performance," in Digital Images and Human Vision (A. B. Watson, ed.), pp. 163–178, Cambridge, MA: The MIT Press, 1993.

18. R. J. Safranek and J. D. Johnston, "A perceptually tuned sub-band image coder with image dependent quantization and post-quantization data compression," in *Proc. ICASSP-89*, vol. 3, (Glasgow, Scotland), pp. 1945–1948, May 1989.

19. A. B.Watson, "DCTune: a technique for visual optimization of dct quantization matrices for individual images," Society for Information Display Digest of Technical Papers, vol. 24, pp. 946–949, 1993.

20. K. Seshadrinathan, R. J. Safranek, J. Chen, T. N. Pappas, H. R. Sheikh, E. P. Simoncelli, Z. Wang and A. C. Bovik. Image quality assessment. In A. C. Bovik, editor, The Essential Guide to Image Processing, chapter 20. Academic Press, 2009.

21. C. J. van den Branden Lambrecht and O. Verscheure, "Perceptual quality measure using a spatiotemporal model of the human visual system," in *Proc. SPIE*, vol. 2668, no. 1. San Jose, CA, USA: SPIE, Mar. 1996, pp. 450–461.

22. S. Winkler, "Perceptual distortion metric for digital color video," *Proc. SPIE*, vol. 3644, no. 1, pp. 175–184, May 1999.

23. E. P. Simoncelli, W. T. Freeman, E. H. Adelson, and D. J. Heeger, "Shiftable multiscale transforms," *IEEE Trans. Inform. Theory*, vol. 38, pp. 587-607, Mar. 1992.

24. A. B. Watson, J. Hu, and J. F. McGowan III, "Digital video quality metric based on human vision," *J. Electron. Imaging*, vol. 10, no. 1, pp. 20–29, Jan. 2001.

25. M. Masry, S. S. Hemami, and Y. Sermadevi, "A scalable wavelet-based video distortion metric and applications," *Circuits and Systems for Video Technology, IEEE Transactions on*, vol. 16, no. 2, pp. 260–273, 2006.

26. H. Peterson, A.J. Ahumada, Jr. and A. Watson,"An Improved Detection Model for DCT Coefficient Quantization," *Human Vision and Electronic Imaging*, Proc. SPIE, 1913, 191–201.

27. M. Carnec, P. Le Callet, and D. Barba, "Objective quality assessment of color images based on a generic perceptual reduced reference," *Signal Processing: Image Communication, Volume 23 , Issue 4, Pages 239-256, April 2008.*

28. K. Seshadrinathan and A. C. Bovik. Video quality assessment. In A. C. Bovik, editor, The Essential Guide to Video Processing, chapter 14. Academic Press, 2009.

29. Z. Wang, A. C. Bovik, H. R. Sheikh, and E. P. Simoncelli, "Image quality assessment: from error visibility to structural similarity," *IEEE Trans. Image Process*, vol. 13, no. 4, pp. 600–612, 2004.

30. Z. Wang and A. C. Bovik, "A universal image quality index," IEEE Signal Processing Letters, vol. 9, no. 3, pp. 81–84, 2002.

31. Z. Wang, E. P. Simoncelli, and A. C. Bovik, "Multiscale structural similarity for image quality assessment," in *Thirty-Seventh Asilomar Conf. on Signals, Systems and Computers*, Pacific Grove, CA, 2003.

32. Z. Wang and E. P. Simoncelli, "Translation insensitive image similarity in complex wavelet domain," in *IEEE Intl. Conf. Acoustics, Speech, and Signal Process.*, Philadelphia, PA, 2005.

33. M. P. Sampat, Z. Wang, S. Gupta, A. C. Bovik and M. K. Markey, "Complex wavelet structural similarity: A new image similarity index," *IEEE Transactions on Image Processing,* to appear 2009.

34. Z. Wang and X. Shang, "Spatial pooling strategies for perceptual image quality assessment," in *IEEE International Conference on Image Processing*, Jan. 1996.

35. A. K. Moorthy and A. C. Bovik, "Visual importance pooling for image quality assessment," *IEEE Journal of Selected Topics in Signal Processing, Special Issue on Visual Media Quality Assessment*, to appear, April 2009.

36. Z. Wang, L. Lu, and A. C. Bovik, "Video quality assessment based on structural distortion measurement," *Signal Processing: Image Communication*, vol. 19, no. 2, pp. 121–132, Feb. 2004.
37. A. Srivastava, A. B. Lee, E. P. Simoncelli, and S.-C. Zhu, "On advances in statistical modeling of natural images," *J. Math. Imag. Vis.*, vol. 18, pp. 17–33, 2003.
38. E. P. Simoncelli and B. A. Olshausen, "Natural image statistics and neural representation," *Annu. Rev. Neurosci.*, vol. 24, pp. 1193–1216, May 2001.
39. H. R. Sheikh and A. C. Bovik, "A visual information fidelity approach to video quality assessment," *First International Workshop on Video Processing and Quality Metrics for Conusmer Electronics*, Jan. 2005.
40. H. R. Sheikh and A. C. Bovik, "Image information and visual quality," *IEEE Trans. Image Process*, vol. 15, no. 2, pp. 430-444, 2006.
41. H. R. Sheikh, A. C. Bovik, and G. de Veciana, "An information fidelity criterion for image quality assessment using natural scene statistics," *IEEE Trans. Image Process.*, vol. 14, no. 12, pp. 2117-2128, 2005.
42. J. Malo, I. Epifanio, R. Navarro, and E. P. Simoncelli, "Non-linear image representation for efficient perceptual coding", *IEEE Transactions on Image Processing*, vol.15(1), pp. 68–80, Jan 2006.
43. J. Portilla and E. P. Simoncelli, " A parametric texture model based on joint statistics of complex wavelet coefficients", *International Journal of Computer Vision*, vol.40(1), pp. 49–71, Dec 2000.
44. J. A. Guerrero Colón, E. P. Simoncelli , and J. Portilla, "Image denoising using mixtures of Gaussian scale mixtures ", *IEEE International Conference on Image Processing*, pp. 565–568, Oct 2008.
45. M. J. Wainwright, E. P. Simoncelli, and A. S. Wilsky, "Random cascades on wavelet trees and their use in analyzing and modeling natural images," *Applied and Computational Harmonic Analysis*, vol. 11, pp. 89–123, 2001.
46. M. J. Wainwright and E. P. Simoncelli, "Scale Mixtures of Gaussians and the statistics of natural images", *Adv. Neural Information Processing Systems (NIPS'99)*, vol.12 pp. 855–861, May 2000.
47. A. P. Hekstra, J. G. Beerends, D. Ledermann, F. E. de Caluwe, S. Kohler, R. H. Koenen, S. Rihs, M. Ehrsam, and D. Schlauss, "PVQM - A perceptual video quality measure," *Signal Proc.: Image Comm.* vol. 17, pp. 781–798, 2002.
48. Opticom. [Online]. Available: http://www.opticom.de/technology/pevq-video-quality-testing.html
49. M. Malkowski and D. Claben, "Performance of video telephony services in UMTS using live measurements and network emulation," *Wireless Personal Comm.*, vol. 1, pp. 19–32, 2008.
50. M. Barkowsky, J. Bialkowski, R. Bitto, and A. Kaup, "Temporal registration using 3D phase correlation and a maximum likelihood approach in the perceptual evaluation of video quality," in *IEEE Workshop on Multimedia Signal Proc.*, 2007.
51. The Video Quality Experts Group. (2000) Final report from the video quality experts group on the validation of objective quality metrics for video quality assessment. [Online]. Available: http://www.its.bldrdoc.gov/vqeg/projects/frtv phaseI
52. Objective perceptual multimedia video quality measurement in the presence of a full reference, International Telecommunications Union Std. ITU-T Rec. J. 247, 2008.
53. M. H. Pinson and S. Wolf, "A new standardized method for objectively measuring video quality," *IEEE Trans. Broadcast.*, vol. 50, no. 3, pp. 312–322, Sep. 2004.
54. The Video Quality Experts Group. (2003) Final VQEG report on the validation of objective models of video quality assessment. [Online]. Available: http://www.ts. bldrdoc.gov/vqeg/projects/frtv phaseII
55. Objective perceptual video quality measurement techniques for digital cable television in the presence of a full reference, International Telecommunications Union Std. ITU-T Rec. J. 144, 2004.

56. "Video quality metric." [Online]. Available: http://www.its.bldrdoc.gov/n3/video/VQM_ software.php
57. M. Yuen and H. R. Wu, "A survey of hybrid MC/DPCM/DCT video coding distortions," *Signal Processing*, vol. 70, no. 3, pp. 247–278, Nov. 1998.
58. J. A. Movshon and W. T. Newsome, "Visual response properties of striate cortical neurons projecting to Area MT in macaque monkeys," *J. Neurosci.*, vol. 16, no. 23, pp. 7733–7741, 1996.
59. Z.Wang and Q. Li, "Video quality assessment using a statistical model of human visual speed perception." *J Opt Soc Am A Opt Image Sci Vis*, vol. 24, no. 12, pp. B61–B69, Dec 2007.
60. A. A. Stocker and E. P. Simoncelli, "Noise characteristics and prior expectations in human visual speed perception," *Nature Neuroscience*, 9, 578-585 (2006).
61. Black, M. J. and Anandan, P., "The robust estimation of multiple motions: Parametric and piecewise-smooth flow fields," *Computer Vision and Image Understanding*, 63, 75-104 (1996).
62. K. Seshadrinathan and A. C. Bovik, "Spatio-temporal quality assessment of natural videos," *IEEE Transactions on Image Processing*, submitted for publication.
63. K. Seshadrinathan and A. C. Bovik, "A structural similarity metric for video based on motion models," *IEEE International Conference on Acoustics, Speech, and Signal Processing*, 2007.
64. D. J. Fleet and A. D. Jepson, "Computation of component image velocity from local phase information," *International Journal of Computer Vision*, vol. 5, no. 1, pp. 77–104, 1990.
65. D. J. Heeger, "Optical flow using spatiotemporal filters," *International Journal of Computer Vision*, vol. 1, no. 4, pp. 279–302, 1987.
66. E. H. Adelson and J. R. Bergen, "Spatiotemporal energy models for the perception of motion." *J Opt Soc Am A*, vol. 2, no. 2, pp. 284–299, Feb 1985.
67. N. J. Priebe, S. G. Lisberger, and J. A. Movshon, "Tuning for spatiotemporal frequency and speed in directionally selective neurons of macaque striate cortex." *J Neurosci*, vol. 26, no. 11, pp. 2941–2950, Mar 2006.
68. E. P. Simoncelli and D. J. Heeger, "A model of neuronal responses in visual area MT," *Vision Res*, vol. 38, no. 5, pp. 743–761, Mar 1998.
69. J. G. Daugman, "Uncertainty relation for resolution in space, spatial frequency, and orientation optimized by two-dimensional visual cortical filters," *Journal of the Optical Society of America A (Optics and Image Science)*, vol. 2, no. 7, pp. 1160–1169, 1985.
70. P. C. Teo and D. J. Heeger, "Perceptual image distortion," in *Proceedings of the IEEE International Conference on Image Processing. IEEE*, 1994, pp. 982–986 vol.2.
71. K. Seshadrinathan and A. C. Bovik, "Unifying analysis of full reference image quality assessment," in *IEEE Intl. Conf. on Image Proc.*, 2008.
72. A. B. Watson and J. Ahumada, A. J., "Model of human visual-motion sensing," *Journal of the Optical Society of America A* (Optics and Image Science), vol. 2, no. 2, pp. 322–342, 1985.
73. H. Frank and S. C. Althoen, "The coefficient of variation," in Statistics: Concepts and Applications. Cambridge, Great Britan: Cambridge University Press., 1995, pp. 58–59.
74. K. Seshadrinathan, "Video quality assessment based on motion models," Ph.D. dissertation, University of Texas at Austin, 2008.
75. H. R. Sheikh, M. F. Sabir, and A. C. Bovik, "A statistical evaluation of recent full reference image quality assessment algorithms," *IEEE Transactions on Image Processing*, vol. 15, no. 11, pp. 3440–3451, Nov. 2006.
76. LIVE image quality assessment database. [Online]. Available: http://live.ece.utexas.edu/research/quality/subjective.html
77. Wang, Z. and Bovik, A. C., "Mean squared error: Love it or leave it? - a new look at fidelity measures." *IEEE Signal Processing Magazine*. January 2009.
78. "Video coding for low bit rate communication", ITU Recommendation H.263.
79. "Generic coding of moving pictures and associated audio information - part 2: Video," 1994, ITU-T and ISO/IEC JTC 1. ITU-T Recommendation H.262 and ISO/IEC 13 818-2 (MPEG-2).
80. "Advanced video coding," 2003, ISO/IEC 14496-10 and ITU-T Rec. H.264.

Chapter 7
Countermeasures for Time-Cheat Detection in Multiplayer Online Games

Stefano Ferretti

Introduction

Cheating is an important issue in games. Depending on the system over which the game is deployed, several types of malicious actions may be accomplished so as to take an unfair and unexpected advantage over the game and over the (digital, human) adversaries. When the game is a standalone application, cheats typically just relate to the specific software code being developed to build the application. It is not a surprise to find (in the Web and in specialized magazines) people that explain cheats on specific games stating, for instance, which configuration files can be altered (and how to do it) to automatically gain some bonus during the game. To avoid this, game developers are hence motivated to build stable code, with related data that should be securely managed and made difficult to alter.

When the game goes online, a number of further issues arise which highly complicate the task of avoiding cheats. Indeed, each node in a Multiplayer Online Game (MOG) has its own, locally installed software, which can be freely altered or substituted by the malicious player. Furthermore, and certainly equally important, the presence of the network and the need for communication among nodes in a MOG can be exploited by some of these nodes to cheat.

It is the best-effort nature of the Internet that allows cheaters to take malicious actions to evade the rules of the game. For instance, they are enabled to alter timing properties of game events in order to mimic that these have been generated at a certain point in (game) time (these are often referred as *time cheats*). Cheaters can delay (or anticipate) the notification of their game events to other nodes in the system. They can also drop some of their game events (i.e. not notify them to other nodes) in order to save their own computational and communication resources (sending a message has a cost) and diminish the amount of updated information provided to other participants.

S. Ferretti (✉)
Department of Computer Science, University of Bologna, Bologna, Italy
e-mail: sferrett@cs.unibo.it

B. Furht (ed.), *Handbook of Multimedia for Digital Entertainment and Arts*,
DOI 10.1007/978-0-387-89024-1_7, © Springer Science+Business Media, LLC 2009

These last classes of cheats must be avoided by devising specific, application-aware communication protocols. In this manuscript, we will deal with *time cheats* and outline two classes of mechanisms to avoid them, i.e. prevention and detection schemes. We will describe some of the existing approaches in a peer-to-peer (P2P) system architecture that exploits a specific game time model. The reason behind the choice of a P2P architecture is that it has been generally recognized as a powerful solution to guarantee a high level of scalability and fault tolerance in MOGs. The adopted game time model is a general framework which ensures a fair management of game events generated at distributed nodes.

In the reminder of this discussion, we will first outline some background on the system architectures employed to support MOGs. We will explain why P2P solutions are generally a better choice with respect to the client/server model. We then present the system model exploited to prevent time cheats and countermeasures to avoid them. A discussion on the framework exploited to model game time advancements is provided in the subsequent section. The idea is that of resorting to a combination of simulation and wallclock times. Some prominent time cheats, which have been considered by the research community, are then discussed. Preventions schemes are explained, focusing on those approaches that prevent the look-ahead time cheat. The discussion continues with detection schemes, together with some simulation results that confirm the viability of these approaches. Finally, some concluding remarks are outlined.

Background on System Architectures

MOGs may be deployed on the Internet, based on different distributed architectures [14]. Besides classical issues concerned with scalability, fault-tolerance and responsiveness, the choice of the architecture to support a MOG is of main importance also on cheating avoidance. Indeed, different game architectures entail different ways to manage the game state, different communication protocols among distributed nodes, different information directly available at (malicious) players. These differences have strong influence also on the way cheats can be accomplished (and contrasted).

For instance, peer-to-peer based approaches represent very promising architectural solutions [15]. Each peer manages its own copy of the game state, which is locally updated based on the messages received by other peers. Communication and synchronization protocols are exploited to be sure that each peer eventually receives all the game events generated by player, hence being able to compute a correct evolution of the game state. P2P architectures and protocols allow a scalable and fault tolerant management of a MOG; they enable self-configuring solutions that face the diverse nature of players' devices and the underlying network. However, the main advantage of P2P in MOGs, i.e. the autonomy of peers, may become an issue when cheaters join the game, since they have a free access to the game state.

Conversely, it is well known that client/server architectures fail to provide scalability, since the server often represents a bottleneck and the single point of failure in the system. In this case, only the server controls the game state which is updated based on the messages sent by clients; the server is then responsible for periodically informing clients about the changes on the game state. This model clearly reduces the possible cheats in the system (without completely avoiding them).

For the reasons mentioned above, it becomes interesting to study whether effective cheating avoidance schemes can be devised on top of P2P architectures. This would enable the provision of fault-tolerant, scalable and secure platforms on top of which games could be played by a multitude of users.

System Model

In the rest of the discussion, we model the game system as composed of several peers organized as a P2P architecture. We assume that each peer maintains a local copy of the game state and keeps it synchronized with others managed by distributed peers, based on notified updates. No assumptions are made here on the exploited synchronization algorithm to maintain game state consistency. There are several possible alternatives, such as, just to mention a few, [8, 19, 26, 28]. For the sake of simplicity, we assume that peers are fully connected, i.e. they can communicate with other nodes directly, without the need to pass through some other node. Needless to say, such assumption is made at the application layer (not at the network layer), just to assert that no overlay network is exploited for the game event dissemination.

We denote with Π the set of peers in the P2P game architecture; p_i identifies a single peer, i.e., $p_i \in \Pi$. With Π_i we indicate all peers but p_i, i.e. $\Pi_i = \Pi - \{p_i\}$. Similarly, notations such as $\Pi_{i,j}$ indicate all peers but p_i and p_j, i.e. $\Pi_{i,j} = \Pi - \{p_i, p_j\}$.

To characterize game events produced at a given peer (i.e. by the same player) we employ an identifier with prime notations, i.e. e^i is an event generated by p_i. Instead, to identify and order events generated (often by the same peer) in different time instants, we employ subscripts, e.g. $e_j, e_k, j < k$. Figure 1 provides a graphical view of the system model, with the associated notation, when only three peers, i.e. p_1, p_2, p_3, constitute the architecture. In the Figure, a game event e^1 is generated and sent from p_1 to p_2. Also the sets Π and Π_1 are represented.

Game events are notified within messages. Typically, MOGs exploit UDP-based delivery solutions to transmit game events [28]. However, for the sake of simplicity,

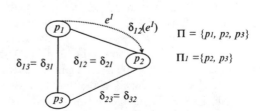

Fig. 1 System model

in our scheme we will assume that transmitted messages can experience different latencies and delay jitters but cannot be lost. We assume the existence of an upper bound UB on the latencies among peers in the system. UB is known by peers. With $\delta_{ij}(e)$ we denote the time needed to transmit a game event e from p_i to p_j. (In Figure 1, the time to send e_1 from p_1 to p_2 is characterized as $\delta_{12}(e^1)$.) With δ_{ij}, instead, we denote the average latency needed for the transmission of a non specified game event from p_i to p_j. We realistically assume that typically $\delta_{ij}(e) \approx \delta_{ij}$. Basically, this last assumption entails that the underlying network over which the game is deployed offers a best-effort service with unpredictable delay latencies and jitters but, on the long run, an average trend of network latencies may be observed. This is in accordance with a plethora of works that model network traffic such as, in the networked gaming literature, [3, 13, 23]. We also assume that transmission latencies are mostly symmetric, i.e. $\delta_{ij} = \delta_{ji}$ (as shown in Figure 1).

Modeling Game Time

Games evolve through events generated by distributed players during time. Time is thus a main characteristic to model in a game. Obviously, several possibilities exist. A first distinction is on who assigns timestamps to the game events. An approach is to leave to a single node (e.g. the server) the task of timestamping and ordering game events. This, however, introduces a high level of unfairness, since transmission latencies to reach that node influence the game event ordering. The other approach is that peers locally assign timestamps to their own generated game events.

It is worth mentioning that most developed games simply adopt the use of a single timestamp to manage the game time. This timestamp is obtained based on the physical clock at the node where the game is executed. However, since the game is played in multiplayer mode, different physical clocks of different nodes timestamp different game events. As a consequence, when these events are processed according to their timestamp order, it is obvious that a fair ordering of game events is obtained only provided that physical clocks of distributed nodes are perfectly synchronized. Yet, this assumption is not realistic, especially when a high number of nodes is involved in the game. Hence, those nodes that have a slow clock are advantaged with respect to other ones.

Trying to provide a fair way to characterize game events produced at distributed nodes in a MOG, a main notion worth of introduction is that of simulation time. *Simulation time* is the abstraction that is used to model when events have been produced within the virtual game timeline. In the context of distributed simulation, Fujimoto defined in [21] simulation time as a *"set of values where each value represents an instant of time in the system being modelled"*. The simulation time measured at a peer p_i is denoted with ST_i. With $ST_i(e)$, we represent the simulation time associated to the game event e, generated by the peer p_i.

Wallclock time, instead, is the time that identifies when the game takes place at a physical node. We denote with WT_i the wallclock time measured at p_i. $WT_i(e)$

represents the wallclock time of generation of the game event e at p_i. We assume that once created, the transmission of the event e from p_i to all other peers $\prod_i$ is instantaneous (unless p_i is a cheater). Moreover, we denote with $WT_j^{rec}(e)$ the wallclock time of reception of e at p_j.

As mentioned, simulation time is an important notion to characterize game events generated by different peers, and then to totally order them. It serves to have a fair way to inject game events in the game world. However, the use of simulation time alone could result as a weakness in terms of cheating avoidance. In fact, in principle each peer is enabled to associate whatever simulation time to its produced game event.

This problem can be reduced in some way, by exploiting ST together with WT and keeping simulation time advancements proportional to wallclock ones (see equation (1) below). A mapping function T_i^W can hence be introduced that transforms a simulation time s into the corresponding wallclock time t at p_i, i.e. $T_i^W(s) = t$. With T_i^S, instead, we represent T_i^W's inverse function. The specific game time model will depend on the definition of T_i^W and T_i^S.

ST and WT can be employed to divide time in coarse intervals, thus adopting a round-based game evolution (i.e. at each round a single move per player is allowed), or mimicking a fluid evolution of time. In particular, in a round-based evolution of the game, ST advances as a step function of WT. In other words, ST increases of a Δs only once all messages from other peers have been received, or a (wallclock) timeout has expired, i.e. $T_i^S(t + h) = T_i^S(t) = s$, for $h < \Delta t$, where Δt is the minimum between time needed to receive all messages from all peers $\prod_i$ and a predefined wallclock timeout. After such Δt, ST advances to $s + \Delta s$.

Conversely, to make the system able to advance in *real-time*, a function T_i^s must be employed to let ST advance in synchrony with WT. A scale factor k may be exploited to identify the pace of game advancements in the simulated world. When $k = 1$, a real-time evolution is implemented; otherwise, i.e. $k \neq 1$, the system is said to advance in scaled real-time [7, 21]. The mapping function to translate WT into ST is thus

$$T_i^s(t_{i,actual}) = T_i^s(t_{i,start}) + k(t_{i,actual} - t_{i,start}), \qquad (1)$$

where $t_{i,actual}$ represents the actual WT at p_i, $t_{i,start}$ represents the wallclock time associated to the beginning of the game at p_i. The mapping $T_i^s(t_{i,start})$ returns a simulation time value, agreed and shared among all nodes, representing the time at which the beginning of game plot takes place, i.e., $T_i^s(t_{i,start}) = s_{start} \in ST$, $\forall p_i \in \Pi$. Using the formula above, the simulation time of a given game event e can be characterized as follows,

$$ST_i(e) = s_{start} + k(WT_i(e) - t_{i,start}). \qquad (2)$$

The binding between these two different timestamps prevent that simulation times are freely altered by cheaters without tampering also wallclock times (in order to respect such mapping between ST and WT). Hence, upon reception of cheated events, based on contained timestamps, honest peers will measure altered network latencies which differ from the real ones. This way, viable detection schemes can be devised, for example, based on statistical methods that measure transmission latencies, as explained in the rest of the work.

Such an approach to model time advancements allows also to cope with the fact that physical clocks of nodes in the system are not synchronized and that nodes cannot start the game at the same, precise instant. In fact, due to the distributed nature of a MOG, with high probability $t_{i,start} \neq t_{j,start}$, $\forall p_i, p_j \in \Pi, i \neq j$. A solution here is to let each peer p_i to associate, at the beginning of the game session, its starting wallclock time $t_{i,start}$ to the agreed constant starting simulation time, i.e. $T_i^s (t_{i,start}) = s_{start}$. Then, each player notifies others with its own $t_{i,start}$.

An important praxis for an efficient delivery protocol is that of exploiting, at the beginning of the game a clock synchronization protocol. This can be accomplished by resorting to an approach that could be devised based on to those presented in literature, e.g. [6, 7, 10, 12, 27]. This would allow to obtain an initial estimation of the average network latencies among peers δ_{ij} and of the drift among physical clocks at p_i and p_j (i.e. $drift_{ij}$). By convention, $drift_{ij} > 0$ if p_j reaches a given wallclock time t^* *before* p_i (i.e., p_j has wallclock times higher than p_i, see Figure 2). We assume that the effects of the drift clock rate at all peers are negligible. Based on such drift, it is easy to characterize the wallclock time at a given peer p_j when an event e^i is generated at p_i, i.e. $WT_i (e^i) + drift_{ij}$. Hence, upon reception of a game event e from p_i to p_j, based on the timestamp included in the message p_j can measure

$$\delta_{ij} (e) = WT_j^{rec} (e) - \left(WT_i (e) - drift_{ij} \right). \tag{3}$$

Of course, such measurement can be considered as a reliable information only provided that $drift_{ij}$ is accurately estimated and that p_i is not cheating (i.e. p_i has not altered the timestamp in its message).

Also a gap_{ij} may be measured representing the (real) time interval between the instants at which p_i and p_j start the game (see Figure 3). A simple equation to measure gap_{ij}, based on the starting point of the beginning time instant (including $drift_{ij}$) is as follows,

$$gap_{ij} = drift_{ij} + t_{i,start} - t_{j,start}. \tag{4}$$

In essence, gap_{ij} takes into account that a drift among clocks of p_i and p_j exists and that they started the game at different times. Clearly, $gap_{ij} = -gap_{ij}$ (as

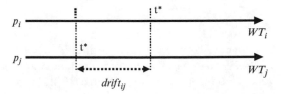

Fig. 2 Drift between p_i and p_j

Fig. 3 Gap between p_i and p_j

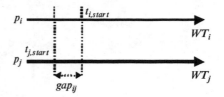

well as $drift_{ij} = -drift_{ij}$). Methods can be adopted to reduce the value of the gap among peers. For instance, an agreement protocol could force peers do determine a certain point in time to start the game session. Alternatively, a peer p_l may be set to broadcast a start message to other ones that begin the game as soon as they receive that message; for each transmitted message, a buffering delay may be utilized at p_l, adapted for each receiver to compensate for different network latencies. This way, the start message is received by all peers within a short time interval.

Time Cheats

Time cheats are those specific cheats which are based on the illegal alteration of game events' timestamp. These cheats are distinctive of Internet-based MOGs and can be profitably exploited by malicious players when the game is hosted on a P2P platform and each peers locally assigns a timestamp to each generated game event [4, 5, 16–18]. The alibi of cheaters is the variable transmission latency that a message may experience when it travels on the Internet.

Needless to say, the simpler the model to characterize game time, the simpler is to alter the communication protocol to gain some malicious advantage. Hence, time cheats vary and depend also on the game time management protocol. When resorting to (1) and (2) to model game time, an important implication is that cheaters which want to alter timing properties of their generated events are forced to alter both ST and WT. Indeed, the communication protocol may impose that for each transmitted event e, both $ST_i(e)$ and $WT_i(e)$ are included (together with a sequence number and other game-related data) within the message transporting e. Thus, given any two game events $e^i{}_h$ and $e^i{}_l$, and based on (2), a check can be made to verify that the following holds,

$$\frac{ST_i\left(e_h^i\right) - ST_i\left(e_l^i\right)}{WT_i\left(e_h^i\right) - WT_i\left(e_l^i\right)} = k. \tag{5}$$

Conversely, it is straightforward to verify that (5) is not respected by p_i, which in this case is a cheater.

In the following, we will define some prominent time cheats presented in the research literature related to MOGs.

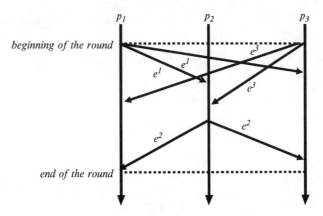

Fig. 4 Look-ahead cheat in a round-based model

Look-Ahead Cheat

The *look-ahead cheat* is a kind of a cheat according to which the cheater waits to see game events generated by other participants before generating its own game event [1]. The idea is that waiting moves from other peers before generating its own one, the malicious player "sees into the future" and can decide which is the best action to take to win the game.

Basically, a cheater p_i waits for events generated by other peers before generating its own events. Then, in order to gain an advantage over other players p_i may determine which is the best action that he could have generated in that specific game context. p_i thus creates such cheated event e and notifies it to others, pretending e has been generated before (or concurrently with) other ones [1, 9, 24].

Most of the existing malicious approaches which exploit this time cheat work over a round based model. Figure 4 provides a graphical representation of look-ahead time cheat in this context, assuming that only three peers are participating to the game i.e. $\Pi = \{p_1, p_2, p_3\}$. In this case, the cheater is p_2. It waits for events coming from p_1 and p_3, decides which the best action to take, and transmits the event to other nodes in Π_2. By doing this, it mimics that the game event has been generated concurrently with other ones. It is clear that in this scenario, altering the game time is quite simple; indeed, it suffices to modify the timestamp $WT_2(e^2)$. Then, the *ST* is advanced by all peers Π only after that all the three messages for that round have been received.

In the following, a formalization of the look ahead cheat in a real-time model is reported.

Let $W(e)$ represent the set of game events p_i waits before generating the cheated event e. The set $W(e)$ obviously depends on the specific game being modelled. In the round-based model considered above, for instance, $W(e)$ simply corresponds to the set of all the game events generated by other players at that round. In a real-time modelling of the game, instead, several solutions are possible. This however does not influence the cheat model. Hence, for the sake of simplicity and without loss of generality, here we consider $W(e)$ to be the set of game events generated by players within a given interval of simulated time Δs, assuming that all these game events may influence the cheater to determine its new cheated game event.

Taking advantage of the knowledge of $W(e)$, e is generated and a cheated simulation time is associated to it based on this formula:

$$ST_i^c(e) = \min\left\{ST_j(e_k) \mid e_k \in W(e), p_j \in \prod_i\right\} - \omega \qquad (\omega \in ST, \omega > 0).$$

Put in words, $ST_i^{\,c}(e)$ is set by p_i so that such timestamp is lower that those associated to game events in $W(e)$, i.e., $ST_i^{\,c}(e) < ST_j(e_k)$, $\forall e_k \in W(e)$. Finally, based on $ST_i^{\,c}(e)$, p_i calculates a cheated wallclock time $WT_i^{\,c}(e)$ and associates these two timestamps to the game event e.

Fast Rate Cheat

A fast rate cheat is a kind of a cheat according to which the cheater mimics a rate of generation of game events which is faster than the real one [16, 17]. In fast-paced MOGs, the faster a player generates game events, the better his game play. For instance, in a sport game, the faster a character moves, the higher the possibility of winning a competition. In role playing or strategic games, instead, the faster the player starts his/her planned activities, the faster he/she may gain resources and power in the game. Hence, fast rate cheat is intended to make believe that the player is more rapid to generate game events than what he actually is. Of course, such a cheat is meant to be activated in specific contexts and short periods of a game session, when a rapid generation of events is required.

Of course, fast rate cheat is possible only when a real-time model is exploited to timestamp game events, since in a round-based model only one move per round is allowed to each player.

Based on it, a cheater (say p_i) timestamps game events at a cheated constant rate k_c. Put in other words, the cheater uses an altered simulation time $ST_i^{\,c}$ and wallclock time $WT_i^{\,c}$, so that once a new event, say $e_h^{\,i}$, must be associated with a simulation time, equation (1) is replaced as follows,

$$ST_i^{\,c}\left(e_h^{\,i}\right) = T_i^{\,s}(t_{i,start}) + k^c k\left(t_{i,actual} - t_{i,start}\right), \quad k^c < 1. \qquad (6)$$

Equation (2) is also modified accordingly. Thus, upon generation of an event e_h^i, p_i timestamps it with an altered simulation time $ST_i^{\,c}\left(e_h^{\,i}\right)$. Then, it also associates to the event a cheated wallclock time $WT_i^{\,c}\left(e_h^{\,i}\right)$ so as to bind timestamps and have that, for any given pair of events $e_h^{\,i}$, $e_j^{\,i}$,

$$\frac{ST_i^c\left(e_h^i\right) - ST^c i\left(e_l^i\right)}{WT_i^c\left(e_h^i\right) - WT_i^c\left(e_l^i\right)} = k. \qquad (7)$$

This way, synchrony among (cheated) simulation and wallclock times is respected [18]. Figure 5 provides a graphical representation of fast rate cheat, assuming that

Fig. 5 Fast rate cheat

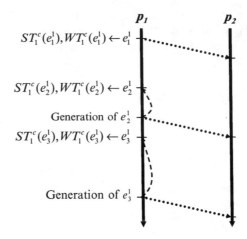

only two peers are participating to the game, i.e. $\prod = \{p_1, \; p_2\}$. In this case, the cheater is p_1.

Suppress-Correct Cheat

Another time-cheat worth of mention is the so called *suppress-correct cheat* [1, 9]. It basically exploits dead reckoning in round-based delivery schemes. According to several gaming systems, a receiving peer is typically set able to dead reckon up to n missing moves from other nodes before assuming that this node has disconnected. This can be exploited by malicious players to gain some advantages. In particular, the cheater can drop $n - 1$ of its game events, without sending them to other nodes. Upon reception of $n - 1$ game events from other nodes, the cheater may builda move based on this information thus gaining an advantage over other nodes. The alibi here is that the cheater has a lossy connection [9].

Figure 6 provides a graphical representation of the suppress correct cheat, assuming that only two peers are participating to the game, i.e. $\Pi = \{p_1, \; p_2\}$. In this case, the cheater is p_1 and n is set equal to 4. p_1 does not send to p_2 the $n - 1$ (i.e. 3) events while receives corresponding events from p_2 and then sends a cheated event at round 4, taking advantage of events received during the previous rounds.

Cheating Prevention

Several communication protocols have been proposed which aim at preventing time cheats. The goodness of these proposals is that it can be formally proved that, upon compliance to the protocol by peers, the game is made cheat-free. However, the problem is that first, the proposed protocols usually guarantee that a specific time cheat is avoided, while no guarantees can be made on other possible time cheats.

Fig. 6 Suppress correct cheat

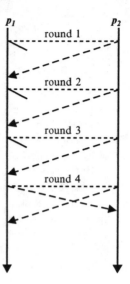

```
1. for each round
2.    e = compute new event
3.    h = generate hash for e
4.    send h to all peers
5.    wait for hash messages from all other peers
6.    send e to all peers
```

Fig. 7 Lockstep pseudo-code at each peer

Second, all the proposed schemes usually require the transmission of a non negligible additional amount of messages among peers and often add synchronization barriers that may reduce the level of responsiveness provided by the system.

In the following, we will look at some specific cheating prevention protocols that cope with the look-ahead time cheat. It is worth mentioning that in the literature, various proposal have been made with respect to this malicious scheme.

For instance, in [1, 2], a seminal scheme has been presented which is fully avoids look-ahead cheat. The scheme (named *lockstep*) works based on a round-based communication protocol. The idea is that players are required to exchange hash values of generated game events before notifying others with the game events. The pseudo-code of the algorithm related to this approach, executed at each peer, is reported in Figure 7.

This guarantees that each event has been generated by all participants before having received any other event at that round. The main limitation of this scheme is that additional messages are distributed among nodes; this augments the network traffic and may have a negative effect on network latencies. In fast paced, real-time MOGs, this represents an important limitation. Moreover, forcing the game to proceed in rounds can slow down the pace of the game evolution, thus jeopardizing responsiveness.

In the same papers, the authors further extend the approach by requiring a synchronous game evolution among players only when they are in the same sphere of influence.

Similar in its philosophy, another round-based protocol has been proposed in [11]. In this case, at each round, generated game events are encrypted and sent to other peers, while keys to decrypt them are sent during the subsequent round. If some game event is received after the round deadline by the majority of peers, it is simply discarded and considered as invalid. To agree on the validity of game events, a voting approach is exploited.

With the aim of diminishing the synchronization barriers of the algorithm presented in [2], in [24] a modification of the approach has been presented which consists in a pipelined version of the lockstep scheme. The idea is that nodes send multiple hashes before the corresponding adversaries' hashes are received and game events are transmitted.

Cronin et al. have further extended the approach above, by presenting an adaptive pipeline protocol [9]. This new scheme is based on the idea of obtaining an estimation of the maximum network latency among peers. Based on it and on the desired event rate to be shown to the user, in order to avoid a jerky and slow rendering of the game evolution, the number of hash messages to send before the message (identified as the pipeline size) is determined. Then, based on such pipeline, a novel hash for the new generated game event is sent, while the event at the end of the pipeline is revealed (i.e. sent to other peers).

Cheating Detection

A main problem with prevention schemes for cheating avoidance is that first, a round-based model of game time advancements is needed. Second, additional messages are to be sent which obviously increase the network traffic. Third and final, there is the need to wait for these messages to have that peers reveal their new move. In fast paced real-time games, these issues represent important limitations, that could make these approaches difficult to employ in practice.

An alternative, viable way to avoid cheating is that of trying to detect cheaters instead of preventing the cheat. The idea is that of finding ways to identify cheaters by simply observing their behavior. This could be a profitable solution, which enables (honest) peers to exploit a simpler communication protocol, with respect to prevention schemes, and freely advance their game in a responsive way. In order to detect time cheats, however, some strategy is required to model the game time advancements.

To provide evidence of the possibility of really detecting time cheaters, we present here a scheme able to cope with look-ahead cheat. In particular, the approach uses the model of game time advancements defined through equations (1) and (2). Then, based on this model, we will show that time cheat detection can be accomplished based on estimations of network latencies and by exploiting the information contained within transmitted messages [17, 18].

The scheme is called *Algorithm for Cheating Detection by Cheating* (AC/DC) [16, 17]. To briefly outline the idea behind the scheme, AC/DC consists on the exploitation of a counterattack to be performed against a suspected node, in order to verify if such a peer can be recognized as a cheater.

More specifically, at a given time only one peer is enabled to perform the counterattack. We call such peer the *leader* peer p_l. Of course, mechanisms should be enabled to make sure that eventually a node chosen as a leader is not a cheater. Hence, such role should be passed among peers, as discussed more in detail in the following.

Once the leader p_l wants to control a suspected node, p_l increases the transmission latency of events generated at p_l for p_i. p_l starts the counterattack by continuously computing a measure of the average latency from p_i to p_l. Such measure is obtained by taking into account values of $\delta_{il}\left(e_k^i\right)$ for events coming from p_i,

$$\delta_{il}\left(e_k^i\right) = WT_l^{rec}\left(e_k^i\right) + drift_{il} - WT_i{}^c\left(e_k^i\right). \tag{8}$$

In (8), $WT_l^{rec}\left(e_k^i\right)$ represents the time of reception of e_k^i at p_l, $WT_i{}^c\left(e_k^i\right)$ is the (possibly cheated) wallclock time at which (p_i claims that) e_k^i has been generated, and $drift_{li}$ is the drift between physical clocks of the two peers. Such values $\delta_{il}\left(e_k^i\right)$ can be averaged (or manipulated through a low-pass filter to smooth the variable behaviour of latencies [20, 22, 25, 28]) so as to have a value of the latency from the suspected node to the leader.

The counterattack that p_l exploits against p_i consists in the delay of the transmission of each novel event e^l generated by p_l towards p_i. Such transmission is delayed for an amount of time λ. Concurrently, new latency values $\delta_{il}\left(e_k^i\right)$ are collected at p_l, for a given time interval. These measurements are averaged to obtain a novel estimation of the average latency from p_i to p_l. The new measure δ_{il}^* is compared with the old value δ_{il} to understand if a statistically significant difference among the two values exists. In particular, when δ_{il}^* is significantly larger than δ_{il}, then the hypothesis that the two measured values are equal must be rejected and hence p_l suspects p_i as a cheater. Conversely, the value of λ is progressively increased and the cheating counterattack mentioned above is iteratively repeated until an upper bound value equal to Δ for $\delta_{il} + \lambda$ is exceeded, where

$$\Delta \geq UB + T_l^W\left(\Delta s\right) + \max\{gap_{il}, p_j \in \Pi_l\}. \tag{9}$$

If such upper bound Δ is reached while a significant difference between δ_{il}^* and δ_{il} has not been noticed, then p_i cannot be considered as a cheater.

The use of such a bound on the increment of λ is due to several reasons. The need to reach UB is due to guarantee that eventually p_l is the peer with the higher (cheated) transmission latency to reach p_i i.e. $\delta_{li} + \lambda > UB \geq \delta_{ji}, \forall\ p_j \in \Pi_{i,l}$. Moreover, cases may arise where some game events e^j, subsequent to e^l but

```
1. pᵢ = peer to control
2. assume δₗᵢ = δᵢₗ                        /*assumption of symmetry*/
3. λ = init value                          /*init value > 0*/
4. while ((δₗᵢ + λ ≤ Δ) ^ (pᵢ is not suspected))
5.    set additional delaying time = λ
6.    observe δᵢₗ* of received game events
7.    if (δᵢₗ* significantly larger than δᵢₗ)
8.       suspect pᵢ
9.    else
10.      λ = increase(λ)
```

Fig. 8 AC/DC Pseudocode

still within $W\left(e_k^i\right)$, can be generated by other peers in $\Pi_{i,l}$. With this in view, the second term $T_l^W(\Delta s)$ accounts for those events $e^j \in W\left(e_k^i\right)$ with simulation times higher than e^l but within a time interval of range Δs. The third term $max\{gap_{jl}, p_j \in \Pi_{il}\}$, instead, accounts for those peers p_j with $gap_{jl} > 0$. Put in other words, it may happen that p_l and p_j generate event s with same simulation times at different real times and p_j reaches such simulation times after p_l. Based on this consideration, the progressive increment of λ, bounded as mentioned above, is meant to guarantee that eventually no event in $W(e_k^i)$ is received by p_i later than e^l. Thus, when the considered peer p_i is a cheater, performing a look-ahead cheat, p_i will eventually stop to wait for game events generated by p_l.

The algorithm related to the scheme described above is reported in Figure 8. Such algorithm is performed at the leader peer.

As mentioned in the pseudo-code, the leader must assume that network latencies between itself and the suspected node are symmetric (i.e., $\delta_{li} = \delta_{il}$). Needless to say, to account for a delay jitter that usually occurs in best-effort networks, a properly tuned number of measurements is needed in order to obtain an accurate value of δ_{il}^*. Moreover, the increment of λ, mentioned with a call of a hypothetical function *increase*() should be implemented using, for instance, a constant increment of λ or some kind of linear growth. Of course, the use of a progressive increment of the value of λ allows a smoother and less intrusive counterattack, since the leader could be able to identify a cheater even before reaching the upper bound for λ [16].

A point worth of mention is that different methods can be devised to suspect a peer for cheating. Probably, a good approach could be to exploit come heuristics based on the combination of diverse factors such that, for instance, i) the degradation of latencies between p_l and p_i, ii) the observation that other peers in the same geographical area of p_i have latencies smaller than p_i, iii) a player that always wins and hence, he is very skilled or he is cheating.

An important assumption is the independence of the generation of game events by a honest peer with those at other peers. In other words, even if certain game events, generated by some peer, will certainly influence the semantics of subsequent game events generated by others (by definition of interactivity in MOGs), in general, the pace of event generation at a given player is mainly influenced by autonomous decisions. From a communication point of view, this means that a honest player generates its own events mostly regardless of the amount, rate and latency of the messages he/she receives. This assumption is supported by the typical use of techniques such as dead reckoning and/or optimistic synchronization, exploited to hide latencies on notifications and local losses of availability on updated information, which provide players with the possibility of independently advance the game [8, 19].

As mentioned, the role of leader should be carefully assigned and managed among peers. First of all, only one leader must be present at a time in the P2P system. In fact, suppose two peers concurrently elect themselves as leaders, and suppose they decide to control each other. In this case, both peers will delay transmission of game events towards the other one. Thus, both peers may erroneously suspect each other. Moreover, each peer should become leader only for a limited amount of time, then another node should be elected. To do this, a token-based scheme should be utilized to determine which is the leader at a given time, i.e. every time a process receives the token, it becomes the leader. A time deadline is set so that each peer is forced to eventually release the token. Thus, after such time deadline the leader could randomly select another peer to be the next leader, pass the token to it and reveal itself to all others. This way, other peers know that a leader as done its job and that it passed the token to another host. However, also in this case, additional mechanisms should be employed in order to guarantee that eventually all peers become leaders, in order to diminish the probability that cheaters collude and, once gained the token, they pass that token only among themselves, thus preventing honest peers to detect cheaters.

Upon identification of a cheater p_i, the leader could pass the token to another, randomly selected peer (not p_i, of course), informing it of its p_i's suspicion. Then, the novel peer will in turn control p_i. Once a majority of peers suspects p_i, then such peer can be considered as a cheater. This solution enables agreement among honest peers (on cheaters detection). Moreover, such a cooperative approach makes harder for the cheater to detect if some other node is monitoring his behavior. Thus, it results more difficult for the cheater to dynamically switch off its cheat as soon as he detects he is being examined.

Just to provide the reader with an idea of the efficacy of a detection scheme to cope with time cheats in a P2P scenario, we report in Figure 9 the percentage of cheaters identified based on the use of AC/DC. In particular, results were based on a simulation performed to mimic a P2P fully connected gaming architecture built over a best effort, reliable network. Based on the literature [3, 13, 16, 19], transmission latencies were based on a lognormal distribution, whose average network latency was set to 100 msec. We varied the value of the delay jitter between 10 and 100 msec, since this parameter may affect the efficacy of our detection schemes.

Starting with an initial estimation of the average latency to reach the controlled peer, the leader was in charge to assess whether, during the counterattack, the newly measured average delay (from the cheater to the leader) grew significantly. It is clear that this initial estimation plays an important role in AC/DC. Indeed, during the game evolution, measured latencies from the cheater to the leader are affected by the

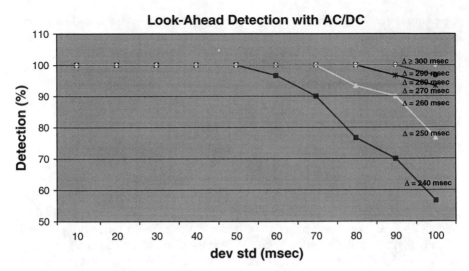

Fig. 9 Look-Ahead Detection Through AC/DC

look-ahead cheat. Thus, if the cheater alters its initialization protocol (where the first estimation of the average latency is measured), the leader may start the counterattack with a delay measure which is higher than the real one [16]. To evaluate the impact of this possible fallacy, we simulated different scenarios with very diverse initial estimations of the average latency from the leader to the peer. Here, we report on the adverse case where the leader starts the counterattack with a false estimation of the average latency, equal to $2\delta_{li}$, i.e. the round trip time from the leader to the cheater. Needless to say, with lower values of the initial estimation, it was easier for our scheme to detect cheaters. The value of λ was initialized to 10 msec and let grow till reaching (if needed) the upper bound Δ. Each curve refers to a different choice of Δ.

For each scenario, 30 different simulations have been run. During each simulation, measurements for different message transmissions were employed to make a statistical test. Among the possible choices on the statistical tests to be employed, due to our interest for measuring average delays and due to the need for viable choices, easily executable on different peers, we decided to employ a classic one-sided t-test ($\alpha = 0.05$). For each test, the number of measurements was set to 40 game events.

As shown in the Figure, while AC/DC detected all cheaters in most of the considered scenarios (all the scenarios when Δ was set greater than 300 msec), some percentage of false negatives (i.e., cheaters not detected) was obtained when high jitters and relatively low upper bounds were set. However, these results suggest that it suffices to augment the upper bound Δ to detect those cheaters.

It is important to notice that no false positives were obtained through AC/DC, even with very high values of the delay jitter (e.g., std.dev. set equal to 100 msec). In other words, no honest peers were erroneously identified as cheaters.

Conclusions and Future Directions

Several malicious mechanisms can be devised to take unfair advantages in multiplayer online games, by exploiting the inadequacies of best-effort networks. We presented here a discussion on time cheats, i.e. those cheats that consist in assigning faked timestamps to game events. Prevention and detection schemes for cheating avoidance have been also outlined, together with some countermeasures to cope with the specific look-ahead time cheat.

The main open question is when it should be wiser to employ a detection, rather than a prevention scheme. Certainly, detection schemes should be taken into consideration when the considered multiplayer game is a fast-paced one, since cases exist when game communication protocols, embodying a cheating prevention scheme, fail to provide that level of responsiveness, which is required to ensure compelling gaming experiences to distributed players.

References

1. Baughman, N.E, Levine, B.N., Cheat-proof Playout for Centralized and Distributed Online Games, in *Proc. of INFOCOM 2001*, Anchorage (USA), IEEE, April 2001, 104-113.
2. Baughman, N. E., Liberatore, M., and Levine, B. N. 2007. Cheat-proof playout for centralized and peer-to-peer gaming. *IEEE/ACM Trans. Netw.* 15, 1 (Feb. 2007), 1-13.
3. Borella, M.S., Source models for network game traffic, *Computer Communications*, 23(4):403-410, February 2000.
4. Cecin, F.R., Real, R., de Oliveira Jannone, R., Resin Geyer, C.F., Martins, M.G., Victoria Barbosa, J.L., FreeMMG: A Scalable and Cheat-Resistant Distribution Model for Internet Games, in *Proc. of International Symposium on Distributed Simulation and Real-Time Applications*, Budapest (Hungary), IEEE, October 2004, 83-90.
5. Chambers, C., Feng, W., Feng, W., and Saha, D. 2005. Mitigating information exposure to cheaters in real-time strategy games. In *Proceedings of the international Workshop on Network and Operating Systems Support For Digital Audio and Video* (Stevenson, Washington, USA, June 13 - 14, 2005). NOSSDAV '05. ACM, New York, NY, 7-12.
6. Cristian, F., Probabilistic clock synchronization, *Distributed Computing*, 3(3):146-158, 1989.
7. Cristian, F., Fetzer, C., The Timed Asynchronous Distributed System Model, *IEEE Transactions on Parallel and Distributed Systems*, 10(6):642-657, 1999.
8. Cronin, E., Filstrup, B., Jamin, S., Kurc, A.R., An efficient synchronization mechanism for mirrored game architectures, *Multimedia Tools and Applications*, 23(1):7-30, May 2004.
9. Cronin, E., Filstrup, B., Jamin, S., Cheat-proofing dead reckoned multiplayer games, in *Proc. of 2nd International Conference on Application and Development of Computer Games*, January 2003.
10. Drummond, R., Babaoglu, O., Low-cost clock synchronization, *Distributed Computing*, 6(3):193-203, 1993.
11. GauthierDickey, C., Zappala, D., Lo, V., and Marr, J. 2004. Low latency and cheat-proof event ordering for peer-to-peer games. In *Proceedings of the 14th international Workshop on Network and Operating Systems Support For Digital Audio and Video* (Cork, Ireland, June 16 - 18, 2004). NOSSDAV '04. ACM, New York, NY, 134-139.
12. Gusella, R., Zatti, S., The accuracy of clock synchronization achieved by tempo in Berkeley Unix 4.3BSD, *IEEE Transactions of Software Engineering*, 15(7):47-53, July 1989.

13. Farber, J., Network game traffic modeling, in Proc. of the 1st Workshop on Network and system support for games, Braunschweig (Germany), ACM, April 2002, 53–57.
14. Ferretti, S., Interactivity Maintenance for Event Synchronization in Massive Multiplayer Online Games, *Ph.D. Thesis, Tech. Rep. UBLCS-2005-05*, University of Bologna (Italy), March 2005.
15. Ferretti, S., A Synchronization Protocol For Supporting Peer-to-Peer Multiplayer Online Games in Overlay Networks, in *Proceedings of the 2nd International Conference on Distributed Event-Based Systems (DEBS'08)*, ACM Press, Rome (Italy), July 2008.
16. Ferretti, S., Cheating Detection Through Game Time Modeling: A Better Way to Avoid Time Cheats in P2P MOGs?, *Multimedia Tools and Applications*, Springer, Volume 37, Number 3, May 2008, 339-363.
17. Ferretti, S., Roccetti, M., AC/DC: an Algorithm for Cheating Detection by Cheating, in *Proceedings of the ACM International Workshop on Network and Operating Systems Support for Digital Audio and Video (NOSSDAV 2006)*, Newport, Rhode Island (USA), ACM Press, May 2006, 136-141.
18. Ferretti, S., Roccetti, M., Game Time Modelling for Cheating Detection in P2P MOGs: a Case Study with a Fast Rate Cheat, in *Proceedings of the 5th ACM SIGCOMM Workshop on Network & System Support for Games 2006 (NETGAMES 2006)*, Singapore, ACM Press, October 2006.
19. Ferretti, S., Roccetti, M., Palazzi, C.E., An Optimistic Obsolescence-Based Approach To Event Synchronization For Massive Multiplayer Online Games, *International Journal of Computers and Applications,* ACTA Press, Vol. 29, No. 1, February 2007, 33-43.
20. Fiedler, U., Bernhard Plattner: Using Latency Quantiles to Engineer QoS Guarantees forWeb Services, in *Proc. of the 11th International Workshop on Quality of Service, (IWQoS 2003)*, LNCS 2707, Springer, Berkeley, CA, USA, June 2003, 345-362.
21. Fujimoto, R., *Parallel and Distribution Simulation Systems*, John Wiley and Sons, Inc., 1999.
22. Gibbon, J.F., Little, T.D.C., The Use of Network Delay Estimation for Multimedia Data Retrieval, *IEEE Journal on Selected Areas in Communications*, IEEE, 14(7):1376-1387.
23. Henderson, T., Bhatti, S., Modeling user behaviour in networked games, in Proc. of the *9th ACM International Conference on Multimedia (ACM Multimedia)*, Ottawa (Canada), October 2001, 212-220.
24. Lee, H., Kozlowski, E., Lenker, S., Jamin, S., Synchronization and Cheat-Proofing Protocol for Real-Time Multiplayer Games, in *Proc. of the International Workshop on Entertainment Computing*, Makuari (Japan), May 2002.
25. Liang, Y.J., Farber, N., Girod, B., Adaptive Playout Scheduling and Loss Concealment for Voice Communication over IP Networks, *IEEE Transactions on Multimedia*, IEEE Signal Processing Society Press, 5(4):532- 543, April 2001.
26. Mauve, M., Vogel, J., Hilt, V., Effelsberg, W., Local-lag and timewarp: Providing consistency for replicated continuous applications, *IEEE Transactions on Multimedia*, 6(1):47-57, February 2004.
27. Mills, D.L., Internet time synchronization: the Network Time Protocol, *IEEE Transactions on Communications*, 39(10):1482-1493, October 1991.
28. Palazzi, C.E., Ferretti, S., Cacciaguerra, S., Roccetti, M., Interactivity-Loss Avoidance in Event Delivery Synchronization for Mirrored Game Architectures, *IEEE Transactions on Multimedia*, IEEE Signal Processing Society, Vol. 8, No. 4, August 2006, 874-879.

Chapter 8
Zoning Issues and Area of Interest Management in Massively Multiplayer Online Games

Dewan Tanvir Ahmed and Shervin Shirmohammadi

Introduction

Game is a way of entertainment, a means for excitement, fun and socialization. Online games have achieved popularity due to increasing broadband adoption among consumers. Relatively cheap bandwidth Internet connections allow large number of players to play together. Since the introduction of Network Virtual Environment (NVE) in 1980s for military simulation, many interesting applications have been evolved over the past few decades. Massively multiplayer online (role-playing) game, MMOG or MMORPG, is a new genre of online games that has emerged with the introduction of Ultima since 1997. It is a kind of online computer game with the participation of hundreds of thousands of players in a virtual world.

Nowadays multiplayer online games are very popular. An MMOG could have millions of subscribers such as *World of Warcraft*, or *Quest*. Interesting is that all subscribers do not play with each other in the same space at the same time. As a consequence, the virtual world is divided into realms or kingdoms which are the clones of the original virtual world, each hosting several thousand registered players. Technically, the realms are geographically distributed across the world. Thus, players from a particular region play together in the same realm. To accommodate millions of subscribers, gaming companies provide many realms across the world as needed. Realms are further divided into separate areas, also known as a zone. Zones can have different themes and different levels of difficulties holding inexperienced players advancing into the next hard level.

MMOGs are similar to generic massively multiuser simulations that have existed for decades, most notably combat training simulations used by *Departments of Defense* (DoD) around the world, and more recently, disaster management applications, emergency planning simulators, etc. These have reached their current state because of their significant impact on virtual training in high-risk situations as well as their

D.T. Ahmed and S. Shirmohammadi (✉)
School of Information Technology and Engineering University of Ottawa, Ottawa, Ontario, Canada
e-mail: dahmed@discover.uottawa.ca

B. Furht (ed.), *Handbook of Multimedia for Digital Entertainment and Arts*, DOI 10.1007/978-0-387-89024-1_8, © Springer Science+Business Media, LLC 2009

ability to interpret the real and the simulated results in extraordinary circumstances such as natural disasters or terrorist attacks.

Commercial MMOGs use the client-server architecture with a single authentic server designed for to support the game logic. The server pool regulates game traffic using the zoning concept and makes its implementation more convenient. Practically, the communication structure within a zone is similar to the Internet multicast structure, not client-server, because of the players' common interest in the game logic. IP multicast, which was originally proposed for group communication, can be an ideal solution for this purpose. But it is a well-known fact that IP Multicast is not deployable on the wide-scale Internet, even in future with IPv6 [1]. Thus, current practices heavily rely on centralized architectures that cause scalability bottlenecks. In addition, the models are costly to adopt and install. Current designs (research oriented), however, try to incorporate client and server side resources in a peer-to-peer fashion to address its different challenges such as scalability, responsiveness, and persistence [2][3].

Challenges and Requirements

The development of an MMOG faces many challenges. A fundamental requirement of any real-time application tool is the exchange of regular update messages among the participants. It is a challenging task while keeping a low data rate without affecting the gaming experience. Scalability is another important concern when designed for large-scale simulators or virtual environments and MMOGs, as it is the function of other gaming components related to the system. However, the amount of data that needs to be exchanged among participants is bounded by server-side resources and other technical conditions such as network bandwidth, processing power and network latencies.

Network Bandwidth - The bandwidth is the amount of data that can be transmitted over a network in a fixed time-slot. It is set by the underlying hardware that connects to the computers. The user's connection to its Internet Service Provider (ISP) and the ISP's hardware and software infrastructures also affect available bandwidth. Practically MMOG players have non-uniform bandwidth. Thus, the amount of data that can be exchanged between two computers is restricted by the bandwidth of the players.

Processing Power - The processing power expresses the computation capability - the amount of computations/instructions executed by a computer in a fixed time-slot. For gaming, higher processing power is required for multiple reasons like physics engine, collision detection, graphic rendering, artificial intelligence, and to send and receive network messages for networked games. But the processing power of all users is not homogenous. Thus, the amount of information that can be exchanged between two computers and the quality of perception also depends on their CPU resources.

Network Latency - Latency is the amount of time a message takes to travel over a network from a source to a destination. The physical limitation of the underlying hardware like routers and switches, and network congestion make it variant from time-to-time. The interaction details of an MMOG player must be sent to all other active participants in time. Because of the networking limitations and the traffic conditions, some of these updates can be lost or delayed. Thus, latency issue cannot be ignored. The updated game states must be forwarded within a time limit so that the responsiveness of game play is maintained. Generally, latency acceptance varies from game-to-game and is restricted to a value between 100ms to 1000ms for online games [4]. The acceptable latency depends on game perspectives (i.e. First-person or Third-person), game genres (i.e. racing or role playing game), and the sensitivity of actions.

MMOG Architecture – An Overview

To accommodate a large number of players, the map is logically divided into multiple zones where each zone encompasses the players that are in the same vicinity. Each zone has a master (e.g. server) that coordinates the interactions of the zone members in a multicast fashion. A set of master nodes regulates the operation of the MMOG and provides overlay services in client-server model. On the other hand, hybrid model incorporates the participation of the players. The system is hybrid as it combines the benefits of both centralized and distributed systems. To overcome the functionality limitations of the IP multicast, application layer multicasting (ALM) can be chosen for intra zonal communication [5].

MMOG Classification

There are many types of massively multiplayer online games. Some popular types are given in the Table 1.

Communication Architecture

The right communication structure is very important for interest management as it regulates message transmission and controls network resource usage. Different packet delivery methods can be used for data communication in multiplayer games. This includes basic unicast communication which is the most popular choice, but broadcast and multicast communications are sometimes also useful.

The proper choice of TCP or UDP protocol for standard unicast communication is important for online games. UDP is a simple best-effort procedure that offers no reliability and no guaranteed packet ordering. On the other hand, it has

Table 1 Types of MMOGs and examples

Types of MMOG	Characteristics	Example
MMORPG	Massively multiplayer online role playing games	EverQuest, Star war galaxies
MMOFPS	Massively multiplayer online first person shooters	World War II Online World: Battleground Europe, 10SIX (known as Project Visitor)
MMORTS	Massively multiplayer online real-time strategy	Ballerium, Time of Defiance, Shattered Galaxy
MMOR	Massively multiplayer online racing games	Darkwind: War on Wheels, Trackmania, Test Drive Unlimited
MMOTG	Massively multiplayer online tycoon games	Starpeace, Industry Player
MMOSG	Massively multiplayer online sports games/social game	Second Life
MMOMG	Massively multiplayer online manager games	Hattrick

little overhead, making it appropriate for highly interactive games (e.g., first-person shooter, car racing) where fast packet delivery is more important. On the other hand, TCP guarantees ordered packet delivery and simplifies programming with additional overhead. Most importantly, TCP can work more transparently across firewalls. Thus, many commercial MMOGs (e.g., *EVE Online, Lineage II, and World of Warcraft*) use TCP for their communication.

Local area networks (LANs) can be restrictively configured to allow broadcast. This can make state dissemination much simpler and efficient. Unfortunately, MMOGs are not able to take the advantages of broadcast in an Internet setting as it is not typically supported across the router boundaries. Another technique is multicast which provides group-based packet delivery. A host can subscribe to one or multiple multicast addresses and receive all messages sent to those addresses. It is usually much more efficient than multiple unicast operations. However, multicasting is not widely available on the global Internet due to technical, business, and practical reasons [1] and is therefore not a practical solution for MMOGs.

There are two general types of MMOG architectures: client-server and peer-to-peer. There are also hybrid architectures that are between these two main paradigms. In client-server architecture, each client has a single connection with the server (Figure 1a). The server is responsible to relay the game states between clients. The main advantage of the client-server architecture is the easy controller which is centralized and autonomous. As a solution for resource limitations multiple servers are deployed. The architecture also facilitates easy implementation of load balancing, fault tolerance, security, and many other concerns. But in client-server architecture, the server is an architectural bottleneck and limits the scalability of the system. Still it is the most popular and practiced approach in the gaming industry.

Commercial NVEs use the client-server architecture which is expensive to deploy and cumbersome to maintain. For example, the virtual world of *Second Life*

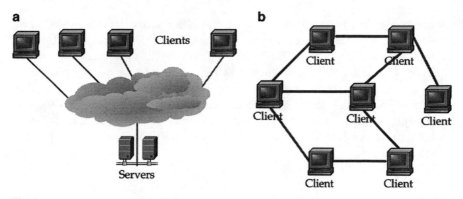

Fig. 1 (**a**) Client-server architecture (**b**) Peer-to-peer architecture

has approximately 5000 servers. Such expensive deployment issue as well as the need for regular maintenance stirs us to an alternative solution. The P2P architecture has a self scalability property, but considering business oriented and practical issues such as quality, cheating, and distributed game logic, it seems that a pure P2P architecture (Figure 1b) is an infeasible and impractical solution. Recently, the hybrid P2P architecture is considered as a good solution both for vendors and end users [6][7]. The P2P community strongly believes that online games over hybrid peer-to-peer architecture have promising prospects considering deployment cost and performance in some sense through reduced latencies.

Virtual Space Decomposition - Zoning

The genre of MMOG is relatively new but popular. The development of MMOGs encompasses many technical challenges. Some of the challenges are

- Ensuring consistency
- Providing fault-tolerance
- Administration of servers and players
- Preventing cheating
- Providing scalability and many others

To achieve these, the concept of *zoning* is typically used. This is what we will describe next.

Zone Definition

For easy state administration, the virtual space is divided into multiple adjacent areas technically called zones. But on what perspective a zone is constructed, is subject to specific implementation. From networking perspective, each LAN can be considered as a zone where several LANs are connected through the Internet forming the whole world. A LAN provides high bandwidth, so it could be easy for the server, i.e. the master, responsible for a zone to construct the overlay network if required, maintain its state, and manage new comers and early leavers. However, this is not a sufficient requirement: other factors such as virtual distance and visibility, and logical partitions need to be taken into consideration when defining a zone. In a nutshell, a zone is a logical partitioning which is usually transparent to the players in the game space.

Multiple Zones and its Space

At its simplest, a zone can be represented by a square or a triangle. Multiple zone definition can be adopted while defining the map of a game space. To accommodate many players, the map is logically divided into multiple zones. Each zone encompasses the players that are in the same vicinity. Henceforth, when a player moves from one zone to another, it gets disconnected from one server and joined to another server. If this multiple-zone layout is considered, more connections and disconnections can be encountered for the same path traversal scenario (Figure 2). Triangular and hexagonal shapes have advantages over other shapes. For example, unlike circles, triangular and hexagonal shapes stick together and maintain regular shapes (Figure 3).

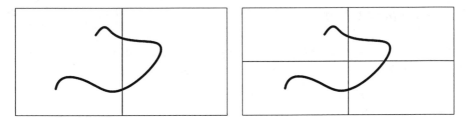

Fig. 2 Two versus multiple zones layout, with a player moving across zones

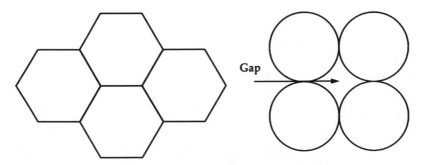

Fig. 3 Hexagonal and circular zone shapes

Area of Interest Management

For online games, *Area of Interest Management* (AoIM) is a technique to reduce communication overhead. AoIM is a method used to determine useful information for a specific player and block all other information. For example, the area of interest of an avatar in an MMOG is the set of avatars and *non-playing components* (NPC) with whom it interacts with in its neighborhood. Since the virtual world is large, filtering out irrelevant information is a fundament requirement for a scalable system.

There are two approaches to model AoIM for MMOGs. The first one is *static geographical partitioning* implemented at the initialization phase of a simulation. This is practical as it describes the structure of a virtual world. For example, a virtual world consists of multiple cities where each city defines a geographical partition: it is the area where most of the interactions take place, and in most cases, the participants are not captivated on what is happening in other cities. *Second Life* has adopted such approach [8]. The virtual world offers uninteresting items around the borders, like cities separated by empty forests or wilderness where players do not want to stay long. Although the static geographic partitioning is good for some cases, it might not be a general solution for all virtual simulators.

The second approach for AoIM is *behavioral modeling*. In military simulations, two different units such as a jeep and an aircraft have different distinctiveness in terms of how fast they can move, how far they can see, and the scope of the interaction space (a jet launching a missile has a larger area of influence than a jeep patrol). Lu et al. argue that, as the mapping of processing resources to the geographic regionalization is straightforward and uncomplicated, the behavioral approach has not been deeply explored [9]. One of the limitations of a geographic regionalization is its unintelligence to prevent inter-server communications. This is because the geographic regionalization does not give enough importance to players' interactions. Even though behavioral modeling is the ideal approach to manage interest of the parties, geographic regionalization is not without merits. Thus, geographic regionalization can be augmented by behavior-based communications for better interest management.

Interest Management Models

An MMOG deals with plenty of information keeping each player's activities and tracking its location. Rationally a player does not need state information of the entire virtual world which is too large. Thus, determining information appropriate to each player is a fundamental requirement of online games. From this perspective, an interest management is a way of determining functional details of a player. So, the performance of a virtual world depends on the cost and effectiveness of an AoIM approach deployed.

Publisher-Subscriber Model

Interest management for an MMOG can be abstracted using a publish-subscribe model. The concept is *publishers create events and subscribers consume events*. In this model, interest management consists of determining when an avatar registers to or gracefully/ungracefully bows out from a publisher's (avatar's) updates. Generally, interest management for online games can have multiple domains. The most common domain is the visibility, although other domains like audible range and radar are also possible. Each interest domain has special properties for the transmission and reception of data, so different sets of publisher-subscribers model might be needed.

Space Model

Interest management can also be categorized into two general groups: space-based and class-based. Space-based interest management can be defined based on the relative position of avatars in a virtual world, while class-based can be determined from an avatar's attributes. Space-based interest management is the most useful for MMOGs because of the relevant information of a player is usually closely related to its position in the environment and is typically based on proximity which can be realized in terms of the aura-nimbus information model given in Figure 4. *Aura* is the area that bounds the existence of an avatar in space, while *nimbus*, i.e. area of interest, is the space in which an object can perceive other objects. In the simplest form, both *aura* and *nimbus* are usually represented by circles around the avatar. This model is more appropriate when a server keeps a connection with each client. The drawback of a pure *aura-nimbus model* is scalability because of the computing cost associated with the determination of intersection between the nimbus and the auras of a large number of players.

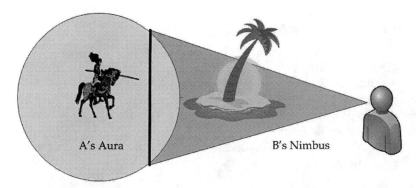

Fig. 4 The aura nimbus model

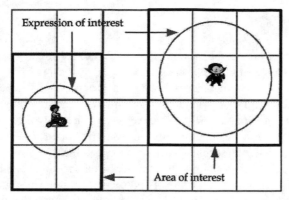

Fig. 5 Region-based area of interest

Region Model

Region-based interest management partitions the game space into several fixed regions. The interest management scheme then determines the regions which intersect with the expression of interest of the players. Thus, an area of interest becomes the union of the intersected regions with respect to the expression of interest as shown in Figure 5. It is an approximation of the true expression-of-interest and generally cheaper to compute but less precise than a pure aura-nimbus model.

Implementation Intelligence

Message Aggregation

Message aggregation is a technique to address MMOG resource limitations [10]. It reduces the overall message update rate by aggregating multiple game messages into a single message. Thus, it rationalizes bandwidth usage by removing redundant message information like the message header. Message aggregation introduces some delay. However updates are piggybacked and could limit game performance if not designed properly.

Message Compression

Simple message compression techniques can be used as a means against strict bandwidth requirement [10]. Although the method is expensive, considering resource constraints it is not without merit.

Dead Reckoning

This method tries to predict the movement of players to help a player take an expert guess in terms of where others players will be in the next short while. Say a player moves from a point P_1 to another point P_2. Each and every discrete step on the path $P_1 P_2$ is required for appropriate rendering as well as for collision detection. If we consider a frame rate of 30 steps per second, which is typical movie quality, each step corresponds to a unique state that needs to be shared among the interested players in every $1/30^{th}$ of a second. Thus, for a large number of moving objects, the total volume of data being shared is high and creates a huge load on network.

Dead reckoning (DR) is a procedure of approximating a player's current position based upon the last known position and velocity, and advancing that position based upon elapsed time. In MMOGs, dead reckoning predicts a remote object's trajectory and locally calculates the next movement to reduce network load.

Interest Management Algorithms

There are several types of interest management algorithms which can be classified into three broad categories: proximity-based, visibility-based, and reachability-based which are explained next.

Proximity Algorithms

Proximity-based interest management algorithms are solely based on the *Euclidean distance* between publishers and subscribers. This type of algorithm ignores the presence of obstacles which could occlude parts of the game space. Algorithms like *Euclidean Distance*, *Square Tiles*, and *Hexagonal Tiles* are some examples of proximity-based interest management. *Euclidean Distance Algorithm* (Figure 6) is purely based on the Euclidean distance among objects while the other two are the approximations that use partitioning concept. In Figure 6, the area of interest is shown with respect to the men at the center of the circle.

Square Tiles Algorithm is a simple region-based interest management where the virtual world is divided into equal-sized squares. Technically, the size of squares is set according to the radius of interest of the players. So, at any location, the subscriber is interested in at most nine tiles: the subscriber's current tile and the eight or less surrounding tiles (Figure 7). Whenever a player performs an action, the action is shared among all players subscribed to the square where the action has taken place.

Like Square Tiles algorithm, *Hexagonal Tiles algorithm* partitions the virtual world into equal-sized hexagons. If a player's radius of interest intersects a tile, the player subscribes to objects in the tiles. So, at any location, the subscriber is

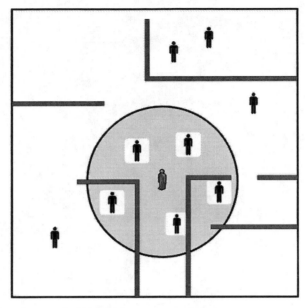

Fig. 6 *Euclidean distance algorithm* for interest management

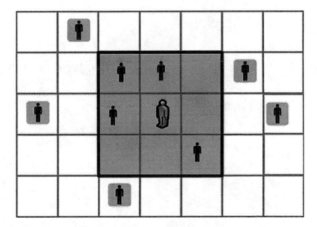

Fig. 7 *Square tile algorithm* for interest management

interested in at most seven tiles: the subscriber's current tile and the six or less surrounding tiles (Figure 8). For each subscriber the algorithm performs a search from its current tile to find all tiles based on the subscriber's radius of interest. The player subscribes to all publishers contained within those tiles. The algorithm could nicely be implemented using a *depth-first search*, and is perhaps the most commonly-used proximity-based algorithm for virtual environments and games.

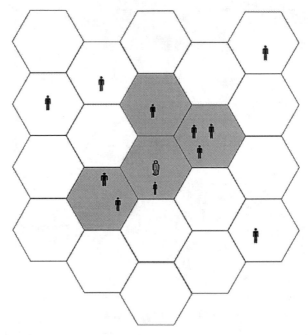

Fig. 8 *Hexagonal tile algorithm* for interest management

Comparison of Euclidean Distance and Hexagonal Tile Algorithms

Euclidean Distance Algorithm

Pros

- Easy to implement
- Computationally inexpensive
- No partitions of the virtual world

Cons

- Less realistic as it does not consider obstacles
- High complexity

Hexagonal Tile Algorithm

Pros

- Easy to implement
- Computationally inexpensive
- A good benchmark

Cons

- Less realistic as it does not consider obstacles
- High complexity

Visibility Algorithms

Visibility-based algorithms consider the occlusion created by obstacles in the virtual world. Theoretically, the area of interest is only limited to the player's visibility scope. In visibility-based algorithms, if a player is out of sight from another player, they are not in the same interest group even if they are physically close. *Ray Visibility* and *Tile Visibility* are two examples of this class. *Ray Visibility* computes the exact visibility between two objects; on the other hand, *Tile Visibility* uses approximation to compute the visibility between static regions.

In *Ray Visibility*, the area of interest is uncovered with respect to the players' visibility scope (Figure 9). To determine an object is visible to a player, it traces a line from the position of the player to the position of the object. If the line does not intersect with any obstacle in the world, they are visible to each other. *Ray Visibility* is a precise interest management algorithm as it accurately determines the area of

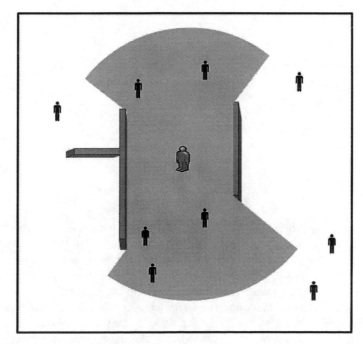

Fig. 9 *Ray visibility algorithm* for interest management

interest of a player. The main advantage is that it provides the lower bound on the number of messages that need to be exchanged between players.

Tile Visibility algorithm is based on the visibility between tiles. The algorithm pre-computes the visibility relationship between each pair of tiles, and the area of interest is projected after the tile visibility for each tile has been pre-computed. A player's area-of-interest is the set of tiles visible from the tile it currently stays.

Comparison of Ray and Tile Visibility Approach

Ray visibility

Pros

- Accurately determines area of interest
- Exchange minimum number of messages between two players
- Efficient approach

Cons

- Harder to implement
- Computationally expensive

Tile visibility

Pros

- Simple as tile visibility relationships are pre-computed
- More realistic than proximity based

Cons

- Dynamic zone shaping is not possible
- Requires supporting algorithms to handle obstacles

Reachability Algorithms

Reachability-based algorithms define area of interest with respect to reachability even though one or more regions are out of sight due to obstacles. It is somewhat similar to proximity-based algorithms, but it discards objects that are unreachable. Unlike visibility-based algorithms, an object that is not visible (e.g., behind an obstacle) may be in the area of interest if there is a path to reach that object within its radius of interest. *Tile Distance* and *Tile Neighbor* algorithms fall into this category.

Tile Distance algorithm uses Euclidean distance between a player and a triangular tile. It runs a *breadth first search* (BFS) algorithm from the current tile to discover the set of connected tiles that intersect the player's radius of interest. Then it discards tiles that are not reachable within the player's area-of-interest.

On the other hand, *Tile Neighbor algorithm* defines area of interest using tile neighbor relationship. The algorithm implements a *breadth-first search* from the current tile of the player and determines all reachable tiles until it reaches a predefined depth. The depth is defined as a number. For example, if depth is one, the set of tiles would be all direct neighbors of the current tile.

Comparison of Tile Distance and Tile Neighbor Algorithms

Tile distance

Pros

- It takes some advantages of both proximity-based and visibility-based approaches
- Smarter than other two approaches

Cons

- Computationally expensive

Tile neighbor

Pros

- Inexpensive compared to Tile Distance approach
- Can be tuned based on applications

Cons

- Less accurate compared to Tile Distance approach

Zone Crossing in P2P MMOGs

A zone crossing occurs when an avatar crosses a zone boundary, i.e. an active node leaves a zone and enters into a neighboring zone. This has an impact on the P2P structure as nodes in the overlay tree are displaced. Synchronous communication depends on how well the protocol handles zone crossings. There are two tasks associated with zone crossing: first, the detection of zone crossing; second, the reconstruction of both departing and entering zone structures. Irrespective of an overlay structure, when a node crosses a zone, all dependent nodes lose the continuity of data as shown in Figure 10. This causes low quality of experience from users' perspective. Most of the cases, it is hard to reduce such zone crossing penalties in a P2P gaming environment.

Fig. 10 Problem of zone
crossing in P2P MMOGs

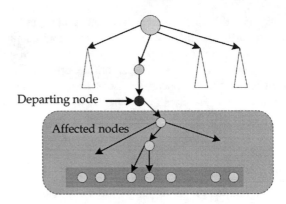

Departing node

Affected nodes

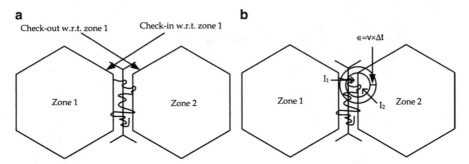

a

Check-out w.r.t. zone 1   Check-in w.r.t. zone 1

Zone 1   Zone 2

b

$\epsilon = v \times \Delta t$

I_1

I_2

Zone 1   Zone 2

Fig. 11 (**a**) Hexagonal regions with check-in and check-out radii with dynamic adjustment of zone marks (**b**) Controlling of frequent zone crossings

As it is difficult to predict players' movements at the boundaries, repeated connections and disconnections may be encountered either among the zone masters (i.e. servers) or among the multiple overlay networks. VELVET's area of interest management can be implemented to avoid the problem of a player's frequent movement around the zone boundary [11]. The interest-driven zone crossing with dynamic shared regions between adjacent zones is a nice solution to regulate such ungraceful events. Here, each zone has two marks namely check-in and check-out (Figure 11a). The area between the two marks is called the buffer region (a.k.a. common area or overlapped area). It can control total number of disconnections and connections between the master and a player by adjusting inner and outer marks. To make it even more effective, an interest vector applicable inside the dynamic shared regions can be used [12]. It would be more realistic if the algorithm relates buffer size with player's velocity, i.e. the overlapped region will be different for different types of players. The interest vector is defined in the weighted form $I_v :< W_1, W_2, ..W_c >$ where W_i represents the weight of the object of type i, c is the number of object types and $\sum W_i = 1$. The logic is as follows: first, if a player is completely inside a zone it is the member of that zone, which is obvious. But if it overlaps two zones and crosses the check-out mark, only then it applies the interest vector. It determines the interest values for both zones. The interest value is determined by the following equation

$$z_j(I) = \sum_{i=1}^{c} w_i \times O_i^j$$

where O_i^j is the number of objects of the type i in *zone I*. These values depend on the number of players that fall inside the circle (i.e. visibility range) of the corresponding regions and weights of interest vector (Figure 11b). So if $I_1 > I_2$, the player is considered to be the member of zone 1, even if it physically lies in zone **2**. For more overlapped zones (at most 3), it follows the same principle. As it is difficult to predict the movement of the player, a safety margin can be considered. Hence it increases radius of the circle by epsilon **(O** which is related to the velocity of the player (*v*) and safety period (*(t)*), i.e (= *v((t* Thus, by controlling the parameters, the protocol changes the circle and hence regulates zone crossings.

Different Interest Management Models – Research Perspectives

Delaunay network is a good solution to NVEs, which organizes players according to their position within the NVE [3]. The maintenance cost of a Delaunay network increases with a large number of players. Thus, players may have considerable volume of traffic to deal with. To address this issue, it proposes a dynamic clustering algorithm where each peer in the network monitors its cost of maintenance and forms a cluster as soon as the volume of traffic exceeds a given threshold. Members of a cluster then expand their coordinates to increase their reciprocal distances. In this way, by decreasing the concentration of players, it tries to achieve a lower maintenance cost.

Scalable multicast-based communication protocol (SCORE) is designed for large-scale virtual environments (LSVE) over the Internet [13]. To handle large number of participants, it supports multiple multicast groups and multiple agents. It dynamically partitions the virtual world into spatial areas and applies planar point processes to determine proper cell size. Thus, it ensures the traffic at the receiver side below a threshold with a given probability.

Knutsson et al. describe P2P support for Massively Multiplayer Games by using *Pastry* and *Scribe*, a P2P overlay and its associated simulated multicast [14]. The virtual world is divided into fixed-size regions. Each region is managed by a coordinator, the root of a multicast tree. Players inside a region subscribe to the address of the root node to receive updates from other players, so neighbors are discovered via the coordinator. Coordinators maintain links with each other, facilitating player transition to other regions. However, this incurs some disadvantages. In Knutsson et al., due to discrete AoI, users cannot see across regions. If players decide to listen to more regions, as suggested, additional messages beyond an AoI must be exchanged. A serious performance penalty can be introduced as the overlay does not consider appropriate area of interest, and messages may need to be relayed by many intermediate nodes.

The model proposed by Hample et al. reuses an architecture capable of exploiting the flexibility and scalability of P2P networks [15]. The main drawback of peer-to-peer networks for games is the lack of a central authority that regulates access and prevents cheating. It introduced a set of controller peers that supervise each other. This kind of redundancy can prevent cheating. The model is based on existing *Pastry*, the extensions of *Scribe*. The key issue is unbounded end-to-end delay that certainly is a problem for synchronization.

Marios et al. present an approach to support Massively Multiplayer Online Role-Playing Games (MMORP) using a centralized distributed architecture [16]. It considers player's locality of interest to reduce bandwidth requirements for both game servers and clients. But it is simply a multiple server based client/server architecture where performance improvement is flat. There is no guarantee for end-to-end delay. Moreover, it completely ignores player's chain effects on node departures in a dynamic P2P environment. The complexity of this approach is also high.

Yamamoto et al. present a load balancing mechanism for crowded sub-space [17]. It proposes a technique to reduce end-to-end event delivery latency through load balancing the tree by replacing one of the intermediate nodes with the backup node incrementally. It gives a technique for efficient and seamless switching of sub-spaces for subscription while a player's view moves in the game space. For each sub-space, a player node called the responsible node is selected. The responsible node forwards events to all players in the same sub space. But it does not mention on what basis such nodes will be chosen. It also ignores nodes' capability of performing such critical task. Here in a sub-space, the events are distributed from one to all nodes. This pattern follows the client-server architecture which has the aforementioned scalability problems.

MOPAR, a peer-to-peer networked game architecture, is a scheme for interest management in NVEs' [18]. It is a combination of both structured and unstructured peer-to-peer system. Here, a master node is chosen in each zone and becomes the parent of all other players in the zone named slaves. Each master node supports all slaves within its zone. Although the architecture is P2P in the sense that the master node is also connected to other master nodes and manages inter-zonal communication, the network architecture within a zone looks like a client-server architecture. So, it has the single point of failure problem that client-server architecture always encounters. One of the main drawbacks of MOPAR is unexploited slaves' bandwidth as salves are only connected to the master node not among themselves.

A. Steed et al. propose a simple but powerful visibility structure called frontier sets [19]. It shows how to construct this set at runtime. For a pair of nodes, a frontier identifies two mutually invisible regions containing nodes. The benefit of frontier sets is to enable scalability of a system. This is possible because, as long as two nodes stay in their respective frontiers, they do not need to send update information to each other. This is an interesting method in theory. However, it would be computationally expensive to implement it in real-time.

To give users a sense of realism in *Collaborative Virtual Environments* (CVE), there is a need for socialization in virtual community. The key issues in CVE research include managing consistency and persistency of distributed information and assuring real-time interactivity. C.T. Fook et al. present *Collaborative Interaction Management* (CIM) and *Task-Oriented Interaction Management* (TIM) methods to resolve extensibility issues in CVE [20]. When multiple interactions occurred at the same time, these approaches can govern and control the message flow. Here *Scene Interaction Manager* (SIM) monitors the network characteristics to prevent network saturation and long network delay.

ATLAS focuses two broad concepts to support users to collaborate in heterogeneous environments. It goes for self-tune-ability rather than for re-configurability where a system automatically configures itself based on current environment. Other concept is the personalized information filtering. Based on human heuristics, application semantics, user preferences and current system status, it filters events to increase the scalability without degrading interactive performance of the users [21]. To support a large number of concurrent participants, Z. Liang proposed a mobile agent-based architecture for *Large-scale Collaborative Virtual Environment* (LCVE) [22]. The software system consists of mobile agents which are responsible for different tasks related to LCVE.

Conclusions and Future Directions

A Distributed Virtual Environment (DVE) is a simulated world that allows people to collaborate in real-time over a network. Possible applications for DVE systems are multiplayer online games, collaborative engineering and military training. In general, a DVE system consists of several servers where each server performs the message relaying task in real-time to let the clients to collaborate.

In MMOG, the area of interest management is a way of determining relevant information related to an avatar in the virtual space. The massively multiuser online game is large and generates plenty of information caused by various events. But, all information is not important to every player. Thus, forwarding relevant information to each player is an effective way to approach message distribution. Dynamic area of interest management for online games is a new direction of research that characterizes the interaction space in real-time and eliminates/reduces inter-AoI communications. To prevent frequent change of AoI, artificial intelligence techniques can be integrated. The commercialization of MMOG over hybrid P2P architecture is another area that needs to be explored and examined.

References

1. A. El-Sayed, V. Roca, and L. Mathy, "A survey of proposals for an alternative group communication service," *IEEE Network Magazine special Issue on Multicasting: An Enabling Technology*, vol. 17, no. 1, pp. 47–54, 2003.
2. S.-Y. Hu, S.-C. Chang, and J.-R. Jiang, "Voronoi state management for peer-to-peer massively multiplayer online games," in *IEEE Consumer Communications and Networking Conference*, 2008, p. 1134–1138.
3. M. Varvello, E. Biersack, and C. Diot, "Dynamic clustering in delaunay-based p2p networked virtual environments," in *ACM SIGCOMM workshop on Network and system support for games*, 2007, pp. 105–110.
4. M. Claypool and K. Claypool, "Latency and player actions in online games," *Entertainment networking SPECIAL ISSUE: Entertainment networking*, pp. 40–45, 2006.
5. M. Hosseini, D. T. Ahmed, S. Shirmohammadi, and N. D. Georganas, "A Survey of Application-Layer Multicast Protocols," *IEEE Communications Surveys & Tutorials*, vol. 9, no. 3, pp. 58–74, 2007.
6. I. Kazem, D. T. Ahmed, and S. Shirmohammadi, "A visibility-driven approach to managing interest in distributed simulations with load balancing," in *IEEE Symposium on Distributed Simulation and Real-Time Applications (DS-RT)*, 2007, pp. 31–38.
7. T. Iimura, H. Hazeyama, and Y. Kadobayashi, "Zoned federation of game servers: a peer-to-peer approach to scalable multi-player online games," in *NetGames '04: Proceedings of 3rd ACM SIGCOMM workshop on Network and system support for games*, 2004, pp. 116–120.
8. B. De Vleeschauwer et al., "Dynamic microcell assignment for massively multiplayer online gaming," in *ACM SIGCOMM workshop on Network and system support for games (NetGames)*, 2005, pp. 1–7.
9. F. Lu, S. Parkin, and G. Morgan, "Load balancing for massively multiplayer online games," in *ACM SIGCOMM workshop on Network and system support for games (NetGames)*, 2006, p. 1.
10. J. Smed, T. Kaukoranta, and H. Hakonen, "Aspects of networking in multiplayer computer games," in *International Conference on Application and Development of Computer Games in the 21st Century*, 2001, pp. 74–81.
11. J. C. d. Oliveira and N. D. Georganas, "VELVET: an adaptive hybrid architecture for very large virtual environments," *Presence: Teleoperators and Virtual Environments*, vol. 12, no. 6, pp. 555–580, 2003.
12. D. T. Ahmed, S. Shirmohammadi, and J. Oliveira, "Improving gaming experience in zonal MMOGs," in *MULTIMEDIA '07: Proceedings of the 15th international conference on Multimedia*, 2007, pp. 581–584.
13. E. Léty, T. Turletti, and F. Baccelli, "SCORE: a scalable communication protocol for large-scale virtual environments," *IEEE/ACM Transactions on Networking (TON)*, vol. 12, no. 2, pp. 247–260, 2004.
14. B. Knutsson, H. Lu, W. Xu, and B. Hopkins, "Peer-to-Peer Support for Massively Multiplayer Games," in *IEEE Conference on Computer Communications (INFOCOM)*, 2004.
15. T. Hampel, T. Bopp, and R. Hinn, "A peer-to-peer architecture for massive multiplayer online games," in *NetGames '06: Proceedings of 5th ACM SIGCOMM workshop on Network and system support for games*, 2006, p. 48.
16. M. Assiotis and V. Tzanov, "A distributed architecture for MMORPG," in *ACM SIGCOMM workshop on Network and system support for games (NetGames)*, 2006, p. 4.
17. S. Yamamoto, Y. Murata, K. Yasumoto, and M. Ito, "A distributed event delivery method with load balancing for MMORPG," in *NetGames '05: Proceedings of 4th ACM SIGCOMM workshop on Network and system support for games*, 2005, pp. 1–8.
18. A. P. Yu and S. T. Vuong, "MOPAR: a mobile peer-to-peer overlay architecture for interest management of massively multiplayer online games," in *international workshop on Network and operating systems support for digital audio and video (NOSSDAV))*, 2005, pp. 99–104.
19. A. Steed and C. Angus, "Supporting Scalable Peer to Peer Virtual Environments Using Fron-

tier Sets," in *VR '05: Proceedings of the 2005 IEEE Conference 2005 on Virtual Reality*, 2005, pp. 27–34.

20. C. T. Fook, L. Qingping, and Z. Liang, "A Novel Approach for Addressing Extensibility Issue in Collaborative Virtual Environment," in *CW '03: Proceedings of the 2003 International Conference on Cyberworlds*, 2003, p. 78.

21. D. Lee, M. Lim, S. Han, and K. Lee, "ATLAS: A Scalable Network Framework for Distributed Virtual Environments," *Presence: Teleoperators and Virtual Environments*, vol. 16, no. 2, pp. 125–156, 2007.

22. Z. Liang, L. Qingping, and C. T. Fook, "Mobile Agent-Based Architecture for Large-Scale CVE," in *CW '03: Proceedings of the 2003 International Conference on Cyberworlds*, 2003, p. 69.

Chapter 9
Cross-Modal Approach for Karaoke Artifacts Correction

Wei-Qi Yan and Mohan S. Kankanhalli

Introduction

A multimedia environment $\Pi(t)$ usually consists of a multiplicity of correlated data streams $\Pi_i(t)$ with $(n \geq 2)$:

$$\Pi(t) = \{\Pi_i(t), i = 0, 1, 2, \cdots, n; t \in (0, +\infty)\} \qquad (1)$$

The correlations R among them can be expressed as:

$$R = \{\sim: \Pi_p(t) \sim \Pi_q(t), 0 \leq p, q \leq n\} \qquad (2)$$

Karaoke ("missing orchestra" in Japanese) is an example of such a multimedia environment. This Japanese entertainment form features a live singer with pre-recorded accompaniment. The user sings into a microphone while the stored music is played simultaneously. Karaoke is tremendously popular in eastern Asia as an avenue for recreation and entertainment. Some of the distinctive characteristics of karaoke are:

- It encourages artistry in which users try to emulate the original singer in terms of timbre and expression;
- The dynamic highlighting of the song caption along with the music provides synchronization cues to the user;
- Its appeal lies in the immediate feedback of the experience to the user;
- It is a vicarious means of experiencing concert singing;
- Users usually have a portfolio of songs to sing and they tend to improve the quality of rendition with practice.

W.-Q. Yan
Department of Computer Science, Queen's University of Belfast, Belfast, UK
e-mail: w.yan@qub.ac.uk

M.S. Kankanhalli (✉)
Department of Computer Science, National University of Singapore, Singapore
e-mail: mohan@comp.nus.edu.sg

B. Furht (ed.), *Handbook of Multimedia for Digital Entertainment and Arts*,
DOI 10.1007/978-0-387-89024-1_9, © Springer Science+Business Media, LLC 2009

The karaoke system is usually based on a CD player. The CD multimedia data includes one video stream and one audio stream which is the musical accompaniment. The system has two audio channels by which the live singing and the accompaniment channels are mixed and played through the speakers. The original rendering of the singing is usually available on the CD.

Given that most users are not professionally trained singers, their rendition often includes some artifacts related to pitch, tempo and tune. There are several reasons for the cause of artifacts [17]:

- Amateurs sometimes cannot sing a song in the proper key and they jump from one scale to another freely. In high key singing, exhaustion often leads to artifacts.
- Some karaoke users are not able to maintain a regular beat, which can vary from being very fast to being too slow.
- The timbre of the singing may be very different from that of the original singer. This is because a singer needs to be trained so as to properly exercise the vocal cords in order to produce a rich timbre. Moreover, accents can also affect the quality of the rendition.
- There can be noise artifacts due to sensitive pickups and feedback. A huffing sound is produced by a sensitive microphone which amplifies the breathing sounds. A piercing screech can sometimes be heard due to amplifier feedback especially when the speakers are close to the microphone.

Such artifacts, which are annoying to the karaoke users and watchers, occur frequently as shown in Fig. 1 and Fig. 2. Our goal of karaoke artifacts handling is to remove or mitigate the effects of the artifacts in the karaoke audio. The key idea is to use the original singer's rendition as a guide to correct the artifacts. Actually, even after the correction, the singing will not sound like that of the professional singer. The main reason is that we are basically doing timing correction. The actual sound quality is determined by the timbre, voice quality, training, emotion, mood etc which is not affected by our processing. Thus, this leaves enough leeway for individuality and creativity in the improvised rendition. Given that there is correlation and redundancy among audio and video streams, we exploit the cross-modal information in order to perform artifact removal. We will thus judiciously employ all of the available information in order to perform the correction.

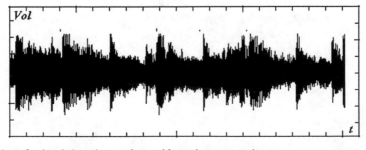

Fig. 1 A professional singer's waveform with music accompaniment

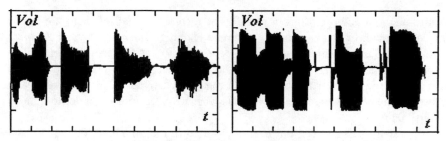

Fig. 2 Two amateur singers' waveforms without music accompaniment

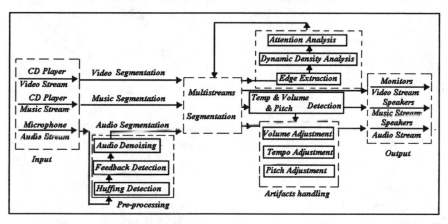

Fig. 3 Flowchart for the cross-modal karaoke correction

In this chapter, we combine adaptive sampling in conjunction with video analogies (VA) to correct the audio stream in the karaoke environment $\kappa = \{\kappa(t): \kappa(t) = (U(t), K(t)), t \in (t_s, t_e)\}$ where t_s and t_e are start time and end time respectively, $U(t)$ is the user multimedia data. We employ multiple streams from the karaoke data $K(t) = (K_V(t), K_M(t), K_S(t))$, where $K_V(t)$, $K_M(t)$ and $K_S(t)$ are the video, musical accompaniment and original singer's rendition respectively along with the user multimedia data $U(t) = (U_A(t), U_V(t))$ where $U_V(t)$ is the user video captured with a camera and $U_A(t)$ is the user's rendition of the song. We analyze the audio and video streaming features $\Psi(\kappa) = \{\Psi(U(t), K(t))\} = \{\Psi(U(t)), \Psi(K(t))\} = \{\Psi_U(t), \Psi_K(t)\}$, to produce the corrected singing, namely output $U'(t)$, which is made as close as possible to the original singer's rendition. Note that Ψ represents any kind of feature processing.

Figure 3 summarizes the research problem tackled in this chapter. In a Karaoke system, the input is video stream $K_V(t)$, music stream $K_M(t)$ and user audio stream $U_A(t)$. After multiple stream segmentation, the tune, tempo and loudness of audio stream are adjusted aligning to the audiovisual information extracted from the original performance. The corrected audio stream is mixed with the music stream together as the output.

Although an audio clip has a plurality of features, not all of them are useful for our purpose. In this chapter, we use three features - *pitch*, *tempo* and *loudness* for removing artifacts in order to produce a rendition as close to the original as possible. We have selected pitch, tempo and loudness as features since they are the primary determinants of the quality of a rendition. Moreover, they are relatively easy to compute and manipulate (which is what we need to do in order to remove the artifacts).

This research is a part of our overall program in multimedia (video, audio and photographs) artifacts handling. We detect and correct those artifacts generated by limitations of either handling skills or consumer-quality equipment. The basic idea is to perform multimedia analysis in order to attenuate the effect of annoying artifacts by feature alteration [13].

Related Work

Given the popularity of karaoke, there has been a lot of work concerning pitch correction, key scoring, gender-shifting, spatial effects, harmony, duet and tempo & key control [5][6][7][8]. What is noteworthy is that most of these techniques work in the analog domain and are thus not applicable in the digital domain.

Interestingly, most of the work has been published as patents. Also, they all attempt to adjust the karaoke output since most karaoke users are amateur singers. The patent [7] detects the actual gender of the live singing voice so as to control the voice changer to select either of the male-to-female and female-to-male conversions if the actual gender differs from the given gender so that the pitch of the live singing voice is shifted to match the given gender of the karaoke song. In the patent [5], a plurality of singing voices are converted into those of the original singers voice signals. In patent [8], the pitches of the user sound input and the music are extracted and compared in order to change it.

Textual lyrics [12] have been automatically synchronized with acoustic musical signals. The audio processing technique uses a combination of top-down and bottom-up approaches, combining the strength of low-level audio features and high-level musical knowledge to determine the hierarchical rhythm structure, singing voice and chorus sections in the musical audio. Actually, this can be considered to be an elementary karaoke system with sentence level synchronization. Our work is distinct from the past work in two ways. First, it works entirely on digital data. Second, we use correlated multimedia streams of both audio and video to effect the correction of artifacts. We believe that this approach of using multiple data streams for artifact removal has wide applications. For example, real-time online music tutoring is one application of these techniques. It can be also used for active video editing as well.

Background

Adaptive Sampling

Given the voluminous nature of continuous multimedia data, it is worth using sampling techniques to filter each media stream $\Pi_i(t) = \{\pi_{ij}, j = 0, 1, 2, \cdots, m\}$, in order to produce relevant samples or frames π_{ij}. We use a simplified version of the experiential sampling technique for doing adaptive sampling [4]. It utilizes $N_S(t)$ number of sensor samples $S(t)$ to deduce $N_A(t)$ number of attention samples $A(t)$ which are the relevant data. The advantage is that we can then focus only on the relevant parts of the stream: $\Pi_i(t) = \{\pi_{ij}, j = 0, 1, 2, \cdots, m\}$ and ignore the rest. i.e.

$$T\left(N_S(t)_{ij}, N_A(t)_{ij}\right) \geq T_{es} \qquad (3)$$

$T(\cdot)$ is the decision function defined by norm L_2 on the domain, such as temporal, spatial or frequency domain, and T_{es} is the sampling threshold. The final samples are obtained by re-sampling: $\Pi_i'(t) = \left\{\pi_{ij}', j = 0, 1, 2, \cdots, m'; m \geq m'\right\}$ which is precisely the relevant data. Adaptive sampling is primarily for the purpose of efficiency given the real-time requirement of the processing. Here is the concise definition of adaptive sampling:

If $\forall t \in [t_s, t_e]$, inquation (3) is true, t_s and t_e are the start time and the end time respectively, then the set $\Pi_i'(t) = \left\{\pi_{ij}', N_A(t)_{ij} > 0; j = 0, 1, 2, \cdots, m'; m \geq m'\right\}$ is the adaptively sampled stream of a multimedia stream $\Pi_i(t) = \{\pi_{ij}, j = 0, 1, 2, \cdots, m\}$; and $\Pi'(t) = \{\Pi_i'(t), i = 0, 1, 2, \cdots, n\}$ is the adaptively sampled multimedia environment $\Pi(t)$.

The adaptive sampling approach (algorithm 1) basically provides a solution for the detection of the dynamically changing data.

Video Analogies

In automatic multimedia editing, we would like to process and transform the existing data into a better form. Video analogies [14] use a two-step operation involving learning and transfer of features: $\Psi(t) = \Psi(\Pi(t)) = \{\Psi(\Pi_i(t)), i = 0, 1, 2, \cdots, n)\} = \{\Psi_i(t), i = 0, 1, 2, \cdots, n\}$. It learns the *ideal* from an exemplar and then *transform* the given data and emulates the exemplar as closely as possible. In order to set up the analogy, the given data and the exemplar data should have at least one common feature that is comparable.

Analogy is a concept borrowed from reasoning. The main idea of an analogy is a metaphor, namely "doing the same thing". For an example, if a real bicycle Fig. 4(a) (from wikipedia) can be drawn as the traffic sign as shown in Fig. 4(b), can we similarly render a real bus Fig. 4(c) (from wikipedia) as the traffic sign as Fig. 4(d)?

Input : Multimedia stream $\Pi_i(t)$
Output : Multimedia samples $\Pi'_{i,m'}$

Procedure:
Initialization: $t = 0$;
$N_s(t) = N_s(0)$;
$N_A(t) = N_A(0) = 0$;
$m' = 0$;
while $t \leq t_e - 1$ do

> for $i = 0, \ldots, n$ do

>> $S_i(t) \leftarrow \Pi_i(t)$; // randomly sample one stream;
>> $\omega_i(t) = \|\Pi_i(t) - \Pi_i(t-1)\| S_i$; // Estimate samples;
>> $\delta(t) = rand(t) > 0$;// Change the attention numbers, $rand(t)$ is a
>> random number;
>> if $\omega_i(t) > T_{es}$ then

>>> $N_{A_i}(t) \leftarrow N_{A_i}(t) + \delta(t)$;

>> else

>>> $N_{A_i}(t) \leftarrow N_{A_i}(t) + \delta(t)$;

>> end
>> if $N_{A_i}(t) > 0$ then

>>> $A_i(t) \leftarrow (A_i(t-1), S_i(t))$; $\Pi'_{i,m'} \leftarrow \Pi_i(t)$;// perform resampling;
>>> $m'++$;//Consider another media stream;

>> else

>>> $N_{A_i}(t) = 0$;

>> end
>> GetTime (t); //Get current time for next iteration;

> end

end

Algorithm 1: Adaptive sampling

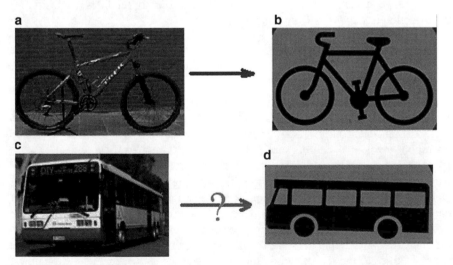

Fig. 4 An example of analogies

Similarly, in video analogies, if we have some desired feature in a source video, we can try to analogously transfer it to the target video.

Definition 1. (Media comparability) If $\bar{\Psi}_p(t) = \bar{\Psi}_q(t)$, $\forall \psi_{pr}(t) \in \Psi_p(t)$, $\exists \psi_{qs}(t) \in \Psi_q(t)$, $d(\psi_{pr}(t), \psi_{qs}(t)) = |\psi_{pr}(t), \psi_{qs}(t)| < \varepsilon$, $\varepsilon > 0, r, s = 0, 1, 2, \cdots m$; then $\Psi_p(t) \subset \Psi(t)$ is *comparable* to $\Psi_q(t) \subset \Psi(t)$, $p, q = 0, 1, 2, \cdots n$; $t \in (-\infty, +\infty)$ denoted as $\Psi_p(t) \approx \Psi_q(t)$ where $\bar{\Psi}_p(t)$ and $\bar{\Psi}_q(t)$ are the rank of the sets. $R_{pq} = \{\approx |\Psi_p(t) \approx \Psi_q(t), \Psi_p \subset \Psi, \Psi_q \subset \Psi, \bar{\Psi}_p(t) = \bar{\Psi}_q(t)\}$.

The underlying idea of video analogies (VA) is that given a source video Π_p and its feature Ψ_p, a target video Π_q and its feature Ψ_q, we seek feature correspondence between the two videos. This learned correspondence is then applied to generate a new video $\Pi'_q(t) = \left\{\pi'_{q,j}, j = 0, 1, \cdots, m\right\}$. Our overall framework is succinctly captured by algorithm 2.

Video analogies have the propagation feature. If the analogy is denoted by Ψ_p^k : $\Psi_q^k :: \Psi_p^j : \Psi_q^j$, then $\Psi_1^k : \Psi_2^k : \cdots : \Psi_m^k :: \Psi_1^j : \Psi_2^j : \cdots : \Psi_m^j$ is true, '::' is the separator, ':' is the comparison symbol. In this chapter, we propagate the video analogies onto the audio channel and use it to automatically correct the karaoke user's singing.

Input :Source video Π_p, target video Π_q
Output :The new target video Π'_q

Procedure:
$\Psi_p \leftarrow \Psi(\Pi_p)$;//extract features;
$\Psi_q \leftarrow \Psi(\Pi_q)$;
$\forall c = 0, 1 \cdots, \Psi_p^=; \Psi_p^= = \Psi_q^=$;
for $s = 0, 1, \cdots, m$ do

   for $k = 0, 1, \cdots, m$ do

      if $d\left(\psi_{p,s}^c, \psi_{q,k}^c\right) \leq d\left(\psi_{p,s}^c, \psi_{q,t}^c\right)$ then

        $\psi_{p,s}^c \approx \psi_{q,k}^c$;//select the comparable feature;

      end

   end

end
$\Psi_p \approx \Psi_q \Leftarrow \psi_{p,s}^c \approx \psi_{q,k}^c$, $\forall s = 0, 1, \cdots, m$;//propagate the feature similarity;
$\Pi_p \sim \Pi_q \Leftarrow \Psi_p \approx \Psi_q$;// comparison;

$f \in \Re_{p,q}; g \in \Re_{p,q}$;//establish mapping functions;
$f : \Psi_p \rightarrow \Psi_q$;
$g : \Psi_q \rightarrow \Psi'_p$;
$\Psi'_q = (g \circ f)(\Psi_p)$;
Ψ'_q and $\Pi_q \Rightarrow \Pi'_q$;//modify date to construct a new video;

Algorithm 2: Video analogies

Our work

Adaptive Sound Adjustment

In this chapter, our main idea is to emulate the performance of the professional singer in a karaoke audio. We simulate them from three key aspects: loudness, tempo and pitch. Although a perfect rendition is dependent upon many factors, these three features play a crucial role in a performance of karaoke song. Thus, we focus our artifact removal efforts on them.

Preprocessing: noise detection and removal. Before we do adaptive audio adjustment for the loudness, tempo and pitch, we consider noise removal first. In a real karaoke environment, if the microphone is near the speakers, a feedback noise is often generated. Also, due to the extreme proximity of the microphone to the singer's mouth, a huffing sound is often generated.

For these two kinds of noise, we find that they have distinctive features after detecting the zero-crossing rate Eq. (4):

$$Z_0 = \frac{1}{2L} \left\{ \sum_{l=1}^{L-1} |sign [u_A (l)] - sign [u_A (l + 1)]| \right\} \cdot 100\% \qquad (4)$$

where L is the window size for the processing and $sign (n)$ is the sign function, $u_A(l)$ is the signal in a window, i.e.:

$$Sign(x) = \begin{cases} 1 & x \geq 0 \\ -1 & x < 0 \end{cases}$$

Normally, zero-crossing rate is the number of X-axis crossings for a signal and is employed to distinguish the vowels and the consonants. It is also used in audio and speech segmentation [2][3]. The zero-crossing rate of the two types of noise are shown in the following graphs (Fig. 5 and Fig. 6).

From the figure, we clearly see the zero-crossing rate of the feedback noise is a straight line since the piercing screeching sound is usually much higher-pitched than human voice. For the detection and removal of the huffing noise, we normally use the short term feature value (STFV). This value is the average in the current window Eq. (5):

$$STFV = \frac{1}{t_s^w - t_e^w} \int_{t_s^w}^{t_e^w} |u_A (t) dt| \qquad (5)$$

where $u_A(t)$ is the audio signal in a window, $L = t_e^w - t_s^w$ is the windowing size. Because the huffing noise always has a high loudness, the average is high. The graphs for huffing and feedback noise are shown in Fig. 7 and Fig. 8.

From Fig. 7, we see that the STFV has a high amplitude and it reflects the features of the huffing noise. What is interesting is that the short time feature value of the

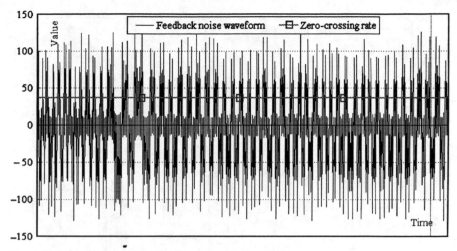

Fig. 5 Zero-crossing rate of feedback noise and its waveform

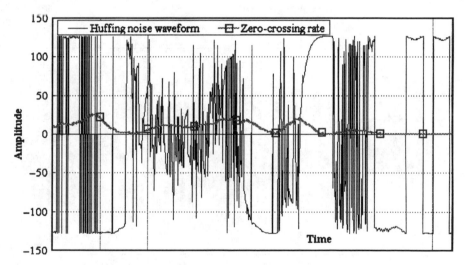

Fig. 6 Zero-crossing rate of huffing noise and its waveform

feedback noise is also a horizontal straight line in Fig. 8. This suggests that the feedback noise is symmetric in an arbitrary window. Using this feature, we replace the signals by silence, because most of time, people will stop singing at this moment.

Tempo handling. We regard the karaoke video music K_M as our baseline for the new rendition. All the features of the new rendition should be aligned to this baseline. The reason is that music generated by instruments is usually more accurate in beat rate, scale and key than human singing. Thus we adaptively sample the

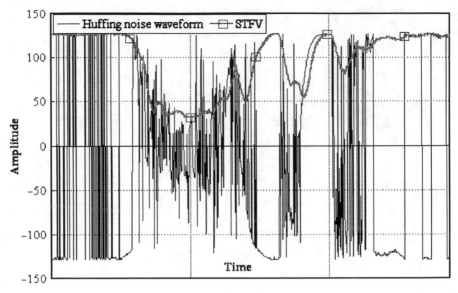

Fig. 7 The huffing noise waveform and its STFV

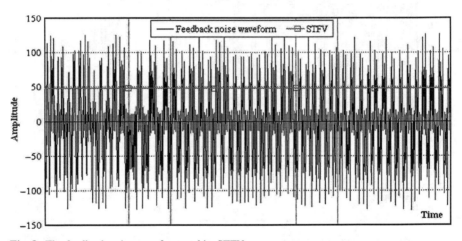

Fig. 8 The feedback noise waveform and its STFV

accompaniment K_M and user audio input U_A first and they are synchronized as shown in Fig. 9.

Then K_M and U_A are segmented again by the tempo or beat rate. The peak of the loudness will appear at constant intervals for a beat. The beat rate is fundamentally characterized by the peaks appearing at regular intervals. For $U_A = \{u_{aj} > 0; \ j = 0, 1, 2, \ldots, m\}$, the start time $t_s^{U_A}$ and the end time $t_e^{U_A}$ are determined by the ends of the duration between two peaks. The peaks are defined by the two conditions shown in Fig. 10:

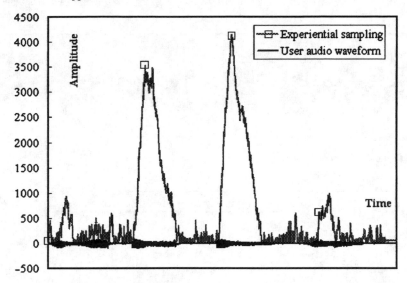

Fig. 9 User audio input and its adaptive sampling

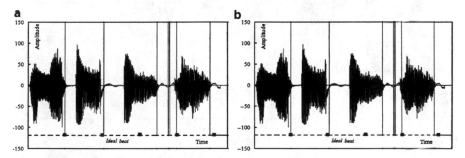

Fig. 10 Windowing based audio segmentation for different people

1. $u_{aj} = \frac{1}{L} \sum_{l=j-L}^{j} u_{al}, L > 0$ is the windowing size.
2. $j \bmod L_b^{U_A} < \delta, L_b^{U_A}/3 > \delta, L_b^{U_A} = t_e^{U_A} - t_s^{U_A}$ is the beat length.

Correspondingly, for $K_M = \{k_{M_j}, j = 0, 1, \cdots, m\}$, the segmented beats are in the interval $\left[t_s^{K_M}, t_e^{K_M}\right]$ shown in Fig. 11. We can see there that the beat rate is fairly uniform.

For audio segmentation, the zero-crossing rate Eq.(4) is a powerful tool in the temporal domain. This can be seen from Fig. 12. The advantage of zero-crossing computation is that it is computationally efficient. We compare the zero-crossing rate of the two singers' audio signals in Fig. 10.

After audio segmentation, the next step is to implement the karaoke audio correction based on analogies. Suppose the exemplar audio after segmentation is: $U_A^S(t) = \{u_A^S(i), i = 0, 1, \cdots, m\}$ and the user's audio after segmentation is $U_A^T(t) = \{u_A^T(i), i = 0, 1, \cdots, m\}$, thus our task is to obtain the following

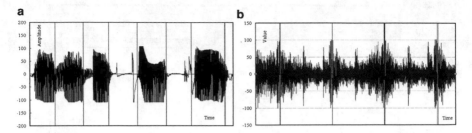

Fig. 11 Windowing based music segmentation

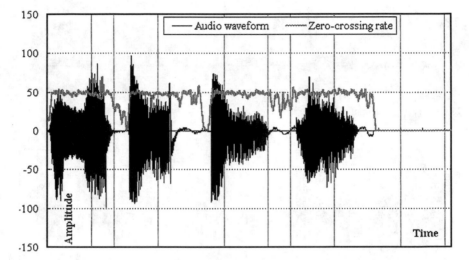

Fig. 12 Zero-crossing rate based audio segmentation

relationship: $U_A^T(0) : U_A^T(1) : \cdots : U_A^T(m) :: U_A^S(0) : U_A^S(1) : \cdots : U_A^S(m)$. For this, we build a mapping in the temporal domain. Subsequently, the centroid point t_τ^{UA} should satisfy:

$$\int_{t_s^{UA}}^{t_\tau^{UA}} |u_a(t)| \, dt = \int_{t_\tau^{UA}}^{t_e^{UA}} |u_a(t)| \, dt \tag{6}$$

where $U_A(t) = \left\{ u_a(t), t \in \left[t_s^{UA}, t_e^{UA} \right] \right\}$. The centroid point t_τ^{KM} should satisfy:

$$\int_{t_s^{KM}}^{t_\tau^{KM}} |k_m(t)| \, dt = \int_{t_\tau^{KM}}^{t_e^{KM}} |k_m(t)| \, dt \tag{7}$$

$K_M(t) = \left\{ k_m(t), t \in \left[t_s^{KM}, t_e^{KM} \right] \right\}$. The corrected audio is then assumed to be:

$$U_A'(t) = \left\{ u_a'(t), t \in \left[t_s^{KM}, t_e^{KM} \right] \right\} \tag{8}$$

We then cut the lagging and leading parts of the user audio input by:

$$\delta^- = \min\left(|t_\tau^{UA} - t_s^{UA}|, |t_\tau^{KM} - t_s^{KM}|\right) \geq 0 \tag{9}$$

$$\delta^+ = \min\left(|t_e^{UA} - t_\tau^{UA}|, |t_e^{KM} - t_\tau^{KM}|\right) \geq 0 \tag{10}$$

We align with the audio stream by using the following shift operation:

$$u_a'(tt) = u_a(t), tt = t_s^{KM} + \left[t - \left(t_\tau^{UA} - \delta^-\right)\right] \tag{11}$$

Where $tt \in \left[t_s^{KM}, t_s^{KM} + \delta^- + \delta^+\right], t \in \left[t_\tau^{UA} - \delta^-, t_\tau^{UA} + \delta^+\right]$.

$$u_a'(tt) = 0, tt \in \left(t_s^{KM} + \delta^- + \delta^+, t_e^{KM}\right) \tag{12}$$

The advantage of such cutting and shifting operations is that the most important audio information is retained and portions such as silences are cut. The basic idea is to automatically cut the redundant parts of the stream by using δ^+ and δ^-.

Tune handling. Tune, as the basic melody of a piece of audio, is closely related to the amplitude of the waveform. Amateur singers easily generate a high key at the initial phase but the performance falters later due to exhaustion. To correct such artifacts in karaoke singing, we should adjust the tune gain by following the professional music and singer's audio.

From the last section, we know the $K_M(t) = \left\{k_m(t), t \in \left[t_s^{KM}, t_e^{KM}\right]\right\}$ and $U_A'(t) = \left\{u_a'(t), t \in \left[t_s^{KM}, t_e^{KM}\right]\right\}$. In order to reduce the tune artifact mentioned above, the average tune is calculated by:

$$A_{avr}^{KM} = \frac{\int_{t_s^{KM}}^{t_e^{KM}} k_m(t)\, dt}{t_e^{KM} - t_s^{KM}} \tag{13}$$

$$A_{avr}^{U_A'} = \frac{\int_{t_s^{KM}}^{t_e^{KM}} u_a'(t)\, dt}{t_e^{KM} - t_s^{KM}} \tag{14}$$

Thus, a multiplicative factor is given by:

$$\sigma = \frac{A_{avr}^{KM} - A_{avr}^{U_A'}}{2^{(Channels \cdot 8)}} \tag{15}$$

where *channels* is the number of interleaved channels. Equation (15) is used to attenuate the high tune and amplify the low ones by using Eq. (16) for the compensation purpose:

$$u_a^*(t) = u_a'(t) * (1.0 - \sigma) + \Delta A \tag{16}$$

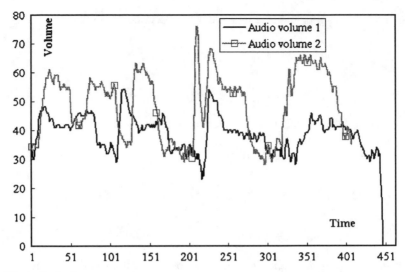

Fig. 13 Audio loudness comparison

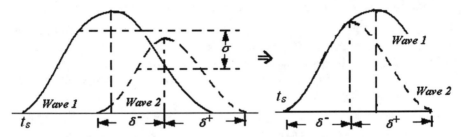

Fig. 14 Core idea for audio analogies based on beat and loudness correction

where $\Delta A = A_{avr}^{K_M} - A_{avr}^{U'_A}$. We show the comparison of loudness for two pieces of audio (Fig. 13), which basically shows tune difference of two different people for the same song rendition. Our core idea for audio analogies based on beat and loudness correction algorithm is illustrated in Fig. 14. In this figure, the music waveform and the audio waveform in a beat are represented by the solid line (wave 1) and the dashed line (wave 2) respectively. We find the minimum effective interval for this beat $\left[t_\tau^{U_A} - \delta^-, t_\tau^{U_A} + \delta^+ \right]$ so that the cropped audio can be aligned to the music track along the start point t_s. Simultaneously, the tune is amplified according to the equation (16).

Pitch handling. Pitch corresponds to the fundamental frequency in the harmonics of the sound. It is normally calculated by auto-correlation of the signal and Fourier transformation, but the auto-correlation is closely related to the windowing size. Thus, a more efficient way is to use the cepstral pitch extraction [2] [3]. In this chapter, cepstrum is used to improve the audio timbre and pitch detection. Figure 15 illustrates music pitch processing. We see that the pitch using auto-correlation is not obvious while the pitch is prominent in the detection relying on

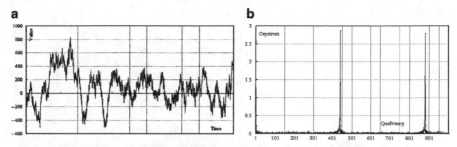

Fig. 15 Pitch detection using auto-correlation and cepstrum

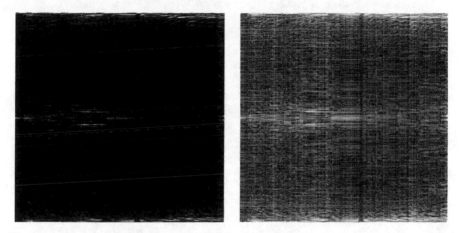

Fig. 16 Left: wave spectrogram; Right: its log spectrogram

cepstrum. The cepstrum is defined as the inverse discrete Fourier transform of the log of the magnitude of the discrete Fourier transform (DFT) of the input signal $U_A^*(x), x = 0, 1, \cdots, N - 1$. The DFT is defined as:

$$Y(\mu) = DFT\left(U_A^*(x)\right) = \sum_{x=0}^{N-1} U_A^*(x) e^{-j\frac{2\pi\mu x}{N}} \tag{17}$$

$Y(\mu)$ is a complex number, $\mu = 0, 1, \cdots, N - 1$. The inverse Fourier transform (IDFT) is:

$$U_A^{DFT}(x) = IDFT\left(Y(\mu)\right) = \frac{1}{N} \sum_{\mu=0}^{N-1} Y(\mu) e^{j\frac{2\pi\mu x}{N}} \tag{18}$$

$x = 0, 1, \cdots, N - 1$. The cepstrum $P(t)$ is:

$$P(t) = IDFT\left(\log_{10}\left(\left|DFT\left(U_A^*(x)\right)\right|\right)\right) \tag{19}$$

where t is defined as the quefrency of the cepstrum signal. Figure 16 shows the spectrogram of a wave and its log spectrogram.

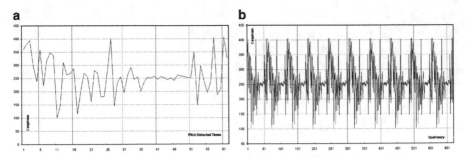

Fig. 17 Pitch varies in a clip but is stable in each window

Normally, females and children have a high pitch while adult males have a low pitch. Pitch tracking is performed by median smoothing: Given windowing size $L > 0$, if

$$\frac{1}{L} \int_{-\frac{L}{2}+t_0}^{\frac{L}{2}+t_0} P(t)dt < P(t_0) \tag{20}$$

then t_0 is the pitch point. However the pitch is not stable throughout the duration of an audio clip. Pitch variations are normal as they reflect the melodic contour of the singing. Therefore we take the average pitch into account and compute the pitch over several windows as shown in Fig. 17(b).

Now we synthesize a new audio $U_A^*(t)$ by utilizing the pitch $P_{U_A^S}(t)$ of

$$U_A^S(t) = \left\{ u_a^S(t), t \in \left[t_s^{U_A^S}, t_e^{U_A^S} \right] \right\} \quad \text{and the pitch} \quad P_{U_A^T}(t) \text{ of } U_A^T(t) =$$

$$\left\{ u_a^T(t), t \in \left[t_s^{U_A^T}, t_e^{U_A^T} \right] \right\}.$$

The pitch is modified by Eq.(21) [2]:

$$U_A^*(x) = IDFT\left(Y\left(\mu - P_0^S + P_0^T \right) \right) \tag{21}$$

where $|Y(\mu)|$ is the amplitude of the μ-th harmonic, P_0^S and P_0^T are the pitch estimation at t_0^s, namely, $P_0^S = P_{U_A^T}(t_0^S), P_0^T = P_{U_A^T}(t_0^T), t_0^S = t_0^T = t_0, IDFT(\cdot)$ is the transformation by using equation (18), $U_A^*(x)$ is the final audio after pitch correction. The expression (21) is visualized as the frequency response of the window, shifted in frequency to each harmonic and scaled by the magnitude of that harmonic.

Detection of Highlighted Video Captions

Karaoke video highlighted caption is a significant cue for synchronizing the singing with the accompaniment and the video. In a karaoke environment, we play the video and accompanying music while a user is singing. The singer looks at the slow moving prompt on the captions with a salient highlight on the video so as to be in synchrony. Thus, the video caption provides a cue for a singer to catch up with the musical progression. Normally, human reaction is accompanied with a lag thus the singing is usually slightly behind the actual required timing. We therefore use the video caption highlighting as a cross-model cue to perform better synchronization.

Although karaoke video varies in caption presentation, we assume the captions exist and have highlight on it. We detect the captions and their highlighting changes in the video frames by using the motion information in the designated region [10] [11] [16]. This is because a karaoke video is very dynamic - its shots are very short and the motion is rather fast. Also, the karaoke video usually is of a high quality with excellent perceptual clarity. We essentially compare the bold color highlighting changes of captions in each clip so as to detect the caption changes. By this segmentation based on caption changes, we can detect when the user should start or stop the singing.

We therefore segment [15] the karaoke video $K_V(t) = \{k_v(x, y, t), x = 1, 2, \cdots, W; y = 1, 2, \cdots, H; t \in [t_s, t_e]\}$ first, where W and H are frame width and height respectively. Then, we detect the caption region. Since a caption consists of static characters of bold font, it is salient and distinguishable from the background. We extract the edges by using the Laplace operator Eq. (22).

$$\Delta k_v(x, y, t) = \frac{\partial k_v(x, y, t)}{\partial x} + \frac{\partial k_v(x, y, t)}{\partial y} \tag{22}$$

Normally, the first order difference is used in place of the partial derivative. With this operator, the image edges are easy to be extracted from a video frame [9]. The extracted edges are used to construct a new frame, we calculate the dynamic densities $I(\Omega, t)$ of those pixels in 8×8 blocks which are less than the threshold T:

$$I(\Omega, t) = \frac{1}{|\Omega|} \int_\Omega \Delta_T k_v(x, y, t)\, dx dy \tag{23}$$

where $\Delta_T k_v(x, y, t) = |k_v(x, y, t + \Delta t) - k_v(x, y, t)|$, Ω is the 8×8 block, $k_v(x, y, t)$ is the pixel value at position (x, y) and time t, x $= 1, 2, \ldots, W$; y $= 1, 2, \ldots, H$. The unions of these blocks are considered to be the caption region. This is also a form of adaptive sampling in video. Figure 18 shows video captions and a detected caption region.

Finally, we detect the precise time of a caption appearance and disappearance. It is apparent that we can see a highlighted prompt moving from one side to the other clearly in a karaoke video, which reflects the progression of the karaoke. Thus, in the detected caption region, we calculate the dynamic changes of the two adjacent frames with the bright cursor moving along a straight line being considered the current prompt. The start time and the end time t are calculated by Eq.(24).

$$t = T_{K_v} \frac{S}{R} \tag{24}$$

where T_{K_v} is the T-th video frame, S is the time scale applicable for the entire video and R is the video playing rate.

Fig. 18 A highlighted and a detected caption region

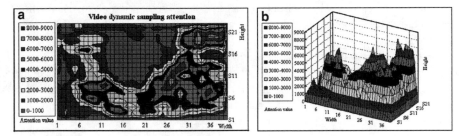

Fig. 19 2D and 3D graphs of dynamic density for a video caption detection

The dynamic density of a video has been calculated and shown in Fig. 19. We would like to point out that in this chapter, we only do the ends synchronization for the singing of each caption. However, a more fine-grained synchronization is possible if required.

Algorithm for Karaoke Adjustment

Algorithm 3 describes the overall procedure for karaoke video adjustment. It is based on the fact that all the data streams in a karaoke are of professional quality except that of the user singing. Because most users are not trained singers, their input has a high possibility of having some artifacts. However, we use the cross-modal information from the video captions and professional audio in order to correct the user's input based on the pitch, tempo and loudness. The overall procedure has been summarized in algorithm 3.

Results

In this section, we present the results of cross-modal approach to karaoke artifacts handling. Figure 20 shows an example for beat and loudness correction in a piece of

Input : Karaoke Stream κ
Output : Corrected Karaoke Stream κ'
Procedure:

1. Initialize the system at $t = t_s < t_e$;
2. Input the karaoke stream $\kappa(t)$ consist of video stream $K_V(t)$, music stream $K_M(t)$ and the audio stream $U_A(t)$;
3. Denoise the input audio stream $U_A(t)$;

   3.1 Detect & remove huffing noise by using Eq.(5);
   3.2 Detect & remove feedback noise by using Eq.(4);

4. Segment the karaoke audio stream employing;

   4.1 Video segmentation [15];
   4.2 Video caption detection by using Eqs:(22) (23);
   4.3 Music tempo detection by using Eq.(5);
   4.4 Audio adaptive sampling by using Eq.(3);
   4.5 Audio segmentation by using Eqs.(4)(5);

5: Modify audio tempo using Eq.(11) (12);
6: Modify audio tune using Eq.(16);
7: Modify audio pitch using Eq.(21);
8: Output the video, music & corrected audio streams;

Algorithm 3. Karaoke artifacts handling

segmented karaoke audio based on audio analogies. Their parameters in bytes are given in Table 1.

We have presented results of experiments for audio analogies in the form of four groups of audio comparisons in Table 2. We employ Peak Signal Noise Ratio (PSNR) (dB), Signal Noise Ratio (SNR) (dB), Spectral difference (SD) and correlation between two audio clips as quality measures. The comparison between the user's singing and the original singer's rendition (which is the exemplar) before (B.) and after (A.) correction is shown in Table 2.

In order to understand the correspondence between numerical values (PSNR, SNR, Correlation) in Table 2 and users' subjective opinion about the quality of the results of audio analogies, we conducted a user study. We polled 11 subjects, with a mix of genders and expertise. The survey was administered by setting up an online site. The users had to listen to four karaoke signing renditions (performed by one child and three adults). The subjects were asked to listen to the original rendition as well as the corrected version using the proposed audio analogies technique. The subjects were asked to rate the quality of the corrected renditions using three numerical labels (corresponding to (1) no change, (2) sounds better & (3) sounds excellent). The mean opinion scores for all participants for the four audio clips were 1.63, 1.80, 1.55 and 1.55 respectively. This indicates that the subject perceived a moderate but definite improvement.

For pitch artifacts, our correction is based on the following analysis shown in Fig. 21. We can easily see that different people have a different pitch and the same person has less amount of variations in his or her pitch. After the pitch handling

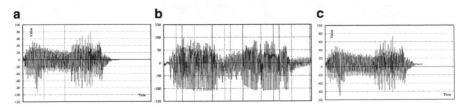

Fig. 20 From up to down: karaoke singer's audio waveform, exemplar music audio waveform and the corrected audio waveform for the singer

Table 1 Audio parameters (Bytes) in analogies based loudness and tempo correction

Audio Parameter	Audio 1	Audio 2	Analogous Audio
Length	24998	32348	24998
Centroid	12480	16034	12480
δ^-	12480	16034	12480
δ^+	12518	16314	12518
BPS	8	8	8
σ	–	–	2.73%
Average amplitude	41	48	46.87

Table 2 Audio comparisons before (B.) and after (A.) analogies

No.	PSNR (B.)	PSNR(A.)	SNR(B.)	SNR(A.)	SD(B.)	SD(A.)	Correlation(B.)	Correlation(A.)
1	9.690989	17.22	−2.509843	−0.253588	0.022842	0.022842	0.003611	0.596143
2	9.581241	11.829815	−2.495654	−5.713023	0.014145	0.055127	0.0105338	0.023705
3	9.511368	15.53444	−2.311739	−0.266603	0.018469	0.023402	0.0161687	0.721914
4	9.581241	15.927253	−3.702734	0.044801	0.016865	0.038852	0.0105338	0.784130

by audio analogies, the pitch is improved as shown in Fig. 22. The cepstrum of the corrected audio is between that of the original singer's audio and the user's audio.

Conclusion

In this chapter, we have presented a cross-modal approach to karaoke audio artifacts handling in temporal domain. Our approach uses adaptive sampling along with the video analogies approach for correcting the artifacts. The pitch, tempo and loudness of the user's singing are synchronized better with video by using audio cues (from original singer's rendition) as well as video cues (caption high-lighting information is extracted to aid proper audio-video synchronization). We also perform the noise removal step prior to artifacts handling. In the future, we plan to extend this cross-modal approach for better video synthesis of karaoke video. There are also applications in active video editing area which can be considered [1].

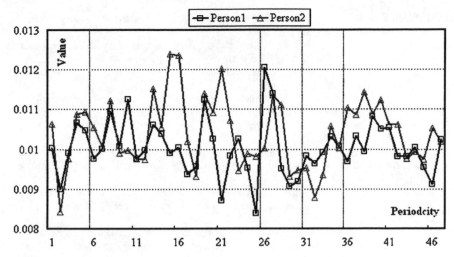

Fig. 21   Pitches for different people

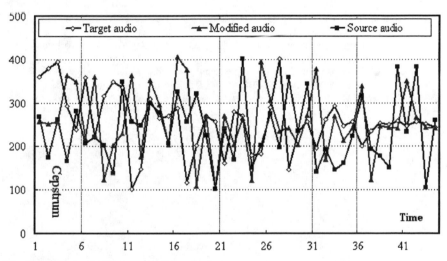

Fig. 22   Pitch comparison after audio analogies

References

1. Marc Davis. Editing out video editing. *IEEE Multimedia*, pages 54{64, Apr.-Jun. 2003.
2. Randy Goldberg and Lance Riek. *A Practical Handbook of Speech Coders*. CRC Press, Floria U.S.A., 2000.
3. Jonathan Harrington and Steve Cassidy. Techniques in Speech Acoustics. Kluwer Academic Press, Dordrecht, The Netherlands, 1999.
4. Mohan S. Kankanhalli, Jun Wang, and Ramesh Jain. Experiential sampling in multimedia systems. *IEEE Transactions on Multimedia*, 8(5):937-946, Sep. 2006.

5. Hirokazu Kato. Karaoke apparatus selectively providing harmony voice to duet singing voices. U.S. Patent 6121531, Sep. 2000.
6. David Kumar and Subutai Ahmad. Method and apparatus for providing interactive karaoke entertainment. U.S. Patent 6692259, Dec. 2002.
7. Shuichi Matsumoto. Karaoke apparatus converting gender of singing voice to match octave of song. U.S. Patent 5889223, Mar. 1998.
8. Kenji Muraki and Katsuyoshi Fujii. Karaoke sound processor for automatically adjusting the pitch of the accompaniment signal. U.S. Patent 5477003, Dec. 1995.
9. Milan Sonka, Vaclav Hlavac, and Roger Boyle. *Image Processing, Analysis, and Machine Vision*. PWS Publishing, 1998.
10. Xiaou Tang, Xinbo Gao, Jianzhuang Liu, and Hongjiang Zhang. A spatial-temporal approach for video caption detection and recognition. *IEEE Transactions on Neural Networks*, 13(4):961-971, Jul. 2002.
11. Xiaou Tang, Bo Luo, Xinbo Gao, Edwige Pissaloux, Jianzhuang Liu, and Hongjiang Zhang. Video text extraction using temporal feature vectors. In *Proc. of IEEE ICME 2002*, pages 85-88, Lausanne, Switzerland, Aug. 2002.
12. Ye Wang, Min-Yen Kan, Tin-Lay Nwe, Arun Shenoy, and Jun Yin. Lyrically: Automatic synchronization of acoustic musical signals and textual lyrics. In *Proc. of ACM Multimedia 2004*, pages 212 - 219, New York, USA, Oct. 2004.
13. Wei-Qi Yan and Mohan S Kankanhalli. Detection and removal of lighting and shaking artifacts in home videos. In *Proc. of ACM Multimedia 2002*, pages 107-116, Juan Les Pins, France, Dec. 2002.
14. Wei-Qi Yan, Jun Wang, and Mohan S. Kankanhalli. Analogies based video editing. *ACM Multimedia Systems*, 11(1):3-18, 2005.
15. HongJiang Zhang, Atreyi Kankanhalli, and Stephen W. Smoliar. Automatic partitioning of full-motion video. *ACM/Springer Multimedia Systems*, 1(1):10-28, 1993.
16. Yi Zhang and Tat-Seng Chua. Detection of text captions in compressed domain video. In *Proc. of ACM Multimedia 2000*, pages 201-204, Marina Del Rey, CA USA, Aug. 2000.
17. Yong-Wei Zhu, Mohan S Kankanhalli, and Chang-Sheng Xu. Music scale modeling for melody matching. In *Proc. of ACM Multimedia 2003*, pages 359-362, Berkeley, U.S., Nov. 2003.

Chapter 10
Dealing Bandwidth to Mobile Clients Using Games

Anastasis A. Sofokleous and Marios C. Angelides

Introduction

Efficient and fair resource allocation is essential in maximizing the usage of shared resources which are available to communication and collaboration networks. Resource allocation aims to satisfy the resource requirements of individual users whilst optimizing average quality and usage of server resources. A number of approaches for resource allocation have been advocated by researchers and practitioners. Bandwidth sharing is often addressed as a resource allocation problem, usually as a multi-client scenario, where more than one clients share network and computational resources, such in the case where many users request content from a single video streaming server. In order to address the bandwidth bottleneck and optimize the overall network utility, researchers focus on management of resources of the usage environment in order to satisfy a collective set of constraints, such as the quality of service [34, 35, 40]. In such cases, the usage environment refers to network resources available to the user on the target server, on the user's terminal and on the servers participating in an interaction. For example, resource allocation can provide better quality of service to a user or a group of users by changing some of the device properties (e.g. device resolution) and/or managing some of the network resources (e.g. allocation of bandwidth).

This chapter exploits a gaming approach to bandwidth sharing in a network of non-cooperative clients whose aim is to satisfy their selfish objectives and be served in the shortest time and who share limited knowledge of one another. The chapter models this problem as a game in which players consume the bandwidth of a video streaming server. The rest of this chapter is organized in four sections: the proceeding section presents resource allocation taxonomies, following that is a section on game theory, where our approach is sourced from, and its application to resource allocation. The penultimate section presents our gaming approach to resource allocation. The final section concludes.

A.A. Sofokleous and M.C. Angelides (✉)
Brunel University Uxbridge, UK
e-mail: marios.angelides@brunel.ac.uk

B. Furht (ed.), *Handbook of Multimedia for Digital Entertainment and Arts*,
DOI 10.1007/978-0-387-89024-1_10, © Springer Science+Business Media, LLC 2009

Resource Allocation Taxonomies

Resource allocation schemes can either be client-centric or server-centric. In a *client-centric scheme*, the objective is to satisfy the user constraints and preferences instead of various resource sharing issues among users. A client-centric algorithm is usually utilized on the client device and may involve management of the last mile bandwidth, prioritization of the client streaming sessions, optimization of the device usage in order to save energy, adaptation of device properties (e.g. display resolution), and management of CPU usage and operating policies [14, 38]. The management of resources on client devices is the most common application of the client-centric scheme. In [22], the authors propose an algorithm that runs on the client and is able to manage the system resources by monitoring the usage of the device, e.g. network traffic, memory and CPU utilization. Similarly, the proposed approach of [32] is embedded as an algorithm on mobile devices and manages the power consumption in order to save energy during its usage and maintain an adequate level on the device's usability.

A *server-centric scheme* takes into account not only the user preferences but also other constraints, such as resource sharing issues on the server, i.e. available bandwidth, memory, CPU [39]. This is the most common scheme followed for managing the network and server resources and providing service differentiation according to user characteristics and analyzing the importance and the content of video packets transmitted via the network [6]. Usually the objective is just to share bandwidth to a number of client request. What makes this a more complex task is where there are deadlines in serving some of the requests. [2], for example, besides addressing the simple bandwidth allocation problem, it also considers the deadlines imposed by each request and the file-size of the requested resource. The work describes fixed policy-based algorithms, dynamic algorithms that consider the network state before allocating the resources, and adaptable algorithms that continuously adapt the bandwidth of new and running requests. In [29], the authors propose a decision algorithm, that works only when the requested resources exceed the available capacity, in order to make some optimal and fair decisions on the resource usage of the network. This approach uses algorithms that can run independently to coordinate and optimize the routing, control flow and resource allocation of the share networks. A different resource sharing scheme is presented in [12]. The authors suggest a scheme for sharing network links. A bandwidth amount is initially allocated to each user and this capacity is guaranteed. However, if the link of a user is unused, then the resource allocation algorithm, in collaboration with the temporary owners of the unused bandwidth, proceeds to short-term contracts, according to which the resource allocation algorithm can use temporarily the unused bandwidth for other requests. The allocation of the unused bandwidth is formulated as an optimization problem, during which the objective is to maximize the total revenue of the network. In [9], the authors present a resource allocation algorithm for a network of peer-to-peer users. Their algorithm takes into account the sharing contribution as users participate by sharing files between each other.

Resource allocation approaches may also incorporate load balancing and storage algorithms on end- or intermediate servers [39], cache-policies and replication algorithms on proxy servers [18, 42] for providing fault tolerant, reliability and improve performance of the servers while, in some cases, personalizing the experience of users [21]. Whilst client-centric schemes determine the resource allocation strategy without involving other users or streaming sessions but only what is best for the current user, server-centric schemes coordinate the computational and network resources usage and provide an average quality of service for more than one user, such as differential services of a server or a network [36].

This chapter addresses the challenge of sharing bandwidth fairly among selfish clients who are requesting video streaming services and will consider a server-centric scheme to guarantee both the satisfaction of the end-user experience and the optimization of usage of shared resources. By sharing the network bandwidth among multiple video streaming requests one can optimize the consumption of bandwidth and satisfy user preferences and other constraints [31]. Bandwidth management has also been addressed in our previous work, e.g. see [34, 35] where we present an algorithm that runs on the client's device and is able to share the last mile bandwidth among multiple concurrent video streaming requests issued by a single user. This approach first analyses and prioritizes the streaming requests, then allocates bandwidth to each request and then collaborates with a remote adaptation engine in order to have the content of streaming requests adapted.

Approaches following any of the aforementioned schemes may require knowledge on the content and usage environment in order to personalize the user experience and maximize the average QoS. To describe the entities involved, such as the user, the content, the terminals and network, international consortiums such as ISO have developed a number normative standards, such as MPEG-7, MPEG-21, W3C and TV-Anytime. These standards enable the deployment and interoperability of media adaptation applications [26]. The MPEG-7 Multimedia Description Scheme (MDS), for example, provides tools for describing general (e.g. title, creator and digital rights), semantic (e.g. who, what, when, where about information on objects and events) and structural (e.g. image, color, histogram) features of the multimedia content [1], which enable content-based searching and filtering of multimedia content [3, 16]. Deploying MPEG-21, for example, applications can describe characteristics of the usage environment (e.g. network, device, user and natural environment).

The resource allocation strategy is either calculated or selected from a discrete or infinite adaptation space. In charge of resource allocation or/and manipulation is a resource management engine, whereas responsible for the decision taking, i.e. to determine the resource allocation strategy, is a decision engine. The two engines are either utilized on the same node or distributed on different nodes, where the latter allows distribution of the load, enables scalability and ensures additional fault tolerance. The strategy depends on end-user experience and the overall network utility and is associated with both the content and the usage environment. Thus, such algorithms can use the MPEG-7 and MPEG-21 information to search and select the optimum strategy, the strategy that specifies how the resource should be manage to optimize a given set of objectives [35]. Note that within the strategy space there is an optimal strategy that maximizes the end-user experience (e.g. the user-perceived quality) and other utilities, such as the server and network usage [8]. Intelligent decision algorithms can search the space and determine an optimal strategy with minimum user feedback [35]. Many researchers have used or developed tools to describe this space. For example MPEG-21 AQoS can be used to specify relationships between constraints, feasible strategies that satisfy these constraints, and associated utilities (e.g. PSNR) [4, 41].

Whether the process is utilized in a single step or as multiple consecutive steps, on a particular node or distributed, the objective it to optimize a set of objectives, e.g. user-perceived quality and bandwidth consumption latency. The problem of searching for the optimum strategy has been formulated by many researchers as an optimization problem and has been addressed widely with computational intelligence including genetic algorithms [17] and artificial Intelligence based planning [19]. The complexity increases where the optimization constraints conflict with each other. In many cases selecting an optimal strategy becomes a multi-optimization problem, which in some cases is solved by a scalar function. An example of resource allocation using a weighted sum of objective values can be found in [5]. The more efficient and objective approach, however, is a multi-optimization algorithm, such as Pareto Optimality, e.g. see [28]. Allocating bandwidth in server-centric schemes, for example, may be formulated to a multi-criteria problem as it is necessary to consider individual constraints, including the maximization of the end-user experience with fairness while optimizing the overall consumption of the server and network resources [30]. The following section discusses game theory and its applications to resource allocation which we deploy in our approach.

Resource Allocation Using Game Theory

Game theory was initially developed to analyze scenarios where individuals are competitive and each individual's success may be at cost of others. Usually, a game consists of more than one player allowed to make moves or strategies and each move or combination of moves has a payoff. Game theory's applications attempt to find equilibrium, a state in which game players are unlike to change their strategies. [15]. The most famous equilibrium concept is the Nash Equilibrium (NE), according to which each player is assumed to know the final strategies of the rest players, and there is nothing to gain by changing only his own strategy. NE is not Pareto Optimal, i.e. it does not necessarily imply that all the players will get the best cumulative payoff, as a better payoff could be gained in a cooperative environment where players can agree on their strategies. NE is established by players following either pure-strategies or mixed-strategies. A pure-strategy defines exactly the player's move for each situation that a player meets, whereas in a mixed-strategy the players selects randomly a pure-strategy according to the probability assigned to each pure-strategy. Furthermore an equilibrium is said to be stable (stability) if by changing slightly the probabilities of a player's pure strategies, then the latter player is now playing with a worse strategy, while the rest of the players cannot improve their strategies. Stability will make the player of the changed mixed-strategy to come back to NE. To guarantee NE, a set of conditions must be assumed including the assumption that the players are dedicated to do everything in their power for maximizing their payoff. Games can be of *perfect information*, if the players know the moves previously made by other players, or *imperfect information*, if not every player knows the actions of the others. An example of the former is a sequential game which allows the players to observe the game, whereas the latter can occur in cases where players make their moves concurrently.

Game theory has been used with mixed success in resource allocation problem. Auctioning is the most common approach for allocating resources to the clients. In an auction, players bid for bandwidth and therefore each player aims to get the a certain bandwidth capacity without any serving latency, both of which are guaranteed according to the player's bid, of which its amount may vary based on the demand. A central agent is responsible for allocating the resources and usually the highest bidder gets the resources as requested and pays the bid. Thus, each player must evaluate the cost of the resources to determine if it is a good offer (or optimum) for biding it; where the player does not get the resources, it may have to wait until the next auction, e.g. until there are available resources. Thus, the cost is the main payoff of this game. It is also assumed that players hold a constrained budget. The main problem with this strategy, however, is that the players can lie and the winner may have to pay more than the true value of the resources [33]. In such a case, NE cannot guarantee a social optimum, i.e. that we can maximize the net benefits for everyone in society irrespective of who enjoys the benefits or pays the cost. According to economic theory, in their attempt to maximize their private benefits, if players pay for any benefits they receive and bear only the corresponding costs (and therefore there aren't any externalities), then the social net benefits are maximized, i.e. they are Pareto Optimal. If such externalities exist, then the decision-maker, as in our case, should not take into account the cost during its decision process.

In [7], the authors use game theory to model selfish and altruistic user behaviors in multi-hop relay networks. Their game uses four type of players which represent four type of elements in a multi-hop network. Despite the fact that the game utility involves the end-user satisfaction, bandwidth and price are used to establish NE. A problem with resource allocation approaches that use only the cost is that the fairness of the game does not take into account the player waiting-time in a queue. This may cause a problem as some players that keep losing may wait indefinitely in the queue. To address the problem, in this chapter we use both the queue length and arrival time to prioritize the players and allow them to adapt their strategy accordingly. Likewise, users in [25] negotiate not only for the bandwidth, but also for the user waiting time in the queue. Their approach addresses the bandwidth bottleneck on a node that serves multiple decentralized users. The users who use only local information and feedback from the remote node need to go to NE so as to be served by the node.

Some researchers classify the game players either as cooperative or non-cooperative. Cooperative players can form binding commitments and communication between each other is allowed. However, the non-cooperative player model is usually more representative of real problems. Examples of both types of players are presented in [10]. The authors apply a game theory in a DVB network of users, who can be either cooperative or non-cooperative. Motivated by environment problems that affect the reliability and performance of satellite streaming, they apply game theory in a distributed satellite resource allocation problem. Game theory is the most appropriate in distributed and scalable models in which conflict objectives exist. The behavior of non-cooperative players is studied in [13]. Specifically, the authors use game theory to model mobile wireless clients in a non-cooperative dynamic self-organized environment. The objective is to allocate bandwidth to network clients, which share only limited knowledge for each other. In our approach we use non-cooperative players as players are not allowed either to cooperative or communication with each other.

Game theory has been also used for solving a variety of other problems, such as for service differentiation and data replication. In service differentiation the objective is to provide quality of service according to a user's class rather than to a user's bid. In [23, 24] the authors present a game-based approach for providing service differentiation to p2p network users according to the service each user is providing to the network. The resource allocation process is modeled as a competition game between the nodes where NE is achieved and a resource distribution mechanism works between the nodes of the p2p network that share content. The main idea, which is to encourage users to share files and provide good p2p service differentiation, is that nodes earn higher contribution by sharing popular files and allowing uploading, and the higher the contribution a node makes the higher the priority the node will have when downloading files. The authors report that their approach promotes fairness in resource sharing, avoids wastage of resources and takes into account the congestion level of the network link. They also argue that it is scalable and can adapt to the conditions of the environment, and can guarantee optimal allocation while maximizing the network utility value. [20] discusses the use of game theory in spectrum sharing for more flexible, efficient and fair spectrum usage and provides an overview of this area by exploiting the behavior of users and analyzing the design and optimality of distributed access networks. Their model defines two types of players: the wireless users whose set of strategies include the choice of a license channel, the price, the transmission power and the transmission time duration, and the spectrum holders, whose strategies include charging for among other the usage and selection of unused channels. The authors provide an overview of current modeling approaches on spectrum sharing and describe an auction-based spectrum sharing game.

Game theory has been also applied for the data replication problem in data grids where the objective is to maximize the objectives of each provider participating in the grid [11]. In [27], game theory has been used for allocating network resources while consuming the minimum energy of battery-based stations of wireless networks. In a non-cooperative environment, a variety of power control game approaches are presented where the utility is modeled as a function of data transmitted over the consumed energy. The following section discusses our gaming approach to dealing bandwidth to mobile clients.

Dealing Bandwidth Using a Game

Our approach addresses bandwidth requests by multiple users who have requested content from a remote video streaming server using heterogeneous devices and who have a diverse set of characteristics and preferences. We use game theory to model the behavior of the users in a five-cards poker game. Players are selfish and act based on their own objectives and constraints. Players formulate their strategy based on their order in the game, which depends on their arrival time, and decisions made during previous rounds of the same game. This decision process takes into account the order of the player in the queue, i.e. the queue length, and players can adapt their strategies based on their constraints and objectives which can be defined in relation to a variety of characteristics, such as the required bandwidth and the estimated time of service. We use both MPEG-7 and MPEG-21, the former to describe semantically and syntactically the video content, the latter -21 to describe the characteristics of usage environment (device, natural environment and network), the characteristics and preferences of users and the constraints which steer the strategies of the players. The proposed approach allocates bandwidth by considering the usage environment properties and user preferences for maximizing the end-user experience. We use MPEG-21 AQoS to describe adaptation strategies in relation to constraints and utilities. The resulting AQoS is used by the video server for selecting the video adaptation according to the bandwidth given to the player.

The Three Phase Bandwidth Dealing Game

A server streams video over the internet. It can serve multiple users concurrently. However, it is constrained by the available bandwidth which may vary over time. To serve the maximum number of users within the given bandwidth and to guarantee quality and fairness, the server employs a game algorithm. The algorithm uses a variation of five card poker draw and repeats a cycle of 3 main phases: k-calculation, three round main game, and streaming-seat reallocation. every 3-phase cycle is a new game where video streaming requests are modeled as players. Thus, from now on, a player refers to a video request made by a user and also has information that can help the satisfaction of the request, such as information about the requested video, the user device, characteristics preferences and constraints that can steer personalization of video streaming. Figure 1 depicts the three phases. In the rest of this section we describe in detail each of the three phases of the game.

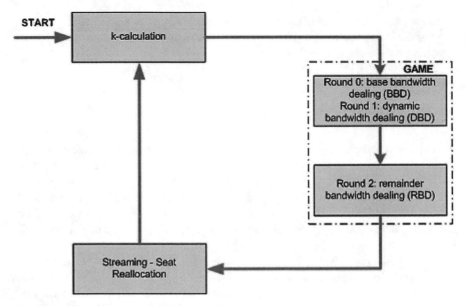

Fig. 1 The Three Phase Bandwidth Dealing Game

k-calculation Phase

Figure 2 shows the process flow of the k-calculation phase. To participate in the game, new players have to enter a FIFO queue, *outerQueue*. This queue is used as a waiting place, where the players can wait until they are invited to participate in the game. Players that exit the *outerQueue*, enter the *gameQueue*, a queue that holds the players playing the actual game. At the end of each game, the server deals the bandwidth to the players participating in the game and starts a new game. Each main game phase consists of two rounds. Whilst the size of *outerQueue* is not fixed and can accept every player interested in joining the game, the size of *gameQueue,* which is also the number of players participating in the actual game, is set dynamically by the server prior to the beginning of each game. *k-calculation* is the first phase of the game and aims to calculates the size of *gameQueue*, i.e. the number of players that will be moved from *outerQueue* to *gameQueue*.

The server's objective is to satisfy the maximum number of players in each game with respect to the available bandwidth and without compromising the quality of service. For each player to be moved from *outerQueue* to *gameQueue*, it will allocate bandwidth fairly calculated based on several values including usage history, and the characteristics, constraints and preferences of the player. Using FIFO, the server can move a player from *outerQueue* to *gameQueue*, as long it can satisfy its estimated minimum bandwidth needs.

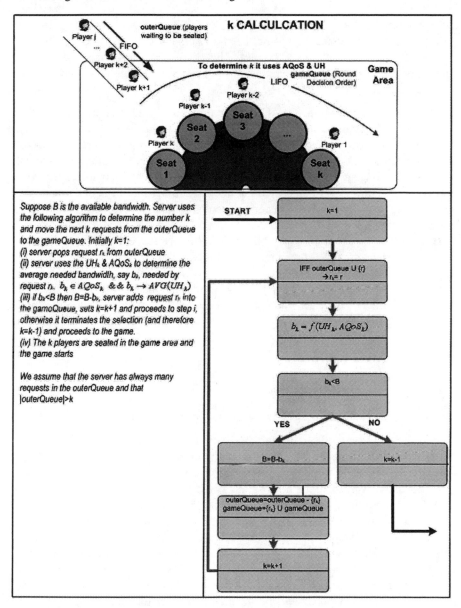

Fig. 2 The k-calculation Phase

In particular, to estimate the bandwidth, say b_k, the server considers:

(i) The user preferences, characteristics and constraints, including minimum and maximum quality/bandwidth values. User preferences and characteristics, and constraints have been described using MPEG-21 UED and UCD, respectively.

(ii) The usage history which shows the consumption details of video V_k over time by player p_k. If video V_k has not been consumed yet, then the usage history, which is empty, is not used. The usage history is described using XML.

(iii) Information regarding all possible ways of consuming video V_k, which is described using MPEG-21 AQoS.

The server searches MPEG-21 AQoS and extracts all the adaptation solutions that satisfy the UCD limit constraints and optimize the UCD optimization constraints. An example of search based algorithms that can determine optimum adaptation solutions can be found in our previous work [36]. If there more than one adaptation solutions, the usage history is used to determine a solution that maximizes the average quality (i.e. the server objectives) but does not compromise the individual one. An example of using the usage history in content adaptation can be found in our previous work [37].

If the player has set minimum acceptable quality, the server starts its initial offer with a solution that matches the minimum expectation of the user. If there is enough bandwidth to satisfy b_k, i.e. $b_k < B$, the player is moved to the *gameQueue*, and the available resources are recalculated, i.e. $B = B - b_k$, and the algorithm processes the next player. Otherwise the selection process terminates and the algorithm proceeds to the main game.

Main Game Phase

The main game phase consists of 3 rounds as shown in Figures 3 and 4.

Round 0 - base bandwidth dealing (BBD): in this round the server announces its initial offer to the k players participating in the current game, i.e. to the players of *gameQueue* (Figure 3) The server offers the players bandwidth and the players will have to make a decision in the next round. The bandwidth is presented to the players as calculated during the k-calculation phase, i.e. a bandwidth value along with an adaptation solution so the player will know what will get, e.g. video quality, video format etc. What will make the players to like a solution depends on their personal game strategy which may depend on individual objectives, and some limit constraints (e.g. minimum acceptable quality) that may not have been announced to the server. The player may choose not to announce something to the server (e.g. the minimum acceptable video quality) if the player believes that this action could bias the server's decision and by not doing this it may lead to a better bandwidth offer.

Round 1 - dynamic bandwidth dealing (DBD): at this round, following a LIFO order and starting from left to right, the k players need to make an initiial decision (Figure 3): either accept the server's offer and receive the bandwidth (i.e. a YES decision) or pass over the offer (i.e. a NO decision). With the latter decision, the server deals this player's bandwidth to the rest of the players waiting in the game to make their initial decision, i.e. the players sitting in the right of the player that made a NO decision. Also with this decision the player knows he may not get another

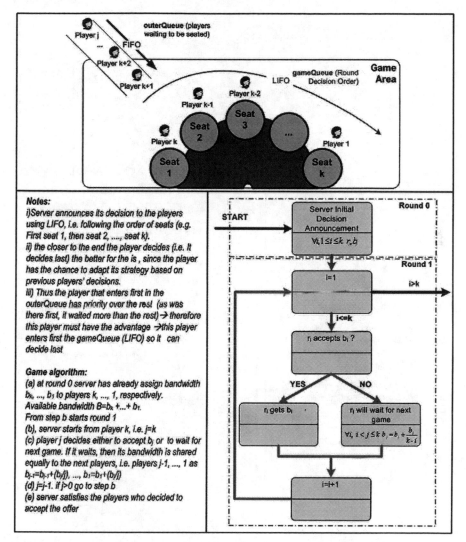

Fig. 3 The Main Game Phase: Round 0 and 1

offer in this game and as a result he may have to wait for the next game. However, the payoff of this player lay in the fact that in the next game he is guaranteed a better offer and also that he may get (be moved to) a better seat in the game. The closer to the end of the round a player gets to make the initial decision the better his position is in relation that of the previous players. This is because only one decision is made at a time using the LIFO order and the players that get to decide last can be benefited from the additional bandwidth that can get from players that do not accept the server's initial offer. Thus, if a player declines the server's offer, the server takes his bandwidth and gives it to the rest of the players waiting in the queue. A player

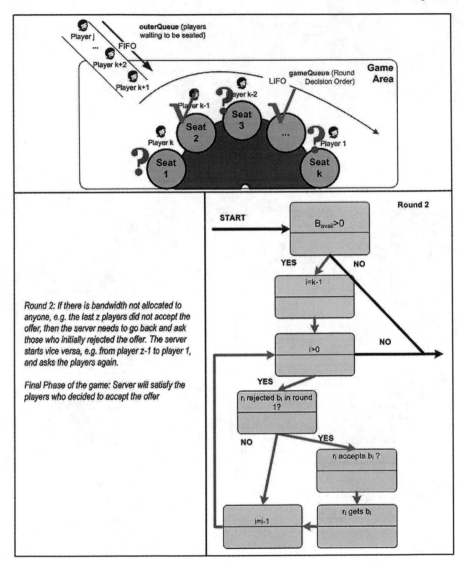

Fig. 4 The Main Game Phase: Round 2

may decide to decline an offer if the offer was not good enough or if he can wait for the next game to get a better offer. The former is calculated from the objectives and constraints set by the player whereas the latter is the payoff of the game to players that give up their bandwidth during a game. The server will take into account their decision and in the next game these players will get at a better offer. Before moving to the next round, all the players must make their initial YES or NO decision. The result of this round is that some players (i.e. with a YES decision) will satisfied in terms of bandwidth, whereas some other will have to wait.

Round 2 - remainder bandwidth dealing (RBD): this round will go ahead only if there is enough bandwidth to satisfy at least one more player (Figure 4). For example, consider the case where the last player declined the server's offer. In figure 4, player 1, who decided last in round 1, declined the offer of server. If b_1, which is the bandwidth offered to player 1, is also the available bandwidth at the end of round 1, in round 2 the objective is to use this bandwidth to make a new offer to the unsatisfied players. Following a vice-versa order, i.e. FIFO on the initial settlement of the *gameQueue* players, the server offers this bandwidth to each one of each one of the players that declined its offers earlier. If one of the players takes the offer then this round terminates and the game proceeds to the next phase. At the end of round 2, the server satisfies the players who accepted the offer, e.g. in figure 4 player $k - 1$ accepted the offer. Players, who have not gone with any of the server's offers, e.g. in figure players k and 1, will play again in the next game and not get any bandwidth from the current game.

Streaming-Seat Reallocation Phase

Figure 5 shows the final phase of the game, where players are either served, if they accepted an offer, or change seat in order to participate in the next game. The new seat arrangement is one of the payoffs of the players who have decided to wait, e.g. player k in Figure 5. In addition, the fact that the server will make a better offer to those players is another payoff of waiting to be served in future games. For example, if the current game is game t, and player j is a player of game t waiting to be served in the next game, then $b_j(t + 1) = b_j(t) + e$, where e is a small additional amount of bandwidth given to these players, e.g. $e = \frac{(B - b_j(t))}{k}$.

Concluding Discussion

This paper describes a game approach to dealing bandwidth. It proposes the modeling of bandwidth allocation based on five-card poker draw, where players are users awaiting to be served sufficient bandwidth. Each player participates in the game under a number of rules for gaining the wanted bandwidth resources. Players have priorities according to the time of arrival. One of the difference of our approach is that it takes into account the length of the queue and the time that a player may need to wait before getting served. Thus, in some cases, the players can sacrifice the quality of the video in order to be served faster, or may choose to wait more in exchange of getting more bandwidth. We are currently extending our algorithm to incorporate content adaptation.

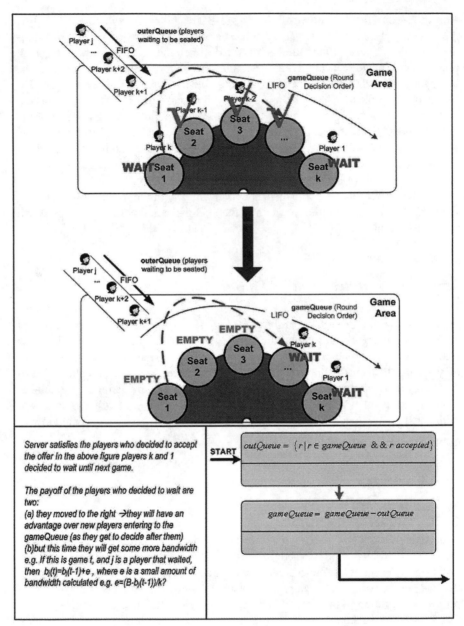

Fig. 5 The Streaming-Seat Reallocation Phase

References

1. H. Agius and M. C. Angelides, "Closing the content-user gap in MPEG-7: the hanging basket model," *Multimedia Systems,* Vol. 13, No. 2, 2007, pp. 155-172.
2. D. Andrei, M. Batayneh, S. Sarkar, C. U. Martel and B. Mukherjee, "Deadline-driven bandwidth allocation with flexible transmission rates in WDM networks," *Proceedings of the IEEE International Conference on Communications (ICC'08),* Beijing, China, 2008, pp. 5354-5358.
3. M. C. Angelides, A. A. Sofokleous and M. Parmar, "Classified ranking of semantic content filtered output using self-organizing neural networks," *Lecture Notes in Computer Science 4132: Proceedings of the 16th International Conference on Artificial Neural Networks (ICANN 2006) Part II,* Athens, Greece, 2006, pp. 55-64.
4. M. C. Angelides, A. A. Sofokleous and C. Schizas, "Implementing the MPEG-21 adaptation quality of service in dynamic environments," *Lecture Notes in Computer Science 3983: Proceedings of the 2006 IEE International Conference on Computational Science and its Applications (ICCSA2006) Part IV,* Glasgow, UK, 2006, pp. 118-127.
5. H. Boche, M. Wiczanowski and S. Stanczak, "On Optimal Resource Allocation in Cellular Networks With Best-Effort Traffic," *Wireless Communications, IEEE Transactions on,* Vol. 7, No. 4, 2008, pp. 1163-1167.
6. J. Chakareski and P. Frossard, "Rate-Distortion Optimized Distributed Packet Scheduling of Multiple Video Streams over Shared Communication Resources," *IEEE Transactions on Multimedia,* Vol. 8, No. 2, 2006, pp. 207-218.
7. S. L. Chao, G. Y. Lin and H. Y. Wei, "Mixed altruistic and selfish users in wireless mesh networks: A game theoretic model for multihop bandwidth sharing," *Proceedings of the 9th ACM International Symposium on Mobile Ad Hoc Networking and Computing,* 2008, pp. 461-462.
8. N. Cranley, P. Perry and L. Murphy, "Optimum adaptation trajectories for streamed multimedia," *Multimedia Systems,* Vol. 10, No. 5, 2005, pp. 392-401.
9. A. Creus-Mir, R. Casadesus-Masanell and A. Hervas-Drane, "Bandwidth allocation in peer-to-peer file sharing networks," *Computer Communications,* Vol. 31, No. 2, 2008, pp. 257-265.
10. E. Del Re, G. Gorni, L. S. Ronga and M. A. Vazquez Castro, "A game theory approach for DVB-RCS resource allocation," *Proceedings of the IEEE 67th Vehicular Technology Conference (VTC'08),* Singapore, 2008, pp. 2937-2941.
11. A. H. Elghirani, R. Subrata and A. Y. Zomaya, "A proactive non-cooperative game-theoretic framework for data replication in data grids," *Proceedings of the 8th IEEE International Symposium on Cluster Computing and the Grid (CCGRID'08),* Lyon, France, 2008, pp. 433-440.
12. J. Elias, F. Martignon, A. Capone and G. Pujolle, "A new approach to dynamic bandwidth allocation in Quality of Service networks: Performance and bounds," *Computer Networks,* Vol. 51, No. 10, 2007, pp. 2833-2853.
13. Z. Fang and B. Bensaou, "Fair bandwidth sharing algorithms based on game theory frameworks for wireless ad-hoc networks," *Proceedings of the 23th Conference of the IEEE Communications Society (INFOCOM'04),* Hong Kong, 2004, pp. 1284-1295.
14. N. Feng, S. C. Mau and N. B. Mandayam, "Pricing and Power Control for Joint Network-Centric and User-Centric Radio Resource Management," *IEEE Transactions on Communications,* Vol. 52, No. 9, 2004, pp. 1547.
15. D. Fotakis, S. Kontogiannis, E. Koutsoupias, M. Mavronicolas and P. Spirakis. "The structure and complexity of nash equilibria for a selfish routing game," *Theoretical Computer Science,* 2008, available online from http://dx.doi.org/10.1016/j.tcs.2008.01.004.
16. M. Gruhne, R. Tous, J. Delgado, M. Doeller and H. Kosch, "MP7QF: An MPEG-7 query format," *Proceedings of the 3rd International Conference on Automated Production of Cross Media Content for Multi-Channel Distribution, (AXMEDIS'07),* Barcelona, Spain, 2007, pp. 15-18.

17. P. Guturu, "Computational intelligence in multimedia networking and communications: Trends and future directions," in *Computational Intelligence in Multimedia Processing: Recent Advances*, vol. 96/2008, A. Hassanien, A. Abraham and J. Kacprzyk, Eds. Springer Berlin / Heidelberg, 2008, pp. 51-76.

18. J. L. Hsiao, H. P. Hung and M. S. Chen, "Versatile Transcoding Proxy for Internet Content Adaptation," *IEEE Transactions on Multimedia*, Vol. 10, No. 4, 2008, pp. 646-658.

19. D. Jannach, K. Leopold, C. Timmerer and H. Hellwagner, "A knowledge-based framework for multimedia adaptation," *Applied Intelligence*, Vol. 24, No. 2, 2006, pp. 109-125.

20. Z. Ji and K. J. R. Liu, "Dynamic Spectrum Sharing: A Game Theoretical Overview," *IEEE Communications Magazine*, Vol. 45, No. 5, 2007, pp. 88.

21. S. Kalasapur, M. Kumar and B. Shirazi, "Personalized service composition for ubiquitous multimedia delivery," *Proceedings of the 6th IEEE-CS International Symposium on a World of Wireless Mobile and Multimedia Networks (WoWMoM'05)*, Taormina, Giardini, Naxos, 2005, pp. 258-263.

22. H. Kung, J. Hua, Y. Chang and C. Lin, "Seamless QoS Adaptation Control for Embedded Multimedia Communications," *IEEE Transactions on Consumer Electronics*, Vol. 52, No. 1, 2006, pp. 240-248.

23. R. T. B. Ma, S. C. M. Lee, J. C. S. Lui and D. K. Y. Yau, "A game theoretic approach to provide incentive and service differentiation in P2P networks," *Proceedings of the Joint International Conference on Measurement and Modeling of Computer Systems*, 2004, pp. 189-198.

24. R. T. B. Ma, S. C. M. Lee, J. C. S. Lui and D. K. Y. Yau, "Incentive and service differentiation in P2P networks: a game theoretic approach," *IEEE/ACM Transactions on Networking (TON)*, Vol. 14, No. 5, 2006, pp. 978-991.

25. R. T. Maheswaran and T. Basar, "Multi-user flow control as a nash game: Performance of various algorithms," *Proceedings of the 37th IEEE Conference on Decision and Control*, Tampa, Florida, USA, 1998, pp. 1090-1095.

26. J. M. Martínez, "MPEG-7 Tools for Universal Multimedia Access," *Journal of the American Society for Information Science and Technology*, Vol. 58, No. 9, 2007, pp. 1374-1376.

27. F. Meshkati, H. V. Poor and S. C. Schwartz, "Energy-efficient resource allocation in wireless networks: An overview of game-theoretic approaches," *IEEE Signal Processing Magazine*, Vol. 24, 2007, pp. 58-68.

28. D. Mukherjee, E. Delfosse, J. Kim and Y. Wang, "Optimal Adaptation Decision-Taking for Terminal and Network Quality-of-Service," *IEEE Transactions on Multimedia*, Vol. 7, No. 3, 2005, pp. 454-462.

29. M. J. Neely, E. Modiano and C. Li, "Fairness and Optimal Stochastic Control for Heterogeneous Networks," *IEEE/ACM Transactions on Networking*, Vol. 16, No. 2, 2008, pp. 396-409.

30. W. Ogryczak, A. Wierzbicki and M. Milewski, "A multi-criteria approach to fair and efficient bandwidth allocation," *Omega*, Vol. 36, No. 3, 2008, pp. 451-463.

31. M. Prangl, T. Szkaliczki and H. Hellwagner, "A Framework for Utility-Based Multimedia Adaptation," *IEEE Transactions on Circuits and Systems for Video Technology*, Vol. 17, No. 6, 2007, pp. 719-728.

32. P. Ranganathan, E. Geelhoed, M. Manahan and K. Nicholas, "Energy-Aware User Interfaces and Energy-Adaptive Displays," *IEEE Computer*, Vol. 39, No. 3, 2006, pp. 31-38.

33. A. Sahasrabudhe and K. Kar, "Bandwidth allocation games under budget and access constraints," *Proceedings of the 42nd Annual Conference on Information Sciences and Systems (CISS'08)*, Princeton, NJ, 2008, pp. 761-769.

34. A. A. Sofokleous and M. C. Angelides, "Client-Centric Usage Environment Adaptation using MPEG-21," *Journal of Mobile Multimedia*, Vol. 2, No. 4, 2006, pp. 297-310.

35. A. A. Sofokleous and M. C. Angelides, "Content Adaptation on Mobile Devices using MPEG-21," *Journal of Mobile Multimedia*, Vol. 2, No. 2, 2006, pp. 112-123.

36. A. A. Sofokleous and M. C. Angelides, "DCAF: An MPEG-21 Dynamic Content Adaptation Framework," *Multimedia Tools and Applications*, Vol. 40, No. 2, 2008, pp. 151-182.

37. A. A. Sofokleous and M. C. Angelides. "Dynamic selection of a video content adaptation strategy from a pareto front," *The Computer Journal,* 2008, available online from http://dx. doi.org/10.1093/comjnl/bxn035.

38. P. J. Teller and S. R. Seelam, "Insights into Providing Dynamic Adaptation of Operating System Policies," *ACM SIGOPS Operating Systems Review,* Vol. 40, No. 2, 2006, pp. 83-89.

39. B. Veeravalli, L. Chen, H. Y. Kwoon, G. K. Whee, S. Y. Lai, L. P. Hian and H. C. Chow, "Design, analysis, and implementation of an agent driven pull-based distributed video-on-demand system," *Multimedia Tools and Applications,* Vol. 28, No. 1, 2006, pp. 89-118.

40. A. Vetro, C. Timmerer and S. Devillers, "Digital item adaptation - tools for universal multimedia access," in *The MPEG-21 Book* I. S. Burnett, F. Pereira, R. Van de Walle and R. Koenen, Eds. Hoboken, NJ, USA: John Wiley, 2006, pp. 282-331.

41. A. Vetro and C. Timmerer, "Digital Item Adaptation: Overview of Standardization and Research Activities," *IEEE Transactions on Multimedia,* Vol. 7, No. 3, 2005, pp. 418-426.

42. F. Yu, Q. Zhang, W. Zhu and Y. Q. Zhang, "QoS-adaptive proxy caching for multimedia streaming over the Internet," *IEEE Transactions on Circuits and Systems for Video Technology,* Vol. 13, No. 3, 2003, pp. 257-269.

Chapter 11
Hack-proof Synchronization Protocol for Multi-player Online Games

Yeung Siu Fung and John C.S. Lui

Introduction

Modern multi-player online games are popular and attractive because they provide a sense of virtual world experience to users: players can interact with each other on the Internet but perceive a local area network responsiveness. To make this possible, most modern multi-player online games use similar networking architecture that aims to hide the effects of network latency, packet loss, and high variance of delay from players. Because real-time interactivity is a crucial feature from a player's point of view, any delay perceived by a player can affect his/her performance [16]. Therefore, the game client must be able to run and accept new user commands continuously regardless of the condition of the underlying communication channel, and that it will not stop responding because of waiting for update packets from other players. To make this possible, multi-player online games typically use protocols based on "dead-reckoning" [5, 6, 9] which allows loose synchronization between players.

However, dead-reckoning protocol is susceptible to some security attack or exploitation. In particular, the type of cheat that exploits this vulnerability is called speed-hack [3] and it has become so widely available and easily accessible because the implementation of a speed-hack is very simple. Speed-hack cheats exist virtually in all popular commercial multi-player online games [15]. Existing countermeasures target on the cheats themselves, i.e. they scan for and block any known cheating software, or observe any abnormal network traffic and ban that player from the game. These methods cannot safeguard against all potential speed-hacks, and honest players may be accidentally recognized as cheaters due to the false positive nature of detection software.

Figure 1a and b are screenshots from a popular commercial massively multiplayer online role-playing game (MMORPG) called *World of Warcraft*. In an

Y.S. Fung and J.C.S. Lui (✉)
Department of Computer Science and Engineering, The Chinese University of Hong Kong,
Ma Liu Shui, China
e-mail: {sfyeung; cslui}@cse.cuhk.edu.hk

B. Furht (ed.), *Handbook of Multimedia for Digital Entertainment and Arts*,
DOI 10.1007/978-0-387-89024-1_11, © Springer Science+Business Media, LLC 2009

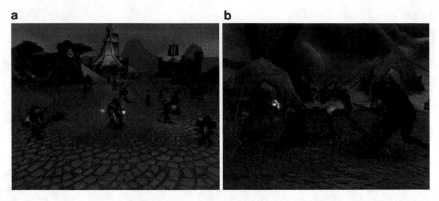

Fig. 1 a Some avatars moving inside a virtual world, each of them is controlled by an individual player. **b** Several avatars attacking each other using different weapons

MMORPG, each player controls the action of an avatar inside a virtual world. For example, the player can move the avatar from one place to another, gather different items by moving the avatar towards them, use different weapons and magic spells to attack other avatars and move the avatar to avoid being attacked. Therefore, a player with a fast moving avatar has definite advantages over players with slower moving avatars. Normally, an avatar can move faster only after it has obtained some particular items. However, when using speed-hack an avatar can move arbitrarily faster. Figure 4 illustrates the effect of using speed-hack in an MMORPG. In Fig. 4c and d, player $\mathcal{P}$ is using a speed-hack. We can see that $\mathcal{P}$'s avatar moves faster than that in Fig. 4a and b.

This paper presents a novel dead-reckoning protocol that is immune from the speed-hack cheats. We assume the cheater can modify any binary code or game data, e.g. the OS's clock speed, the memory data, the incoming and outgoing packets, etc. However, we will prove that the invulnerability of our protocol does not depend on what the cheater can do and even the cheater can modify the outgoing packets, only very limited advantages can be gained. Since our protocol is based on the conventional dead-reckoning protocol, existing games can easily be modified to become resistant to speed-hack. Our protocol can be adapted to both client-server architecture and P2P architecture in a very similar way.

Backgrounds

Dead-reckoning

In most multi-player online games, before the game starts, a player is able to select among a number of avatars, each having different abilities and characteristics, such as appearance, health point, magic point, speed, etc. When the game begins, or when a player joins an existing game session, the avatar will be given an initial speeding capability. This speeding capability may be different according to which avatar the player has chosen. This speeding capability limits how fast the avatar can move in the virtual world. The avatar can be moving or stationary at any moment during the game, but while it is moving, its speed is fixed. Throughout this paper, we call this speed the *legal speed* of the avatar. The legal speed of the avatar can be changed when the game is in progress. It can be achieved by either gaining enough experience points to upgrade the avatar's abilities or by obtaining special items which will affect the avatar's abilities. In a client-server architecture, the change of an avatar's legal speed needs to be granted by the game server and the game server will broadcast the new legal speed of that avatar to all clients. In a peer-to-peer architecture, the change of an avatar's legal speed needs to be verified by all peers. For example, all peers must agree that the avatar has obtained the specific item successfully and so they will update its legal speed accordingly. Therefore, the change of the legal speed of an avatar works under a tight synchronization requirement.

Synchronization protocols based on dead-reckoning are commonly used in multiplayer online games because they do not require synchronization at every state change. In a game using dead-reckoning, each client sends update packet to the server (in client-server architecture) or to the peers (in peer-to-peer architecture) at a constant interval called timeframe, instead of at each state change. An update packet consists of a timestamp of the game states and a dead-reckoning vector while a dead-reckoning vector consists of the current coordinates and moving direction of the avatar. Using the latest received update packet, each client can predict the movement of another player before the next packet arrives. When a new packet arrives, correction will be made if there is any deviation induced by the prediction. Therefore, players do not maintain strictly synchronized views at every state change. Instead, their views will only be re-synchronized each time when the synchronization takes place.

An important advantage of this loose synchronization is that the rate of graphics rendering at each client side can be made independent to the rate of synchronization. In order to produce smooth display, the graphics should be rendered at a rate no less than 30 frames per seconds (fps). However, synchronization in MMORPGs typically takes place in a much slower rate. This is because synchronization can consume a significant amount of processing power and network bandwidth the server since the number of connected clients are typically in the order of thousands. The situation is even more severe in peer-to-peer games, since IP multicast is still not yet widely available, a peer-to-peer game client may resort to sending separate update packets to every peer. Because of this, synchronizations in MMORPGs typically take place at a rate less than 10 updates per second, i.e. a timeframe of 100 ms. If a client only renders moving objects to their new coordinates each time when an update packet arrives, i.e. it renders the graphics at a rate of 10 fps, the animation will look choppy and jittery, which will definitely destroy the game's playability. However, under dead-reckoning, since prediction is carried out before any newer packet is available, each client can render the movement of objects at the fastest rate which only depends on the processing power of the client machine.

In order to predict an object's movement from its previous game states, simple linear extrapolation can be used. Using the dead-reckoning vector in the last received packet, the client can extrapolate a linear movement from the object's last known coordinates which head towards the last known direction. When a new update packet arrives, the accurate coordinates may be different from the current coordinates predicted by the extrapolation. Algorithms such as [1] and [11] can be used to hide the effect of any extrapolation error emerged in rendering the movements. Under the dead-reckoning protocol with the use of extrapolation, all clients can render the movement of all avatars at the fastest possible rate, which only depends on the computational power of the client side. If an update packet is late on arrival or is even lost, the graphics rendering will still not be affected and therefore smooth gameplay can be ensured.

Linear Extrapolation

We give an example to illustrate a simple linear extrapolation algorithm. Referring to Fig. 2, when a client sends an update packet at time t_1, it is reported that avatar $\mathcal{P}$ is at (x_1, y_1) heading at an angle r. Before the next synchronization scheduled at time t_2 occurs, other clients render $\mathcal{P}$'s movement by linearly extrapolating the position of $\mathcal{P}$ based on $\mathcal{P}$'s dead-reckoning vector sent at time t_1, as follows:

$$\left. \begin{array}{l} x(t) = x_1 + (t - t_1) * \textit{legal speed of } \mathcal{P} * \sin(r) \\ y(t) = y_1 + (t - t_1) * \textit{legal speed of } \mathcal{P} * \cos(r) \end{array} \right\} \text{ for } t \geq t_1$$

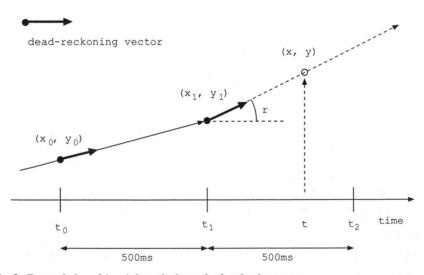

Fig. 2 Extrapolation of (x, y) from the latest dead-reckoning vector

Dead-reckoning protocol provides a means of loose synchronization among players. It is especially necessary when a massive number of concurrent players are interacting with each other. The larger the number of concurrent players the higher the change of having someone's update packet congested or lost in the network. Without dead-reckoning, at the end of each timeframe, all game clients must be halted and wait for update packets from all other players. This will cause significant amount of jitter to the graphics rendering and slow down the response to the player's control, and therefore implies unpleasant gaming experiences. However, by using dead-reckoning protocol, late arrived packets or lost packets can simply be ignored. To fill in the missing packets, extrapolation is used to predict the missing game states, therefore the game clients will never be required to halt at any circumstance.

Speed-hack

Dead-reckoning protocol is popular because of its advantage listed above, that is, all players can have a perception of smooth gameplay even though the underlying communication channel is in fact error-prone, congested and has high delay variance. However, it hints the potential vulnerability to a form of very popular and highly available cheat called *speed-hack*. When using a speed-hack, a cheater can speed up all movements of his/her avatar and thus gain an unfair advantage over other honest players.

A speed-hack essentially speeds up the timing of the cheating game client, and this can be done quite easily, especially under the dead-reckoning protocol. This is due to the fact that most of the game clients depend on a time source, such as software programmable timer or system library calls, to count the time elapsed and then applies it to the Newton's first law of motion to project the movements of moving objects in the virtual world. Here, we illustrate how most online games handle player movement. According to Fig. 3, the avatar is at position p_0 at time t_0. The player moves the avatar by clicking the mouse at the point d_0 in the virtual world. The game client then stores this coordinates into memory and initiates the avatar to

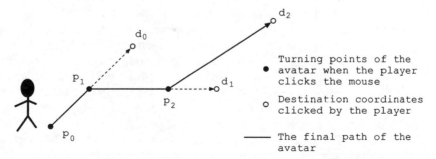

Fig. 3 Movement of an avatar in typical massively multiplayer online games

move towards this destination. However, before the avatar reaches the destination d_0, if the player issues another mouse click at the point d_1 when the avatar is at coordinates p_1 at time t_1, the game client will initiate a new movement towards d_1 from p_1. Similarly, at time t_2, when the player issues another mouse click at d_2 before the avatar reaches d_1, therefore, the avatar will change its direction at p_2 and moves towards d_2. At any time t' after the player issues a destination point d_i at time t_i, but before the avatar reaches there from p_i, the game client will update the avatar's position as follows. Let T_j be the journey time of an avatar,

$$T_j = journey\ time$$
$$= \frac{\sqrt{(x_{d_i} - x_{p_i})^2 + (y_{d_i} - y_{p_i})^2}}{legal\ speed\ of\ the\ avatar}$$

and the computation of the new coordinates will be:

$$x(t) = x_{p_i} + (x_{d_i} - x_{p_i})\frac{t - t_i}{T_j}$$
$$y(t) = y_{p_i} + (y_{d_i} - y_{p_i})\frac{t - t_i}{T_j}$$

In order to speed up a game client, a speed-hack alters its own time source to count time faster, or intercepts the genuine time source and injects a malicious one that counts time faster, i.e. it makes the value of t advances at a faster rate. All local objects in the hacked game client will therefore move faster in the cheater's local view. Under dead-reckoning protocol, the game client simply reports in its update packet about the coordinates of the cheater's avatar computed in the cheater's local view. Upon receiving the cheater's update packet, a client will move the cheater's avatar to that new position as reported in the update packet. Therefore, all players will perceive that the cheater's avatar moves at a faster speed.

Figure 4a and b illustrate the views of two interacting honest players $\mathcal{P}$ and $\mathcal{Q}$ respectively. In the figures, $\mathcal{P}$'s avatar is moving upward while $\mathcal{Q}$'s avatar stays motionless. $\mathcal{P}$ sends two updates at time t_n and t_{n+1} respectively, giving $\mathcal{Q}$ the information to render the two opaque avatars corresponding to $\mathcal{P}$'s position at time t_n and t_{n+1} respectively. However, when rendering $\mathcal{P}$'s position between time t_n and t_{n+1}, where no exact information about $\mathcal{P}$'s position is available, $\mathcal{Q}$ extrapolates it from the position at time t_n to fill in the positions between time t_n and t_{n+1}.

Figure 4c and d illustrate the views of two interacting players $\mathcal{P}$ and $\mathcal{Q}$ respectively, where $\mathcal{P}$ is using a speed-hack. In the figures, $\mathcal{P}$'s avatar is moving upward while $\mathcal{Q}$'s avatar stays motionless. The speed-hack speeds up $\mathcal{P}$'s game client so that $\mathcal{P}$ is able to move at a faster speed and therefore travels farther at time t_{n+1} compared to that in Fig. 4a. When synchronization takes place at t_{n+1}, $\mathcal{P}$'s dead-reckoning vector reports the same position as what $\mathcal{P}$ perceives locally. Therefore $\mathcal{Q}$ updates $\mathcal{P}$'s avatar to that farther position and therefore perceives $\mathcal{P}$'s avatar moving at a faster speed compared to the scenario shown at Fig. 4b.

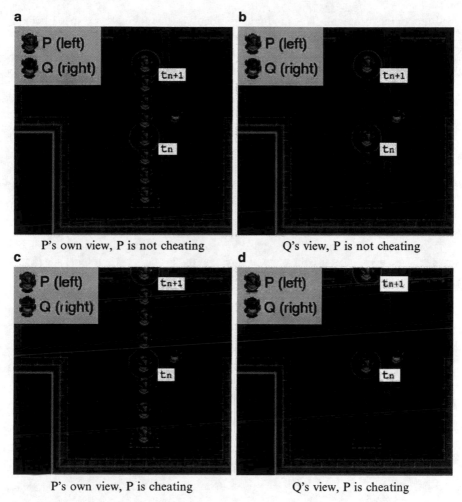

Fig. 4 Overlapped successive frames observed by two interacting players $\mathcal{P}$ (*left*) and $\mathcal{Q}$ (*right*) (**a–d**). Opaque avatars represent accurate positions given by the dead-reckoning vectors. Transparent avatars represent positions predicted by extrapolations

Hack-proof Synchronization Protocol

In this section, we present a dead-reckoning protocol that is invulnerable to speed-hacks. The invulnerable protocol completely preserves the latency-hiding characteristic of conventional dead-reckoning protocol. Extrapolations are still allowed to smooth out the graphics rendering under the enhanced protocol.

We first describe a baseline countermeasure to act against the speed-hack. Inspired by this baseline countermeasure, we can then propose a modified dead-reckoning protocol which is a slightly modified version of the conventional dead-reckoning protocol. The modified protocol is invulnerable to speed-hack; however, it cannot handle some synchronization scenarios which are common in real games. Therefore, we will propose another enhanced version of the invulnerable protocol which is based on the modified protocol but is more sophisticated and is able to handle all possible synchronization scenarios.

Countermeasure

The first countermeasure to act against speed-hack under dead-reckoning protocol is to verify the new coordinates of the avatar during each synchronization before accepting them so as to ensure that the avatar has only moved within a legitimate displacement since the last synchronization.

To verify the new coordinates stated in a dead-reckoning update packet, the server (or the peers) can use the elapsed time and the avatar's current legal speed to compute the maximum possible displacement of the avatar as

$$d_{\max} = (t_i - t_{i-1}) * \text{legal speed}$$

Under this simple approach, a game client can detect if a player is using speed-hack and hence restrict the movement of an avatar within its maximum possible displacement in each timeframe. To illustrate, we should have a look at Fig. 5. The cheater uses a speed-hack so that the avatar's displacement between each synchronization is larger than its maximum possible displacement $d_{\max}$ in the cheater's local view. However, when other clients receive the cheater's update packet, they will compute the displacement of the avatar of the last synchronization as

$$d = \sqrt{(x_i - x_{i-1})^2 + (y_i - y_{i-1})^2}$$

and conclude that

$$d > d_{\max}$$

If d is much greater than $d_{\max}$ in several consecutive timeframes, then obviously the player is using a speed-hack and the server can consider to kick that cheater out of the game. However, sometimes a cheater may only speed up a little bit just to gain an advantage over honest players. A conservative scheme is to accumulate the excess displacements over an extended period of time. For example, if an avatar moves on average 10% faster than its legal speed in a period of 10 s, then the player should be kicked out of the game. To avoid a cheater from gaining enough advantage within the grace period, such as successfully obtaining an important item because he/she moves faster than other honest players, we should limit the actual displacement of an avatar within each timeframe to its maximum value $d_{\max}$, and this is illustrated in Fig. 5.

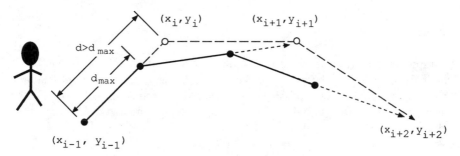

— — — — — Path in cheater's local view

───────── Path perceived by other players
           limited to d $_{max}$ in each timeframe

- - - - - - - ► Direction of the path

Fig. 5 Limiting the displacement of any avatar within its maximum possible value in each time-frame

Referring to the figure, it is seen that when the server (or the peers) verifies that the displacement of a certain avatar is larger than its maximum possible value d_{max}, the avatar's position stated in the update packet will be ignored. Instead, the recipient will compute a restricted position along the same path but with a shortened displacement, by linearly extrapolating from the last synchronized position as follows,

$$x'_i = x_{i-1} + (t_i - t_{i-1}) * \text{legal speed} * \sin(r)$$
$$= x_{i-1} + (t_i - t_{i-1}) * \text{legal speed} * \frac{y_i - y_{i-1}}{\sqrt{(x_i - x_{i-1})^2 + (y_i - y_{i-1})^2}}$$

and

$$y'_i = y_{i-1} + (t_i - t_{i-1}) * \text{legal speed} * \cos(r)$$
$$= y_{i-1} + (t_i - t_{i-1}) * \text{legal speed} * \frac{x_i - x_{i-1}}{\sqrt{(x_i - x_{i-1})^2 + (y_i - y_{i-1})^2}}$$

Invulnerability

The only possible way for a cheater to spoof other players is by tagging a larger timestamp t_i in the latest update packet, resulting in a larger d_{max} for the cheater. However, the exaggeration in t_i is limited by the traveling time of the update packet from the sender to the server (or the peers) which is the network latency. For example, if a game client sends out an update packet at time t_i, and the network latency between it and the server is 20 ms. The server will receive the update packet at time $t_i + 20$ ms and the cheating client cannot replace the timestamp with a value larger than $t + 20$ ms or otherwise it will be detected and the packet may be treated as corrupted and simply being ignored. Moreover, when the next synchronization starts, the corresponding elapsed time will be counted from $t_i + 20$ ms and thus the exaggeration cannot be accumulated over time.

Handling Missing Packets

An important feature of the dead-reckoning protocol is that it allows packet loss. Therefore, the above countermeasure should also preserve this important feature. Assume that there are some missing packets before an update packet arrives with timestamp t_j, we can generalize the maximum displacement $d_{\max}$ used for the verification as

$$d_{\max} = (t_j - t_i) * \text{legal speed},$$

where t_i is the timestamp of the last valid dead-reckoning position received. If the position is verified to be invalid, the recipient will compute a restricted position by the generalized equations as follows,

$$x'_j = x_i + (t_j - t_i) * \text{legal speed} * \sin(r)$$
$$= x_i + (t_j - t_i) * \text{legal speed} * \frac{y_j - y_i}{\sqrt{(x_j - x_i)^2 + (y_j - y_i)^2}}$$

and

$$y'_j = y_i + (t_j - t_i) * \text{legal speed} * \cos(r)$$
$$= y_i + (t_j - t_i) * \text{legal speed} * \frac{x_j - x_i}{\sqrt{(x_j - x_i)^2 + (y_j - y_i)^2}}$$

Modified Dead-reckoning Protocol

Under the above countermeasure, all dead-reckoning vectors in update packets have to be verified at first. If a dead-reckoning position is found to be illegal, additional computation will then be required to adjust the position. In fact, we can modify the protocol so that we can eliminate any client from sending illegal dead-reckoning vectors out in the first place.

Instead of computing the maximum possible displacement and verifying the integrity of the coordinates in each synchronization, we modify the dead-reckoning protocol so that the position vector will not be transmitted directly. Synchronization parameters are computed from the position vectors and a recipient can reveal the position vector from these parameters. The computation of the synchronization parameters and the reverse computation do not depend on the timing of any single machine, but only depend on a global clock. We assume the cheater can modify any binary code or game data, e.g. the OS's clock speed, the memory data, the incoming and outgoing packets, etc. We will show that the cheater can only gain very few advantages under the modified protocol, and the advantages cannot be accumulated over time.

We assume that the game server and all game clients are synchronized to a global clock, the Network Time Protocol (NTP) [14] or similar protocols [18] can be used to achieve this purpose. A client must firstly be synchronized to an appointed NTP time source before joining a game session. Otherwise, the game server will reject the connection if the client's clock differs too much from the server's. During the game, the clients and the server are only required to synchronize with the NTP server at a moderate interval, but their clocks will be incremented locally. The synchronization is only used to ensure that each clock is always kept within an acceptable amount of deviation. Since the clock of an innocent client normally will not diverge from the NTP server significantly within several minutes, a synchronization interval of 1 min is typically sufficient.

Moreover, the invulnerability of our protocol does not depend on the strictly synchronized clocks. Instead, when a client's clock diverges too much from the NTP server, it will generate malicious timestamps in its update packets and the server and other clients will consider it as cheating. However, if the cheater tries to modify the packets to pretend generating correct timestamping, only very limited advantages can be gained under our protocol and the advantages cannot be accumulated over later updates. Therefore, under our protocol, a synchronized clock is not a requirement for the invulnerability but is only necessary for a client to manifest its honesty.

Here we present the details of our modified dead-reckoning protocol. Instead of providing the current coordinates directly in the update packet, several parameters are provided such that the recipients can compute the corresponding avatar's new coordinates accordingly. Attempts to modify these parameters will not give the cheater any advantage. The parameters are the *tangent of angle r*, where r is the angular coordinates of the current dead-reckoning coordinates with respect to the previous dead-reckoning coordinates. The parameter r is transmitted in the update packet in the form of (T_y, T_x) where $\tan(r) = \frac{T_y}{T_x}$. Therefore, we can simply take (T_y, T_x) as the offset from the previous dead-reckoning coordinates to the current dead-reckoning coordinates. Figure 6 shows an example that illustrates the idea. The avatar is at (x_n, y_n) at time t_n. When synchronization takes place at time t_{n+1}, and the avatar has moved to (x_{n+1}, y_{n+1}). The angular coordinates of (x_{n+1}, y_{n+1}) with respect to (x_n, y_n) is 45°. The parameter (T_y, T_x) is given by $(y_{n+1} - y_n, x_{n+1} - x_n)$ or $(1, 1)$, since $tan(45°) = \frac{1}{1}$. Upon receiving this update packet, the server (or the peers) can compute that avatar's new coordinates from (x_n, y_n), the timestamp tagged on the packet and the avatar's current legal speed, as follows:

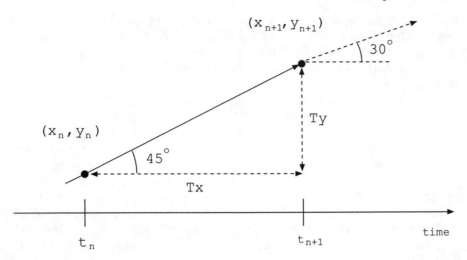

Fig. 6 The parameter (T_y, T_x) and the current direction when synchronization takes place at time t_{n+1}

$$\cos(r) = \frac{x_{n+1} - x_n}{\text{legal speed} * \text{elapsed time}}$$

$$x_{n+1} = x_n + (\text{legal speed} * \text{elapsed time}) * \cos\left(\arctan\left(\frac{T_y}{T_x}\right)\right)$$

and

$$\sin(r) = \frac{y_{n+1} - y_n}{\text{legal speed} * \text{elapsed time}}$$

$$y_{n+1} = y_n + (\text{legal speed} * \text{elapsed time}) * \sin\left(\arctan\left(\frac{T_y}{T_x}\right)\right)$$

Invulnerability

Suppose a cheater wants to gain an advantage by maliciously tagging a larger timestamp on the packet, and he/she intents to produce a farther displacement from the above computations. The exaggeration in the timestamp is limited by the traveling time of the update packet from the sender to the server (or the peers) which is the network latency. Since an over-large timestamp can be detected easily as all machines are synchronized to the same global clock. Moreover, since at each update the elapsed time is computed against the timestamp of the previous update, the exaggerated elapsed time cannot be accumulated over time but will be bounded within only one single-trip latency in general. We will prove it in Section "Proof of Invulnerability".

Extension

If the avatar does not have any movement since the last synchronization, then $(T_y, T_x) = (0, 0)$ can be used to indicate such a special case. However, this simple protocol can only express either completely motionless or completely nonstop movement in the whole timeframe. Every movement must start or stop at the beginning of a timeframe, and then keep moving or motionless until the next timeframe begins. This may be impractical for real games because it impedes the game's responsiveness to player's control. Hence, in the next section we propose an enhanced version of this invulnerable protocol which is more sophisticated in handling various situations.

Handling Missing Packets

The new dead-reckoning protocol still allows late packet arrival. Extrapolation is used to predict the avatar's movement until an update packet arrives, just as it is used in conventional dead-reckoning protocol. However, since the synchronization parameters in each synchronization is based on the previous synchronized position, any lost packets must be re-transmitted or otherwise the path of the avatar's movement cannot be reconstructed. A simple approach can be used to overcome this problem. When there is only a single packet being dropped, i.e. a sending client does not receive any acknowledgment until the next synchronization takes place, the client may simply re-transmit the last parameters along with the new parameters so that the recipient can compute the two latest dead-reckoning positions at once.

If there is more than one packet being dropped, i.e. the sending client does not receive any acknowledgment for several consecutive timeframes, re-transmission of all of the parameters may induce additional loads to the network. In this situation, the protocol have to allow packets to be dropped permanently. To realize it, the sender includes an extra parameter t_{ack} in its update packet, which is the timestamp of the latest acknowledged update packet. For example, in Fig. 7, the sending client does not receive acknowledgments of the synchronizations at t_{n+1} to t_{n+3}. At t_{n+4} the sender computes the synchronization parameters based on the avatar's position at t_n, so that the recipients can determine the corresponding dead-reckoning position based on the position synchronized at t_n. Therefore, all of the parameters in the dropped packets can be ignored.

Enhanced Invulnerable Protocol

In this section, we enhance the above invulnerable protocol so that it becomes more sophisticated and can tolerate malicious timestamping.

In each update packet, a game client sends the current timestamp and three parameters F, R_1 and R_2 to the server (or the peers) as illustrated in Fig. 8. The solid arrowed line represents the actual path taken by avatar $\mathcal{P}$; the two points

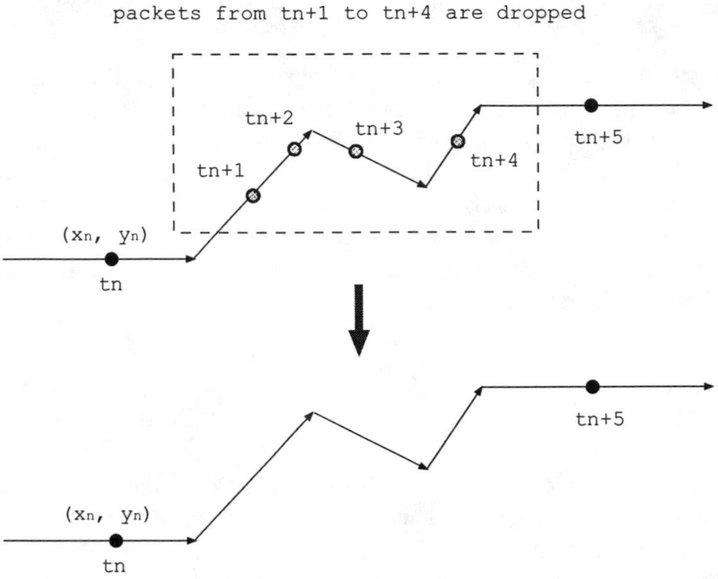

packets from tn+1 to tn+4 are dropped

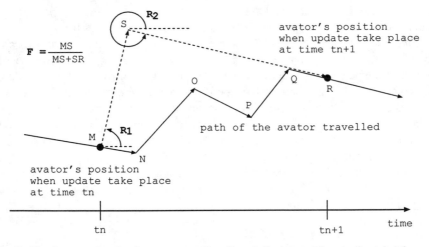

Fig. 7 When more than one packet is dropped, the sender includes an extra parameter $t_{ack} = t_n$ in its update packet and computes the synchronization parameters at t_{n+4} based on the latest synchronized position (x_n, y_n) at t_n

Fig. 8 The three synchronization parameters R_1, R_2 and F when synchronization take places at time t_{n+1}

$M(x_1, y_1)$ and $R(x_2, y_2)$ on the path indicate $\mathcal{P}$'s coordinates when update packets are sent at time t_n and t_{n+1} respectively.

To illustrate how to compute the three parameters for the update packet at time t_{n+1}, we construct a triangle MST as shown in Fig. 9. The line SRT is extended from

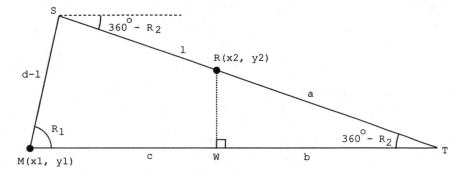

R2 is the current angular velocity
a, b and c can be computed from (x1, y1), (x2, y2) and R2
d is the total displacement of the avator along the path MNOPQR

Fig. 9 Computation of the three parameters in the hack-proof dead-reckoning protocol

the avatar's velocity vector. The line MT is constructed such that the angle included with the line SRT equals to $360° - R_2$, where R_2 is the current direction of $\mathcal{P}$'s movement. Let d be the length of the path $MNOPQR$ taken by $\mathcal{P}$ and the length of the line segment SR be l, we need to find out l such that the total length of the two line segments MS and SR equals to d.

The value of l is given by

$$\cos(\angle STM) = \frac{ST^2 MT^2 - MS^2}{2(ST)(MT)}$$

$$\cos(360° - R_2) = \frac{(l+a)^2 + (b+c)^2 - (d-l)^2}{2(l+a)(b+c)}$$

$$\cos(R_2) = \frac{(l+a)^2 + (b+c)^2 - (d-l)^2}{2(l+a)(b+c)}$$

$$2(l+a)(b+c)\cos(R_2) = l^2 + 2al + a^2 + b^2 + 2bc + c^2 - d^2 + 2dl - l^2$$

$$2l(b+c)\cos(R_2) = 2l(a+d) + (a^2 + b^2 + 2bc + c^2 - d^2)$$
$$-2a(b+c)\cos(R_2)$$

$$2l(b+c)\cos(R_2) - 2l(a+d) = (a^2 + b^2 + 2bc + c^2 - d^2) - 2a(b+c)\cos(R_2)$$

$$2l\{(b+c)\cos(R_2) - (a+d)\} = (a^2 + b^2 + 2bc + c^2 - d^2) - 2a(b+c)\cos(R_2)$$

$$l = \frac{(a^2 + b^2 + 2bc + c^2 - d^2) - 2a(b+c)\cos(R_2)}{2\{(b+c)\cos(R_2) - (a+d)\}}$$

Having l, we can then compute the parameter F by

$$F = \frac{MS}{MS + SR}$$
$$= \frac{d - l}{d}$$

Finally, we can compute R_1 by

$$\frac{MS}{\sin(\angle MTS)} = \frac{ST}{\sin(\angle SMT)}$$
$$\frac{d - l}{\sin(360° - R_2)} = \frac{l + a}{\sin(R_1)}$$
$$\sin(R_1) = \frac{(l + a)\sin(R_2)}{l - d}$$

Working Example. We now use an example to illustrate the computation of the synchronization parameters and illustrate how a server (or the peers) can compute the new coordinates and direction from the received synchronization parameters. Referring to Fig. 10, let $\mathcal{P}$ was at $M(15, 18)$ at time $t_n = 14900$ ms. At time $t_{n+1} = 15000$ ms $\mathcal{P}$ was moved $d = 8$ units to $R(20, 20)$ and was heading at an angle of 315°. The host of $\mathcal{P}$ computes that $R_2 = 315°, c = x_2 - x_1 = 20 - 15 = 5, b = \frac{RW}{\tan 45°} = y_2 - y_1 = 2, a = \frac{b}{\cos 45°} = \sqrt{8}$. Therefore, we get

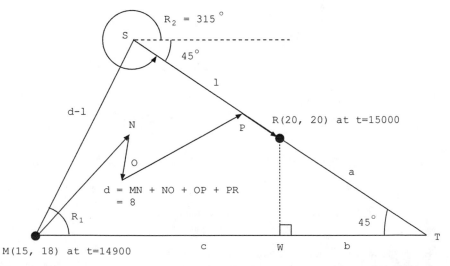

Fig. 10 Working example of the enhanced invulnerable dead-reckoning protocol where the host of $\mathcal{P}$ computes its synchronization parameters

$$l = \frac{(a^2 + b^2 + 2bc + c^2 - d^2) - 2a(b + c)\cos(R_2)}{2\{(b + c)\cos(R_2) - (a + d)\}}$$

$$= \frac{(\sqrt{8}^2 + 2^2 + 2 * 2 * 5 + 5^2 - 8^2) - 2\sqrt{8}(2 + 5)\cos(45°)}{2\{(2 + 5)\cos(45°) - (\sqrt{8} + 8)\}}$$

$$= \frac{(8 + 4 + 20 + 25 - 64) - 2\sqrt{2}(7)\frac{1}{\sqrt{8}}}{2\left\{(7)\frac{1}{\sqrt{8}} - (\sqrt{8} + 8)\right\}}$$

$$= 2.9768589$$

hence

$$F = \frac{d - l}{d} = \frac{8 - 2.9768589}{8}$$
$$= 0.6278926375$$

and

$$\sin(R_1) = \frac{(l + a)\sin(R_2)}{l - d} = \frac{(2.9768589 + \sqrt{8})\sin(45°)}{2.9768589 - 8}$$
$$R_1 = 54.8063918°$$

On receiving the update packet (*timestamp, F, R_1, R_2*), the server (or the peers) computes the elapsed time between $\mathcal{P}$'s two latest synchronizations as $t_{n+1} - t_n = 15000 - 14900 = 100$ ms, and use the legal speed of $\mathcal{P}$, i.e. 0.08 units/ms, to compute that $d = 0.08 * 100 = 8$ units. To illustrate the computation of $\mathcal{P}$'s new co-ordinates, we construct two triangles as shown in Fig. 11. First, the server computes the coordinates of S by

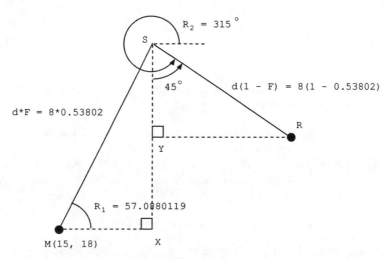

Fig. 11 Working example of the hack-proof dead-reckoning protocol where the server determines $\mathcal{P}$'s coordinates and the direction from $\mathcal{P}$'s synchronization parameters

$$S = (15 + MX, \ 18 + XS)$$
$$= (15 + \cos R_1 * MS, \ 18 + \sin R_1 * MS)$$
$$= (15 + \cos R_1 * (d * F), \ 18 + \sin R_1 * (d * F))$$
$$= (15 + \cos 54.8063918 * 8 * 0.6278926375, \ 18 + \sin 54.8063918 * 8$$
$$*0.6278926375)$$
$$= (17.8950429, \ 22.1049571)$$

and then computes the coordinates of R by

$$R = (17.8950429 + \sin(R_2 - 270°) * SR,$$
$$22.1049571 - \cos(R_2 - 270°) * SR)$$
$$= (17.8950429 + \sin(45°) * d(1 - F),$$
$$22.1049571 - \cos(45°) * d(1 - F))$$
$$= (17.8950429 + \sin(45°) * 8(1 - 0.6278926375),$$
$$22.1049571 - \cos(45°) * 8(1 - 0.6278926375))$$
$$= (20, 20)$$

which is the correct new coordinates of $\mathcal{P}$ at $t = 14900$ ms, and the new direction of $\mathcal{P}$'s movement can be simply given by $R_2 = 315°$.

Handling Missing Packets

The enhanced protocol can handle missing packets in the same way as the modified dead-reckoning protocol. Readers can refer to previous section on "Handling Missing Packets".

Extensions

In this section, we use different scenarios to illustrate some additional issues and how we can extend the protocol to handle these cases.

Scenario 1. Referring to Fig. 12, suppose player $\mathcal{P}$ has moved and stopped occasionally, or has accelerated and decelerated occasionally, between time t_n and t_{n+1} so that the total length of the path $\mathcal{P}$ taken is shorter than the maximum possible displacement if $\mathcal{P}$ moves continuously with its legal speed. We re-define the value of d for a greater generality:

$$d = \text{legal speed of } \mathcal{P} * \text{elapsed time}$$

Therefore, when the host of $\mathcal{P}$ computes its synchronization parameters and when the server (or the peers) computes $\mathcal{P}$'s new coordinates from the

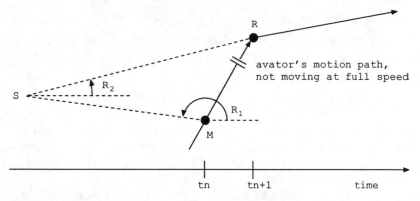

Fig. 12 Player $\mathcal{P}$ has stopped or decelerated occasionally between time t_n and t_{n+1}, therefore the path *MR* taken by $\mathcal{P}$ is shorter than $d = MS + SR$

synchronization parameters, they will always have the same value of d and therefore the correct coordinates of $\mathcal{P}$ can be determined even if $\mathcal{P}$ has stopped or deccelerated occasionally since the last synchronization.

Scenario 2. Suppose player $\mathcal{P}$ has not moved since the last synchronization at time t_n and remains stationary until time t_{n+1}, i.e. the final displacement is zero, but the direction may or may not have changed. In this scenario, the client may simply use $F = 0.5$ and $R_1 = NULL$ to report the server (or the peers) to render no movement in this synchronization. Notice that the synchronization parameter R_2 is still useful in this scenario, because $\mathcal{P}$ may have changed the direction, i.e. it has local motion since time t_n but without having any global motion. The value of R_2 tells other players to render $\mathcal{P}$ turning to the direction given by R_2.

Proof of Invulnerability

Theorem. *Let a cheater be capable of modifying the content of the update packets, the extra displacement that an avatar $\mathcal{P}$ can gain over the whole game session is bounded by*

$$single\text{-}trip\ latency * legal\ speed\ of\ \mathcal{P}.$$

Proof. In Fig. 11, the largest displacement that avatar $\mathcal{P}$ can travel between two successive synchronizations is given by

$$displacement = MS + SR = d * F + d(1 - F) = d$$
$$= legal\ speed\ of\ \mathcal{P} * elapsed\ time.$$

Therefore, the overall displacement that an avatar can travel over the whole game session is bounded by *overall displacement*

$\leq displacement_1 + displacement_2 + \ldots + displacement_n$

$= legal\ speed\ of\ \mathcal{P} * (elapsed\ time_1 + elapsed\ time_2 + \ldots +$

$elapsed\ time_n)$

$= legal\ speed\ of\ \mathcal{P} * \{(t_1 - t_0) + (t_2 - t_1) + \ldots + (t_n - t_{n-1})\}.$

Note that the legal speed of an avatar $\mathcal{P}$ is authorized on either the server side (client-server architecture), or on the peers (P2P architecture), its value only changes when it is granted by the server or agreed by all peers in particular game events. Therefore, its value cannot be spoofed by the cheater.

The only way to spoof a larger elapsed time is to provide a larger timestamp in an update packet. However, a large value of timestamp can be detected easily since all machines are synchronized to the same global clock. Therefore, the exaggeration on the elapsed time is bounded by a single-trip latency from the sender to the recipient where

$$t_{exaggerated} \leq t_{loyal+single\text{-}trip\ latency},$$

or else $t_{exaggerated}$ will be larger than the system time of the recipient when receiving this malicious packet. Moreover, this exaggeration cannot be accumulated since

$$elapsed\ time_n = t_{exaggerated_n} - t_{exaggerated_{n-1}}$$

$$\leq (t_{loyal_n} + single\text{-}trip\ latency) - t_{loyal_{n-1}}$$

$$= t_{loyal_n} - t_{loyal_{n-1}}.$$

That is, when the timestamp in the previous update packet is already exaggerated, the exaggerated timestamp in the current update packet will not be able to produce an enlarged elapsed time again. By induction, the exaggerated timestamp in any later update packets cannot produce any enlarged elapsed time, too. Therefore, the illegal overall displacement is bounded by

illegal overall displacement

$\leq legal\ speed\ of\ \mathcal{P} * \{(t_1 - t_0) + (t_2 - t_1) + \ldots + (t_n + single\text{-}trip$

$latency - t_{n-1})\}$

$= legal\ speed\ of\ \mathcal{P} * (t_n + single\text{-}trip\ latency - t_0)$

$= legal\ speed\ of\ \mathcal{P} * (t_n - t_0) + legal\ speed\ of\ \mathcal{P} * single\text{-}trip\ latency$

$= legal\ displacement + (legal\ speed\ of\ \mathcal{P} * single\text{-}trip\ latency)$

The extra displacement is *legal speed of $\mathcal{P}$ * single-trip latency* and the theorem is hence proved.

Implementation

We have implemented a prototype server and a prototype client to demonstrate the feasibility of our proposed protocol. The prototype server only acts as a broadcaster which forwards dead-reckoning packets to all clients. The prototype client automatically generates random moves continuously and sends out dead-reckoning parameters at an interval of 1 s. Both client and server are coded with Visual C++ using Windows Socket API. We tested our prototype on Windows XP platforms.

All clients are synchronized to the same NTP time server. In our implementation, we used the public NTP server available at stdtime.gov.hk. Each client queries the NTP server at a 30-s interval to ensure that the clocks of all clients are loosely synchronized throughout the whole game session. However, between successive NTP updates, a client increments its time with its local system clock.

Rounding error may occur when a sender converts a position vector to dead-reckoning parameters and when a recipient converts back the parameters to a position vector. Since at each synchronization, the position vector is computed based on the previous one, the errors will accumulate over time. To overcome this, a sender simply runs the same routine used by the recipients with the parameters it sends out, and adjust the position of its local avatar accordingly. The position of the local avatar is hence adjusted with an amount equals to the rounding errors emerged from the computations which is a very small value that will not be noticeable on the rendered graphics. Using this simple scheme, the accumulation of the rounding errors is eliminated.

Figures 13 and 14 shows the rendered paths of two connected clients in a duration of 10 min. The paths are generated by the clients randomly. There is no boundary on the movements (clients can move freely to any direction at every moment), and collision test was omitted (clients may overlap together at the same coordinates). These two requirements are necessary for real games, standard boundary and collision test for conventional dead-reckoning protocol are appropriate for our new protocol; however, missing these details does not disprove the correctness of our protocol.

The thicker lines are the actual paths of the 2 avatars on their local machines respectively. The thinner lines represent the extrapolated paths of non-local avatars. The extrapolated paths are projected from the dead-reckoning vectors computed from the received synchronization parameters. The dead-reckoning vectors are illustrated as dashed lines with circled tails. Only some of the dead-reckoning vectors are displayed on the figures for a clear view of the paths. Figures 15 and 16 zoom into the last 60 s of Figs. 13 and 14 respectively. We can see that the clients are still synchronized correctly after 10 min of simulation.

Speed-hacking on a client is achieved with generic over-clocking software together with a spoofed NTP source. However, doing so produced invalid synchronization parameters which resulted in invalid computation on the recipients. The recipients simply discarded all invalid updates and the cheater was regarded as disconnected.

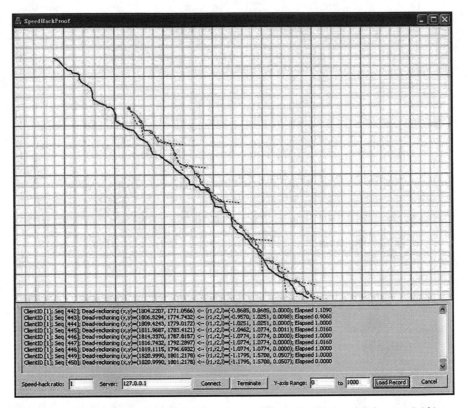

Fig. 13 The path of the local avatar $\mathcal{P}$ (*thicker line*) and the path of the non-local avatar $\mathcal{Q}$ (*thinner line*) rendered on $\mathcal{P}$'s local machine. The *circled tails* represent the dead-reckoning positions computed from the received synchronization parameters and the *dashed lines* represent the directions of the dead-reckoning vectors

Network Overhead

In conventional dead-reckoning protocol, the exchange of location information requires four parameters: x-coordinate, y-coordinate, angle, and the timestamp. Typically, a game divides the whole map into smaller areas called zones. Assuming a two-bytes integer is used for a single coordinate, a floating point number for the angle in radian, and a double precision timestamp, the total payload for the location information is therefore

$$2 + 2 + 4 + 8 = 16 bytes.$$

In our proposed protocol, the required synchronization parameters F, R_1, R_2 and the timestamp requires four double precision numbers implies a total of 32 bytes. Since 25 frame-per-second or above is enough for a fluent video display, we assume 25 synchronizations per second (in practical 5–10 is usually enough) concurrently

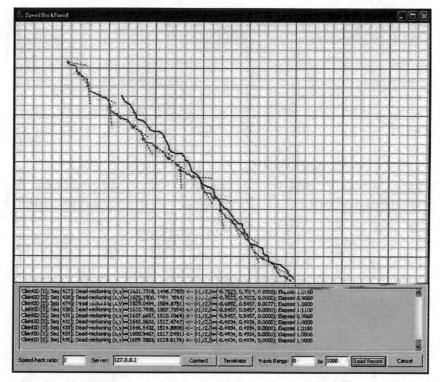

Fig. 14 The path of the local avatar Q (*thicker line*) and the path of the non-local avatar P (*thinner line*) rendered on Q's local machine. The *circled tails* represent the dead-reckoning positions computed from the received synchronization parameters and the *dashed lines* represent the directions of the dead-reckoning vectors

which implies a total overhead of

$$(32 - 16)25 = 400bps$$

which is a small value compares to the 40 Kbps average bandwidth requirement for some commercial multiplayer online games [8]. Therefore, we expect the overhead of our protocol will not induce significant impact on the network traffic.

Related Works

In [4], the authors proposed the use of runtime verification to verify game codes. This approach mainly targets on cheats that exploit implementation bugs. But this approach is not applicable to cheats that involve modification of client code loading into the memory at runtime. Where most speed-hacks fall into the category of runtime cheats.

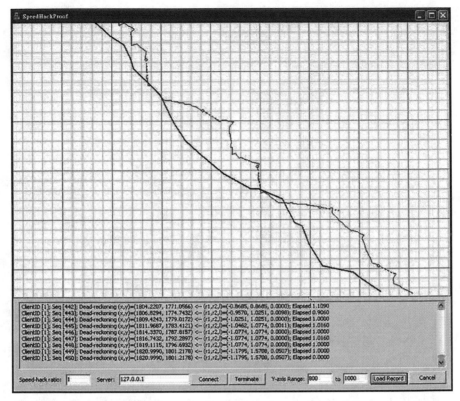

Fig. 15 The path of the local avatar $\mathcal{P}$ (*thicker line*) and the path of the non-local avatar $\mathcal{Q}$ (*thinner line*) rendered on $\mathcal{P}$'s local machine which zoomed into the last 60 s

PunkBuster [7] is the first client-side cheat prevention system for commercial online games. HLGuard [20], formerly called CSGuard, is a free server-side anti-cheat system for a famous commercial FPS game, Half-Life, and many variations of Half-Life. Besides PunkBuster and HLGuard, there are a few other commercial anti-cheating software [21]. Basically, they are pattern scanners that scan for known cheats in the client machine. The anti-cheating software must be kept up-to-date from time to time since new cheats exist frequently. Cheating still cannot be completely prevented and these anti-cheating software themselves are also vulnerable to hacks.

In [2], the authors describe a type of cheat called *suppress-correct cheat* and propose a cheat-proof protocol that resists this type of cheat. Suppose a cheater S uses the suppress-correct cheat and S purposefully drops n packets while receiving n packets from each of other players, other players will be forced to extrapolate the movement of S for n timeframes but cannot confirm where S really is. S then can construct the $n + 1$th packet based on the knowledge of the previous n timeframes and it provides him with some advantages. To eliminate suppress-correct cheat, the authors propose a synchronization technique called asynchronous syn-

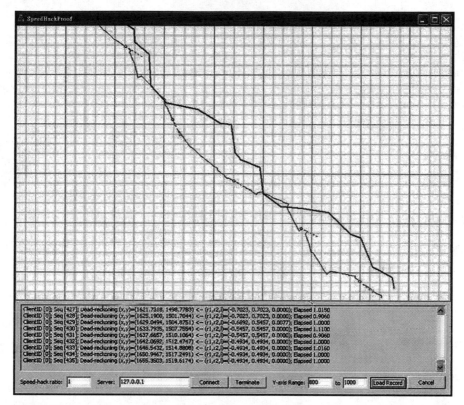

Fig. 16 The path of the local avatar Q (*thicker line*) and the path of the non-local avatar P (*thinner line*) rendered on Q's local machine which zoomed into the last 60 s

chronization (AS). Using AS, each host advances in time asynchronously from the other players but enters into the lockstep mode when interaction occurs. When entering the lockstep mode, in every timeframe t each involved player must wait for all packets from other players before advancing to timeframe $t + 1$. Because this is a stop-and-wait protocol, extrapolation cannot be used to smooth out any delay caused by the network latency.

In [12], the authors improve the performance of the lockstep protocol by adding pipelines. Extrapolation is still not allowed under the pipelined lockstep protocol. Therefore, if there is an increased network latency and packets are delayed, the game will be stalled.

In [10], the authors propose a sliding pipeline protocol that dynamically adjusts the pipeline depth to reflect current network conditions. The authors also introduce a send buffer to hold the commands generated while the size of the pipeline is adjusted. The sliding pipeline protocol allows extrapolation to smooth out jitters.

Although these protocols are designed to defend against the suppress-correct cheat, it can also prevent speed-hacks when entering into the lock-step mode because players are forced to synchronize within a bounded amount of timeframes.

However, speed-hack can still be effective when lock-step mode is not activated. And since these protocols do not allow packets to be dropped, any lost packet must be retransmitted until they are finally sent and acknowledged. Therefore, the minimum timeframe of the game cannot be shorter than the maximum latency of the player with the slowest connection and all clients must run the game at a speed that even the slowest client can support. Furthermore, any sudden increase in the latency will cause jitters to all players.

Our protocol does not incur any lock-step requirement to game clients while the advantage of loose synchronization in conventional dead-reckoning protocol is completely preserved. Thus, smooth gameplay can be ensured. As we have proved in Section "Proof of Invulnerability", a cheater can only cheat by generating malicious timestamps and it can be detected easily and immediately. Therefore, the speed-hack invulnerability of our protocol will be enforced throughout the whole game session so that any action of cheating can be detected immediately.

Moreover, the AS protocol requires a game client to enter the lock-step mode when interaction occurs which requires a major modification of the client code to realize it. However, existing games can be modified easily to adapt our proposed protocol. One can simply add a plugin routine to convert a dead-reckoning vector to the synchronization parameters before sending out the update packets, and add another plugin routine to convert back the synchronization parameters to a dead-reckoning vector on receiving the packets.

The *NEO* protocol [13] is based on [2], the authors describe five forms of cheating and claim that the *NEO* protocol can prevent these cheating.

In [17], the authors show that for the five forms of cheating [13] designed to prevent, it prevents only three. They propose another Secure Event Agreement (*SEA*) protocol that prevents all five forms of cheating which the performance is at worst equal to *NEO* and in some cases better.

In [19], the authors show that both *NEO* and *SEA* suffer from the *undo* cheat. Let P_H denote an honest player and P_C denote a cheater, and M_H, K_H and M_C, K_C represent the message and its key from P_H and P_C respectively. The cheater P_C performs the undo cheat as follows: both players send their encrypted game moves (M_H and M_C) normally in the commit phase. Then, P_H sends key K_H in the reveal phase. However, P_C delays K_C until K_H is received and M_H is revealed. If P_C find that M_C is poor against M_H, P_C will purposely drop K_C and therefore undoing the move M_C. The authors then propose another anti-cheat scheme for P2P games called *RACS* which relies on the existence of a trusted *referee*. The referee is responsible for T1 - receiving player updates, T2 - simulating game play, T3 - validating and resolving conflicts in the simulation, T4 - disseminating updates to clients and T5 - storing the current game state.

The *referee* used in *RACS* works very likely to a traditional game server in conventional client-server architecture. The security of *RACS* completely depends on the referee. For example, speed-hack can be prevented with validating every state updates by the referee. Although *RACS* is more scalable than client-server architecture, it suffers from the same problem that the involvement of a trusted third party is required.

Conclusion

In this paper, we presented a synchronization protocol for multi-player online games that support dead-reckoning. Meanwhile, it is invulnerable to a very common type of cheat called speed-hack. The general idea is that the server or peer players can use the legal speed of an avatar to compute its position from a set of update parameters. This eliminates the need to state the avatar's position directly in the update packets. Even if the cheater is able to modify the data in the update packets, the cheater cannot spoof other players to render a faster moving avatar because the displacement an avatar can travel is now bounded by the legal speed of the player that is authorized by the server (in client-server architecture) or among all peers (in P2P architecture). We have used various examples to illustrate our protocol and proved the security feature of our proposal. We have carried out simulations to demonstrate the feasibility of our protocol.

References

1. Banavar H, Aggarwal S, Khandelwal A (2004) Accuracy in dead-reckoning based distributed multi-player games. In: Proceedings of NetGames 2004, Portland, August 2004, pp 161–165
2. Baughman NE, Levine BN (2001) Cheat-proof playout for centralized and distributed online games. In: Proceedings of IEEE INFOCOM. IEEE, Piscataway, pp 104–113
3. Counter Hack (2007) Types of Hacks. http://wiki.counter-hack.net/CategoryGeneralInfo
4. DeLap M et al (2004) Is runtime verification applicable to cheat detection. In: Proceedings of NetGames 2004, Portland, August 2004, pp 134–138
5. Diot C, Gautier L (1999) A distributed architecture for multiplayer interactive applications on the internet. In: IEEE Networks magazine, Jul–Aug 1999
6. Diot C, Gautier L, Kurose J (1999) End-to-end transmission control mechanisms for multiparty interactive applications on the internet. In: Proceedings of IEEE INFOCOM, IEEE, Piscataway
7. Even Balance (2007) Official PunkBuster website. http://www.evenbalance.com
8. Feng WC, Feng WC, Chang F, Walpole J (2005) A traffic characterization of popular online games. IEEE/ACM Trans Netw 13(3):488–500
9. Gautier L, Diot C (1998) Design and evaluation of mimaze, a multiplayer game on the Internet. In: Proceedings of IEEE Multimedia (ICMCS'98). IEEE, Piscataway
10. Jamin S, Cronin E, Filstrup B (2003) Cheat-proofing dead reckoned multiplayer games (extended abstract). In: Proc. of 2nd international conference on application and development of computer games, Hong Kong, 6–7 January 2003
11. Lee FW, Li L, Lau R (2006) A trajectory-preserving synchronization method for collaborative visualization. IEEE Trans Vis Comput Graph 12:989–996 (special issue on IEEE Visualization'06)
12. Lenker S, Lee H, Kozlowski E, Jamin S (2002) Synchronization and cheat-proofing protocol for real-time multiplayer games. In: International Worshop on Entertainment Computing, Makuhari, May 2002
13. Lo V, GauthierDickey C, Zappala D, Marr J (2004) Low latency and cheatproof event ordering for peer-to-peer games. In: ACM NOSSDAV'04, Kinsale, June 2004
14. Mills DL (1992) Network time protocol (version 3) specification, implmentation and analysis. In: RFC-1305, March 1992
15. MPC Forums (2007) Multi-Player Cheats. http://www.mpcforum.com
16. Pantel L, Wolf L (2002) On the impact of delay on real-time multiplayer games. In: ACM

NOSSDAV'02, Miami Beach, May 2002

17. Schachte P, Corman AB, Douglas S, Teague V (2006) A secure event agreement (sea) protocol for peer-to-peer games. In: Proceedings of ARES'06, Vienna, 20–22 April 2006, pp 34–41
18. Simpson ZB (2008) A stream based time synchronization technique for networked computer games. http://www.mine-control.com/zack/timesync/timesync.html
19. Soh S, Webb S, Lau W (2007) Racs: a referee anti-cheat scheme for p2p gaming. In: Proceedings of NOSSDAV'07, Urbana-Champaign, 4–5 June 2007, pp 34–42
20. The Z Project (2007) Official HLGuard website. http://www.thezproject.org
21. Wikipedia (2007) Category: Anti-cheat software. http://en.wikipedia.org/wiki/Category:Anti-cheat_software

Chapter 12
Collaborative Movie Annotation

Damon Daylamani Zad and Harry Agius

Introduction

Web 2.0 has enjoyed great success over the past few years by providing users with a rich application experience through the reuse and amalgamation of different Web services. For example, YouTube integrates video streaming and forum technologies with Ajax to support video-based communities. Online communities and social networks such as these lie at the heart of Web 2.0. However, while the use of Web 2.0 to support collaboration is becoming common in areas such as online learning [1], operating systems coding [2], e-government [3], and filtering [4], there has been very little research into the use of Web 2.0 to support multimedia-based collaboration [5], and very little understanding of how users behave when undertaking multimedia content-based activities collaboratively, such as content analysis, semantic content classification, annotation, and so forth. At the same time, spurred on by falling resource costs which have reduced limits on how much content users can upload, online communities and social networking sites have grown rapidly in popularity and with this growth has come an increase in the production and sharing of multimedia content between members of the community, particularly users' self-created content, such as song recordings, home movies, and photos. This makes it even more imperative to understand user behaviour.

In this paper, we focus on metadata for self-created movies like those found on YouTube and Google Video, the duration of which are increasing in line with falling upload restrictions. While simple tags may have been sufficient for most purposes for traditionally very short video footage that contains a relatively small amount of semantic content, this is not the case for movies of longer duration which embody more intricate semantics. Creating metadata is a time-consuming process that takes a great deal of individual effort; however, this effort can be greatly reduced by harnessing the power of Web 2.0 communities to create, update and maintain it.

D.D. Zad and H. Agius (✉)
School of Information Systems, Computing and Mathematics, Brunel University,
Uxbridge, Middlesex, UK
e-mail: damon.zad@brunel.ac.uk; harryagius@acm.org

B. Furht (ed.), *Handbook of Multimedia for Digital Entertainment and Arts,*
DOI 10.1007/978-0-387-89024-1_12, © Springer Science+Business Media, LLC 2009

Consequently, we consider the annotation of movies within Web 2.0 environments, such that users create and share that metadata collaboratively and propose an architecture for collaborative movie annotation. This architecture arises from the results of an empirical experiment where metadata creation tools, YouTube and an MPEG-7 modelling tool, were used by users to create movie metadata. The next section discusses related work in the areas of collaborative retrieval and tagging. Then, we describe the experiments that were undertaken on a sample of 50 users. Next, the results are presented which provide some insight into how users interact with existing tools and systems for annotating movies. Based on these results, the paper then develops an architecture for collaborative movie annotation.

Collaborative Retrieval and Tagging

We now consider research in collaborative retrieval and tagging within three areas: research that centres on a community-based approach to data retrieval or data ranking, collaborative tagging of non-video files, and collaborative tagging of videos. The research in each of these areas is trying to simplify and reduce the size of a vast problem by using collaboration among members of a community. This idea lies at the heart of the architecture presented in this paper.

Collaborative Retrieval

Retrieval is a core focus of contemporary systems, particularly Web-based multimedia systems. To improve retrieval results, a body of research has focused on adopting the collaborative approach of social networks. One area in which collaboration has proven beneficial is that of reputation-based retrieval, where retrieval results are weighted according to the reputation of the sources. This approach is employed by Chen et al. [4] who propose adaptive community-based multimedia retrieval using an agent reputation model that is based on social network analysis methods. Sub-group analysis is conducted for better support of collaborative ranking and community-based search. In social network analysis, relational data is represented using 'sociograms' (directed and weighted graphs), where each participant is represented as a node and each relation is represented as an edge. The value of a node represents an importance factor that forms the corresponding participant's reputation. Peers who have higher reputations should affect other peers' reputations to a greater extent, therefore the quality of data retrieval of each peer database can be significantly different. The quality of the data stored in them can also be different. Therefore, the returned results are weighted according to the reputations of the sources. Communities of peers are created through clustering.

Koru [6] is a search engine that exploits Web 2.0 collaboration in order to provide knowledge bases automatically, by replacing professional experts with thousands or even millions of amateur contributors. One example is Wikipedia, which can be directly exploited to provide manually-defined yet inexpensive knowledge bases, specifically tailored to expose the topics, terminology and semantics of individual document collections. Koru is evaluated according to how well it assists real users in performing realistic and practical information retrieval tasks.

Collaboration in filtering is common. For example, Chen et al. [7] provide a framework for collaborative filtering that circumvents the problems of traditional memory-based and model-based approaches by applying orthogonal nonnegative matrix tri-factorization (ONMTF). Their algorithm first applies ONMTF to simultaneously cluster the rows and columns of the user-item matrix, and then adopts the user-based and item-based clustering approaches respectively to attain individual predictions for an unknown test rating. Finally, these ratings are fused with a linear combination. Simultaneously clustering users and items improves on the scalability problem of such systems, while fusing user-based and item-based approaches can improve performance further. As another example, Yang and Li [8] propose a collaborative filtering approach based on heuristic formulated inferences. This is based on the fact that any two users may have some common interest genres as well as different ones. Their approach introduces a more reasonable similarity measure metric, considers users' preferences and rating patterns, and promotes rational individual prediction, thus more comprehensively measuring the relevance between user and item. Their results demonstrate that the proposed approach improves the prediction quality significantly over several other popular methods.

Collaborative Tagging of Non-Video Media

Collaborative tagging has been used to create metadata and semantics for different media. In this section, we review some examples of research concerning collaborative tagging of non-video media. SweetWiki [9] revisits the design rationale of wikis, taking into account the wealth of new Web standards available, such as for the wiki page format (XHTML), for the macros included in pages (JSPX/XML tags), for the semantic annotations (RDFa, RDF), and for the ontologies it manipulates (OWL Lite). SweetWiki improves access to information with faceted navigation, enhanced search tools and awareness capabilities, and acquaintance networks identification. It also provides a single WYSIWYG editor for both metadata and content editing, with assisted annotation tools (auto-completion and checkers for embedded queries or annotations). SweetWiki allows metadata to be extracted and exploited externally.

There is a growing body of research regarding the collaborative tagging of photos. An important impetus for this is the popularity of photo sharing sites such as Flickr. Flickr groups are increasingly used to facilitate the explicit definition of communities sharing common interests, which translates into large amounts of content (e.g. pictures and associated tags) about specific subjects [10]. The users of Flickr have created a vast amount of metadata on pictures and photos. This large number of images has been carefully annotated for the obvious reason they were accessible to all users and therefore the collaboration of these users has resulted in producing an impossible amount of metadata that is not perceivable without such collaboration. Zonetag [11] is a prototype mobile application that uploads camera phone photos to Flickr and assist users with context-based tag suggestions derived from multiple sources. A key source of suggestions is the collaborative tagging activity on Flickr, based on the user's own tagging history and the tags associated with the location of the user. Combining these two sources, a prioritized suggested tag list is generated. They use several heuristics that take into account the tags' social and temporal context, and other measures that weight the tag frequency to create a final score. These heuristics are spatial, social and temporal characteristics; they gather all tags used in a certain location regardless of the exact location, tags the users themselves applied in a given context are more likely to apply to their current photo than tags used by others, and finally tags are more likely to apply to a photo if they have been used recently. CONFOTO [12] is a browsing and annotation service for conference photos which exploits sharing and collaborative tagging through RDF (Resource Description Framework) to gain advantages like unrestricted aggregation and ontology re-use. Finally, Bentley et al. [13] performed two separate experiments: one asking users to socially share and tag their personal photos and one asking users to share and tag their purchased music. They discovered multiple similarities between the two in terms of how users interacted and annotated the media, which have implications for the design of future music and photo applications.

Collaborative Tagging of Video Media

We now review some examples of research concerning collaborative tagging of video media. Yamamoto et al. [14] present an approach for video scene annotation based on social activities associated with the content of video clips on the Web. This approach has been demonstrated through assisting users of online forums associate video scenes with user comments and through assisting users of Weblog communications generate entries that quote video scenes. The system extracts deep-content-related information about video contents as annotations automatically, allowing users to view any video, submit and view comments about any scene, and edit a Weblog entry to quote scenes using an ordinary Web browser. These user comments and the links between comments and video scenes are stored in annotation databases. An annotation analysis block produces tags from the accumulated annotations, while an application block has a tag-based, scene-retrieval system.

IBM's Efficient Video Annotation (EVA) system [15] is a server-based tool for semantic concept annotation of large video and image collections, optimised for collaborative annotation. It includes features such as workload sharing and support in conducting inter-annotator analysis. Aggregate-level user data may be collected during annotation, such as time spent on each page, number and size of thumbnails, and statistics about the usage of keyboard and mouse. EVA returns visual feedback on the annotation. Annotation progress is displayed for the given concept during annotation and overall progress is displayed on the start page.

Ulges et al. [16] present a system that automatically tags videos by detecting high-level semantic concepts, such as objects or actions. They use videos from on-line portals like YouTube as a source of training data, while tags provided by users during upload serve as ground truth annotations.

Elliot and Ozsoyoglu [17] present a system that shows how semantic metadata about social networks and family relationships can be used to improve semantic annotation suggestions. This includes up to 82% recall for people annotations as well as recall improvements of 20-26% in tag annotation recall when no anno-tation history is available. In addition, utilising relationships among people while searching can provide at least 28% higher recall and 55% higher precision than keyword search while still being up to 12 times faster. Their approach to speed-ing up the annotation process is to build a real-time suggestion system that uses the available multimedia object metadata such as captions, time, an incomplete set of related concepts, and additional semantic knowledge such as people and their relationships.

Finally, Li and Lu [18] suggest that there are five major methods for collaborative tagging and all systems and applications fit into one of these five categories:

- *Ontology approaches:* FolksAnnotation, a system that extracts tags from del.ici.ous and maps them to various ontology concepts, has helped to demon-strate that semantics can be derived from tags. However, before any ontological mapping can occur, the vocabulary usually must be converted to a consistent format for string comparison.
- *Statistical and pattern approaches:* These approaches allow researchers to control and manipulate inconsistency and ambiguity in collaborative tagging. Statistical and pattern methodologies work well in general Internet indexing and searching, such as Google's PageRank or Amazon's collaborative filtering system.
- *Social network approaches:* These approaches attempt to incorporate social net-work knowledge into collaborative tagging to improve the understanding of tag behaviours.
- *Visualization approaches*: Some researchers have incorporated the help of visu-alization, such as showing a navigation map or displaying the social network relations of the users.
- *User consensus formation approaches:* These approaches focus on the incon-sistency and ambiguity issues associated with collaborative tagging which stem from a lack of user consensus. Prominent applications, such as those offered by Wikipedia that ask users to contribute more extensive information than tags, have placed more focus on this issue. Given the complexity of the content being con-tributed, collaborative control and consensus formation is vital to the usability of a wiki and is driving extensive research.

Summary

This section considered example research related to collaborative retrieval and tagging. There is a great deal of research focused on retrieval that exploits user collaboration to improve results. Mostly, user activity is utilised rather than information explicitly contributed or annotated; consequently, there tends to be less useful, general purpose metadata produced that could be exploited by other systems. There is also a rising amount of research being carried out on collaborative annotation of non-video media, especially photos, spurred on by websites such as Flickr and del.icio.us. Such sites provide the means for users to collaborate within a community to produce extensive and comprehensive annotations. However, the static nature of the media makes it less complicated and time-consuming to annotate than video, where there are a much greater number of semantic elements to consider which can be intricately interconnected due to temporality. There is far less understanding of how users behave collaboratively when annotating video; consequently, a body of research is starting to emerge here, some examples of which were reviewed above, where user comments in blogs and other Web resources, tags in YouTube, sample data sets, and power user annotations have been the source for annotating the videos. Since the majority of systems rely on automatic annotation or manual annotation from power users, the power of collaboration from more typical 'everyday' users, who are far greater in number, to tackle this enormous amount of data is underexplored. As a result, we undertook an experiment with a number of everyday users in order to ascertain their typical behaviour and preferences when annotating video, in particular, when annotating user-created movies (e.g. those found on sites like YouTube). The experiment design and results are described in the following sections.

Experiment Design

In order to better understand how users collaborate when annotating movies, we undertook an experiment with 50 users. This experiment is now described and the results presented in the subsequent section.

Users were asked to undertake a series of tasks using two existing video metadata tools and their interactions were tracked. The users were chosen from a diverse population in order to produce results from typical users similar to the ZoneTag [11] average user approach. The users were unsupervised, but were communicating with other users via an instant messaging application, e.g. Windows Live Messenger, so that transcripts of all conversations could be recorded for later analysis. These transcripts contain important information about the behaviour of users in a collaborative community and contain metadata information if they are considered as comments on the videos. This is similar to the approach of Yamamoto et al. [14] who tried to utilise user comments and blog entries as sources for annotations. Users were also interviewed after they completed all tasks.

Video Metadata Tools and Content

The two video metadata tools used during the experiment were:

- *YouTube:* This tool provides a community for sharing video content on the Web. YouTube enables users to upload their videos, set age ratings for the videos, enter a description of the video, and also enter keywords.
- *COSMOSIS:* This system provides the means for more advanced content-based annotation with MPEG-7. With this system, users can model video content and define the semantics of their content such as objects, events, temporal relations and spatial relations [19, 20].

The video content used in the experiment was categorised according to the most popular types of self-created movies found on sites such as YouTube and Google Video. The categories were as follows:

- *Personal content:* This type of content is personal to users, e.g. videos of family, friends and work colleagues. Content is typically based around the people, occasion or location.
- *Business content:* This type of content has been created and is used for commercial purposes. It mainly includes videos created for advertising and promotion, such as video virals.
- *Academic content:* This type of content serves academic purposes, e.g. teaching and learning or research.
- *Recreational content:* This type of content has been created and is used for purposes other than personal, business or academic, such as faith, hobbies, amusement or filling free time.

In addition, the video content exhibits certain content features. We consider the key content features in this experiment as follows:

- *Objects:* People, animals, inanimate objects, and properties of these objects.
- *Events:* Visual or aural occurrences within the video, e.g. a car chase, a fight, an explosion, a gunshot, a type of music. Aural occurrences include music, noises and conversations.
- *Relationships:* Temporal, spatial, causer (causes another event or object to occur), user (uses another object or event), part (is part of another object or event), specialises (a sub-classification of an object or event), and location (occurs or is present in a certain location).

The video content used in the experiment was chosen for its ability to richly exhibit one or more of these features within one or more of the above content categories. Each segment of video contained one or more of these features but was rich in a particular category, e.g. one video might be people-rich while another is noise-rich. In this way, all the features are present throughout the entire experiment and participants' responses and modelling preferences, when presented with audiovisual content that includes these features, can be discovered.

User Groups and Tasks

Users were given a series of tasks, requiring them to tag and model the content of the video using the tools above. Users were assigned to groups (12-13 per group), one for each of the four different content categories above, but were not informed of this. Within these category groups, users worked together in smaller experiment groups of 3-6 users to ease the logistics of all users in the group collaborating together at the same time. Members of the same group were instructed to communicate with other group members while they were undertaking the tasks, using an instant messaging application, e.g. Windows Live Messenger. The collaborative communication transcripts were returned for analysis using grounded theory [21]. Consequently, group membership took into account user common interests and backgrounds since this was likely to increase the richness and frequency of the communication. The importance of user communication during the experiment was stressed to users.

The four user category groups were given slightly different goals as a result of differences between the categories. The personal category group (Group 1) was asked to use their own videos, the business category group (Group 2) was provided with business-oriented videos, the academic category group (Group 3) was provided with videos of an academic nature, and the recreational category group (Group 4) were provided with a set of recreational videos. The videos for each category group differed in which features they were rich in, with other features also exhibited. Table 1 summarises the relationships between the content categories, user category groups and content rich features.

Each user was required to tag and model the content of 3-5 mins worth of videos in YouTube and COSMOSIS. This could be one 5 min long video or a number of

Table 1 Mapping of content categories to user category groups to content features

	Content Category: User Category Group:	Personal 1	Business 2	Academic 3	Recreation 4
Content Features	People	X	X	X	X
	Animals	X	X	X	X
	Inanimate Objects	X	X	X	X
	Properties	X	X	X	X
	Events	X	X	X	X
	Music	X			X
	Noise	X		X	X
	Conversation		X		X
	Temporal Relations			X	
	Spatial Relations	X		X	
	Causer Relations			X	X
	User Relations		X	X	
	Part Relations		X	X	X
	Specialises Relations		X	X	
	Location Relations	X			X

videos that together totalled 5 mins. This ensured that users need not take more than about 15 mins to complete the tasks, since more time than this would greatly discourage them from participating, either initially or in completing all tasks. At the same time, the video duration is sufficient to accommodate meaningful semantics. Users did not have to complete all the tasks in one session and were given a two week period to do so. YouTube tags, COSMOSIS metadata and collaborative communication transcripts were collected post experiment.

After the users had undertaken the required tasks, a short, semi-structured interview was performed with each user. The focus of the interviews was on the users' experiences with, and opinions regarding, the tools.

Experiment Results

This section presents the results from the experiment described in the above section. The experiment produced three types of data from four different sources: the metadata from tagging videos in YouTube, the MPEG-7 metadata created by COSMOSIS, the collaborative communication transcripts, and the interview transcripts. The vast amount of textual data generated by these sources called for the usc of a suitable qualitative research method to enable a thorough but manageable analysis of all the data to be performed.

Research Method: Grounded Theory

A grounded theory is defined as theory which has been "systematically obtained through social rescarch and is grounded in data" [22]. Grounded theory methodology is comprised of systematic techniques for the collection and analysis of data, exploring ideas and concepts that emerge through analytical writing [23]. Grounded theorists develop concepts directly from data through its simultaneous collection and analysis [24]. The process of using this method starts with *open coding* which includes theoretical comparison and constant comparison of the data, up to the point where conceptual saturation is reached. This provides the *concepts*, otherwise known as *codes*, that will build the means to tag the data in order to properly *memo* it and thus provide meaningful data (dimensions, properties, relationships) to form a theory. Conceptual saturation is reached when no more codes can be assigned to the data and all the data can be categorised under one of the codes already available, with no room for more codes. In our approach, we include an additional visualisation stage after memoing in order to assist with the analysis and deduction of the grounded theory. Figure 1 illustrates the steps taken in our data analysis approach.

As can be seen in the figure, the MPEG-7 metadata and the metadata gathered from YouTube tagging, along with the collaborative communication transcripts and

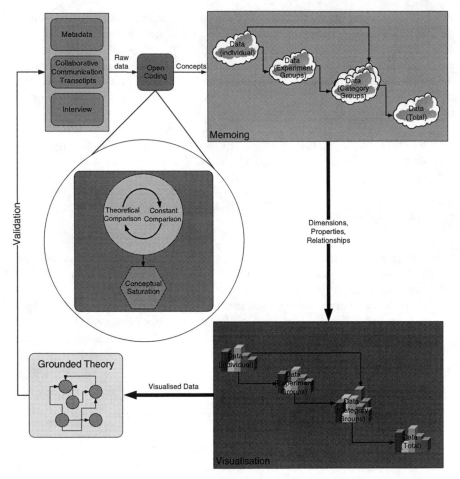

Fig. 1 Grounded theory as applied to the collected data in this experiment

interviews, form the basis of the open coding process. The memoing process is then performed on a number of levels. The process commences on the individual level where all the data from the individual users is processed independently. Then the data from users within the same experiment group are memoed. Following this, the data for entire user category groups is considered (personal, academic, business and recreational) so that the data from all the users who were assigned to the same category are memoed together to allow further groupings to emerge. Finally, all the collected data is considered as a whole. All of the dimensions, properties and relationships that emerge from these four memoing stages are then combined together and visualised. Finally, the visualised data is analysed to provide a grounded theory concerning movie content metadata creation and system feature requirements.

The most important results are presented in the following two sub-sections and are then used to form the basis of an architecture for a collaborative movie annotation system.

Movie Content Metadata Creation

This section presents the key metadata results from the grounded theory approach. We first consider the most commonly used tags; then we discuss the relationships between the tags.

Most Commonly Used Tags

According to Li and Lu [18], recognising the most common tags used by different users when modelling a video can assist with combining the ontology approach with the social networking approach (described earlier) when designing a collaborative annotation system. Our results indicate that there were some inconsiderable differences in the use of tags for movies in different content categories and that, overall, the popularity of tags remains fairly consistent irrespective of these categories. Figure 2 to Figure 5 represent the visualisation of the tags used in YouTube in different categories and show all of the popular tags. The four most commonly used tags in YouTube concerned:

1. inanimate objects
2. events
3. people
4. locations

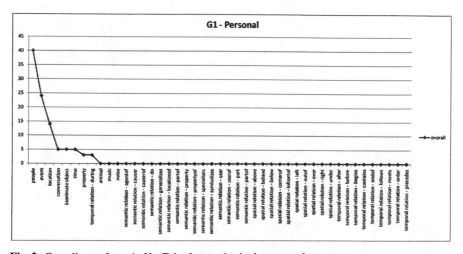

Fig. 2 Overall use of tags in YouTube for movies in the personal category

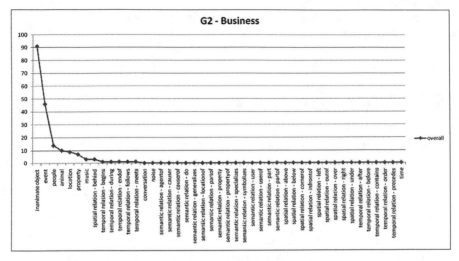

Fig. 3 Overall use of tags in YouTube for movies in the business category

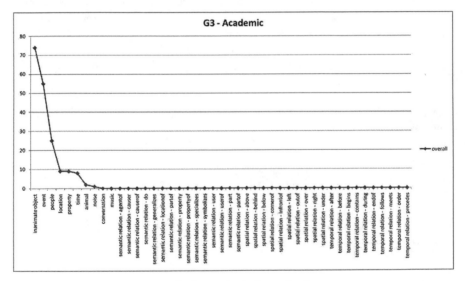

Fig. 4 Overall use of tags in YouTube for movies in the academic category

Figure 6 to Figure 9 illustrate the tags used in COSMOSIS within each category and their popularity. In this case, the four most commonly used tags overall concerned:

1. time
2. events
3. inanimate objects
4. people

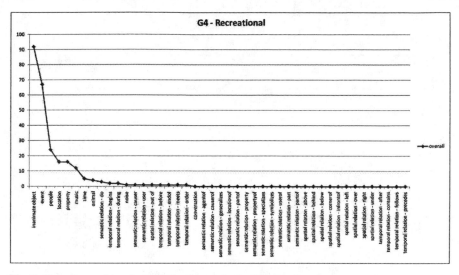

Fig. 5   Overall use of tags in YouTube for movies in the recreational category

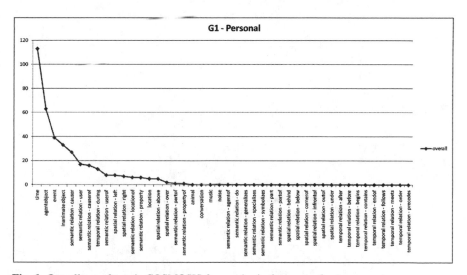

Fig. 6   Overall use of tags in COSMOSIS for movies in the personal category

The peak use of time in COSMOSIS is explained by the fact that it allows tags to be associated with time points (start points and/or end points), which is not possible in YouTube, and asks users if they wish to add time points after each tag is added. As a consequence, users added time points to most tags. This suggests that users will add time points for tags if the means to do so is easily provided.

Consequently, a collaborative movie annotating system should fully support these commonly used tags and prioritise their accessibility.

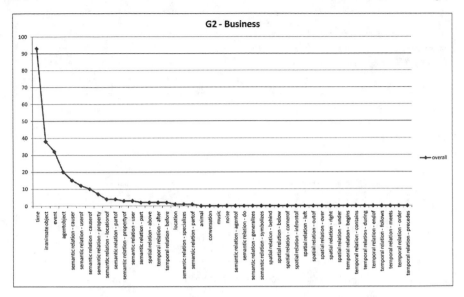

Fig. 7 Overall use of tags in COSMOSIS for movies in the business category

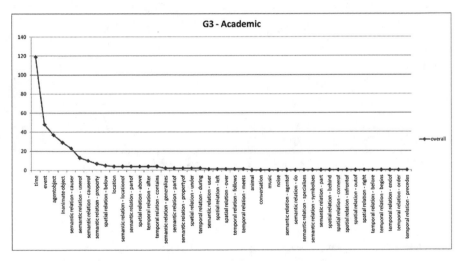

Fig. 8 Overall use of tags in COSMOSIS for movies in the academic category

Relationships between Tags

Another set of key results from the experiment concerned relationships between the tags. This shows which tags are used with each other more often; that is, if an object is tagged in a scene which tag also tends to be used in conjunction with it. The bar diagrams in Figure 10 and Figure 11 show the relationships between tags for YouTube and COSMOSIS respectively (tags that were not used at all have been removed to improve readability). One immediate observation is that as users are not

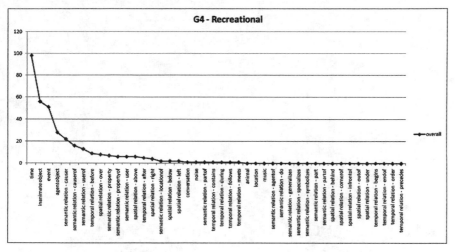

Fig. 9 Overall use of tags in COSMOSIS for movies in the recreational category

able to provide time points in YouTube, the relation between time and other tags is considerably low while for COSMOSIS it is extremely high, for the reasons stated above. Overall, the most common relationships between tags discovered from the experiment data were:

- Inanimate Object – Time
- Inanimate Object – Property
- Inanimate Object – People

- Event – Time
- Event – Property
- Event – Inanimate Object

- People – Time
- People – Property
- People – Event

The strong relationships between time and other tags suggests that a collaborative movie annotating system should allow and encourage users to add time points for their tags and make the process of it as simple as possible. Similarly, users tend to add properties for inanimate objects, events and people quite frequently; therefore it is imperative that this process be supported in an accessible fashion.

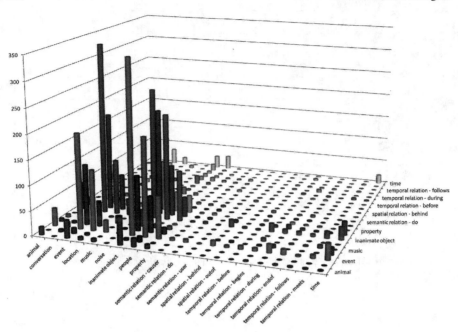

Fig. 10 Overall relationships between tags used in YouTube

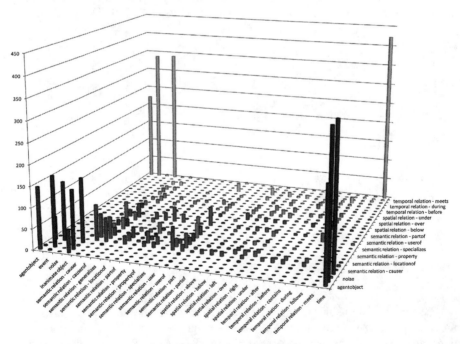

Fig. 11 Overall relationships between tags used in COSMOSIS

System Features

The collected data also provided results pertaining to system features and functionality. On the whole, users found YouTube easier and less confusing to use than COSMOSIS due to the wealth of tagging options caused by the MPEG-7 focus in the latter. For example, the great deal of different semantic relations available in MPEG-7 can overwhelm unfamiliar and inexperienced users. This suggests that including schemes such as MPEG-7 in their entirety, while very helpful to a power user, may not be useful for typical, everyday users and may actually impede them. The metadata, collaborative communication transcripts and interviews all suggest that users found inanimate objects, events, people, properties and the overall topic of the movie easiest to model, while temporal relations and spatial relations proved to be the most difficult. Users also reported differences in difficulty creating metadata for different types of movies. Users found that home videos, eventful, sport and factual movies were the easiest to create metadata for, while dull content, content with too many visual stimulants, academic content and lectures were the most difficult to create metadata for.

Working in groups forms the essence of any collaborative system and during the interviews, 80% of users stated that they found working in a group useful. They generally found that working in groups and collaborating with others helped them to better observe and create metadata for the movies since content features they may have missed were frequently 'caught' by other users. Some users also stated that working in a group allowed them to better express themselves as they were helped by other users in how best to represent certain features. This suggests that collaborative annotation has the potential to produce more meaningful and comprehensive metadata. However, while participants were encouraged to use an instant messenger to converse with other users while undertaking the experiment, all users found this to be very distracting and perceived little or no value in taking part in real-time conversations. All users stated a preference for non-real-time communication, such as a forum-based system, explaining that the useful parts of conversations could have been held asynchronously with the same accuracy and results and without a lot of unwanted and unnecessary conversations that distracted them from focusing on the task at hand.

During the interviews in particular, users suggested a number of additional system features that they felt they would benefit from when creating metadata collaboratively. These are summarised in Table 2.

An Architecture for a Collaborative Movie Annotation System

This section proposes an architecture for a collaborative movie annotation system based on the results presented in the previous section. We consider first the underlying metadata scheme and then the overall system architecture.

Table 2 Additional system features

Feature	Purpose
Predictive tags	Similar tags may be automatically determined and exploited within the metadata.
Predefined tags	Speed up tagging of common features. Hierarchical organisation to enable selection of sub-tags particularly beneficial.
Discover similar users or groups	Assists users to work collaboratively with like-minded and similarly-experienced individuals to improve accuracy and productivity.

Metadata Scheme

A metadata scheme lies at the heart of any annotation system, determining which tags may be employed by users when creating metadata, specifying how the metadata is represented, and influencing system functionality accordingly. This section presents the metadata scheme used within the proposed collaborative movie annotation architecture. The most common tags and tag relationships employed by users during the experiment were given primacy within this scheme while also taking into account user behaviour with the metadata tools.

The metadata scheme is illustrated in Figure 12. At the core of the scheme are events, objects and people, shown at the top of the figure, which were the most commonly used tags by users during the experiment. Time, which featured most prominently during COSMOSIS usage, is represented within each of these three templates so that users are able to add time points for the events, objects and people, as well as represent semantic time concepts such as morning, midday, October, and so forth. Properties and location are also incorporated for events, objects and people as these were found to be commonly used together. For example, a user can add an event such as *sword fight* where this event has been *ferocious* (property), *violent* (another property) and took place in *Camelot* (location) during the *Middle Ages* (Time). The user may then add a *sword* inanimate object, specifying its properties as *bright* and *sharp*, while also specifying the time as *Middle Ages* and location as *Camelot's Armoury*. Similarly, a person such as *King Arthur* could be added, who is *wise* and *just* (properties), and who is also located in *Camelot* (location) during the *Middle Ages* (time).

Relationships, while not as commonly used as other tags because users found them confusing, are also included since they are essential for providing structure to the metadata and can be made more accessible for users through an improved user interface (in the same way as with the time points). For example, the *sword* object can be specified as being *owned* by *King Arthur* through the use of a semantic relation.

Movies include noise, conversation and music and while these were not the most popular tags used during the experiment, these tags were used not insignificantly and thus they are accommodated within the scheme. These tags are related to other

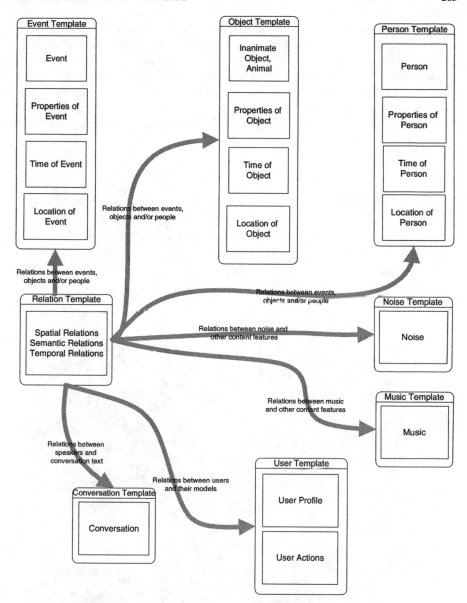

Fig. 12 Metadata scheme for a collaborative movie annotation system

content features through the relation template. For example, a noise (*clank*) can be generated from an object (*sword*) due to an event (*sword fight*) that was initiated by a person (*King Arthur*). Similarly, conversation can be related directly to the speakers (people) involved. Music can have a very distinct effect on the emotions, particularly during movies, and users showed interest in modelling musical metadata such as genre, singers, composers and song names.

Finally, in order to associate users with their metadata activity and allow users to identify similar users or user groups to improve collaboration, a user template is included which incorporates a profile for the user and a set of user actions. The user profile incorporates descriptive information about the user such as their username, real name, interests, and so on, while the user actions represent the metadata activity that they have undertaken, such as tags added, modified or removed. Recording such data enables patterns in user actions and similarities between different users to be determined.

System Architecture

From the output of the grounded theory, we determine a collaborative movie annotation system to require four key components, which form the basis of the architecture proposed in Figure 13: *Resources*, *Annotation*, *Retrieval*, and *Community Interaction and Profiling*. Each component is now discussed in turn.

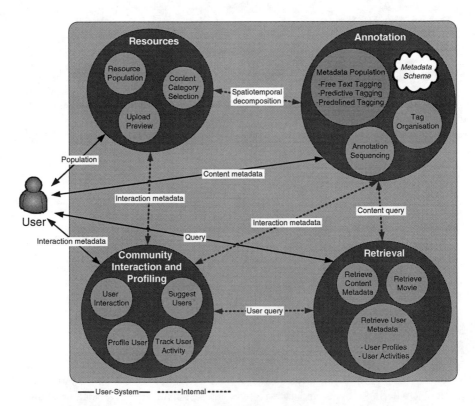

Fig. 13 A collaborative movie annotation system architecture

Resources

This component facilitates population of the system with the raw movie streams and is required so that new movies are able to be uploaded to the system and existing movies may be modified or removed. A content category selection function enables the user to specify that the movie belongs to a certain category (such as those categories used in the experiment) either pre or post upload, which helps to initially bring the movie to the attention of users that tend to tag those types of movies. A preview function enables the user to check that the movie has uploaded correctly.

Annotation

This component is the cornerstone of the architecture and incorporates the metadata scheme described above. It enables the creation and maintenance of content metadata for the movie streams contained within the Resources component and user metadata for the Community Interaction and Profiling component. It is related to the movie resources through spatiotemporal decompositions of the content, i.e. demarcations of the streams in time and/or space, while interaction metadata from the Community Interaction and Profiling component enables the user profiles and activities to be created according to the metadata scheme. This component also provides content and user metadata to the Retrieval component so that it can service queries.

The experiment results revealed that users have a preference for some predefined tags in order to speed the creation of metadata, but without sacrificing the ability to add tags freely, thus both are provided for within the architecture. In addition, experiment participants also stated a preference for predictive functionality such that the system would suggest additional tags with similar meanings when they add or edit a tag. Since the number of predefined and predictive tags offered could potentially be quite large, there is a need to organise them for presentation to the user. As was seen in Figure 2 to Figure 9, there were some differences in the order of popularity of tags for different categories and therefore tags could be organised according to their relevance to a particular category. This may take the form of a simple sort or something more complex like a hierarchical organisation.

Finally, an annotation sequencing function enables the support of common metadata 'patterns', whereby certain tags or sets of tags are frequently used in sequence, such as creating objects and then adding properties for them or adding time points after adding an event, object or person. This is sequenced for the user automatically to ease metadata input.

Retrieval

This component enables the retrieval of movie content and content and user metadata based on internal and user-system queries. It supports the retrieval of content metadata and movie streams from the Annotation component via internal content queries and the retrieval of user metadata (the user profiles and user activities) via internal user queries to the Community Interaction and Profiling component. In this way, the architecture enables users to search for particular content or users.

Community Interaction and Profiling

This component facilitates interaction within the community. An important part of a collaborative community is the communication of the users with one another. The experiment results revealed that participants disliked real-time communications and preferred a more traditional forum-based approach and this is provided for by the user interaction function. Such a forum should enable users to comment on movies and tags and engender general discussion, both in the community and on a one-to-one asynchronous basis, e.g. private messages. This component also provides functions for profiling the user and keeping track of their activities within the system, with the actual storage of this user metadata handled by the Annotation component. Interaction metadata from this component also works with the Annotation component to enable the user metadata to be related to content metadata. Finally, experiment participants expressed a preference for being able to find similar users or user groups and therefore a suggest users function caters for this aspect.

Concluding Discussion

Users are now empowered with easily accessible technology for producing, uploading and distributing movies that they have created themselves. As a result, the sharing of such movies on Web 2.0 sites has rocketed, bringing about a need for non-trivial metadata so that the movies may be searched effectively. Exploiting the online communities in which such movies are shared is an effective means for reducing the sheer effort involved in annotating the movies with metadata, by distributing the effort among a large number of members of the community. In support of this, this paper has proposed an architecture for collaborative movie annotation. Research in collaborative retrieval, collaborative tagging of non-video media, and collaborative tagging of video media was considered. Then, the paper described an experiment that was undertaken with 50 users to determine how users collaborate when annotating movies using existing tools (YouTube and an MPEG-7-based tool). The experiment revealed the tags most commonly used by users, these being those related to inanimate objects, events and people. Users appeared to exhibit slight differences in annotation behaviour based on the type of content they were modelling which affected which tags were most likely to be used. It was also found that some tags are more likely to be used closely with each other and users tended to include start and end time points for inanimate objects, events and people during a video if the means were easily provided. Another important relationship observed in the results was the use of properties with inanimate objects, events and people. From these results, an architecture for collaborative movie annotation was proposed, consisting of Resources, Annotation, Retrieval, and Community Interaction and Profiling components. Underlying the Annotation component is a general metadata scheme, which was designed to take into account the most common tags and tag relationships employed by users during the experiment as well as user behaviour with the metadata tools. The metadata scheme can be implemented using a suitable standard such as MPEG-7.

Acknowledgement This research is supported by the Engineering and Physical Sciences Research Council, grant no. EP/E034578/1.

References

1. J.J. Jung, "Social grid platform for collaborative online learning on blogosphere: A case study of eLearning@BlogGrid," Expert Systems with Applications, Vol. 36, No. 2, Part 1, 2009, pp. 2177-2186.
2. N. Del Conte, "Can eyeOS Succeed Where Desktop.com Failed?," TechCrunch, 27 November 2006. <http://www.techcrunch.com/2006/11/27/eyeos-open-source-webos-for-the-masses/trackback/>.
3. J.P. Zappen, T.M. Harrison, and D. Watson, "A new paradigm for designing e-government: web 2.0 and experience design," in Proceedings of the 2008 international conference on Digital government research, 2008, pp. 17-26.
4. W. Chen, J. Chen, and Q. Li, "Adaptive community-based multimedia data retrieval in a distributed environment," in Proceedings of the 2nd international conference on Ubiquitous information management and communication, 2008, pp. 20-24.
5. S. Boll, "MultiTube–Where Web 2.0 and Multimedia Could Meet," IEEE MultiMedia, Vol. 14, No. 1, 2007, pp. 9-13.
6. D.N. Milne, "Exploiting web 2.0 for all knowledge-based information retrieval," in Proceedings of the ACM first Ph.D. workshop in Conference on Information and Knowledge Management (CIKM), 2007, pp. 69-76.
7. G. Chen, F. Wang, and C. Zhang, "Collaborative filtering using orthogonal nonnegative matrix tri-factorization," Information Processing & Management, In Press, Corrected Proof, 2009.
8. J.-M. Yang and K.F. Li, "Recommendation based on rational inferences in collaborative filtering," Knowledge-Based Systems, Vol. 22, No. 1, 2009, pp. 105-114.
9. M. Buffa, F. Gandon, G. Ereteo, P. Sander, and C. Faron, "SweetWiki: A semantic wiki," Web Semantics: Science, Services and Agents on the World Wide Web, Vol. 6, No. 1, 2008, pp. 84-97.
10. R.A. Negoescu and D. Gatica-Perez, "Analyzing Flickr groups," in Proceedings of the 2008 international conference on Content-based image and video retrieval, 2008, pp. 417-426.
11. M. Naaman and R. Nair, "ZoneTag's Collaborative Tag Suggestions: What is This Person Doing in My Phone?," IEEE MultiMedia, Vol. 15, No. 3, 2008, pp. 34-40.
12. B. Nowack, "CONFOTO: Browsing and annotating conference photos on the Semantic web," Web Semantics: Science, Services and Agents on the World Wide Web, Vol. 4, No. 4, 2006, pp. 263-266.
13. F. Bentley, C. Metcalf, and G. Harboe, "Personal vs. commercial content: the similarities between consumer use of photos and music," in Proceedings of the SIGCHI conference on Human Factors in computing systems, 2006, pp. 667-676.
14. D. Yamamoto, T. Masuda, S. Ohira, and K. Nago, "Video Scene Annotation Based on Web Social Activities," IEEE MultiMedia, Vol. 15, No. 3, 2008, pp. 22-32.
15. T. Volkmer, J.R. Smith, and A. Natsev, "A web-based system for collaborative annotation of large image and video collections: an evaluation and user study," in Proceedings of the 13th annual ACM international conference on Multimedia, 2005, pp. 892-901.
16. A. Ulges, C. Schulze, D. Keysers, and T. Breuel, A System That Learns to Tag Videos by Watching YouTube, in Computer Vision Systems, Lecture Notes in Computer Science, Vol. 5008, Springer, Berlin, Heidelberg, 2008, pp. 415-424.
17. B. Elliott and Z.M. Ozsoyoglu, "Annotation suggestion and search for personal multimedia objects on the web," in Proceedings of the 2008 international conference on Content-based image and video retrieval, 2008, pp. 75-84.

18. Q. Li and S.C.Y. Lu, "Collaborative Tagging Applications and Approaches," IEEE MultiMedia, Vol. 15, No. 3, 2008, pp. 14-21.
19. H. Agius and M. Angelides, "MPEG-7 in action: end user experiences with COSMOS-7 front end systems," in Proceedings of the 21st Annual ACM Symposium on Applied Computing (SAC '06), Vol. 2, 2006, pp. 1348-1355.
20. M. Angelides and H. Agius, "An MPEG-7 scheme for semantic content modelling and filtering of digital video," Multimedia Systems, Vol. 11, No. 4, 2006, pp. 320-339.
21. J. Corbin and A. Strauss, "Basics of Qualitative Research: Techniques and Procedures for Developing Grounded Theory," 3rd ed., Sage Publications, 2008.
22. C. Goulding, "Grounded theory: the missing methodology on the interpretivist agenda," Qualitative Market Research, Vol. 1, No. 1, 1998, pp. 50-57.
23. K. Charmaz, "Constructing Grounded Theory: A Practical Guide through Qualitative Analysis," Sage Publications, 2006.
24. R. Matavire and I. Brown, "Investigating the use of "Grounded Theory" in information systems research," in Proceedings of the 2008 annual research conference of the South African Institute of Computer Scientists and Information Technologists on IT research in developing countries: riding the wave of technology, 2008, pp. 139-147.

Part II
DIGITAL AUDITORY MEDIA

Chapter 13
Content Based Digital Music Management and Retrieval

Jie Zhou and Linxing Xiao

Introduction

With thousands of songs in personal collection, and millions of songs available via Internet, managing large scale music data becomes more and more challenging. Traditional tools which utilize only text tags (title, artist and etc.), such as the file browser and iTunes, provide little information to assist this process. To address this challenge, considerable approaches have been explored to facilitate the procedure of browsing and retrieving music in large scale dataset, which can be classified into three research areas:

- Music visualization: get to know a song without listening to it.
- Music summarization: just listen to the most representative part of a song.
- Music similarity measure: listen to one single song and get the songs similar to it.

Music visualization maps music content information to 2D or 3D space, and makes eyes another channel to perceive music. Just like viewing a picture, the user is able to obtain some attributes of a song within a glance. Music summarization extracts the most informative and impressive part of song. Since the length of such part is usually less than 30s, this technique will save a lot of time for a user checking if the song matches his preference. And the last research field tries to calculate the perceived music similarity which is the essential part of music retrieval. With such technique, instead of manually checking songs one by one, a user can get an automatically generated playlist by providing just one preferred song.

This chapter will introduce the three research fields mentioned above. For each fields, we briefly review the attempts and take one of them as an example. Then we describe the mechanism, and the performance of each example to show the effectiveness of these techniques. And at last, we will show a music archive management system realized by us which utilizes the techniques described in this chapter.

J. Zhou (✉) and L. Xiao
Department of Automation, Tsinghua University, Beijing, China
e-mail: jzhou@tsinghua.edu.cn; xiaolx02@mails.tsinghua.edu.cn

B. Furht (ed.), *Handbook of Multimedia for Digital Entertainment and Arts*,
DOI 10.1007/978-0-387-89024-1_13, © Springer Science+Business Media, LLC 2009

Music Visualization: Tension Visualization Approach

The purpose of music visualization is to take advantage of the strong pattern-recognition abilities of the human visual system to reveal similarities, patterns and correlations among a large collection of music. The typical procedure of music visualization is as follows:

1. Automatically extract content information from music stored in digital audio format.
2. Render the extracted information visually.

Currently, in the 1st step, low level features are used to represent the content information of music. For example, the Mel-Frequency Cepstral Coefficients (MFCCs) is frequently employed to describe the timbre related information and the Fluctuation Pattern is utilized to represent the rhythm information [1]. And in the second step, the extracted features' dimensionality is linearly (e.g. PCA-based techniques [2]) or non-linearly (e.g. SOM-based techniques [1]) reduced so that they can be displayed in a 2D (or 3D) space.

One problem of such visualization techniques, which would lower the users' experience of interacting, is that, users don't know what the x-axis and the y-axis represent. When the SOM-based techniques are applied, since the mapping is non-linear, it's not possible to label the axes. And when the PCA-based techniques are used, although we know the two dimensions would correspond to the first two principal components of the extracted low level feature, users still can't understand the meaning because they cannot be explained semantically.

To solve this problem, high level features should be mapped to the axes instead of low level features. The tension visualization is just such a highlevel mapping technique. It derives the content information which could affect the tension of listener, and then map them to x and y axes respectively.

One of the most important characteristics of music is the powerful emotional effect. Humans often react to music emotionally. A study about the effect of different type of music on emotion [3] indicates that, when listening to grunge rock music which has quite noisy background and large tempo value, listeners are detected with significant increase in tension; while listening to songs with quiet background and small tempo value, listeners show significant decrease in tension. Therefore, the noisy level and tempo value could be useful tension descriptors. More importantly, these two descriptors could be easily understood by listeners and thus improve the interacting experience when used for visualization.

Noisy Level Calculation

Apparently the noisy level of a song with heavy background (e.g. rock) should be higher than that of a song with quiet background. Figure 1 compares the time-frequency distributions of two piece of music, one of which is extracted from a

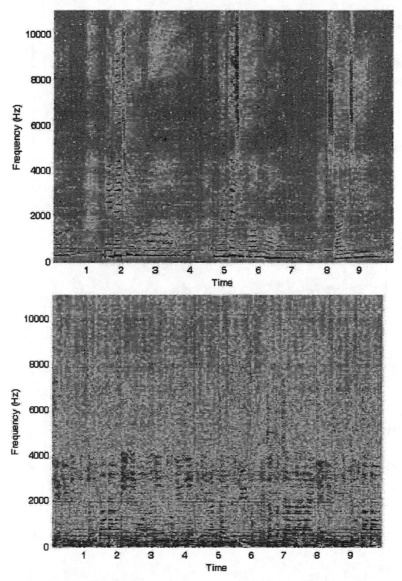

Fig. 1 The time-frequency distribution comparison of two kinds of songs. The left is from a lyrics song and the right is from a rock song

lyric song and the other from a rock song. They differ a lot. The spectrums extracted from the time-frequency distributions, shown in Figure 2, clearly illustrate the difference between the two kinds of music. The spectrum from the lyric song has several high and sharp resonance peaks while the spectrum of the rock song is much flatter. Thus, the noisy level of a piece of music could be determined by the flatness of the spectrum, which can be computed using the Spectrum Flatness Measure (SFM) [4]. The definition of SFM is:

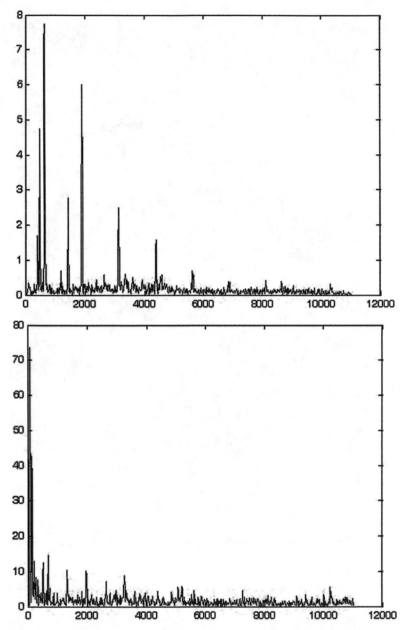

Fig. 2 The spectrum comparison of two different songs. The left is from a lyrics song and the right is from a rock song

$$\text{SFM} = \frac{\exp\left(\frac{1}{2\pi}\int\limits_{-\pi}^{\pi}\ln P(\omega)d\omega\right)}{\frac{1}{2\pi}\int\limits_{-\pi}^{\pi}\ln P(\omega)d\omega}, \tag{1}$$

where $P(\omega)$ is the spectrum. It also could write in a discrete form:

$$\text{SFM} = \frac{\exp\left(\frac{1}{N}\sum\limits_{i}\ln P(\omega_i)\right)}{\frac{1}{N}\sum\limits_{i}P(\omega_i)} = \frac{\left(\prod\limits_{i=1}^{N}P(\omega_i)\right)^{\frac{1}{N}}}{\frac{1}{N}\sum\limits_{i}P(\omega_i)}. \tag{2}$$

In the tension visualization system, the noisy level is determined as follows:

1. Segment a song into frames with 100ms duration.
2. Calculate the SFM of each frame.
3. Use the median of the SFM of all frames as the noisy level of the song.

Other statistics such as mean, max and min have also been tested in step 3, but the median outperforms all of them.

Tempo Estimation

The perceived tempo is an apparent and descriptive feature of songs, and it gives the listener a direct impression of the music emotion. Consequently, one can search for songs with his expectant speed quickly.

Considerable approaches have been proposed for automatic tempo estimation. Most of them are optimization model based algorithms [5], which search the best tempo estimation of a song under the constraints of the rhythm patterns, like periodicity and strength of onsets. For example, [6] uses dynamic programmings to find the set of beat times that optimize both the onset strength at each beat and the spacing between beats (tempo). The formulation of tempo estimation in terms of a constraint optimization problem requires a clear understanding of the inherent mechanisms of tempo perception. However, people barely know what factors and how these factors affect the perceived tempo. And that is why sometimes, the most salient tempo estimation is not the perceived tempo but half or double of it is.

Instead of using the optimization model based algorithm, the tension visualization system employs a two stage tempo estimation algorithm [7], which incorporates a statistics model to improve the estimation accuracy. We not only consider the information of rhythm patterns, but also utilize the timbre information based on an observation that, songs with high perceived tempo are usually quite noisy while those with low perceived tempo are usually quiet. The correlation between timbre and perceived tempo is captured by a statistic model via a training procedure. To detect the tempo of a song, a state-of-the-art method is first employed to generate several tempo candidates. Then, the likelihood of each candidate is computed based on the statistic model. Finally, the candidate with the highest likelihood is regarded as the tempo of the song.

Following are the detailed procedures for training and detecting part.

To train the statistic model of the correlation between timbre and tempo, we need to: (1) For each song in the training set, divide it into several 10-second segments, with neighboring segments overlapping 1/2 of the length. (2) Each 10-second segment is further windowed into 0.1-second frames. After extracting a 12-dimensional MFCC vector from each frame, the mean MFCC vector of each 10-second segment is computed. Then the annotated tempo is combined with the mean MFCC vector to form a 13-dimensional tempo-timbre feature. (3) Finally, the aggregate of tempo-timbre features of all songs in the training set is used to train a GMMs model, which describes the probability distribution of tempo-timbre feature.

And to detect the tempo, one need to:

1. Partition a testing song into several 10-second segments with 5-second overlapping.
2. For each segment, use the algorithm described in [6] to get a possible tempo. Then, four additional tempi are generated by multiplying the original tempo with factor 0.33, 0.5, 2 and thus, there are five candidate tempi for a piece of music, denoted as Ti, i = 1, . . . , 5.
3. Compute the 12-dimensional mean MFCC vector of each segment, denoted as M.
4. For each 10-second segment, compute the probability of the combination of Ti and M in the pre-trained statistic model. The candidate with the highest probability is determined as the tempo of the segment:

$$T^* = \arg \max_{T_i} P(T_i|M),$$

   where P(x|y) is the likelihood of x with respect to y.
5. Select the median of the tempi of all segments as the estimated tempo of the testing song.

The employed statistic model of this technique significantly improves the tempo estimation accuracy compared with the state-of-the-art method [6]. Furthermore, this technique outperforms all optimization based algorithms described in [5].

Music Summarization: Key Segment Extraction Approach

The aim of music summarization is to extract the most representative part of a song. While most existing approaches [8–11] regard the most repeated segment as the summary and extract it based on the self-similarity of a song, Zhang and Zhou [12] formulates the music summarization task from a quite novel perspective. It treats the so-called key-segment (chorus most of the time) as the most representative part of a song and models the key-segment extraction to a binary classification problem.

Description of Key Segment

People almost enjoy music every day, among all kinds of music we are known, popular songs may be the most familiar one. Generally, a popular song can be roughly divided into four parts: a beginning part, which is usually a pure accompanying segment; a developing part, a long and slow singing segment; a climactic part, which is usually an ardent singing segment; and an ending part, fading out to end the whole song. Among all the parts, most people like the climactic part more. We have such an experience that there is always a special segment which attracts and moves us strongly in a popular song. Once the song is mentioned, this segment will bring to our mind first. Zhang [12] call such kind of segment as the key segment of the whole music. For example, the song, "my heart will go on" is a song from a famous English movie, "Titanic", sung by Miss Celine Dion. The sentence, "you are here, there's nothing I fear, and I know that my heart will go on; we'll stay forever this way, you are safe in my heart, and my heart will go on and on", is usually regarded as the most impressive part in it. Taking the song, "right here waiting" sung by Mr. Richard Marx as another example, its key segment can be regarded as the sentence like "wherever you go, whatever you do, I will be right here waiting for you" or "whatever it takes, or how my heart breaks, I will be right here waiting for you".

Generally speaking, the key segment should be a singing segment rather than a pure instrumental one. It always exits in the climactic part of the whole song. It is highly possible that the title of the song is contained in the lyric of the key segment. Obviously, the length of the key segments varies according to different popular songs, but it usually cannot be too long or too short. The length distribution of key segments manually extracted from the training database is showed in Figure 3. We can see that the length of most key segments is between 20s and 40s.

Key-Segment Extraction

The Key-Segment Extraction problem is actually a binary classification problem. Based on the observation that key-segment of a song differs from its non-key-segment, [12] assumes that the distributions of all key and non-key segments in some particular feature space could be quite different. Therefore classical binary classification techniques could be directly utilized for music summarization.

The architecture of key-segment extraction is shown in Figure 4, which consists of an off-line training part and an online extraction part. In the training part, the key segments of songs are labeled as positive samples and the other segments are

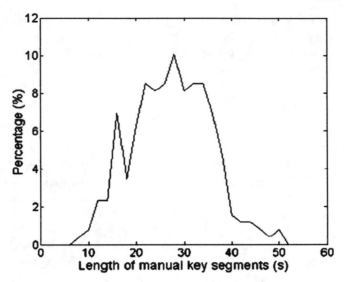

Fig. 3 The length distribution of key segments

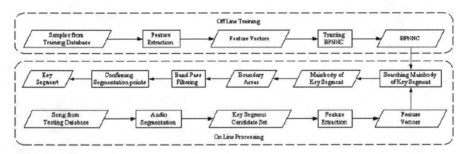

Fig. 4 Flowchart of the key segment extraction algorithm

regards as negative samples. Then, the system trains a binary classifier with the carefully designed 17-dimensional features extracted from the samples. Ref. [12] tests several typical classifiers and indicates that, the back propagation neural network classifier (BPNNC) outperforms others like k-nearest neighbor (KNN), minimum mahalanobis distance (MMD) and support vector machine (SVM). Therefore this system employs the trained BPNNC as its key segment discriminator.

In the online extraction part, things become a little complicated since the length and start point of the key segment are unknown when given an unknown song. The only thing we know is the length distribution as shown in Figure 3. Ref. [12] solves this problem by producing a collection of key segment candidates from the song. With a time resolution of 2 seconds, all segments whose length is from 20s to 40s are cut out to generate the key segment candidate collection. From each candidate, its 17-dimensional feature is extracted. Supposing the length of input popular song is L seconds, the number of candidates will be:

$$S = \sum_{i=0}^{10} \left\lfloor \frac{L - 20 - 2i}{2} \right\rfloor. \tag{3}$$

Using the well trained BPNNC, we can select a music segment which is most likely to be the key segment of this song from all of the candidates. In this system, the BPNNC has two output neurons which are corresponding to the class of "key segment" and the class of "non key segment", respectively. The sum of these two output values is 1. For an input feature vector, if the value of the output neuron corresponding to the class of "key segment" is larger than 0.5, the corresponding candidate will be labeled as "key segment". The larger the value is, the higher the reliability is. And the candidate with the largest value is finally chosen as the key segment.

The last step of this system is to refine the boundary to guarantee that the key segment locates at the clearance of singing. Since the energy of human voice mainly concentrates in the band of 100Hz to 3500Hz [13], a band pass filter is used to strengthen the human voice. And then, the lowest energy points around the boundary are regarded as the refined starting and ending points.

The performance of this system is tested on a dataset containing 130 songs in [12]. Six volunteers are invited to evaluate both the automatically generated and manually labeled key segment in the same song. The average rating score over the whole test set shows that the quality of automatically extracted key segment is comparable to manually selected one.

Music Similarity Measure: Chroma-Histogram Approach

Subjective similarity between musical pieces is an elusive concept, but one must be pursued in support of application to provide automatic organization of large music collections. The aim of music similarity measure is to automatically compute the similarity between songs which matches the subjective similarity as well as possible.

Works in music similarity mainly focus on three areas: symbolic representations [14], subjective information [15] and acoustic properties [16]. The symbolic representation of music, such as MIDI music data or score, is hard to obtain without human effort. Thus such technique is not very suitable for automatic system. The subjective information, which is the human opinions about songs, is beyond the concept of "content based". Therefore, in this chapter we only focus on the acoustic property based one, which analyzes the music content directly.

All acoustic property based techniques have common components as:

1. Feature extraction: extract low level features from audio content;
2. Model construction: build a model for the song from the extracted feature;
3. Distance measures: design a proper distance to measure the similarity between different models representing songs.

Among the three components, the first one determines the music factor on which one particular technique will measure the similarity. For example, Ref. [17] measures the timbre similarity by extracting the feature Mel-Frequency Cepstral Coefficients (MFCCs) and Ref. [18] measures the rhythm similarity by extracting the feature emphasizing the percussion sound.

Chroma-histogram approach [19] is a technique attempting to measure the melody/chord similarity between songs. Generally speaking, the melody/chord pattern is the prior factor when people compare different pieces of music. One typical case is that different interpretations of the same piece of music, such as the two versions of "when I fall in love" sung by Celine Dion and Julio Iglesias respectively, are regarded very similar. Melody and chord are also efficient features for people to distinguish songs from different genres such as Blues, Jazz and Folk. Furthermore, melody/chord pattern contains rich information related to human feelings. Thus, it can be used to measure the high-level music similarity such as emotion. The goals of the Chroma-histogram approach are to design a model which is able to capture the melody/chord pattern of music, and to find a matching method to simulate the human's perception. To implement such a system, one has to account for the following fundamental issues. First, melody/chord pattern is very robust to variations of parameters such as timbre and tempo. Second, the human's perception of melody/chord pattern is irrelevant to the key transposition. For example, people usually think there is little difference between a song in C and its counterpart in G.

The three components of Chroma-histogram are described in the remainder of this section.

Feature Extraction

Since this approach aims to measure the melody/chord similarity, the chroma [20] is chosen to be extracted from an audio music file. Chroma is a short term acoustic feature which records the energy distribution on 12 pitch classes of a small duration music signal.

The first step of feature extraction is to segment a song into a series of small duration frames (usually around 100ms). Then, the 12-element chroma vector is calculated to capture the dominant note as well as the broad harmonic accompaniment. Thus, a song is represented by a sequence of chroma vectors. Figure 5(a) is a sample of a chroma sequence extracted from a piece of Robbie Williams' song "Better man".

In Chroma-histogram approach [19], the chroma calculation algorithm provided by Dan Ellis [21] is utilized. The major advantage of Ref. [21] is that, it uses instantaneous frequency thus get a higher resolution estimation of the frequency.

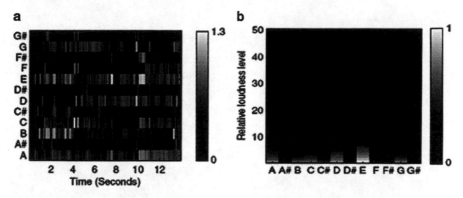

Fig. 5 (a) A sample of a chroma sequence and (b) its corresponding Chroma-histogram

Model Construction

Denote the chroma vector sequence as $CM = \{c(1), c(2), \ldots, c(l)\}$, where l is the total number of frames and $c(i)$ is a chroma feature. A CM uniquely characterizes a piece of music. However it is too specific for individual songs and cannot represent the common properties of a group of music. Therefore, the Chroma-histogram is designed as the model to capture the common pattern of similar music. The process of building the model is given as:

1. Elements of CM are normalized in [0, 1], and quantized with a loudness resolution of 50. For example we assign the value 20 to $CM(i, j)$ if $0.38 < CM(i, j) < 0.42$. We denote this quantized chroma feature matrix as CM_q.
2. Partition CM_q into 2^N sub-sequences of chroma features with overlaps.
3. For each sub-sequence, we use a chroma histogram to summarize the melody and chord pattern. A chroma histogram has 12 columns for 12 chroma bands and 50 rows for loudness resolution. The histogram counts how many times a specific loudness in a specific chroma band was reached or exceeded. The sum of histogram is normalized to 1. Figure 5(b) is the chroma histogram derived from the chroma matrix (Figure 5(a)). In the end, a piece of music is represented by 2^N chroma histograms.

It is necessary to bring Step2 for further discussion. Compared with computing only one chroma histogram for one song, using a series of chroma histograms is more reasonable. First of all, a series of chroma histograms can preserve both the structure information and the sequence information of CM_q. Second, it is often the case that a song is performed in more than one key. Step2 guarantees that every sub-sequence is in only one key (e.g. C Major) and facilitates the transposition-invariant matching in next section. Choosing the parameter N is crucial. If N is too small, the aforementioned advantages are not apparent. On the other hand if N is too large, the feature will fail to describe the common characteristics shared by a group of songs. Ref. [19] reports that N = 3 is a good choice.

Distance Measure

As mentioned above, we obtain a series of chroma histogram for every song, denoted as $S = \{CH^1, CH^2, \ldots, CH^8\}$. We then compare the chroma histograms of two different songs. Since similar songs usually have similar structure (e.g. ABAB), to take advantage of structure information, we sequentially compute the distance between 2 corresponding chroma histograms. The formula is as following:

$$Dist(S_1, S_2) = \sum_{i=1}^{8} D(CH_1^i, CH_2^i), \tag{4}$$

where $S_1 = \{CH^i_1\}$, $S_2 = \{CH^i_2\}$. And $D(.)$ is the transposition-invariant distance, which will be introduced below.

In a general sense, human's perception of a piece of music is irrelevant to its key. For example, people usually think there is little difference between a song in C and its counterpart in G. If we cyclically shift the C version rightwards by 7 semitones, the chroma histograms of these two versions will be exactly the same. Thus, [my] derives a transposition-invariant distance measure by using this property of chroma histogram.

For a chroma histogram $CH = \{v(1), v(2), \ldots, v(12)\}$, where $v(i)$ corresponds to the *ith* column of CH, the transposition function is defined as:

$$f^1(v(1), v(2), \ldots, v(12)) = \{v(12), v(1), \ldots, v(11)\}, \tag{5}$$

Accordingly, the i-transposed version of CH is $f^i(CH)$, and $f^{12}(CH) = CH$. In the end, the transposition-invariant distance of two chroma histograms is defined as:

$$D(CH_1, CH_2) = \min_{i \in [0:11]} d(CH_1, f^i(CH_2)), \tag{6}$$

where $d(x, y)$ is the Euclidean distance between x and y.

The performance of chroma-histogram approach is evaluated through two preliminary objective experiments [19]. It is first used to identify the *Cover Songs*, the alternate interpretations of the same underlying piece of music. Cover songs typically keep the essence of the melody and the chord, but may vary greatly in other aspects such as timbre, tempo and key. And then it is tested by a *Genre Classification* task. The results of chroma-histogram approach in two experiments outperform other timbre and rhythm related similarity measures.

An Realized Music Archive Management System

We build a music archive management system using these techniques described above. Figure 6 illustrates the User Interface (UI), which consists of two panels: the

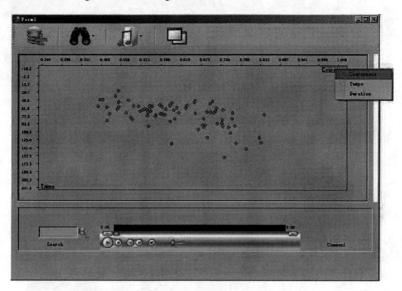

Fig. 6 The UI of the music archive management system

upper one (display panel) is used for music collection visualization and the lower one (function panel) is used to play, retrieve and comment individual songs.

In this system, currently three music attributes can be used for visualization, which are Coarseness (the Noisy Level), Tempo and Duration. And Coarseness and Tempo are selected in Figure 6, which are mapped to x-axis and y-axis respectively. The green circles on the display panel represent songs. With such visualization system, suffering in large scale dataset is convenient. When the user wants quiet and slow songs such as lyrics song, he/she can choose songs in the left-top corner and when one wants noisy and fast songs, he/she should select songs in the right-bottom corner. Figure 7 shows how to construct a playlist with little human effort. A zoom-in/out function is provided thus one can check the detail information of songs in a small region. A snapshot of the display panel after zoom-in is shown in Figure 8.

And when clicking on one green circle, the structure of the corresponding song will be shown in the function panel. As shown in Figure 9, the selected circle becomes red and the summary of the song show up as the orange block. Then the user could skim the song by only listen to the orange region of it. The blue and yellow colors are used to distinguish vocal and non-vocal part of the song respectively. Considerable techniques could be used for vocal part detection; here we use the algorithm in Ref. [22]. With such technique, the user can locate the singing part, which is the more informative than non-vocal part like prelude and interlude.

The similarity measure approach described above is utilized as the core component of the searching function. When the user encounters a wonderful song, he/she could immediately get all songs similar to it by typing the title into the "Search"

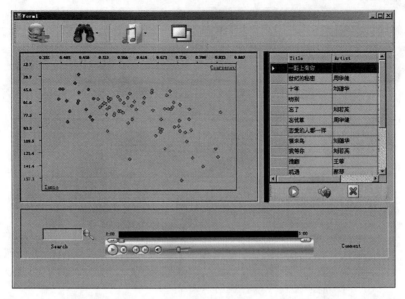

Fig. 7 An illustration of building a playlist with songs quiet and slow. The title and artist information in Chinese is listed in the right panel

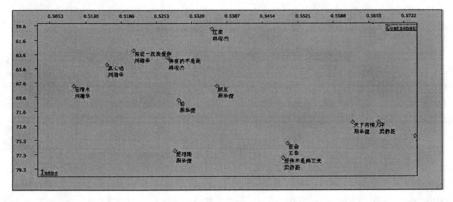

Fig. 8 The snapshot of the display panel after zoom in. The information about title and artist in Chinese shows up

blank. Without such function, the only way to obtain those songs is to listen to all songs in the dataset.

Conclusion and Future Directions

This chapter describes the content-based music management and retrieval techniques from the research areas of music visualization, music summarization and

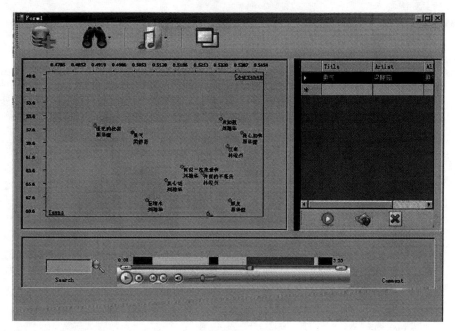

Fig. 9   The structure of a selected song displayed on the function panel

music similarity measure. The realized music archive management system demonstrates the effectiveness of those content-based techniques in facilitating user to surf in large scale music dataset. There are potential directions to improve the performance of such system. In our opinion, the following directions will make the system much smarter:

The first one is similarity fusion. Currently, there are many attempts proposed to measure similarities corresponding to different attributes of music, such as timbre, rhythm and melody. However, none of them could precisely describe the subjective similarity perceived by human, since music contains so many kinds of information. With the similarity fusion technique, we could combine different similarity measures together to approximate the subjective similarity.

The second one is relevance feedback retrieval. Starting with the query (generally one or more songs with label "prefer" or "not prefer"), such technique iterates to ask user to give feedback on some automatically selected "most informative" songs. And after a small number of rounds, it will generate result much better than that generated solely using the starting query. Mandel et al. [23] applies the active SVM classifier for relevance feedback retrieval and gets quite promising result.

And the last one is the personalized music recommendation. Difference users have different appetites. By recording the frequencies of the listened songs, the system could learn the preference of individual user and is able to automatically recommend songs based on the learned preference.

References

1. E. Pampalk, A. Rauber, and D. Merkl, "Content-Based Organization and Visualization of Music Archives," Proceedings of ACM Multimedia, pp. 570–579, 2002
2. G. Tzanetakis, and P. Cook, "3D Graphics Tools for Sound Collections," the 3rd International Conference on Digital Audio Effects, pp. 1–4, 2000
3. R. McCraty, B. Barrios-Choplin, M. Atkinson, and D. Tomasino, "The Effects of Different Types of Music on Mood, Tension, and Mental Clarity," Alternation Therapies in Health and Medicine, 4(1): 75–84, 1998
4. N. Jayant, and P. Noll. Digital Coding of Waveforms, Prentice-Hall, Englewood Cliffs, NJ, 1984
5. F. Gouyon, A. Klapuri, S. Dixon, M. Alonso, G. Tzanetakis, C. Uhle and P. Cano, "An experimental comparison of audio tempo induction algorithms," IEEE Transactions on Audio, Speech and Language processing, vol.14, no. 5, pp. 1832–1844, 2006
6. D.P.W. Ellis, "Beat Tracking with Dynamic Programming," MIREX'06, 2006
7. L. Xiao, A. Tian, W. Li and J. Zhou, "Using A Statistic Model to Capture the Association Between Timbre and Perceived Tempo," Proceedings of the International Conference on Music Information Retrieval, pp. 659–662, 2008
8. B. Logan and S. Chu, "Music summarization using key phrases" Proceeding of IEEE International Conference on Signal and Speech Processing, vol. 2, pp. 749–752, 2000
9. C. S. Xu, Y. W. Zhu and Q. Tian, "Automatic Music Summarization Based on Temporal, Spectral and Cepstral Features", Proceedings of IEEE International Conference on Multimedia and Expo., vol.1, pp. 117–120, 2002
10. M. Cooper and J. Foote, "Automatic Music Summarization via Similarity Analysis", Proceedings of Internation Symposium on Music Information Retrieval (ISMIR), 2002
11. C. Wei and V. Barry, "Music Thumbnailing via Structural Analysis", Proceedings of ACM International Conference on Multimedia, pp. 223–226, 2003
12. Y. Zhang, J. Zhou and Z. Bian, "Sample-Based Automatic Key Segment Extraction for Popular Songs", Proceedings of International Conference on Machine Learning and Cybernetics, pp. 4891–4897, 2005
13. F. G. Owens, Signal Processing of Speech, Macmillan: London, pp. 3–7, 1993
14. A. Ghias, J. Logan, D. Chamberlin and B. Smith, "Query by Humming: Music Information Retrieval in An Audio Database", Proceedings of ACM Multimedia, pp. 231–236, 1995
15. D.P. Ellis, B. Whitman, A. Berenzweig and S. Lawrence, "The Quest for Ground Truth in Musical Artist Similarity" Proceedings of International Conference on Music Information Retrieval, pp. 170–177, 2002
16. E. Pamoak, S. Dixon, and G. Widmer, "On the evaluation of perceptual similarity measures for music," Proceedings of the 6th conference on Digital Audio Effects, pp. 7–13, 2003
17. B. Logan and A. Salomon, "A music similarity function based on signal analysis," Proceedings of IEEE International Conference on Multimedia and Expo, pp. 745–748, 2001
18. E.D. Scheirer, "Tempo and beat analysis of acoustic musical signals," Journal of Acoustical Society of America, vol. 103, no.1, pp. 588–601, 1998
19. L. Xiao and J. Zhou, "Using Chroma Histogram to Measure the Perceived Similarity of Music," Proceedings of IEEE International Conference of Multimedia and Expo., pp. 1317–1320, 2008
20. Mark A. Bartsch and Gregory H. Wakefield, "Audio thumbnailing of popular music using chroma-based representations," IEEE Transactions on multimedia, vol. 7, no. 1, pp. 96–104, 2005
21. D.P. Ellis, www.ee.columbia.edu/dpwe/resources/matlab/chromaansyn
22. L. Xiao, J. Zhou and T. Zhang, "Using DTW Based Unsupervised Segment to Improve the Vocal Part Detection in Pop Music," Proceedings of IEEE International Conference of Multimedia and Expo., pp. 1193–1196, 2008
23. M. Mandel, G.E. Poliner and D.P. Ellis, "Support Vector Machine Active Learning for Music Retrieval," Multimedia Systems, Vol. 12, No. 1, pp. 3–13, 2006

Chapter 14
Incentive Mechanisms for Mobile Music Distribution

Marco Furini and Manuela Montangero

Introduction

Music anywhere and anytime is a desire of most of the people that legally download digital music from the Internet. The number of these people is growing at an exceptional speed and today, according to the International Federation of the Phonographic Industry [17], it generates the 15% of the entire music revenues. As an example, the number of legal downloads grew from 156 millions in 2004 to 420 millions in 2005 to 795 millions in 2006. The speed of this success is expected to further increase with the involvement of the mobile scenario.

The mobile digital world is seen as an important business opportunity for two main reasons: the widespread usage of cellphones (more than two billions [30], most of them with sound features) and the pervasiveness of mobile technologies. As a result, music industry and telecoms are bringing the successful Internet-based music market strategy into the mobile scenario: record labels are setting up agreements with cellphone network providers (Sprint, Verizon, Vodafone, Orange just to name a few) to offer a download music service also in the mobile scenario. The strategy is to use wireless channels to distribute music contents in the attempt of replicating the success of the Internet-based download scenario.

Although mobile music distribution is expected to play an important role in the future music business, the employed distribution strategy might be compromised by the differences between the current mobile and Internet-based scenario. In fact, according to [11, 12, 23], the success of any distribution strategy depends on three main factors: the characteristics of the communication infrastructure, the pricing strategy applied to the distribution model and the copyright protection method used to secure the distributed contents.

M. Furini (✉)
Faculty of Communication and Economic Sciences, University of Modena and Reggio Emilia, Italy
e-mail: marco.furini@unimore.it

M. Montangero
Dipartimento di Ingegneria dell'Informazione, University of Modena and Reggio Emilia, Italy
e-mail: manuela.montangero@unimore.it

B. Furht (ed.), *Handbook of Multimedia for Digital Entertainment and Arts*,
DOI 10.1007/978-0-387-89024-1_14, © Springer Science+Business Media, LLC 2009

The first contribution of this paper is an analysis of the current mobile music scenario. The analysis shows that the communication infrastructure is inadequate for music files download (the available transfer data rate is still too far from the wired scenario, causing the download time to be too long); the pricing strategy can be questioned (the use of the expensive cellphone data network causes users to pay much more to downloaded a song in the mobile environment than in the wired scenario); the copyright protection is a burden (it usually denies customers to listen to legally acquired music over different mobile devices).

The second contribution of this paper is to propose and analyze a multi-channel distribution strategy to ameliorate the problems of the current mobile music scenario. The idea is to involve customers in music distribution, so that distribution can be done using both the traditional cellphone network and the free-of-charge communication technology (e.g., Bluetooth and Wi-Fi, provided in recent cellphones). To be successful, distribution is based on a license security mechanism and on an effective incentive mechanism that financially compensates customers that participate to the music distribution. In essence, customers can acquire music from the music store using the cellphone network, but can also receive song files from other customers through the faster free-of-charge communication technology. Song files are locked and can be unlocked only through license files. To avoid the sharing of licenses, a license file is bounded to the customer's mobile device and is released only by the music store. Hence, customers can buy license files only through the cellphone data network. To stimulate cooperation among customers we design an incentive mechanism and three different reward policies, with the goal of financially compensating the cooperating users.

To evaluate the multi-channel distribution strategy we investigate its effects on the entities involved in the mobile music distribution (i.e., customers, mobile music store and cellphone providers). Results show that the usage of an incentive mechanism can ameliorate the problems of the current distribution strategy and produces benefits to all the entities involved in the mobile music market.

In the following, we first analyze the current mobile music market and then we outline a possible multi-channel distribution strategy along with an incentive mechanism that stimulates cooperation in a mobile environment. We proceed by presenting the evaluation of the multi-channel distribution strategy and by overviewing related works in the area of content distribution.

The Current Mobile Music Market

Thanks to the pervasiveness of the mobile technologies, music can be sold anywhere and anytime. To this aim, record labels and telecoms operators are opening mobile music stores, with the goal of replicating the success of the Internet-based music distribution strategy also in the mobile scenario.

In this section, we analyze the differences between the two scenarios, by focusing on communication infrastructure, pricing strategy and copyright protection. These aspects are in fact, according to [11, 12, 23], the key-factors of any digital distribution strategy.

Communication Infrastructure

The fastest available data rate for the mobile scenario is provided by 3G networks, which offer three different transfer data rates: vehicular (144Kbps), pedestrian (384Kbps) and fixed (2Mbps). Unfortunately, the real situation is very different [22] and actual tests show that the downloading speed ranges from 264 Kbps to 360 Kbps (a 264 Kbps leads to a download time of 120 seconds for a 4MB song). Not to mention that 3G networks are available only in some areas (usually big cities) and where 3G networks are not available, the transfer data rate is the one of EDGE or GPRS; if the service scales down to EDGE (the 384 Kbps maximum transfer data rate is usually a 80 Kbps actual connection), a 4MB song can be downloaded in 390 seconds, more than 6 minutes; if the service is GPRS (the maximum 170 Kbps connection is usually a 50 Kbps actual connection), around 15 minutes are necessary to download a 4MB song.

Needless to say, this may be a shock for users accustomed to residential xDSL broadband connection, where different Mbps are commonly available.

Pricing Strategy

The pricing strategy plays a fundamental role in the success of a distribution channel, as the song price should be sufficiently attractive to entice customers to buy music from the new distribution channel.

In the Internet scenario, the most successful business model is the a-la-carte model, which accounts for 86% of the on-line sales. In this model each song is priced around one dollar and users choose and pay song by song. Thanks to low prices, many left the illegal P2P world in favor of legal music stores.

In the mobile scenario, although using the same a-la-carte model, the song is priced much higher, ranging from 1.5 to 2.50 dollars. The reason of this high price is mainly due to the usage of the expensive cellphone data network. In fact, although some flat rate data plans are becoming available, data service to mobile phones are often metered, with users paying by the megabyte. It is to point out that, for music download, mobile providers charge a *forfeit* (from 1.5 to 2.5 dollars), regardless of the amount of bits that compose the song (otherwise the song price would be much higher).

Needless to say, it is likely that most of the customers will wait to be home to download the song.

Copyright Protection

A Digital Right Management (DRM) scheme allows content providers (e.g., record labels or artists) to protect their data by wrapping a media file with a control mechanism that specifies user rights (e.g., a collection of permissions and constraints) and discloses the material only to authorized users. Although employed extensively to fight piracy, DRM schemes are questioned for intrusion in user privacy, as they impose restrictions on what customers can do (e.g., using the content over several devices and/or deny the *fair use*, which is the possibility for the user to legally perform a number of personal copies without incurring in violation of copyright) [5].

In the Internet scenario, the proliferation of proprietary DRM systems is making things difficult for customers since a song acquired legally cannot be played over all the user's devices. Furthermore, in addition to privacy concerns, DRM schemes are also questioned for security issues, since they are employed on un-trusted environments (the play out device is under the user's control).

In the mobile scenario, the security level can be increased as cellphones provide a more secure environment, by offering reliable information regarding both the device and the user (e.g., the IMEI and the IMSI code) [20]. Unfortunately, the increase of security affects user privacy: most of the DRMs currently used allow the song play out only on the device used to acquire and to download the song. To mitigate this burden, some mobile providers offer two versions of the same song: one is designed to be played out on the cellphone, while the other is to be used over a computer, allowing customers to burn their music on CDs.

Needless to say, this lack of flexibility limits the attractiveness of the mobile music market.

A Multi-Channel Distribution Approach

In this section, we present a multi-channel distribution strategy coupled with an effective incentive mechanism, in order to mitigate the problems of the current mobile music scenario. Our goal is to show that an additional opportunity is available for the mobile music market and hence, instead of focusing on implementation details, we outline a possible distribution strategy focusing on its effects on such a music market.

We start by presenting a possible mobile scenario, depicted in Figure 1. Customers access to a wireless music store through the cellphone network and share music files using the cellphone free-of-charge communication technology (e.g., Bluetooth and Wi-Fi). Despite the price is high and the download time is considerable, Alice acquires a song from the mobile music store and downloads both the song and the license through the cellphone network. She decides to share the song with Bob and Marc, so she Wi-Fis them the song. Marc is curios about the song and thinks about buying the license. Since the license file size is much smaller than the song file, the price is reasonable (more similar to the price that Marc would pay

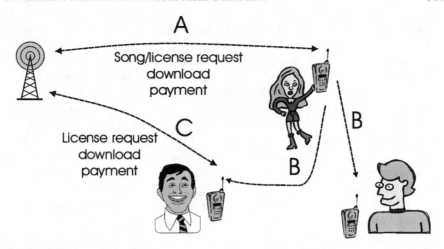

Fig. 1 Multi-channel distribution strategy: customers are authorized to re-distribute music contents

at home to download the same song) and hence he acquires the license song using the cellphone network. After Marc acquired the license, Alice receives a financial compensation for her cooperation in the song distribution. Bob, on the other hand, decides to ignore the message and does nothing.

The scenario just described shows that music distribution among customers can be used to decrease both the usage of the expensive cellphone data network and the time necessary to download a song in the wireless environment. In addition, customers can get commissions back for their cooperation. To be effective, the multi-channel distribution needs customers cooperation and hence, in the following we also propose an incentive mechanism to stimulate such cooperation.

Multi-Channel Mobile Distribution

The main goal of a multi-channel distribution is to reduce costs and the download time of a song. To meet these two goals without penalizing the music store and the cellphone provider, we propose the following multi-channel distribution.

A customer can browse, acquire and download songs directly from the mobile music store using the cellphone network. Once the song has been downloaded, he/she can share the song with other customers using the free-of-charge communication technologies of the cellphone. Since these technologies offer a higher data transfer rate than the one of the cellphone network, the time for song download is highly reduced (e.g., few seconds to download a 4MB song with a Wi-Fi enable cellphone like the Nokia N91). Customers who receive the song can play it out only upon license acquisition, released by the music store through the cellphone network.

Since the license file is much smaller than the song file, the cellphone network is used (and paid) much less than for the entire song transfer. This leads to a final song price that is much smaller than the cost of the same song if downloaded from the cellphone network (the customer-to-customer song transfer is free-of-charge).

It is worth pointing out that, to be effective and successful, a multi-channel distribution has to deal with piracy and customers cooperation. Piracy can be fought with a license-based DRM system. Since the design of a DRM system goes out of the scope of this paper, we refer the reader to [5] for an interesting survey about security, effectiveness and desirability of DRM systems. Here, without loss of generality, we assume that a license-based DRM system is employed so that sharing music files does not compromise security (see the just released PlayReady Microsoft DRM [21]). In such a system, the media song is encrypted with a key (a piece of data that locks and unlocks the song file). Once the song file is encrypted, a customer can only play out the protected file with a separate license. This license contains both the key that decrypts the song file and the rights that specify how the song file can be used. Customers cannot share or copy licenses (a license is released for a specific device/customer and is useless if used over/by a different one); however, copying and sharing protected digital media files with others is allowed, as the only way to play the song is by acquiring the license. Therefore, copying protected files does not compromise their security.

Another important aspect of a multi-channel distribution is related to customers cooperation: without cooperation the multi-channel distribution cannot take place. Unfortunately, by analyzing the behavior of customers in cooperative scenarios like P2P networks, it has been shown that customers tend to consume resources while providing little (or none) to others [4]. This selfish behavior, better known as the *free-riders* problem, can be mitigated by stimulating customers cooperation with incentive mechanisms [1, 7, 9, 15, 24, 27]. In the following, we show how such an incentive mechanism can be used and we propose three different reward policies to financially compensate users for their cooperation.

An Incentive Mechanism

In literature, mechanisms to stimulate users cooperation, can be *reputation/payment* based and *centralized/distributed*. A reputation scheme punishes/rewards the peers on the basis of the observed behavior [9, 15, 24] (Ebay uses this mechanism to attach a feedback rating to each seller), while a payment scheme provides a commission to users that provide a service [1, 7, 27]. Since in the multi-channel strategy, customers are asked to provide a service to other customers (the song transfer), we consider the payment-based mechanism more suited. In a distributed scheme, cooperation activity information is stored directly on the peer, while a centralized scheme requires a central entity to store these information. Since the difficulty in using incentive mechanisms lies in ensuring that they are robust against malicious entities [10] (and special tamper resistant software would be necessary at the wireless terminal to avoid malicious modifications of the customer behavior [4]), we propose using a centralize incentive mechanism.

The main idea is to give a financial compensation to those customers that success- fully distribute a song (meaning that the song has been delivered to another customer and this one acquired the song license). This mechanism is easy to implement, as it is sufficient to attach an additional financial cost to the license price, with the requirement that this additional cost has to be partially or totally recouped by re- distributing the song to other customers. Our findings further suggest that not only customers can fully recover the additional financial cost, but they can also have ad- ditional incomes if the re-distribution mechanism takes place. Before presenting the details of the proposed mechanism, it is worth describing all the components that affect the price of a song.

The final price of a song is determined by: the cost of the license, the cost for transmitting the license and the cost for transmitting the song through the cellphone network. It is worth pointing out that when a customer buys a song from the Internet with the computer at home, the price paid for the song is merely the license song price (data traffic is not included and is usually negligible due to broadband flat residential plans). Conversely, the cost of the data traffic plays an important role in mobile distribution.

By considering the additional financial cost that is attached to the final price for incentive purposes, the parameters that participate to the song price are the following:

- C_L = Cost of the License;
- C_{LT} = Cost of transmitting the License;
- C_{ST} = Cost of transmitting the Song;
- C_I = Cost for the incentive scheme.

and the final song price, P, is given by

$$P = C_L + C_{LT} + C_{ST} + C_I. \tag{1}$$

Quantity C_L is the same for all customers, decided once for all by the music store; C_I depends on the used network (either the cellphone data network or the free-of-charge one); C_{LT}, C_{ST} might differ from customer to customer, according to their subscription plans and/or to their cellphone providers. Depending on the network used to download, two cases are possible:

- Cellphone Network. The additional financial cost is not charged to the customers ($C_I = 0$), as the song is directly downloaded through the cellphone network; The song price is $P = C_L + C_{LT} + C_{ST}$.
- Bluetooth/Wi-Fi Network. The additional financial cost is charged to the cus- tomer ($C_I > 0$), while the cost for transmitting the song through the cellphone network is not charged ($C_{ST} = 0$). The song price is $P = C_L + C_{LT} + C_I$.

The amount C_I is the additional cost introduced in the multi-channel distribution for incentive purposes, but it is also the reward that the mobile music store will give back to customer(s)[1]. The decision about the amount of C_I is up to the mobile music store, but it is strongly recommended that $0 \leq C_I \ll C_{ST}$, otherwise it would be more convenient to download the song using the cellphone network, leading to the current situation and to the problems already mentioned.

How C_I is subdivided among customers depends on the reward policy. Usually, this policy falls into one of the following categories:

- *Single reward*: The amount C_I is given only to the customer who just delivered the song;
- *Multiple reward*: The amount C_I is shared among some of the customers who distributed the song, from the one who originally downloaded the song from the store, to the one who just delivered the song.

With respect to Figure 2, let us suppose that F, after receiving the song from E, buys the license song. The cost C_I can be given only to E (single reward policy) or can be shared among all the customers that cooperated to the song distribution, from E up to the one who bought he song from the cellphone network (in the example, C_I would be shared by A, B and E).

The reward policy requires the mobile music store to know who distributed the song. This information can be easily obtained during the license acquisition procedure. In fact, since a sign-up procedure is always required to access a music store, a user identifier is sufficient to the store to know which customer delivered the song (with respect to Figure 2, when F acquires the license, it tells the music store that E delivered the song).

Although the single reward policy is very simple to implement, it presents a fairness issue: the reward given to a customer does not make a distinction between the customer that bought the song from the expensive cellphone network and the one that received the song from another customer. This is quite unfair, as the former

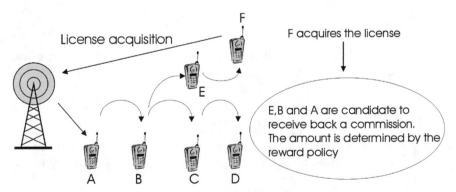

Fig. 2 Multi-channel distribution. After F acquires the license, E, B and A can receive a commission back. The amount depends on the reward policy

---

[1] The form of the reward can be either digital cash, coupons, future credits, etc, and it's up to the mobile music store.

paid much more than those who simply re-distribute the song. Hence, customers may avoid direct song acquisitions from cellphone networks, and this may slow down the expansion of the mobile music market. For this reason, the multi-channel strategy should be coupled with a multiple reward policy.

We propose three different natural multiple reward policies, namely *selfish, equal* and *proportional*, to regulate the redistribution, among several users, of the income of a sale. Each policy has different advantages and disadvantages for the ones involved in the redistribution. The store might decide which one to apply according to its needs/predilection. The selfish policy divides the amount C_I in two quotas: one for customer that bought the song from the store, one for the customer that delivers the song directly to another one. The second policy equally divides the amount C_I among all the customers along the song distribution path. The last policy proportionally assigns a quota of C_I to customers along the song distribution path, where the proportion is done according to how far a customer is to the one delivering the song.

A final remark relates to hypothetical cheating peers spreading files with illegal names and/or invalid content. Without entering into details, observe that the validity of the music file can be checked in cooperation with the music store or using techniques like the one proposed in [19]. Hence this phenomenon should be minor, as spreading invalid contents will not lead to a financial compensation. Moreover, whenever the song is distributed thanks to social connections, the seller has no interest in getting a bad name among friends, as he/she will not be able to use these connections again in the future.

Evaluation of the Multi-Channel Distribution Strategy

In this section we evaluate the multi-channel distribution strategy, analyzing the effects of such distribution on the wireless music store, cellphone network operators and customers.

Wireless Music store

A first observation is that a wireless music store gets revenues for song-license sales and not for cellphone data traffic; hence the multi-channel distribution strategy does not affect its revenues. Furthermore, the approach allows reducing the workload of the music store since music distribution is done by others (the customers). Another important benefit is related to *impulsive buying*. Music is considered an experience good, and new music is often discovered through friends [6]. Hence, when a customer receives a song (usually from a known person), he/she is stimulated to buy [8, 26]. Needless to say, if customers are stimulated to buy, it is likely that the wireless music store will sell more songs, increasing its revenues.

Cellphone Network Operators

Cellphone network operators may seem penalized by the multi-channel strategy, as customers are allowed to re-distribute the songs through free-of-charge technologies. However, it is worth highlighting that: (1) the approach reduces the song price, in a context in which high price is considered a burden for the success of the mobile music market, and (2) customers are forced to use the cellphone network to acquire the license. Hence, with the expansion of the mobile music market, the data traffic generated by license downloads may also increase the revenues of the cellphone operators.

Customer Point of View

The multi-channel distribution strategy provides an additional opportunity for mobile customers to directly download media contents over their devices using the cellphone network only partially (*i.e.*, just to get the song license). Price reduction is, hence, the major benefit for customers. As mentioned, the multi-channel distribution strategy uses an incentive mechanism that attaches an additional financial cost to the license price; cost that can be regained by song re-distribution.

Before presenting a detailed investigation of benefits that customers might have, observe that the set of customers cooperating to a song distribution can be seen as a tree, where the root is the customer who bought the song from the store (using the cellphone network) while the others are organized in hierarchical levels: customers at level 1 are the customers that directly bought the song from the root; customers at level 2 are those who bought it from customers at level 1 and so on (*e.g.*, see Figure 2).

For each proposed reward policy (selfish, equal and proportional), our goal is to investigate the best and the worst scenario with respect to the amount of reward that a customer can have. Given the best possible scenario, we will determine which customers will never have a full refund of the cost C_I. Given the worst possible situation, we compute, for any given customer, the minimum number of people that has to acquire the license in order to get a full refund of the cost C_I. In general, the higher the number of nodes in subtrees rooted at a customer, the higher the revenue of the customer will be. To make a better analysis, we will examine the shape of such subtrees (with the exception of the selfish policy, where the entire subtree is not important).

Formally (see Figure 3.a for notation), we consider a tree T with $k + 1$ levels (*i.e.*, height $h = k$) where the root r is at level zero, its sons at level one and so on, and some leaves are at level k. Given a node v at level $0 \leq j \leq k$ with $c_v \geq 0$ children, let T_v be the subtree rooted in v and $h_v \leq k - j$ be the height of T_v. We denote the level (in T) of the furthest leaf of T_v with k_v (*i.e.*, $k_v = h_v + j$). The maximum degree of the tree, $\max_{v \in T} c_v$, is denoted by m, and we will assume that $m \geq 1$ (as $m = 0$ means the tree is only the root, not an interesting case). Finally, R_v is the revenue of node v.

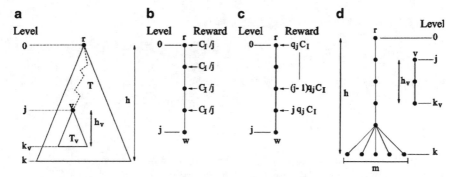

Fig. 3 (**a**) Notation used in this section. (**b**) Rewards according to equal distribution. (**c**) Rewards according to proportional distribution. (**d**) Shape of tree in worst-case scenario

Selfish distribution. When a node w buys a song from a node $v \in T$, the incentive cost C_I paid by w is equally divided between the root r and v. In this policy, the node that gets the greatest reward is the root, getting the entire C_I from its children and half C_I from any other node. Thus, if T has n nodes, then $R_r = (n - 1 + c_r)C_I/2$. For a node v, different from the root, the reward R_v is determined only by the number of its children:

$$R_v = c_v C_I/2.$$

With only two children, node v has repaid exactly the price for the incentive mechanism and it will receive a profit starting at the third child.

Equal distribution. When a node w at level $0 < j \leq k$ pays C_I, each node at level $0 \leq j' < j$ on the path form r to w, receives a reward equal to C_I/j (see Figure 3.b). For the root it is enough to have just one node $v \neq r$ in the tree to get a reward equal to C_I (but observe that the root paid much more than C_I to download the song). On the other side, if a node v is at level k (the last) it has no reward at all.

Higher Reward. The maximum reward for node v, at level $0 \leq j \leq k$, comes when tree T_v has the maximum number of nodes; *i.e.*, each node has exactly the maximum number m of children. Hence, in T_v there are m^i nodes at level $i + j$, for each $1 \leq i \leq h_v$, each contributing to the revenue R_v by $C_I/(j + i)$:

$$R_v = C_I \sum_{i=1}^{h_v} \frac{m^i}{j + i}. \tag{2}$$

Who might have C_I back, in the best case. The reward of node v depends on the height of the tree T_v: the higher the tree, the higher the reward (here we assume that $m \geq 2$, otherwise we fall in the worst case, treated in the following). The terms of the summation in (2) increase with increasing i, hence, $R_v \geq C_I$ if at least the last term of the summation is greater than one, *i.e.*, if

$$m^{h_v} \geq j + h_v$$
$$h_v \log m \geq \log(j + h_v) \tag{3}$$

Node v regains C_I as soon as $h_v \geq j \geq 1$, as equation (3) holds:

$$h_v \log m \geq h_v \geq \log h_v + \log 2 = \log(2h_v) \geq \log(j + h_v).$$

In particular, this is true for each node v at level above $h/2$ having subtree T_v high enough. Otherwise, if $1 \leq h_v < j$, v re-gains C_I if $h_v \geq \log(2j)/\log m$:

$$h_v \log m \geq \log(2j) \geq \log(j + h_v).$$

The ratio $\log(2j)/\log m$ grows much slower than levels, hence even nodes low in the tree (approximatively above level $h\text{-}\log h/\log m$) might regain C_I in the best case.

Who will not have C_I back, not even in the best case. Analogously, we can prove that for $h_v < \log(1 + j/h_v)/\log m \approx \log(j/h_v)/\log m$ then $R_v < C_I$ (because the summation in (2) is smaller than $(h_v + 1)$ times the biggest -the last-term). Thus, for j close to k, h_v is very close to one and we can conclude that, as expected, nodes at lower levels (approximatively below level $h\text{-}\log h/\log m$) will not, even in the best case, regain the price spent for C_I.

Minimum Reward. The minimum reward for v comes when the subtree T_v is a (possibly empty) chain. We distinguish the cases in which v is the root or not (see Figure 3d). In the former there must be, at some level $0 \leq j \leq k - 1$ along the chain, a node w with m children. Each node at level i along the chain contributes to the root's revenue R_r with C_I/i, while each of the m children of w contributes with $C_I/(j + 1)$:

$$R_r = \sum_{i=1}^{k} \frac{C_I}{i} + (m - 1)\frac{C_I}{j + 1}. \tag{4}$$

Equation (4) is minimized for maximum j (*i.e.*, for $j = k - 1$). Hence, the worst case is the one depicted in Figure 2.d and R_r can be computed by substituting $k - 1$ to j into equation (4).

If v is not the root, then it might happen that the node with m children is not in subtree T_v, but somewhere else in T, hence, its subtree is just a chain with h_v nodes (Figure 3.d) and the reward of v is given by:

$$R_v = C_I \sum_{i=j+1}^{k_v} \frac{1}{i}. \tag{5}$$

Who will surely have C_I back, even in the worst case (*i.e.*, always). What is the minimum k_v that makes v sure that $R_v \geq C_I$ in the worst scenario? We will use the following (well known) facts: let $H(n) = \sum_{i=1}^{n} 1/i$ be the partial sums of the harmonic series, then we have:

$$\log(n + 1) \leq H(n) \leq \log n + 1$$
$$H(n) - \log(n + 1) < 0.57,$$

where 0.57 is the Eulero-Mascheroni constant. From (5) we have

$$
\begin{aligned}
\frac{R_v}{C_I} = \sum_{i=j+1}^{k_v} \frac{1}{i} &= H(k_v) - H(j) \\
&= H(k_v) - H(j) + \log(j+1) - \log(j+1) \\
&> \log(k_v+1) - 0.57 - \log(j+1) \\
&= \log \frac{k_v+1}{j+1} - 0.57 \geq 1
\end{aligned}
$$

when $(k_v+1)/(j+1) \geq 2^{1.57}$, that is $k_v \geq 2^{1.57}(j+1) - 1$. As $h_v = k_v - j$, if $h_v \geq (2^{1.57} - 1)(j+1)$ then $R_v \geq C_I$. This means that whenever there are at least $\lceil (2^{1.57} - 1)(j+1) \rceil$ nodes in subtree T_v, then v is sure he got C_I back, no matter how these nodes are arranged in the subtree.

Who might not have C_I back, in the worst case. For which k_v we have $R_v \leq C_I$ in the worst-case scenario?

$$
\begin{aligned}
\frac{R_v}{C_I} = \sum_{i=j+1}^{k_v} \frac{1}{i} &= H(k_v) - H(j) \\
&= H(k_v) - \log(k_v+1) + \log(k_v+1) - H(j) \\
&< 0.57 + \log(k_v+1) - \log(j+1) \\
&= 0.57 + \log \frac{k_v+1}{j+1} \leq 1
\end{aligned}
$$

when $(k_v+1)/(j+1) \leq 2^{0.43}$, that is $k_v \leq 2^{0.43}(j+1) - 1$. Again, as $h_v = k_v - j$, if $h_v \leq (2^{0.43} - 1)(j+1)$ then $R_v \leq C_I$. This means that a node v at level $j \geq 2^{-0.43}(h+1) - 13h/4$ will not be able to regain C_I.

In conclusion, the exact number of nodes N in T_v needed to repay v for C_I is bounded by:

$$
\lceil (2^{0.43} - 1)(j+1) \rceil \leq N \leq \lfloor (2^{1.57} - 1)(j+1) \rfloor.
$$

Proportional distribution. When a node w at level $0 < j \leq k$ pays C_I, a quota $q_j = j(j+1)/2$ is determinate and each other node, at level $j' < j$ on the path from r to w, gets $j'+1$ quotas (see Figure 3c). Also under this policy, the root gains C_I as soon as it sells the song to its first child. Given a node v at level $0 \leq j \leq k-1$, it is easy to see that the shapes of the trees in the best and worst case are the same as in the case of the equal distribution.

Higher Reward. T_v is a m-regular tree and the revenue coming from any of the m^{i-j} nodes at level $j < i \leq k_v$ is $(j+1)C_I/q_i$. Hence,

$$
R_v = C_I \sum_{i=j+1}^{k_v} m^{i-j} \left(\frac{j+1}{q_i} \right) = 2(j+1)C_I \sum_{i=j+1}^{k_v} \frac{m^{i-j}}{i(i+1)} \tag{6}
$$

Who will get C_I back, in the best case. With proofs analogous to the ones done for the equal policy, we state that, given a node v at level j we have: (a) if $h_v \geq j/2$ then, as the rightmost summation in (6) is greater than h_v times its first term (the smallest), v has regained C_I; (b) if $\log(9j/8)/\log m \leq h_v < j/2$, as the rightmost summation in (6) is greater than just its last term (the greatest), v has regained C_I.

Who might not get C_I back, not even in the best case. It is possible to prove that, if $h_v < [\log(1 + j/h_v) - 1]/\log m \approx (\log(j/h_v) - 1)/\log m$, then R_v is smaller than C_I.

Observe that these three bounds are slightly better than the ones in the case of the equal distribution, resulting sometimes in one extra level of satisfied customers.

Minimum Reward. Again, we distinguish the cases in which v is the root or not (Figure 3.d). In the first case we have:

$$R_r = C_I \left(\frac{m}{q_k} + \sum_{i=1}^{k-1} \frac{1}{q_i} \right).$$

For any other node v at level $0 < j < k$:

$$R_v = C_I(j+1) \sum_{i=j+1}^{k_v} \frac{1}{q_i} = 2(j+1)C_I \sum_{i=j+1}^{k_v} \frac{1}{i(i+1)} \qquad (7)$$

Who will get exactly C_I back, even in the worst case. If $k_v = 2j + 1$, then the rightmost quantity in expression (7) is exactly C_I. In fact, using $\sum_{i=1}^{n} 1/i(i+1) = 1 - 1/(n+1)$, we have

$$2(j+1) \sum_{i=j+1}^{k_v} \frac{1}{i(i+1)} = 2(j+1) \left(\sum_{i=1}^{k_v} \frac{1}{i(i+1)} - \sum_{i=i}^{j} \frac{1}{i(i+1)} \right)$$

$$= 2(j+1) \left(1 - \frac{1}{k_v + 1} - 1 + \frac{1}{j+1} \right)$$

$$= 2(j+1) \frac{k_v - j}{(k_v+1)(j+1)}$$

$$= 2 \frac{k_v - j}{k_v + 1} = 1$$

As $h_v = k_v - j$, we conclude that, whenever there are at least $j + 1$ nodes in T_v (this might happen only for nodes above level $h/2$) then $R_v \geq C_I$ and v gets the incentive cost back, no matter how these nodes are arranged in T_v. Conversely, if v is at level below $h/2$, in the worst case, it will not get C_I back.

Figure 4(a) presents the results obtained from analyzing the minimum number of costumers that has to buy a license in order to provide a full refund of C_I to

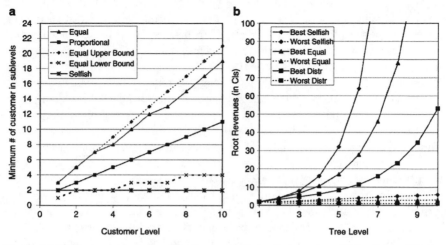

Fig. 4 (**a**) Minimum number of customer to get back the C_I incentive additional cost. (**b**) Root revenues in best and worst case assuming a maximum tree degree of 2

a node located in a particular tree level, with respect to the three reward policies. The root node (at level zero) is not present as this node does not pay the amount C_I (it acquires the song through the cellphone network). In the case of the equal distribution, we present both theoretical and experimental results. We can see that the experimental results lie in between the theoretical bounds, but much closer to the upper bound than to the lower bound. Hence the upper bound can be used as a better measure to estimate the real value. For what concerns the selfish and proportional distribution, experimental and theoretical results coincide.

Figure 4(b) shows the revenue of the customer that bought the song form the store (*i.e.*, the root), in the best and in the worst case (assuming, without loss of generality, a maximum degree of $m = 2$), where the reward is expressed in C_I units. Note that, since $C_I \ll C_{ST}$ the root may need several C_I to recoup the price paid for downloading the song through the cellphone data network (C_{ST}). The number of C_Is depends on the ratio between C_{ST} and C_I, decided by the mobile store. For example, if C_I is too close to C_{ST}, customers will preferably buy music directly from the store, if too close to zero, customers may avoid direct buying from the store; in both cases, this leads to a starvation of music distribution among customers.

From the customer point of view, observe that in the selfish policy the customer who bought from the store has the higher revenue, independently of how the song spreads among customers, but depending on the number of customers involved in the song distribution. For the other customers, only the number of direct deliveries causes revenue. This means that the costumer knows exactly how much income it will get, as it depends only on its actions and *things are completely under control*. As a backside, customers are not really encouraged to distribute the song, as he/she knows he/she gets repaid for the incentive cost with just two sales, and the multi-channel distribution philosophy gets lost. On the contrary, in the case of the two other policies, the revenue of a customer depends on the number of customers that receive the song directly and indirectly from him/her. Thus, the way in which the song spreads among customers greatly influences their revenue; *e.g.*, a customer might have a big income with little effort if the customers to whom the song is delivered put a lot of effort in reselling the song; customers might get an unexpected reward also after a long period of time from the moment he/she sold the song. The proportional reward policy produces better results than the equal distribution, as a customer needs a smaller number of customers in its subtree, even if to get a full refund of C_I, the minimum number of customers is reasonable in both cases.

Moreover, although we analyzed the worst-case scenario, this is unlikely to happen in reality, especially if we think that music is distributed according to social relationships. Hence, with a multi-channel distribution strategy, in average, even a smaller number of customers has to be reached and it is likely that many customers (the higher they are in the tree, the better) might have a revenue grater than C_I.

From the store point of view, the choice of the policy depends on which, among the customers, the store wants to favor: the selfish policy favors the ones that buy from the store; the equal favors the customers that join the music distribution earlier; the proportional favors the customers that actually distribute the song.

Related Work

Content distribution in a mobile environment is a subject investigated in recent literature: some are experiencing the development of ad-hoc P2P networks in a mobile environment [13, 14], others are proposing to disseminate contents in Wi-Fi based ad-hoc networks through epidemic algorithms [18, 29].

The multi-channel distribution outlined in this paper does not require a real P2P network, as the song delivery simply requires the cooperation of two customers, making the operation more similar to what happens when a friend text-messages or sends an MMS to another friend. In this case, the message content is the song and the network used is other than the cellphone network.

Many of the approaches present in literature are designed to stimulate users cooperation in a P2P networks [2, 3, 25, 28]; for example, peers are asked to route queries or are limited in the use of bandwidth according to the amount of bandwidth they provided to the system. For scalability reasons, most of these mechanisms are distributed, requiring only local information available at each peer. This might lead to malicious modification of peer local information by the peer itself, and hence tamper resistant software should be employed at the user side. Our mechanism is simple to implement because it comes with a centralized control mechanism at no cost: the store can always keep track of the spreading of the song and is always able to correctly assign revenues. Whenever a user wants to play a song he/she just bought, he/she needs to buy the license from the store. At this stage, the store can easily record who sold and who bought the song, updating the information about song spreading.

We are not aware of any distribution strategy that couples cellphone networks and free-of-charge technologies to distribute contents, and that makes use of incentive mechanisms to stimulate the customer cooperation in content distribution.

Conclusions

In this paper we analyzed the characteristics of the current mobile music scenario, investigating the communication infrastructure, the pricing strategy and the copyright protection scheme currently used. The analysis highlighted that a replication of the strategy used to distribute contents in the Internet-based music market is not worth applying in the mobile scenario, as it presents critical problems (excessive download time and high cost).

To mitigate such problems, we show that a multi-channel distribution strategy can be successful. In such a strategy, customers can re-distribute the song acquired by using the free-of-charge communication technologies provided in cellphones. We showed that by using a smart protection scheme, music sharing could avoid piracy. We also present an incentive mechanism, coupled with three different reward policies, which stimulates customers cooperation by providing a financial compensation to those customers who help distributing music files.

The evaluation of the multi-channel distribution strategy equipped with the proposed incentive mechanism showed that considerable benefits may be received by all the entities involved in the mobile music distribution, from music stores to customers, to cellphone network providers.

References

1. K. C. Almeroth and A. Garyfalos. Coupons: Wide scale information distribution for wireless ad hoc networks. In *Proc. of IEEE Globecom*, December 2004.
2. K. G. Anagnostakis and M. B. Greenwald, Exchange-based incentive mechanisms for peer-to-peer file sharing. In International Conference on Distributed Computing Systems, 2004.
3. K. G. Anagnostakis, M. B. G. Yang, T. Condie, S. Kamvar, and H. Garcia-Molina, Non-cooperation in competitive p2p networks. In International Conference on Distributed Computing Systems, 2004.
4. P. Antoniadis, C. Courcoubetis and B. Strulo, Incentives for content availability in memory-less peer-to- peer file sharing systems. *SIGecom Exch.*, Vol.5, No. 4, pp. 11–20, 2005, ACM press.
5. K. Biddle, P. England, M. Peinado, and B. Willman. The darknet and the future of content distribution. In *Proc. of the ACM Workshop on DRM*, 2002.
6. B. Brown, A. J. Sellen, and E. Geelhoed. Music sharing as a computer supported collaborative application. In *Proceedings of ECSCW 2001*, Bohn, Germany, 2001. Kluwer academic publishers.
7. L. Buttyan and J. P. Hubaux. Stimulating cooperation in selforganizing mobile ad hoc networks. *ACM/Kluwer Mobile Networks and Applications (MONET)*, 8(5):579–592, October 2003.

8. C. J. Cobb and W. D. Hoyer. Planned versus impulse purchase behavior. *Journal of Retailing*, 62, April 1986.

9. R. Dingledine and P. Syverson. Reliable mix cascade networks through reputation. In *Proceedings of the Sixth International Financial Cryptography Conference (FC02)*, March 2002.

10. M. Feldman, K. Lai, I. Stoica and J. Chuang, Robust incentive techniques for peer-to-peer networks, Proceedings of the 5th ACM conference on Electronic commerce, pp. 102–111, 2004.

11. M. Furini, M. Montangero, "The Impact of Incentive Mechanisms in Multi-Channel Mobile Music Distribution", Multimedia Tools and Applications, Vol. 37. No. 3, pp. 365–382, March 2008. Springer Netherlands Editor.

12. M. Furini, M. Montangero, "The Use of Incentive Mechanisms in Multi-Channel Mobile Music Distribution", Proceedings of 2nd IEEE International Conference on Automated Production of Cross Media Content for Multi-Channel Distribution (AXMEDIS 2006), Leeds, UK, December 12–15. IEEE Computer Press 2006.

13. E. Harjula, M. Ylianttila, J. Ala-Kurikka, J. Riekki, J. Sauvola, *Plug-and-play application platform: towards mobile peer-to-peer*, Proceedings of the 3rd international conference on Mobile and ubiquitous multimedia MUM, October 2004.

14. N. Hatt *BlueFramework - Application Framework for Bluetooth Enabled Mobile Phones*, TIK-MA-2005-16, ETH ZÃ¹/₄rich, Switzerland, 2005.

15. T. H.-T. Hu, K. Wongrujira, and A. Seneviratne. Reputation in peer-to-peer networks. In *Proceedings of the IEEE International Conference on Communications (ICC 2004)*, pages 1411Â–1415, Paris, France, June 2004.

16. D. Hughes, G. Coulson, J. Walkerdine, *Free Riding on Gnutella Revisited: The Bell Tolls?*, IEEE Distributed Systems online, Vol. 6, No. 6, June 2005.

17. IFIP. Digital music report 2008 – Summary. Research report, International Federation of the Phonographic Industry, 2008. [on-line] Available at http://www.ifpi.org/content/library/DMR2008-summary.pdf

18. A. Khelil, C. Becker, J. Tian, K. Rothermel, *An epidemic model for information diffusion in MANETs*, Proceedings of the 5th ACM International Workshop on Modeling, Analysis and Simulation of Wireless and Mobile Systems, September 2002.

19. J. Liang, R. Kumar, Y. Xi, and K. Ross, Pollution in P2P File Sharing Systems. In *IEEE Infocom*, Miami, FL, USA, March 2005.

20. T.S. Messerges and E.A. Dabbish, *Digital Rights Management in a 3G Mobile Phone and Beyond* Proceedings of Digital Right Management (DRM), Washington, October 2003. ACM Press.

21. Microsoft Corporation, *Microsoft PlayReady powers next-generation media experiences on mobile networks*, http://www.microsoft.com/presspass/press/2007/feb07/02-123GSMNewTechnologyPR.mspx

22. M. J. O'Grady and G. M. P. OÂ'Hare Just-In-Time Multimedia Distribution in a Mobile Computing Environment. *IEEE Multimedia*, 62–74, 2004.

23. G. P. Premkumar. Alternative distribution strategies for digital music. *Communication of the ACM*, 9(9):89–95, September 2003.

24. P. Resnick, K. Kuwabara, R. Zeckhauser, and E. Friedman. Reputation systems. *Communications of the ACM*, 43(12):45–48, 2000.

25. A. Roczniak and A. El Saddik, Impact of incentive mechanisms on quality of experience. Proceedings of the 13th annual ACM international conference on Multimedia, pp. 311–314, 2005.

26. D. Rook. The buying impulse. *Journal of Consumer research*, 14(2):189–199, September 1987.

27. N. B. Salem, M. J. L. Buttyan, and J. P. Hubaux. A charging and rewarding scheme for packet forwarding. In *Proceedings of MobiHoc*, June 2003.

28. Q. Sun and H. Garcia-Molina, Slic: A selfish link based incentive mechanism for unstructured peer-to-peer networks. In International Conference on Distributed Computing Systems, 2004.

29. Paul Tennent, Malcolm Hall, Barry Brown, Matthew Chalmers, Scott Sherwood, Toward social mobility: Three applications for mobile epidemic algorithms Proceedings of the 7th international conference on Human computer interaction with mobile devices & services MobileHCI '05.
30. Wireless-Intelligence. World cellular connection. Research report, Wireless Intelligence, 2005. [on-line] Available at https://www.wirelessintelligence.com

Chapter 15
Pattern Discovery and Change Detection of Online Music Query Streams

Hua-Fu Li

Introduction

In recent years, many applications generate large amount of data streams in real time. For example, sensor data generated from sensor networks, online transaction flows in retail chains, stream Web click-sequences and records in Web services and applications, performance measurement in network monitoring and traffic management, call records in telecommunications. Mining data streams differs from mining traditional static data sets in two main aspects [2]:

- The volume of a continuous data stream over its lifetime could be huge and fast changing.
- The queries require timely answers, and the response time is short.

Hence, it is not possible to store all the streaming data in main memory or even in secondary storage. This motivates the design for in-memory summary data structure with small memory footprints that can support both one-time and continuous queries. Furthermore, online approach of mining such data has to sacrifice the correctness of their analysis results by allowing some counting errors, i.e., it generates approximate results, and only has single pass over the data [8].

Recently, online music downloading is a hot Web service. Many companies, such as Apple's iTunes [18], Napster [16], Loudeye, Yahoo's MusicMatch [17], Kuro [20], KKBox [19], and EasyMusic.com, provide this Web service. According to the reports of IFPI (International Federation of the Phonographic Industry; IFPI: http://www.ifpi.org/), there are more than 60 hundred millions of online music downloads at 2006. For example, the amount of online music downloading of Apple's iTune is about 50 hundred millions from 2004 to 2007. Hence, knowledge discovery of such online music downloading behaviors of customers is an important research and a practical issue for data mining.

H.-F. Li (✉)
Department of Computer Science, Kainan University, Taoyuan, Taiwan
e-mail: hfli@mail.knu.edu.tw

B. Furht (ed.), *Handbook of Multimedia for Digital Entertainment and Arts*,
DOI 10.1007/978-0-387-89024-1_15, © Springer Science+Business Media, LLC 2009

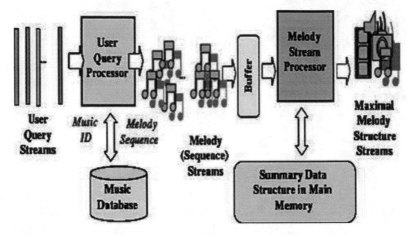

Fig. 1 Computation model for music query streams

The issue comes from the context of online music-downloading services (such as Apple's iTunes, Napster, Loudeye, Yahoo's MusicMatch, Kuro, KKBox, and EasyMusic. com), where the stream in question are streams of queries, i.e., music-downloading requests, sent to the server, and we are interested in finding the useful music melody structures requested by most customers during some period of time. The discovered patterns can be used to predict the future trend of online music styles and to personalize the Web services of online music downloading. With the processing model of music query streams presented in Fig. 1 [11, 12], the melody stream processor and the summary data structure are two major components in such a streaming environment. The user query processor receives user queries in the form of *<Timestamp, Customer-ID, Music-ID>*, and then transforms the queries into music data (i.e., melody sequences) in the form of *<Timestamp, Customer-ID, Music-ID, Melody-Sequence>* by querying the music database. Note that the component Buffer can be optionally set for temporary storage of recent music melody sequences from the music query streams.

Among various techniques of data mining, frequent pattern mining is one of the most popular data mining approaches used to discover the customers' behaviors from large data sets. However, traditional data mining techniques for discovering frequent patterns are not feasible for mining frequent patterns from such application of online music downloading. Because such data characteristic is streaming, the proposed methods for mining such streaming data need new capabilities such as using limited memory to maintain the essential information embedded in an unbound data stream, one-pass data scan and real time processing of each incoming data element.

Mining music data is one of the most important research issues in multimedia data mining. Although several techniques have been developed for discovering and analyzing the content of static music data [3, 9, 10, 14, 15], new techniques are needed to analyze and discover the content of streaming music data. Recently, two efficient one-pass mining algorithms, FCS-stream [11] and MMS$_{LMS}$ [12], were proposed by Li et al. for discovering the closed frequent melody structures and the maximal frequent melody structures over the entire history of a continuous music query stream. Both algorithms are stream mining methods of a landmark window. However, the knowledge embedded in streaming data is likely to be changed as time goes by. Identifying the recent changes of data streams quickly can provide valuable information for the analysis of the streaming data [5]. Hence, we need new single-pass approaches for mining frequent patterns from the streaming online music downloading requests within a sliding window.

Several one-pass mining methods [5, 6] were proposed for finding frequent patterns over data streams within a sliding window. The baseline method, called SWFI-stream, for mining frequent patterns over transaction data streams within a sliding window was proposed by Chang and Lee [5]. In the framework of SWFI-stream algorithm, there are two phases for mining frequent patterns over stream sliding windows. One is a window initialization phase. The phase is activated while the number of incoming data transactions generated so far is less than or equal to a predefined window size. The other is a window sliding phase. The second phase is activated after the window becomes full. The SWFI-stream algorithm is composed of four steps. First, all sub-patterns of a transaction are extracted. Second, these sub-patterns are inserted into a prefix-tree lattice structure. Third, all in-frequent patterns are pruned from the lattice structure. Finally, all frequent patterns are generated form the lattice structure. The first two steps are performed in the window initialization phase and the last two steps are performed in the window sliding phase.

There are several performance bottlenecks of the typical solution. First, SWFI-stream needs the extra memory to maintain the original window in a temporal list and a prefix-tree lattice structure for storing the frequent patterns and semi-frequent patterns. Second, the processing complexity of enumerating each incoming transaction is exponential, i.e., $O(k^2)$, where k is the length of transaction. Third, the cost of maintaining the prefix-tree lattice structure of this typical solution is also exponential.

Chi et al. [6] proposed a sliding window based algorithm, called Moment, which might be the first method to find frequent closed itemsets from transaction data streams. A summary data structure, called CET (Closed Enumeration Tree), is used in the Moment algorithm to maintain a dynamically selected set of itemsets over a sliding window. These selected itemsets consist of closed frequent itemsets and a boundary between the closed frequent itemsets and the rest of the itemsets. CET covers all necessary information because any status changes of itemsets (e.g. from infrequent to frequent or from frequent to infrequent) must be through the boundary in CET. Whenever a sliding occurs, it updates the counts of the related nodes in CET and modifies CET. Experiments of Moment algorithm show that the boundary in CET is stable so the update cost is little. However, Moment must maintain huge CET nodes for a closed frequent itemset. The ratio of CET nodes and closed frequent itemsets is about 30:1. If there are a large number of closed frequent itemsets, the memory requirement of Moment algorithm will be inefficient.

In this paper, an efficient stream mining algorithm, called FTP-stream (*Frequent Temporal Pattern* mining of *streams*), is proposed to find the frequent temporal patterns over melody sequence streams. In the framework of our proposed algorithm, an effective bit-sequence representation is used to reduce the time and memory needed to slide the windows. The FTP-stream algorithm can calculate the support threshold in only a single pass based on the concept of bit-sequence representation. It takes the advantage of "left" and "and" operations of the representation. Experiments show that the proposed algorithm only scans the music query stream once, and runs significant faster and consumes less memory than existing algorithms, such as SWFI-stream and Moment.

The proposed FTP-stream algorithm is an exact stream mining method. That means the FTP-stream algorithm can generate the set of frequent patterns over music query streams without any information loss. It is because that the proposed algorithm uses bit-sequence representation of chord-sets to record the exact frequency of each chord-set. Then, the algorithm constructs the set of frequent patterns by using these bit-sequence representations of chord-sets. Consequently, generating exact results is one of the benefits of our proposed algorithm.

After mining frequent temporal patterns from online music query streams, the next issue of this work is that how to use these frequent patterns to predict the future trend of online music styles and to personalize the Web services of online music downloading. Hence, we need new information, i.e., changes of patterns, to assist the domain experts to predict the Web user behaviors and personalize the Web services.

The second research issue of this paper is change detection of frequent patterns across data streams. With data streams, people are more often interested in mining queries such like "*Compared to the history, what are the distinct features of the current status?*", "*What are the most popular melody structures in the last four hours?*" and "*What are the relatively stable factors over time?*" To answer such queries, we have to examine the changes of streaming data to assist the domain experts to predict the future trend of popular online music styles [7, 13]. Therefore, a simple single-pass algorithm, called MQS-change (*changes* of *Music Query Streams*), is proposed to detect the changes of frequent patterns across music query streams. Experiments show that the proposed MQS-change algorithm is an effective method to detect the changes of data streams efficiently. Based on our best knowledge, the proposed MSQ-change algorithm is the first stream mining algorithm for discovering the changes of frequent patterns over music query data streams. Furthermore, for answering such above example query "*What are the most popular melody structures in the last four hours?*", the definitions of MFI (maximal frequent itemset), MFS (maximal frequent item-string), ICI (increasing changed itemset) and ICS (increasing changed item-string) can be used as popular melody structures in this paper although there are many other definitions of most popular melody structures depend on domain knowledge of experts. Note that MFI, MFS, ICI, ICS are defined in concluding Section. Hence, if the sliding window can be modified to contain the melody sequences generated from last four hours, we can use the proposed MQS-change to mine the most popular melody structures from last four hours.

Problem Definition of Pattern Discovery of Music Query Streams

In this section, several features of music data are described and the problem
definition of pattern discovery of music query streams is described. The basic terminologies on music used in this paper are referred to [9, 10, 14]. A *chord* is the
sounding combination of three or more notes at the same time. A *note* is a single
symbol on a musical score, indicating the pitch and duration of what is to be sung
and played. A *chord-set* is a set of chords.

Let $\Psi = \{i_1, i_2, \ldots, i_n\}$ be a set of *chord-sets*, called **items** for simplicity,
where n is the total number of chord-sets used for pattern mining. An **itemset** is
a subset of items, i.e., a set of chord-sets. A k-**itemset** is an itemset with k items,
denoted as $(x_1, x_2, \ldots, x_k)$, where k is the *length* of that itemset. For brevity, the
commas are omitted. For example, a 3-itemset (a, b, c) is written as (abc), where
a, b, c are chord-sets, and the length of (a, b, c) is 3. A **melody sequence stream**
(MSS) is a sequence of incoming melody sequences, $[m_1, m_2, \ldots, m_N)$, where a
melody sequence m_i is an itemset and N is an unknown large number of melody
sequences that will arrive. Note that, in the representation of $[m_1, m_2, \ldots, m_N)$,
the symbol "[" is the starting point of incoming melody sequence of the data stream
and the symbol ")" is the current point of the data stream. Hence, it means that m_1
is the first melody sequence and m_N is latest incoming melody sequence of the data
stream.

The sequence of w recent melody sequences of MSS is called the **sliding window**
(SW) of MSS, where w is the *size* of the SW. The **support** of an itemset X, denoted
as $\textbf{sup}(X)$, is the number of melody sequences in SW containing X as a subset.
An itemset X is a **frequent temporal pattern** (FTP), if and only if $\textbf{sup}(X) \geq s \cdot w$,
where s is a user-defined minimum support threshold in the range of [0, 1]. An
itemset X is called **infrequent temporal pattern** (ITP), if and only if $\textbf{sup}(X) < s \cdot w$.
A frequent temporal pattern is called **maximal frequent temporal pattern** (MFTP)
if and only if it is not a subset of any other frequent temporal patterns.

Definition of Problem 1 Given a melody sequence stream MSS and the size of sliding window w, the problem of online mining of user-centered music query streams is
to discover the set of frequent temporal patterns by one scan of the w recent melody
sequences of MSS with an adjustable user-defined minimum support threshold s in
the range of [0, 1].

Example 1. Let the first four melody sequences of a stream of melody sequences
be $<m_1, (acd)>$, $<m_2, (bce)>$, $<m_3, (abce)>$, and $<m_4, (be)>$, where m_1,
m_2, m_3, and m_4 are the identifiers of melody sequences and a, b, c, d and e are the
identifiers of chord-sets, i.e., item identifiers. Let the size w of sliding window be 3
and the user-specified minimum support threshold s be 0.5. The stream of first four
melody sequences is composed of two sliding windows, i.e., $SW_1 = [m_1, m_2, m_3]$
and $SW_2 = [m_2, m_3, m_4]$, where first window SW_1 contains the sequences m_1, m_2
and m_3, and the second window SW_2 contains the sequences m_2, m_3 and m_4. Thus,

A Melody Sequence Stream	FTPs of SW_1	FTPs of SW_2
$<m_1, (acd)>$	(a), (b), (c), (e)	(b), (c), (e)
$<m_2, (bce)>$	(ac), (bc), (be), (ce)	(bc), (be), (ce)
$<m_3, (abce)>$	(bce)	(bce)
$<m_4, (be)>$		

A melody sequence stream is formed by melody sequences arriving in series

Fig. 2 An example melody sequence stream and the frequent temporal patterns in two consecutive sliding windows SW_1 and SW_2

the number of melody sequences of FTPs must have at least two sequences (0.5 of $w = 3$ is 1.5). The result of example 1 is shown in the right side of Fig. 2, and the explanation on how to get the FTPs in Fig. 2 is given in Section "The Proposed Algorithm FTP-stream".

In Fig. 2, the discovered FTPs in SW_1 are four 1-itemsets, $\{(a), (b), (c), (e)\}$, four 2-itemsets, $\{(ac), (bc), (be), (ce)\}$, and one 3-itemset, $\{(bce)\}$. The discovered FTPs in SW_2 are three 1-itemsets, $\{(b), (c), (e)\}$, three 2-itemsets, $\{(bc), (be), (ce)\}$, and one 3-itemset, $\{(bce)\}$. In this example, we can find that $\{(a), (ac)\}$ are FTPs in SW_1, but are not FTPs in SW_2.

Mining of Frequent Temporal Patterns in Music Query Streams

Data Processing: Bit-sequence Representation

In the proposed algorithm, for each item X in the current sliding window, a *bit-sequence* with w bits, denoted as **Bit**(X), is constructed. If an item X is in the i-th music sequence of current sliding window, the i-th bit of **Bit**(X) is set to be 1; otherwise, it is set to be 0. The process is called **bit-sequence transform**.

Example 2. Consider an example melody sequence stream in Fig. 2 and assume that sliding window is composed of three melody sequences. Five items (chord-sets), *a, b, c, d,* and *e*, are used in this example. The first window SW_1 consists of three consecutive melody sequences: $<m_1, (acd)>$, $<m_2, (bce)>$, and $<m_3, (abce)>$. Because the item *a* appears in the 1st and 3rd melody sequences of SW_1, the bit-sequence of *a* is 101, i.e., **Bit**$(a) = 101$. Finally, a set of bit-sequences of 1-itemsets, i.e., **Bit**$(b) = 011$, **Bit**$(c) = 111$, **Bit**$(d) = 100$ and **Bit**$(e) = 011$, is generated by using bit-sequence transform for each new item of SW_1.

The Proposed Algorithm FTP-stream

In this section, based on the representations of appearing items, an efficient steam mining algorithm, called FTP-stream (*F*requent *T*emporal *P*attern mining of *streams*), is introduced. In the framework of FTP-stream algorithm, an effective list structure, called **2C-list** (a *list* of *2-C*andidates), is constructed after performing bit-sequence transform of each incoming item. Therefore, each item has its unique 2C-list. Each entry in the 2C-list consists of two fields: X and **sup**(X), where X is the item identifier of the item being inserted and **sup**(X) registers the number of sequences containing the item X. The process of stream mining is composed of three phases: *window initialization* phase, *window sliding* phase, and *frequent temporal pattern generation* phase.

Window Initialization Phase of FTP-stream Algorithm

The window initialization phase is activated while the number of melody sequences generated so far in a melody sequence stream is less than or equal to a user-predefined sliding window size w. In this phase, each item in the new incoming melody sequence is transformed into its bit sequence representation by using the bit-sequence transform.

Example 3. Consider the melody sequence stream in Fig. 2. The first sliding window SW_1 contains three melody sequences: m_1, m_2, and m_3. The bit-sequences of items and 2C-lists of sliding window SW_1 in the initialization phase of FTP-stream algorithm are shown in Fig. 3.

ID	Melody Sequence	Bit-Sequences and 2C-lists in current SW_1	
m_1	(*acd*)	**Bit**(*a*)=100 → [c:1, d:1]	**Bit**(*c*)=100 → [d:1]
		Bit(*d*)=100 → [ ]	
m_2	(*bce*)	**Bit**(*a*)=100 → [c:1, d:1]	**Bit**(*c*)=110 → [d:1, e:1]
		Bit(*d*)=100 → [ ]	**Bit**(*b*)=010 → [c:1, e:1]
		Bit(*e*)=010 → [ ]	
m_3	(*abce*)	**Bit**(*a*)=101 → [b:1, c:2, d:1, e:1]	**Bit**(*c*)=111 → [d:1, e:2]
		Bit(*d*)=100 → [ ]	**Bit**(*b*)=011 → [c:2, e:2]
		Bit(*e*)=011 → [ ]	

Fig. 3 Bit-sequences and 2C-lists of items of SW_1 after window initialization phase (from m_1 to m_3)

Window Sliding Phase of FTP-stream Algorithm

The window sliding phase is activated after the sliding window becomes full. A
new incoming melody sequence is appended to the current sliding window, and the
oldest melody sequence is removed from the window.

For removing oldest information, an effective pruning method is used in the FTP-
stream algorithm. Based on the bit-sequence representation, FTP-stream uses the
bitwise-left-shift operation to remove the aged melody sequences from the set of
items in the current sliding window. After sliding the window, an effective pruning
method, called **Item-Prune**, is used to improve the memory requirement of FTP-
stream. The pruning approach is that *an item X in the current sliding window is
dropped if and only if* $sup(X) = 0$. Note that the support of an item(-set) is computed by counting the number of ones from its bit sequence representation. For
example, **sup**(a) is 2 and **sup**(c) is 3 since **Bit**$(a) = 101$ and **Bit**$(c) = 111$.

Example 4. Consider the melody sequence stream in Fig. 2. Before the fourth
melody sequence $<m_4, (be)>$ is processed, the first melody sequence m_1 must
be removed from the current sliding window using the bitwise-left-shift operation
on the set of items. Hence, **Bit** (a) is modified from 101 to 010 by using bitwise-
left-shift operation. After performing bitwise-left-shift operation for each item, we
got **Bit**$(c) = 110$, **Bit**$(d) = 000$, **Bit**$(b) = 110$, and **Bit**$(e) = 110$. Then, the new
melody sequence $<sm_4, (be)>$ is processed by using bit-sequence transform. The
result is shown in Fig. 4. Note that the item d is dropped since **Bit**$(d) = 000$, i.e.,
sup$(d) = 0$, based on **Item-Prune** method.

Frequent Temporal Pattern Generation Phase of FTP-stream

The frequent temporal pattern phase is performed only when the up-to-date set
of FTPs is requested. In this phase, the FTP-stream algorithm uses a level-wise

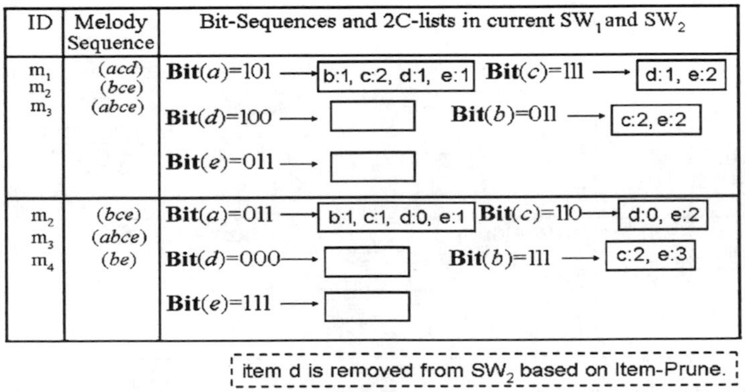

Fig. 4 Bit-sequences and 2C-lists of items after sliding SW_1 to SW_2

method to generate the set of candidate temporal patterns CTP_k (candidate *temporal patterns* with k items) from the pre-known frequent temporal patterns FTP_{k-1} (*frequent temporal patterns* with $k - 1$ items) according to the *Apriori* property, where $k > 2$. The step is called **CTP-Gen-W2C** (*Candidate Temporal Pattern Generation Without 2-Candidates*). Then, FTP-stream uses the *bitwise AND* operation to compute the supports of these candidates in order to find the frequent ones FTP_k. The generation-then-test process is stopped until no new candidates with $k + 1$ items (CTP_{k+1}) are generated. One of the benefits of the proposed algorithm is that the FTP-stream algorithm generates candidates from 3-candidates to l-candidates, where l is the size of largest itemset. It is because the set of frequent 2-itemsets can be determined by the 2C-lists and its bit-sequences. Consequently, it overcomes the performance bottleneck of 2-candidate generation of the level-wise frequent pattern mining algorithms.

Example 5. Consider the bit-sequences and 2C-lists of items of SW_2 in Fig. 4, and let the minimum support threshold s be 0.5. Hence, a temporal pattern X is *frequent* if $\mathbf{sup}(X) \geq 0.5 \cdot 3 = 1.5$. In the following, we discuss the mining steps of frequent temporal patterns of SW_2.

First, the FTP-stream algorithm checks the bit-sequence of each item to find the frequent 1-itemsets, i.e., (b), (c) and (e). Then, FTP-stream generates **frequent 2-itemsets**, (bc), (be) and (ce), by combining frequent 1-item (c) with item e where $\mathbf{sup}(e) = 2$ in 2C-list of item e and frequent 1-item (b) with items c and e in 2C-list of item b. After that we find that $\mathbf{sup}(ce) = 2$, $\mathbf{sup}(bc) = 2$, and $\mathbf{sup}(be) = 3$. Then, the algorithm generates one candidate 3-itemset (bce) from 2C-list of item b according to Apriori property. After that FTP-stream uses bitwise AND operation to count the $\mathbf{sup}(bce) = 2$, i.e., $\mathbf{Bit}(b)$ AND $\mathbf{Bit}(c)$ AND $\mathbf{Bit}(e) = 110$. Because no new candidates are generated, the generation-then-test process is stopped. Hence, there are six frequent temporal patterns, (b), (c), (bc), (be), (ce), (bce), generated by FTP-stream in SW_2.

Experimental Evaluation of Pattern Discovery of Music Query Streams

In this section, the experiments are performed to compare the proposed algorithm FTP-stream with the algorithms SWFI-stream [5] and Moment [6]. The source code of Moment algorithm, denoted as MomentFP, is provided by Dr. Yun Chi [5]. In this paper, we focus on the problem of mining frequent itemsets from stream sliding window, but MomentFP algorithm is a closed frequent itemset mining method. Hence, we modified the MomentFP algorithm by enumerating each closed frequent itemset into a subset of frequent itemsets. The new MomentFP algorithm for mining *frequent itemsets* is called MomentFP+ in this paper.

All the programs are implemented using Microsoft Visual C + + Version 6.0 and performed on a 1.80 GHz Pentium® PC machine with 512 MB memory running on Windows 2000. For testing frequent temporal patterns mining of melody sequence streams, we generate melody sequence streams using IBM synthetic data generator proposed by Agrawal and Srikant [1]. One synthetic melody sequence stream, denoted by T5.I4. D1000K, of size 1 million melody sequences each are used to evaluate the performance of the proposed FTP-stream algorithm. T5.I4.D1000K, with 1,000 unique items, has an average melody sequence size of five items with an average maximal frequent temporal pattern size of four items. The minimum support threshold s used in the following experiments is set to 0.001.

The comparisons of memory usages of the existing algorithms with the proposed FTP-stream algorithm are shown in Figs. 5, 6 and 7. Figure 5 shows the memory usage of the window initialization phase. As shown in Fig. 5, FTP-stream consumes only about 2.9 MB in window initialization phase, but the memory consumption of original data is increased linearly from 0.3 MB to 4.2 MB. From the figure, we can see that as the number of incoming melody sequences increases, the memory requirements of all algorithms grow. However, the memory requirement of

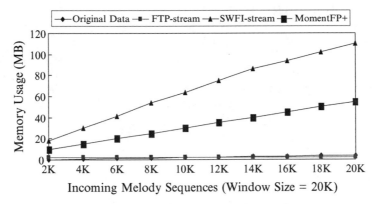

Fig. 5 Comparisons of memory usages in the window initialization phase

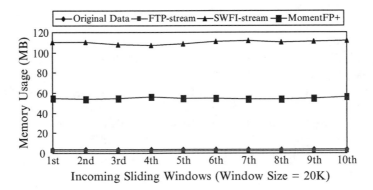

Fig. 6 Comparisons of memory usages in the window sliding phase

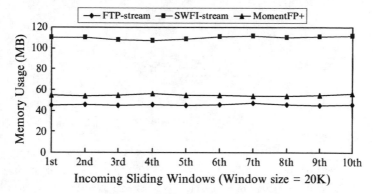

Fig. 7 Comparisons of memory usages in frequent temporal patterns generation phase

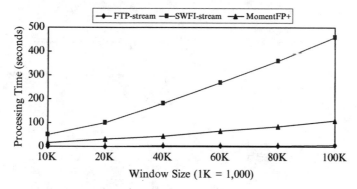

Fig. 8 Comparisons of processing time of window initialization phase under different window sizes

our FTP-stream algorithm is significant less than that of algorithms SWFI-stream and MomentFP+.

Figure 6 shows the memory usage of the window sliding phase. In the window sliding phase, the memory usage of FTP-stream is approximately a half of original data. The memory requirements of algorithms SWFI-stream and MomentFP+ are significant larger than that of FTP-stream algorithm. Figure 7 shows the memory usage of the frequent temporal pattern generation phase. In this phase, the memory usage of FTP-stream is between 43 MB to 48 MB but the memory requirement of FTP-stream is still less than that of algorithms SWFI-stream and MomentFP+. Consequently, the memory requirement of the proposed FTP-stream algorithm is less than that of the existing well-known algorithms SWFI-stream and MomentFP+.

The comparisons of processing time of these algorithms are given in Figs. 8, 9, and 10. Figure 8 shows the processing time of window initialization phase of algorithms, FTP-stream, SWFI-stream and MomentFP+, under different window sizes from 10 K melody sequences to 100 K melody sequences. From the figure,

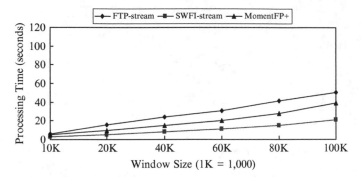

Fig. 9 Comparisons of mining time of frequent temporal patterns under different window sizes

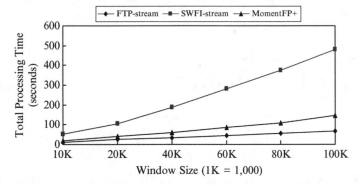

Fig. 10 Comparisons of total processing time (=window initialization time+window sliding time+pattern generation time) under different window sizes

the processing time of FTP-stream is less than that of algorithms SWFI-stream and MomentFP+.

Figure 9 shows the mining time of frequent temporal patterns under different window sizes from 20,000 melody sequences to 100,000 melody sequences. From this figure, we can find that the frequent pattern generation time of FTP-stream is greater than that of algorithms SWFI-stream and MomentFP+. The reason is that the FTP-stream algorithm uses a level-wise method to generate all frequent patterns in this phase. Although the processing time of FTP-stream in this phase is greater than the existing algorithms, the total processing time (included window initialization time, window sliding time and pattern generation time) is less than that of algorithms SWFI-stream and MomentFP+. The result is shown in Fig. 10. Consequently, the proposed FTP-stream algorithm is faster than the existing algorithms SWFI-stream and MomentFP+.

Change Detection of Online Music Query Streams

Problem Definition

In this section, we describe several features of music data used in this paper and define the problem of detecting changes of user-centered music query streams. For the basic terminologies on music, we refer to [8, 12].

Definition 1. The *type I melody structure* is represented as a set of chord-sets.

Definition 2. The *type II melody structure* is represented as a string of chord-sets.

Note that the difference between sets and strings is the order of elements. The order of chord-sets in a set (type I melody structure) is not necessary, but it is important in a string (type II melody structure). For example, given a set of chord-sets $\{a,\ b,\ c\}$, there are one set of chord-set (abc) with 3 chord-sets, but there are six strings of chord-sets with 3 chord-sets, i.e., $<abc>$, $<acb>$, $<bac>$, $<bca>$, $<cab>$, and $<cba>$.

Definition 3. A string Z is called an *item-string*, i.e., *a string of chord-sets*. A *k-item-string* is represented by $<x_1 x_2 \ldots x_k>$, where $x_i \in \Psi$, $\forall i = 1, 2, \ldots, k$. The *support* of an item-string Z, denoted as $\mathbf{sup}(Z)$, is the number of melody sequences containing Z as a *substring* in the MSS so far. An item-string is *frequent* if $\mathbf{sup}(Z) \geq s \cdot |\text{MSS}|$.

Definition 4. A frequent itemset is called a *maximal frequent itemset* (**MFI**) if it is not a subset of any other frequent itemsets.

Definition 5. A frequent item-string is called a *maximal frequent item-string* (**MFS**) if it is not a substring of any other item-strings.

Definition 6. A maximal frequent itemset P is called *positive itemset burst* (**PIB**) if its $\mathbf{sup}(P)^z - \mathbf{sup}(P)^{z-1} \geq \partial_{\text{MFI}}$, where ∂_{MFI} is a user-specified itemset burst threshold in the range of [0, 1], $\mathbf{sup}(P)^z$ is the estimated support of P from window w_1 to window w_z, and z is the window identifier of current window.

Definition 7. A maximal frequent itemset P is called *negative itemset burst* (**NIB**) if its $\mathbf{sup}(P)^{z-1} - \mathbf{sup}(P)^z \geq \partial_{\text{MFI}}$.

Definition 8. A maximal frequent item-string Q is called *positive item-string burst* (**PSB**) if its $\mathbf{sup}(Q)^z - \mathbf{sup}(Q)^{z-1} \geq \partial_{\text{MFS}}$, where ∂_{MFS} is a user-specified item-string burst threshold in the range of [0, 1], $\mathbf{sup}(Q)^z$ is the estimated support of Q from window w_1 to window w_z.

Definition 9. A maximal frequent item-string Q is called *negative item-string burst* (**NSB**) if its $\mathbf{sup}(Q)^{z-1} - \mathbf{sup}(Q)^z \geq \partial_{\text{MFS}}$.

Definition 10. A maximal frequent itemset P is called *increasing changed itemset* (**ICI**) if $\partial_{\mathrm{MFI}} > (\mathbf{sup}(P)_{i+1} - \mathbf{sup}(\mathrm{P})_i) \geq \varepsilon_{\mathrm{MFI}}$, $\forall i$, $i = z - h_1 + 1$, $z - h_1 + 2$, $\dots, z$, where $\varepsilon_{\mathrm{MFI}}$ is a user-specified increasing changed itemset threshold in the range of $[0, 1]$, and h_1 is a number of basic windows defined by user.

Definition 11. A maximal frequent item-string Q is called *increasing changed item-string* (**ICS**) if $\partial_{\mathrm{MFS}} > (\mathbf{sup}(Q)_{j+1} - \mathbf{sup}(Q)_j) \geq \varepsilon_{\mathrm{MFS}}$, $\forall j$, $j = z - h_2 + 1$, $z - h_2 + 2$, $\dots, z$, where $\varepsilon_{\mathrm{MFS}}$ is a user-specified increasing changed item-string threshold in the range of $[0, 1]$, and h_2 is a number of basic windows defined by user.

Definition 12. A maximal frequent itemset P is called *decreasing changed itemset* (**DCI**) if $\partial_{\mathrm{MFI}} > (\mathbf{sup}(Q)_j - \mathbf{sup}(Q)_{j+1}) \geq \gamma_{\mathrm{MFI}}$, $\forall j$, $j = z - h_1 + 1$, $z - h_1 + 2$, $\dots, z$, where γ_{MFI} is a user-specified decreasing changed item-string threshold in the range of $[0, 1]$, and h_1 is a number of basic windows defined by user.

Definition 13. A maximal frequent item-string Q is called *decreasing changed item-string* (**DCS**) if $\partial_{\mathrm{MFS}} > (\mathbf{sup}(Q)_j - \mathbf{sup}(Q)_{j+1}) \geq \gamma_{\mathrm{MFS}}$, $\forall j$, $j = z - h_2 + 1$, $z - h_2 + 2$, $\dots, z$, where γ_{MFS} is a user-specified decreasing changed item-string threshold in the range of $[0, 1]$, and h_2 is a number of basic windows defined by user.

Definition of Problem 2 Given a MSS, s, ∂_{MFI}, ∂_{MFS}, $\varepsilon_{\mathrm{MFI}}$, $\varepsilon_{\mathrm{MFS}}$, γ_{MFI}, and γ_{MFS}, the problem of detecting changes in user-centered music query streams is to maintain the set of MFI and MFS, and to detect the set of PIB, NIB, PSB, NSB, ICI, ICS, DCI, and DCS, by one scan of a continuous user-centered music query stream.

Detecting Changes from User-centered Music Query Streams

In this section, we developed an effective algorithm, called MQS-change (changes of Music Query Streams), to detect the changes of maximal frequent melody structures in current user-centered music query streams. Two music melody structures (set of chord-sets and string of chord-sets) are maintained and four melody structure changes (positive burst, negative burst, increasing change and decreasing change) are monitored in a new summary data structure, called MSC-list (a list of Music Structure Changes).

The Proposed Summary Data Structure MSC-list

The proposed summary data structure, called MSC-list, consists of two temporal lists, MFI-list and MFS-list, where MFI-list is a list of entries which contains current maximal frequent itemsets, and MFS-list is a list of entries which maintains maximal frequent item-strings so far. Each entry of MFI-list consists of two fields: *pattern-id Y* and *support-list $Y.support\text{-}list$*, where pattern-id is a unique identifier of this maximal frequent itemset, and support-list is composed of a list of $(\mathbf{sup}(Y), i)$, where i is the window identifier of window w_i containing the itemset e.

For example, an entry $<abcd, (30\%, 1), (37\%, 2), (46\%, 3), (70\%, 4)>$ of MFI-list indicates that the itemset $abcd$ is a maximal frequent itemset and its estimated support is 30% in window w_1, 37% in w_2, 46% in w_3, and 70% in w_4. Assume that the ∂_{MFI} is 0.2 (i.e., 20%), $\varepsilon_{MFI} = 0.05$ (i.e., 5%), and h_1 be 3 (i.e., three consecutive windows). Hence, the pattern $abcd$ is an *increasing changed itemset* from windows w_1 to w_3, and has a *positive itemset burst* in window w_4.

Each entry of MFS-list also consists of two fields: *pattern-id Z* and *support-list Z. support-list*, where pattern-id is a unique identifier of this maximal frequent item-string, and support-list is composed of a list of $(\mathbf{sup}(Z), i)$, where i is the identifier of window w_i containing the item-string Z.

In the following, we use the term *maximal frequent pattern* (**MFP**) to substitute the maximal frequent itemset and maximal frequent item-string.

Two operations are used to maintain the MSC-list:

1. **Update MSC-list**: For each entry *<pattern-id, support-list>* of MSC-list, MQS-change algorithm updates the support-list of this entry, i.e., append a new support record to the support-list. If an entry e is not a MFP, i.e., $\mathbf{sup}(e) < s \cdot |MSS|$, the entry is deleted from the current MSC-list.
2. **New MSC-list**: if MQS-change finds a maximal frequent pattern P from the current window w_z and $P \notin$ MSC-list, and $\mathbf{sup}(P) \geq s \cdot w$, where s is the minimum support threshold in the range of [0, 1], and w is the window size, a new entry of the form $<P, (\mathbf{sup}(P), z)>$, where z is the current window identifier, is created in the current MSC-list.

In this section, a new summary data structure, called **MSC-list** (a list of Music Structure Changes), is developed to maintain the essential information about MFI, MFS, PIB, NIB, PSB, NSB, ICI, ICS, DCI, and DCS with their supports embedded in the individual window of the current MSS. A simple single-pass algorithm, called *MQS-change* (changes of Music Query Streams), is proposed to mine the changes from user-centered music query streams.

The Proposed MQS-change Algorithm

The proposed **MQS-change** (changes of Music Query Streams) algorithm is composed of four steps. First, MQS-change repeatedly reads a window of melody sequences into available main memory. Second, the maximal frequent itemsets and maximal frequent item-strings in the current window are mined using the proposed FTP-stream algorithm, and added into MSC-list with their potential supports computed. Third, the set of MFIs and MFSs are maintained in the current MSC-list, and the changes are verified by MQS-change. Finally, MQS-change will return the changed patterns immediately if the user-centered music query stream has a change.

For discovering each change of patterns, the proposed MQS-change algorithm is divided into five mining procedures, called MQS-change-MFIS (MQS-change for MFI and MFS, as shown in Fig. 11), MQS-change-PNIB (MQS-change for PNI and

Procedure MQS-change-MFIS (maximal frequent itemsets and item-string mining of MQS-change algorithm)

Input: (1) MSS, (2) s.

Output: a MSC-list which is composed of MFI and MFS.

Begin
  MSC-list = NULL;
  Repeat:
   foreach window w_i in MSS **do** /*$\forall i$ =1,2, ..., z, and z is the current window id */
     Mine MFPs from w_i by using **FTP-stream** algorithm;
    foreach MFP of w_i **do**
     if MFP∈ MSC-list **then**
      Update MSC-list;
     else
      New MSC-list;
     endif
    endfor
    foreach entry e in the MSC-list **do** /* Pruning of MSC-list */
     foreach sup(e) in e.*support-list* **do**
      if $\mathbf{sup}(e)^i < s \cdot (z-i+1)$ **then**
    /* i is the window identifier and $\mathbf{sup}(e)^i$ is the estimated support of e from w_1 to w_i */
       Delete the entry (sup(e), i) from e.*support-list*;
      endif
      endfor
      if sup(e) < s $\cdot$ | MSS | **then** /* entry e is not a MFP */
       Delete e from MSC-list;
     endif
    endfor
   endfor
End

Fig. 11 Procedure MQS-change-MFIS of MQS-change algorithm

Procedure MQS-change-PNIB (positive and negative itemset burst mining of MQS-change)

Input: (1) a MSC-list (2) ∂_{MFI}.

Output: Discovered Changes (PIB and NIB).

Begin
  foreach entry e in the MSC-list **do**
   if $(\mathbf{sup}(e)^z - \mathbf{sup}(e)^{z-1} \geq \partial_{MFI})$ **then** /* sup(e)^z is the estimated support of e from w_1 to w_z */
    Output pattern e as a *PIB* (positive itemset burst);
   elseif $(\mathbf{sup}(e)^{z-1} - \mathbf{sup}(e)^z \geq \partial_{MFI})$ **then**
    Output pattern e as a *NIB* (negative itemset burst);
   endif
  endfor
End

Fig. 12 Procedure MQS-change-PNIB of MQS-change algorithm

PNS, as shown in Fig. 12), MQS-change-PNSB (MQS-change for PNS and PNB, as shown in Fig. 13), MQS-change-ICIS (MQS-change for ICI and ICS, as shown in Fig. 14), and MQS-change-DCIS (MQS-change for DCI and DCS, as shown in

Procedure MQS-change-PNSB (positive and negative item-string burst mining of MQS-change)

Input: (1) a MSC-list (2) ∂_{MFS}.

Output: Discovered Changes (PSB and NSB).

Begin

   foreach entry e in the MSC-list **do**

      if $(\text{sup}(e)^z - \text{sup}(e)^{z-1} \geq \partial_{MFS})$ **then** /* $\text{sup}(e)^z$ is the estimated support of e from w_1 to w_z */

         Output pattern e as a *PSB* (positive item-string burst);

      elseif $(\text{sup}(e)^{z-1} - \text{sup}(e)^z \geq \partial_{MFS})$ **then**

         Output pattern e as a *NSB* (negative item-string burst);

     endif

   endfor

End

Fig. 13 Procedure MQS-change-PNSB of MQS-change algorithm

Procedure MQS-change-ICIS (increasing changed itemset and item-string mining of MQS-change)

Input: (1) a MSC-list, (2) ∂_{MFI} (∂_{MFI}), (3) ε_{MFI} (ε_{MFS}), (4) h_1.

Output: Discovered Changes (ICI and ICS).

Begin

   foreach entry e in the MSC-list **do**

      if $(\partial_{MFI} \geq (\text{sup}(e)_{i+1} - \text{sup}(e)_i))$ **AND** $((\text{sup}(e)_{i+1} - \text{sup}(e)_i) \geq \varepsilon_{MFI})$ **then**

      /* h_1 is the number of windows defined by user */

         Output pattern e as a *ICI* (increasing changed itemset);

      elseif $(\partial_{MFS} \geq (\text{sup}(e)_{i+1} - \text{sup}(e)_i))$ **AND** $((\text{sup}(e)_{i+1} - \text{sup}(e)_i) \geq \varepsilon_{MFS})$ **then**

         Output pattern e as a *ICS* (increasing changed item-string);

     endif

   endfor

End

Fig. 14 Procedure MQS-change-ICIS of MQS-change algorithm

Fig. 15). Furthermore, each procedure of MQS-change algorithm accepts about two to four parameters and generates two changes. The connection between FTP-stream and MQS-change is given in Fig. 16.

Connection Between FTP-stream and MQS-change

After mining frequent temporal patterns from online music query streams, the second problem is that how to use these discovered patterns to predict the future trend of online music styles and to personalize the Web services of online music

Procedure MQS-change-DCIS (decreasing changed itemset and item-string mining of MQS-change)

Input: (1) a MSC-list, (2) ∂_{MFI} (∂_{MFI}), (3) γ_{MFI} (γ_{MFS}), (4) h_2.

Output: Discovered Changes (DCI and DCS).

Begin

    foreach entry e in the MSC-list **do**

        if ($\partial_{MFI} \geq$ (**sup**$(e)_{i+1}$ - **sup**$(e)_i$)) **AND** ((**sup**$(e)_{i+1}$ - **sup**$(e)_i$) $\geq \gamma_{MFI}$) **then**

        /* h_2 is the number of windows defined by user */

            Output pattern e as a *DCI* (decreasing changed itemset);

        elseif ($\partial_{MFS} \geq$ (**sup**$(e)_{i+1}$ - **sup**$(e)_i$)) **AND** ((**sup**$(e)_{i+1}$ - **sup**$(e)_i$) $\geq \gamma_{MFS}$) **then**

            Output pattern e as a *DCS* (decreasing changed item-string);

        endif

    endfor

End

Fig. 15 Procedure MQS-change-DCIS of MQS-change algorithm

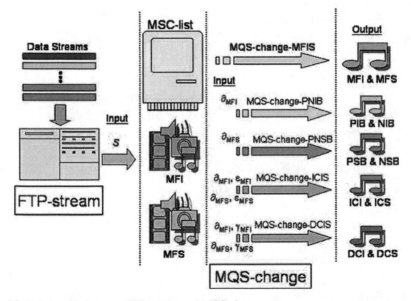

Fig. 16 Relationship between FTP-stream and MQS-change

downloading. We need new patterns, i.e., changes of discovered patterns, to assist the domain experts to predict the Web user behaviors and personalize the Web services. The relationship between first issue, i.e., mining of maximal frequent temporal patterns, and second issue, change detection of discovered patterns, is given in Fig. 16. From this figure, we can find that each discovered changes is determined by at most three parameters by using suitable procedure of MQS-change algorithm. For example, we can set parameters s, and to find out the PSB by using MQS-change-ICIS. Consequently, user does not need to set 10 predefined parameters to run the MQS-change algorithm.

Experimental Results of MQS-change Algorithm

The performance of MQS-change algorithm is analyzed by a synthetic music query stream *T5.I4.D1000K-AB*, where three parameters denote the average melody sequence size (T), the average maximal frequent pattern size (I), and the total music melody sequences (D), respectively. The data is generated by the IBM synthetic data generator proposed by Agrawal and Srikant [1]. *T5.I4.D1000K-AB* consists of two consecutive subparts TA and TB. TA denotes a set of melody sequences generated by a set of chord-sets A while TB denotes a set of sequences generated by a set of chord-sets B. There are no common chord-sets between TA and TB. TA-100,000 indicates that the size of the tested window in TA is 100,000 melody sequences. In this section, we discuss the adaptability of the proposed MQS-change algorithm.

In order to illustrate how rapidly the MQS-change algorithm can adapt the change of information over a data stream, we use the *coverage rate* (CR) [4] to evaluate the adaptability of the MQS-change algorithm. It denotes the ratio of frequent itemsets induced by an itemset X in all frequent patterns as follows:

$$CRX = ((\text{\# of frequent itemsets induced by an itemset } X)/|R|) \times 100(\%),$$

where $|R|$ denotes the total number of frequent itemsets in a MSC-list. The result is shown in Fig. 17. As the size of a window becomes smaller, the MQS-change adapts more rapidly the change of recent information between the two different subparts of *T5.I4.D1000K-AB*.

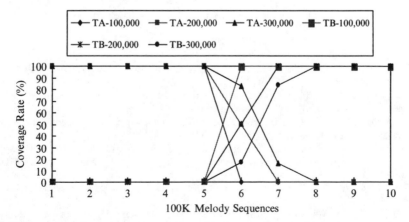

Fig. 17 Coverage rate for *T5.I4.D1000K-AB*

Conclusions

In this paper, we study the problems of mining frequent temporal patterns and detecting changes of patterns from recent music query streams. One new online algorithm, called FTP-stream (Frequent Temporal Pattern mining of streams), is proposed to mine the frequent temporal patterns over music query streams without any information loss. An effective bit-sequence representation is developed to maintain the essential information of recent frequent temporal patterns. Experiments show that the proposed algorithm is efficient single-pass algorithm for mining music query streams. Moreover, we propose a simple online algorithm, called MQS-change (changes of Music Query Streams), to maintain two music melody structures (sets of chord-sets and string of chord-sets) and to detect three changes of music melody structures (significant pattern bursts, increasing changed patterns and decreasing changed patterns) from a continuous user-centered music query stream. A new summary data structure, called MSC-list (a list of Music Structure Changes), is developed to maintain the essential information about the maximal melody structures of music query streams so far. Based on our knowledge, MQS-change algorithm is the first online, single-pass method to detect the changes in a continuous user-centered music query stream.

Acknowledgements The authors thank the reviewers' precious comments for improving the quality of the paper. We would like to thank Dr. Yun Chi for contributing the source codes of Moment algorithm (MomentFP). The research is supported in part by the National Science Council, Project No. NSC 96-2218-E-424-001-, Taiwan, Republic of China.

References

1. Agrawal R, Srikant R (1994) Fast algorithms for mining association rules. In: Proc. VLDB, pp 487–499
2. Babcock B, Babu S, Data M, Motwani R, Widom J (2002) Models and issues in data stream systems. In: Proc. PODS, pp 1–16
3. Bakhmutora V, Gusev VU, Titkova TN (1997) The search for adaptations in song melodies. Comput Music J 21(1):58–67. doi:10.2307/3681219
4. Chang JH, Lee WS (2003) Finding recent frequent itemsets adaptively over online data streams. In: Proc. KDD, pp 487–492
5. Chang JH, Lee WS (2004) A sliding window method for finding recently frequent itemsets over online data streams. J Inform Sci Eng (JISE) 20(4):753–762
6. Chi Y, Wang H, Yu P, Muntz R (2004) MOMENT: maintaining closed frequent itemsets over a stream sliding window. In: Proc. ICDM, pp 59–66
7. Dong G, Han J, Lakshmanan LVS, Pei J, Wang H, Yu PS (2003) Online mining of changes from data streams: research problems and preliminary results. In: Proc. ACM SIGMOD-MPDS
8. Gaber MM, Zaslavsky A, Krishnaswamy S (2005) Mining data streams: a review. SIGMOD Rec 34(1): 18–26
9. Hsu J-L, Liu C-C, Chen ALP (2001) Discovering nontrivial repeating patterns in music data. IEEE Trans Multimed 3(3):311–325. doi:10.1109/6046.944475

10. Jones GT (1974) Music theory. Harper & Row, New York
11. Li H-F, Lee S-Y, Shan M-K (2004) Mining frequent closed structures in streaming melody sequences. In: Proc. ICME
12. Li H-F, Lee S-Y, Shan M-K (2005) Online mining maximal frequent structures in continuous landmark melody streams. Pattern Recognit Lett 26(11):1658–1674. doi:10.1016/j.patrec.2005.01.016
13. Li H-F, Lee S-Y, Shan M-K (2005) Online mining changes of items over continuous append-only and dynamic data streams. J Univers Comput Sci 11(8):1411–1425
14. Shan M-K, Kuo F-F (2003) Music style mining and classification by melody. IEICE Trans Inform Syst E 86-D(4):655–659
15. Yoshitaka A, Ichikawa T (1999) A survey on content-based retrieval for multimedia databases. IEEE Trans Knowl Data Eng 11(1):81–93. doi:10.1109/69.755617
16. http://free.napster.com/
17. http://new.music.yahoo.com/
18. http://www.apple.com/itunes/
19. http://www.kkbox.com.tw
20. http://www.music.com.tw

Chapter 16
Music Search and Recommendation

Karlheinz Brandenburg, Christian Dittmar, Matthias Gruhne, Jakob Abeßer, Hanna Lukashevich, Peter Dunker, Daniel Gärtner, Kay Wolter, Stefanie Nowak, and Holger Grossmann

Introduction

In the last ten years, our ways to listen to music have drastically changed: In earlier times, we went to record stores or had to use low bit-rate audio coding to get some music and to store it on PCs. Nowadays, millions of songs are within reach via on-line distributors. Some music lovers already got terabytes of music on their hard disc. Users are now no longer desparate to get music, but to select, to find the music they love. A number of technologies has been developed to adress these new requirements. There are techniques to identify music and ways to search for music. Recommendation today is a hot topic as well as organizing music into playlists.

For online music shops, recommendation is a way to significantly improve accessibility of music, therefore helping them to sell music. For users, play list generation helps them to find their favorite track in a much more convenient way than just to search for artists or title. Casual users can broaden their knowledge about music by finding new tracks in the style they are looking for. Expert users can find their way in the millions of tracks available including new releases without having to search through music magazines or listen to thousands of new tracks. Thus, automatic recommendation seems to pose a possible solution for the so called long-tail phenomenon that has been detailed in [4].

Basically, organizing music can be done using Web 2.0 methods, i.e. the knowledge of thousands of other music lovers, or using local, digital signal processing based methods. For well known mainstream music, huge amounts of user generated browsing traces, reviews, play-lists and recommendations are available in different online communities. They can be analyzed through collaborative filtering methods in order to reveal relations between artists, songs and genres. For novel or niche content one obvious solution to derive such data is content based similarity search. Since the early days of Music Information Retrieval (MIR) the search for items related to a specific query song or a set of those (Query by Example) has been a consistent focus of scientific interest. Thus, a multitude of different approaches with varying

K. Brandenburg (✉), C. Dittmar, M. Gruhne, J. Abeßer, H. Lukashevich, P. Dunker,
D. Gärtner, K. Wolter, S. Nowak, and H. Grossmann
Fraunhofer IDMT, Ehrenbergstr. 31, 98693 Ilmenau, Germany
e-mail: dmr@idmt.fraunhofer.de

B. Furht (ed.), *Handbook of Multimedia for Digital Entertainment and Arts*,
DOI 10.1007/978-0-387-89024-1_16, © Springer Science+Business Media, LLC 2009

degree of complexity has been proposed [110], [43], [85]. Many publications have addressed suitable modelling methods that represent the musical gist whilst keeping the description blurry enough to account for small but irrelevant differences [8]. Since the human perception of music and their similarities is subjective, context dependent and mulidimensional, mathematical models can always only be an imprecise estimate of reality.

Acoustic Features for Music Modeling

In order to make a computer understand music, it must be translated into numbers. Though partly mathematical in it's original nature, the music as we hear it is a seemingly random series of different air pressure levels. When sampled and quantized, these continuous functions of time become vectors of discrete digits. These vectors still reveal almost no information about their content. Instead, further signal processing operations are necessary to derive the meaning of these data. These operations are called *feature extraction* and their result is called *feature vectors*.

As depicted in Figure 1, acoustic feature vectors can be roughly distinguished into three categories based on their degree of semantic meaning. The low-level features can be extracted from the audio signal via few basic signal processing operations. Mid-level features intend to bridge the gap between low-level features and a full music annotation and transcription. They present an intermediate semantic layer that combines signal processing techniques with a-priori musical knowledge. High-level features carry a high degree of semantic information, since a human listener is able to understand their meaning. They bear a close relation to the musicological vocabulary and can be used as features for special MIR tasks. Prominent examples of these three categories are described in the following subsections.

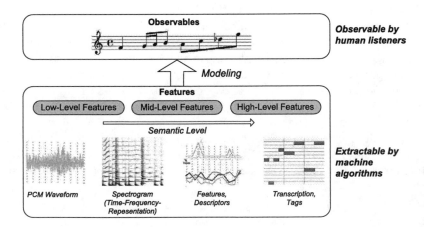

Fig. 1 Different semantic layers of acoustic features for music modeling

Low-level Audio Features

Low-level acoustic features are directly extracted from the digitized audio signal. Therefore, the signal is divided into adjacent or overlapping frames with a typical size of 10 to 100 milliseconds. Each of the frames is processed independently and the feature extraction results in a feature vector with the length (or dimension) N. Numerous different proposals for computing the various feature vectors have been described in literature. The work of [114], [121] and [79] provide a good overview on low-level features commonly used in MIR-applications. It should be stressed that already slight implementation differences in the signal processing chain for low-level feature extraction can result into huge numerical differences in the feature vectors. Thus, the MPEG-7 standard [53] describes a number of standardized low-level features and an interface that is open to the public. Since it is impossible to detail the vast variety of features that has been introduced during the last years, the focus will be on features that have been most commonly and successfully been used in MIR systems.

Figure 2 shows the common processing blocks for the acoustic low-level feature extraction. The starting point of this processing chain is always an audio frame. For the different low-level features, one or more of these blocks are applied. The following paragraphs describe each of these blocks in detail:

- *Windowing:* If a time-frequency transformation is applied to the single audio frames, the discontinuities at the edges of each frame lead to erroneous high frequencies. Therefore, a windowing function is usually multiplied with the audio frame before the transformation. Several different windowing functions are used in signal processing, the most common ones are Hamming and Hann windows.

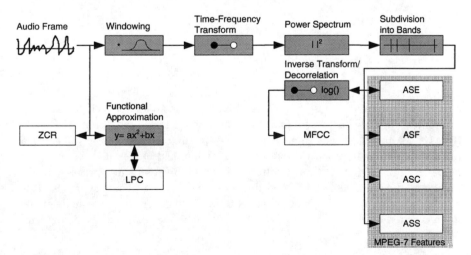

Fig. 2 Processing blocks for the acoustic low-level feature extraction

- *Time-Frequency Transformation:* In order to transfer the signal from the time domain into the frequency domain, usually the Discrete Fourier Transform (DFT), respectively the more efficient Fast Fourier Transform (FFT), is applied. Since the human perception of the frequency scale is nonlinear, methods like Constant-Q, Multiresolution-FFT or Warped FFT are often utilized.
- *Squaring:* As most of the features are based on the spectrum magnitude while the output of the DFT is a complex-valued vector, all elements of vector are squared. The resulting vector is called the *power spectrum*.
- *Subspacing:* In general, the number of coefficients, respectively dimensions N should be kept as low as possible, in order to guarantee for efficient search and retrieval later on. Therefore, the raw spectra are commonly subdivided into adjacent or overlapping frequency bands and a single value is calculated per band depending on the underlying feature extraction algorithm. Commonly, a logarithmic frequency spacing is used. Mel scale is another option.
- *Decorrelation:* Some features perform a decorrelation in order to reduce the number of coefficients in the feature vector. This is often realized by a Karhunen Loéve (KL)-Transform (see 16), which results in a linear combination of the original feature vector elements, sorted by decreasing significance. Thus, the number of elements in the feature vector can be limited, according to the requirements of the system. Logan [70] compared the usage of DCT instead of the KL Transform in the area of music information retrieval and came to the conclusion, that a DCT is adequate for decorrelation.
- *Functional Approximation:* Some features are based on a functional approximation of the original signal. The resulting functional parameters can either be used for parametric coding or as a feature vector. An efficient implementation method is given by Levinson-Durbin algorithm.

The following itemization describes the most common low-level features. Their necessary extraction blocks are depicted in Figure 1 and their specific purpose is described below:

Mel-Frequency Cepstral Coefficients

The *Mel-Frequency Cepstral Coefficients* (MFCC) low-level feature is one of the most commonly used acoustic low-level feature in the area of speech recognition, where it has already been used almost 30 years ago [51] and later on in MIR [70], [8], [108]. Although speech signals are quite different to audio signals, [70] showed that MFCC are appropriate for music classification, and numerous other publications have proven that. The most noticeable blocks in the extraction process are the logarithm and the inverse DFT after the summation of the frequency bands. This process transfers any multiplication into additions and decorrelates the audio signal in order to reduce the dimensions (see 16) and to facilitate statistical modeling later on (see 16).

Audio Spectrum Envelope

The *Audio Spectrum Envelope* (ASE) low-level feature is a very basic feature that has been applied, e.g., in [13] for audio classification. In order to allow interoperability, ASE is also described as AudioSpectrumEnvelope low-level feature in the MPEG-7 standard (ISO/IEC 15938-4) [53]. The necessary extraction blocks are described in Figure 2. The final step is the summation of the power-spectrum magnitudes inside the logarithmically spaced frequency bands. The disadvantage of this feature is it's dependence on the global level of the signal. If the feature is extracted from exactly the same song with two different amplification factors, the resulting feature vectors will differ significantly. Thus, this feature is often post-processed in MIR systems.

Audio Spectrum Flatness

The feature *Audio Spectrum Flatness* (ASF) is also a standardized low-level feature in the MPEG-7 audio standard [53]. It has originally been used for calculating the noise masking threshold in audio coding [55] and later for several MIR tasks, such as audio identification [3] and audio similarity search [2]. The feature extraction is conducted similar to ASE. The difference is, that the values between the band edges are not accumulated. Instead, the audio spectrum flatness factor is estimated by dividing the geometric mean by the arithmetic mean. This factor indicates the tonality of the signal. The factor ranges from 0 to 1. A value of "1" indicates, that the spectrum is completely noise-like and a value of "0" indicates, that the spectrum is sinusoidal-like.

Linear Predictive Coding

One of the fundamentals for digital speech communication is the compression of the speech signal in order to reduce the amount of transmitted data and hence, to save bandwidth. The digital speech compression often bases on the principle of *Linear Predictive Coding* (LPC). This principle optimizes a set of filter coefficients in a manner, that the residual error is minimized when applied on the speech signal. For speech coding, only the filter coefficients and the quantized residual error signal are transmitted from the sender to the receiver, where the original signal is reconstructed by a synthesis filter. These coefficients turned out to be suitable as low-level features for automatic speech recognition. LPC coefficients have also been successfully used in MIR especially when dealing with vocals in music. Kim and Whitman [56] described an algorithm, where conventional LPC have been utilized as features for identifying the performing artist of a popular song. Furthermore, Shao et al. published a paper [99] on automatic music genre classification based on LPC.

Zero Crossing Rate

The *Zerocrossing Rate* (ZCR) simply counts the number of changes of the signum in audio frames. Since the number of crossings depends on the size of the examined window, the final value has to be normalized by dividing by the actual window size. One of the first evaluations of the zerocrossing rate in the area of speech recognition have been described by Licklider and Pollack in 1948 [63]. They described the feature extraction process and resulted with the conclusion, that the ZCR is useful for digital speech signal processing because it is loudness invariant and speaker independent. Among the variety of publications using the ZCR for MIR are the fundamental genre identification paper from Tzanetakis et al. [110] and a paper dedicated to the classification of percussive sounds by Gouyon [39].

Audio Spectrum Centroid

The *Audio Spectrum Centroid* (ASC) is another MPEG-7 standardized low-level feature in MIR [88]. As depicted in [53], it describes the center of gravity of the spectrum. It is used to describe the timbre of an audio signal. The feature extraction process is similar to the ASE extraction. The difference between ASC and ASE is, that the values within the edges of the logarithmically spaced frequency bands are not accumulated, but the spectrum centroid is estimated. This spectrum centroid indicates the center of gravity inside the frequency bands.

Audio Spectrum Spread

Audio Spectrum Spread (ASS) is another feature described in the MPEG-7 standard. It is a descriptor of the shape of the power spectrum that indicates whether it is concentrated in the vicinity of its centroid, or else spread out over the spectrum. The difference between ASE and ASS is, that the values within the edges of the logarithmically spaced frequency bands are not accumulated, but the spectrum spread is estimated, as described in [53]. The spectrum spread allows a good differentiation between tone-like and noise-like sounds.

Mid-level Audio Features

Mid-level features ([11]) present an intermediate semantic layer between well-established low-level features and advanced high-level information that can be directly understood by a human individual. Basically, mid-level features can be computed by combining advanced signal processing techniques with a-priori musical knowledge while omitting the error-prone step of deriving final statements about semantics of the musical content. It is reasonable to either compute mid-level features on the entire length of previously identified coherent segments (see section "Statistical Models of The Song") or in dedicated mid-level windows that virtually sub-sample the original slope of the low-level features and squeeze their most important properties into a small set of numbers. For example, a window-size of of approximately 5 seconds could be used in conjunction with an overlap of 2.5 seconds. These numbers may seem somewhat arbitrarily chosen, but they should be interpreted as the most suitable region of interest for capturing the temporal structure of low-level descriptors in a wide variety of musical signals, ranging from slow atmospheric pieces to up-tempo Rock music.

Rhythmic Mid-level Features

An important aspect of contemporary music is constituted by its rhythmic content. The sensation of rhythm is a complex phenomenon of the human perception which is illustrated by the large corpus of objective and subjective musical terms, such as tempo, beat, bar or shuffle used to describe rhythmic gist. The underlying principles to understanding rhythm in all its peculiarities are even more diverse. Nevertheless, it can be assumed, that the degree of self-similarity respectively periodicity inherent to the music signal contains valuable information to describe the rhythmic quality of a music piece. The extensive prior work on automatic rhythm analysis can (according to [111]) be distinguished into *Note Onset Detection*, *Beat Tracking and Tempo Estimation*, *Rhythmic Intensity and Complexity* and *Drum Transcription*. A fundamental approach for rhythm analysis in MIR is onset detection, i.e. detection of those time points in a musical signal which exhibit a percussive or transient event indicating the beginning of a new note or sound [22]. Active research has been going on over the last years in the field of beat and tempo induction [38], [96], where a variety of methods emerged that aim intelligently estimating the perceptual tempo from measurable periodicities. All previously described areas result more or less into a set of high-level attributes. These attributes are not always suited as features in music retrieval and recommendation scenarios. Thus, a variety of different methods for extraction of rhythmic mid-level features is described either frame-wise [98], event-wise[12] or beat-wise [37]. One important aspect of rhythm are rhythmic patterns, which can be effectively captured by means of an auto-correlation function (ACF). In [110], this is exploited by auto-correlating and accumulating a number of successive bands derived from a Wavelet transform of the music signal. An alternative method is given in [19]. A weighted sum of the ASE-feature serves a so called *detection function* and is auto-correlated. The challenge is to find suitable distance measures or features, that can further abstract from the raw ACF-functions, since they are not invariant to tempo changes.

Harmonic Mid-level Features

It can safely be assumed that the melodic and harmonic structures in music are a very important and intuitive concept to the majority of human listeners. Even non-musicians are able to spot differences and similarities of two given tunes. Several authors have addressed chroma vectors, also referred to as harmonic pitch class profiles [42] as a suitable tool for describing the harmonic and melodic content of music pieces. This octave agnostic representation of note probabilities can be used for estimation of the musical key, chord structure detection [42] and harmonic complexity measurements. Chroma vectors are somewhat difficult to categorize, since the techniques for extraction are typical low-level operations. But the fact that they already take into account the 12-tone scale of western tonal music places them halfway between low-level and mid-level. Very sophisticated post-processing can be performed on the raw chroma-vectors. One area of interest is the detection and alignment of cover-songs respectively classical pieces performed by different conductors and orchestras. Recent approaches are described in [97] and [82], both works are dedicated to matching and retrieval of songs that are not necessarily identical in terms of their progression of their harmonic content.

A straightforward approach to use chroma features is the computation of different histograms of the most probable notes, intervals and chords that occur throughout a song ([19]). Such simple post-processing already reveals a lot of information contained in the songs. As an illustration, Figure 3 shows the comparison of chroma-based histograms between the well known song "I will survive" by "Gloria Gaynor" and three different renditions of the same piece by the artists "Cake", "Nils Landgren" and "Hermes House Band" respectively. The shades of gray in the background indicate the areas of the distinct histograms. Some interesting phenomena can be observed when examining the different types of histograms. First, it can be seen from the chord histogram (right-most), that all four songs are played in the same key. The interval histograms (2nd and 3rd from the left) are most similar between the first

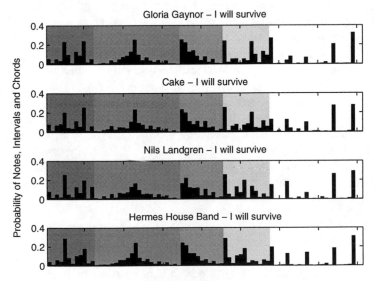

Fig. 3 Comparison of chroma-based histograms between cover songs

and the last song, because the last version stays comparatively close to the original. The second and the third song are somewhat sloppy and free interpretations of the original piece. Therefore, their interval statistics are more akin.

High-level Music Features

High-level features represent a wide range of musical characteristics, bearing a close relation to musicological vocabulary. Their main design purpose is the development of computable features being capable to model the music parameters that are observable by musicologists (see Figure 1) and that do not require any prior knowledge about signal-processing methods. Some high-level features are abstracted from features on a lower semantic level by applying various statistical pattern recognition methods. In contrast, transcription-based high-level features are directly extracted from score parameters like onset, duration and pitch of the notes within a song, whose precise extraction itself is a crucial task within MIR. Many different algorithms for drum [120], [21], bass [92], [40], melody [33], [89] and harmony [42] transcription have been proposed in the literature, achieving imperfect but remarkable detection rates so far. Recently, the combination of transcription methods for different instrument domains has been reported in [20] and [93]. However, modeling the ability of musically skilled people to accurately recognize, segregate and transcribe single instruments within dense polyphonic mixtures still bears a big challenge.

In general, high-level features can be categorized according to different musical domains like rhythm, harmony, melody or instrumentation. Different approaches for the extraction of rhythm-related high-level features have been reported. For instance, they were derived from genre-specific temporal note deviations [36] (the so-called *swing ratio*), from the percussion-related instrumentation of a song [44] or from various statistical spectrum descriptors based on periodic rhythm patters [64]. Properties related to the notes of single instrument tracks like the dominant grid (e.g. 32th notes), the dominant feeling (down- or offbeat), the dominant characteristic (binary or ternary) as well as a measure of syncopation related to different rhythmical grids can be deduced from the *Rhythmical Structure Profile* ([1]). It provides a temporal representation of all notes that is invariant to tempo and the bar measure of a song. In general, a well-performing estimation of the temporal positions of the beat-grid points is a vital pre-processing step for a subsequent mapping of the transcribed notes onto the rhythmic bar structure of a song and thereby for a proper calculation of the related features.

Melodic and harmonic high-level features are commonly deduced from the progression of pitches and their corresponding intervals within an instrument track. Basic statistical attributes like mean, standard deviation, entropy as well as complexity-based descriptors are therefore applied ([25], [78], [74] and [64]).

Retrieval of rhythmic and melodic repetitions is usually achieved by utilizing algorithms to detect repeating patterns within character strings [49]. Subsequently, each pattern can be characterized by its length, incidence rate and mean temporal distance ([1]). These properties allow the computation of the pattern's relevance as a measure for the recall value to the listener by means of derived statistical descriptors. The instrumentation of a song represents another main musical characteristic which immediately affects the timbre of a song ([78]). Hence, corresponding high-level features can be derived from it.

With all these high-level features providing a big amount of musical information, different classification tasks have been described in the literature concerning meta-data like the genre of a song or its artist. Most commonly, genre classification is based on low- and mid-level features. Only a few publications have so far addressed this problem solely based on high-level features. Examples are [78], [59] and [1], hybrid approaches are presented in [64]. Apart from different classification methods, some major differences are the applied genre taxonomies as well as the overall number of genres.

Further tasks that have been reported to be feasible with the use of high-level features are artist classification ([26], [1]) and expressive performance analysis ([77], [94]). Nowadays, songs are mostly created by a blending of various musical styles and genres. Referring to a proper genre classification, music has to be seen and evaluated segment-wise. Furthermore, the results of an automatic song segmentation can be the source of additional high-level features characterizing repetitions and the overall structure of a song.

Statistical Modeling and Similarity Measures

Nearly all state-of-the-art MIR systems use low-level acoustic features calculated in short time frames as described in Section "Low-level Audio Features". Using these raw features results in an $K \times N$ dimension feature matrix $\mathbf{X}$ per song, where K is the number of the time frames in the song, and N is the number of feature dimensions. Dealing with this amount of raw data is computationally very inefficient. Additionally, the different elements of the feature vectors could appear strongly correlated and cause information redundancy.

Dimension Reduction

One of the usual ways to suppress redundant information in the feature matrix is utilization of dimension reduction techniques. Their purpose is to decrease the number of feature dimension N while keeping or even revealing the most characteristic data properties. Generally, all dimension reduction methods can be divided into supervised and unsupervised ones. Among the unsupervised approaches the one most often used is *Principal Component Analysis* (PCA). The other well-established unsupervised dimension reduction method is *Self-Organizing Maps* (SOM), which is often used for visualizing the original high-dimensional feature space by mapping it into a two dimensional plane. The most often used supervised dimension reduction method is *Linear Discriminant Analysis* (LDA), it is successfully applied as a pre-processing for audio signal classification.

Principal Component Analysis

The key idea of PCA [31] is to find a subspace whose basis vectors correspond to the maximum-variance directions in the original feature space. PCA involves an expansion of the feature matrix into the eigenvectors and eigenvalues of its covariance matrix, this procedure is called the *Karhunen Loéve expansion*. If $\mathbf{X}$ is the original feature matrix, then the solution is obtained by solving the eigensystem decomposition $\lambda_i v_i = \mathbf{C} v_i$, where $\mathbf{C}$ is a covariance matrix of $\mathbf{X}$, and λ_i and v_i are the eigenvalues and eigenvectors of $\mathbf{C}$. The column vectors v_i form the PCA transformation matrix $\mathbf{W}$. The mapping of original feature matrix into new feature space is obtained by the matrix multiplication $\mathbf{Y} = \mathbf{X} \cdot \mathbf{W}$. The amount of information of each feature dimension (in the new feature space) is determined by the corresponding eigenvalue. The larger the eigenvalue the more effective the feature dimension. Dimension reduction is obtained by simply discarding the column vectors v_i with small eigenvalues λ_i.

Self-Organizing Maps

SOM are special types of artificial neural networks that can be used to generate a low-dimensional, discrete representation of a high-dimensional input feature space by means of unsupervised clustering. SOM differ from conventional artificial neural networks because they use a neighborhood function to preserve the topological properties of the input space. This makes SOM very useful for creating low-dimensional views of high-dimensional data, akin to *multidimensional scaling* (MDS). Like most artificial neural networks, SOM need training using input examples. This process can be viewed as vector quantization. As will be detailed later (see 16), SOM are suitable for displaying music collections. If the size of the maps (the number of neurons) is small compared to the number of items in the feature space, then the process essentially equals k-means clustering. For the emergence of higher level structure, a larger so-called *Emergent SOM* (ESOM) is needed. With larger maps a single neuron does not represent a cluster anymore. It is rather an element in a highly detailed non-linear projection of the high dimensional feature space to the low dimensional map space. Thus, clusters are formed by connected regions of neurons with similar properties.

Linear Discriminant Analysis

LDA [113] is a widely used method to improve the separability among classes while reducing the feature dimension. This linear transformation maximizes the ratio of between-class variance to the within-class variance guaranteeing a maximal separability. The resultant $N \times N$ matrix $\mathbf{T}$ is used to map an N-dimensional feature row vector $\mathbf{x}$ into the subspace $\mathbf{y}$ by a multiplication. Reducing the dimension of the transformed feature vector $\mathbf{y}$ from N to D is achieved by considering only the first D column vectors of $\mathbf{T}$ (now $N \times D$) for multiplication.

Statistical Models of The Song

Defining a similarity measure between two music signals which consist of multiple feature frames still remains a challenging task. The feature matrices of different songs can be hardly compared directly. One of the first works on music similarity analysis [30] used MFCC as a feature, and then applied a supervised tree-structured quantization to map the feature matrices of every song to the histograms. Logan and Salomon [71] used a song signature based on histograms derived by unsupervised k-means clustering of low-level features. Thus, the specific song characteristics in the compressed form can be derived by clustering or quantization in the feature space. An alternative approach is to treat each frame (row) of the feature matrix as a point in the N-dimensional feature space. The characteristic attributes of a particular song can be encapsulated by the estimation of the *Probability Density Function* (PDF) of these points in the feature space. The distribution of these points is a-priori unknown, thus the modeling of the PDF has to be flexible and adjustable to different levels of generalization. The resulting distribution of the feature frames is often influenced by the various underlying random processes. According to the central limit theorem, the vast class of acoustic features tends to be normally distributed. The constellation of these factors leads to the fact, that already in the early years of MIR the *Gaussian Mixture Model* (GMM) became the commonly used statistical model for representing a feature matrix of a song [69], [6]. Feature frames are thought of as generated from various sources and each source is modeled by a single Gaussian. The PDF $p(\mathbf{x} \mid \lambda)$ of the feature frames is estimated as a weighted sum of the multivariate normal distributions:

$$p(\mathbf{x} \mid \lambda) = \sum_{i=1}^{M} \omega_i \frac{1}{(2\pi)^{N/2} |\Sigma|^{1/2}} \exp\left(-\frac{1}{2}(\mathbf{x} - \mu_i)^T \Sigma_i^{-1} (\mathbf{x} - \mu_i) \right) \quad (1)$$

The generalization properties of the model can be adjusted by choosing the number of Gaussian mixtures M. Each single i-th mixture is characterized by its mean vector μ_i and covariance matrix Σ_i. Thus, a GMM is parametrized in $\lambda = \{\omega_i, \mu_i, \Sigma_i\}$, $i = \overline{1, M}$, where ω_i is the weight of the i-th mixtures and $\sum_i \omega_i = 1$. A schematic representation of a GMM is shown in Figure 4. The parameters of the GMM can be estimated using the Expectation-Maximization algorithm [18]. A good overview of applying various statistical models (ex. GMM or k-means) for music similarity search is given in [7].

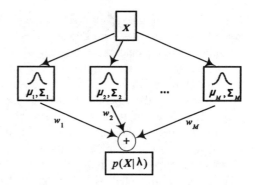

Fig. 4 Schematic representation of Gaussian Mixture Model

The approach of modeling all frames of a song with a GMM is often referred as a "bag-of-frames" approach [5]. It encompasses the overall distribution, but the long-term structure and correlation between single frames within a song is not taken into account. As a result, important information is lost. To overcome this issue, Tzanetakis [109] proposed a set of audio features capturing the changes in the music "texture". For details on mid-level and high-level audio features the reader is referred to the Section "Acoustic Features for Music Modeling".

Alternative ways to express the temporal changes in the PDF are proposed in [28]. They compared the effectiveness of GMM to *Gaussian Observation Hidden Markov Models* (HMM). The results of the experiment showed that HMM better describe the spectral similarity of songs than the standard technique of GMM. The drawback of this approach is a necessity to calculate the similarity measure via log-likelihood of the models.

Recently, another approach using semantic information about song segmentation for song modeling has been proposed in [73]. Song segmentation implies a time-domain segmentation and clustering of the musical piece in possibly repeatable semantically meaningful segments. For example, the typical western pop song can be segmented into "intro", "verse", "chorus", "bridge", and "outro" parts. For similar songs not all segments might be similar. For the human perception, the songs with similar "chorus" are similar. In [73], application of a song segmentation algorithm based on the Bayesian Information Criterion (BIC) has been described. BIC has been successfully applied for speaker segmentation [81]. Each segment state (ex. all repeated "chorus" segments form one segment state) are modeled with one Gaussian. Thus, these Gaussians can been weighted in a mixture depending on the durations of the segment states. Frequently repeated and long segments achieve higher weights.

Distance Measures

The particular distance measure between two songs is calculated as a distance between two song models and therefore depends on the models used. In [30] the distance between histograms was calculated via *Euclidean distance* or *Cosine distance* between two vectors. Logan and Salomon [71] adopted the *Earth mover's distance* (EMD) to calculate the distance between k-means clustering models.

The straight forward approach to estimate the distance between the song modeled by GMM or HMM is to rate the log-likelihood of feature frames of one song by the models of the others. Distance measures based on log-likelihoods have been successfully used in [6] and [28]. The disadvantage of this method is an overwhelming computational effort. The system does not scale well and is hardly usable in real-world applications dealing with huge music archives. Some details to its computation times can be found in [85].

If a song is modeled by parametric statistical model, such as GMM, a more appropriate distance measure between the models can be defined based on the parameters of the models. A good example of such parametric distance measure is a *Kullback-Leibler divergence* (KL-divergence) [58], corresponding to a distance between two single Gaussians:

$$D(f \| g) = \frac{1}{2} \left(log\frac{|\Sigma_g|}{|\Sigma_f|} + Tr\left[\Sigma_g^{-1}\Sigma_f\right] + \left(\mu_f - \mu_g\right)^T \Sigma_g^{-1} \left(\mu_f - \mu_g\right) - N \right)$$

(2)

where f and g are single Gaussians with the means μ_f and μ_g and covariance matrices Σ_f and Σ_g correspondingly, and N is the dimensionality of the feature space. Initially, KL-divergence is not symmetric and needs to be symmetrized

$$D_2(f_a \| g_b) = \frac{1}{2} [D(f_a \| g_b) + D(g_b \| f_a)].$$

(3)

Unfortunately, the KL-divergence for two GMM is not analytically tractable. Parametric distance measures between two GMM can be expressed by several approximations, see [73] for an overview and comparison.

"In the Mood" – Towards Capturing Music Semantics

Automatic semantic tagging comprises methods for automatically deriving meaningful and human understandable information from the combination of signal processing and machine learning methods. Semantic information could be a description of the musical style, performing instruments or the singer's gender. There are different approaches to generate semantic annotations. Knowledge based approaches focus on highly specific algorithms which implement a concrete knowledge about a specific musical property. In contrast, supervised machine learning approaches use a large amount of audio features from representative training examples in order to implicitly learn the characteristics of concrete categories. Once trained, the model for a semantic category can be used to classify and thus to annotate unknown music content.

Classification Models

There are two general classification approaches, a generative and a discriminative one. Both allow to classify unlabeled music data into different semantic categories with a certain probability, that depends on the training parameters and the underlying audio features. Generative probabilistic models describe how likely a song belongs to a certain pre-defined class of songs. These models form a probability distribution over the classes' features, in this case over the audio features presented in Section "Acoustic Features for Music Modeling", for each class. In contrast, discriminative models try to predict the most likely class directly instead of modeling the class' conditional probability densities. Therefore, the model learns boundaries between different classes during the training process and uses the distance to the boundaries as an indicator for the most probable class. Only two classifiers that are most often used in MIR will be detailed here, since space is not enough to describe the large number of classification techniques which has been introduced in the literature.

Classification Based on Gaussian Mixture Models

Apart from song modeling described in 16, GMM are successfully used for probabilistic classification because they are well suited to model large amounts of training data per class. One interprets the single feature vectors of a music item as random samples generated by a mixture of multivariate Gaussian sources. The actual classification is conducted by estimating which pre-trained mixture of Gaussians has most likely generated the frames. Thereby, the likelihood estimate serves as some kind of confidence measure for the classification.

Classification Based on Support Vector Machines

A support vector machine (SVM) attempts to generate an optimal decision margin between feature vectors of the training classes in an N-dimensional space ([15]). Therefore, only a part of the training samples is taken into account called *support vectors*. A hyperplane is placed in the feature space in a manner that the distance to the support vectors is maximized. SVM have the ability to well generalize data actually in the case of few training samples. Although the SVM training itself is an optimization process, it is common to accomplish a cross validation and grid search to optimize the training parameters ([48]). This can be a very time-consuming process, depending on the number of training samples.

In most cases classification problems are not linear separable in the actual feature space. Transformed into a high-dimensional space, non-linear classification problems can become linear separable. However, higher dimensions deal with an increase of the computation effort. To overcome this problem, the so called *kernel trick* is used to get non-linear problems separable, although the computation can be performed in the origin feature space ([15]). The key idea of the kernel trick is to replace the dot product in a high-dimensional space with a kernel function in a original feature space.

Mood Semantics

Mood as an illustrative example for semantic properties describes a more subjective information which correlates not only to the music impression but also to individual memories and different music preferences. Furthermore, we need a distinction between mood and emotion. Emotion describes an affective perception in a short time frame, whereas mood describes a deeper perception and feeling. In the MIR community sometimes both terms are used for the same meaning. In this article the term mood is used to describe the human oriented perception of music expression.

To overcome the subjective impact, generative descriptions of mood are needed to describe the commonality of different user's perception. Therefore, mood characteristics are formalized in mood models which describe different peculiarities of the property "mood".

Mood Models

Mood models can be categorized into category-based and dimension-based descriptions. Furthermore, combinations of both descriptions are defined to combine the advantages of both approaches. The early work on music expression concentrates on category based formalization e.g. Hevner's adjective circle [45] as depicted in Fig. 5(a). Eight groups of adjectives are formulated whereas each group describes

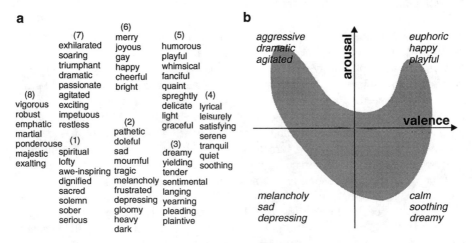

Fig. 5 Category and Dimension based Mood Models based on [45]

a category or cluster of mood. All groups are arranged on a circle and neighbored groups are consisting of related expressions. The variety of adjectives in each group gives a better representation of the meaning of each group and depicts the different user perceptions. Category based approaches allow the assignment of music items into one or multiple groups which results in a single- or multi-label classification problem.

The dimension based mood models focus on the description of mood as a point within a multi-dimensional mood space. Different models based on dimensions such as valence, arousal, stress, energy or sleepiness are defined. Thayers model [103] describes mood as a product of the dimensions energy and tension. Russels circumplex model [91] arrange the dimensions pleasantness, excitement, activation and distress in a mood space with 45° dimension steps. As base of its model, Russel defines the dimensions pleasantness and activation. The commonality of different theories on dimension based mood descriptions is the base on moods between positive and negative (valence) and intensity (arousal) as depicted in Fig. 5(b). The labeled area in Fig. 5(b) shows the affect area which was evaluated in physiological experiments as the region that equates a human emotion [41]. Mood models that combine categories and dimensions, typically place mood adjectives in a region of the mood space, e.g. the Tellegen-Watson-Clark model [102]. In [23] the valence and arousal model is extend with mood adjectives for each quadrant, to give a textual annotation and dimensional assignment of music items.

Mood Classification

Scientific publications on mood classification use different acoustic features to model different mood aspects, e.g. timbre based features for valence and tempo and rhythmic features for high activation.

Feng et al. [27] utilize an average silence ratio, whereas Yang et al. [117] use a beats per minute value for the tempo description. Lu et al. [72] incorporate various rhythmic features such as rhythm strength, average correlation peak, average tempo and average onset frequency. Beyond others Li [62] and Tolos [105] use frequency spectrum based features (e.g. MFCC, ASC, spectral flux or spectral rolloff) to describe the timbre and therewith the valence aspect of music expression. Furthermore, Wu and Jeng [116] setup a complex mixture of a wide range of acoustical features for valence and arousal expression: rhythmic content, pitch content, power spectrum centroid, inter-channel cross correlation, tonality, spectral contrast and Daubechies wavelet coefficient histograms.

Next to the feature extraction process the introduced machine learning algorithms GMM and SVM are often utilized to train and classify music expression. Examples for GMM based classification approaches are Lu [72] and Liu [68]. Publications that focus on the discriminative SVM approach are [61, 62, 112, 117]. In [23] GMM and SVM classifiers are compared with a slightly better result of the SVM approach. Liu et al. [67] utilize a nearest-mean classifier. Trohidis et al. [107] compare different multi-label classification approaches based on SVM and k-nearest neighbor.

One major problem of the comparison of different results for mood and other semantic annotations is the lack on a golden standard for test data and evaluation method. Most publication use an individual test set or ground-truth. A specialty of Wu and Jeng's approach [116] is based on the use of mood histograms in the ground truth and the results beeing compared by a quadratic-cross-similarity, which leads to a complete different evaluation method then a single label annotation.

A first international comparison of mood classification algorithms was performed on the MIREX 2007 in the Audio Music Mood Classification Task. Hu et al.[50] presented the results and lessons learned from the first benchmark. Five mood clusters of music were defined as ground truth with a single label approach. The best algorithm reach an average accuracy in a three cross fold evaluation of about 61 %.

Music Recommendation

There are several sources to find new music. Record sales are summarized in music charts, the local record dealers are always informed about new releases, and radio stations keep playing music all day long (and might once in a while focus on a certain style of music which is of interest for somebody). Furthermore, everybody knows friends who share the same musical taste. These are some of the typical ways how people acquire recommendations about new music. Recommendation is recommending items (e.g., songs) to users. How is this performed or (at least) assisted by computing power?

There are different types of music related recommendations, and all of them use some kind of similarity. People that are searching for albums might profit from artist recommendations (artists who are similar to those these people like). In song recommendation the system is supposed to suggest new songs. Playlist generation is some kind of song recommendation on the local database. Nowadays, in times of the "social web", neighbor recommendation is another important issue, in which the system proposes other users of a social web platform to the querying person - users with a similar taste of music.

Automated systems follow different strategies to find similar items[14].

- Collaborative Filtering. In collaborative filtering (CF), systems try to gain information about similarity of items by learning past user-item relationships. One possible way to do this is to collect lots of playlists of different users and then suggesting songs to be similar, if they appear together in many of these playlists. A major drawback is the cold start for items. Songs that are newly added to a database do not appear in playlists, so no information about them can be collected. Popular examples for CF recommendation are last.fm[1] and amazon.com[2].

---

[1] http://www.last.fm

[2] http://www.amazon.com

- Content-Based Techniques. In the content-based approach (CB), the content of musical pieces is analyzed, and similarity is calculated from the descriptions as result of the content analysis. Songs can be similar if they have the same timbre or rhythm. This analysis can be done by experts (e.g., Pandora[3]) , which leads to high quality but expensive descriptions, or automatically, using signal processing and machine learning algorithms (e.g., Mufin[4]). Automatic content-based descriptors cannot yet compete with manually derived descriptions, but can be easily created for large databases.
- Context-Based Techniques. By analyzing the context of songs or artists, similarities can also be derived. For example, contextual information can be acquired as a result of web-mining (e.g., analyzing hyperlinks between artist homepages) [66], or collaborative tagging [100].
- Demographic Filtering Techniques. Recommendations are made based on clusters that are derived from demographic information, e.g. "males at your age from your town, who are also interested in soccer, listen to...".

By combining different techniques to hybrid systems, drawbacks can be compensated, as described in [95], where content-based similarity is used to solve the item cold start of a CF system.

A very important issue within recommendation is the user. In order to make personalized recommendations, the system has to collect information about the musical taste of the user and contextual information about the user himself. Two questions arise: How are new user profiles initialized (user cold start), and how are they maintained? The user cold start can be handled in different ways. Besides starting with a blank profile, users could enter descriptions of their taste by providing their favorite artists or songs, or rating some exemplary songs. Profile maintenance can be performed by giving feedback about recommendations in an explicit or implicit way. Explicit feedback includes rating of recommended songs, whereas implicit feedback includes information of which song was skipped or how much time a user spent on visiting the homepage of a recommended artist.

In CB systems, recommendations can be made by simply returning the most similar songs (according to computed similarity as described in 16) to a reference song. This song, often called "seed song" represents the initial user profile. If we just use equal weigths of all features, the same seed song will always result in the same recommendations. However, perceived similarity between items may vary from person to person and situation to situation. Some of the acoustic features may be more important than others, therefore the weighting of the features should be adjusted according to the user, leading to a user-specific similarity function.

Analyzing user interaction can provide useful information about the user's preferences and needs. It can be given in a number of ways. In any case, usability issues should be taken into account. An initialization of the user profile by manually labeling dozens of songs is in general not reasonable. In [10], the music signal is analyzed

---

[3] http://www.pandora.com
[4] http://www.mufin.com

with respect to semantically meaningful aspects (e.g., timbre, rhythm, instrumentation, genre etc.). These are grouped into domains and arranged in an ontology structure, which can be very helpful for providing an intuitive user interface. The user now has the ability to weight or disable single aspects or domains to adapt the recommendation process to his own needs. For instance, similarities between songs can be computed by considering only rhythmic aspects. Setting the weights of aspects or domains by for example adjusting the corresponding sliders is another way to initialize a user profile.

The settings of weights can also be accomplished by collecting implicit or explicit user feedback. Implicit user interaction can be easily gathered by, e.g., tracing the user's skipping behavior ([86], [115]). The recommendation system categorizes already recommended songs as disliked songs, not listened to, or liked songs. By this means, one gets three classes of songs: songs the user likes, songs the user dislikes and songs, that have not yet been rated and therefore lack a label. Explicit feedback is normally collected in form of ratings. Further information can be collected explicitly by providing a user interface, in which the user can arrange already recommended songs in clusters, following his perception of similarity. Machine learning algorithms can be used to learn the "meaning" behind these clusters and classify unrated songs following the same way. This is analogous to 16, where semantic properties are learned from exemplary songs clustered in classes. In [76], explicit feedback is used to refine the training data. An SVM classifier is used for classification. The user model, including seed songs, domain weighting or feedback information, can be interpreted as a reflection of the user's musical taste. The primary use is to improve the recommendations. Now songs are not further recommended solely based on a user-defined song, instead the user model is additionally incorporated into the recommendation process. Besides, the user model can also serve as a base for neighbor recommendation in a social web platform.

Recommendation algorithms should be evaluated according to their usefulness for an individual, but user-based evaluations are rarely conducted since they require a lot of user input. Therefore, large scale evaluations are usually based on similarity analysis (derived from genre similarities) or the analysis of song similarity graphs. In one of the few user-based evaluations [14] is shown that CF recommendations score better in terms of relevance, while CB recommendations have advantages regarding to novelty. The results of another user-based evaluation [75] supports the assumption that automatic recommendations are yet behind the quality of human recommendations.

The acceptance of a certain technique further depends on the type of user. People who listen to music, but are far from being music fanatics (about 3/4 of the 16-45 year old, the so called "Casuals" and "Indifferents", see [54]) will be fine with popular recommendations from CF systems. By contrast the "Savants", for which "Everything in life seems to be tied up with music" ([54]) might be bored when they want to discover new music.

Apart from that, hybrid recommender systems, which combine different techniques and therefore are able to compensate for some of the drawbacks of a standalone approach, have the largest potential to provide good recommendations.

Visualizing Music for Navigation and Exploration

With more and more recommendation systems available, there is a need to visualize the similarity information and to let the user explore large music collections. Often an intuitively understandable metaphor is used for exploration. As already illustrated in Section "Music Recommendation", there are several ways to obtain similarities between songs. The visualization of a music archive is independent from the way the similarity information was gathered from the recommenders. There exist visualization interfaces that illustrate content-based, collaborative-based or web-based similarity information or that combine different sources for visualization.

This section deals with approaches and issues for music visualization. First, a brief overview of visualizing musical work is given. The next subsection deals with visualizing items in music archives followed by a description of browsing capabilities in music collections.

Visualization of Songs

Early work on visualizing songs was performed by [29]. Self-similarity matrices are used to visualize the time structure in music. Therefore, the acoustic similarity between any two instances of a musical piece is computed and plotted as a two-dimensional graph. In [65], Lillie proposes a visualization technique based on acoustic features for the visualization of song structure. The acoustic features are computed based on the API of EchoNest[5]. In the 2-dimensional plot, the x-axis represents the time of the song and the y-axis the chroma indices. Additionally, the color encodes the timbre of the sound. An example is given in Figure 6. The acoustic features for the *Moonlight Sonata* of Beethoven are displayed on the left and the song *Cross the Breeze* from Sonic Youth is displayed on the right.

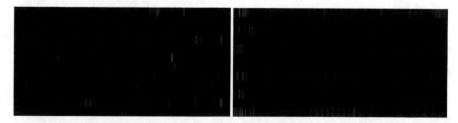

Fig. 6 Visualizing the structure of songs. Left: Visualization of the *Moonlight Sonata* of Beethoven, Right: Visualization of the song *Cross the Breeze* from Sonic Youth (http://www.flyingpudding.com/projects/viz_music/)

---

[5] http://developer.echonest.com/pages/overview

In [118], Yoshii et al. propose the visualization of acoustic features through image thumbnails to let the user guess the music content through the appearance of the thumbnail and decide if he wants to listen to it. The mapping between the acoustical space and the visual space is performed via an optimization method, additionally taking some constraints into account. Hiraga et al. [47] propose a 3-D visualization technique for MIDI data. They visualize the performance of musical pieces by focusing on the musical expression like articulation, tempo, dynamic change and structure information. For further reading, the interested reader is referred to [52], where an overview of visualization techniques for musical work with MIR methods is given.

Most work done in song visualization is independent of the work performed in visualization of music archives. From the next subsection it becomes apparent, that visualization of music archives mainly concentrates on the arrangement of songs in the visualization space. One main focus is to realize the paradigm of *closeness encodes similarity* rather than a sophisticated visualization of the song itself. Nevertheless one has to keep in mind that music archives consist of songs. Combined visualization techniques that also stress the musical characteristics of each song in a music archive are still an open research issue.

Visualization of Music Archives

The key point when visualizing music archives is how to map the multidimensional space of music features per song to a low dimensional *visualization space*. Usually a 2-D plot or a 3-D space are used as visualization spaces. The placement of a song in the visualization space is depending on the similarity of this song to neighbored songs. Therefore a mapping of the acoustic features to a spatial distance is performed. For the user it is intuitive and easy to understand that closely positioned songs have similar characteristics. Next to the placement of the songs in this visualization space, additional features can be encoded via the color or the shape of the song icon.

Islands of Music [87] is a popular work for visualizing music archives. The similarities are calculated with content-based audio features and organized in a SOM. Continents and islands in the geographic map represent genres. The *MusicMiner* system [80] uses ESOM to project the audio features onto a topographic map. An example is illustrated in Figure 7.

Kolhoff et al. [57] use glyphs to represent each song based on its content. The songs are projected into a 2-D space by utilizing a PCA for dimension reduction with a special weighting and relaxation for determining the exact position. Also in [84], a PCA is used to determine the three most important principal components and project the feature vectors onto the three resulting eigenvectors. The feature vectors are deskewed and the resulting vectors are reduced to two dimensions via a second PCA. Torrens et al. [106] propose different visualization approaches based on metadata. Interesting is their *disc visualization*. Each sector of the disc represents

Fig. 7 MusicMiner: 700 songs are represented as colored dots

a different genre. The songs are mapped to the genres while tracks in the middle are the oldest. They use this visualization technique to visualize playlists.

Requirements for the visualization of music archives are the scalability to large numbers of songs and computational complexity. Even for music archives containing hundreds of thousands of songs, the algorithm has to be able to position every song in the visualization space quickly.

Navigation and Exploration in Music Archives

Digital music collections are normally organized in folders, sorted corresponding to artists or genres, forcing the user to navigate through the folder hierarchy to find songs. They only allow for a text-based browsing in the music collection. A completely different paradigm for exploring music collections is the comprehensive search for similar music by browsing through a visual space. In this section, a short review about navigation and browsing capabilities is given. There are some overlaps to the section about visualization of music archives since most visualization scenarios also offer a browsing possibility. Here the focus is on approaches that concentrate more on browsing.

A popular method is the use of metaphors as underlying space for visualization. A metaphor provides an intuitive access for the user and an immediate understanding of the dimensions. There were already examples of geographic metaphors in the previous section. In [35] the metaphor of a *world of music* is used. The authors focus on compactly representing similarities rather than on visualization. The similarities are obtained with collaborative filtering methods, a graph from pairwise similarities is constructed and mapped to Euclidean space while preserving distances. [46] uses a *radar system* to visualize music. Similar songs are located closely to each other and the eight directions from the radial plot denote different oppositional music characteristics like calm vs. turbulent or melodic vs. rhythmic. The actual chosen song is placed in the middle of the radar. *MusicBox* is a music browser that organizes songs in a 2D-space via a PCA on the music features [65]. It combines browsing techniques, visualization of music archives and visualization of the song structure in one application.

In Figure 8 we show an example of the metaphor *stars universe*. The 2-D universe is representing the musical space and stars are acting as visual entities for the songs. The user can navigate through this universe finding similar songs arranged closely to each other, sometimes even in star concentrations. The visualization space is subdivided into several semantic regions. On the x-axis there are the rhythmic characteristics from slow to fast subdivided in five gradations and the y-axis contains the instrument density from sparse to full in three gradations. To position a song in the universe, a similarity query on a rhythmic and an instrument density reference set is performed. Each reference set contains the feature vectors of three songs per gradation. For both reference sets the winning song determines the subregion in the visualization space, the rhythmic one for the x-axis and the other for the y-axis. The exact position in the subregion is influenced by locally translating each song in the subspace in dependence from the mean and standard deviations of the song positions belonging to the same region (cp. [84]).

A quite different approach is performed in [9]. Here, the *collaging technique*, emerged from the field of digital libraries, is used to visualize music archives and enable browsing based on metadata. Other research focuses on visualizing music archives on mobile devices, e.g., [83]. In [17] a music organizer and browser for children is proposed. The authors stress the needs from children for music browsing and provide a navigation software.

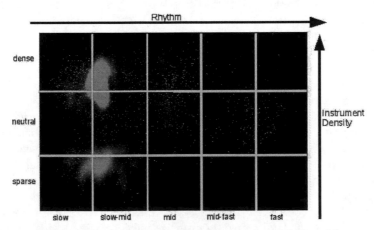

Fig. 8 Semantic browsing in a stars universe. The x-axis encodes the rhythm of the songs and the y-axis the instrument density. For illustration purposes the semantic regions are marked in yellow

Summary and Open Issues

We presented a number of approaches for visualizing the song structure, music archives and browsing. They all offer the user a different insight into his music collection and allow for a discovery of new, unknown songs, that match to the preferences of the user. The main drawback of visualization and browsing methods that project the high-dimensional feature space of acoustic features into a low (2-D or 3-D) visualization space with dimension reduction methods, is the lack of *semantic browsing*. For the user it is not apparent which semantic entity changes by navigating along one axis. Although nearly located songs are most similar to each other, it is not intuitive which musical characteristic changes when browsing through the visualization space. As a solution many approaches introduce semantic entities like genre mountains. These can serve as a landmark for the user and describe which musical characteristics are typical for a specific direction. Another possibility is the use of high-level features. One example from Section "Navigation and Exploration in Music Archives" is the radar system, where each radial direction refers to a change in a special semantic characteristic. Another example is the stars universe, also presented in Section "Navigation and Exploration in Music Archives". Problems with these approaches are due to the fact that music is not eight-dimensional or two-dimensional, but multidimensional. So it is not possible to define the holistic impression of music along a few semantic dimensions. One has to abstract that the songs are similar in the mentioned dimensions but regarding other musical aspects, neighbored songs can sound very differently.

Applications

Today both physical products (records and CDs) as well as virtual goods (music tracks) are sold via Internet. To find the products, there is an increasing need for search functionalities. This need has been addressed by a number of search paradigms. Some just work, even without scientific foundation, others use elaborated models like the ones described in this book.

During the last years, a large amount of MIR-based applications and services appeared. Some of them generated quite some attention in online communities. Some of the underlying techniques are still subject to basic research and not yet understood to the utmost extent. However, the competition for unique features incited many small start-up companies as well as some innovation-oriented big players to push immature technologies to the market. Below we list some applications, that integrate automatic CB methods to enable retrieval and recommendation of music. The focus is clearly on CB based systems. Beyond the applications below, there are a large number of strictly CF-based systems around. Applications that are merely scientific showcases without significant commercial ambitions will not be mentioned here. Furthermore, a distinction is made between projects that make their applications publicly available and companies that approach other entities and offer them their services. In the latter case, it is difficult to assess whether the capabilities of the real product can live up to their marketing promises. It should be noted, that this section does not claim to be absolutely comprehensive. There are probably some more projects and companies on the Asian market which we do not know due to language-barriers. Furthermore, the market for MIR-applications is quite volatile, so the examples in the following sections can only provide a snapshot of the current situation.

Business to Business Applications

The American company Gracenote[6] is probably best known for providing the CDDB CD identification service. Today, they have added different solutions for music identification and recommendation to their portfolio. Their recommendation service "Discover" is based on editorial recommendations, content-based and collaborative filtering.

The Canadian company Double V3[7] provides audio identification services to the music and entertainment industry.

The US-based company One Llama[8] can rely on a core team with long experience in academic MIR research. One Llama's flagship is called 'Artificial Ear' and is said to have extracted hundreds of music features from millions of songs. Their music discovery tools are based on a combination of CB and CF techniques.

The Echo Nest's[9] APIs are based on the so-called "Musical Brain". Following their description, the MIR-platform combines CB-recommendation with web-crawling and knowledge extraction. The founders of the company have a history with the MIT Media Lab.

The San Francisco based company Music Intelligence Solutions[10] and its Barcelona based predecessor Polyphonic Human Media Interface (PHMI) are offering diverse solutions for music discovery. They are especially well known for the "Hit Song Science" tool that claims to reliably measure the hit potential of novel songs.

The New York based company Music Xray[11] has a common history with aforementioned Music Intelligence Solutions. Their portfolio comprises a web service that allows artists and music industry professionals to measure, monitor, stimulate the demand for novel artists and their songs. They have teamed up with Queen Mary University's Centre For Digital Music.

The Spanish company BMAT[12] is a commercial spin-off of the Music Technology Group, the music and audio research lab of the Universidad Pompeu Fabra in

---

[6] http://www.gracenote.com/business_solutions/discover/

[7] http://www.doublev3.com/

[8] http://onellama.com/

[9] http://the.echonest.com/

[10] http://www.uplaya.com/company.html

[11] http://www.musicxray.com/music-xray

[12] http://bmat.com/

Barcelona. BMAT generated quite some public attention when they powered the casting of a Spanish idol show with a web application that automatically evaluated the singing.

The Norwegian company Bach Technology[13] benefits from a long tradition with related projects in the digital content domain. Bach Technology develops and distributes audio search and annotation technology to stimulate sales in the "Long Tail" of music catalogues.

Business to Consumer Applications

The goal of the German company mufin[14] is to foster music consumption and sales by helping end-users to discover new music that is relevant to their personal preferences. Their products enable discovery and management in large-scale music collections. In addition, mufin delivers several applications for free download, such as a recommender Plug-In for Apple iTunes and a stand-alone media player.

The California based company MusicIP[15] was one of the pioneers that made MIR-applications accessible to end users. Their flagship application is called "MyDJ Desktop". It allows the creation of CB based similarity playlists. Additionally, their music identification service "MusicDNS" has an extensive database of reference music fingerprints available. It is the basis for the community music metadatabase MusicBrainz[16].

Midomi[17] is a melody search engine combined with a community portal. Midomi circumvents the typical problems of how to acquire melody information in a clever way. They let their end-users maintain and update the melody database. The input can be either singing, humming or whistling. The company behind the service is MELODIS, based in Silicon Valley. Their goal is the development of next generation of search and sound technologies for global distribution on a wide range of mobile platforms and devices.

The U.K. based company Shazam[18] started their business in audio identification in 2002 and emerged as the leading mobile music identification service provider. They claim to have a fingerprint database of over 6 million tracks. The integration of their service into the Apples iPhone 3G made the service very well known among technology-affine communities.

The Berlin based company aupeo[19] is one of the first that combine a music-lovers social network with a mood-based personalized internet radio. The mood

---

[13] http://www.bachtechnology.com/

[14] http://www.mufin.com/us/software

[15] http://www.musicip.com/

[16] http://musicbrainz.org/

[17] http://www.midomi.com/

[18] http://www.shazam.com/music/web/home.html

[19] http://www.aupeo.com/

annotations of their music catalogue are computed by CB methods. Their unique business idea is the integration of their service into hardware devices, such as inexpensive internet-radios.

Future Directions and Challenges

The former chapters of this article presented important aspects and first results of state-of-the-art MIR research. However, it seems that many available technologies are just in their infancy as it was summarised in a mentionable survey by Lew [60] for the whole multimedia information retrieval sector. Despite considerable research progress and the astonishing amount of different projects and applications already on the market, there is no final solution to be seen that would solve the aforementioned problems related to music recommendation sufficiently. Even worse, there is a lack of adequate business models to make MIR-technologies an indispensible helper for modern and technology-oriented lifestyle. The very first MIR-based applications to become publicly available seemed like toys. This situation is changing slowly with the integration of recommendation technologies into mobile devices and other consumer electronics hardware. This takes originally strictly web-based applications directly into everybodies living room or car. This article shall be concluded with a brief overview of possible future directions and challenges.

Context-Sensitivity: Purely content based methods for music recommendation and retrieval know very little about the real world. Learning systems can be taught some semantics about music, styles and moods. But there are complex interdependencies between sociocultural aspects, the users' current condition as well as environmental factors. In [16] some future directions are proposed that are promising with respect to mobile applications. In fact, new interactive devices (positional tracking, health, inclination sensors) may provide new possibilities, such as human emotional state detection and tracking.

Semantic Web and Music Ontologies: A body of formally represented knowledge is based on a conceptualization: the objects, concepts, and other entities that exist in some area of interest and the relationships that hold among them. A conceptualization is an abstract, simplified view of the world. Every knowledge-based system is committed to some conceptualization, explicitly or implicitly. An ontology is an explicit specification of a conceptualization. The term is borrowed from philosophy, where an Ontology is a systematic account of Existence. The Music Ontology Specification[20] provides main concepts and properties for describing music (i.e. artists, albums, tracks, but also performances, arrangements, etc.) on the Semantic Web. This initiative shall enable the interlinking of music related databases on the semantic level [90].

Folksonomies: It's unnecessary to state once again how difficult it is to extract descriptive and relevant information from music content. Consequently, the majority

---

[20] http://www.musicontology.com/

of the existing search engines are using simple keyword based approaches. Large heterogeneous collections of music can probably not be sufficiently described using a rigid, pre-defined taxonomy. Since it is easier to develop inverted file structures to search for keywords in large collections, tagging became more attractive. By freely assigning tags, unstructured files can be made searchable. This is strongly connected to concepts like wisdom of the crowds or crowd-sourcing. This is based on the assumption that tags assigned by a number of human listeners will result in "wise tags" (because they are assigned by the crowd) and this will be a better approach than the rigid taxonomy defined by experts. This idea is appealing and made LastFM[21] and MP3.com[22] useful and popular. In [101], it can be found that taxonomies created by experts are useful for cataloguing and hierarchical browsing while the flat view of folksonomies allows better organization and access of a personal collection. Thus, it can be assumed that a combination of taxonomy and folksonomy will be a promising future direction. Furthermore, adaptive MIR models can be trained using the music examples labeled with tags in order to assign such tags automatically afterwards [24]

Hybrid Systems: According to first published work ([119], [104]) the combination of automatic content based and collaborative filtering methods might be beneficial for the further developments of music retrieval and recommendation systems. One intuitive advantage is the possibility to avoid the cold-start problem inherent to collaborative filtering based systems, by recommending novel or unknown songs based on their acoustic properties. More advantages are to be expected from merging social and content-based music metadata with musicological knowledge as introduced before. Such systems should then be able to derive the importance of given or computed information for a certain task in a certain context in order to optimise the decision process or to assess the precision of data sources in order to autonomously suppress uncertain information. As another example content-based similarity measures can probably utilised to automatically correlate the meaning of differnt tags given by users.

Scaleability: There are different approaches to deal with large amounts of music content in identification scenarios which have proven to work reliably in real-world applications. However, it is still an open problem how to deal with millions of songs in more fuzzy retrieval and recommendation tasks. As an example, currently music similarity lists in catalogues of several million songs have to be pre-computed. This however collides with the demand for personalized music recommendations tuned to the listeners very own preferences. It is an interesting question whether the consideration of musical knowledge in hybrid recommenders will be able to improve the scalability problem.

Scientific exchange: For the future development of the MIR research scientific exchange is an essential issue. In that regard the Music Information Retrieval Evaluation eXchange (MIREX)[23] is a very commendable initiative of the University

---

Urbana at Champaign, Illinois, USA. The big problem for such contests is the struggle with the limited availability of common music test beds. In the past some independent labels have released content for certain competitions, but most researchers have originally started with their own test sets, often ripped from commercial CDs. These sets are annotated, but may not be shared due to copyright issues. There exists some databases (e.g., [34], [32]) that are intended to be shared among researchers. Unfortunately, their usage is not as widespread as it could be.

Both, content of a song and context of the user are important to understand why a user likes or dislikes a song. The decoding of this relation will indeed require lots of further research. And once it is done, it remains to be shown that knowledge about the "why" will help finding other songs that satisfy these conditions. This will be a step towards high-quality individual recommendations that are independent from what other users feel. As a conclusion it can be clearly stated, that most problems in content-based MIR are still far from being finally solved. The only task that has matured to real-world applicability is probably the audio identification task, as the very successful examples in Section on "Applications" show. Generally speaking, all of the tasks described in this chapter need significant further research.

References

1. Abeßer, J., Dittmar, C., Großmann, H.: Automatic genre and artist classification by analyzing improvised solo parts from musical recordings. In: Proceedings of the Audio Mostly Conference (AMC). Piteå, Sweden (2008)
2. Allamanche, E., Herre, J., Hellmuth, O., Kastner, T., Ertel, C.: A multiple feature model for music similarity retrieval. In: Proceedings of the 4th International Symposium of Music Information Retrieval (ISMIR). Baltimore, Maryland, USA (2003)
3. Allamanche, E., Herre, J., Helmuth, O., Froba, B., Kastner, T., Cremer, M.: Content-based identification of audio material using MPEG-7 low level description. In: Proceedings of the 2nd International Symposium of Music Information Retrieval (ISMIR). Bloomington, Indiana, USA (2001)
4. Anderson, C.: The Long Tail: Why the Future of Business is Selling Less of More. Hyperion, New York, NY, USA (2006)
5. Aucouturier, J.J., Defreville, B., Pachet, F.: The bag-of-frame approach to audio pattern recognition: A sufficient model for urban soundscapes but not for polyphonic music. Journal of the Acoustical Society of America 122(2), 881–891 (2007)
6. Aucouturier, J.J., Pachet, F.: Music similarity measures: What's the use? In: Proceedings of the 3rd International Conference on Music Information Retrieval (ISMIR). Paris, France (2002)
7. Aucouturier, J.J., Pachet, F.: Improving timbre similarity: How high is the sky? Journal of Negative Results in Speech and Audio Sciences 1(1), 1–13 (2004)
8. Aucouturier, J.J., Pachet, F., Sandler, M.: The way it sounds: timbre models for analysis and retrieval of music signals. IEEE Transactions on Multimedia 7(6), 1028–1035 (2005)
9. Bainbridge, D., Cunningham, S., Downie, J.: Visual collaging of music in a digital library. In: Proceedings of the International Conference on Music Information Retrieval (ISMIR). Barcelona, Spain (2004)
10. Bastuck, C., Dittmar, C.: An integrative framework for content-based music similarity retrieval. In: Proceedings of the 35th German Annual Conference on Acoustics (DAGA). Dresden, Germany (2008)

11. Bello, J.P., Pickens, J.: A robust mid-level representation for harmonic content in music signals. In: Proceedings of the 6th International Conference on Music Information Retrieval (ISMIR). London, UK (2005)
12. Brown, J.: Determination of the meter of musical scores by autocorrelation. Journal of the Acoustical Society of America **94**(4), 1953–1957 (1993)
13. Casey, M.: MPEG-7 sound recognition. IEEE Transactions on Circuits and Systems Video Technology, special issue on MPEG-7 **11**, 737–747 (2001)
14. Celma, O.: Music recommendation and discovery in the long tail. Ph.D. thesis, Universitat Pompeu Fabra, Barcelona, Spain (2008)
15. Chen, P.H., Cheh-Jen, L., Schölkopf, B.: A turorial on ν-support vector machines. Tech. rep., Department of Computer Science and Information Engineering, Taipei, Max Planck Institute for Biological Cybernetics, Tübingen (2005)
16. Cunningham, S., Caulder, S., Grout, V.: Saturday night or fever? Context aware music playlists. In: Proceeding of the Audio Mostly Conference (AMC). Piteå, Sweden (2008)
17. Cunningham, S., Zhang, Y.: Development of a music organizer for children. In: Proceedings of the 9th International Conference on Music Information Retrieval (ISMIR). Philadelphia, Pennsylvania (2008)
18. Dempster, A.P., Laird, N.M., Rdin, D.B.: Maximum likelihood from incomplete data via the em algorithm. Journal of the Royal Statistical Society, Series B **39**, 1–38 (1977)
19. Dittmar, C., Bastuck, C., Gruhne, M.: Novel mid-level audio features for music similarity. In: Proc. of the Intern. Conference on Music Communication Science (ICOMCS). Sydney, Australia (2007)
20. Dittmar, C., Dressler, K., Rosenbauer, K.: A toolbox for automatic transcription of polyphonic music. In: Proceedings of the Audio Mostly Conference (AMC). Ilmenau, Germany (2007)
21. Dittmar, C., Uhle, C.: Further steps towards drum transcription of polyphonic music. In: Proceedings of the AES 116th Convention (2004)
22. Dixon, S.: Onset detection revisited. In: Proceedings of the 9th International Conference on Digital Audio Effects (DAFx06). Montréal, Québec, Canada (2006)
23. Dunker, P., Nowak, S., Begau, A., Lanz, C.: Content-based mood classification for photos and music: A generic multi-modal classification framework and evaluation approach. In: Proceedings of the International Conference on Multimedia Information Retrieval (ACM MIR). Vancouver, Canada (2008)
24. Eck, D., Bertin-Mahieux, T., Lamere, P.: Autotagging music using supervised machine learning. In: Proceedings of the 8th International Conference on Music Information Retrieval (ISMIR). Vienna, Austria (2007)
25. Eerola, T., North, A.C.: Expectancy-based model of melodic complexity. In: Proceedings of the 6th International Conference of Music Perception and Cognition (ICMPC). Keele, Staffordshire, England (2000)
26. Ellis, D.: Classifying music audio with timbral and chroma features. In: Proceedings of the 8th International Conference on Music Information Retrieval (ISMIR). Vienna, Austria (2007)
27. Feng, Y., Zhuang, Y., Pan, Y.: Music information retrieval by detecting mood via computational media aesthetics. International Conference onWeb Intelligence (IEEE/WIC) pp. 235–241 (2003)
28. Flexer, A., Pampalk, E., Widmer, G.: Hidden markov models for spectral similarity of songs. In: Proceedings of the 8th International Conference on Digital Audio Effects (DAFX'05). Madrid, Spain (2008)
29. Foote, J.: Visualizing music and audio using self-similarity. In: Proceedings of the seventh ACM international conference on Multimedia (Part 1). New York, NY, USA (1999)
30. Foote, J.T.: Content-based retrieval of music and audio. In: Proceeding of SPIE Conference on Multimedia Storage and Archiving Systems II. Dallas, TX, USA (1997)
31. Fukunaga, K.: Introduction to Statistical Pattern Recognition, Second Edition (Computer Science and Scientific Computing Series). Academic Press (1990)

32. Gillet, O., Richard, G.: Enst-drums: an extensive audio-visual database for drum signals processing. In: Proceedings of the 7th International Conference on Music Information Retrieval (ISMIR). Victoria, BC, Canada (2006)
33. Goto, M.: A real-time music-scene-description system - predominant-f0 estimation for detecting melody and bass lines in real-world audio signals. Speech Communication **43**, 311–329 (2004)
34. Goto, M.: AIST annotation for the RWC music database. In: Proceedings of the 7th International Conference on Music Information Retrieval (ISMIR). Victoria, BC, Canada (2006)
35. Goussevskaia, O., Kuhn, M., Lorenzi, M., Wattenhofer, R.: From Web to Map: Exploring the World of Music. In: Proceedings of IEEE/WIC/ACM International Conference on Web Intelligence and Intelligent Agent Technology (WI-IAT). Sydney, Australia (2008)
36. Gouyon, F., Fabig, L., Bonada, J.: Rhythmic expressiveness transformations of audio recordings - swing modifications. In: Proceedings of the 60th International Conference on Digital Audio Effects (DAFx). London, UK (2003)
37. Gouyon, F., Herrera, P.: Determination of the meter of musical audio signals: Seeking recurrences in beat segment descriptors. In: Proceedings of the 114th AES Convention. Amsterdam, Netherlands (2003)
38. Gouyon, F., Klapuri, A., Dixon, S., Alonso, M., Tzanetakis, G., Uhle, C., Cano, P.: An experimental comparison of audio tempo induction algorithms. IEEE Transactions on Speech and Audio Processing **14**, 1832–1844 (2006)
39. Gouyon, F., Pachet, F., Delerue, O.: The use of zerocrossing rate for an application of classification of percussive sounds. In: COST G-6 Conference on Digital Audio Effects (DAFx). Verona, Italy (2000)
40. Hainsworth, S.W., Macleod, M.D.: Automatic bass line transcription from polyphonic music. In: Proceedings of the International Computer Music Conference (ICMC). Havana, Cuba (2001)
41. Hanjalic, A.: Extracting moods from pictures and sounds. IEEE Signal Processing Magazine **23**(2), 90–100 (2006)
42. Harte, C.A., Sandler, M.B.: Automatic chord identification using a quantised chromagram. In: Proceedings of the 118th AES Convention. Barcelona, Spain (2005)
43. Herre, J., Allamanche, E., Ertel, C.: How similar do songs sound? In: Proceedings of the IEEE Workshop on Applications of Singal Processing to Audio and Acoustics (WASPAA). Mohonk, New York, USA (2003)
44. Herrera, P., Sandvold, V., Gouyon, F.: Percussion-related semantic descriptors of music audio files. In: Proceedings of the 25th International AES Conference. London, UK (2004)
45. Hevner, K.: Experimental studies of the elements of expression in music. American Journal of Psychology **48**(2), 246–268 (1936)
46. Hilliges, O., Holzer, P., Kluber, R., Butz, A.: AudioRadar: A metaphorical visualization for the navigation of large music collections. Lecture Notes in Computer Science **4073**, 82 (2006)
47. Hiraga, R., Mizaki, R., Fujishiro, I.: Performance visualization: a new challenge to music through visualization. In: Proceedings of the 10th ACM international conference on Multimedia. New York, NY, USA (2002)
48. Hsu, C., Chang, C., Lin, C., et al.: A practical guide to support vector classification. Tech. rep., National Taiwan University, Taiwan (2003)
49. Hsu, J.L., Liu, C.C., Chen, A.L.P.: Discovering nontrivial repeating patterns in music data. IEEE Transactions on Multimedia **3**(3), 311–325 (2001)
50. Hu, X., Downie1, J.S., Laurier, C., Bay, M., Ehmann, A.F.: The 2007 MIREX Audio Mood Classification Task: Lessons Learned. In: Proceedings of the 9th International Conference on Music Information Retrieval (ISMIR). Philadelphia, Pennsylvania, USA (2008)
51. Hunt, M.J., Lennig, M., Mermelstein, P.: Experiments in syllable-based recognition of continuous speech. In: Proceedings of the International Conference on Acoustics and Signal Processing (ICASSP). Denver, Colorado, USA (1980)

52. Isaacson, E.: What you see is what you get: on visualizing music. In: Proceedings of the International Conference on Music Information Retrieval. London, UK (2005)
53. ISO/IEC: ISO/IEC 15938-4 (MPEG-7 Audio). ISO (2002)
54. Jennings, D.: Net, Blogs and Rock 'n' Roll: How Digital Discovery Works and What it Means for Consumers. Nicholas Brealey Publishing (2007)
55. Johnston, J.: Transform coding of audio signals using perceptual noise criteria. IEEE Journal on Selected Areas in Communications 6(2), 314–322 (1988)
56. Kim, Y., Whitman, B.: Singer identification in popular music recordings using voice coding features. In: Proceedings of 3rd International Symposium on Music Information Retrieval (ISMIR). Paris, France (2002)
57. Kolhoff, P., Preuß, J., Loviscach, J.: Content-based icons for music files. Computers & Graphics 32(5), 550–560 (2008)
58. Kullback, S.: Information Theory and Statistics (Dover Books on Mathematics). Dover Publications (1997)
59. de León, P.J.P., Inesta, J.M.: Pattern recognition approach for music style identification using shallow statistical descriptors. IEEE Transactions on System, Man and Cybernetics - Part C : Applications and Reviews 37(2), 248–257 (2007)
60. Lew, M.S., Sebe, N., Lifl, C.D., Jain, R.: Content-based multimedia information retrieval: State of the art and challenges. ACM Transactions on Multimedia Computing, Communications, and Applications (2006)
61. Li, T., Ogihara, M.: Detecting emotion in music. Proceedings of the Fifth International Symposium on Music Information Retrieval pp. 239 240 (2003)
62. Li, T., Ogihara, M.: Content-based music similarity search and emotion detection. Proceedings IEEE International Conference on Acoustics, Speech, and Signal Processing (ICASSP). 5 (2004)
63. Licklider, J., Pollack, I.: Effects of differentiation, integration, and infinite peak clipping on the intelligibility of speech. Journal Acoustical Society of America 20, 42–51 (1948)
64. Lidy, T., Rauber, A., Pertusa, A., Iesta, J.M.: Improving genre classification by combination of audio and symbolic descriptors using a transcription system. In: Proceedings of the 8th International Conference on Music Information Retrieval (ISMIR). Vienna, Austria (2007)
65. Lillie, A.S.: Musicbox: Navigating the space of your music. Master's thesis, Massachusetts Institute of Technology, USA (2008)
66. Liu, B.: Web Data Mining: Exploring Hyperlinks, Contents, and Usage Data. Springer, New York, NY, USA (2008)
67. Liu, C., Yang, Y., Wu, P., Chen, H.: Detecting and classifying emotion in popular music. In: 9th Joint International Conference on Information Sciences (2006)
68. Liu, D., Lu, L., Zhang, H.: Automatic mood detection from acoustic music data. In: Proceedings International Symposium Music Information Retrieval (ISMIR), pp. 81–87 (2003)
69. Liu, Z., Huang, Q.: Content-based indexing and retrieval-by-example in audio. In: Proceedings of IEEE International Conference on Multimedia and Expo (ICME). New York City, NY, USA (2000)
70. Logan, B.: Mel frequency cepstral coefficients for music modeling. In: Proceedings of 1st International Symposium on Music Information Retrieval (ISMIR). Plymouth, Massachusetts, USA (2000)
71. Logan, B., Salomon, A.: A music similarity function based on signal analysis. In: Proceedings of IEEE International Conference on Multimedia and Expo (ICME). Tokyo, Japan (2001)
72. Lu, L., Liu, D., Zhang, H.: Automatic mood detection and tracking of music audio signals. IEEE Transactions on Audio, Speech & Language Processing 14(1), 5–18 (2006)
73. Lukashevich, H., Dittmar, C.: Applying statistical models and parametric distance measures for music similarity search. In: Proceedings of the 32nd Annual Conference of German Classification Society. Hamburg, Germany (2008)
74. Madsen, S.T., Widmer, G.: A complexity-based approach to melody track identification in midi files. In: Proceedings of the International Workshop on Artificial Intelligence and Music (MUSIC-AI). Hyderabad, India (2007)

75. Magno, T., Sable, C.: A comparison of signal-based music recommendation to genre labels, collaborative filtering, musicological analysis, human recommendation, and random baseline. In: Proceedings of the 9th International Conference on Music Information Retrieval (ISMIR). Philadelphia, USA (2008)

76. Mandel, M.I., Poliner, G.E., Ellis, D.P.: Support vector machine active learning for music retrieval. Multimedia Systems 12, 1–11 (2006)

77. de Mántaras, R.L., Arcos, J.L.: AI and music: From composition to expressive performances. AI Magazine 23, 43–57 (2002)

78. McKay, C., Fujinaga, I.: Automatic genre classification using large high-level musical feature sets. In: Proceedings of the International Conference in Music Information Retrieval (ISMIR). Barcelona, Spain (2004)

79. Mierswa, I., Morik, K.: Automatic feature extraction for classifying audio data. Machine Learning Journal 58, 127–149 (2005)

80. Mörchen, F., Ultsch, A., Nöcker, M., Stamm, C.: Databionic visualization of music collections according to perceptual distance. In: Proceedings of the 6th International Conference on Music Information Retrieval (ISMIR). London, UK (2005)

81. Moschou, V., Kotti, M., Benetos, E., Kotropoulos, C.: Systematic comparison of BIC-based speaker segmentation systems. In: Proceedings of IEEE 9th Workshop on Multimedia Signal Processing (MMSP). Crete, Greece (2007)

82. Müller, M., Appelt, D.: Path-constrained partial music synchronization. In: Proc. International Conference on Acoustics, Speech, and Signal Processing (ICASSP). Las Vegas, USA (2008)

83. Neumayer, R., Dittenbach, M., Rauber, A.: PlaySOM and PocketSOMPlayer, alternative interfaces to large music collections. In: Proceedings of the 6th International Conference on Music Information Retrieval (ISMIR). London, UK (2005)

84. Nowak, S., Bastuck, C., Dittmar, C.: Exploring music collections through automatic similarity visualization. In: Tagungsband der DAGA Fortschritte der Akustik. Dresden, Germany (2008)

85. Pampalk, E.: Computational models of music similarity and their application in music information retrieval. Ph.D. thesis, Vienna University of Technology, Vienna, Austria (2006)

86. Pampalk, E., Pohle, T., Widmer, G.: Dynamic playlist generation based on skipping behaviour. In: Proceedings of the 6th International Conference on Music Information Retrieval (ISMIR). London, UK (2005)

87. Pampalk, E., Rauber, A., Merkl, D.: Content-based organization and visualization of music archives. In: Proceedings of the 10th ACM international conference on Multimedia. New York, NY, USA (2002)

88. Peeters, G.: A large set of audio features for sound description (similarity and classification) in the CUIDADO project. Tech. Rep. CUIDADO I.S.T. Project, Institut de Recherche et Coordination Acoustique/Musique (IRCAM), Paris, France (2004)

89. Poliner, G.E., Ellis, D.P.W., Ehmann, A.F., Gómez, E., Streich, S., Ong, B.: Melody transcription from music audio: Approaches and evaluation. IEEE Transactions on Audio, Speech, and Language Processing 15, 1247–1256 (2007)

90. Raimond, Y.: A distributed music information system. Ph.D. thesis, Queen Mary, University of London, London, UK (2008)

91. Russell, J.: A circumplex model of affect. Journal of Personality and Social Psychology 39(6), 1161–1178 (1980)

92. Ryyänen, M., Klapuri, A.: Automatic bass line transcription from streaming polyphonic audio. In: Proceedings of the IEEE International Conference on Acoustics, Speech, and Signal Processing (ICASSP). Honolulu, Hawaii, USA (2007)

93. Ryynnen, M.P., Klapuri, A.P.: Automatic transcription of melody, bass line, and chords in polyphonic music. Computer Music Journal 32, 72–86 (2008)

94. Saunders, C., Hardoon, D.R., Shawe-Taylor, J., Widmer, G.: Using string kernels to identify famous performers from ther playing style. In: Proceedings of the 15th European Conference on Machine Learning (ECML). Pisa, Italy (2004)

95. Schein, A.I., Popescul, R., Ungar, L.H., Pennock, D.M.: Methods and metrics for cold-start recommendations. In: Proceedings of the 25th Annual International ACM SIGIR Conference on Research and Development in Information Retrieval. Tampere, Finland (2002)
96. Schuller, B., Eyben, F., Rigoll, G.: Tango or waltz?: Putting ballroom dance style into tempo detection. EURASIP Journal on Audio, Speech, and Music Processing (JASMP) **2008**(6), 1–12 (2008)
97. Serra, J., Gomez, E.: Audio cover song identification based on tonal sequence alignment. In: Proceedings of the IEEE International Conference on Acoustics, Speech and Signal processing (ICASSP). Las Vegas, USA (2008)
98. Sethares, W., Staley, T.: Meter and periodicity in musical performance. Journal of New Music Research **30**(2), 149–158 (2001)
99. Shao, X., Xu, C., Kankanhalli, M.: Unsupervised classification of music genre using hidden markov model. In: Proceedings of the IEEE International Conference on Multimedia and Expo (ICME). Edinburgh, Scotland,United Kingdom (2004)
100. Smith, G.: Tagging: People-Powered Metadata for the Social Web. New Riders, Berkeley, CA, USA (2008)
101. Sordo, M., Celma, Ó., Blech, M., Guaus, E.: The quest for musical genres: Do the experts and the wisdom of crowds agree? In: Proceedings of the Ninth International Conference on Music Information Retrieval (ISMIR). Philadelphia, Pennsylvania, USA (2008)
102. Tellegen, A., Watson, D., Clark, L.: On the dimensional and hierarchical structure of affect. Psychological Science **10**, 297–303 (1999)
103. Thayer, R.: The Biopsychology of Mood and Arousal. Oxford University Press (1989)
104. Tiemann, M., Pauws, S., Vignoli, F.: Ensemble learning for hybrid music recommendation. In: Proceedings of the 8th International Conference on Music Information Retrieval (ISMIR). Vienna, Austria (2007)
105. Tolos, M., Tato, R., Kemp, T.: Mood-based navigation through large collections of musical data. In: 2nd IEEE Consumer Communications and Networking Conference. Las Vegas, Nevada, USA (2005)
106. Torrens, M., Hertzog, P., Arcos, J.: Visualizing and exploring personal music libraries. In: Proceedings of the International Conference on Music Information Retrieval (ISMIR). Barcelona, Spain (2004)
107. Trohidis, K., Tsoumakas, G., Kalliris, G., Vlahavas, I.: Multilabel classification of music into emotions. In: Proceedings of the 9th International Conference on Music Information Retrieval (ISMIR). Philadelphia, Pennsylvania, USA (2008)
108. Tsai, W., Wang, H.: Automatic singer recognition of popular music recordings via estimation and modeling of solo vocal signals. IEEE Transactions on Audio, Speech, and Language Processing **14**(1), 330–431 (2006)
109. Tzanetakis, G.: Manipulation, analysis and retrieval systems for audio signals. Ph.D. thesis, Princeton University, NJ, USA (2002)
110. Tzanetakis, G., Cook, P.: Musical genre classification of audio signals. IEEE transactions on Speech and Audio Processing **10**(5), 293–302 (2002)
111. Uhle, C.: Automatisierte extraktion rhythmischer merkmale zur anwendung in music information retrieval-systemen. Ph.D. thesis, Ilmenau University, Ilmenau, Germany (2008)
112. Wang, M., Zhang, N., Zhu, H.: User-adaptive music emotion recognition. In: 7th International Conference on Signal Processing, vol. 2, pp. 1352–1355 (2004)
113. Webb, A.: Statistical Pattern Recognition, 2nd edn. John Wiley and Sons Ltd. (2002)
114. West, K., Cox, S.: Features and classifiers for the automatic classification of musical audio signals. In: Proceedings of the 5th International Conference on Music Information Retrieval (ISMIR). Barcelona, Spain (2004)
115. Wolter, K., Bastuck, C., Gärtner, D.: Adaptive user modeling for content-based music retrieval. In: Proceedings of the 6th Workshop on Adaptive Multimedia Retrieval (AMR). Paris, France (2008)
116. Wu, T., Jeng, S.: Probabilistic estimation of a novel music emotion model. In: 14th International Multimedia Modeling Conference. Springer (2008)

117. Yang, D., Lee, W.: Disambiguating music emotion using software agents. In: Proc. of the International Conference on Music Information Retrieval (ISMIR). Barcelona, Spain (2004)
118. Yoshii, K., Goto, M.: Music thumbnailer: Visualizing musical pieces in thumbnail images based on acoustic features. In: Proceedings of the 9th International Conference on Music Information Retrieval (ISMIR). Philadelphia, Pennsylvania, USA (2008)
119. Yoshii, K., Goto, M., Komatani, K., Ogata, T., Okuno, H.G.: Hybrid collaborative and content-based music recommendation using probabilistic model with latent user preferences. In: Proceedings of the 7th International Conference on Music Information Retrieval (ISMIR). Victoria, BC, Canada (2006)
120. Yoshii, K., Goto, M., Okuno, H.G.: Automatic drum sound description for real-world music using template adaption and matching methods. In: Proceedings of the 5th International Music Information Retrieval Conference (ISMIR). Barcelona, Spain (2004)
121. Zils, A., Pachet, F.: Features and classifiers for the automatic classification of musical audio signals. In: Proceedings of the 5th International Conference on Music Information Retrieval (ISMIR). Barcelona, Spain (2004)

Chapter 17
Automated Music Video Generation Using Multi-level Feature-based Segmentation

Jong-Chul Yoon, In-Kwon Lee, and Siwoo Byun

Introduction

The expansion of the home video market has created a requirement for video editing tools to allow ordinary people to assemble videos from short clips. However, professional skills are still necessary to create a music video, which requires a stream to be synchronized with pre-composed music. Because the music and the video are pre-generated in separate environments, even a professional producer usually requires a number of trials to obtain a satisfactory synchronization, which is something that most amateurs are unable to achieve.

Our aim is automatically to extract a sequence of clips from a video and assemble them to match a piece of music. Previous authors [8, 9, 16] have approached this problem by trying to synchronize passages of music with arbitrary frames in each video clip using predefined feature rules. However, each shot in a video is an artistic statement by the video-maker, and we want to retain the coherence of the video-maker's intentions as far as possible.

We introduce a novel method of music video generation which is better able to preserve the flow of shots in the videos because it is based on the multi-level segmentation of the video and audio tracks. A shot boundary in a video clip can be recognized as an extreme discontinuity, especially a change in background or a discontinuity in time. However, even a single shot filmed continuously with the same camera, location and actors can have breaks in its flow; for example, actor might leave the set as another appears. We can use these changes of flow to break a video into segments which can be matched more naturally with the accompanying music.

Our system analyzes the video and music and then matches them. The first process is to segment the video using flow information. Velocity and brightness

J.-C. Yoon and I.-K. Lee (✉)
Department of Computer Science, Yonsei University, Seoul, Korea
e-mail: media19@cs.yonsei.ac.kr; iklee@yonsei.ac.kr

S. Byun
Department of Digital Media, Anyang University, Anyang, Korea
e-mail: swbyun@anyang.ac.kr

B. Furht (ed.), *Handbook of Multimedia for Digital Entertainment and Arts*,
DOI 10.1007/978-0-387-89024-1_17, © Springer Science+Business Media, LLC 2009

features are then determined for each segment. Based on these features, a video segment is then found to match each segment of the music. If a satisfactory match cannot be found, the level of segmentation is increased and the matching process is repeated.

Related Work

There has been a lot of work on synchronizing music (or sounds) with video. In essence, there are two ways to make a video match a soundtrack: assembling video segments or changing the video timing.

Foote et al. [3] automatically rated the novelty of segment of the metric and analyzed the movements of the camera in the video. Then they generated a music video by matching an appropriate video clip to each music segment. Another segment-based matching method for home videos was introduced by Hua et al. [8]. Amateur videos are usually of low quality and include unnecessary shots. Hua et al. calculated an attention score for each video segment which they used to extract the more important shots. They analyzed these clips, searching for a beat, and then they adjusted the tempo of the background music to make it suit the video. Mulhem et al. [16] modeled the aesthetic rules used by real video editors; and used them to assess music videos. Xian et al. [9] used the temporal structures of the video and music, as well as repetitive patterns in the music, to generate music videos.

All these studies treat video segments as primitives to be matched, but they do not consider the flow of the video. Because frames are chosen to obtain the best synchronization, significant information contained in complete shots can be missed. This is why we do not extract arbitrary frames from a video segment, but use whole segments as part of a multi-level resource for assembling a music video.

Taking a different approach researches, Jehan et al. [11] suggested a method to control the time domain of a video and to synchronize the feature points of both video and music. Using timing information supplied by the user, they adjusted the speed of a dance clip by time-warping, so as to synchronize the clip to the background music. Time-warping is also a necessary component in our approach. Even the best matches between music and video segments can leave some discrepancy in segment timing, and this can be eliminated by a local change to the speed of the video.

System Overview

The input to our system is an MPEG or AVI video and a .wav file, containing the music. As shown in Fig. 1, we start by segmenting both music and video, and then analyze the features of each segment. To segment the music, we use novelty scoring

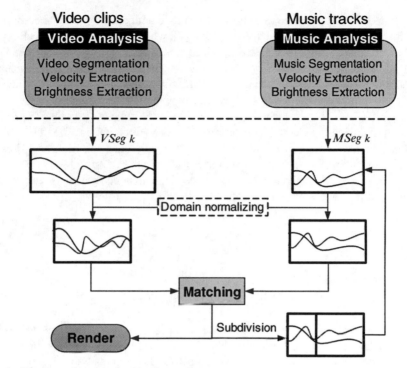

Fig. 1 Overview of our music video generation system

[3], which detects temporal variation in the wave signal in the frequency domain. To segment the video, we use contour shape matching [7], which finds extreme changes of shape features between frames. Then we analyze each segment based on velocity and brightness features.

Video Segmentation and Analysis

Synchronizing arbitrary lengths of video with the music is not a good way to preserve the video-maker's intent. Instead, we divide the video at discontinuities in the flow, so as to generate segments that contain coherent information. Then we extract features from each segment, which we use to match it with the music.

Segmentation by Contour Shape Matching

The similarity between two images can be simply measured as the difference between the colors at each pixel. But that is ineffective for a video only to detect short boundaries because the video usually contains movement and noise due to compression. Instead, we use contour shape matching [7], which is a well-known technique for measuring the similarities between two shapes, on the assumption that one is a distorted version of the other. Seven Hu-moments can be extracted by contour analysis, and these constitute a measure of the similarity between video frames which is largely independent of camera and object movement.

Let $V_i (i = 1, \ldots, N)$ be a sequence of N video frames. We convert V_i to an edge map F_i using the Canny edge detector [2]. To avoid obtaining small contours because of noise, we stabilize each frame of V_i using Gaussian filtering [4] as a preprocessing step. Then, we calculate the Hu-moments h_g^i, $(g = 1, \ldots, 7)$ from the first three central moments [7]. Using these Hu-moments, we can measure the similarity of the shapes in two video frames, V_i and V_j, as follows:

$$I_{i,j} = \sum_{g=1}^{7} \left| 1/c_g^i - 1/c_g^j \right|$$

where

$$c_g^i = \text{sign}\left(h_g^i\right) \log_{10} \left| h_g^i \right|, \tag{1}$$

and h_g^i is invariant with translation, rotation and scaling [7]. $I_{i,j}$ is independent of the movement of an object, but it changes when a new object enters the scene. We therefore use large changes to $I_{i,j}$ to create the boundaries between segments. Figure 2a is a graphic representation of the similarity matrix $I_{i,j}$.

Foote et al. [3] introduced a segmentation method that applies the radial symmetric kernel (RSK) to the similarity matrix (see Fig. 3). We apply the RSK to the diagonal direction of our similarity matrix $I_{i,j}$, which allows us to express the flow discontinuity using the following equation:

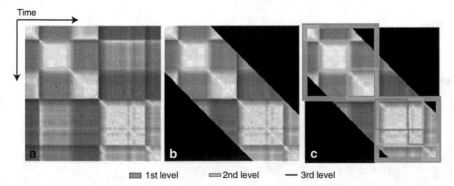

Fig. 2 Video segmentation using the similarity matrix: **a** is the full similarity matrix $I_{i,j}$, **b** is the reduced similarity matrix used to determine maximum kernel overlap region, and **c** is the result of segmentation using different sizes of radial symmetric kernel

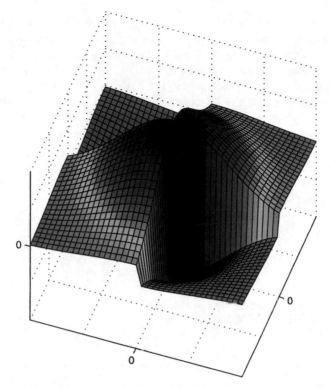

Fig. 3 The form of a radially symmetric Gaussian kernel

$$EV(i) = \sum_{u=-\delta}^{\delta} \sum_{v=-\delta}^{\delta} \text{RSK}(u, v) \cdot I_{i+u,i+v}, \qquad (2)$$

where δ is the size of the RSK. Local maxima of $EV(i)$ are taken to be boundaries of segments. We can control the segmentation level by changing the size of the kernel: a large δ produces a coarse segmentation that ignores short variations in flow, whereas a small δ produces a fine segmentation. Because the RSK is of size δ and only covers the diagonal direction, we only need to calculate the maximum kernel overlap region in the similarity matrix $I_{i,j}$, as shown in Fig. 2b. Figure 2c shows the result of for $\delta = 32$, 64 and 128, which are the values that we will use in multi-level matching.

Video Feature Analysis

From the many possible features of a video, we choose velocity and brightness as the basis for synchronization. We interpret velocity as a displacement over time derived from the camera or object movement, and brightness is a measure of the visual impact of luminance in each frame. We will now show how we extract these features.

Because a video usually contains noise from the camera and the compression technique, there is little value in comparing pixel values between frames, which is what is done in the optical flow technique [17]. Instead, we use an edge map to track object movements robustly. The edge map F_i, described in the previous section can be expected to outline. And the complexity of edge map, which is determined by the number of edge points, can influence the velocity. Therefore, we can express the velocity between frames as the sum of the movements of each edge-pixel. We define a window $\phi_{x,y}(p,q)$ of size $w \times w$, on edge-pixel point (x, y) as its center, where p and q are coordinates within that window. Then, we can compute the color distance between windows in the ith and $(i + 1)^{\text{th}}$ frames as follows:

$$D^2 = \sum_{p,q \in \phi_{x,y}^i(p,q)} \left(\phi_{x,y}^i(p,q) - \phi_{(x,y)+vec_{x,y}^i}^{i+1}(p,q) \right)^2, \tag{3}$$

where x and y are image coordinates. By minimizing the squared color distance, we can determine the value of $vec_{x,y}^i$. We avoid considering pixels which are not on an edge, we assign a zero vector when $F_i(x, y) = 0$. After finding all the moving vectors in the edge map, we apply the local Lucas-Kanade optical flow technique [14] to track the moving objects more precisely.

By summing the values of $vec_{x,y}^i$, we can determine the velocity of the ith of the video frames. However, this measure of velocity is not appropriate if a small area outside the region of visual interest makes a large movement. In the next section, we will introduce a method of video analysis based on the concept of significance.

Next, we determine the brightness of each frame of video using histogram analysis [4]. First, we convert each video frame V_i into a grayscale image. Then we construct a histogram that partitions the grayscale values into ten levels. Using this histogram, we can determine the brightness of the ith frame as follows:

$$V_{bri}^i = \sum_{e=1}^{10} B(e)^2 B_{mean_e}, \tag{4}$$

where $B(e)$ is the number of pixels in the eth bucket and B_{mean_e} is the representative value of the eth bucket. Squaring $B(e)$ means that a contrasty image, such as a black-and-white check pattern, will be classified as brighter than a uniform tone, even if the mean brightness of all the pixels in each image is the same.

Detecting Significant Regions

The tracking technique, introduced in the previous section, is not much affected by noise. However, an edge may be located outside the region of visual interest.

This is likely to make the computed velocity deviate from a viewer's perception of the liveliness of the videos. An analysis of visual significance can extract the region of interest more accurately. We therefore construct a significance map that represents both spatial significance, which is the difference between neighboring pixels in image space, and temporal significance, which measures of differences over time.

We use the Gaussian distance introduced by Itti [10] as a measure of spatial significance. Because this metric correlates with luminance [15], we must first convert each video frame to the YUV color space. We can then calculate the Gaussian distance for each pixel, as follows:.

$$G_{l,\eta}^{i}(x, y) = G_{l}^{i}(x, y) - G_{l+\eta}^{i}(x, y), \tag{5}$$

where G_l is the lth level in the Gaussian pyramid, and x and y are image coordinates. A significant point is one that has a large distance between its low-frequency and high-frequency levels. In our experiment, we used the $l = 2$ and $\eta = 5$.

The temporal significance of a pixel (x, y) can be expressed as the difference in its velocity between the ith and the $(i + 1)^{\text{th}}$ frames, which we call its acceleration. We can calculate the acceleration of a pixel from $vec_{x,y}^{i}$, which is already required for edge-map, as follows:

$$T^{i}(x, y) = N \left(\left\| vec_{x,y}^{i} - vec_{x,y}^{i+1} \right\| \right), \tag{6}$$

where N is a normalizing function which normalizes the acceleration so that it never exceeds 1. We assume that a large acceleration brings a pixel to the attention of the viewer. However, we have to consider the camera motion: if the camera is static, the most important object in the scene is likely to be the one making the largest movement; but if the camera is moving, it is likely to be chasing the most important object, and then a static region is significant. We use the ITM method introduced by Lan et al. [12] to extract the camera movement, with a 4-pixel threshold to estimate camera shake. This threshold should relate to the size of the frame, which is 640×480 in this case. If the camera moves beyond that threshold, we use $1 - T^{i}(x, y)$ rather than $T^{i}(x, y)$ as the measure of temporal significance.

Inspired by the focusing method introduced by Ma et al. [15], we then combine the spatial and temporal significance maps to determine a center of attention that should be in the center of the region of interest, as follows:

$$x_{f}^{i} = \frac{1}{CM} \sum_{x=1}^{n} \sum_{y=1}^{m} G^{i}(x, y) T^{i}(x, y) x. \tag{7}$$

$$y_{f}^{i} = \frac{1}{CM} \sum_{x=1}^{n} \sum_{y=1}^{m} G^{i}(x, y) T^{i}(x, y) y,$$

where

$$CM = \sum_{x=1}^{n} \sum_{y=1}^{m} G^i(x,y) T^i(x,y) \qquad (8)$$

and where x^i_f and y^i_f are the coordinates of the center of attention in the ith frame.

The true size of the significant region will be affected by motion and color distribution in each video segment. But the noise in a home video prevents the calculation of an accurate region boundary. So we fix the size of the region of interest at 1/4 of the total image size. We denote the velocity vectors in the region of interest by $\overline{vec}^i_{x,y}$ (see Fig. 4d), which those outside the region of interest are set to 0. We can then calculate a representative velocity V^i_{vel}, for the region of interest by summing the pixel velocities as follows:

$$V^i_{vel} = \sum_{x=1}^{n} \sum_{y=1}^{m} \left\| \overline{vec}^i_{x,y} \right\|, \qquad (9)$$

where $n \times m$ is the resolution of the video.

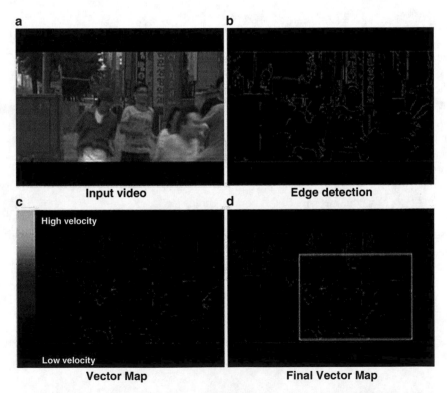

Fig. 4 Velocity analysis based on edge: **a** is a video segment; **b** is the result of edge detection; **c** shows the magnitude of tracked vectors; and **d** shows the elimination of vectors located outside the region of visual interest

Home video usually contains some low-quality shots of static scenes or discontinuous movements. We could filter out these passages automatically before starting the segmentation process [8], but we actually use the whole video, because the discontinuous nature of these low-quality passages means that they are likely to be ignored during the matching step.

Music Segmentation and Analysis

To match the segmented video, the music must also be divided into segments. We can use conventional signal analysis method to analyze and segment the music track.

Novelty Scoring

We use a similarity matrix to segment the music, which is analogous to our method of video segmentation combined with novelty scoring, which is introduced by Foote et al. [3] to detect temporal changes in the frequency domain of a signal. First, we divide the music signal into windows of 1/30 second duration, which matches that a video frame. Then we apply a fast Fourier transform to convert the signal in each window into the frequency domain.

Let i index the windows in sequential order and let A_i be a one-dimensional vector that contains the amplitude of the signal in the ith window in the frequency domain. Then the similarity of the ith and j^{th} windows can be expressed as follows:

$$SM_{i,j} = \frac{A_i \cdot A_j}{\|A_i\| \|A_j\|}. \tag{10}$$

The similarity matrix $SM_{i,j}$ can be used for novelty scoring by applying the same radial symmetric kernel that we used for video segmentation as follows:

$$EA(i) = \sum_{u=-\delta}^{\delta} \sum_{v=-\delta}^{\delta} RSK(u, v) \cdot SM_{i+u, j+v}, \tag{11}$$

where $\delta = 128$. The extreme values of the novelty scoring $EA(i)$ form the boundaries of the segmentation [3]. Figure 5 shows the similarity matrix and the corresponding novelty score. As in the video segmentation, the size of the RSK kernel determines the level of segmentation (see Fig. 5b). We will use this feature in the multi-level matching that will follow in Section on "Matching Music and Video".

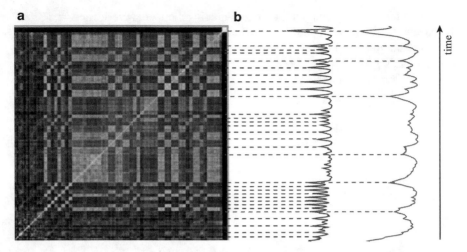

Fig. 5 Novelty scoring using the similarity matrix in the frequency domain: **a** is the similarity matrix in the frequency domain; **b** the novelty scores obtained with different size of RSK

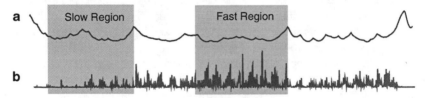

Fig. 6 **a** novelty scoring and **b** variability of RMS amplitude

Music Feature Analysis

The idea of novelty represents the variability of music (see Fig. 6a). We can also introduce a concept of velocity for music, which is related to its beat. Many previous authors have tried to extract the beat from a wave signal [5, 18], but we avoid confronting this problem. Instead we determine the velocity of each music segment from the amplitude of the signal in the time domain.

We can sample the amplitude $S_i(u)$ of a window i in the time domain, where u is a sampling index. Then we can calculate a root mean square amplitude for that window:

$$RMS_i = \frac{1}{U} \sum_{u=1}^{U} (S_i(u))^2, \tag{12}$$

where U is the total number of samples in the window. Because the beat is usually set by the percussion instruments, which dominate the amplitude of the signal, we can estimate the velocity of the music from the RMS of the amplitude. If a music segment has a slow beat, then the variability of the amplitude is likely to be relatively low; but if it has a fast beat then the amplitude is likely to be more variable. Using this assumption, we extract the velocity as follows:

$$M_{vel}^i = |RMS_i - RMS_{i-1}|. \tag{13}$$

Figure 6a shows the result of novelty scoring and Fig. 6b shows the variability of the RMS amplitude. We see that variability of the amplitude changes as the music speeds up, but the novelty scoring remains roughly constant.

Popular music is often structured into a pattern, which might typically consist of an intro, verse, and chorus, with distinct variations in amplitude and velocity. This characteristic favors our approach.

Next, we extract the brightness feature using the well-known spectral centroid [6]. The brightness of music is related to its timbre. A violin has a high spectral centroid, but a tuba has a low spectral centroid. If $A_i(p)$ is the amplitude of the signal in the ith window in the frequency domain, and p is the frequency index, then the spectral centroid can be calculated as follows:

$$M_{hri}^i = \frac{\Sigma p\,(A_i(p))^2}{\Sigma\,(A_i(p))^2}. \tag{14}$$

Matching Music and Video

In previous sections, we explained how to segment video and music and to extract features. We can now assemble a synchronized music video by matching segments based on three terms derived from the video and music features, and two terms obtained from velocity histograms and segment lengths.

Because each segment of music and video has a different length, we need to normalize the time domain. We first interpolate the features of each segment, especially velocity, brightness, and flow discontinuity, using a Hermite curve and then normalize the magnitude of the video and music feature curves separately. The flow discontinuity was calculated for segmentation and velocity and brightness features were extracted both videos and music in previous sections. Using Hermite interpolation, we can represent the kth video segment as a curve in a three-dimensional feature space, $V^k(t) = (cv_{ext}^k(t),\ cv_{vel}^k(t),\ cv_{bri}^k(t))$, ever the time interval $[0, 1]$. The features of a music segment can be represented by a similar multidimensional curve, $M^k(t) = (cm_{ext}^k(t),\ cm_{vel}^k(t),\ cm_{bri}^k(t))$. We then compare the curves by sampling them at the same parameters, using these matching terms:

– **Extreme boundary matching** $Fc_1(V^y(t), M^z(t))$.
   The changes in Hu-moments $EV(i)$ in Eq. 2 determine discontinuities in the video, which can then be matched with the discontinuities in the music found by novelty scoring $EA(i)$ in Eq. 11. We interpolate these two features to create the continuous functions $cv_{ext}^k(t)$ and $cm_{ext}^k(t)$, and then calculate the difference by sampling them at the same value of the parameter t.

- **Velocity matching** $Fc_2(V^y(t), M^z(t))$.
  The velocity feature curves for video, $cv_{vel}^k(t)$, and the music, $cm_{vel}^k(t)$ can be interpolated by V_{vel}^i and M_{vel}^i. These two curves can be matched to synchronize the motion in the video with the beat of the music.
- **Brightness matching** $Fc_3(V^y(t), M^z(t))$.
  The brightness feature curves for the video, $cv_{bri}^k(t)$, and the music, $cm_{bri}^k(t)$ can be interpolated by V_{bri}^i and M_{bri}^i. These two curves can be matched to synchronize the timbre of the music to the visual impact of the video.

Additionally, we used match the distribution of the velocity vector. We can generate a histogram $VH^k(b)$ with K bins for the kth video segment using the video velocity vector $\overline{vec}_{x,y}$. We also construct a histogram $MH^k(b)$ of the amplitude of the music in each segment, in the frequency domain A_k. This expresses the timbre of the music, which determines its mood. We define the cost of matching each pair of histogram as follows:

$$Hc(y,z) = \sum_{b=1}^{K} \left(\frac{VH^y(b)}{N_y} - \frac{MH^z(b)}{N_z} \right)^2, \tag{15}$$

where y and z are the indexes of a segment, and N_y and N_z are the sum of the cardinality of the video and music histograms. This associates low-timbre music with near-static video, and high-timbre music with video that contains bold movements. Finally, the durations of video and music should be compared to avoid the need for excessive time-warping. We therefore use the difference of duration between the music and video segments as the final matching term, $Dc(y,z)$. Because the range of $Fc_i(V^y(t), M^z(t))$ and $Hc(y,z)$ are [0,1], we normalize the $Dc(y,z)$ by using the maximum difference of duration.

We can now combine the five matching terms into the following cost function:

$$Cost_{y,z} = \sum_{i=1}^{3} w_i Fc_i(V^y(t), M^z(t)) + w_4 Hc(y,z) + w_5 Dc(y,z), \tag{16}$$

where y and z are the indexes of a segment, and w_i is the weight applied to each matching terms. The weights control the importance given to each matching term. In particular, w_5, which is the weight applied to segment length matching, can be used to control the dynamics of the music video. A low value of w_5 allows more time-warping.

We are now able to generate a music video by calculating $Cost_{y,z}$ for all pairs of video and music segments, and then selecting the video segment which matches each music segment at minimum cost. We then apply time-warping to each video segment so that its length is exactly the same as that of the corresponding music segment. A degree of interactivity is provided by allowing the user to remove any displeasing pair of music and video segments, and then regenerate the video. This facility can be used to eliminate repeated video segments. It can also be extended, so that the user is presented with a list of acceptable matches form which to choose a pair.

We also set a cost threshold to avoid low-quality matches. If a music segment cannot be matched with a cost lower than the threshold, then we subdivide that segment by reducing the value of δ in the RSK. Then we look for a new match to each of the subdivided music segments. Matching and subdivision can be recursively applied to increase the synchronization of the music video; but we limit this process to three levels to avoid the possibility of runaway subdivision.

Experimental Results

By trial and error, we selected (1, 1, 0.5, 0.5, 0.7) for the weight vector in Eq. 16, set $K = 32$ in Eq. 15, and set the subdivision threshold to $0.3 \times mean(Cost_{y,z})$.

For an initial test, we made a 39-min video (Video 1) containing sequences with different amount of movement and levels of luminance (see Fig. 7). We also composed 1 min and 40 s of music (Music 1), with varying timbre and beat. In the initial segmentation step, the music was divided into 11 segments. In the subsequent matching step, the music was subdivided into 19 segments to improve synchronization.

We then went on to perform more realistic experiments with three short films and one home video (Videos 2, 3, 4 and 5: see Fig. 8), and three more pieces of music which we composed. From this material we created three sets of five music videos. The first set was made using Pinnacle Studio 11 [1]; the second set was made using

Fig. 7 Video filmed by the authors

Fig. 8 Example videos: **a** Short film "Someday", directed by Dae-Hyun Kim, 2006; **b** Short film "Cloud", directed by Dong-Chan Kim; **c** Short film "Father", directed by Hyun-Wook Moon; **d** Amateurs home video "Wedding"

Foote's method [3]; and the third was produced by our system. The resulting videos can all be downloaded from URL.[1]

We showed the original videos to 21 adults who had no prior knowledge of this research. Then we showed the three sets of music videos to the same audience, and asked them to score each video, giving marks for synchronization (velocity, brightness, boundary and mood), dynamics (dynamics), and the similarity to the original video (similarity), meaning the extent to which the original story-line is presented. The 'mood' term is related to the distribution of the velocity vector and 'dynamics' term is related to the extent to which the lengths of video segments are changed by time-warping. Each of the six terms was given a score out of ten. Figure 9 shows that our system obtained better than Pinnacle Studio as Foote's methods on five out of the six terms. Since our method currently makes no attempt to preserve the original orders of the video segments, it is not surprising that the result for 'similarity' were more ambiguous.

Table 1 shows the computation time required to analyze the video and music. We naturally expect the video to take much longer to process than the music, because of its higher dimensionality.

---

[1] http://visualcomputing.yonsei.ac.kr/personal/yoon/music.htm

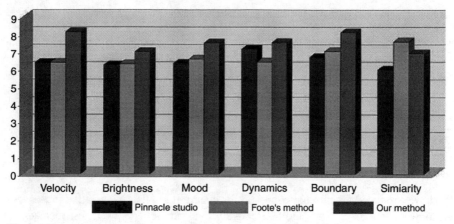

Fig. 9 User evaluation results

Table 1 Computation times for segmentation and analysis of music and video

Media	Length	Segmentation	Velocity	Brightness
Video 1	30 min	50 min	84 min	3 min
Video 2	23 min	44 min	75 min	2.5 min
Video 3	17 min	39 min	69 min	2.1 min
Video 4	25 min	46 min	79 min	2.6 min
Video 5	45 min	77 min	109 min	4.1 min
Music 1	100 s	7.2 s	4.2 s	2.1 s

Table 2 A visual count of the numbers of shots in each videos, and the number of segments generated using different values of δ in the RSK

Media	Visually counted num. of shots	$\delta = 128$	$\delta = 64$	$\delta = 32$
Video 1	44	49	63	98
Video 2	34	41	67	142
Video 3	36	50	57	92
Video 4	43	59	71	102
Video 5	79	92	132	179

Table 2 shows how the number of video segments was affected by the value of δ in the RSK. We also assessed the number of distinct shots in each video by inspection. This visual count tallies quite well with the results when $\delta = 128$. By reducing δ to 32, the number of distinct shots are approximately doubled.

Table 3 shows computation times for matching the music and video. Because the matching is takes much less time than analysis, we stored the all the feature curves for both video and music to speed up the calculations.

Table 3 Computation times
for matching Music 1 to the
five videos

Media	Time (s)
Video 1	6.41
Video 2	8.72
Video 3	6.22
Video 4	7.48
Video 5	10.01

Conclusion

We have produced an automatic method for generating music videos that preserves the flow of video segments more effectively than previous approaches. Instead of trying to synchronize arbitrary regions of video with the music, we use multi-level segment matching to preserve more of the coherence of the original videos. Provided with an appropriate interface to simplify selection of the weight terms, this system would allow music video to be made with very little skill.

The synchronization of segments by our system could be improved. Although each segment is matched in terms of features, it is possible for points of discordancy between music and video to remain within a segment. We could increase the level of synchronization by applying time-warping within each segment using features [13]. Another area of concern is the time required to analyze the video, and we are working on a more efficient algorithm.

Many home videos have a weak story-line, so that the original sequence of the video may not be important. But this will not be true for all videos, and so we need to look for ways of preserving the story-line, which might involve a degree of user annotation.

Acknowledgements This research is accomplished as the result of the promotion project for culture contents technology research center supported by Korea Culture & Content Agency (KOCCA).

References

1. Avid Technology Inc (2007) User guide for pinnacle studio 11. Avid Technology Inc, Tewksbury
2. Canny J (1986) A computational approach to edge detection. IEEE Trans Pattern Anal Mach Intell 8(6):679–698
3. Foote J, Cooper M, Girgensohn A (2002) Creating music videos using automatic media analysis. In: Proceedings of ACM multimedia. ACM, New York, pp 553–560
4. Gose E, Johnsonbaugh R, Jost S (1996) Pattern recognition and image analysis. Prentice Hall, Englewood Cliffs
5. Goto M (2001) An audio-based real-time beat tracking system for music with or without drum-sounds. J New Music Res 30(2):159–171
6. Helmholtz HL (1954) On the sensation of tone as a physiological basis for the theory of music. Dover (translation of original text 1877)

7. Hu M (1963) Visual pattern recognition by moment invariants. IRE Trans Inf Theo 8(2): 179–187
8. Hua XS, Lu L, Zhang HJ (2003) Ave—automated home video editing. In: Proceedings of ACM multimedia. ACM, New York, pp 490–497
9. Hua XS, Lu L, Zhang HJ (2004) Automatic music video generation based on temporal pattern analysis. In: 12th ACM international conference on multimedia. ACM, New York, pp 472–475
10. Itti L, Koch C, Niebur E (1998) A model of saliency-based visual attention for rapid scene analysis. IEEE Trans Pattern Anal Mach Intell 20(11):1254–1259
11. Jehan T, Lew M, Vaucelle C (2003) Cati dance: self-edited, self-synchronized music video. In: SIGGRAPH conference abstracts and applications. SIGGRAPH, Sydney, pp 27–31
12. Lan DJ, Ma YF, Zhang HJ (2003) A novel motion-based representation for video mining. In: Proceedings of the IEEE international conference on multimedia and expo. IEEE, Piscataway, pp 6–9
13. Lee HC, Lee IK (2005) Automatic synchronization of background music and motion in computer animation. In: Proceedings of eurographics 2005, Dublin, 29 August–2 September 2005, pp 353–362
14. Lucas B, Kanade T (1981) An iterative image registration technique with an application to stereo vision. In: Proceedings of 7th international joint conference on artificial intelligence (IJCAI), Vancouver, August 1981, pp 674–679
15. Ma YF, Zhang HJ (2003) Contrast-based image attention analysis by using fuzzy growing. In: Proceedings of the 11th ACM international conference on multimedia. ACM, New York, pp 374–381
16. Mulhem P, Kankanhalli M, Hasan H, Ji Y (2003) Pivot vector space approach for audio-video mixing. IEEE Multimed 10:28–40
17. Murat Tekalp A (1995) Digital video processing. Prentice Hall, Englewood Cliffs
18. Scheirer ED (1998) Tempo and beat analysis of acoustic musical signals. J Acoust Soc Am 103(1):588–601

Chapter 18
Real-Time Content Filtering for Live Broadcasts in TV Terminals

Yong Man Ro and Sung Ho Jin

Introduction

The growth of digital broadcasting has lead to the emergence and wide spread distribution of TV terminals that are equipped with set-top boxes (STB) and personal video recorders (PVR). With increasing number of broadcasting channels and broadcasting services becoming more personalized, today's TV terminal requires more complex structures and functions such as picture-in-picture, time-shift play, channel recording, etc. The increasing number of channels also complicates the efforts of TV viewers in finding their favorite broadcasts quickly and efficiently. In addition, obtaining meaningful scenes from live broadcasts becomes more difficult as the metadata describing the broadcasts is not available [1]. In fact, most live broadcasts cannot afford to provide related metadata as it must be prepared before the broadcast is aired.

Until now, many scene detection and content-indexing techniques have been applied to video archiving systems for video summarization, video segmentation, content management, and metadata authoring of broadcasts [2–7]. Some of them have been applied in STB or PVR after recording entire broadcasts [8–10]. Current broadcasting systems provide simple program guiding services with electronic program guides, but do not provide meaningful scene searching for live broadcasts [11, 12]. In order to provide a user-customized watching environment in digital broadcasting, meaningful scene search in real-time is required in the TV terminal. N. Dimitrova et al. [13], studied video analysis algorithms and architecture for abstracted video representation in consumer domain applications and developed a commercial tool for skipping through the detection of black frames and changes in activity [14]. Our work, however, focuses on establishing a system that enables the indexing and analyzing of live broadcasts at the content-level.

The goal of this chapter is to develop a service that provides content-level information within the limited capacity of the TV terminal. For example, a TV viewer

Y.M. Ro (✉) and S.H. Jin
IVY Lab, Information and Communications University, Daejon, Korea
e-mail: yro@icu.ac.kr

B. Furht (ed.), *Handbook of Multimedia for Digital Entertainment and Arts*,
DOI 10.1007/978-0-387-89024-1_18, © Springer Science+Business Media, LLC 2009

watches his/her favorite broadcasts (*e.g.*, a drama or sitcom) on one channel, while the other channels broadcast other programs (*e.g.*, the final round of a soccer game) that also contain scenes of interest to the viewer (*e.g.*, shooting or goal scenes). To locate these scenes of interest on other channels, a real-time filtering technique, which recognizes and extracts meaningful contents of the live broadcast, should be embedded in the TV terminal. In this chapter, a new real-time content filtering system for a multi-channel TV terminal is proposed. The system structure and filtering algorithm have been designed and verified. The system's filtering requirements such as, the number of available input channels, the frame sampling rate, and buffer size were analyzed based on queueing theory, and filtering performance was calculated so as to maintain a stable filtering system.

The chapter is organized as follows. We first give an overview of the proposed system and general filtering procedure in Section II. Section III shows the analysis of filtering system based on the queue model. Section IV presents experiments in which soccer videos were tested in the proposed system and shows the experimental results of five soccer videos. Realization of the proposed system is discussed in Section V, and concluding remarks are drawn in Section VI.

Real-time Content Filtering System

In this section, we explain the structure of a real-time broadcasting content filtering system in a TV terminal. In addition, a filtering algorithm for multiple broadcasts is proposed, which is simplified for real-time processing and shows a promising filtering performance. Typical processing of face-name association is as follows:

Filtering System Structure

The system structure of a TV terminal for the real-time content filtering function is illustrated in Fig. 1. In this work, the terminal is assumed to have more than two TV tuners. One of the tuners receives a broadcast stream from the main channel to be watched, and the rest receive streams from the selected channels to be filtered. It is assumed that the TV viewer is interested in the selected channels as well as the main channel.

As shown in Fig. 1, a selected broadcast from the main channel is conveyed to the display unit after passing through demux, buffer, decoder, and synchronizer. In the content filtering part, meaningful scenes are extracted from input broadcasts and filtered results are sent to the display unit. The receiver components, *i.e.* the demux and the decoder, before the content filtering part, are supposed to be able to support the decoding of multi-streams.

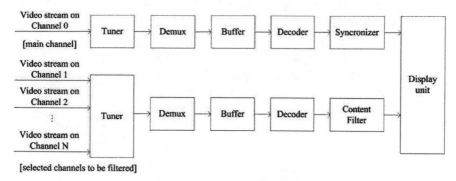

Fig. 1 System structure of TV terminal for real-time content filtering

The number of allowable input channels required to guarantee real-time filtering depends on frame sampling rate, buffer condition, etc. (these are discussed in detail in Section III).

Real-Time Content Filtering Algorithm

In the terminal of Fig. 1, the content filtering part monitors channels and selects meaningful scenes based on the TV viewer's preference. As soon as the terminal finds the selected scenes, that is, the viewer's desired scenes filtered from his/her channels referred to as "scenes of interest," it notifies this fact by means of the channel change or channel interrupt function. The picture-in-picture function currently available in TVs is useful for displaying the filtering results.

To filter the content of the broadcast, sampling and processing of multiple input broadcasts should be performed without delay. Figure 2 shows the proposed filtering algorithm through which a TV viewer not only watches the broadcast of the main channel, but also obtains meaningful scenes of broadcasting content from other channels. The procedure of the filtering process is as follows.

Step 1: A viewer logs on to a user terminal.

Step 2: After turning on the real-time filtering function, the TV viewer chooses filtering options such as scenes of interest. Simultaneously, the viewer's preference database is updated with new information on the selected scenes.

Step 3: In a TV decoder, the filtering part in Fig. 1 receives video streams of broadcasts and acquires frames by sampling in regular intervals.

Step 4: The sampled frames are queued in a buffer followed by feature extraction. This step is repeated during the filtering process.

Step 5: Image and video features such as color, edge, and motion from the sampled frame are extracted to represent the spatial information of the frame.

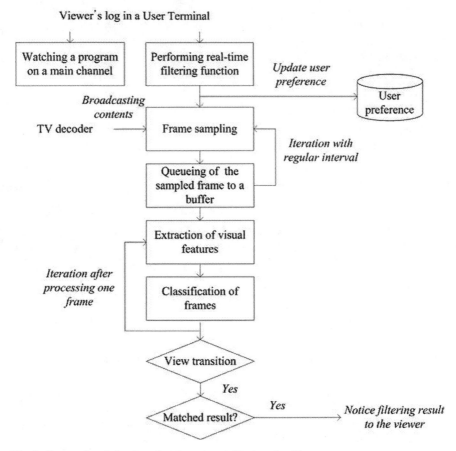

Fig. 2 Proposed real-time broadcasting content filtering algorithm

Step 6: The view type of the input frame is decided according to visual features. After completing this step, a new frame is fetched for the next feature extraction.
Step 7: Desired scenes are detected by the pattern of temporal frame sequences such as view type transition or continuity.
Step 8: Finally, the filtering process is concluded with the matched filtering result.

In *Step 5*, the feature extraction time depends on the content characteristics of the input frame. Broadcasting video consists of various types of frames represented by various features (*e.g.*, color, edge. etc.). Therefore, we need to avoid the overflow problem at the buffer caused by the feature extraction time.

Filtering System Analysis

Since real-time filtering should be performed within a limited time, frame sampling rate to filter, buffer size to input frames, and the number of allowable input channels, should be suitably determined to achieve real-time processing.

Modeling of a Filtering System

In Fig. 2, the inputs of the filtering part are the sampled frames from the decoder in regular sampling rate. The frames waiting for filtering should be buffered because the filtering processing time is irregular. Thus, filtering can be modeled by queueing theory. Figure 3 illustrates the queue model for the proposed filtering system for N input channels. The frames sampled from the input channels are new customers in the buffer and the filtering process is a server for customers. Before being fetched to the server, the frames wait for their orders in the buffer. In the figure, f is the sampling rate which denotes the number of sampled frames per second from one channel.

As shown in the Fig. 3, frames are acquired by sampling periodically arriving video streams at the buffer. After filtering a frame, the next frame in the buffer is taken out irregularly in the order of its arrival at the buffer. Note that the filtering time for the video frame is irregular and depends on the content characteristics of the frame.

The proposed filtering system is designed as a queue model with the following characteristics: 1) arrival pattern of new customers into the queue, 2) service pattern of servers, 3) the number of service channels, 4) system capacity, 5) number of service stages, and 6) the queueing policy [15–18].

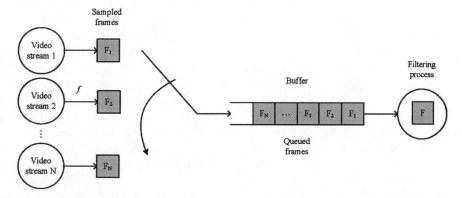

Fig. 3 Queue model of content filtering for multiple channels

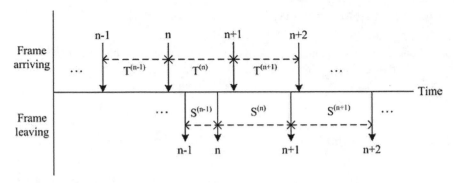

Fig. 4 Queueing process for successive frames

First, we consider the distributions of the buffer in terms of inter-arrival time between sampled frames and service time between filtered frames. In Fig. 4, let $T(n)$ represent the inter-arrival time between nth and $(n + 1)$st customers (sampled frames), and $S(n)$ represent the service time of the nth customer. As seen in Fig. 3, the inter-arrival time is determined by a regular sampling rate, i.e. the inter-arrival time is constant. We can see that the probability distribution describing the time between successive frame arrivals is deterministic.

Given that the view types of the frames in a queue are statistically independent, follow a counting process, and have different service times (filtering times), we assume that the number of filtering occurrences within a certain time interval becomes a Poisson random variable. Then, the probability distribution of the service time is an exponential distribution. A D/M/1 queue model can be applied to model the proposed filtering system, which covers constant inter-arrivals to a single-server queue with exponential service time distribution, unlimited capacity and FCFS (first come, first served) queueing discipline.

However, the D/M/1 model may cause buffer overflow and decrease filtering performance by frame loss when the buffer is feed with frames of the same type, a situation which has the longest processing time. Thus, if the service (filtering) time of one frame is longer than the inter-arrival time, the waiting frames pile within the buffer. Therefore, filtering policies such as frame skipping or dropping of sampling rate are required.

To find a sufficient condition in which the filtering system remains stable, the worst case is considered. We assume the worst case is one in which the buffer is occupied by frames with the longest filtering time sampled from multiple channels. The pattern of filtering times for successive similar frames is constant. Therefore, the two probability patterns can be established as deterministic distributions.

In the above model, the number of filtering processes and the length of buffer are 1 and 1(I don't understand why it is 1 and 1?), respectively; and the queueing discipline for filtering is FCFS. Thus, the stable filtering system in which the worst case is considered can be explained as a D/D/1 queue model in a steady state.

Requirements of Stable Real-Time Filtering.

From the established queue model, the first condition is established so that the proposed filtering system can perform steadily in real-time. Let λ denote the average arrival rate (the number of sampled frames per second), and μ be the average filtering rate, which is the inverse of the average filtering time in the filtering process. The arrival rate can be written as

$$\lambda = N \cdot f \tag{1}$$

where N is the number of channels, and f represents the sampling rate, which denotes the number of sampled frames per second from one channel.

For the case in which only the frames with the longest processing time are been feed into the buffer, we can assume that the average filtering time is equal to the maximal value among filtering times for various frames. Then, the filtering rate can be written as

$$\mu = \frac{1}{\max_{x \in V}\{PT(x)\}} \tag{2}$$

where V means a set of frame view types for the input video, and PT(x) represents the filtering processing time for frame type x.

Let ρ denote the traffic intensity of the model which is equal to the arrival rate over the service rate (λ/μ). Given that the proposed queue model is always stable if $\rho \leq 1$, the first condition can be established as follows,

$$\begin{aligned} \rho &= \lambda/\mu \\ &= N \cdot f \cdot \max_{x \in V}\{PT(x)\} \leq 1. \end{aligned} \tag{3}$$

The second condition can be established from the trade-off between the sampling rate and the filtering performance. The filtering performance depends on the sampling rate and decreases as the frame sampling rate decreases. The relationship between filtering performance and frame sampling rate (f) is denoted by the function of FP(f). Thus, an appropriate sampling rate can satisfy the confidence limit of the filtering performance. The confidence limit denotes the minimum value of filtering performance that TV viewers can accept; in other words, the minimum value the filtering system should maintain during changes in the sampling rate or number of channels. This can lead to the second condition as

$$f_s = \arg \min_f \{FP(f) \geq T_{fp}\}, \tag{4}$$

where FP means the filtering performance, T_{fp} is the confidence limit of the filtering performance, and f_s is the sampling rate that satisfies the specific performance.

By Eq. (4), we get the range of the sampling rate, f, as

$$f > f_s. \tag{5}$$

If these two conditions are satisfied, the proposed filtering system can guarantee stable filtering in live broadcasts. We apply these two conditions to the content filtering system for soccer videos to verify the effectiveness of the model.

Experiments

Experiments were performed with soccer videos to verify the proposed queue model and the requirements of content filtering. The test videos consist of five soccer videos of about 90 minutes in length. In order to evaluate the filtering requirements with regards to computing power of a system, we used three different terminals (T_1, T_2, T_3) comprising 650 MHz CPU and 128 MByte memory, 1.7 GHz and 512 MByte, and 3 GHz and 2 GByte, respectively. Actually, the terminal with 650 MHz CPU has the same computing power currently available in set-top boxes.

Applied Filtering Algorithm for Soccer Videos

In our experiments, we applied the proposed real-time content filtering method to live soccer videos. Sport is an appropriate genre for live broadcasting since sporting events consist of meaningful scenes that occur repeatedly. Thus, sports videos have suitable broadcasting contents that can be filtered on the air. Object-based features (*e.g.*, object motions) in sports video indexing enable high-level domain analysis, but their extraction may be computationally costly for real-time implementation [19, 20]. To minimize computational complexity, we employ cinema features, made up of common video composition and production rules (*e.g.*, replay), as well as the threshold methods used in previous works [21–23].

We first analyzed the soccer videos to extract meaningful scenes. The meaningful scenes refer to shooting scenes including goal scenes. The frame view types in soccer are divided into four categories: 1) global view with goal post (G_p), 2) global view without goal post (G), 3) medium view (M), and 4) close-up view (C).

The filtering algorithm used in this chapter to detect the shooting scenes of soccer videos is shown in Fig. 5.

The algorithm is divided into two parts, *i.e.*, view detection and replay detection. A temporal pattern of view sequence is used to decide shooting scene candidates among goal scenes. The replay function verifies the detection of a shooting scene.

View detection is performed according to the following steps

Step 1: The input frame is divided into 9 sub-blocks as shown in Fig. 6 (a).
Step 2: The soccer field has one dominant color which represents the grass on the field. The dominant color is then checked by hue values (from 70° to 105°) as shown in Fig. 6 (b). To examine the existence of the audience, players, referees, and grass, we check hue values in sub-block R_2, R_5, R_6, and R_8. In each sub-block, we count the pixels of hue values that belong to values between 70° and

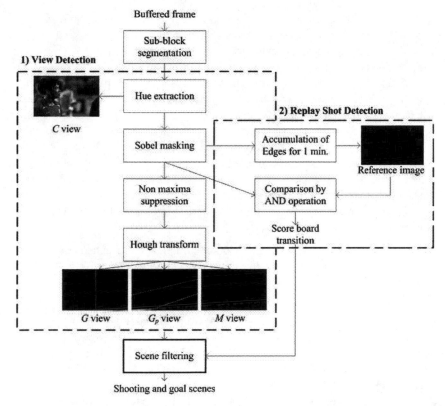

Fig. 5 Filtering algorithm used for soccer videos

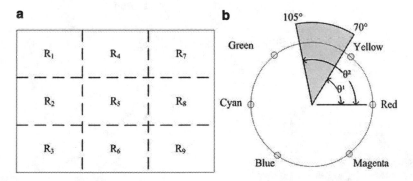

Fig. 6 (a) 9 sub-blocks segmented in the input frame and (b) Hue region representing the dominant color of grass in the field

$105°$. We then normalize the counted pixels by the total number of pixels in a sub-block and define it as *Hue Ratio*.

Step 3: Close-up view is detected if the *Hue Ratio*s of sub-block R_5 and R_6 in Fig. 6 (a) are less than 0.6 and 0.55, respectively, which means the usually dominant color of grass becomes sparse in the center area of the frame when the broadcasting camera focuses on objects such as players and referees.

Step 4: Edge components are extracted by Sobel operator with a 3×3 mask.

Step 5: The non maxima suppression method thins the edges [25].

Step 6: The lines of the soccer field are detected from the $\theta\gamma$-plane of the Hough transform. With the length constraint ($\gamma \geq$ threshold), we denote horizontal lines for ($80° < \pm\theta \leq 90°$), vertical lines for ($0° \leq \pm\theta < 10°$), and diagonal lines for ($20° < \pm\theta \leq 80°$), respectively. Using the detected lines, we resolve the billboard, goal post and penalty box lines, as well as the center line.

Step 7: Other view types are classified according to the results of *Step 2* and *6*. Global views with goal post are classified if the frame has more than 3 diagonal lines. Global views without goal post are classified if the frame contains one center line or the *Hue Ratios* in sub-block R_2 and R_8 are more than 0.8. Otherwise, it is classified as a medium view.

For replay detection in Fig. 5, we use scoreboard analysis. The text characters in a frame form a regular texture containing vertical and horizontal strokes [26]. Input frames are compared with the reference frame which has the scoreboard. The replay shot detection is given by the following steps.

Step 1: Reference frames with the scoreboard are obtained from given interval (in this work, one minute frames) at the beginning of the video. To find the regions of the scoreboard, we accumulate the edges of Sobel masking for the reference frames. The scoreboard regions are then decided around dominant parts with values of more than 0.7 as shown in Fig. 7 (a).

Step 2: Edges of the input frames are compared with the reference edges obtained in *Step 1*. If the edges around the scoreboard region are varied, we believe that a change in the scoreboard has occurred and the replay starts.

Finally, scene filtering is performed with extracted view sequences and detected replay. The filtering of shooting scenes is organized by specific view types. Figure 7

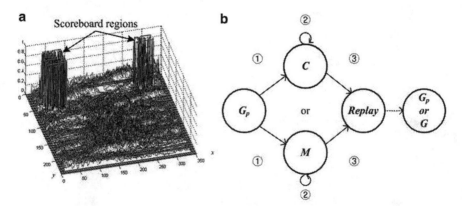

Fig. 7 (a) Accumulated edges in the region of a scoreboard; (b) Temporal view patterns of frames for shooting scenes in soccer games

(b) shows the temporal sequences of the scenes modeled in this work: ① denotes view transition, ② refers to the sequence of close-up views or medium views, and ③ denotes the replay of the scene.

The view transition from the global view with goal post to the close-up view or medium view shows the beginning of a meaningful scene in sports broadcasts. As well, a replay occurring just after a meaningful scene verifies the detection of a shooting scene.

In the experiments, we observed the time consumed and filtering performance, and obtained the filtering requirements by applying them to the proposed queue model in Fig. 3.

Experimental Results with Soccer Videos

We established a TV terminal playing a video on one channel while another video from another channel was being filtered using the proposed filtering system. We then measured the performances of view decision scene detection and processing time in the filtering.

Figure 8 shows the performance of the proposed view decision with three frames per second sampling rate and one channel of interest. In the experiment, the total average recall rate was over 93.5 % and the total average precision rate was approximately 89.5%.

The filtering performance of the shooting scenes (including goals scenes) showed an average recall rate of 81.5 % and an average precision rate of 76.4 % in the test videos. The detection of goal scenes is more accurate than that of the shooting scenes because goal scenes have replay shots without exception.

The processing time for content filtering is dependent on the detection of view type. We calculated the expected filtering time as depicted in Eq. (1). As mentioned

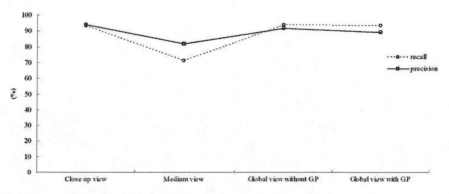

Fig. 8 Performance of the proposed view type decision

above, the frames of soccer videos were categorized into four view types, *i.e.*, $V = \{C, M, G, G_p\}$. The processing time for the view decision in soccer videos was measured.

Table 1 shows the time measured for the view type decision for different terminal computing power. As shown, the longest time is taken to detect the global view with goal post.

From the experimental results, the first condition of the soccer video, meaning its stability in real-time for the proposed filtering system, can be found by substituting these results to Eq. (3). For the soccer video, the first condition can be described as,

$$\rho = N \cdot f \cdot PT(G_p) \leq 1,$$

$$\text{therefore, } N \cdot f \leq 1/PT(G_p). \tag{6}$$

The second condition is verified by evaluating the filtering performance of the proposed filtering algorithm. Figure 9 shows the variation of the filtering performance with respect to sampling rate. As shown, the performance (recall rate in the figure) decreases as the sampling rate decreases. From Fig. 9, it is shown that the maximum permissible limit of sampling rate is determined by the tolerance (T_{fp}) of filtering performance. When the system permits about 80% filtering performance of T_{fp}, it is observed that the sampling rate, f_s, becomes 2.5 frames per second by the experimental result.

As a result of the experiments, we obtain the system requirements for real-time filtering of soccer videos as shown in Fig. 10. Substituting $PT(G_p)$s of Table 1 into

Table 1 Processing time for the view type decision

View \ Terminal	T_1	T_2	T_3
$E[PT(C)]$	0.170 sec.	0.037 sec.	0.025 sec.
$E[PT(M)]$	0.270 sec.	0.075 sec.	0.045 sec.
$E[PT(G)]$	0.281 sec.	0.174 sec.	0.088 sec.
$E[PT(G_p)]$	0.314 sec.	0.206 sec.	0.110 sec.

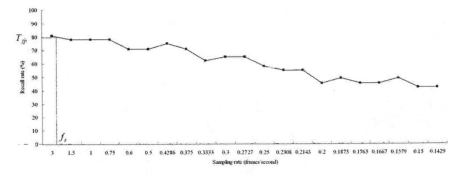

Fig. 9 Variation of filtering performance according to sampling rate

Eq. (6), we acquire the number of input channels and frame sampling rates available in the used filtering system. As shown, the number of input channels depends on both sampling rate and terminal capability. By assuming the confidence limit of the filtering performance, T_{fp}, we also get the minimum sampling rate from Fig. 10.

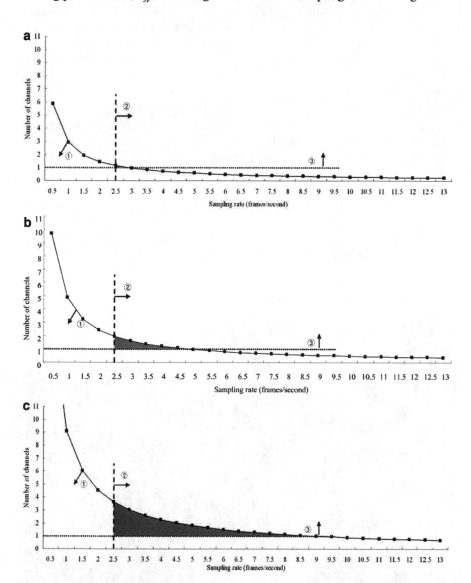

Fig. 10 The number of input channels enables the real-time filtering system to satisfy the filtering requirements in (**a**) Terminal 1, (**b**) Terminal 2, and (**c**) Terminal 3. ① and ② lines indicate the conditions of Eq. 6 and Fig. 9, respectively. ① line shows that the number of input channels is inversely proportional to b with the processing time of G_p. ② line is the range of sampling rate required to maintain over 80% filtering performance. And ③ line (the dotted horizontal line), represents the minimum number of channels, *i.e.*, one channel

To maintain stability in the filtering system, the number of input channels and the sampling rate should be selected in the range where the three conditions by ①, ②, and ③lines meet. Supposing that the confidence limit of the filtering performance is 80%, Figure 10 illustrates the following results: one input channel is allowable for real-time filtering in Terminal 1 at sampling rates between 2.5 and 3 frames per second. In Terminal 2, one or two channels are allowable at sampling rates between 2.5 and 4.5 frames per second. Terminal 3 can have less than four channels at sampling rates between 2.5 and 9 frames per second. The results show that Terminal 3, which has the highest capability, has a higher number of input channels for real-time filtering than the others.

We implemented the real-time filtering system on our test-bed [27] as shown in Fig. 11. The main screen shows a drama channel assumed to be the favorite station of the TV viewer. And the screen box at the bottom right in the figure shows the filtered broadcast from the channel of interest. In this case, a soccer video is selected as the channel of interest and "Shooting" and "Goal" scenes are considered as the meaningful scenes.

To perform the filtering algorithm on the soccer video, the CPU usage and memory consumption of each terminal should remain stable. Each shows a memory consumption of between 32 and 38 Mbytes, and an average of 85% (T_1), 56% (T_2), and 25% (T_3) CPU usage time by a Window's performance monitor.

Fig. 11 Screen shot to run real-time content filtering service with a single channel of interest

Discussion

For practical purposes, we will discuss the design, implementation and integration of the proposed filtering system with a real set-top box. To realize the proposed system, computing power to calculate and perform the filtering algorithm within the limited time is the most important element. We expect that TV terminals equipped with STB and PVR will evolve into multimedia centers in the home with computing and home server connections [28, 29]. The terminal also requires a digital tuner enabling it to extract each broadcasting stream time-division, or multiple tuners for the filtering of multiple channels Next, practical implementation should be based on conditions such as buffer size, the number of channels, filtering performance, sampling rate, etc., in order to stabilize filtering performance. Finally, the terminal should know the genre of the input broadcasting video because the applied filtering algorithm depends on video genre. This could be resolved by the time schedule of an electronic program guide.

The proposed filtering system is not without its limitations. As shown in previous works [21–24], the filtering algorithm requires more enhanced filtering performance with real-time processing. As well, it is necessary that the algorithm be extendable to other sport videos such as baseball, basketball, golf, etc; and, to approach a real environment, we need to focus on the evaluation of the corresponding system utilization, e.g., CPU usage and memory consumption as shown in [13] and [30].

Conclusion

In this chapter, we introduced a real-time content filtering system for live broadcasts to provide personalized scenes, and analyzed its requirements in TV terminals equipped with set-top boxes and personal video recorders. As a result of experiments based on the requirements, the effectiveness of the proposed filtering system has been verified. By applying queueing theory and a fast filtering algorithm, it is shown that the proposed system model and filtering requirements are suitable for real-time content filtering with multiple channel inputs. Our experimental results revealed that even a low-performance terminal with 650 MHz CPU can perform the filtering function in real-time. Therefore, the proposed queueing system model and its requirements confirm that the real-time filtering of live broadcasts is possible with currently available set-top boxes.

References

1. TVAF, "Phase 2 Benchmark Features," SP001v20, http://www.tv-anytime.org/, 2005, pp. 9.
2. N. Dimitrova, H.-J. Zhang, B. Shahraray, I. Sezan, T. Huang, and A. Zakhor, "Applications of Video-Content Analysis and Retrieval," IEEE Multimedia, Vol. 9, No. 3, 2002, pp. 42–55.

3. S. Yang; S. Kim; Y. M. Ro, "Semantic Home Photo Categorization," IEEE Trans. Circuits and Systems for Video Technology, Vol. 17, 2007, pp. 324–335.
4. C.-W. Ngo, Y.-F. Ma, and H.-J. Zhang, "Video Summarization and Scene Detection by Graph Modeling," IEEE Trans. Circuits and Systems for Video Technology, Vol. 15, No. 2, 2005, pp. 296–305.
5. H. Li, G. Liu, Z. Zhang, and Y. Li, "Adaptive Scene-Detection Algorithm for VBR Video Stream," IEEE Trans. Multimedia, Vol. 6, No. 4, pp. 624–633, 2004.
6. Y. Li, S. Narayanan, and C.-C. Jay Kuo, "Content-Based Movie Analysis and Indexing Based on AudioVisual Cues," IEEE Trans. Circuits and System for Video Technology, Vol. 14, No. 8, 2004, pp. 1073–1085.
7. J. M. Gauch, S. Gauch, S. Bouix, and X. Zhu, "Real Time Video Scene Detection And Classification," Information Processing and Management, Vol.35, 1999, pp. 381–400.
8. I. Otsuka, K. Nakane, A. Divakaran, K. Hatanaka and M. Ogawa, "A Highlight Scene Detection and Video Summarization System using Audio Feature for a Personal Video Recorder," IEEE Trans. Consumer Electronics, Vol. 51, No. 1, 2005, pp. 112–116.
9. S. H. Jin, T. M. Bae, Y. M. Ro, "Intelligent Broadcasting System and Services for Personalized Semantic Contents Consumption" Expert system with applications, Vol. 31, 2006, pp. 164–173.
10. J. Kim, S. Suh, and S. Sull, "Fast Scene Change Detection for Personal Video Recorder," IEEE Trans. Consumer Electronics, Vol. 49, No. 3, 2003, pp. 683–688.
11. J. S. Choi, J. W. Kim, D. S. Han, J. Y. Nam, and Y. H. Ha, "Design and implementation of DVB-T receiver system for digital TV," IEEE Trans. Consumer Electronics, Vol. 50, No. 4, 2004, pp. 991–998.
12. M. Bais, J. Cosmas, C. Dosch, A. Engelsberg, A. Erk, P. S. Hansen, P. Healey, G. K. Klungsoeyr, R. Mies, J.-R. Ohm, Y. Paker, A. Pearmain, L. Pedersen, A. Sandvand, R. Schafer, P. Schoonjans, and P. Stammnitz, "Customized television: standards compliant advanced digital television," IEEE Trans. Broadcasting, Vol. 48, No. 2, 2002, pp. 151–158.
13. N. Dimitrova, T. McGee, H. Elenbaas, and J. Martino, "Video content management in consumer devices," IEEE Trans. Knowledge and Data Engineering, Vol. 10, Issue 6, 1998, pp. 988–995.
14. N. Dimitrova, H. Elenbass, T. McGee, and L. Agnihotri, "An architecture for video content filtering in consumer domain," in Proc. Int. Conf. on Information Technology: Coding and Computing 2000, 27–29 March 2000, pp. 214–221.
15. D. Gross, and C. M. Harris, Fundamentals of Queueing Theory, John Wiley & Sons: New York, NY, 1998.
16. L. Kleinrock, Queueing System, Wiley: New York, NY, 1975.
17. K. Lee, and H. S. Park, "Approximation of The Queue Length Distribution of General Queues," ETRI Journal, Vol. 15, No. 3, 1994, pp. 35–46.
18. Jr. A. Eckberg, "The Single Server Queue with Periodic Arrival Process and Deterministic Service Times," IEEE Trans. Communications, Vol. 27, No. 3, 1979, pp. 556–562.
19. Y. Fu, A. Ekin, A. M. Tekalp, and R. Mehrotra, "Temporal segmentation of video objects for hierarchical object-based motion description," IEEE Trans. Image Processing, vol. 11, Feb. 2002, pp. 135–145.
20. D. Zhong, and S. Chang, "Real-time view recognition and event detection for sports video," Journal of Visual Communication & Image Representation, Vol. 15, No. 3, 2004, pp. 330–347.
21. A. Ekin, A. M. Tekalp, and R. Mehrotra, "Automatic Soccer Video Analysis and Summarization," IEEE Trans. Image Processing, Vol. 12, No. 7, 2003, pp. 796–807.
22. A. Ekin and A. M. Tekalp, "Generic Play-break Event Detection for Summarization and Hierarchical Sports Video Analysis," in Proc. IEEE Int. Conf. Multimedia & Expo 2003, 2003, pp. 27–29.
23. M. Kumano, Y. Ariki, K. Tsukada, S. Hamaguchi, and H. Kiyose, "Automatic Extraction of PC Scenes Based on Feature Mining for a Real Time Delivery System of Baseball Highlight Scenes," in Proc. IEEE Int. Conf. Multimedia and Expo 2004, 2004, pp. 277–280.

24. R. Leonardi, P. Migliorati, and M. Prandini, "Semantic indexing of soccer audio-visual se-
    quences: a multimodal approach based on controlled Markov chains," IEEE Trans. Circuits
    and Systems for Video Technology, Vol. 14, No. 5, 2004, pp. 634–643.
25. P. Meer and B. Georgescu, "Edge Detection with Embedded Confidence," IEEE Trans. Pattern
    Analysis and Machine Intelligence, Vol. 23, No. 12, 2001, pp. 1351–1365.
26. C. Wolf, J.-M. Jolion, and F. Chassaing, "Text localization, enhancement and binarization in
    multimedia documents," in Proc. 16th Int. Conf. Pattern Recognition, Vol. 2, 2002, pp. 1037–
    1040.
27. S. H. Jin, T. M. Bae, Y. M. Ro, and K. Kang, "Intelligent Agent-based System for Personalized
    Broadcasting Services," in Proc. Int. Conf. Image Science, Systems and Technology'04, 2004,
    pp. 613–619.
28. S. Pekowsky and R. Jaeger, "The set-top box as multi-media terminal," IEEE Trans. Consumer
    Electronics, Vol. 44, Issue 3, 1998, pp. 833–840.
29. J.-C. Moon, H.-S. Lim, and S.-J. Kang, "Real-time event kernel architecture for home-network
    gateway set-top-box (HNGS)," IEEE Trans. Consumer Electronics, Vol. 45, Issue 3, 1999,
    pp. 488–495.
30. B. Shahrary, "Scene change detection and content-based sampling of video sequences," in
    Proc. SPIE, Vol. 2419, 1995, pp. 2–13.

Chapter 19
Digital Theater: Dynamic Theatre Spaces

Sara Owsley Sood and Athanasios V. Vasilakos

Introduction

Digital technology has given rise to new media forms. Interactive theatre is such a new type of media that introduces new digital interaction methods into theatres. In a typical experience of interactive theatres, people enter cyberspace and enjoy the development of a story in a non-linear manner by interacting with the characters in the story. Therefore, in contrast to conventional theatre which presents predetermined scenes and story settings unilaterally, interactive theatre makes it possible for the viewer to actually take part in the plays and enjoy a first person experience.

In "Interactive Article" section, we are concerned with embodied mixed reality techniques using video-see-through HMDs (head mounted display). Our research goal is to explore the potential of embodied mixed reality space as an interactive theatre experience medium. What makes our system advantageous is that we, for the first time, combine embodied mixed reality, live 3D human actor capture and Ambient Intelligence, for an increased sense of presence and interaction.

We present an Interactive Theatre system using Mixed Reality, 3D Live, 3D sound and Ambient Intelligence. In this system, thanks to embodied Mixed Reality and Ambient Intelligence, audiences are totally submerged into an imaginative virtual world of the play in 3D form. They can walk around to view the show at any viewpoint, to see different parts and locations of the story scene, and to follow the story on their own interests. Moreover, with 3D Live technology, which allows live 3D human capture, our Interactive Theatre system enables actors at different places all around the world play together at the same place in real-time. Audiences can see the performance of these actors/actresses as if they were really in front of them. Furthermore, using Mixed Reality technologies, audiences can see both virtual objects

S.O. Sood
Department of Computer Science, Pomona College, 185 East Sixth Street, Claremont, CA 91711
e-mail: sara@cs.pomona.edu

A.V. Vasilakos (✉)
Department of Theatre Studies, University of Peloponnese, 21100 Nafplio, Greece
e-mail: vasilako@ath.forthnet.gr

B. Furht (ed.), *Handbook of Multimedia for Digital Entertainment and Arts*,
DOI 10.1007/978-0-387-89024-1_19, © Springer Science+Business Media, LLC 2009

and the real world at the same time. Thus, they can see not only actors/actresses of the play but the other audiences as well. All of them can also interact and participate in the play, which creates a unique experience.

Our system of Mixed Reality and 3D Live with Ambient Intelligence is intended to bring performance art to the people while offering performance artists a creative tool to extend the grammar of the traditional theatre. This Interactive Theatre also enables social networking and relations, which is the essence of the theatre, by supporting simultaneous participants in human-to-human social manner.

While Interactive Theater engages patrons in an experience in which they drive the performance, a substantial number of systems have been built in which the performance is driven by a set of digital actors. That is, a team of digital actors autonomously generates a performance, perhaps with some input from the audience or from other human actors.

The challenge of generating novel and interesting performance content for digital actors differs greatly by the type of performance or interaction at hand. In cases where the digital actor is interacting with human actors, the digital actor must understand the context of the performance and respond with appropriate and original content in a time frame that keeps the tempo or beat of the performance in tact. When performances are completely machine driven, the task is more like creating or generating a compelling story, a variant on a classic set of problems in the field of Artificial Intelligence. In section "Automated Performance by Digital Actors" of this article, we survey various systems that automatically generate performance content for digital actors both in human/machine hybrid performances, as well as in completely automated performances.

Interactive Theater

The systematic study of the expressive resources of the body started in France with Francois Delsarte at the end of the 1800s [4, 5]. Delsarte studied how people gestured in real life and elaborated a lexicon of gestures, each of which was to have a direct correlation with the psychological state of man. Delsarte claimed that for every emotion, of whatever kind, there is a corresponding body movement. He also believed that a perfect reproduction of the outer manifestation of some passion will induce, by reflex, that same passion. Delsarte inspired us to have a lexicon of gestures as working material to start from. By providing automatic and unencumbering gesture recognition, technology offers a tool to study and rehearse theatre. It also provides us with tools that augment the actor's action with synchronized digital multimedia presentations.

Delsarte's "laws of expression" spread widely in Europe, Russia, and the United States. At the beginning of the century, Vsevolod Meyerhold at the Moscow Art Theatre developed a theatrical approach that moved away from the naturalism of Stanislavski. Meyerhold looked to the techniques of the Commedia dell'Arte, pantomime, the circus, and to the Kabuki and Noh theatres of Japan for inspiration, and created a technique of the actor, which he called "Biomechanics." Meyerhold was fascinated by movement, and trained actors to be acrobats, clowns, dancers, singers, and jugglers, capable of rapid transitions from one role to another. He banished virtuosity in scene and costume decoration and focused on the actor's body and his gestural skills to convey the emotions of the moment. By presenting to the public properly executed physical actions and by drawing upon their complicity of imagination, Meyerhold aimed at a theatre in which spectators would be invited to social and political insights by the strength of the emotional communication of gesture. Meyerhold's work stimulated us to investigate the relationship between motion and emotion.

Later in the century Bertold Brecht elaborated a theory of acting and staging aimed at jolting the audience out of its uncritical stupor. Performers of his plays used physical gestures to illuminate the characters they played, and maintained a distance between the part and themselves. The search of an ideal gesture that distills the essence of a moment (Gestus) is an essential part of his technique. Brecht wanted actors to explore and heighten the contradictions in a character's behavior. He would invite actors to stop at crucial points in the performance and have them explain to the audience the implications of a character's choice. By doing so he wanted the public to become aware of the social implications of everyone's life choices. Like Brecht, we are interested in performances that produce awakening and reflection in the public rather than uncritical immersion. We therefore have organized our technology to augment the stage in a way similar to how "Mixed Reality" enhances or completes our view of the real world. This contrasts work on Virtual Reality, Virtual Theatre, or Virtual Actors, which aims at replacing the stage and actors with virtual ones, and to involve the public in an immersive narration similar to an open-eyes dream.

English director Peter Brook, a remarkable contemporary, has accomplished a creative synthesis of the century's quest for a novel theory and practice of acting. Brook started his career directing "traditional" Shakespearean plays and later moved his stage and theatrical experimentation to hospitals, churches, and African tribes. He has explored audience involvement and influence on the play, preparation vs. spontaneity of acting, the relationship between physical and emotional energy, and the usage of space as a tool for communication. His work, centered on sound, voice, gestures, and movement, has been a constant source of inspiration to many contemporaries, together with his thought-provoking theories on theatrical research and discovery. We admire Brook's research for meaning and its representation in theatre. In particular we would like to follow his path in bringing theatre out of the traditional stage and perform closer to people, in a variety of public and cultural settings. Our Virtual theatre enables social networking by supporting simultaneous participants in human-to-human social manner.

Flavia Sparacino at the MIT Media Lab created the Improvisational TheatreSpace [1], [2], which embodied human actors and Media Actors to generate an emergent story through interaction among themselves and the public. An emergent story is one that is not strictly tied to a script. It is the analog of a "jam session" in music. Like musicians who play together, each with their unique musical personality, competency, and experience, to create a musical experience for which there is no score, a group of Media Actors and human actors perform a dynamically evolving story. Media Actors are autonomous agent-based text, images, movie clips, and audio. These are used to augment the play by expressing the actor's inner thoughts, memory, or personal imagery, or by playing other segments of the script. Human actors use full body gestures, tone of voice, and simple phrases to interact with media actors. An experimental performance was presented in 1997 on the occasion of the Sixth Biennial Symposium on Arts and Technology [3].

Interactive Theater Architecture

In this section, we will introduce the design of our Interactive Theatre Architecture. The diagram in Fig. 3 shows the whole system architecture.

Embodied mixed reality space and Live 3D actors

In order to maintain an electrical theatre entertainment in a physical space, the actors and props will be represented by digital objects, which must seamlessly appear in the physical world. This can be achieved using the full mixed reality spectrum of physical reality, augmented reality and virtual reality. Furthermore, to implement human-to-human social interaction and physical interaction as essential features of the interactive theatre, the theory of embodied computing is applied in the system. As mentioned above, this research aims to maintain human-to-human interaction such as gestures, body language and movement between users. Thus, we have developed a live 3D interaction system for viewers to view live human actors in the mixed reality environment. In fact, science fiction has presaged such interaction in computing and communication. In 2001: A Space Odyssey, Dr. Floyd calls home using a videophone an early on-screen appearance of 2D video-conferencing. This technology is now commonplace.

More recently, the Star Wars films depicted 3D holographic communication. Using a similar philosophy in this paper, we apply computer graphics to create real-time 3D human actors for mixed reality environments. One goal of this work is to enhance the interactive theatre by developing a 3D human actor capture mixed reality system. The enabling technology is an algorithm for generating arbitrary novel views of a collaborator at video frame rate speeds (30 frames per second). We also apply these methods to communication in virtual spaces. We render the image of the collaborator from the viewpoint of the user, permitting very natural interaction.

Hardware setup

Figure 1 represents the overall structure of the 3D capture system. Eight Dragonfly FireWire cameras, operating at 30 fps, 640 by 480 resolution, are equally spaced around the subject, and one camera views him/her from above. Three Sync Units

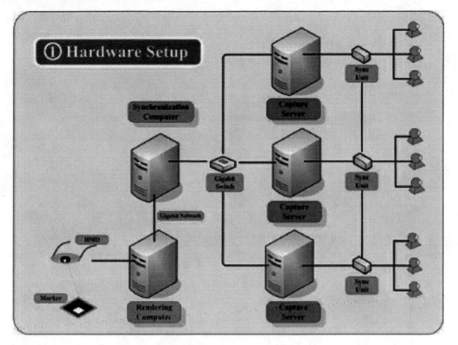

Fig. 1   Hardware architecture [8]

from Point Grey Research are used to synchronize image acquisition of these cameras across multiple FireWire buses [6]. Three Capture Server machines receive the three 640 by 480 video streams in Bayer format at 30 Hz from three cameras each, and pre-process the video-streams. The Synchronization machine is connected with three Capture Sever machines through a Gigabit network. This machine receives nine processed images from three Capture Server machines, synchronizes them, and sends them also via gigabit Ethernet links to the Rendering machine. At the Rendering machine, the position of the virtual viewpoint is estimated. A novel view of the captured subject from this viewpoint is then generated and superimposed onto the mixed reality scene.

Software components

All of the basic modules and the processing stages of the system are represented in Figure 2. The Capturing and Image Processing modules are placed at each Capture Server machine. After the Capturing module obtains raw images from the cameras, the Image Processing module will extract parts of the foreground objects from the background scene to obtain the silhouettes, compensate for the radial distortion component of the camera mode, and apply a simple compression technique. The Synchronization module, on the Synchronization machine, is responsible for

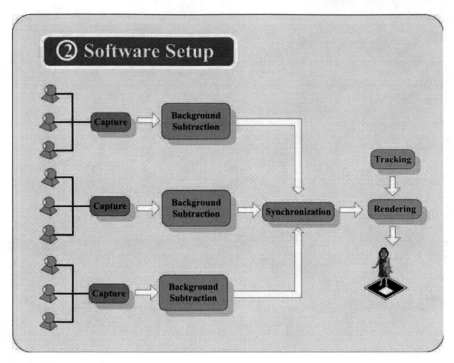

Fig. 2 Software architecture [8]

getting the processed images from all the cameras and checking their timestamps to synchronize them. If those images are not synchronized, based on the timestamps, the Synchronization module will request the slowest camera to continuously capture and send back images until all these images from all nine cameras appear to be captured at nearly the same time.

The Tracking module will calculate the Euclidian transformation matrix between a live 3D actor and the user's viewpoint. This can be done either by marker-based tracking techniques [7] or other tracking methods, such as IS900. After receiving the images from the Synchronization module and the transformation matrix from the Tracking module, the Rendering module will generate a novel view of the subject based on these inputs. The novel image is generated such that the virtual camera views the subject from exactly the same angle and position as the head mounted camera views the marker. This simulated view of the remote collaborator is then superimposed on the original image and displayed to the user. In the interactive theatre, using this system, we capture live human models and present them via the augmented reality interface at a remote location. The result gives the strong impression that the model is a real three-dimensional part of the scene.

Interactive Theatre system

In this section, we will introduce the design of our Interactive Theatre system. The diagram in Figure 3 shows the whole system architecture.

3D Live capture room

3D Live capture rooms are used to capture the actors in real-time. Basically, these are the capturing part of 3D Live capture system, which has been described in the previous section. The actors play inside the 3D Live recording room, and their images are captured by nine surrounding cameras. After subtracting the background, those images are streamed to the synchronization server using RTP/IP multicast, the well-known protocols to transfer multimedia data streams over the network in real-time. Together with the images, the sound is also recorded and transferred to the synchronization server using RTP in real-time. This server will synchronize those sound packets and images, and stream the synchronized data to the render clients by also using RTP protocol to guarantee the real-time constraint. While receiving the synchronized streams of images and sounds transferred from the synchronization server, each render client buffers the data and uses it to generate the 3D images and playback the 3D sound for each user. One important requirement of this system

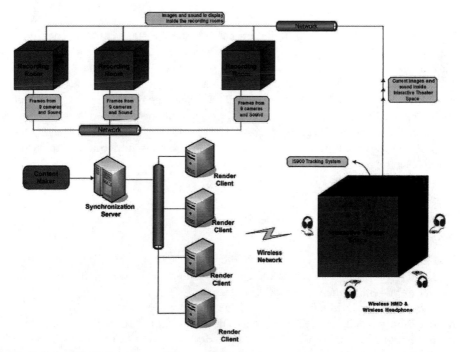

Fig. 3 Interactive Theatre system [8]

Fig. 4 Actor playing Hamlet is captured inside the 3D Live recording room

is that the actors at one recording room need to see the story context. They may need to follow and communicate with actors from other recording rooms, with the virtual characters generated by computers, or even with the audiences inside the theatre to interact with them for our interactivity purpose. In order to achieve this, several monitors are put at the specific positions inside the recording room to reflect the corresponding views of other recording rooms, the virtual computer generated world, and the current images of the audiences inside the theatre. Those monitors are put at fixed positions so that the background subtraction algorithm can easily identify their fixed area in the captured images and eliminate them as they are parts of the background scene. Figure 4 shows an example of the recording room, where an actor is playing Hamlet.

Interactive Theatre Space

The Interactive Theatre Space is where the audiences can view the story in high resolution 3D MR and VR environments. Inside this space, we tightly couple the virtual world with the physical world.

The system uses IS900 (InterSense) inertial-acoustic hybrid tracking devices mounted on the ceiling. While visitors walk around in the room-size space, their head positions are tracked by the tracking devices. We use the user's location information to interact with the system, so that the visitors can actually interact with the theatre context using their bodily movement in a room-size area, which incorporates the social context into the theatre experience. The Interactive Theatre Space supports two experience modes, VR and MR modes. Each user wears a wireless HMD and a wireless headphone connected to a render client. Based on the user's head position in 3D, which is tracked IS900 system, the render client will render the image and sound of the corresponding view of the audience so that the audience can view the MR/VR environment and hear 3D sound seamlessly embedded surrounding her.

In VR experience mode, featured with fully immersive VR navigation, the visitors will see they are in the virtual castle and they need to navigate in it to find the story performed by the 3D live actors. For example, in Figure 5, we can see the live 3D images of the actor playing Hamlet in the Interactive Theatre Space in VR mode with the virtual grass, boat, trees and castle. The real actors can also play with imaginative virtual characters generated by the computers, as shown in Figure 6. As a result, in VR mode, the users are surrounded by characters and story scenes. They are totally submerged into an imaginative virtual world of the play in 3D form. They can walk or turn around to view the virtual world at any viewpoint, to see different parts and locations of the story scene, and to follow the story on their own interests.

Besides the VR mode, users can also view the story in MR mode, where the virtual and the real world mixed together. For example, the real scene is built inside the room, with real castle, real chairs, tables, etc., but the actors are 3D live characters being captured inside the 3D Live recording rooms at different places.

Moreover, our Interactive Theatre system enables actors at different places play together on the same place in real-time. With the real-time capturing and rendering feature of 3D Live technology, using RTP/IP multicast to stream 3D Live data in real-time, people at different places can see each other as if they were in the same location. With this feature, dancers from many places all over the world can dance together via internet connection, and their 3D images are displayed at the Interactive Theatre Space corresponding to the users' viewpoints, tracked by IS900 system. The Content Maker module in Figure 3 defines the story outline and scene by specifying the locations and interactions of all 3D Live and virtual characters. In order to enable the interaction of the audiences and the actors at different places, several cameras and microphone are put inside the Interactive Theatre Space to capture the images and voice of the audiences. Those images and voice captured by the camera and microphone near the place of a 3D Live actor, which is pre-defined by the

Fig. 5 Interactive Theatre Space in VR mode: 3D Live actor as Hamlet in virtual environment

Fig. 6 Interactive Theatre Space in VR mode: 3D Live actor as Hamlet playing with virtual character

Content Maker, will be transferred to one of the display of that corresponding actor's recording room. Consequently, the actors can see the audiences' interactions and give the responses to them following the pre-defined story situations. As a result, the users can walk around inside the Interactive Theatre Space to follow the story, interact with the characters, and use their own interactions to change the story within the scope of the story outline pre-defined by the Content Maker module.

Automated Performance by Digital Actors

Human/machine collaborative performance

There have been numerous projects that bring both human and digital actors together to create a theatrical performance. Many of these projects exist in the realm of improvisational theater, likely due to the group/team-based nature of the style. In the task of creating a digital actor that is capable of performing alongside humans in an improvisational performance, several challenges must be addressed. The digital actor must understand the context of the ongoing performance, it must generate novel and appropriate responses within this context, and it must make these contributions in a timely manner, keeping the beat or tempo of the performance.

The Association Engine [9, 10, 11] was a troupe of digital improvisers that attempted these three tasks in autonomously generating a creative and entertaining experience. A team of five digital actors, with animated faces and voice generation, could autonomously perform a series of improvisational warm-up games with one or more human participants, followed by a performance.

While there are many published guidelines of improvisational theater, many of the great improvisers say that they don't follow these rules. Improvisation is about connecting with and reacting to both the other actors and your audience [12]. It is largely about the associations that each actor has to words and phrases, which are based on their own life experiences. It's hard to imagine how creating a digital improviser would be possible. How can a system embody the experiences and associations from one's life, and access them? How could the system's experiences grow in order to provide novel associations? How could it scale to represent different personalities and characters?

The Pattern Game

In improvisational comedy, troupes generally gather before performances to warm up, and get on the same contextual page. There are a variety of ways that troupes do this. One common way is a game called the *pattern game*, also known as *free association, free association circle*, or *patterns*. There are many variations to this game, but there are some very basic rules that are common across all variations. The actors stand in a circle. One actor begins the game by saying a word. The actor to the right of this actor says the first word that comes to their mind, and this continues around the circle. The actors try to make contributions on a strict rhythm to ensure that the associations are not thoughtful or preconceived. Some variations of the game encourage the actors to only associate from the previous word, while others require that the associations are in reference to all words contributed so far. In some cases, the actors attempt to bring their associations full circle and return to the original word. The goal of all variations of this game is to get actors warmed up on the same contextual page and in tune with each other before a performance.

The first step towards creating a digital improviser was the modest goal of creating a system that could participate in a *pattern game*. If we are able to create a digital improviser that can participate in a *pattern game* with other human and digital actors, then we can build a team of improvisers that can generate a shared context, and eventually do a full performance. If we assume that the digital actor has a way to communicate with the other actors (speech recognition and generation and simple sockets for digital actor to digital actor communication), the most challenging issue that remains is to generate novel associations and contributions for the game.

We began by providing the system with access to some set of possible associations to words. We used an online connected thesaurus, Lexical FreeNet [13], as a source of word associations, with association types ranging from "Synonyms" to "Occupation of" for a vast set of words. Given a single word, Lexical FreeNet provides a vast set of related words. Many of the words and associations in Lexical

FreeNet are very obscure. For example, in Lexical FreeNet, there are 508 words related to the word "cell." Included in this set are "cytoplasm," "vacuole," "gametocyte," "photovoltaic cell" and "bozell." In human improvisation troupes, actors would not contribute a word like "gametocyte" to the *pattern game* for a few reasons. They are warming up with the intent of generating a context from which to do a performance. Because this is aimed towards a future performance, they will not use words that would be unfamiliar to their audience as this would result in the audience becoming disengaged [14]. Just as we use vocabulary that is familiar to someone we are engaged in a conversation with, the content of a performance must be familiar and understandable to the audience. Additionally, they would not make associations that the other actors might not understand as that is counter productive to the goal of getting them on the same page. An actor can't be expected to free associate from a word they are not familiar with. Similarly, overly common words are not advantageous as they are generally uninteresting, and don't provide a rich context for a show.

For these reasons, we enabled the digital improvising agency with the ability to avoid words that are overly obscure or too common from the related word set provided by Lexical FreeNet. While WordNet [15] provides a familiarity score for each word, it did not appear to us that these scores gave an accurate reflection of how commonly the word is used. To generate an accurate measure of familiarity, we looked to the web as an accessible corpus of language use, using the frequency of a term's occurrence on the web (as gauged through the size of a search engine's result set) as a measure of its familiarity [16].

In addition to the familiarity of contributions, actors also consider the context of previous words contributed. As mentioned previously, there are several different varieties of the *pattern game*. We chose to implement a version where the actors associate not only from the previous word, but from the context of all previous words being contributed. This keeps the actors on point, and tied into a space of words. When one word space is exhausted, they can jump out of it with an association into a different space or set of words. The ending result is that the team has one or multiple clear topic areas within which they will do their performance. To emulate this behavior within our digital improvisers, we use a sliding window of context. Contributions are chosen not merely from the set of words related to the previous word contributed, but from the intersection of the sets of words related to the last n words contributed, where n is decreased when the intersection set of related words is sparse or empty. This method resulted in selection of words that stays within a context for some time and then jumps to a new word space when the context is exhausted, much like how human improvisers perform in this game.

To maintain novelty and flow in the *pattern game*, human improvisers will not make redundant associations. For example, six rhyming words will not be contributed in a row. Conversely, some improvisers might lean towards particular relation types. For example, an actor might contribute antonyms whenever possible. To take these two characteristics into account, the digital improvisers use memory of previous relations and tendencies to guide their decisions. Remembering the previous n associations made, they can avoid those relation types where possible. They can also be seeded with tendencies towards particular types of relations, "kind of," "synonym," etc., using these relationship types whenever possible.

The final backend system is one that uses all the methods described above in order to choose a related word to contribute to the *pattern game*. The system first takes a seed from the audience through speech recognition. To make a contribution, the digital improviser first finds the intersection set of the sets of related words to the previous n words. Then, from that set, it eliminates those words which are too familiar or too obscure. It then takes into account its own tendencies towards relation types and the recent history of relation types used in order to choose a word to contribute to the game.

Here is an example string of associations made the digital improvisers given the input word "music." "Music, fine art, art, creation, creative, inspiration, brainchild, product, production, magazine, newspaper, issue, exit, outlet, out."

Here is a second example, starting with the input word "student." "Student, neophyte, initiate, tyro, freshman, starter, recruit, fledgling, entrant, beginner, novice, learner, apprentice, expert, commentator."

One Word Story

Improvisational games and performances can take many different forms. A common game is the *one word story*, also known as *word at a time story*. To do this game, the troupe again stands in a circle. One actor starts by saying a word to begin the story. Moving around the circle, each actor contributes one word at a time until the story is complete. At the end of sentences, one actor may say "period." Like any other performance, this game is usually done after a warm-up so that the troupe is on the same contextual page from which the story can be told. While simplistic in interaction, this game is surprisingly hard for new actors.

Our next step in building a digital improviser was creating a team that could participate in and create a compelling performance of the *one word story* game. Given the complexity of the task, we chose to create a purely digital *one word story* performance. Using the collaborative context created between digital and human actors in a *pattern game*, the goal is then for the digital actors to take that context to tie it together into a cohesive story. To do so, we used a template-based approach, choosing and filling story templates based on the resulting context of the pattern game. Taking a template based approach to story generation; we first generated a library of story templates which indicate how different types of stories are told. For this system, we chose to generate stories similar to the types of stories in Aesop's fables [17] as they are short and simple, yet still have a moral or lesson. We generated a set of twenty-five story templates, somewhat similar to the children's word game "MadLibs" [18]. The goal was to be able to generate stories which were both original or novel and interesting. This was done by making the templates simple, with parameterized actors, locations, objects, and emotions.

Below are two of the twenty-five parameterized templates used by the system. The types of each blank or parameter for the story are defined above each story.

For example, in Story Template #1, the system must fill in the blank labeled "<0>" with a "female-name." This name will be used again throughout the story whenever the "<0>" is referenced. While games such as "MadLibs" reference the parameters by parts of speech and the like, we found that more specific parameter types could result in a more coherent story.

Story Template #1

#	0	female-name
#	1	employee
#	2	employee
#	3	building
#	4	emotion
&		

There once was a woman named <0>. <0> wanted very much to be a <1>, but no one thought she could do it. To become a <1>, <0> went to the <3>, where all of the <1> people gather. Unfortunately when <0> got to the <3>, she found out that all of the <1> people had become <2> people. <0> felt <4>.

Story Template #2

#	0	male-name
#	1	material
#	2	school-subject
#	3	tool
#	4	material
&		

<0> was taking a class in <2>. For his <2> class, <0> had to build a project. <0> had planned to use a <3> to build his project out of <1>. It turned out that his <3> did not work on <1>, so he had to use <4> instead.

One important feature of these templates is the notion of "call backs." In performing a *one word story*, human actors often make reference to actors, objects, locations, or actions that were previously mentioned in the story by another performer. To include this concept in our digital improvisers performance of a *one word story*, the templates include places where the type based parameters are repeated, using "call backs" to give the story a cohesive feel. The *one word story*, by the nature of its implementation, will also make call backs to the topics mentioned in the *pattern game*.

In a performance, the agency took a generated pattern game performance context, found the most relevant template, and filled that template with words from or related to the pattern game context. The details of this process have been omitted for brevity, but can be found in [9]. The final backend system is one that uses all the methods described above in order to generate a *one word story*. The system begins with the set of words generated in a *pattern game* performance. From there, it chooses the most appropriate template using the method described above. To fill the template, it chooses the words from the type based list that are most closely matched to the set of words from the *pattern game*, often using those exact words. When faced with a decision between words to choose, it uses selectional restriction to find the most appropriate word to fill a blank.

Below is a table containing two examples of *pattern games* and *one word stories*, both generated by *the Association Engine*:

Pattern Game	One Word Story
"Music, fine art, art, creation, creative, inspiration, brainchild, product, production, magazine, newspaper, issue, exit, outlet, out."	"An artist named Colleen called her friend Alicia. Colleen wanted to go to the production at the music hall. Colleen and Alicia met up at the music hall. To their surprise there was no production at the music hall. Instead the women decided to go to the stage."
"Student, neophyte, initiate, tyro, freshman, starter, recruit, fledgling, entrant, beginner, novice, learner, apprentice, expert, commentator."	"There once was a woman named Lauren. Lauren wanted very much to be a student, but no one thought she could do it. To become a student, Lauren went to the institution, where all of the student people gather. Unfortunately, when Lauren got to the institution, she found out that all of the student people had become scholar people. Lauren felt diffidence."

The Association Engine

To exhibit the backend content creation, and create a compelling interactive performance, we chose to embody the digital actors with animated faces (see Figure 7 – complements of Ken Perlin's Responsive Face Project [19, 20]). Using speech generation and lip syncing, we now have a team of five digital improvisers that are capable of voicing their contributions in an embodied avatar. In addition to the five embodied digital actors, we chose to supplement the performance with a collective word space, representing the collection of words chosen so far, and the association space around them. For this, we used a word cloud to display previously contributed words. An image of the full installation including the five actors and supplemental display is shown in Figure 8.

Fig. 7 Four faces, adapted from Perlin's original Responsive Face

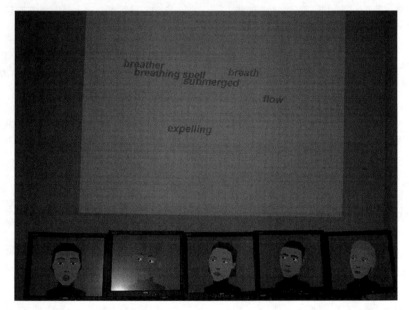

Fig. 8 *The Association Engine* in action

Given our set of embodied actors, it soon became evident that using an embodied actor put more constraints on making the improvisers' interaction seem realistic. Things like timing, expression, turning, and tilting of the heads become much more meaningful. The digital actor must be empowered with some reasoning for how to act like a human improviser would.

The system not only addressed the task of generating a novel contribution to the team, given the context of the warm-up thus far; it had to make this contribution in a timely manner that kept the flow of the warm-up and beat of the team in tact. In our first pass at building an embodied troupe of digital improvisers, we found that the associations were unrealistically quick, too fast for a human actor to possibly consider the association space and make a contribution. Our first step at improving this involved a change made to the presentation of the *one word story*. Instead of presenting just one word at a time, each actor would contribute a phrase to the story. The phrase consisted of one uncommon word (non stop word), and the remaining words before the uncommon word. For example, "up the hill" and "into the forest" are sample phrases. "Hill" and "forest" are uncommon words, while "up," "the," and "into" all occur on a list of common terms.

In addition to this improvement, we instilled the actors with a notion of beats, that is, moments which have a meaning in the performance. The moments that became important or evident in the troupe were: listening to others, thinking of an association, and speaking an association. When listening to others, the digital actors are attentive by looking at the actor currently speaking, that is, their eyes and head are turned to face them, and their head is tilted to the side in a thoughtful position. While thinking of an association, it's important that the actors pause long enough to convey a genuine thought process. When speaking an association, the actor turns forward to face the audience.

Experiencing a Performance

Finally, the *Association Engine* in its final form was capable of interacting with an audience member in order to generate a performance autonomously. The user would approach the system picture in Figure 8 and suggest a seed word for the performance. Following this suggestion, the digital improvisers would perform a pattern game and one word story from the viewer's seed word. The performance could be experienced through the digital improvisers voices, but was also supplemented with the visual word cloud to emphasize/remind viewers of the performance space.

The *Association Engine* was exhibited at the 2004 *Performing Imagination Festival* at Northwestern University. It was shown in its full form, as pictured in Figure 5. Viewers interacted with the system by typing in a seed word which began the *pattern game*, followed by a *one word story*. Feedback from the Festival was positive and grounded in a larger community including professors and students of film, studio art, theater, and performance art.

The *Association Engine's* pattern game backend was also exhibited as part of a larger installation in the 2004 *PAC (Performing Arts Chicago) Edge Festival*. The installation was called Handle with Care: Direct Mail and the American Dream. The leading artist of the piece was GirlCharlie. The installation was set up as a staged living room with two recliners, a table, and walls covered in "direct mail." In the headrests of the recliners were installed sets of speakers. The speakers played the sounds of *the Association Engine*, computer generated voices, doing free association from seed words such as "urgency," "danger," "accusation," "patriots," "outraged," "sick," "homosexuals," "vicious," and "imminent," all highly evocative and emotional words manually extracted from the real hate mail the lined the walls. *The Association Engine* was used to heighten the feelings of fear and fraud that one may feel when reading such mail.

Completely Automated Performances

Through work on *the Association Engine*, we became interested in stories, and the task of artificially generating them. Researchers in the field of Artificial Intelligence have been attempting to build machines that can generate stories for decades. Since much of Artificial Intelligence is concerned with understanding human intelligence, many researchers study how knowledge is acquired, represented and stored in our minds. Some theories of knowledge representation cite stories, also called cases, as the core representation schema in our minds [21, 22]. They explain that these stories are indexed in our memory by their attributes (locations, situations, etc.). Stories are sometimes thought to be how memories are represented; so the ability to understand, learn from, and tell stories could be seen as a measure of intelligence. From that metric, it's clear why many Artificial Intelligence researchers have focused their careers on building machines that are able to both understand and tell stories.

In the 1970s, many researchers began to build story generation systems, the most famous of which was Tale-Spin. Tale-Spin [23, 24, 25] used a world simulation model and planning approach for story generation. To generate stories, Tale-Spin triggered one of the characters with a goal and used natural language generation to narrate the plan for reaching that goal. The stories were simplistic in their content (using a limited amount of encoded knowledge) as well as their natural language generation. Klein's Automatic Novel Writer [26] uses a world simulation model in order to produce murder novels from a set of locations, characters, and motivating personality qualities such as "dishonest" or "flirty." The stories follow a planning system's output as the characters searched for clues. Dehn's Author system [27] was driven by the need for an "author view" to tell stories, as opposed to the "character view" found in world simulation models. Dehn's explanation was that "the author's purpose is to make up a good story" whereas the "character's purpose is to have things go well for himself and for those he cares about" [27]. These three systems are a good representation of the early research done in story generation. They cover both approaches that are structuralist, in the case of the Automatic Novel Writer where a predefined story structure is encoded, and transformationalist, in the cases of Tale-Spin and Author [28] which generated stories based on a set of rules or goals.

Over the past several decades, research in story generation has continued. Recent work has taken a new spin; using various modern approaches in an attempt to solve this classic AI problem [29, 30, 31]. Make-Believe [28] makes use of the structure and content of Open Mind Commonsense (OMCS), a large-scale knowledge base, in order to form stories. It extracts cause-effect relationships from OMCS and represents them in an accessible manner. After taking a sentence from the user to start the story, it forms a causal chain starting with the state represented in the sentence. The end result is a simple story that represents a chain of events. Similar to Make-Believe, many others have taken the approach of interactive story telling systems, which take advantage of the creativity of their users in providing seed sentences and on going interactions [32, 33, 34]. Brutus [35, 36] uses a more knowledge representation intensive method to tell stories with literary themes, such as betrayal. The stories often intentionally omit some key details to leave the reader with a bit of mystery. The stories are more interesting, but at the cost of being less automated since each portrayal of an interesting theme must be represented for the system.

Some recent systems have taken a Case Based Reasoning approach to story and plot generation [37]. Minstrel [38, 39] uses case based reasoning, still within the confines of a problem-solving approach to story generation. The case base is a hand coded based of known stories, which is used to extract plot structures. The goals for the problem solving system are devised from an author view (as Dehn proposed) as opposed to a character point of view. These goals exist across four categories: dramatic, presentation, consistency and thematic. This system, along with Brutus, seem to be a huge step closer to generating stories that are interesting to a reader and that embody many of the traits of good stories.

Story Discovery

In general, previous story generation systems faced a trade-off between a scalable system, and one that can generate coherent stories. Besides Dehn's Author, early systems in this area did not employ a strong model of the aesthetic constraints of story telling. More recent work on story generation has taken a more interactive approach, leverage input from humans, or taking a case based approach to achieve greater variance.

In facing the task of enabling *the Association Engine* to generate a story, we began to examine how people tell stories. They don't create them out of thin air, they typically take pieces of experiences, or stories that they have heard, and adapt them. Taking the notion of leveraging input from humans a step further, it is possible to use the vast internet itself as "human input" – shifting the goal from story generation to story discovery. The emergence of weblogs (blogs) and other types of user-generated content has transformed the internet from a professionally produced collection of sites into a vast compilation of personal thoughts, experiences, opinions and feelings. The movement of the production of online news, stories, videos and images beyond the desks of major production companies to personal computers has provided internet users with access to the feelings and experiences of many as opposed to merely professionally edited content.

While this collection of blogs is vast, only a subset of blog entries contains subjectively interesting stories. Using what we know from previous story generation systems to inform story discovery, we define a stronger model for the aesthetic elements of stories and use that to drive retrieval of stories, and to filter and evaluate results. *Buzz* is a system that exemplifies this notion of story discovery [11, 40]. *Buzz* is a digital theater installation consisting of four digital actors that autonomously find and extract their performance content. Specifically, they discover compelling stories from the blogosphere, and perform those stories.

The *Buzz* backend is enabled with a representation of the qualities of compelling stories. These qualities range from high-level qualities such as the topic and emotional impact of the story to simply qualities such as its length. In addition to these qualities, *Buzz* was also encoded with a set of terms that appear frequently within

Table 1 A set of stories retrieved and presented by *Buzz* [11, 40]

my husband and i got into a fight on saturday night; he was drinking and neglectful, and i was feeling tired and pregnant and needy. it's easy to understand how that combination could escalate, and it ended with hugs and sorries, but now i'm feeling fragile. like i need more love than i'm getting, like i want to be hugged tight for a few hours straight and right now, like i want a dozen roses for no reason, like a vulnerable little kid without a saftey blankie. fragile and little and i'm not eating the crusts on my sandwich because they're yucky. i want to pout and stomp until i get attention and somebody buys me a toy to make it all better. maybe i'm resentful that he hasn't gone out of his way to make it up to me, hasn't done little things to show me he really loves me, and so the bad feeling hasn't been wiped away. i shouldn't feel that way. it's stupid; i know he loves me and is devoted and etc. yet i just want a little something extra to make up for what i lost through our fighting. i just want a little extra love in my cup, since some of it drained.

I have a confession. It's getting harder and harder to blindly love the people who made George W Bush president. It's getting harder and harder to imagine a day when my heart won't ache for what has been lost and what we could have done to prevent it. It's getting harder and harder to accept excuses for why people I respect and in some cases dearly love are seriously and perhaps deliberately uninformed about what matters most to them in the long run.

I had a dream last night where I was standing on the beach, completely alone, probably around dusk, and I was holding a baby. I had it pulled close to my chest, and all I could feel was this completely overwhelming, consuming love for this child that I was holding, but I didn't seem to have any kind of intellectual attachment to it. I have no idea whose it was, and even in the dream, I don't think it was mine, but I wanted more than anything to just stand and hold this baby.

interesting stories such as "I had a dream last night" or "I have a confession to make." Using these queries as a starting point, Buzz spans the blogosphere looking for blog posts that include one of these phrases. For each post it finds, it extracts the full text of the post, and then packages this post as a "candidate story." The candidate stories are then passed through a filtering and modification engine driven by the encoded "qualities of compelling stories" listed above. Posts that do not match these qualifications are discarded – resulting in a 2% acceptance rate for candidate stories. The remaining stories are modified according to the needs of the performance (shortened, punctuation inserted, etc). Table 1 shows examples of stories retrieved by the *Buzz* story discovery system.

As *Buzz* is a digital theater installation, the performance itself is just as important as the generation of compelling content. The *Buzz* performance engine was informed by the work with beats and believable actions in the Association Engine. It included the same set of four virtual actors, as well as a word cloud that displayed the most emotionally evocative words fro the current story being performed (see Figure 9). The actors would trade of telling complete stories; while one actor is telling a story, all the other actors are attentive, turning to look at the actor speaking. For more information on the performance side of *Buzz*, see [11]. *Buzz* created a performance through retrieving content from the web. As the web and the blogosphere continue to grow, the abundance of online content will enable more and more automated theatrical performance such as *Buzz*.

Fig. 9   An installation of *Buzz* at Northwestern University

Conclusions

In this article, we presented work that encompasses the goals of modern digital theater systems. These systems both engage the audience in an interactive theatrical
experience and employ the machine to generate novel and compelling performance
content. As our society trend away from broadcast experiences towards highly
personalized entertainment continues, so too does the likely large-scale impact of
digital theater systems. While digital theater systems are not yet ubiquitous, it is
clear that there is a strong potential for compelling interactive experiences that will
have a large impact on the future of theater.

References

1. Sparacino F. DirectIVE: Choreographing Media for Interactive Virtual Environments. Master
   Thesis, MIT Media Lab, 1996.
2. Sparacino F., Devenport G., and Pentland A. Media in performance: Interactive spaces for
   dance, theater, circus and museum exhibits. IBM Systems Journal, 39(3–4), 2000.
3. Sparacino F., Hall K., Wren C., Davenport G., and Pentland A. Improvisational theaterspace.
   In The Sixth Biennal Symposium for Arts and Technology, Connecticut College, New London,
   CT, 1997.
4. Carlson M. Theories of the Theatre: A historical and critical survey, from Greeks to the
   Present. Cornell University Press, 1984.
5. Brockett O. The History of the theater. Allyn and Bacon, Inc., 5th edition, 1987.

6. Point Grey Research Inc. [Online]. Available from: <http://www.ptgrey.com>
7. ARToolKit [Online]. Available from: <http://www.hitl.washington.edu/artoolkit/>
8. Vasilakos, A., Cheok, A.D., Nguyen, T.H.D., Qui, T.C.T. and Chen, L.C. (2008) 'Interactive theater via wearable computers and mixed reality with ambient intelligence' *Information Sciences* (Elsevier), Vol. 178, pp.679–663.
9. Owsley Sara, Shamma D. A., Hammond K., Bradshaw S., Sood S., "The Association Engine: A Free Associative Digital Improviser." An Art Demonstration. ACM Multimedia 2004.
10. Shamma, D. A., S. Owsley, et al. (2004). Network Arts: Exposing Cultural Reality. The International World Wide Web Conference. New York.
11. Sood, Sara Owsley. Compelling Computation: Strategies for Mining the Interesting. PhD Thesis, 2007.
12. Napier, M. (2004). Improvise: Scene From The Inside Out. Portsmouth, NH, Heinemann.
13. Beeferman, D. (1998). Lexical discovery with an enriched semantic network. Workshop on Applications of WordNet in Natural Language Processing Systems, ACL/COLING.
14. Csikszentmihalyi, M. (1991). Flow: The Psychology of Optimal Experience, Harper Perennial.
15. WordNet. (1997). "WordNet." 2004, from http://wordnet.princeton.edu/
16. Shamma, D., S. Owsley, et al. (2004). Using Web Frequency Within Multimedia Exhibitions. ACM Multimedia. New York, ACM Press.
17. Pinkney, J. (2000). Aesop's Fables, SeaStar.
18. Price, R. and L. Stern (1974). The Original Mad Libs 1, Price Stern Sloan.
19. Perlin, K. (1996). "Responsive Face Project.
20. Perlin, K. and A. Goldberg (1996). "Improv: A System for Scripting Interactive Actors in Virtual Worlds." Computer Graphics 29(3).
21. Schank, R. C. (1990). Tell Me A Story. Evanston, IL, Northwestern University Press.
22. Schank, R. C. (1999). Dynamic Memory Revisited. Cambridge, United Kingdom, Cambridge University Press.
23. Schank, R. C. and R. Abelson (1977). Scripts Plans Goals and Understanding: An Inquiry into Human Knowledge Structures. Hillsdale, New Jersey, Lawrence Erlbaum Associates, Publishers.
24. Meehan, J. R. (1977). Tale-spin, an interactive program that writes stories. the 5th IJCAI.
25. Meehan, J. R. (1981). TALE-SPIN and Micro TALE-SPIN. Inside Computer Understanding. R. Schank and C. Riesbeck. Hillsdale, NJ, Erlbaum: 197 to 258.
26. Klein, S., J. Aeschlimann, et al. (1973). Automatic novel writing., University of Wisconsin Madison.
27. Dehn, N. (1981). Story Generation after Tale-Spin. Seventh Internation Joint Conference on Artificial Intelligence. University of British Columbia.
28. Liu, H. and P. Singh (2002). MakeBelieve: Using commonsense knowledge to generate stories. Eighteenth National Conference on Artificial Intelligence and Fourteenth Conference on Innovative Applications of Artificial Intelligence.
29. Smith, S. and J. Bates (1989). Towards a theory of narrative for interactive fiction. Pittsburgh, PA, Carnegie Melon University.
30. Murray, J. (1997). Hamlet on the Holodeck: The Future of Narrative in Cyberspace, The Free Press.
31. Mateas, M. and P. Sengers (1999). Narrative Intelligence. AAAI 1999 Fall Symposium Series.
32. Mateas, M. (2001). "Expressive AI: A hybrid art and science practice." Leonardo: Journal of the International Society for Arts, Sciences, and Technology 34(2): 147–153.
33. Mateas, M., S. Domike, et al. (1999). Terminal time: An ideologically-biased history machine. AISB Symposium on Artificial Intelligence and Creative Language: Stories and Humor.
34. Domike, S., M. Mateas, et al., Eds. (2003). The recombinant history apparatus presents: Terminal Time. Narrative Intelligence. Amsterdam, John Benjamins.
35. Bringsjord, S. and D. A. Ferrucci (2000). Artificial Intelligence and Literary Creativity. Mahwah, NJ, Erlbaum.

36. Sousa, R. d. (2000). "Artificial Intelligence and Literacy Creativity: Inside the Mind of BRUTUS, a Storytelling Machine." Computational Linguistics 26(4): 642–647.
37. Gervas, P., B. Diaz-Agudo, et al. (2005). "Story plot generation based on CBR." Knowledge based systems 18(4–5): 235–242.
38. Oatley, K. (1994). "The Creative Process: A computer model of storytelling and creativity." Computational Linguistics 21(4): 579–581.
39. Turner, S. R. (1994). The Creative Process: A computer model of storytelling and creativity. Hillsdale, NJ, Lawrence Erlbaum Associates.
40. Sood, Sara Owsley. Buzz: Mining and Presenting Interesting Stories. The International Journal of Art and Technology V1 N1, 2008.

Chapter 20
Video Browsing on Handheld Devices

Wolfgang Hürst

Introduction

Recent improvements in processing power, storage space, and video codec development enable users now to playback video on their handheld devices in a reasonable quality. However, given the form factor restrictions of such a mobile device, screen size still remains a natural limit and – as the term "handheld" implies – always will be a critical resource. This is not only true for video but any data that is processed on such devices. For this reason, developers have come up with new and innovative ways to deal with large documents in such limited scenarios. For example, if you look at the iPhone, innovative techniques such as flicking have been introduced to skim large lists of text (e.g. hundreds of entries in your music collection). Automatically adapting the zoom level to, for example, the width of table cells when double tapping on the screen enables reasonable browsing of web pages that have originally been designed for large, desktop PC sized screens. A multi touch interface allows you to easily zoom in and out of large text documents and images using two fingers.

In the next section, we will illustrate that advanced techniques to browse large video files have been developed in the past years, as well. However, if you look at state-of-the-art video players on mobile devices, normally just simple, VCR like controls are supported (at least at the time of this writing) that only allow users to just start, stop, and pause video playback. If supported at all, browsing and navigation functionality is often restricted to simple skipping of chapters via two single buttons for backward and forward navigation and a small and thus not very sensitive timeline slider.

One might assume that more advanced and complex browsing techniques are just not needed for mobile video. However, recent studies indicate that such functionality might actually be even more important in a mobile context. In the following, we will review some of these evaluations and identify examples that illustrate the importance of video browsing techniques for mobile video usage. Offering such functionality given the small form factor of the screen and the limited interaction

W. Hürst (✉)
Faculty of Science, Utrecht University, Utrecht, The Netherlands
e-mail: huerst@cs.uu.nl

B. Furht (ed.), *Handbook of Multimedia for Digital Entertainment and Arts*,
DOI 10.1007/978-0-387-89024-1_20, © Springer Science+Business Media, LLC 2009

capabilities of handheld devices is a difficult task that is yet unsolved. In the remainder of the article, we summarize our ongoing work in developing better interfaces that offer a richer browsing experience and therefore better usability of mobile video.

A Short Review of Video Browsing Techniques for Larger Displays

When browsing video, for example, to get an overview of the content of a file or to localize a specific position in order to answer some information need, there are normally two major problems. First, video is a continuous medium that changes over time. With a static medium such as text, people always see some context at a time and can decide themselves at which speed they look at it. In contrast to this, for video only a single frame of a sequence of time-ordered frames is shown for a time slot that depends on the playback speed (e.g. 1/25 sec for a typical video playback rate). Second, there is often not much meta-information available to support users in their search and browsing tasks. Again, think about browsing the pages of a book. Besides the actual content, there is meta-information encoded, for example, in the header and footer. Spatial information such as the separation in different paragraphs illustrates related parts with regards to content. Headlines give a short summary of the following content. Different font styles, such as bold face or italic, are used to highlight important information, and so on. In addition, higher level meta-information exists such as an abstract printed on the cover of the book, the content list at its beginning, etc. All of this meta-information supports users in various browsing task. For video however, comparable information is usually missing.

Not surprisingly, most existing research in digital video browsing tries to make up for this lack of meta-information by automatically extracting comparable information from videos and representing it in an appropriate way that supports users in their browsing tasks (cf. Figure 1). For example, automatic segmentation techniques are often used to identify content-related parts of a video [13, 17]. This structure information can be displayed and used for navigation (e.g. jumping from scene to scene using dedicated buttons) in order to make up of the missing structure information encoded in paragraphs and spaces between them in printed text. Single key frames can be extracted from a scene and represented as a storyboard, that is, a visual arrangement of thumbnails containing the key frames where the spatial order represents the temporal alignment in the video [4, 16]. This static representation can be used to get a rough idea of the video's content, similarly to the content list in a book. One variation, so called Video Mangas, represent different scenes in a comic book style where thumbnail sizes depend on the relevance of the related scene, thus resembling the hierarchical structure of a content list [2, 18]. Another variation of storyboards, so called video skims or moving storyboards pay tribute to the dynamic nature of video. Here, the static thumbnail representation is replaced with a short video clip that offers a glimpse into the related scene [3]. On a higher level,

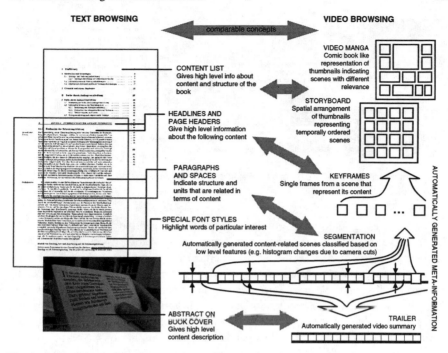

Fig. 1 Comparing content-based video browsing approaches with text skimming

automatically generated trailers offer a high level overview of a video's content and can thus be compared to the abstract often found on the back side of a book's cover [11]. Because all of these approaches are based on the actual structure or content of a file, we will subsequently refer to them as *content-based approaches*. Figure 1 summarizes how they relate to text browsing thus illustrating the initial claim that most of the work on video browsing aims at making up for the missing meta-information commonly available for text.

The usefulness of such content-based approaches for video browsing has been confirmed by various evaluations and user studies. However, when browsing text, people do not only look at meta-data, but also skim the actual content at different speeds and levels of detail. For example, when grabbing a new book, they often skim it in flip-book style in order to get a rough overview. They browse a single page by quickly moving their eyes over it and catch a glimpse of a few single words allowing them to get a rough idea of the content. If they run over something that might be of particular interest, they quickly move their eyes back, read a few sentences, and so on. Hence, they skim text by moving their eyes over the content at different speeds and in random directions. Their visual perception allows them to make sense of the snatches of information they are picking up by filtering out irrelevant information and identifying parts of major interest.

Unfortunately, such intuitive and flexible ways for data browsing are not possible for a dynamic medium such as video. Due to its continuous nature, people can not

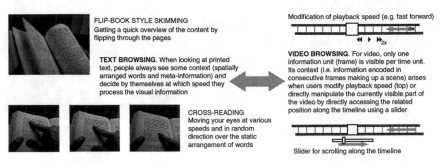

Fig. 2 Comparing timeline-based video browsing approaches with text skimming

move their eyes spatially over a video. However, comparable to how readers are able to make sense of the snatches of information they grasp when moving their eyes quickly over a printed text, the visual perception of the human brain is able to classify certain parts of the content of a video even if played back at higher speeds or in reverse direction. We call video browsing approaches that try to take advantage of this characteristic subsequently *timeline-based approaches*. In related techniques, users control what part of the video they see at a particular time by manipulating the current position on the timeline. This is comparable to implicitly specifying which part of a text is currently seen by moving ones eyes over the printed content.

Figure 2 illustrates how such temporal movements along the timeline when skimming a video relate to spatial movements of your eyes over printed text. The most obvious approach to achieve something like this is to enable users to manipulate playback speed. This technique is well known from analog VCRs where fast forward and backward buttons are provided to skim forward or backward. Since digital video is not limited by the physical characteristics of an actual tape, but only by the time it takes to decode the encoded signal, we are usually able to provide users with a much larger variety of different browsing speeds. Alternatively to manipulation of playback speed, people can often also navigate a video by dragging the thumb of a slider representing the video's timeline. If visual feedback from the file is provided in real-time, such an approach can be used to quickly skim larger parts of a file, abruptly stop and change scrolling speed and direction, and so on, thus offering more flexibility than modification of replay speed. On the other hand, increasing or decreasing playback speed seems to be a better and more intuitive choice when users want to continuously browse larger parts of a document at a constant speed or if the information they are looking for is encoded into the temporal changes of an object in the video.

Both approaches enable users to perceive visual information from a video in a comparably flexible way to moving their eyes over text when browsing the content of a book. It should also be noted that in both cases, browsing of static media such as text as well as dynamic media such as video, the content-based browsing approaches summarized in Figure 1 also differ from the timeline-based ones illustrated in Figure 2 in a way that for content-based approaches, users generally browse some meta-data that was preprocessed by the system (e.g. headlines or extracted

key frames), whereas for timeline-based approaches, they usually manipulate themselves what part of the content they see at a particular point in time (either by moving
their eyes over text at random speed or by using interface elements to manipulate
the timeline of a video). Hence, none of the two concepts is superior to the other but
they both complement each other and it depends on the actual browsing task as well
as personal preference which approach is preferred in a particular situation.

Mobile Video Usage and Need for Browsing

Even though screen sizes are obviously a limiting factor for mobile video, improvements in image quality and resolution have recently led to a viewing experience
that in many situations seems reasonable and acceptable for users. In addition, techniques for automatic panning and scanning [12] and adequate zooming [10] offer
great potential for video viewing on handhelds although they have not made it to
the market yet. Recent reports claim that mobile video usage, although still being
small, is facing considerable rates of growth with "continued year-over-year growth
of mobile video consumption"[1].

Observing that mobile video finally seems to take of, it is interesting to notice
that so far, most mobile video players only offer very limited browsing functionality, if supported at all. Given that we can assume that established future usage
patterns for mobile video will differ from watching traditional TV (a claim shared
by Belt et al. [1]), one might wonder if intensive mobile video browsing might not
be needed or required by the users. Indeed, a real-life study on the usage of mobile TV presented by Belt at al. [1] indicated little interest in interactive services.
However, the authors themselves claim that this might also be true do to a lack of
familiarity with such advanced functions. In addition, the study focused on live TV
where people obviously have different expectations for its consumption on mobiles.
In contrast to this, the study on the usage of mobile video on handheld devices
presented by O'Hara et al. [14] did report several mobile usage scenarios and situations that already included massive video browsing or would most likely profit
from improved navigation functionality. For example, in one case, a group of four
kids gathered around on PSP (Sony's PlayStation®Portable) in order to watch and
talk about the scenes of their favorite movie that each of them liked the most. Such
an activity does not only require massive interaction to find the related scene, but
also continuously going backwards in order to replay and watch particular parts
again to discuss them or because they have not been well perceived by some of the

---

[1] The quote was taken from an online article from November 4, 2008, that was posted at http://
www.cmswire.com/cms/mobile/mobile-video-growing-but-still-niche-003453.php (accessed Feb
1, 2009) and discussed a related report by comScore. On January 8, 2009, MediaWeek reported
comparable arguments from a report issued by the Nielsen Company, cf. http://www.mediaweek.
com/mw/content_display/news/media-agencies-research/e3i746   3e6c2968d742bad51c7faf7439
adc (accessed Feb 1, 2009).

participants due to the small screen size. Ojala et al. [15] present a study in which several users experimented with multimedia content delivered to their device in a stadium during hockey games. According to their user study, the "most desired content was video footage from the ongoing match". Reasonable applications of such data streams would be to get a different view of the game (e.g., a close up of the player closest to the puck that complements the overview sight of the hockey field they have from their seat) but also the opportunity to re-watch interesting scenes (e.g. replays of goals or critical referee decisions) – a scenario that would require significant interaction and video browsing activity.

At this rather early stage of video usage on handhelds, we can only speculate what kind of browsing activities users would be willing and interested to really do on their mobiles once given the opportunity. However, the examples given above demonstrate that there are indeed lots of scenarios where users in a mobile context would be able to take advantage of advanced browsing functionality, or which would only be feasible if their system offers such technologies in an intuitive and useful way. In the following section, we present an example that is related to the study in a hockey stadium done by Ojala et al. [15] but extends the described scenario to a fictional case illustrating the possibilities advanced browsing functionalities could offer in order to increase the mobile video user experience.

Timeline-Based Mobile Video Browsing and Related Problems

In order to motivate the following interface designs and illustrate the most critical problems for timeline-based mobile video browsing, let's look at a simple example. Assume you are watching a live game in a soccer stadium. The game is also transmitted via mobile TV onto your mobile phone. In addition, live streams from different cameras placed in the stadium are provided. Having a large storage space (common newer multimedia smart phones already offer storage of up to 16GB, for example), you can store all these live streams locally and then have instant access to all videos on your local device. The study related to hockey games presented by Ojala et al. [15] (cf. previous section) confirmed that such a service might be useful and would most likely be appreciated and used intensively by many sports fans. But what kind of browsing functionality would be necessary? What could and would many people like to do (i.e. search or browse for)? We can think of many interesting and useful scenarios. For example, it would be good to have some system generated labels indicating important scenes, goals, etc. that users might want to browse during halftime. During the game, people might want to quickly go back in a video stream in order to review a particular situation, such as a clever tactical move leading to a goal or an offside situation, a foul, a critical decision from the referee, etc. In the latter case, it can be useful to be able to navigate through the video at a very fine level of detail – even frame by frame, for example to identify the one single frame that best illustrates if a ball was indeed outside or not. Such a scenario would require easy and intuitive but yet powerful and ambitious browsing functionality.

For example, people should be able to quickly switch between browsing on a larger scale (e.g. to locate a scene before the ball went outside of the playfield) and very sensitive navigation along the timeline (e.g. to locate a single frame that illustrates best which player was the last to touch it). It is also important to keep in mind that the related interactions are done by a user who is standing in a soccer stadium (and probably quite excited about the game or a questionable decision by the referee) and thus neither willing nor able to fully concentrate on a rather complex and sensitive interaction task. Given the small form factor and the limited interaction possibilities of handheld devices this clearly makes high demands on the interface design and the integration of the offered browsing functionality.

Obviously, the content-based approaches known from traditional video browsing could be quite useful for some higher level semantic browsing, for example when users want to view all goals or fouls during halftime. For a more advanced interaction, for example to check if a ball was outside of the field or not, timeline-based approaches seem to be a good choice. For example, by moving a slider thumb quickly backwards along the timeline, a user can identify a critical scene (e.g. an offside) that is then further explored in more detail (e.g. by moving the slider thumb back and forth in a small range in order to identify a frame confirming that it was indeed an offside).

However, one significant problem with this approach is that sliders do not scale to large document files. Due to the limited space that is available on the screen, not every position from a long video can be mapped onto a position on the slider. Thus, even the smallest possible movement of a slider's thumb (i.e. one pixel on the screen) will result in a larger jump in the file, making it impossible to do a detailed navigation and access individual frames. In addition, grabbing and manipulating the tiny icon of a slider's thumb on a mobile is often considered hard and unpleasant. Interfaces that allow users to browse a video by manipulating its playback speed often provide a slider-like interaction element as well in order to let users select from a continuous range of speed values. Although the abovementioned scaling problem of sliders might appear here as well, it is usually less critical because normally, not that many values, that is, levels of playback speed need to be mapped to the slider's length. However, the second problem, that is, targeting and operating a very tiny icon during interaction remains (and becomes especially critical in situations such as standing in a crowded soccer stadium).

In the following, we will present different interface designs for handheld devices that deal with these problems by providing an interaction experience that is explicitly optimized for touch screen based input on mobiles. The first four approaches realize timeline-based approaches – both navigation along the timeline at different levels of granularity and skimming the file by using different playback rates (cf. Fig. 2) – whereas the fifth approach presents a content-based approach that also takes into account another important characteristic we often observe in mobile scenarios: that often, people only have one hand available for operating the device. Research on interfaces for mobile video browsing is just at its beginning and an area of active investigation. The question of how both interaction concepts can seamlessly be integrated into one single interface is yet unanswered and thus part of our ongoing and future research.

Implementation

All interfaces presented in the next two sections are optimized for pen-based interaction with a touch sensitive display. Touch screen based interaction has become an
important trend in mobile computing due to the tremendous success of the iPhone.
So far, we restricted ourselves to pen-based operation in our research, although
some of the designs presented below might be useful for finger-based interaction as
well. All proposed solutions have been implemented on a Dell AXIM^{TM} X51v PDA
which was one of the high end devices at the time we started the related projects.
Meanwhile, there are various other mobile devices (PDAs as well as cell phones)
offering similar performance. Our Dell PDA features an Intel XScal, PXA 270,
624 MHz processor, 64 MB SDRAM, 256 MB FlashROM, and an Intel 2700g co-
processor for hardware-side video encoding. The latter one is particularly important
for advanced video processing as it is required by our browsing applications. The device has a 3.7-inch screen with a resolution of 640×480 pixels and a touch sensitive
surface for pen-based operation. Our interfaces have been implemented in C + + on
the Windows Mobile 5 platform on top of TCPMP (The Core Pocket Media Player)
which is a high-performance open source video player. The implementation was
based on the Win32 API using the Graphics Device Interface for rendering.

   For all approaches we present below, audio feedback is paused when users start
browsing the visual information of a video stream. We believe that there are lots of
situations where approaches to browse the audio stream are equally or sometimes
maybe even more important than navigation in the visual part of a video. However,
at the time we started these projects, technical limitations of the available devices
prevented us from addressing related issues. With newer, next generation models,
this issue certainly becomes interesting and therefore should be addressed as part of
future work (cf. the outlook at the end of this article). All our implementations have
been evaluated in different user studies. In the following, we will only summarize
the most important and interesting observations. For a detailed description of the
related experiments as well as further implementation details and design decisions
we refer to the articles that are cited in the respective sections.

Flicking vs. Elastic Interfaces

As already mentioned in the introduction, the iPhone uses a technique called *flicking* to enable users to skim large lists of text, for example all entries of your music
collection. For flicking, users touch the screen and move their finger in the direction
they want to navigate as if they want to push the list upwards or downwards. Upon
releasing the finger from the screen, the list keeps scrolling with a speed that slowly
decreases till it comes to a complete stop. The underlying metaphor can be explained
with two rolls each of which holding one end of the list (cf. Figure 3). Pushing the
rolls faster increases scrolling speed in the respective direction. Releasing the finger

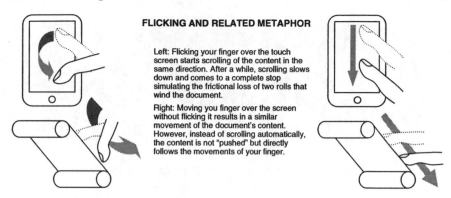

FLICKING AND RELATED METAPHOR

Left: Flicking your finger over the touch screen starts scrolling of the content in the same direction. After a while, scrolling slows down and comes to a complete stop simulating the frictional loss of two rolls that wind the document.

Right: Moving you finger over the screen without flicking it results in a similar movement of the document's content. However, instead of scrolling automatically, the content is not "pushed" but directly follows the movements of your finger.

Fig. 3   Scrolling text lists on the iPhone by flicking

By flicking their fingers over the touch screen, users can "push" the video along the timeline.

Fig. 4   Applying flicking to video browsing

causes scrolling to slow down due to frictional loss. If the user does not push the content but the finger rests on the screen while moving it, the list can be moved directly thus allowing some fine adjustment. By modifying how often and how fast the finger is flicking over the touch screen or by changing between flicking and continuous moving users can achieve different scrolling speeds thus giving them a certain variety for fast and slow navigation in a list. Transferring this concept to video browsing is straightforward if we assume the metaphor illustrated in Figure 4. Although the basic idea is identical, it should be noted that it is by no means clear that we can achieve the same level of usability when transferring such an interaction approach to another medium, that is, from text to video. With text, we always see a certain context during browsing, allowing us, for example, to identify paragraph borders and new sections easily even at higher scrolling speeds. With video on the other hand, scene changes are pretty much unpredictable in such a browsing approach. This might turn out to be critical for certain browsing tasks. Based on an initial evaluation that to some degree confirmed these concerns, we introduced an indication of scrolling speed that is visualized at the top of the screen during browsing. In a subsequent user study it turned out that such information can be quite useful in order to provide the users a certain feeling for the scrolling speed which is otherwise lost because of the missing contextual information. Figure 5 shows a snapshot of the actual implementation on our PDA.

Fig. 5 Implementation of flicking for video browsing on a PDA. The bar at the top of the display illustrates the current scrolling speed during forward and backward scrolling

Our second interface design, which also enables users to navigate and thus browse through a video at different scrolling speeds, is based on the concept of elastic interfaces. For elastic interfaces, a slider's thumb is not dragged directly but instead pulled along the timeline using a virtual rubber band that is stretched between the slider thumb and the mouse pointer (or pen, in our case). The slider's thumb follows the pointer's movements at a speed that is proportional to the length of the virtual rubber band. A long rubber band has a high tension, thus resulting in a faster scrolling speed. Shortening the band's length decreases the tension and thus scrolling slows down. Using a clever mapping from band length to scrolling speed, such interfaces allow users to scroll the content of an associated file at different levels of granularity. The concept is illustrated in Figure 6 (left and center). Similarly to flicking, transferring this approach from navigation in static data to scrolling along the timeline of a video is straightforward. However, being forced to hit the timeline in order to drag the slider's thumb can be critical on the small screen of a handheld device. In addition, the full screen mode used per default on such devices prevents us from modifying the rubber band's length at the beginning and the end of a file when scrolling backward and forward, respectively. Hence, we introduced the concept of *elastic panning* [5] which is a generalization of an elastic slider that works without explicit interface elements. Here, scrolling functionality is evoked by simply clicking anywhere on the screen, that is, in our case, the video. This initial clicking position is associated with the current position in the file. Scrolling along the timeline is done by moving the pointer left or right for backward and forward navigation, respectively. Vertical movements of the pointer are ignored. The (virtual) slider thumb and the rubber band are visualized by small icons in order provide maximum feedback without interfering with the actual content. Figure 6 (right) illustrates the elastic panning approach. Photos from the actual interface on the PDA can be found in Figure 7. For implementation details of this approach we refer to [5, 9].

With both implementations we did an initial heuristic evaluation in order to identify design flaws and optimize some parameters such as appropriate levels for frictional loss and a reasonable mapping of rubber band length to scrolling speed. With the resulting interfaces, we did a comparative evaluation with 24 users. After making themselves familiar with the interface, each participant had to solve three

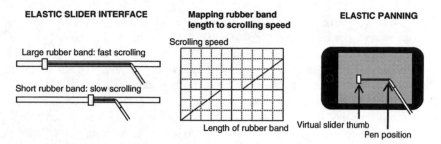

Fig. 6   Elastic interface concepts: slider (left) and panning (right)

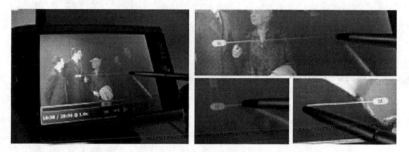

Fig. 7   Implementation of elastic panning for video browsing on a PDA

browsing tasks that required navigation in the file at different levels of granularity: First, on a rather high level (getting an overview by identifying the first four news messages in a new show recording), second, a more specific navigation (finding the approximate beginning of one particular news message), and finally, a very fine granular navigation (finding one of the very few frames showing the map with the temperature overview in the weather forecast).

Flicking and elastic panning are comparable interaction approaches insofar as both can be explained with a physical metaphor – the list or tape on two rolls in one case vs. the rubber band metaphor in the other case. Both allow users to skim a file at different granularity levels by modifying the scrolling or playback speed – in the first case by flicking your finger over the screen with different speeds, in the second case by modifying the length of the virtual rubber band. In both cases it is hard, however, to keep scrolling the file at a constant playback speed similar to the fast forward mode of a traditional VCR due to the frictional loss and the effect of a slowing down slider thumb in result of a shorter rubber band. Despite these similarities, both concepts also have important differences. Dragging the slider thumb by pulling the rubber band usually gives people more control over the scrolling speed than flicking because the can, for example, immediately slow down once they see something interesting. In contrast to this, flicking always requires a user to stop first and then push the file again with a lower momentum. However, being able to do a fine adjustment by resting the finger on the screen is much more flexible, for example, to access single frames than using the slow motion like behavior that results from a very short rubber band. The most interesting and surprising result in the evaluation was therefore that we were not able to identify a significant difference in the average time it took for the users to solve the three browsing tasks. Similarly, average grades calculated from the subjective user ratings given after the evaluation also showed minimum differences. However, when looking at the distribution, it turned out that the ratings for elastic panning were mostly centered around the average whereas for flicking, they were much more distributed, that is, many people rated it as much better or much worse. Given that both interfaces performed equally well in the objective measure, that is, the time to solve the browsing tasks, we can assume that personal preference and pleasure of use played an important role for users when giving their subjective ratings. In addition, flicking is often associated with the iPhone and thus, personal likes or dislikes of the Apple brand might have influenced these ratings as well.

Linear vs. Circular Interaction Patterns

When comparing the flicking and elastic panning approaches from the previous section, it becomes clear that the latter only supports manipulation of playback speed. In contrast to this, flicking also allows a user to modify the actual position of a file, similar to moving a slider's thumb along the timeline of a video, by resting and moving a finger over the screen. However, this kind of position-based navigation along the timeline is only possible in a very short range due to the small size of the device's screen. In the following, we present two approaches that enable users to scroll along the timeline and offer more control over the scrolling granularity, that is, the resolution of the timeline.

Similarly to flicking and elastic panning, scrolling functionality in both cases is evoked without the explicit use of any widget but by doing direct interactions on top of the video. In the first case, clicking anywhere on the screen creates a virtual horizontal timeline. Moving the pointer to the left or right results in backward and forward navigation along the timeline in a similar way as if the slider thumb icon is grabbed and moved along the actual timeline widget. However, the resolution of the virtual timeline on the screen depends on the vertical position of the pen. At the bottom, close to the original slider widget, the timeline has the same coarse resolution. At the very top of the screen, the virtual timeline has the smallest resolution supported by the system, for example, one pixel is mapped to one frame in the video. The resolutions of the virtual timelines in between are linearly interpolated as illustrated in Figure 8. Hence, users have a large variety of different timeline resolutions from which to choose from by moving the pen horizontally at an appropriate vertical level. The resulting scrolling effect is similar to zooming in or out of the original timeline in order to do a finer or coarser, respectively, navigation. Hence, we called this approach the *Mobile ZoomSlider*.

Navigation along the timeline offers certain advantages over manipulation of playback speed in certain situations. For example, many users consider it easier to access individual frames by moving along a fine granular timeline in contrast to

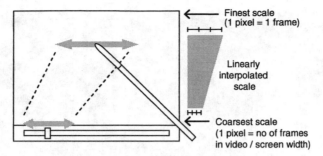

Fig. 8 Mobile ZoomSlider design for timeline scrolling at different granularities

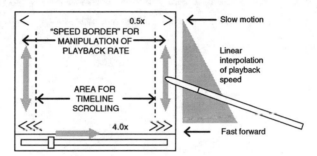

Fig. 9 Modification of playback speed in the Mobile ZoomSlider design

using a slow motion like approach. However, there are also cases where playback speed manipulation might be more useful, for example, when users want to skim a whole file at a constant speed. In the Mobile ZoomSlider design this kind of navigation is supported at the left and right screen border. If the user clicks on the right side of the screen, constant scrolling starts with a playback speed that is proportional to the vertical position of the pen. At the bottom, you get a fast forward like feedback. At the top, video is played back in slow motion. In between, the level of playback speed is linearly interpolated between these two extremes. On the left screen border, you get a similar behavior for backward scrolling. Figure 9 illustrates this behavior. It should be noted that in both cases – the navigation along the timeline in the center of the screen and the modification of playback speed on the screen borders – finer navigation is achieved at the top of the screen whereas the fastest scrolling is done when the pen is located at its bottom. Therefore, users can smoothly switch between both interaction styles by moving the pen horizontally, for example, from the right region supporting playback speed based navigation to the position-based navigation in the center of the screen.

An initial evaluation with 20 users that verified the usability and usefulness of this design can be found in [6]. Figure 10 shows the actual implementation of this interface on our PDA. Similarly to the flicking and elastic panning approaches described above, visualization of additional widgets is kept to a minimum in order to not interfere with the actual content of the video.

Fig. 10 Implementation of the Mobile ZoomSlider design on a PDA.

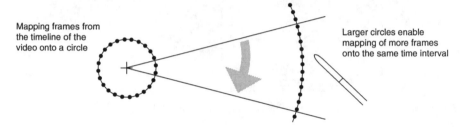

Fig. 11 Basic idea of the ScrollWheel design: mapping timeline onto a circle

The second approach is called the *ScrollWheel* design. Its basic idea is to map the timeline onto a circle. Despite being an intuitive concept due to the similarity to the face of an analog clock, a circle shaped timeline as an important advantage over a linear timeline representation: a circle has no beginning or end and thus, arbitrarily file lengths can be mapped onto it. Not surprisingly, using hardware with knob-like interfaces is very popular for video editing. In our case, we implemented a software version of the circular timeline that can be operated via the PDA's touch screen. Once a user clicks on the screen, the center of the circle is visualized by a small icon in the center of the screen. A specific interval of the video's timeline, for example, five minutes, is then mapped to one full rotation. Compared to a hardware solution, such an implementation has the additional advantage that users can implicitly manipulate the resolution of the timeline and thus scrolling granularity by modifying the radius of their circular movements when navigating the file. Larger circles result in slower movements along a finer timeline whereas smaller circles can be done to quickly skim larger parts of the file as illustrated in Figure 11. The resulting behavior is somehow comparable to the functionality in the center of the Mobile ZoomSlider. Here, users can get a finer scrolling granularity by increasing the distance from the center. With the Mobile ZoomSlider, a similar effect is achieved by increasing the distance between the bottom of the screen and the pen position.

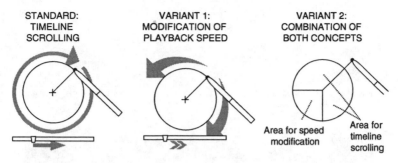

Fig. 12 Different variants of the ScrollWheel design

In an initial heuristic evaluation we compared the ScrollWheel implementation described above with two variations which are illustrated in Figure 12. In the first option, we did not map the actual timeline on the circle but different values for playback speed. Turning the virtual scroll wheel on the screen clockwise results in an increase in scrolling speed. Turning it counterclockwise results in a decrease. Once the initial clicking point is reached, scrolling switches from forward to backward navigation and vice versa. The second variant combines both approaches. The two thirds of the circle around the initial clicking position on the screen are associated with the timeline before and after the current position in the file, thus supporting slider-like navigation in a certain range of the file. The remaining part of the circle is reserved for playback speed manipulation. Depending on from which side this area is entered, playback speed in forward and backward direction, respectively, is increased. It should be noted that users have to actively make circular movements in order to navigate along the timeline whereas for the second variant and the part of the circle in the third version that supports playback speed manipulation they have to stay at a fixed point on the circle in order to keep scrolling with the associated playback rate.

Since our initial heuristic evaluation indicated that it might be to confusing for users to integrate two different interaction styles in one interface (variant 3) and that just playback speed manipulation without navigation along the timeline (variant 2) might not be powerful enough compared to the functionality offered by the Mobile ZoomSlider design, we decided to provide both interaction styles separately from each other. In the final implementation, the ScrollWheel represents a continuous timeline as illustrated in Figure 11. Playback speed manipulation is achieved by grabbing the icon in the center of the screen and moving it horizontally. Pen movements to the right result in forward scrolling, movements to the left in backwards navigation. Playback speed is proportional to the distance between pen and center of the screen with longer distances resulting in faster replay rates. This final concept is illustrated in Figure 13. Figure 14 shows the actual implementation.

In a user study with 16 participants we compared the Mobile ZoomSlider with the ScrollWheel design. All users had to solve tree browsing tasks with each of the two interfaces. The tasks were similar to the ones used in the comparative evaluation

By grabbing the icon, users can modify playback rate

Moving the pen to the right increases playback rate

Playback rate is proportional to the distance between pointer and icon

Fig. 13 Integration of playback speed modification into the ScrollWheel design

Fig. 14 Implementation of the ScrollWheel design on a PDA

of flicking with elastic panning described in the previous section. They included one overview task, one scene searching task, and one exact positioning task. However, they were formulated more informally and thus we did not do any qualitative time measurement in this experiment but solely relied on the users' feedback and our observation of their behavior during the studies. Therefore the results of these experiments should not be considered as final truth but more as general trends which are nevertheless quite interesting and informative. Both interfaces had a very good reception by the users and allowed them to solve the browsing talks in an easy and successful way. One important observation with both interfaces was a tendency by many participants to use different interaction styles for more complex browsing tasks thus confirming our initial assumption that it is indeed useful for a system designer to support, for example, navigation along the timeline and playback speed manipulation in one interface. Considering the direct comparison between the two interface designs, there was no clear result. However, for the navigation along the timeline we could identify a slight trend for people often preferring the ScrollWheel approach compared to the horizontal navigation in the screen center supported by the Mobile ZoomSlider. However, for manipulation of playback speed, the situation was reversed, that is, more people preferred to modify the replay rate by moving the pen along the left and right border of the screen in contrast to grabbing the icon in the screen's center as required in the ScrollWheel implementation. In contrast to our expectations, the seamless switch between both interaction styles provided by the Mobile ZoomSlider implementation did not play an important role for the majority of users. In contrast, we had the impression that most preferred a strict separation of both interaction styles. Another major reason for the common preference towards speed manipulation at the screen borders is obviously that users do not need to grab a rather small icon but can just click in a reasonably large area on the side of the screen in order to access the associated functionality. Further details and results of the evaluation can be found in [7].

One-handed Content-Based Mobile Video Browsing

The interfaces discussed in the preceding two sections can be operated mostly without having to target small widgets on the screen. This characteristic takes account of the small screen sizes that make it usually hard to hit and manipulate the tiny icons that are normally associated with regular graphical user interfaces. Another issue that is typical for a mobile scenario and we have not addressed so far is that often people have just one hand free for operation of the device. A typical example includes holding on to the handrail while standing in a crowded bus. Our premise for the design discussed in this section was therefore to create an interface that can easily be operated with a single hand. In contrast to the previous designs we assumed finger-based interaction with the touch screen because obviously pen-based operation with one hand is not practical. In addition, we decided not to address timeline-based navigation in this design, but to focus on a more structured, content-based browsing approach. As already mentioned above, we believe that both interaction concepts complement each other and are thus equally important. Integrating them in a reasonable interface design is part of our future work. Here, we decided to take a storyboard-like approach (cf. Figure 1), that is, use a pre-generated segmentation in content related scenes which are then represented by one representative static thumbnail. However, due to the small screen size, the common trade off for storyboards between overview and level of detail becomes even more critical. Representing too many scenes results in a thumbnail size that is too small for recognizing any useful information. Representing too few scenes can guarantee a reasonable thumbnail size but at the cost of a loss of overview of the whole file's content. Hence, we decided that in the final implementation only a few thumbnails should be visible but the user should be able to easily modify them, that is, easily navigate through the spatially ordered set of thumbnails that represent the temporally ordered scenes from the video.

From experimenting with different ways to hold the device in one hand while still being able to reach and operate the touch screen it resulted that the only reasonable approach seems to hold the PDA as illustrated in Figure 15 and operate it using your thumb. This allows us to support three possible interaction modes: circular movements of the thumb in the lower right area of the screen, horizontal movements at the lower screen border, and vertical movements on the right side of the screen. Other thumb movements, such as moving it from the screen's lower right corner towards its center or moving it horizontally over the center of the screen, seemed too unnatural or not feasible without the risk of dropping the device. As a consequence, the design decision for the thumbnail representation was to place them on the left

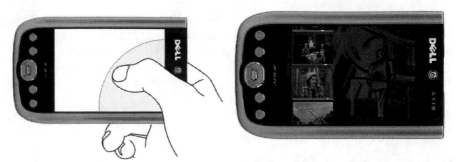

Fig. 15 Interface design for one-handed video browsing (left: interaction concepts, right: interface design)

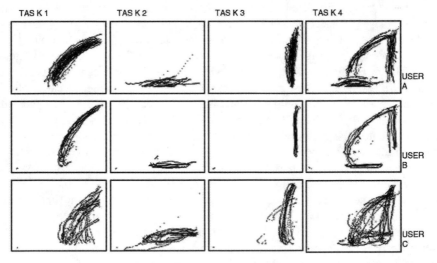

Fig. 16 Logged interaction data from the initial evaluation of possible motion ranges when holding the device with one hand and operating it with your thumb

side of the screen in order to not interfere with the operation. Thumb movements should be used to manipulate the currently visible subset of thumbnails. Clicking on the screen is reserved for starting replay at the position of the currently selected thumbnail.

In order to evaluate if and within which range people are able to perform such thumb movements without feeling uncomfortable and still being able to solidly hold the device, we set up an initial experiment with 18 participants. Each of them had to do four simple scrolling tasks (navigation within a list of text entries) by doing each of the following interactions with their thumb while holding the device like depicted in Figure 16: horizontal thumb movements at the bottom of the screen, vertical thumb movements at the right side of the screen, circular-shaped thumb movements in the center of the screen, and finally a combination of all three. Figure 16 depicts some examples of the logged interactions. Similar visualizations for the remaining participants as well as more detailed information about the experiments can be found in [8].

The evaluation revealed some interesting and important observations for the final interface design. First and most important, it proved that this way of holding and operating the device is feasible and that most users find it useful to support this kind of interaction. Only two users had problems holding it and said that they would always prefer to use two hands. Considering the actual interactions, we observed that horizontal movements are the hardest to do, followed by vertical thumb movements on the right screen border, whereas circular-shaped interaction was considered easiest and most natural. Variations in the circular movements were much lesser than expected. However, for the horizontal and vertical ones, a larger variety could be observed. Especially for the interactions at the lower screen border, people used different lengths and different areas to move their thumbs. Because of this, we concluded that in the final design, manipulation of values (e.g. the interval of thumbnails that is currently visible) should not be associated with absolute positions on the screen but relative ones (e.g. an initial click associates with the currently visible interval and left or right movements modify the range in backward and forward direction, respectively). Functionalities requiring intensive interactions should be associated with the most natural thumb movement pattern, that is, circular shapes, whereas horizontal movements, which have been identified as most uncomfortable and hardest to control, should only be used occasionally and not for very sensitive data manipulation. In addition, there have been two users who did not feel comfortable operating the device with one hand at all and some others expressed that they see a need for one-handed operation, think that it is useful, but only would take advantage of it if they have to. Otherwise, they would always use both hands. Therefore, the final design, although being optimized for one-handed operation, should also support interaction with both hands.

Figure 17 illustrates how we mapped different functionalities to the described interaction styles considering the previously discussed requirements. Because perceptibility of the thumbnails depends on the actual content, it is important to enable uses to modify their sizes. This functionality is provided at the bottom of the screen. Clicking anywhere and moving your thumb to the left or right decreases and increases, respectively, the thumbnail size. It should be noted that this functionality is most likely not used very often during browsing and that only a fixed discrete set of sizes needs to be supported thus limiting the amount of interaction that is required. Modification of scrolling speed of the thumbnails requires a much more sensitive input and therefore is associated with the right screen border where interactions are usually considered to be easier and more intuitive. Clicking on the right screen border and moving your thumb up or down starts scrolling the thumbnail overview in opposite direction. This reverse scrolling direction has been chosen in order to resemble scrolling with a regular scrollbar where interaction and resulting scrolling direction also behave complementary. In the related evaluation (cf. below), it was noted that some users might consider the opposite association to be more intuitive, but it was not seen as a critical issue that might negatively affect usability. The most

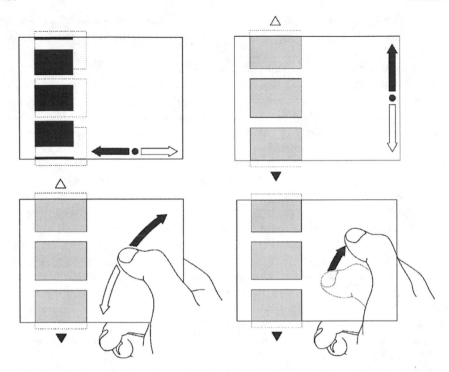

Fig. 17 Illustrations of different interaction functionalities. Top left: horizontal thumb movements on lower screen border to modify thumbnail sizes, top right: vertical thumb movements on right screen border to scroll through thumbnails at constant speed, bottom left and right: flicking on the center of the screen for interactive navigation through the list of thumbnails

sensitive interaction was mapped to the circular movements in the center of the screen. Similarly to flicking text lists on the iPhone or the flicking along the timeline of a video introduced above, users can navigate through the list of thumbnails by flicking their thumbs in circular-shaped movements over the screen. Scrolling direction again behaves complementary to the direction of the flick. Moving your thumb over the screen without flicking allows you to move the thumbnail list in order to do some fine adjustment. The center thumbnail of the list on the left is always marked as current and double taping on the screen starts replay at the associated scene. It should be noted that flicking requires much more interaction than modification of scrolling speed on the right side of the screen because users have to constantly flick to skim a larger set of thumbnails due to the frictional loss that would otherwise force the thumbnail list to slow down. Hence, it is important to associate it with the more natural and intuitive interaction pattern that also enables users to do a more sensitive input. The internal classification algorithm that is used to classify the circular thumb movements is robust enough to also correctly interpret up and down movements done with another finger as flicking interactions, thus fulfilling the requirement that users should also be able to operate the interface with two hands.

Fig. 18   Implementation of one-handed video browsing interface design on a PDA

Figure 18 shows examples for the implementation of the proposed design on our PDA. In addition to the functionality and visualization described above, there is a timeline-like bar placed below each thumbnail with a highlighted area indicating the relative position of the associated scene within the video (cf. Fig. 1). This implementation was shown to four users who did a heuristic evaluation of the interface design. In addition, they participated in an experiment where they had to solve different search tasks while walking around and operating the device with one hand. This setup was different than the pure lab studies used for the interface evaluations described in the two preceding sections and aimed at creating a more realistic test environment. The heuristic evaluation gave some hints about small improvements of the design and for parameter optimization. Overall, it could confirm the usefulness and usability of the interface. This also became apparent in the mobile experiment where all participants were able to solve the provided search tasks easily and without any major problems. It should be noted that the main focus of this study was on the evaluation of one-handed interaction, which is why we limited the provided video browsing functionality to pure navigation in scene-based thumbnails. In a final implementation, we could replace one of the two options to browse the thumbnail list with a timeline-based approach. For example, we could use the right screen border to modify playback speed in order to enable users to skim the actual content. This would make sense because first, not much of the content would be blocked by your thumb during browsing. Second, this kind of navigation does usually not require much interaction. The motion intensive flicking interaction in the center of the screen could then be used to navigate the thumbnails similarly to the current implementation.

Summary and Outlook

In this article, we addressed the problem of video browsing on handheld devices. We started by reviewing traditional video browsing approaches created for larger screens and then motivated the mobile scenario. It became clear that we can not just transfer existing approaches but have to come up with new techniques and interface designs that consider certain issues that are characteristic for a mobile context. For example, the first four interfaces we summarized in this article take into account the small screen sizes and thus limited interaction capabilities of handheld devices. They all offer a rich interaction experience without taking too much space away from the actual video content and, for example, do not force the user to target tiny icons and small interaction elements on the screen. Another characteristic of mobile interaction is that people are often in an environment that does not allow them to fully concentrate on the interaction with their device, are easily distracted, and, for example, might only be able to use one hand for operation. This was taken into account by the last interface presented here which, in contrast to the other ones, also supported some content-based browsing approach. Combining such a technique with the other, more interactive timeline-based navigation techniques is an important issue and it is yet unclear how to solve this in the best possible way. While screen size will always remain a limited resource for handheld devices, other performance issues are quickly disappearing. Continuous acoustic and visual feedback during scrolling along the timeline is still to challenging for most devices currently on the market. However, we expect this issue to change soon, thus offering a variety of new opportunities for better video browsing. In addition, newer devices might also feature additional interaction possibilities. For example, the iPhones multi touch feature that enables to do more advanced gestures than the rather simple ones used in our designs could be very useful for browsing not single videos but larger collections of different video files.

References

1. S. Belt, J. Saarenpää, A. Elsilä, J. Häkkilä, "Usage Practices with Mobile TV - A Case Study," Mobile Multimedia – Content Creation and Use workshop at MobileHCI 2008, Amsterdam, The Netherlands, September 2008, available at http://research.nokia.com/files/Belt_MMworkshop2008.pdf (accessed Feb 1, 2009).
2. J. Boreczky, A. Girgensohn, G. Golovchinsky, S. Uchihashi, "An Interactive Comic Book Presentation for Exploring Video," Proceedings of the SIGCHI conference on Human factors in computing systems, The Hague, The Netherlands, April 2000, pp. 185–192.
3. M. G. Christel, A. G. Hauptmann, A. S. Warmack, S. A. Crosby, "Adjustable Filmstrips and Skims as Abstractions for a Digital Video Library," Proceedings of the IEEE Forum on Research and Technology Advances in Digital Libraries, March 1999, pp. 98.
4. M. G. Christel, A. S. Warmack, "The Effect of Text in Storyboards for Video Navigation," Proceedings of the Acoustics, Speech, and Signal Processing, 2001. on IEEE International Conference - Volume 03, May 2001, pp. 1409–1412.
5. W. Hürst, G. Götz, T. Lauer, "New Methods for Visual Information Seeking Through Video Browsing," Proceedings of the 8th International Conference on Information Visualisation, London, UK, July 2004, pp. 450–455.
6. W. Hürst, G. Götz, M. Welte, "Interactive Video Browsing on Mobile Devices," Proceedings of the 15th international conference on Multimedia, Augsburg, Germany, September 2007, pp. 247–256.
7. W. Hürst, G. Götz, "Interface Designs for Pen-Based Mobile Video Browsing," Proceedings of the 7th ACM conference on Designing interactive systems, Cape Town, South Africa, February 2008, pp. 395–404.

8. W. Hürst, P. Merkle, "One-Handed Mobile Video Browsing," Proceeding of the 1st international conference on Designing interactive user experiences for TV and video, Silicon Valley, California, USA, October 2008, pp. 169–178.
9. W. Hürst, K. Meier, "Interfaces for Timeline-based Mobile Video Browsing," Proceeding of the 16th ACM international conference on Multimedia, Vancouver, British Columbia, Canada, October 2008, pp. 469–478.
10. H. Knoche, M. Papaleo, M. A. Sasse, A. Vanelli-Coralli, "The Kindest Cut: Enhancing the User Experience of Mobile TV Through Adequate Zooming," Proceedings of the 15th international conference on Multimedia, Augsburg, Germany, September 2007, pp. 87–96.
11. R. Lienhart, S. Pfeiffer, W. Effelsberg, "Video abstracting," Communications of the ACM, Vol. 40, No. 12, 1997, pp. 54–62.
12. F. Liu, M. Gleicher, "Video retargeting: automating pan and scan," Proceedings of the 14th annual ACM international conference on Multimedia, Santa Barbara, California, USA, October 2006, pp. 241–250.
13. A. Miene, N. Luth, "Segmentation and Content Based Indexing of Video Sequences," Proceedings of the IFIP IC2/WG2.6 Eigth Working Conference on Database Semantics (DS-8), January 1999, pp. 65–84.
14. K. O'Hara, A. S. Mitchell, A. Vorbau, "Consuming Video on Mobile Devices," Proceedings of the SIGCHI conference on Human factors in computing systems, San Jose, California, USA, April-May 2007, pp. 857–866.
15. T. Ojala, J. Korhonen, T. Sutinen, P. Parhi, L. Aalto, "Mobile Kärpät – A Case Study in Wireless Personal Area Networking," Proceedings of the 3rd international conference on Mobile and ubiquitous multimedia, College Park, Maryland, USA, October 2004, pp. 149–156.
16. D. Ponceleon, S. Srinivasan, A. Amir, D. Petkovic, D. Diklic, "Key to Effective Video Retrieval: Effective. Cataloguing and Browsing," Proceedings of the 6th ACM international conference on Multimedia, Bristol, United Kingdom, September 1998, pp. 99–107.
17. M. A. Smith, "Video Skimming and Characterization through the Combination of Image and Language Understanding Techniques," Proceedings of the 1997 Conference on Computer Vision and Pattern Recognition (CVPR '97), June 1997, pp. 775.
18. S. Uchihashi, J. Foote, A. Girgensohn, J. Boreczky, "Video Manga: Generating Semantically Meaningful Video Summaries," Proceedings of the 7th ACM international conference on Multimedia, Orlando, Florida, USA, October-November 1999, pp. 383–392.

Chapter 21
Projector-Camera Systems in Entertainment and Art

Oliver Bimber and Xubo Yang

Introduction

Video projectors have evolved tremendously in the last decade. Reduced costs and increasing capabilities (e.g. spatial resolution, brightness, dynamic range, throwratio) have led to widespread applications in entertainment, art, visualization and in other areas.

In this chapter we summarize fundamental visualization and interaction techniques for projector-camera systems that are being used to display interactive content on everyday surfaces - without the need for optimized canvases. Coded projections and camera feedback allows measurement of the projected light on these complex surfaces and compensates the modulation, while also enabling computer vision based interaction techniques.

Section "Visualization and Projector-Camera Systems" reviews basic image correction techniques for projector-camera systems, such as geometric and photometric image correction, and defocus compensation. It also outlines off-line as well as imperceptible on-line structured light calibration techniques that can be used for measuring image distortions on geometrically complex, colored and textured surfaces.

Section "Interaction with Projector-Camera Systems" discusses near- and far-distance interaction techniques that can be supported with spatially fixed projector-camera systems. In particular, the real-time camera-feedback enables different forms of interaction that are based on computer vision methods. It also describes interaction possibilities for handheld projector-camera systems.

O. Bimber (✉)
Faculty of Media Bauhaus-University Weimar, Germany
e-mail: bimber@uni-weimar.de

X. Yang
School of Software Shanghai Jiao Tong University, Shanghai, China
e-mail: yangxubo@cs.sjtu.edu.cn

B. Furht (ed.), *Handbook of Multimedia for Digital Entertainment and Arts*,
DOI 10.1007/978-0-387-89024-1_21, © Springer Science+Business Media, LLC 2009

Section "Application Examples" outlines different professional applications of projector-camera systems in commercial and research fields. The examples include museums installations, multimedia presentations at historic sites, on-stage projection in theaters, architectural visualization, visual effects for film and broadcasting, and interactive attraction installations for exhibitions and other public environments.

Finally, section "The Future of Projector-Camera Systems" gives a brief outlook of the technological future of projector-camera systems that will become widespread many more application fields.

Visualization with Projector-Camera Systems

For conventional applications, screen surfaces are optimized for a projection. Their reflectance is usually uniform and mainly diffuse (although with possible gain and anisotropic properties) across the surface, and their geometrical topologies range from planar and multi-planar to simple parametric (e.g., cylindrical or spherical) surfaces. In many situations, however, such screens cannot be applied, such as for example, to the applications explained in section. Instead, projections onto arbitrary everyday surfaces are required for visualization with projector camera systems. The modulation of the projected light on such surfaces, however, can easily exceed a simple diffuse reflection modulation. In addition, blending with different surface pigments and complex geometric distortions can degrade the image quality significantly.

The light of the projected images is modulated on the surface together with possible environment light. This leads to a color, intensity and geometry distorted appearance. The intricacy of the modulation depends on the complexity of the surface. The modulation may contain interreflections, diffuse and specular reflections, regional defocus effects, refractions, and more.

Recently, numerous projector-camera approaches that enable seamless projections onto non-optimized everyday surfaces have been developed. An overview of these approaches can be found in [1]. These techniques enable unconstrained visualization for a variety of different applications. Therefore, two tasks are important. First, scanning techniques must measure the modulation of light on the surfaces. This can be arbitrarily complex – ranging from simple local diffuse and specular reflection, over refraction, defraction, and defocusing, to global inter-reflections. Second, the detected modulation effects need to be compensated in real-time to make projected images appear undistorted. An overview over basic techniques will be described below. The interested reader is referred to [1] for more details.

Inverting the Light Transport

One fundamental possibility of pre-correcting images before projecting them onto non-optimized surfaces is to measure the transport of light from projector over the

surface to the camera and invert it, as described in [2]. The light transport represents a 4D slice of the 8D reflectance field. The forward light transport and its inverse can be expressed as linear equation systems:

$$c_\lambda = T_\lambda p_\lambda + e_\lambda, T_\lambda^{-1}(c_\lambda - e_\lambda) = p_\lambda$$

where c_λ is a single color channel λ of a camera image with resolution $m \times n$. The projector pattern p_λ has a resolution of $p \times q$, and e_λ is the environment light including the projector's blacklevel captured from the camera. Thereby, T_λ contains all global and local modulation effects that can be detected with the camera, and the multiplication with T_λ^{-1} neutralizes these effects.

Essentially, there are several challenges in the equation above: acquiring T_λ in an acceptable amount of time, acquiring T_λ with a high quality, and finding a numericallystable solution for its inverse T_λ^{-1}. Both problems are compounded by the fact that T_λ and T_λ^{-1} have the enormous size of $m \times n \times p \times q$ entries for a single projector-camera pair (even more if multiple cameras or projectors are involved).

Although, the inverse light transport represents a general solution for demodulating projected light –and therefore for compensating all detectable modulations on the surface– it is not very efficient in terms of quality, performance, and storage requirements. Many specialized techniques exist that scan and compensate individual modulation effects one by one, instead of scanning and compensating all of them at once. These techniques will be described briefly below. More details are presented in [1]. Note that, in theory, the inverse light transport unifies all of these individual techniques. In practice, however, it leads to a lower compensation quality that is mainly due to the limited memory and computational power of today's graphics hardware?

Geometric Image Correction

The amount of geometric distortion of projected images depends on how much the projection surface deviates from a plane, and on the projection angle itself. The goal of the geometric image correction is to warp the projected image in such a way that it appears, from the perspective of the camera which is frequently placed at a sweet spot position of the viewers, undistorted. Once the registration between projector and camera is known, the image is defined for the camera's perspective and warped into the perspective of the projector. Different geometric registration techniques are applied for individual surface topologies.

For planar screen surfaces, homographies are suitable for representing the geometric mapping between camera pixels and projector pixels over the common screen plane:

$$p_{[x,y,1]} = H_{3x3}c_{[x,y,1]}$$

where $c_{[x,y,1]}$ is a given homogeneous coordinate of a camera pixel, $p_{[x,y,1]}$ is the projector pixel that corresponds to c (i.e., maps onto the same surface point), and H_{3x3} is a 3x3 homography matrix that can be determined if sufficient correspondences between c and p are known. While simple homographies are suited for registering projectors with planar surfaces, projective texture mapping [4] can be used for non-planar surfaces of known geometry. For geometrically complex and textured surfaces of unknown geometry, image warping based on real-time look-up operations has frequently been used to achieve a pixel-precise mapping [5]. In this case, the correspondences between $p_{[x,y,1]}$ and $c_{[x,y,1]}$ have to be measured individually.

Photometric Image Correction

Once projector pixels and camera pixels are registered on a common surface, the projected image can be corrected in such a way that it appears geometrically undistorted from the perspective of the camera. However, if the projection surface is colored and textured, the projected image is color distorted. Furthermore, the modulation of the light from the surrounding environment on the same surface adds additional color and intensity shifts. This color distortion can be compensated as can geometric image correction also be compensated. It is relatively easy if the surface is Lambertian (i.e., perfectly diffuse).

The color transform and its inverse between each camera pixel and projector pixel can be expressed as a 3x3 color mixing matrix V_{3x3} [6]:

$$c_{[r,g,b]} = V_{3x3}p_{[r,g,b]}, \, p_{[r,g,b]} = V_{3x3}^{-1}c_{[r,g,b]}$$

where $p_{[r,g,b]}$ is the color of a projected pixel and $c_{[r,g,b]}$ is the color of the corresponding pixel as detected by the camera (after being modulated by the surface color). As for the homographies, the parameters of the color mixing matrix V_{3x3} can be determined by measuring an adequate number for corresponding color modulations between $p_{[r,g,b]}$ and $c_{[r,g,b]}$. Once V_{3x3} has been measured, its inverse V_{3x3}^{-1} can be computed to compensate for the color and intensity modulation on the surface. Note, that in this case individual forward and inverse color mixing matrices V_{3x3} and V_{3x3}^{-1} exist for each pixel.

Different extensions to this simple linear color transformation, and a variety of acquisition techniques for V exist. Using a 3x4 matrix, for instance, additionally allows for the consideration and compensation of light from the immediate environment [6]. The limited dynamic range and brightness of projectors, however, is problematic for photometric compensation techniques. Compensation strong absorptions of projected light on the surface in all, or in particular color channels, would require projection intensities that cannot be reached by conventional projectors. The relatively high blacklevel of projectors, nonetheless, prevents the production of very low light intensities. These limitations will lead to imperfect compensation results, and consequently to remaining color and intensity artifacts.

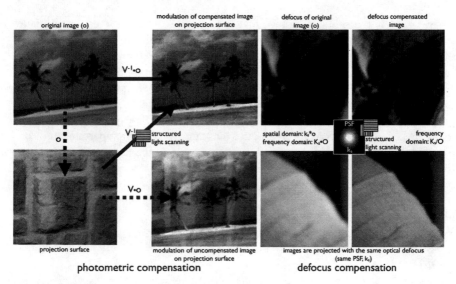

Fig. 1 Image compensation examples: photometric compensation when projecting on a tex-tured/colored surface (left) and defocus compensation when projecting onto a non-planar surface (right). Both examples are geometry corrected

Therefore, contemporary approaches consider limitations of human visual percep-tion as part of the photometric compensation process to overcome some of the technical limitations of projectors [8, 9]. Using multiple projectors, highlights on specular surfaces [10] or shadow casts [11, 12] can also be compensated. Details on such extensions are summarized in [1]. An example is illustrated in figure 1.

In contrast to the photometric compensation techniques that are explained above, similar methods boost the contrast of existing surfaces rather than fitting arbitrary image content into their limited contrast range [19]. Such structured illumination techniques can be used if a low contrast reflection or transmission an under ordinary uniform illumination is problematic, since they enhance existing surface features.

Defocus Compensation

Conventional projectors trade focal depth in favor of high light throughput. This can lead to regional defocussing of images projected onto surfaces, planar or non-planar, that are not aligned to the optically adjusted focal plane. Besides geometric and photometric image distortions, defocussing is a further source of error when projecting onto non-optimized surfaces.

Optical defocus is often described as convolution with a filter kernel that corre-sponds to an image of the applied aperture:

$$c_{defocus} = k_s * p_{focus}$$

where p_{focus} is the projected image that is focused to one particular focal plane, $c_{defocus}$ is the camera frame that captures the projected image on a non-planar surface that varies locally from the adjusted focal plane of the projector, k_s represents the scaled (by s) filter kernel that contains the defocus related point spread function at a corresponding focal distance, and $*$ denotes convolution. The point spread function that is represented by the kernel depends on the shape of the aperture that is used by projector. It is Gaussian, if a circular aperture is applied. If no aperture is used, then the boundaries of the projector's objective lens acts as a circular aperture.

Thus, the degree of defocus correlates to the scale of the kernel. Convolving an image with the inverse aperture kernel will digitally sharpen the image and consequently compensate optical defocus. This is referred to as deconvolution or inverse filtering. In the frequency domain, the filter kernel's reciprocal is its own inverse, and deconvolution reduces it the following division:

$$C = K_s P, P = C / K_s$$

where, C, K_s, P are in frequency domain (i.e., Fourier transforms of c, k_s, p). Thus, deconvolving the original image $c = o$ with the locally varying filter kernel (depending on the measured amount of defocus at a particular position) leads to a defocus compensated projected image p (after an inverse Fourier transform of P). Projecting p instead of the original image o compensates the optical defocus up to a certain degree. An example is illustrated in figure 1. How well this works depends on the amount of defocus and on the image content. If Gaussian point spread functions are compensated, as in [13, 14, 15], and if the amount of defocus becomes too high, the result can quickly show ringing artifacts. The reason for this is, that circular apertures are optical low pass filters, and high image frequencies are difficult to recover through inverse filtering. Since they are more broadband in frequency domain, the application of coded apertures in conjunction with deconvolution [16] is better suited than simple circular apertures. Thus ringing artifacts are reduced after inverse filtering.

Alternative defocus composition techniques exist that apply multiple projectors with overlapping images at different focal planes [17]. Ringing artifacts are not produced by such techniques, since inverse filtering is not applied. Instead, the focal depth changes with the number of applied projection units.

Structured Light Scanning

The above sections explained how images can be corrected to compensate geometric (i.e., image warping), photometric (i.e., color and intensity blending) and defocus artifacts that result from projections onto non-optimized surfaces. However, not explained was how the necessary parameters that are required for solving the above equations are determined. Correct matrix parameters for either homography, color mixing, light transport matrices, or point spread functions and their scales for de-convolution have to be known before the images can be corrected.

Projector-camera systems apply structured light projections [3] for measuring these parameters automatically. Well established codes, such as Gray codes (e.g., for measuring pixel correspondences) or point impulses (e.g., for measuring point spread functions) are applied for scanning.

For a static scenery (i.e., fixed surface and projector-camera system), structured light scanning can be carried our as part of a one-time calibration process. Once they are measured, the image correction process itself is normally performed in real-time. Precise scanning, however, is normally time-consuming. Therefore, real-time adaptations to dynamic situations (e.g., moving projector-camera systems or surfaces) are difficult to achieve – mainly due to constrains of surface scanning, and not of the image correction itself.

For a single projector-camera system, both devices can be optically co-aligned (i.e., they share the same optical axis). In this special case, the pixel correspon-dence between projector and camera remains static –regardless of the surface depth– and a geometric re-calibration is not necessary for dynamic situations, as in [18].

In cases where projector and camera cannot be co-aligned (e.g., because multiple projectors are applied simultaneously, or the viewers' sweet spot cannot match the projector's position), an parameter scanning in real-time is not possible at that time. However, some modern scanning approaches integrate structured code patterns directly into the projected image content in such a way that an imperceptible calibration can be performed during run-time. Thus, the calibration code cannot be perceived by humans, but can be extracted from the projection with a synchronized camera. Binary codes can be seamlessly embedded into the mirror-flip sequence of DLP projectors [20] which supports a geometric re-registration of projector and camera at interactive (yet not real-time) rates. More complex intensity and color codes can also be embedded into projected images that are compensated on a tem-poral basis to remain invisible [21]. This enables an imperceptible geometric and photometric re-calibration at interactive rates. More details on these and similar techniques are summarized in [1].

Interaction with Projector-Camera Systems

By measuring the main factors of projectors and surfaces that cause different types of distortions, projector-camera system can correct the output images accordingly and produce undistorted visuals on arbitrary surfaces. However, if such a projec-tion is purely passive, its applicability is clearly limited. It is therefore desirable to further let the projector-camera system be aware of users' actions within the sys-tem's scanning range, and respond accordingly. An interaction ability is especially important for interactive media art and entertainment applications.

Possible projector-camera configurations may be classified by the types of projectors used and the display surfaces in question. On one hand, projectors can be classified by mobility, ranging from static spatial projectors fixed in closed installations to location-fixed but direction-adjustable and steerable projectors that can project images on different surfaces in a room, to automated projectors mounted on robots that can move in a building, and to hand-held or eye-worn projectors that can be carried almost anywhere. On the other hand, projection surfaces can be classified by their generality, ranging from specially designed ideal (white, diffuse, planar) projection screens, to near-ideal everyday flat surfaces such as papered walls, floors, ceilings and tabletops, to non-optimized arbitrary surfaces that may be multi-faced, non-planar, curved, colored, textured and discontinuous. On another dimension of mobility, projection surfaces may also vary from static to movable, to foldable and deformable surfaces.

Different types of projector-camera system interaction techniques exist. One common method is interactive visualization from different angles and distances, where natural physical interaction abilities can be exploited or where viewpoint tracking is necessary. Finger touching and hand gesture techniques are suitable for near-field interaction with the projection surfaces. Pointing and selecting techniques are often useful for middle-range interaction, where detailed interaction tasks are required but the projection surface is beyond arm distance. Limb gesture and body pose can be used for large scale interaction, where the interaction accuracy is less important. Besides, spontaneous interaction and multiple user interaction are featured in portable projectors.

Since projectors are often used for visualization applications, the emphasis, in above configurations, has been on projectors, not cameras, despite the fact that cameras often act as facilitating devices. However, in other applications, cameras may instead be dominant, where the main task may be recording the environment. In such a case projectors become secondary to the recording process. The following subsections will focus on key issues and approaches for interaction with projector-dominant systems.

Interaction with Spatial Projector

Spatial projectors are installed at fixed locations, and are either static, steerable or automated. Static spatial projectors are the most common installations for virtual environment and for commercial usage, and recently are increasingly used for home entertainment systems. A large number of interaction techniques has been proposed for projected virtual environments. Interested readers are referred to [25]. However, these systems are mainly concerned with ideal projection screens. Instead, the main focus, here, will be on interaction with projector-camera systems that display onto everyday surfaces.

Physically Viewing Interaction

By projecting images directly onto everyday surfaces, a projector-camera system may be used for creating augmentation effects, such as virtually painting the object surface with a new color, new texture, or even an animation. Users can interact directly with such projector-based augmentations. For example, they may observe the object from different sides, while simultaneously experiencing consistent occlusion effects and depth, or they can move nearer or further from the object, to see local details and global views. Thus, the intuitiveness of physical interaction and advantages of digital presentation are combined.

This kind of physically interactive visualization ability is suitable for use in situations when virtual content is mapped as a texture on real object surfaces. View-dependent visual effects such as highlighting to simulate virtually shiny surfaces require tracking of the users' view. Multi-user views can also be supported by time-multiplexing the projection for multiple users, with each user wearing a synchronized shutter glass allowing the selection of individual views. But this is only necessary for view-dependent augmentations. Furthermore, view tracking and stereoscopic presentation ability enables virtual objects to be displayed not only on the real surface, but also in front of or behind the surface. A general geometric framework to handle all these variants is described in [26].

The techniques described above, only simulate the desired appearance of an augmented object which is supposed to remain fixed in space. To make the projected content truly user-interactive, more information apart from viewpoint changes is required. After turning an ordinary surface into a display, it is further desirable to extend it to become a user interface with an additional input channel. Thereby, cameras can be used for sensing. In contrast to other input technologies, such as embedded electronics for touch screens, tracked wand, or stylus and data gloves often used in virtual environments; vision-based sensing technology has the flexibility to support different types of inputting techniques without modifying the display surface or equipping the users with different devices for different tasks. Differing from interaction with special projection screens such as electronically enabled multi-touch or rear-projected screens, some of the primary issues associated with vision-based interaction with front-projected interfaces are the illuminations on the detected hand and object, as well as cast of shadows.

In following subsections, two types of typical interaction approaches with spatial projector-camera systems will be introduced, namely near distance interaction and far distance interaction. Vision based interaction techniques will be the main focus and basic interaction operations such as pointing, selecting and manipulation will be considered.

Near Distance Interaction

In near-distance situations where the projection surface is within arm's length of the user, finger touching or hand gestures are intuitive ways to select and manipulate the interface. Apart from this, the manipulation of physical objects can also be detected and used for triggering interaction events.

Vision-based techniques may apply a visible light or infrared light camera to capture the projected surface area. To detect finger touching on a projected surface a calibration process, similar to the geometric techniques presented in section "Geometric Image Correction", is needed to map corresponding pixels between projector and camera.

Next, fingers, hands and objects need to be categorized as part of the foreground in order to separate them from the projected surface background. When interactions take place on a front-projected surface, the hand is illuminated by the displayed images and thus the appearance of a moving hand changes quickly. This renders segmentation methods, based on skin color or region-growing methods as useless. Frequently, conventional background subtraction methods are also unreliable, since the skin color of a hand may become buried in the projected light.

One possible solution to this problem is to expand the capacity of the background subtraction. Despite, its application to an ideal projection screen which assumes enough color differences from skin color as in [27], the background subtraction can also be used to take into account different background and foreground reflectance factors. When the background changes significantly, a segmentation may fail. An image update can be applied to keep the segmentation robust, where an artificial background may be generated from the known input image for a projector with geometric and color distortions corrected between the projector and camera.

Another feasible solution is to detect the changing pixel area between the frames of the captured video to obtain a basic shape of the moving hand or object. Noise can then be removed using image morphology. Following this, a fingertip can be detected by convolution with a fingertip-shaped template over the extracted image, as in [28].

To avoid the complex varying illumination problem for visible light, an infrared camera can be used instead, together with an infrared light source to produce invisible shadow of a finger on the projected flat surface, as shown in [29]. The shadow of the finger can then be detected by the infrared camera and can thus be singularly used to detect the finger region and fingertip. To enable screen interation by finger touching, the positioning of the finger, either touching the surface or hovering above it, can be further determined by detecting the occlusion ratio of the finger shadow. When the finger is touching the surface, its shadow is fully occluded by the finger itself; while the finger is hovering over the surface, its shadow is larger.

It is also possible to exclude the projected content from the captured video by interlacing the projecting images and captured camera frames using synchronized high-speed projectors and cameras, so that more general gesture recognition algorithms can be adopted as those reviewed in [30]. To obtain more robust detection results, specific vision hardware can also be utilized, such as real-time depth cameras that are based on the time-of-flight principle [31].

Far Distance Interaction

In a situation where the projection surface is beyond the user's arm length, laser pointer interaction is an intuitive way to select and manipulate projected interface components. Recently, laser pointer interaction has used for interacting with large scale projection display or tiled display at a far distance [32].

To detect and track a laser dot on a projection surface in projector-camera systems, a calibrated camera covering the projecting area is often used. The location and movement of a laser dot can be detected simply by applying an intensity threshold to the captured image – assuming that the laser dot is much brighter than the projection. Since the camera and the projector are both geometrically calibrated, the location of the laser dot on the camera image can be mapped to corresponding pixels on projection image. The "on" and "off" status of the laser pointer can be mapped to mouse click events for selecting particular operations. One or more virtual objects that are supposed to be intersected with the laser dot or a corresponding laser ray can be further calculated from the virtual scene geometry.

More events for laser pointer interaction can be triggered by temporal or spatial gestures, such as encircling, or simply by adding some hardware on laser pointers, such as buttons and embedded electronics for wireless communication. Multiple user laser pointer interaction can also be supported for large projection areas where each user's laser pointer is distinguishable. This can be supported by time-multiplexing the laser or by using different laser colors or patterns. User studies have been carried out to provide optimized design parameters for laser pointer interaction [33].

Although laser pointing is an intuitive technique, it also suffers from issues such as hand-jittering, inaccuracy and slow interaction speeds. To overcome the hand-jittering problem, which is compounded at greater distances, filtering-based smoothing techniques can be applied, though may lead to discrepancy between the pointing laser dot and the estimated location. Infrared laser pointers may solve this problem, but according to user study results, visible laser lights are still found to be better for interaction.

Apart from laser pointing, other tools such as a tracked stylus or specially designed passive vision wands [34] tracked by a camera have proven to be flexible and efficient when interacting with large scale projection displays over distances.

Gesture recognition provides a natural way for interaction in greater distances without using specific tools. It is mainly based on gesture pattern recognition with or without hand model reconstruction. Evaluating body motions is also an intuitive way for large scale interaction, where the body pose and motion are estimated and behavior patterns may be further detected. When gesture and body motion are the dominant modes of interaction with projector-camera systems, shadows and varying illumination conditions are the main challenges, though shadows can also be utilized for detecting gesture or body motion.

In gesture or body interaction, background subtraction is often used for detecting the moving body from the difference between the current frame and a reference background image. The background reference image must be regularly updated so as to adapt to the varying luminance conditions and geometry settings. More complex models have extended the concept of background subtraction beyond its literal meaning. A thorough review of the background extraction methods is presented in [35].

Vision-based human action recognition approaches can be generally divided into four phases. The model initialization phase ensures that a system commences its operation with a correct interpretation of the current scene. The tracking phase segments and tracks the human bodies in each camera frame. The pose estimation phase estimates the pose of the users in one or more frames. The recognition phase can recognize the identity of individuals as well as the actions, activities and behaviors performed by one or more user. Details about video based human action detection techniques are reviewed in [36].

Interaction with Handheld Projectors

Hand-held projectors may display images on surfaces anywhere at anytime while they are being moved by the user. This is especially useful for mobile projector-based augmentation, which superimposes digital information in physical environments. Unlike other mobile displays such as provided by PDAs or mobile phones, hand-held projectors offer a consistent visual combination of real information gather from physical surfaces with virtual information. This is possible without context switching between information space and real space, thus seamlessly blurring the virtual and real world. They can be used, for instance, as interactive information flashlights [37] – displaying registered image content on surface portions that are illuminated by the projector.

Although hand-held projectors provide great flexibility for ubiquitous computing and spontaneous interaction, there are fundamental issues to be addressed before a fluid interaction between the user and the projector is possible. When using a hand-held projector to display on various surfaces in a real environment, the projected image will be dynamically modulated and distorted by the surfaces as the user moves. When the user stops moving the projector, the presented image still suffers from shaking by the user's unavoidable hand-jitter. Thus, a basic requirement for hand-held projector interaction is to produce stable projection.

Image Stabilizing

One often desired form of image stabilization is to produce a rectangular 2D image on a planar surface – independently of the projector's actual pose and movement. In this case, the projected image must be continuously warped to keep the correct aspect ratio and to remain undistorted. The warping process is similar to the geometric correction techniques described earlier. The difference, however, is that the target viewing perspective is usually pointing towards the projection surface along its normal direction, while the position of the hand-held projector may keep on changing.

To find the geometric mapping between the projector and the target perspective, the projector's six degrees of freedom may be obtained from an attached tracking device. The homography is an adequate method to represent this geometric mapping when the projection surface is planar. Instead of using the detected four vertices of the visible projection area to calculate the homography matrix, another practical technique is to identify laser spots displayed from laser-pointers that are attached to the projector-camera system. The laser spots are brighter and therefore easier to detect.

In [38], hand-jittering was compensated together with the geometry correction, by continuously tracking the projector's pose and warping the image at each time-step. A camera attached to the projector detects visual markers on the projection surface, that are used for warping the projected image accordingly. In [42] a similar stabilization approach is described. Here, the projector pose relative to the display surface is recovered up to an unknown translation in the display plane.

Pointing Techniques

After the stabilization of the projector images, several techniques can be adopted to interact with the displayed content. Controlling a cursor by laser pointing (e.g., with a projector-attached laser pointer) represents one possibility. In this case, common desktop mouse interaction techniques can be mapped directly to hand-held projectors. The projector's center pixel ray can also be used instead of a laser pointer to control the mouse cursor. One of the biggest problems associated with these methods are size reductions and cropping of the display area, caused by the movement of the projector when controlling the cursor. Using a secondary device such as a tracked stylus or a separate laser pointer can overcome these limitations, however the user needs both hands for interaction. Mounting a touch pad or other input devices on the projector is also possible, but might not be as intuitive as a direct pointing with the projector itself.

Selection and Manipulation

Based on the display and direct pointing ability described above, mouse like interaction can be emulated such as selecting a menu or performing a cut-and-paste operation by pointing the cursors on the projected area and pressing buttons mounted on the projector. However, in this scenario, the hand jitter problem, similar to laser pointer interaction, also exists – making it difficult to locate the cursor in specific and small areas. The jitter problem is intensified when cursor pointing is combined with mouse button-pressing operations. Adopting specially designed interaction techniques rather than emulating common desktop GUI methods, can alleviate this problem.

One proven and efficient interaction technique for hand-held projectors is the crossing based widget technique [37]. Crossing based widget is operated by moving the cursor to cross the widget in a specific direction (e.g. from outside to inside, or from top to bottom), while holding the mouse button. This technique avoids pointing the cursor and pressing a button at the same time. Crossing widget can be used for hand-held projectors to support commonly used desktop GUI elements, such as menus and sliders. Crossing based menu items can be activated by crossing from one direction; and deactivated by crossing from the opposite direction. All actions are executed by releasing the mouse button. Different colors can be used to indicate the crossing directions. Hierarchical menus can also be supported. Similarly, the crossing based slider is activated by crossing the interface in one direction, deactivated by crossing it in the opposite direction, and adjusted according to the cursor movement parallel to the slider.

Another specially designed interaction technique is called zoom-and-pick widget, proposed by [39]. It was designed to implement the simultaneous use of stable high-resolution visualization and pixel-accurate pointing for hand-held projectors. The widget is basically a square magnification area, located around the current pointing cursor position. A circular dead zone is defined within this area. The center of the dead zone is treated as an interaction hot-spot. The widget remains static when the pointing cursor is moving within the dead zone. To gain pixel-accurate pointing ability, a rim is defined around the dead zone. Each crossing of the cursor from the dead zone into the rim triggers a single pixel movement of the widget in the direction of the pointer movement. If the pointer is moving beyond the dead zone and the rim, the widget will be relocated to include the pointer in its dead zone again.

Multi-user Interaction

Hand-held projectors also pose new chances and challenges for multi-user interaction. In contrast to other multi-user devices such as tabletop displays, primarily used for sharing information with others, or other mobile devices such as personal mobile phones; hand-held projectors, due to their portability, and personal usage, are suitable both for shared and individual use. Multiple hand-held projectors combine the advantages of public and personal display systems.

The main issues associated with multi-user interaction and hand-held projectors are primarily concerned with design for ownership, privacy control, sharing, and so on. The name of the owner of a displayed object can be represented by specially designed label widgets placed on the object and operated using crossing based operations. The overlap of two or more cursors can signify consent from multiple users to accomplish collaborative interactive task, such as coping a file or blending two images between the users. Snapping and docking actions can be performed by multiple users in order to quickly view or modify connected information between multiple objects. Multiple displayed images from more than one user can be blended directly or semantically. By displaying high resolution images when the user moves closer to the display surface, a focus-and-context experience can be achieved by providing refined local details. More details can be found in [40].

Environment Awareness

Due to their portability, hand-held projectors are mainly used spontaneously. Therefore, it is desirable to enhance the hand-held projectors with environment awareness abilities. Geometric and photometric measurement and object recognition and tracking capacities, would enable the projector to sense and respond to the environment accordingly.

Geometric and photometric awareness can be implemented using, for example, structured light techniques, as described in section "Structured Light Scanning". For object recognition and tracking, the use of a passive fiducial marker (e.g., supported with open source computer vision toolkits such as ARToolkit[41]) is a cheap solution. However, it is not visually attractive which may disturb the appearance of the object and may fail as a result of occlusion or low illumination. Unpowered passive RFID tags can be detected via a radio frequency reader without being visible. They represent another inexpensive solution for object identification. However, they do not support pose tracking. The combination of RFID tags with photo-sensors, called RFIG, has been developed in order to obtain both – object identification and object position. The detection of the object position is implemented by projecting Gray codes onto the photo-sensors. In this way the Gray code is sensed by each photo-sensor and allows computing the projection of the sensors to the projector image plane, and consequently enables projector registration. More details about RFIG are referred to [42].

Interaction Design and Paradigm

In the sections above, techniques for human interaction with different configurations of projector-camera systems were presented. This subsection, however, will introduce higher level concepts and methods for interaction design and interaction paradigms for such devices. Alternative configurations such as steerable projector and moveable surfaces will also be discussed briefly.

Projector-based systems for displaying virtual environments assume high quality, large field of view, and continuous display areas which often evoke feelings of immersion and presence, and provide continuous interaction spaces. In contrast, spatial projector-camera systems that display on everyday surfaces may produce blended and warped images with average quality and a cropped field of view. The cropped view occurs as a result of the constricted display area, discontinuous images on different depth levels, and surfaces with different modulation properties. Due to these discrepancies, it is not always possible to directly adopt interaction techniques from immersive virtual environments or from conventional augmented reality applications.

For example, moving a virtual object using the pointing-and-drag technique, which is often adopted in virtual environments, may not be the preferred method in a projector-based augmented environment, since the appearance of the virtual object may vary drastically as it is moved and displayed on discontinuous surfaces with different depths and material properties. Instead, grasp-and-drop techniques may be better suited to this situation, as discussed in [43].

Furthermore, the distance between the user and display surface is important for designing and selecting interaction techniques. It was expected that pointing interaction is more suitable for manipulating far distance objects, while touching is suitable for near distance objects. However, contradictory findings, derived from user studies for interaction with projector-camera systems aimed for implementing augmented workspace [43], have proven otherwise. Users were found unwilling to touch the physical surfaces even at close range distances after they learned distance gestures such as pointing. Instead, users frequently continued using the pointing method, even for surfaces located in close proximity to them. The reason for this behavior may be two-fold. Firstly, users may prefer to use a consistent technique for manipulation such as pointing. Secondly, it seems that the appearance and materials of the surfaces affect the user's willingness to interact with them [44].

Several interaction paradigms have been introduced with or for projector-camera systems. Tangible user interfaces were developed to manipulate projected content using physical tangible objects [45]. Vision based implicit interaction techniques have also been applied to support subtle and persuasive display concepts derived from ubiquitous computing [46]. The peephole paradigm is discussed as a concept to describe the projected display as a peephole for the physical environment [47]. Varying bubble-like free-form shapes of the projected area based on the environment enables a new interface that moves beyond regular fixed display boundaries [48].

Besides hand-held projectors which enable ubiquitous display, steerable projectors also bring new interaction concepts, such as everywhere displays. Such systems enable projections on different surfaces in a room, and to turn them into an interaction interfaces. The best way to control a steerable projector during the interaction, however still needs to be determined. Body tracking can be combined with steerable projections to produce a paradigm called user-following display [49], where the user's position and pose are tracked. Projection surfaces are then dynamically selected and modulated accordingly, based on a measured and maintained three-dimensional model of the surfaces in the room. Alternatively, laser pointers can be used and tracked by a pan/tilt/zoom camera to control and interact with a steerable projector unit [50]. Another issue for interaction with steerable projectors is the question of how to support a dynamic interfaces which can change form and location on the fly. A vision-based approach can solve this problem by decoupling interface specifications from its location in space and in the camera image [51].

Besides the projectors themselves, projection surfaces might also be moveable rather than remain static in the environment. They may be rigidly moveable flat screens, semi-rigidly foldable objects such as a fan or an umbrella, or deformable objects such as paper and cloth. Moveable projection surfaces can provide novel interfaces and enable unique interaction paradigms such as foldable displays or organic user interfaces [52]. Tracking the pose or deformation of such surfaces, however, is an issue that still needs to be addressed. Cheap hardware trackers have been used recently to support semi-rigid surfaces [53]. Vision-based deformation detection algorithms may be useful in future for supporting deformable display surfaces.

Application Examples

The basic visualization and interaction techniques that have been presented in the sections above enable a variety of new applications in different domains. In general, projector-camera systems can be applied to interactive or non-interactive visual presentations in situations where the application of projection screens is not possible, or not desired. Several examples are outlined below.

Embedded Multimedia Presentations

Many historic sites, such as castles, caves, or churches, are open to public. Flat panel displays or projection screens are frequently being used for presenting visual information. These screens, however, are permanently installed features and unnecessarily cover a certain amount of space. They cannot be temporally disassembled to give the visitors an authentic impression of the environment's ambience when required.

Being able to project undistorted images onto arbitrary existing surfaces offers a potential solution to this problem. Projectors can display images that are much larger than the device itself. The images can be seamlessly embedded, and turned off any time to provide an unconstrained experience. For these reasons, projector-camera systems and image correction techniques are applied in several professional domains, such as historic sites, theater, festivals, museums, public screen presentations, advertisement displays, theme parks, and many others. Figure 2 illustrates two examples for a theater stage projection at the Karl-May Festival in Elspe (Germany), and an immersive panoramic projection onto the walls of the main tower of castle Osterburg in Weida (Germany). Both are used for displaying multimedia content which is alternately turned on and off during the main stage performance and the museum presentation respectively. Other examples of professional applications can be found at www.vioso.com.

Superimposing Museum Artifacts

Projector-camera systems can also be used for superimposing museum artifacts with pictorial content. This helps to communicate information about the displayed objects more efficiently than secondary screens.

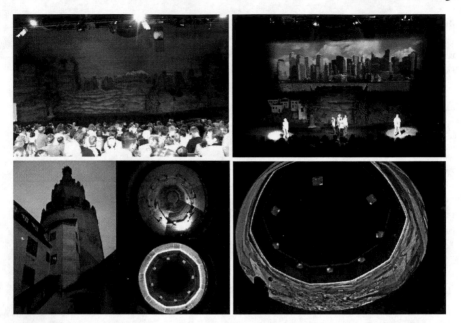

Fig. 2 Projection onto physical stage setting (top), and 360 degree surround projection onto natural stone walls in castle tower (bottom). Image courtesy: VIOSO GmbH, www.vioso.com

In this case, a precise registration of the projector-camera system is not only necessary to ensure an adequate image correction (e.g., geometrically, photometrically, and focus), but also for displaying visual content that is geometrically registered to the corresponding parts of the object.

Figure 3 illustrates two examples for superimposing visual content, such as color, text and image labels, interactive visualizations of magnifications and underdrawings, and visual highlights on replicas of a fossil (primal horse displayed by Senckenberg Museum Frankfurt, Germany) and paintings (Michaelangelo's Creation of Adam, sanguine and Pontormo's Joseph and Jacob in Egypt, oil on wood) [22].

In addition to augmenting an arbitrary image content, it is also possible to boost the contrast of low contrast objects, such as paintings whose colors have faded after a long exposure to sun light. The principle techniques describing how this can be achieved are explained in [19].

Spatial Augmented Reality

Projector-camera systems cannot only acquire parameters that are necessary for image correction, but also higher level information, such as the surrounding scene geometry. This, for instance, enables corrected projections of stereoscopic images

Fig. 3 Fossil replica superimposed with projected color (top), and painting replicas augmented with interactive pictorial content (bottom) [22]

onto real-world surfaces which allows the augmentation of three-dimensional interactive content. Active stereoscopic shutter glasses and head-tracking technology supports correct depth viewing of virtual content in precise alignment with the physical environment. This is a projector-based variation of what is referred to as spatial augmented reality [23]. In contrast to mobile augmented realities, the display technology for spatial augmented reality applications is not hand-held or head-worn, but fixed in the environment. This has several technological advantages, but also limits the applications to non-mobile ones.

Figure 4 illustrates two projector-based spatial augmented reality examples: An architectural global lighting simulation is projected directly within the real environment enabling a more realistic and immersive visualization than possible with only a monitor. Stereoscopically projected game content can interact with real objects. A physical simulation of the virtual car allows realistic collisions with real items. This is possible through the scanned scene geometry, which also enables correct occlusion effects. Object recognition techniques that are applied to the acquired scene geometry and to the captured camera image enable the derivation of contextual information that is used in the game logic. Motorized pan-tilt projector-camera units allow using large parts of an entire room as playground for such spatial augmented reality games. More information on spatial augmented reality can be found in [23]. A free e-book is available at www.SpatialAR.com.

Fig. 4 Examples for spatial augmented reality applications with projector camera systems. An immersive in-place visualization of an architectural lighting simulation (left), and a stereoscopically projected spatial augmented reality game (right). Door, window, illumination and the car are projected

Flexible Digital Video Composition

Blue screens and chroma keying technology are essential for digital video composition. Professional studios apply tracking technology to record the camera path for perspective augmentations of original video footage. Although this technology is well established, it does not offer a great deal of flexibility.

For shootings at non-studio sets, physical blue screens can be installed and takes might have to be recorded twice (with and without blue screens), or parts have to be re-recorded in a studio.

In addition, virtual studio technology itself still faces limitations. Chroma-keying and studio illumination, for instance, are difficult to harmonize. Moderators or actors have to spend a fair amount of practice time before interacting with invisible virtual components naturally. Spill on the foreground and disadvantageous foreground colors lead to low-quality or even unusable keying results.

Temporally synchronized projector-camera systems can be used to project corrected keying patterns and other spatial codes onto arbitrary diffuse (real-world) surfaces. Therefore the reflectance of the underlying real surface is widely neutralized by applying the image correction techniques that have been explained above. The main difference to the application examples that have been described so far, is that projector-camera systems are used for recording visual effects, and not for presenting corrected visual content directly to human observers.

A temporal multiplexing between projection (p-frames) and flash illumination (i-frames) allows capturing the fully lit scene, while still being able to key the foreground objects. This is illustrated in figure 5.

Since the entire scene is recorded when physical blue screens do not block the view, the footage of the full background scene can be used for video composition. Thus, recordings need not be taken twice, and keying is invariant to foreground colors. In addition, other spatial codes can be embedded into the projected images to enable tracking of the camera, environment matting, and displaying in-place

Fig. 5 VirtualStudio2Go: Odd (i-) frames record the fully illuminated scene. Even (p-) frames record the non-illuminated scene with projected images that neutralize the appearance of a real background surface and display code patterns. Repeating this at HD scanning speed (59.94Hz) and registering both sub-frames during post-processing supports high quality digital video composition effects for real (non-studio) environments

moderator information. Furthermore, the reconstruction of the scene geometry is implicitly supported, and allows special composition effects, such as shadow casts, occlusions and reflections.

A concept that combines all of these techniques into one single compact and portable system that is fully compatible with common digital video composition pipelines, and offers an immediate plug-and-play applicability is presented in [24]. It enables professional digital video composition effects in real indoor environments.

Interactive Attraction Installations

Today, the most popular applications of projector-camera systems are perhaps interactive attractions as public installations. By projecting interactive graphics onto everyday surfaces in public places, such as walls in museums, floors in shopping mall, subway tunnels, and even dining tables in restaurants, projector-camera systems emerge as an effective attraction tool by creating vivid interactive art, entertainment, and advertisement experience for people. Vision based sensing technology can be mainly adopted in such interactive art systems to detect people's presence and activity in an unobtrusive way, and implicitly engaging people with the artificially augmented environment through large scale human body motions, hand gesture, or finger touching interactions with such installations.

Figure 6 illustrates two projector-based interactive attraction installations. In the left example, a realistically rendered water pool is projected directly onto the ground of the Lou Dong Chinese Painting Museum at Tai Cang (China) with a physically built pool boundary, where the rendered water, lotus, and fishes in the pool are all responsive to the visitors who step into it. Ripple effects in the water, blooming lutoses, and escaping fishes, have been rendered in this way [54]. A Chinese painting is mapped as texture on the ground of the pool to compliment the artwork. Since this system has been installed in the museum, its realistic appearance and vivid

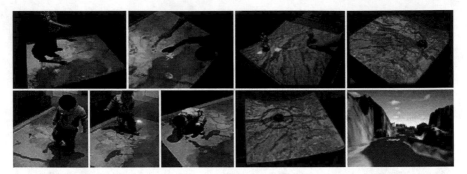

Fig. 6 Examples for interactive attraction installations. An interactive water pool installed in a traditional art museum (left) and an interactive augmented physical map installation for tourist attraction (right)

interactivity have attracted many visitors, especially young children who have little contact with traditional culture.

In another installation which was exhibited for an art-science festival in Shanghai's Oriental Pearl Tower (China), a shining icon is projected onto a traditional physical tourist map. The tourists can select different sites by hands or props on the map to see related video information. A tour guide can then create a touring path on the map with a laser pointer, or a visitor could produce a path by walking on a projected map on the ground. A three dimensional walk-through of the tour scene can then be triggered along the created path [55]. By integrating the traditional tangible map with the augmented digital information, and enabling vision-based and tangible interaction techniques, the projector-camera system can provide tourists and tour guides with a fresh sightseeing experience.

The Future of Projector-Camera Systems

Projector-camera systems have already found practical applications in theater, museums, historic sites, open-air festivals, trade shows, advertisement, visual effects, theme parks, and art installations. With advances in technology and techniques, they will be applied in many more areas in future.

Future projectors will become more compact in size and will require little power and cooling. Reflective technology (such as DLP or LCOS) will increasingly replace transmissive technology (e.g., LCD). This will leads to an increased brightness and extremely high update rates. GPUs for real-time graphics and vision processing will also be integrated. While resolution, contrast and speed will keep increasing, production costs and market prizes will continue to fall. Conventional UHP lamps will be replaced by powerful LEDs or multi-channel lasers. This will make them suitable for mobile applications. Projector-camera technology is currently being integrated into mobile devices, such as cellphones, and supports truly flexible presentations methods. Image correction techniques, such as the ones explained above are essential for these devices, since projection screens will most likely not become mobile.

But projector-camera systems will not only be used as display devices. In future, they will also enable intelligent, spatially and temporally controllable light sources. Projector-based illumination techniques will not only solve problems in professional domains, such as microscopy or endoscopy, but -one day- might also be applied in more general contexts.

Imagine that networked projector-camera systems become as cheap and as compact as light bulbs. They could not only be turned on and off, but would allow to offer synthetic room illumination and interactive display capabilities everywhere. For instance, they could produce individual mood profile and ambient light situations, as well as to enable internet access wherever you stand.

References

1. O. Bimber, D. Iwai, G. Wetzstein, and A. Grundhoefer, "The Visual Computing of Projector-Camera Systems," Computer Graphics Forum, Vol. 27, No. 8, pp. 2219–2245, 2008.
2. G. Wetzstein and O. Bimber, "Radiometric Compensation through Inverse Light Transport," Proceedings of Pacific Graphics, pp. 391–399, 2007.
3. J. Salvi, J. Pagés, and J. Batlle, "Pattern Codification Strategies in Structured Light Systems," Pattern Recognition, Vol. 37, No.4, pp.827–849, 2004.
4. R. Raskar, G. Welch, M. Cutts, A. Lake, L. Stesin, and H. Fuchs, "The Office of the Future: A Unified Approach to Image-Based Modeling and Spatially Immersive Displays," Proceedings of ACM SIGGRAPH, pp. 179–188, 1998.
5. O. Bimber, A. Emmering, and T. Klemmer, "Embedded Entertainment with Smart Projectors," IEEE Computer, Vol.38, No.1, pp.56–63, 2005.
6. S. K. Nayar, H. Peri, M. D. Grossberg, and P. N. Belhumeur, "A Projection System with Radiometric Compensation for Screen Imperfections," Proceedings of IEEE International Workshop on Projector-Camera Systems (ProCams), 2003.
7. T. Yoshida, C. Horii, and K. Sato, "A Virtual Color Reconstruction System for Real Heritage with Light Projection," Proceedings of International Conference on Virtual Systems and Multimedia (VSMM), pp. 161–168, 2003.
8. M. Ashdown, T. Okabet, I. Sato, and Y. Sato, "Robust Content-Dependent Photometric Projector Compensation," Proceedings of IEEE International Workshop on Projector-Camera Systems (ProCams), 2006.
9. A. Grundhoefer and O. Bimber, "Real-Time Adaptive Radiometric Compensation," IEEE Transactions on Visualization and Computer Graphics (TVCG), Vol. 14, No. 1, pp. 97–108, 2008.
10. H. Park, M.-H. Lee, S.-J. Kim, and J.-I. Park, "Specularity-Free Projection on Nonplanar Surface," Proceedings of Pacific-Rim Conference on Multimedia (PCM) (2005), pp. 606–616.
11. R. Sukthankar, C. Tat-Jen, and G. Sukthankar, "Dynamic Shadow Elimination for Multi-Projector Displays," Proceedings of IEEE Conference on Computer Vision and Pattern Recognition (CVPR), Vol. II, pp. 151–157, 2001.
12. C. Jaynes, S. Webb, and R. M. Steele, "Camera-Based Detection and Removal of Shadows from Interactive Multiprojector Displays," IEEE Transactions on Visualization and Computer Graphics (TVCG), Vol. 10, No. 3, pp. 290–301, 2004.

13. M. S. Brown, P. Song, and T. - J. Cham, "Image Pre-Conditioning for Out-of-Focus Projector Blur," Proceedings of IEEE Conference on Computer Vision and Pattern Recognition (CVPR), Vol. II, pp. 1956–1963, 2006.

14. Y. Oyamada and H. Saito, "Focal Pre-Correction of Projected Image for Deblurring Screen Image," Proceedings of IEEE International Workshop on Projector-Camera Systems (ProCams), 2007.

15. L. Zhang and S. K. Nayar, "Projection Defocus Analysis for Scene Capture and Image Display," ACM Trans. Graph. (Siggraph), Vol. 25, No. 3, pp.907–915, 2006.

16. M. Grosse and O. Bimber, "Coded Aperture Projection," Proceedings of Emerging Display Technologies and Immersive Projection Technologies 2008 (EDT IPT08), 2008.

17. O. Bimber and A. Emmerling, "Multifocal Projection: A Multiprojector Technique for Increasing Focal Depth," IEEE Transactions on Visualization and Computer Graphics (TVCG), Vol. 12, No. 4, pp. 658–667, 2006.

18. K. Fuji, M. Grossberg, and S. Nayar, "A Projector-Camera System with Real-Time Photometric Adaptation for Dynamic Environments," Proceedings of IEEE Conference on Computer Vision and Pattern Recognition (CVPR), Vol. I, pp. 814–821, 2005.

19. O. Bimber and D. Iwai, "Superimposing Dynamic Range," ACM Transactions on Graphics (ACM Siggraph Asia), Vol. 27, No. 5, article 150, 2008.

20. D. Cotting, M. Naef, M. H. Gross, and H. Fuchs, "Embedding Imperceptible Patterns into Projected Images for Simultaneous Acquisition and Display," Proceedings of IEEE/ACM International Symposium on Mixed and Augmented Reality (ISMAR), pp. 100–109, 2004.

21. S. Zollmann and O. Bimber, "Imperceptible Calibration for Radiometric Compensation," Proceedings of Eurographics, pp. 61–64, 2007.

22. O. Bimber, F. Coriand, A. Kleppe, E. Bruns, S. Zollmann, and T. Langlotz, "Superimposing Pictorial Artwork with Projected Imagery," IEEE MultiMedia, Vol. 12, No.1, pp. 16–26, 2005.

23. O. Bimber and R. Raskar, "Spatial Augmented Reality: Merging Real and Virtual Worlds," A K Peters LTD (publisher), ISBN: 1-56881-230-2, free e-book: www.SpatialAR.com, July 2005.

24. A. Grundhoefer and O. Bimber, "VirtualStudio2Go: Digital Videocomposition for Real Environments," ACM Transactions on Graphics (ACM Siggraph Asia), Vol. 27, No. 5, article 151, 2008.

25. D. A. Bowman, E. Kruijff, J. J. Laviola, and I. Poupyrev, "3D User Interfaces: Theory and Practice," Addison-Wesley, 2005.

26. R. Raskar and K. L. Low, "Interacting with spatially augmented reality," Proceedings of the 1st international conference on Computer graphics, virtual reality and visualisation(AFRIGRAPH '01), pp. 101–108, 2001.

27. A. Licsar and T. Sziranyi, "Hand gesture recognition in camera-projector system," Proceedings of the ECCV 2004 Workshop on HCI - Computer Vision in Human-Computer Interaction, pp. 83–93, 2004.

28. R. Kjeldsen, C. Pinhanez, G. Pingali, J. Hartman, T. Levas, and M. Podlaseck, "Interacting with Steerable Projected Displays," Proceedings of the 5th International Conference on Automatic Face and Gesture Recognition, pp. 12–17, 2002.

29. A. D. Wilson, "Playanywhere: a compact interactive tabletop projection-vision system," Proceedings of the 18th annual ACM symposium on User interface software and technology (UIST '05), pp. 83–92, 2005.

30. Y. Wu, T. S. Huang, and N. Mathews, "Vision-based gesture recognition: A review," Proceedings of the International Workshop on Gesture-Based Communication in Human-Computer Interaction, pp. 103–115, 1999.

31. G. Yahav, G. Iddan, and D. Mandelboum, "3d imaging camera for gaming application," International Conference on Consumer Electronics (ICCE 2007) - Digest of Technical Papers, pp. 1–2, 2007.

32. D. R. Olsen and T. Nielsen, "Laser pointer interaction," Proceedings of the SIGCHI conference on Human factors in computing systems (CHI '01), pp. 17–22, 2001.

33. B. Myers, R. Bhatnagar, J. Nichols, C. Peck, D. Kong, R. Miller, and A. Long, "Interacting at a distance: measuring the performance of laser pointers and other devices," Proceedings of the SIGCHI conference on Human factors in computing systems (CHI '02), pp. 33–40, 2002.

34. X. Cao and R. Balakrishnan, "Visionwand: interaction techniques for large displays using a passive wand tracked in 3d," Proceedings of the 16th annual ACM symposium on User interface software and technology (UIST '03), pp. 173–182, 2003.

35. M. Piccardi, "Background subtraction techniques: a review," Proceedings of the IEEE International Conference on Systems, Man and Cybernetics, Vol. 4, pp. 3099–3104, 2004.

36. T. Moeslund, A. Hilton, and V. Krüger, "A survey of advances in vision-based human motion capture and analysis," Computer Vision and Image Understanding, Vol. 104, No. 2–3, pp. 90–126, 2006.

37. X. Cao and R. Balakrishnan, "Interacting with dynamically defined information spaces using a handheld projector and a pen," Proceedings of the 19th annual ACM symposium on User interface software and technology (UIST '06), pp. 225–234, 2006.

38. P. Beardsley, J. Van Baar, R. Raskar, and C. Forlines, "Interaction using a handheld projector," IEEE Computer Graphics and Applications, Vol. 25, No. 1, pp. 39–43, 2005.

39. C. Forlines, R. Balakrishnan, P. Beardsley, J. van Baar, and R. Raskar, "Zoom-and-pick: facilitating visual zooming and precision pointing with interactive handheld projectors," Proceedings of the 18th annual ACM symposium on User interface software and technology (UIST '05), pp. 73–82, 2005.

40. X. Cao, C. Forlines, and R. Balakrishnan, "Multi-user interaction using handheld projectors," Proceedings of the 20th annual ACM symposium on User interface software and technology (UIST '07), pp. 43–52, 2007.

41. H. Kato and M. Billinghurst, "Marker Tracking and HMD Calibration for a Video-based Augmented Reality Conferencing System," Proceedings of the 2nd IEEE and ACM International Workshop on Augmented Reality, Vol. 99, pp. 85–94, 1999.

42. R. Raskar, P. Beardsley, J. van Baar, Y. Wang, P. Dietz, J. Lee, D. Leigh, and T. Willwacher, "RFIG Lamps: interacting with a self-describing world via photosensing wireless tags and projectors," Proceedings of SIGGRAPH 2004, pp. 406–415, 2004.

43. S. Voida, M. Podlaseck, R. Kjeldsen, and C. Pinhanez, "A study on the manipulation of 2D objects in a projector/camera-based augmented reality environment," Proceedings of the SIGCHI conference on Human factors in computing systems, pp. 611–620, 2005.

44. M. Podlaseck, C. Pinhanez, N. Alvarado, M. Chan, and E. Dejesus, "On interfaces projected onto real-world objects," Proceedings of the SIGCHI Conference on Human Factors in Computing Systems, pp. 802–803, 2003.

45. J. Underkoffler, B. Ullmer, and H. Ishii, "Emancipated pixels: real-world graphics in the luminous room," Proceedings of the 26th annual conference on Computer graphics and interactive techniques (SIGGRAPH '99), pp. 385–392, 1999.

46. P. Dietz, R. Raskar, S. Booth, J. van Baar, K. Wittenburg, and B. Knep, "Multi-projectors and implicit interaction in persuasive public displays," Proceedings of the working conference on Advanced visual interfaces, pp. 209–217, 2004.

47. A. Butz and A. Krüger, "Applying the Peephole Metaphor in a Mixed-Reality Room," IEEE Computer Graphics and Applications, Vol. 26, No.1, pp. 56–63, 2006.

48. D. Cotting and M. Gross, "Interactive environment-aware display bubbles," Proceedings of the 19th annual ACM symposium on User interface software and technology (UIST '06), pp. 245–254, 2006.

49. G. Pingali, C. Pinhanez, T. Levas, R. Kjeldsen, and M. Podlaseck, "User-Following Displays," Proceedings of IEEE International Conference on Multimedia and Expo, 2002.

50. D. Kurz, F. Hantsch, M. Grobe, A. Schiewe, and O. Bimber, "Laser pointer tracking in projector-augmented architectural environments," Proceeding of the 6th IEEE and ACM International Symposium on Mixed and Augmented Reality (ISMAR), pp.1–8, 2007.

51. R. Kjeldsen, A. Levas, and C. Pinhanez, "Dynamically reconfigurable vision-based user interfaces," Machine Vision and Applications, Vol. 16, No. 1, pp. 6–12, 2004.

52. R. Vertegaal and I. P. Poupyrev, "Introduction to Special Issue of Organic user interfaces," Communications of ACM, Vol. 51, No. 6, 2008.
53. J. C. Lee, S. E. Hudson, and E. Tse, "Foldable interactive displays," Proceedings of the 21st annual ACM symposium on User interface software and technology (UIST '08), pp. 287–290, 2008.
54. M. Jin, H. Zhang, X. Yang, and S. Xiao, "A Real-Time ProCam System for Interaction with Chinese Ink-and-Wash Cartoons," Proceedings of IEEE International Workshop on Projector-Camera Systems (ProCams), 2007.
55. Y. Yuan, X. Yang, and S. Xiao, "A Framework for Tangible User Interfaces within Projector-based Mixed Reality," Proceedings of the 6th IEEE and ACM International Symposium on Mixed and Augmented Reality (ISMAR), 2007.

Chapter 22
Believable Characters

**Magy Seif El-Nasr, Leslie Bishko, Veronica Zammitto, Michael Nixon,
Athanasios V. Vasiliakos, and Huaxin Wei**

Introduction

The interactive entertainment industry is one of the fastest growing industries in
the world. In 1996, the U.S. entertainment software industry reported $2.6 billion
in sales revenue, this figure has more than tripled in 2007 yielding $9.5 billion in
revenues [1]. In addition, gamers, the target market for interactive entertainment
products, are now reaching beyond the traditional 8–34 year old male to include
women, Hispanics, and African Americans [2]. This trend has been observed in
several markets, including Japan, China, Korea, and India, who has just published
their first international AAA title (defined as high quality games with high budget),
a 3D third person action game: *Ghajini – The Game* [3].

 The topic of believable characters is becoming a central issue when designing
and developing games for today's game industry. While narrative and character were
considered secondary to game mechanics, games are currently evolving to integrate
characters, narrative, and drama as part of their design. One can see this pattern
through the emergence of games like *Assassin's Creed* (published by Ubisoft 2008),
Hotel Dusk (published by Nintendo 2007), and *Prince of Persia series* (published
by Ubisoft), which emphasized character and narrative as part of their design.

M.S. El-Nasr (✉)
School of Interactive Arts and Technology, Simon Fraser University, Vancouver, BC, Canada
e-mail: magy@sfu.ca

L. Bishko
Department of Animation, Emily Carr University of Art and Design, Vancouver, BC, Canada
e-mail: lbishko@ecuad.ca

V. Zammitto, M. Nixon, and H. Wei
School of Interactive Arts and Technology, Simon Fraser University, Vancouver, BC, Canada
e-mail: vzammitt@sfu.ca; mna32@sfu.ca; huaxinw@sfu.ca

A.V. Vasiliakos
University of Peloponnese, Nauplion, Greece
e-mail: vasilako@ath.forthnet.gr

B. Furht (ed.), *Handbook of Multimedia for Digital Entertainment and Arts*,
DOI 10.1007/978-0-387-89024-1_22, © Springer Science+Business Media, LLC 2009

Beyond the entertainment industry, the use of virtual environments for learning, health therapy, cultural awareness, and training is increasingly becoming a reality. In the recent years, there has been an increase in the number of research initiatives that use simulations and interactive 3D environments for a wide variety of applications [4–11]. Several great examples are displayed in the projects developed by Institute of Creative Technologies at University of Southern California, where they utilize 3D environments with rich characters to teach cultural norms and foreign language, among other subjects. These applications provide a safe and comfortable environment for participants to interact within and learn at their own pace. In order to achieve their goals, however, such applications require realistic simulation of culture, people, and space. Thus, again the topic of believable characters is gaining more attention as a central topic that deserves further attention.

Since the above mentioned applications are typically interactive, animated believable characters are often required to adapt based on the interaction. Current industry methods, however, rely on heavy scripting, where voice acting, dialogue scripts, hand-coded animation routines, and hard-coded behaviors are used to portray the desired character; To mention a few examples of games that employ very detailed motion-captured characters, readers are referred to *Assassins' Creed* and *Prince of Persia* (developed by Ubisoft) and *Façade* (developed by Mateas and Stern [12]), see Figure 1. In these games, artists work very diligently to detail characters' mannerisms and body motion to exhibit the right character characteristics [3]. Such attention to detail of the non-verbal behaviors is a crucial element for character believability [4].

As one can guess, this kind of scripting is labor intensive and rigid, as it does not adapt to all variations induced by interaction. An alternative is to use artificial intelligent algorithms and graphics techniques to adapt character behaviors to variations in context induced by interaction. This alternative, however, is not as simple as it sounds, as it has been under research for many years and is still an open problem. Researchers have been working on several fronts to create believable expressive characters that can dynamically adapt within interactive narratives. Graphics researchers, for example, explored the integration of emotions and personality as parameters to modify virtual character animations [5–7]. Researchers working on developing conversational agents focus on building articulate virtual characters that can automatically synchronize gesture and speech [8]. Artificial intelligence

Fig. 1 Screenshots from games and interactive media featuring characters

researchers focus on integrating models of emotion and personality to build characters that have the ability to improvise [9–11].

As researchers tackle different aspects of this open problem, gaps between these different directions start to appear. One important gap is the gap between character models or attributes, such as personality, physical appearance, and emotions, and how characters use nonverbal behaviour to portray these attributes. In order for a character to adapt, it needs to not only be able to automatically select its motions and execute its actions, but to also select nonverbal behaviours that convey and maintain its attributes. Let's take a character within a soccer game, for example. Such a character is required to adapt and blend between different actions, such as dribbling, diving, running, walking, scoring, yelling, and arguing with the referee, to mention a few actions. This character should be able to select its actions based on the current context and its own goals. In choosing how to blend between actions and how to execute the animations, it needs to convey and maintain its own personality and emotions. The important open problem here is how to enable characters to do this without hand coding all different variations given all different contexts? This is the central question and problem that this chapter deals with. The aim is to review ongoing research that may provide readers with a good starting point to tackle this problem.

To start discussing this problem, we will first define believability, or believable characters. Believability is gauged by the extent to which a viewer engages and empathizes with an animated character [13–15]. In the context of believability, it is important to note the theory of the Uncanny Valley. Proposed in 1970 by Japanese roboticist Masahiro Mori, the theory explains human reactions towards increasing levels of realism to non-human entities, e.g., robots. The theory suggests that humans may develop feelings of repulsion or negativity towards non-human entities as the level of realism increases. In recent years, the application of the Uncanny Valley theory broadened to areas of animation. In the context of this chapter, we look towards believability over realism, focusing on broader concepts of nonverbal communication that may contribute to future efforts to solve the Uncanny Valley problem.

Character believability can be approached from several perspectives, including personality theories, movement theories, emotion and cognitive theories. Each of these perspectives have been studied in different fields of inquiry, including psychology, kinesiology, animation, and acting. This chapter attempts to discuss many of these perspectives. However, due to space limitations several notable works are left out, such as the narrative and literature perspective.

In this chapter we study two concepts: *non-verbal behavior* and their relation to *character attributes*. We define non-verbal behavior as a single or pattern of movements and postures that are exhibited in the body, such as hand movement, or leg movement. For example, the motion of quickly glancing at a character then at the ground is considered a non-verbal behavior pattern. We use the terms character attributes, character characteristics, and character model to mean a list of parameters that define a character, including age, physique, personality, behavior tendencies, quirks, and habits.

We specifically explore believable character through personality models (e.g., Factor theories from psychology [16, 17]), nonverbal character behavior models (e.g., Ekman's Facial experession [18]), motion analysis models (e.g., Laban Movement Analysis [19, 20]), improvisational theatre character models (e.g., Johnstone's impro [21, 22]) and animation techniques, including Disney's animation methods [13]. In discussing these models, we will discuss theories as well as practical applications of these models within the computer science or believable agents field. We will conclude by discussing the current state of the art of interactive believable characters, identifying open problems that need to be addressed in order for the field to move forward.

We specifically explore believable character through personality models such as Factor theories from psychology [16, 17], nonverbal character behavior models such as Ekman's Facial experession [18], motion analysis models such as Laban Movement Analysis [19, 20], improvisational theatre character models such as Johnstone's impro [21, 22] and animation techniques, including Disney's animation methods [13]. In discussing these models, we will discuss theories as well as practical applications of these models within the computer science or believable agents field. We will conclude by discussing the current state of the art of interactive believable characters, identifying open problems that need to be addressed in order for the field to move forward.

Character Personality

The term personality has its origin in the Ancient Greek literature; it comes from the role played by actors who wore a mask and read aloud the script from their characters' scroll. Character as a synonym of personality comes from this same theatrical origin; the word *persona* was used for *mask*. Personality is a psychological concept that has been widely used inside and outside this field. Aiken [23] (page xi) describes that:

> The term personality refers to the organized totality of the qualities, traits, and behaviors that characterize a person's individuality and by which, together with his or her physical attributes, the person is recognized as unique.

This definition reached consensus. However, Aiken [23] also warns that this definition is open and abstract, and hence difficult to operationalize. Different theories define personality with different terms and emphasize certain characteristics on top of others. Nevertheless, all of them agree that uniqueness is a key of personality, and that personality is a combination of variables that composes a unique pattern of behavior.

Personality is an important concept that is related to character believability. Characters seen in movies, theatre productions, animations, and video games all inhabit a particular personality. This personality is what makes them distinct and memorable. We expect characters to have personality and subject such personality through their goals, behaviors, and expressions. But what is personality and how can it be operationalized for computational representation of an adaptive believable character? In this section, we will look at previous work from psychology and theatre to try to conceptualize an appropriate computational representation. We will also discuss previous computational models of personality within fields such as graphics and artificial intelligence.

Through the literature, two theoretical perspectives of personality are assumed: *nomothetic* and *idiographic*. The *nomothetic* perspective approaches personality from a general perspective trying to compose personality models which can explain all different types of personalities. The *idiographic* perspective emphasizes the uniqueness of personality structure with the belief that every person has his own system, such as in phenomenological theories [24]. In this section, we discuss different personality models that fall within the nomothetic perspective, because we believe this approach is most appropriate for the development of computational models.

Body Type Theories

Theories on body-types have typically collected their data from physiological characteristics and made assumptions based on generalizations. Since there are many exceptions to their classifications, these theories do not enjoy academic popularity, yet they could offer physical cues for modeling characters. Major body-type researchers and theorists were criminologists, such as Cesare Lombroso [25], Ernst Kretschmer [26], and William Sheldon and S. S. Stevens [27].

Lombroso studied the body constitution of criminals. He stated that their physiological development is in a lower stage, and that their physiognomy is different from other people. Lombroso presumed that there was a born-criminal conception; however, since many other criminals don't possess such features, his idea didn't receive much popularity. Repeated identified atavistic characteristics were: large jaws, high cheekbones, receding foreheads, handle-shape ears, long arms, and other primitive physical traits [25].

Ernst Kretschmer [26] created the first scientific theory describing personality types based on body build. However, his research had low validity and applications of it were relegated. He collected different data measuring bodily constitution of mental patients and others, which he used to formulate four categorizations of body types:

1) *Asthenic or Leptosomic* physique: tall, thin, lanky, angular body build. People in this type are characterized as introverts, withdrawing behavior, and 'schizoid temperament'. This type of mental patient has schizophrenic symptoms.
2) *Pyknic* physique: round, stocky body build. People in this type are associated with emotional instability. Mental patients with this body complex develop bipolar disorder (manic-depressive).
3) *Athletic* physique: broad shoulders and slim hips. People in this type are prone to develop either a maniac-depressive disorder or schizophrenia.

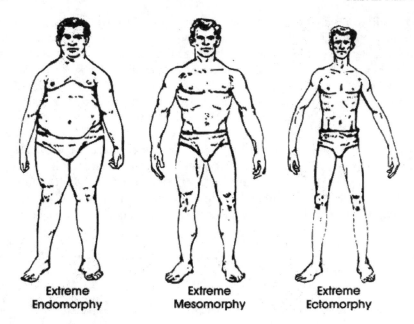

Fig. 2 Sheldom's body types

4) *Dysplastic* physique: any other body build that does not fit into any of the three other categories.

Similar to Kretschmer, Sheldon and Stevens [27] developed a quantitative classification of personality along three dimensions of body types: *Endomorphy* (fatness), *mesomorphy* (muscularity), and *ectomorphy* (thinness), where each dimension was defined on a score from 1 to 7. For example, a person with 7 for *endomorphy*, 1 for *mesomorphy*, and 1 for *ectomorphy* represents an extremely fat person who lacks other characteristics (see Figure 2). Their classification method is fuzzy as it is hard to score measures such as fatness or thinness. They found correlations between high scores of body types to temperament types which also ranged in a 7-point scale. The temperament types are:

1) *Viscerotonics*: associated to the endomorphy type. This temperament is characterized by being gregarious, friendly, and the enjoyment of comfort and eating.
2) *Somatotonics*: correlated to the mesomorphy type. This temperament is characterized by enjoying physical exercise, dominance, being loud and assertive, but not empathetic.
3) *Cerebrotonics*: linked to ectomorphy. This temperament is characterized by being quiet and reserved, reacting quickly, but over-sensitive to pain and have sleeping difficulties.

Body type theories are interesting to explore further for believable characters. They represent an important construct for character designs, concepts, and development. However, we see this type of approach to be in the hand of a designer rather than a decision of an adaptive system. The development of this approach could be a useful tool for designers as they develop their own characters, as well as a method for training character design artists.

Psychodynamic Theories

Freud, known for pioneering the psychoanalysis approach to therapy, developed a theory of personality where each individual was described to have three levels of awareness: unconscious, preconscious and conscious [28]. Personality was then categorized as three entities: id, ego, and superego. The id is full of animal instincts and operates by prioritizing pleasure satisfaction, but is purely unconscious. The ego mediates between the id, the superego, and the external world by evaluating the consequences of actions. The superego is formed by the mandates that have been internalized, and the ideal image of oneself. The ego and superego have unconscious, preconscious, and conscious levels. According to Freud the human personality is a struggle of power among id, ego, and superego.

Freud also asserts that personality is shaped through the progress of the psychosexual stages [23, 29]. During each stage a part of the body is the primary source of satisfaction and psychoenergetical (libidinal) stimulation. The first stage is oral, from birth to eighteen months, in which the mouth brings gratification as in eating and sucking. The second stage is anal, from the eighteen months to three years old, in which the anus provides satisfaction by retaining and defecating, and sphincter control is achieved. The third stage is phallic, from three to six years old, in which genitals are the focus in a rudimentary and egocentric way. The fourth stage is latency, from six to twelve years old, and is characterized by a decrease in the concentration of the genital organs. Finally is the genital stage, from the age of twelve, when genitals are the center of gratification, sexual instincts are fully developed, and sexual maturity is achieved. However, the libidinal energy that flows might get stuck in certain psychosexual stages. This fixation can be the result of traumatic or stressful experiences; it might also lead to regression of behaviors. For instance, fixation in the oral stage could be the cause of verbosity, gorging, smoking, nail biting, sarcasm or hostility. These characteristics originate from gratification of the mouth and lips through sucking, eating, and chewing. Whereas fixation in the anal stage can develop into an obsessive-compulsive personality, stubbornness, stinginess, stuttering, and petulance, having to do with the satisfaction of eliminating and controlling feces.

There are a lot of different theories that emerged based on psycho-analysis. One such research was the work of Carl Jung [29–31]. Jung detached from Freud's work; he analyzed the personality through different ways of orientation towards the external world. He identified two attitudes and four functions of thoughts shown in

Table 1 The components of
Jung's personality types

	Introversion	Extroversion
Rational	Thinking	Thinking
	Feeling	Feeling
Irrational	Sensation	Sensation
	Intuition	Intuition

Table 2 Myers-Briggs Type Indicator Personality Inventory

I	T	N	J
Introversion	Thinking	iNtuition	Judging
Extraversion	Feeling	Sensation	Perceiving
E	F	S	P

Table 1. The attitudes were *extroversion*, which looks towards the outside world, and *introversion*, which leans towards the internal world. The functions were based on the functions of the Ego: Thinking, Feeling, Sensation, and Intuition. *Thinking* and *Feeling* were considered *Rational* functions (where Jung accepts some emotions as Rational and others Irrational), and *Sensation* and *Intuition* were *Irrational*. The Rational and Irrational pairings were considered polar opposites. Jung's theory is of particular importance to us here as it has influenced much of the work in animation and motion analysis theories. These theories and approaches will be discussed below.

Based on his theory, the Myers-Briggs Type-Indicator personality inventory was developed [23, 32]. The Myers-Briggs typology places Introversion and Extraversion alongside the Ego Functions, adding an additional pairing: *Judging* and *Perceiving*. Individuals are typed as having characteristics of, and abilities within all eight functions, yet will exhibit dominant preferences among them.

Personality types according the MBTI are labeled following the letter coding, for example ESTJ (Extraversion-Sensation- Thinking -Judging), shown in Table 2. The main characteristics for each type are as follows:

- I: The interest resides in ideas, and analysis. Internal reasons are the source of motivation, and privacy is appreciated. One-to-one relationships are preferred. Related professions are librarians, anesthesiologists, and accountants.
- E: the environment and interacting with it are the major interests. People with high E are sociable, demonstrative, impulsive, and eager to lead. Linked occupations to this type are travel guides, and actors.
- T: objective observations and logical thinking are prioritized. People are identified as analytical, skeptical, and fair. Professions identified with high Thinking scores are engineers and computer scientists.
- F: values objects, people, and ideas. People with high F are emphatic and altruists. Occupations linked to F are nursing, teaching and religious clerking.
- N: the emphasis is on the upcoming possibilities, the associations that can be generated, and the interpretation of meanings. People with high score on

intuition like complexity and creativity. They are related to academic or artistic professions.

- S: attention to what is actually perceived by the senses, emphasizing the present. This type defines people as realistic, conventional, good observers, attention to and memory for detail, use common sense, dislike complexity, and enjoy the present. Typical professions associated to this type are accountant, banker, and managers.
- J: the interaction with the world is mainly through T or F functions, and having a plan of action. It is associated with rules, obedience and self-control. Occupations related to J are governmental and educational managers.
- P: interaction in the external world is characterized by using N or S functions, adapting as the situations change. It provides the ability to cope with new situations; it is also linked to autonomy and procrastination.

An important aspect of interpreting the sixteen variations is called *Type Dynamics*. One preference will have the strongest influence, and is called the *dominant function*. The second strongest preference is called the *auxiliary function*, which supports and balances the dominant. The *tertiary function* is the function opposite from an individual's auxiliary function, and tends to develop importance later in one's life. The fourth function is called the *inferior function*. It can surface unconsciously when an individual is stressed and one's dominant and auxiliary resources are exhausted. For instance, if the *dominant function* is T (a judgment type) the *auxiliary function* is a perceiving type, like S the *tertiary function* would be N, and the *inferior function* would be F, for the ESTJ type.

Traits Theories

Gordon Allport developed the first personality trait theory [23, 29]. Trait theories surpass the body type theories discussed above. The former introduces a continuum where a personality is defined as a point in the continuum. In contrast, Allport's trait theory defined three different groups of traits:

- *Cardinal traits*: highly present across situations. It is expected that a person only has a few of the following traits: despotism, humanitarianism, power striving, sadism, narcissism.
- *Central traits*: likely present in a range of situations. They are more common than cardinal traits. For example: assertiveness, honesty, gregariousness, trustworthiness.
- *Secondary traits*: related to certain situations, such as food or musical preferences.

Allport's conception of personality [23, 29] stands apart from psychoanalysis, he considered it over-concerned with unconscious mechanisms that manifest as drives. Allport embraced an idiographic approach advocating that personalities are unique, and that they change throughout our lives. Although certain patterns might remain, motivations during childhood are different from those in adulthood; their functions are independent since they serve different purposes. Therefore, there is no need to look into a person's past. He also considered intentions as the shapers of personality.

Factor Theories

Personality factor theories were constructed from statistical analysis. Several factor theories were proposed. One of the early models was Eysenck's three factor model, in which the factors were 'super-traits' [23, 29] represented as a bi-dimensional chart: y-axis representing introversion-extroversion and the x-axis representing emotional stability-instability (see Figure 3). According to Eysenck, introverts are quiet, reliable, planners, intellectual rather than social, and tend to have the ability to control their own emotions. Extraverts, on the other hand, are social, impulsive, and look for excitement. People with high scores in emotional instability are referred as neurotics and are anxious, moving constantly, and temperamental, while people who score high on the emotional stability dimension are calm and mood stable. The third factor, Psychoticism was added later, and thus does not have a graphical representation. It is linked to aggression, impulsivity, and inability to establish rapport.

Based on Eysenck's work, Cattell [23, 33] developed a multifactor theory describing personality in 16 Factors, which were:

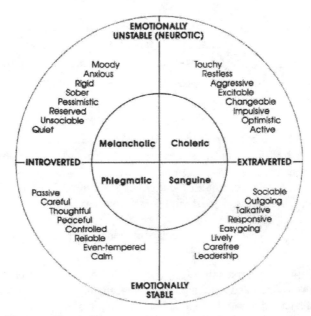

Fig. 3 Eysenck's personality model

- Warmth
- Intellect
- Emotional Stability
- Dominance
- Liveliness
- Rule-Consciousness
- Social Assertiveness
- Sensitivity
- Paranoia
- Abstractedness
- Introversion
- Anxiety
- Open-Mindedness
- Independence
- Perfectionism
- Tension

Several years later, Costa et al. [34] developed the Five Factor Model (also known as FFM, Big Five, or OCEAN) which is one of the most widely accepted personality models as it presents high dimensional consistency in different situations and across cultures [17]. The five factors are: Openness, Consciousness, Extroversion, Agreeableness, and Neuroticism (see Table 3). A personality is then defined as a score in the each factor representing a point in this 5-dimentional space [35].

For computational models, the factor theories are probably the most promising models of all others described in this section so far. They are the easiest to formalize algorithmically. It is to no one's surprise that several agent models have used these theories, as will be discussed later, for creating personality based characters. However, factor theories only examine the character attributes aspect of character representation with little information on how such personalities are manifested

Table 3 Five Factor Model

Dimension	Refers to	If low score
Openness	Imaginative, prefer variety, independent, intellectual sensitive	Down-to-earth, conventional, conforming, low aesthetical appreciation
Conscientiousness	Well-organized, careful, reliable, self-discipline, consistent	Disorganized, careless, weak-willed, aimless
Extraversion	Sociable, warmth, affectionate, optimistic, active	Reserved, sober, retiring
Agreeableness	Trusting, helpful, softhearted, modesty	Suspicious, cynical, ruthless, uncooperative
Neuroticism	Anxiety, experience negative emotions, vulnerability, worrying, impulsiveness	Secure, calm, self-satisfied

through nonverbal behaviors or mannerisms. Thus, most computational models based on factor theories, as we shall see later, fail to truly develop a believable character due to their inability to represent or develop the link between personality and behavior models.

Johnstone's Fast Food Stanislavsky Model

Stanislavisky [36, 37] is a famous Russian director who composed a theory for acting that is currently used by many acting schools to teach actors how to build and develop their characters. In his teachings, he discussed the importance of purpose for a character. Thus, instead of an actor playing an emotion, the actor would develop his actions depending on his character's goals, tactics, and purpose.

Johnstone [21, 22] is a professor emeritus at the University of Calgary and former founding Artistic Director of the Loose Moose Theatre. Johnstone is well known for his training courses on improvisational theatre techniques. In his teachings, he uses several improvisational tools that students can use to start role playing. Johnstone took the Stanislavsky model and developed several exercises (examples are shown in Table 4) defined in terms of purpose. One such exercise of interest is Fast-Food Stanislavsky based on Stanislavsky's model [21, 22].

Johnstone identified several parameters of character representation that can affect non-verbal behaviors. One such parameter is *status*. He identified *status* as a major signifier defining posture, gaze, and use of space in movement. A person of high status, for example, occupies more space, with erect posture, and always looks people in the eye. A person of low status, on the other hand, tends to occupy less space, with more inward posture, hunched back, and always looks away from people. Johnstone stated that characters often identify their status in comparison to other characters in the space, and behave relatively low or high by modifying their posture, gaze, and use of space in opposition to other characters in the space.

These models are indeed interesting to verify in terms of their computational significance. It is also of interest to verify their relation to believability and utility in developing adaptive believable characters. We will discuss two studies related

Table 4 Fast Food Stanislavsky

To Give Someone a Bad Time	To be Thought a 'Computer'
Invade their space.	Be cold and distant.
Be restless, tap fingers.	Be insensitive to pain or pleasure.
Cross your legs away from them.	Dislike physical contact.
Frown; sigh; 'tut'.	Other people are slow.
Glare at them.	Pause before answering.
Laugh at wrong time.	Be efficient – everything in its right place.
Poke them with finger.	

to this idea. The first is a simulation by Harger to show the role of status on body movement (see next section). The second is a study we conducted to verify the use of FFM as a character model and develop a set of nonverbal behaviour patterns that are linked with the different character models defined by Johnstone.

Personality and Believable Characters

Several research projects used the personality models discussed above to develop virtual animated believable characters. In this section we discuss some of these projects. Table 5 summarizes these believable character models and the personality models they used.

André et al. [38] have employed personality as a variable to achieve fine control on affect. They used the Five Factor Model, but only implemented the extraversion and agreeableness dimensions. They created three different environments to try their implementation: *Virtual Puppet Theater*, *Inhabited Market Place*, and *Presence*. *Puppet* is a virtual learning environment specially designed for kids. The setting for this project is in a farmyard, where the user can interact through different modes. He can, through his avatar, interact with the environment and other characters, such as pigs and cows. He can also observe interactions among the autonomous characters representing the animals in the zoo. Alternatively, he can play as a director and set up the story and characters' interactions. The objective of the project is to teach children to recognize how emotions and personalities influence behaviors. *Inhabited* is a virtual market place where personalized agents interact among each other providing information. The scripts were given special attention towards depicting personality. *Presence* is a kiosk application, where users interact with characters to get certain kinds of information. They used believable characters extensively in all these experiences. The goal was to create a more engaging experience through such

Table 5 Computational models for believable characters that embedded personality

Authors	Personality Model	Applications
André et al.	FFM, but only implemented extraversion and agreeableness	*Puppet* – kids as users, to recognize emotions and personalities *Inhabited Market Place* – to improve sales presentation by simulated dialogues *Presence* – kiosk, to improve user interface
Chittaro & Serra	FFM	*Cybertherapy*
Campos et al.	FFM Jung	*SimOrg*
Vick	FFM, 4 dimensions	*Game Space*
Brenda Harger	Johnstone's Status parameter	*This is my Space* simulation

believable characters that exhibit different personalities. While much work has been done on these simulations to represent personality and express it through visual and audio output (through the agents depicted in the simulations), the link between personality and nonverbal behavior are hand coded and thus less formalized.

Chittaro and Serra [39] developed another model for believable characters, where the goal was to create realistic characters that can be used for a psychotherapy application. Although they are aware of the aspects for creating believable characters, they pursued 'realism' without addressing the uncanny valley problem. Like Andre et al., Chittaro and Serra also used the Five Factor model for depicting personality, where each dimension was represented on a scale of 0 to 100. They used probability to model unpredictability; they also used several heuristics to establish a link between the personality type and animation parameters; for example they used neuroticism as a measure of animation speed. Like Andre et al.'s work, Chittaro and Serra did an incredible job representing personality. However, they focused on realism rather than believability. They also derived the link between animation and personality based on best guesses or heuristics approach. This chapter calls for a formal model to derive such a link.

Campos et al. [40] aimed to develop autonomous agents. They used personality as a function that allows each agent to be unique and different from the other. They created a software company simulation, called *SimOrg*, to experiment with the use of personality; developing two different personality models based on the Five Factor model and Jung's model. They collected information describing how different personality models performed on prototypical tasks within a software company. Based on this data, they derived the link between personality and job performance. Although this work presents an interesting model to show job performance and personality, it did not explain or integrate a model of nonverbal behavior as a factor of personality.

Vick [41] developed a testing bed for integrating personality and emotions within game characters. To model personality he used the Five Factor Model. However, he implemented only four dimensions: extraversion, openness, consciousness, and neuroticism. He used a text-based interface to show character behaviors. His simulation showed interesting effects where knowledge, emotional and personality states of one character were refined by other characters. The work deserves more exploration on the use and representation of visual and audio output, via animation and mannerisms.

In addition to this work, Harger proposed a preliminary study that used improvisational theatre models to develop believable characters. Harger is herself an improvisational theatre actor who teaches at the Carnegie Mellon University, Entertainment Technology Center. Her teaching emphasizes the use of improvisational techniques for creating and conceptualizing character models and animation for interactive entertainment. With help from several graduate students at the Entertainment Technology Center, she developed a simple personality simulation where several characters enter a room and say the statement "This is my Space." The users of this simulation have the ability to define characters' personality through one quantitative parameter: status. Through this parameter one can see different ways that characters can perform the entrance action [42, 43]. This simulation was meant as a proof of concept-an exploration of the use of improvisational techniques as a base for character models. Harger's work is important as it defines personality in terms of behavior and attributes rather than attributes alone.

This section has concentrated on character attributes, but has not addressed behavior in any detail. The topic of behavior is of special importance to the industry as it tries to develop not only character attributes but visual representations of characters. As such industry designers have developed their own approximations of character personalities which rely primarily on how characters are portrayed visually or aurally. Different game designers defined character personalities using a single adjective, not necessarily basing their choices on the psychological models described above, e.g. [44]. These professionals are more influenced by practice and art. For instance, George Broussard discusses personality through how the character reacts to situations. He defines Max Payne's personality, for example, through the way he speaks. Toby Gard, creator of Lara Croft, states that the characters' personality comes from the drawings. A similar declaration was made by Michael Ancel about Rayman, stating that the animations unveiled the personality.

Unfortunately, the industry has not developed any formal techniques or models for developing nonverbal behaviors. Theoretical frameworks that target this area are very few and tend to tackle some isolated parameter, such as facial expressions [18]. Nevertheless, in the next sections, we will discuss these topics in detail outlining some of the most prominent work developed in the area of nonverbal behavior.

Nonverbal Behavior Theory and Models

The topic of nonverbal behaviors received some attention within several disciplines, including psychology, communication, and acting. One of the earliest nonverbal behavior systems was developed by Francios Delsarte. Delsarte was born in France in 1811. He developed a formalized system describing the expressive parameters of motion, which till this day is the best comprehensive work that specifically explores the expressiveness of nonverbal behavior [45, 46]. His nonverbal method has been used to train many famous actors, including Kirk Douglas. The method was very popular during the turn of the century, but then received much criticism caused by misinterpretations of the aim and details of the technique.

An interest in analyzing movement was revived during the Industrial Revolution. During this era, the mechanization of labor influenced a scientific, analytic approach to efficiency in the workplace. The photographic studies of Eadweard Muybridge (1830–1904) gave people a new way to understand human and animal movement. Muybridge's techniques were improved upon by Etienne Jules Marey (1830–1904), who equalized the intervals between photographs, providing an accurate space/time analysis of motion [47].

The field of ergonomics also bloomed during this era, with the work of Frederick Winslow Taylor (1856–1915), followed by Frank (1868–1924) and Lillian Gilbreth

(1878–1972). Taylor developed Scientific Management, and conducted studies that resulted in the standardization of shovel sizes. The Gilbreth's work emphasized eliminating unnecessary steps needed to achieve tasks [47].

During World War II, Rudolph Laban (1879–1958), an established movement theorist and choreographer, collaborated with F. C. Lawrence on ergonomic studies of factory workers. As women worked in factories while male laborers were on the battlefield, they were required to operate machinery designed for men. These studies resulted in the refinement of Laban's Effort theory, which addressed the rhythmic phrasing of movement qualities as a key element of biomechanical functioning that also awakened the pure joy of moving by connecting motivation to movement [19].

These theories led to the development of motion theories that had great influence beyond the area where they were originally applied. For example, Laban's movement models have been applied in areas such as dance, acting, and recently animation. In this section, we look at these theories in more depth. We also discuss their application to believable characters research.

In psychology and linguistics, there has been some work that explored the use of nonverbal behavior as a communication mechanism, exploring its link to emotions, social power and structure, and its relation to speech. Many studies within psychology and sociology relied on observation of human actions. One fundamental issue that comes into play with such observation studies is the measurement and understanding of human actions. In 1978 Harper et al. [48] published a review of notation systems used for this purpose. They first defined non-verbal communication borrowing from Dittman [49] who defined nonverbal communication as:

> The sending person (source), having an idea to get across, transforms his idea in linguistic forms (source encoding); ... he shapes these linguistic forms by means of his vocal apparatus and articulators into sounds (channel) encoding ... The receiving person hears the sounds through the air between them (channel) and groups them together into linguistic forms (channel decoding), which he finally translates centrally (user decoding) into the idea the sending person had wished to communicate, thus understanding what was said (user).

They diagram this as:

Source -> source encoder -> channel encoder -> channel -> channel decoder -> user decoder -> user

Looking at this from the point of view of developing a computational theory of communication, there are four important aspects:

a) The information contained in the message.
b) The coding process that takes place on both sides.
c) The channels employed; their capacities and limitations.
d) The effects of noise on accurate transmission.

One of the main works that Harper et al. [48] focused on in their review is the structural approach adopted by the early pioneer Birdwhistell [50] and the later external variable approach developed by Ekman and others [18].

Structural Approach

Birdwhistell [50] was a linguist, and sought to find in movement studies (*kinesics*) the same basic unit of measurement that exists in linguistics, the *morpheme*. He identifies these as *kinemes*, the smallest set of body movements with the same differential meaning, which are in turn composed of *allokines*, similar to *phonemes*. These last from 1/50 of a second to over 3 seconds. This means that observers need to be able to capture or play the motion in slow-motion to be able to detect such subtle details. Birdwhistell hypothesizes that there are 50–60 *kinemes*, which he groups into *kinemorphic* classes and illustrates using a pictorial notation system called *kinegraphs*, which chart motion using symbols. Birdwhistell would observe speakers and link kinemes with verbal meaning. He believed all behaviors had meaning in the context of verbal communication and could not be separated from it. There were several criticisms of this approach. For example, Dittmann [49] attacked the entire idea that movements are atomic and undermined the whole analogy.

Spiegel and Machotka [51] also criticized the structural approach proposed by Birdwhistell and presented a new formal system for classifying behavior. They classified motion into the following categories:

1) The somatotactical categories of body movement: these categories are a way of classify motion based on its "somatotaxis" or the arrangement of the body in space. A coding system is proposed that is concerned with the formal pattern of movement in body space rather than with the anatomical program of movement that produces the pattern. (127) Patterns of movement are given codes according to their movement within body space, their range in the approach-separation continuum, and their syntropic positioning.
2) An activity series capable of giving the sequence of movements: people learn behavior in an algorithmic way. Harkening back to Darwin's findings, many body movements are the result of cognitive triggers that meet specific needs, even if the action is not completed fully.
3) A set of social roles to provide interpersonal context: a role is a "sequence of acts moving toward a target outcome - the goal - which also describes the function of the role." According to Spiegel and Machotka everyone possesses at least one role, likely more, and these provide cultural context for many behaviors.
4) An event structure or scenario: body motion occurs within a continuous flow of events that has been overlooked in the past. Such a scenario provides valuable contextual information such as a specific social occasion, cultural meaning, and the scale of the vent in terms of people and size of location.

In order to find some validation for their formal system, they performed a series of experiments which involved showing observers a variety of portrayals of interpersonal activity. These range from a nude and clothed Venus, then Apollo, to sketched figures demonstrating various gazes and arm positions. Another series of experiments asked participants to stage wooden figures in response to a described male-female encounter. These experiments provide some validity for the general concepts described in the first part of this work by providing evidence for the claims about physical body space and context they made earlier. Nonetheless, their methodology involves mostly reasonable observations and statistical inference. However, they did not present any notation system that can be formalized.

Descriptive Approach

What followed was a more descriptive rather than structural approach to nonverbal behavior. Ekman and Friesen [18] present an exhaustive description of the types of non-verbal behavior that people perform. In their 1969 paper [18], they lay out a descriptive system for non-verbal behavior. They discuss three characteristics of an action: (a) origin: how it became part of one's repertoire, (b) usage: the regular external conditions, and (c) coding the type of information conveyed. These behaviors then fulfill one of five general functions in relation to verbal communication: repetition, contradiction, complementing, accenting, or regulating. They reveal five types of acts:

1) Emblems: culture specific, learned behaviors that represent meaning.
2) Illustrators: socially learned behaviors that complement or contrast verbal messages.
3) Affect Displays: Ekman and Friesen argue that the facial display of emotion is universal for the seven primary affects: happiness, surprise, fear, sadness, anger, disgust, and interest. They base their argument on the underlying muscles and physical responses in the face. They also describe various culturally-obtained display rules that modify displays of emotion within various contexts.
4) Regulators: conversational flow gestures that control the back and forth within a dyad.
5) Adaptors: learned actions based on satisfying bodily needs, based on childhood experience. These are then fragmented in adult-hood and experienced in response to buried triggers. These include self-adaptors such as grooming and eating, alter-adaptors such as attacking and flirting, and object-adaptors which are tool-based learned behaviors.

These categories allow the identification and classification of non-verbal acts, as well as helping to clarify why they are performed. They are referenced and used quite frequently by later literature to refer to non-verbal behavior. However, Ekman and Friesen [18] conclude that it "[is] difficult to conceive of non-verbal behavior as a simple unified phenomenon, best explained by a single model of behavior, whether that model be neurophysiologic, linguistic, or psychoanalytic."

Social and Communication

In contrast, Scheflen [52] examines non-verbal communication from the "communicational" point of view, which holds "body movement as a traditional code which maintains and regular human relationships without reference to language and conscious mental processes" and examines it "in relation to social processes like group cohesion and group regulation." This examination starts by focusing on primate communication and mankind's territoriality that is common to the great apes as well. It also examines bonding behavior and the use of body movement in so-called reciprocals such as aggressive behavior and acts of dominance. As well as identifying the usual body movements such as symbolic gestures and postures and spacing behaviors that frame and punctuate the verbal transaction, Scheflen recognizes verbal discourse as more than a symbolic system for conveying new information; that is, it serves to maintain and make agreeable the existing order. Body language thus becomes a form of human communication that occurs in small, face-to-face groups that employs conventional utterances, facial displays, hand gesture, and touch to keep the couple or group bonded. In addition, Scheflen examines non-verbal behavior in the context of social order. Through the use of examples, he shows how people can live in heavily-bound situations where body language serves to reinforce attitudes of control that aren't being expressed in language. Many family situations can develop in this way: e.g. the overprotective mother who emotionally curtails the development of her child, or the threatening manner in which aggressive racist men might confront a black man while speaking normally.

This work reinforces the idea that body language can be used in a character system to reinforce the role a character plays in a small group, as well as express personal emotion. Since Scheflen's claims are based on observation and psychiatric interviews, these mechanisms are observable in the wild, regardless of whether the theory behind them is conventionally agreed upon. Body language that regulates verbal communication, as well as reciprocals which maintain territory should intuitively make sense. It can also speak to the kinds of social contexts a character may exist within.

Gesture

On another spectrum, there has been much work on the use of body for speech and communication, specifically gesture. McNeill [53] defines gesture as "movements of the arms and hands which are closely synchronized with the flow of speech." An important work in this area is the work of McNeill and Cassell [53–55], who explored the use of communicative gestures by observing and analyzing many cases of people talking about specific subjects, such as real estate, etc. They categorized gestures into the following categories:

- *Iconic gestures*: gestures that represent some features of the subject that a person is speaking about, such as space or shape.
- *Metaphoric gestures*: gestures that represent an abstract feature of the subject that a person is speaking about, such as exchange or use.
- *Deictic gestures*: these gestures indicate or refer to some point in space.
- *Beat gestures*: they are hand movements that occur with accented spoken words.

- *Emblem gestures*: are gestural patterns that have specific meaning within the culture, such as hello or ok.

Our emphasis here is on nonverbal behaviors that represent personality and mannerisms rather than gesture and speech. Thus, we are satisfied by just mentioning this work here rather than elaborating further on it.

Delsarte

During the 19th century, François Delsarte spent over thirty years making observations of the human experience in terms of emotions and movement and comparing them to the principles which guided the sculpting of ancient Greek statuary. According to Stebbins, a student of Delsarte's protégé Steele MacKaye, Delsarte believed that nonverbal behavior is more important than the verbal words as it conveys the inner intent and state more clearly. Based on this belief, he developed an acting style that attempted to connect the inner emotional experience with a systematic set of gestures and movements. Delsarte's work makes much of the Swedenborgian "Law of Correspondence, in the trinity, applied to the art of human expression." [45, p. 397] It should be noted that he himself has never published his work. He trained many people using his system. This training was passed from one student to another. His work was published by his students and his students' students. The best descriptions of his work are in [45, 46]. According to the available literature, Delsarte grounded his work in systematic observations categorizing nonverbal behavior into the following forms:

1. the habitual bearing of the agent of expression
2. the emotional attitudes of the agent
3. the passing inflections of the agent

Delsarte's system divides the body into zones, which are further subdivided into three parts, the mental, moral, and vital subsections. These zones are seen as significant points of arrival or departure for the gesture. Motion which starts from yourself as a centre is termed "excentric"; to yourself as a centre "concentric", and well balanced motion is termed "normal." Delsarte provides meaning for motion made in any of these three ways for each zone of the body. Beyond his sets of laws of motion and form that dictate how and why movement occurs, he provides a practical provision of meaning to each systematic gesture that could be performed. If this system was to be adopted by a human artist, then a system of flexibility exercises is described to allow for limber movement; alternatively, an application to posing statuary is described.

Delsarte's system for human expression, based as it is upon observation of human interaction as well as ancient art, provides a most intriguing basis for systematizing the movement of believable characters. Being systematic, it lends itself to being adopted by a rule-based system - in fact, it was criticized as artificial and mechanical by some - and stands in need of further empirical testing to determine its overall validity. So while Stebbins concludes that understanding Delsarte' metaphysics did not bring her commensurate reward, she finds that "Practical Delsartism" lays "the solid foundations of art in expression on which others can build in safety."

Marsella et al.'s saw in Delsarte an exquisite system for believable characters' nonverbal behaviors. They set out to first validate his theory. They started with hand movements [56]. They developed a set of animations that portrayed the hand movements Delsarte suggested and asked participants to interpret them. They then later compared the participant's interpretation with Delsarte's associate meaning of the animation. They concluded that Delsarte's model showed considerable consistency in the subjects' interpretation of a given set of animated hand movements. The next step is to validate other zones he identified and perhaps to develop a model based on his system.

Laban Movement Analysis

Rudolf Laban is considered one of the most important movement theorists of the twentieth century and the founding father of modern dance in central Europe. His lifelong study of movement gave rise to an integrated and holistic system for observing, describing and notating movement and it's inseparability from human expression. Delsarte was among Laban's influences, along with Free Masonry and Rosicrucianism. Laban Movement Analysis (LMA) [57, 58] is an open theory of movement that is applicable to any area of human movement investigation. The body of material known as LMA is an expansion of Laban's original theories through the work of Irmgard Bartenieff, Warren Lamb, Judith Kestenberg and Bonnie Bainbridge-Cohen.

Five categories of movement delineate the full spectrum of LMA's movement parameters: **Body, Effort, Shape, Space** and **Phrasing**. For the purposes of this chapter, we will focus on Effort, which links inner intent to movement qualities and is associated with C.G. Jung's four ego functions: Feeling, Sensing Thinking, and Intuiting (described above). The corresponding Effort factors of Flow, Weight, Space, Time, do not indicate specific actions or gestures, but rather, various ways in which inner intent influences the quality of the gesture. As such, Effort represents a broad parameter space that includes groupings called States and Drives.

The Effort category has become the most widely known aspect of LMA due to its extensive practice within theater. Effort delineates qualities of movement as ongoing fluctuations between Light and Strong Weight, Indirect or Direct Space, Sustained or Sudden Time, and Free or Bound Flow. From these associations, we observe that a mover's Flow of Weight in Space and Time communicates information about physical sensations and the agency to mobilize one's weight with delicacy or force, the broadness or focus of thought, the intuitive leisureliness or urgency of decisions, and the release or control of feelings [47]. The eight Effort qualities emerge in combinations of two elements, forming "states," three elements, creating "drives," and in the rare case of an extreme and compelling movement, four elements combine in a "full Effort action."

Of particular importance for animation and virtual environments is the weight parameter. LMA delineates three Weight parameters: the sensing of one's body weight, and the Passive Weight components of Limp and Heavy.

Effort Overview

FLOW Feeling, Progression, "How": Feeling for how movement progresses

- Free: external releasing or outpouring of energy, going with the flow
- Bound: contained and inward, controlled, precise, resisting the flow

WEIGHT Sensing, Intention, "What": How you sense and adjust to pulls of gravity

- Light: delicate, sensitive, buoyant, easy intention
- Strong: bold, forceful, powerful, determined intention
- Weight Sensing: the sensation of your body's weight, buoyancy
- Passive Weight – surrendering to gravity

  - Limp: weak, wilting, flaccid
  - Heavy: collapse, giving up

SPACE Thinking, Attention, "Where": Thinking, or attention to spatial orientation

- Indirect: flexibility of the joints, three-dimensionality of space, all-around awareness
- Direct: linear actions, focused and specific, attention to a singular spatial possibility

TIME Intuition, Decision, "When": Intuitive decisions concerning when

- Sustained: continuous, lingering, indulging in time, leisurely
- Sudden: urgent, unexpected, isolated, surprising

In animated movement, the illusion of the qualities of weight provides information about the materiality of form in motion. Materiality is intricately bound with intent because the motivation to move and act requires us to mobilize our body mass in constant negotiation with the affects of gravity. One may recognize this negotiation in the difference between the struggle to rise up out of bed in the morning, verses the way one feels on the tennis court later that day swinging an energetic serve.

Another concept of importance is phrasing. Phrasing describes how we sequence and layer the components of movement over time. A movement phrase is analogous to a verbal sentence, or to a phrase of music, in which a complete idea or theme is represented. A phrase unit involves three main stages: Preparation, Action and Recuperation. Our uniqueness is expressed through our movement phrases: individualized rhythmic patterns and preferences of Body, Effort, Shape and Space. How one initiates a phrase of movement organizes intent and patterns the neuromuscular coordination of the action [57].

Every person has his or her own unique patterns of movement. These patterns are deeply embedded movement habits that are integrated with our emotions and self-expression. A Movement Signature describes the unique movement habits and phrasing patterns of an individual using the descriptive language of LMA. It articulates baseline patterns, as well as what movement choices are made when the mover responds to various stimuli in their environment: interactions and relationships with others, places, memories, problem solving and creativity, play and work, relaxation, exertion, etc. Among his colleagues, Rudolf Laban was known for his ability to intuitively "read" a person based on their Movement Signature.

Warren Lamb worked closely with Laban in the late 1940's [19], and later developed the Shape category of LMA. His interest in behavioral analysis led him to create a theoretical model and assessment technique called Movement Pattern Analysis (MPA), which relates decision-making to non-verbal behavioral styles. These styles are based on the way individuals integrate, or merge Posture and Gesture through rhythmic phrasing of Effort and Shape. Developed as a tool for personnel management, MPA applies a specific interpretive framework to the LMA language.

MPA regards the decision making process as occurring in Stages of Attention (Space Effort, and Horizontal Shaping), to Intention (Weight Effort, and Vertical Shaping) to Decision/Commitment (Time Effort, and Sagittal Shaping). Effort Qualities are indicative of styles of energy Assertion, and Shaping Qualities indicate initiative given to gaining Perspective. The way one changes his/her body shape in space reveals a Perspective within one of the three Planes of movement, and viewed alongside Effort as "complementary aspects of the decision making process" [47], reveals ones interactive style with others as shown in Table 6. For example, an action such as greeting someone with integrated Spreading, then Enclosing them in a hug occurs in the Horizontal plane, and is associated with an Exploring Perspective in the Stage of Attention. Integrated Spreading is complemented with Indirect Space Effort (as if opening one's Attention to a wide-lens focus), while Enclosing is complemented with Direct Space Effort (a singular focus). When these complements occur together, the movement is Sharing in Interaction with others. Laban and Lamb observed that these typical or complementary combinations generally

Table 6 Effort/Shape Affinities associated with the Decision Making Process [47]

ASSERTION		PERSPECTIVE
Investigating	**ATTENDING**	**Exploring**
Correlates with	⇓	Correlates with
Space Effort		**Shaping in the Horizontal Plane**
(directing and indirecting)		(enclosing and spreading)
Determining	**INTENDING**	**Evaluating**
Correlates with	⇓	Correlates with
Weight Effort		**Shaping in the Vertical Plane**
(increasing and decreasing pressure)		(descending and rising)
Timing	**COMMITTING**	**Anticipating**
Correlates with	⇓	Correlates with
Time Effort		**Shaping in the Sagittal Plane**
(accelerating and decelerating)		(retreating and advancing)

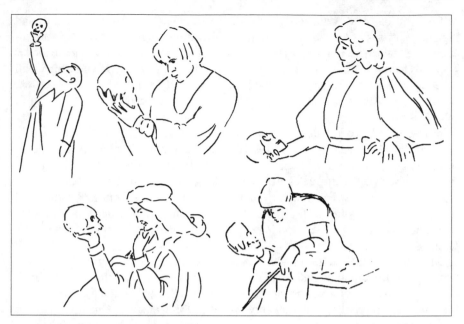

Fig. 4 Illustrations showing Posture Gesture Mergers

supported ease and naturalness in movement, and in that sense invited others in. The dynamics of expression in Effort/Shape could also lead to dis-affined combinations such as Indirectness with Enclosing, or Directness with Spreading, which would signal a preference for more privacy in interaction.

The process of shape change in the body occurs through the relationship of Posture (whole body action) and Gesture (action of one body part). Fleeting, unconscious moments of posture-gesture congruence, where postural adjustment supports, or is simultaneous with gestural action, reveal authenticity in one's communication.

The illustrations shown in Figure 4 depict Act 3, Scene 1 from William Shakespeare's Hamlet, in which Hamlet contemplates suicide. Here Hamlet delivers his soliloquy while addressing a skull, held in one hand. Each variation shows a different postural relationship to the gesturing hand, yet the integration of posture and gesture clearly communicates the authenticity of Hamlet's plight during this passionate scene.

These are the baseline movement parameters on which the MPA system is based. Individuals are assessed based on their movement patterns and preferences; the resulting profile reveals which phase of the decision making process they prefer and put most of their energy towards. As Shape is about relating to others, it also reveals the way individuals make decisions as part of a team. This enables managers to employ MPA towards creating effective teams, bringing together employees who compliment each other's approach to achievement [47].

Others have developed applications based on LMA in the areas of psychology and movement re-education based on developmental patterns. Grounding her

work in the observation of infants, Judith Kestenberg developed the Kestenberg
Movement Profile, basing her interpretive system in Anna Freud's developmental psychoanalytic metapsychology [59]. Katya Bloom, also working with infants,
applies LMA as an observation and communication tool in a movement based
psychoanalytic therapy practice. Bonnie Bainbridge Cohen developed Body Mind
Centering ®, blending neurodevelopmental therapy with developmental movement
patterns that were inherent in Irmgard Bartenieff's rehabilitative movement sequences.

Understanding the Subtle Meaning of Nonverbal Behaviors

Several research projects attempted to explore non-verbal behavior patterns and
their links to one particular character attribute: emotion. Wallbott and Scherer [60]
present a seminal work in this area. They studied a sample of 224 videos, in
which actors portrayed a variety of emotions in a scenario. Through this study,
they found that some body movements and postures can be specifically mapped
to certain emotions. For example, the posture 'arms crossed in front of chest'
is typical of pride, confirmed by Tracy's experiments on pride [61]. In addition,
Tom Calvert et al. investigated how emotion is expressed through animation, particularly hand movement [62]. The development of a comprehensive model for
understanding the link between nonverbal behavior and emotions is still an open
problem.

In our previous study [63], we aimed to extend the studies discussed above in
search for a model that links non-verbal behavior to character attributes not limited to emotions. We developed a study to explore the link between the personality
models presented in Section 22 and nonverbal behavior described in Section [64].
In particular, we used Fast Food Stanislavsky's model developed by Keith Johnstone (described in Section 22), and set out to explore two questions: (1) how well
does this model describe distinct characters? And (2) are there any unique mappings between these character variations and nonverbal movements? To this end,
we recruited three animators from the School of Interactive Arts and Technology.
We gave them the task of animating ten variations of a simple two-character scenario, where the variations constituted variations in character definitions using the
model. The results were mixed. There were some consistencies among the portrayal
of specific characters, which indicates a coherent understanding of some of the character attributes used. However, there were also some inconsistencies with specific
character descriptions. Nonetheless, the study led us to identify specific nonverbal
behavior patterns and led to several lessons on the process and methods for conducting this kind of study. More work is needed to understand the meanings of
nonverbal behaviors. We believe the models presented in sections and provide some
utility.

Nonverbal Behavior and Adaptive Believable Character

There are several proposed believable character models that fall within the area of conversational agents, such as [55, 65, 66]. The algorithms for these characters specifically focus on the use of gesture and synchronizing it with speech. Readers who are interested in computational models for gestural functionality should start with the references stated above.

There has been a lot of work within the area of believable characters. All such work employed a heuristic based model linking nonverbal behaviors to character attributes, which was usually a best guess model that a researcher came up with or a mixture of motion capture data and some common sense knowledge simulating behavioral patterns that make sense for the developer. For example, one of the earliest and most profound work on believable agents is the Oz project, which was presented in the 90s [67, 68]. In the Oz project, they simulated creatures called Woggles which are circular in shape. For these creatures they developed their own nonverbal behaviors which include a combination of squash and stretch of the entire body or parts of the body, such as the eyes, a model influenced by animation techniques. They also developed an authoring language for encoding character attributes, such as emotions, personality, and attitudes [68]. The nonverbal behavior and their link to character attributes was mostly encoded through this authoring system and mostly based on artistic sense rather than a formal model. Mateas and Stern later extended this system by developing ABL (A Behavior Language), which was used to encode behaviors for their interactive drama Façade. For Façade, Mateas and Stern developed a very expressive set of nonverbal behaviors including patterns of eye movements, posture changes, and hand gestures. All these patterns were also encoded based on artistic sense rather than a formal model [69]. Therefore, the link between these behaviors and the character model is required to be authored by the developer or artist, leading to a very tedious and often static encoding.

To date we only know of one work, the work by Zhao [20] at University of Pennsylvania, that applied movement analysis to animation of adaptive believable characters. Zhao developed a system called EMOTE (Expressive MOTion Engine) which uses Effort and shape qualities from Laban Movement Analysis model as a base model for their character animation. They used motion capture data to acquire and abstract effort and shape parameters from actor motions. They then developed an algorithm that will manipulate these parameters in an already developed key frame or motion captured animation based on the autonomous agents' situation. In particular, Zhao focused on limb and torso movements extracting key pose and timing information of motion capture data. Zhao's work is the only work we found that used LMA in an animated agent architecture. This by itself is a great step forward. However, the model is still limited to limb and torso movements, as discussed by Delsarte hand and head are two other zones that also add towards the mannerisms and aesthetics of body movement. The work also did not establish or explore the link between movement and personality, which is important for a believable character as argued earlier. However, a relationship to personality is inherent in the work, as it is based in LMA, which can be linked to Jungian personality types as described above.

Animation Techniques

The evolution of animated movement at the Walt Disney Animation Studios during the 1930's is key to the formalization of movement parameters for animation. During this era, a core team of animators began to experiment with animated movement. As reported by Frank Thomas and Ollie Johnston in *The Illusion of Life: Disney Animation* [13], Walt Disney pushed the animators to develop their skills and create a more physically believable animated world. Gradually, a terminology, or language of animated movement evolved, which became known as the Principles of Animation. As these precepts are widely known and can be referenced in *The Illusion of Life*, they are listed here with brief definitions:

- Squash and Stretch – elasticity of shapes, maintaining consistency of inner volume.
- Anticipation – the preparation before an action: inclining backwards before moving forwards.
- Staging – posing the action graphically and compositionally for readability and style.
- Straight Ahead Action and Pose to Pose – animating the action chronologically, from the beginning forwards, vs. creating the beginning and ending, then filling in the middle with "inbetween" drawings.
- Follow Through and Overlapping Action – action that sequences from one part to the next. Nothing starts and ends at the same time.
- Slow In and Slow Out – acceleration and deceleration.
- Arcs – use of curved spatial pathways to create actions that maintain volume and form between key poses.
- Secondary Action – movement that happens as the result of the main action.
- Timing – how varied speeds of the same action communicate different meanings.
- Exaggeration – making selected features very pronounced.
- Solid Drawing – maintaining a volumetric quality through all key pose and inbetween drawings.
- Appeal – character designs that support a character's personality and hold the interest of the audience – a character we can empathize with on some level.

Through action analysis classes held on-site, the Disney animators scrutinized live-action footage frame by frame and honed their craft. A richly detailed, full animation style evolved that promoted the physical properties of objects and characters in motion as the basis for believability. The goal was to bring drawings to life and create believable characters through realistic characterization and acting. While the Principles of Animation can be applied to non-character movement, they are specifically geared to support the illusion of life. Note that as soon as you move an inanimate object with Anticipation or Squash and Stretch, it acquires characteristics of motivation and intent.

In recent years, several people have theorized additional Principles of Animation in an attempt to reflect continued developments in animation practice, as well as the limitations of the original twelve. Walt Stanchfield taught life drawing classes for animators from 1970–1990. He is well known for his expanded 28 Principles of Animation which have been published informally on the internet [70, 71].

While the Principles of Animation have become core concepts used by animators, they do not represent formal models that can be easily computationally formalized. They are also time consuming and inflexible for interactive environments where characters need to be malleable and adaptive as narrative and behaviors change over time induced by users' actions.

In the past few years, there has been a move towards the use of motion capture data as well as tools and algorithms that modify motion captured data. Motion capture is a system usually involving several cameras or sensors placed in strategic positions within the body to capture all intricate details of motion. Such techniques have been extensively used within animation. However, they have also shown great utility within the interactive entertainment industry. Motion capture provides an easy and quick solution to creating animations and encoding expressive behaviors as studios tend to hire professional actors who act out different actions using directions from a director. These animations are then made available for artists to manipulate using algorithms and tools available to them. Thus, most animation techniques within the research community are now targeting the development of routines and tools that take in motion capture data and allow artists to manipulate them. This technique makes use of nonverbal behavior patterns that are encoded in our subconscious without requiring us to uncover or understand these patterns are or what they mean, it is really up to the actor to encode them within the motion captured data that artists can manipulate.

This technique has several disadvantages. First, it is hard to develop animations for creatures other than figures that you can motion capture in real life. Second, while there have been many techniques that adapt the motion capture data depending on the scenario, there are still many open problems within this direction, including naturally blending motion, keeping the personality while blending or transitioning between motions, etc. Third, even though actors are phenomenal at impersonating characters in action, most of the time they do not get the right expression or personality. This is due to the method of acting that is currently taught, namely method acting. This method dictates that actors need to stimulate their emotions from action within a scenario. Since interactive narrative is not set based on specific scenarios and the number of scenarios and contexts differ depending on interaction, a motion capture technique will necessitate capturing motions for all different scenarios that the authors or designers can predict. This was in fact the process used in creating Façade (based on our conversation with the developers). This technique also limits the scenarios within the interactive narrative to the ones that are accounted for. An alternative is to build a model for nonverbal behavior and its link to personality as suggested in this chapter, but the road to this alternative is long.

Animation and Adaptive Believable Character

Several graphics researchers focused on developing real-time algorithms that modify animation routines, such as walk, run, jump, by adding mannerisms, emotions, and personality [62, 72–74]. For example, Perlin created a framework for procedural emotion shaders [75, 76]. The goal of his work is to allow designers to dynamically encode mannerisms for their character animations, and thereby convey mood, emotions, and very simple personalities through the base movements and actions the animators create. An example is adding 'sexy' modification for a 'walk' animation developed by the animator.

One interesting alternative work that made use of specifically Anticipation from the Disney model described above was presented by Bruce Blumberg at the Game Developers conference [77]. His work on Silas is an exciting example of how a simple model of nonverbal behavior can add fluidity and believability to characters. He developed a model that emphasizes on patterns of gaze movement and body movements for a dog based on anticipation. This model was developed based on observation of dog behaviors. The resulting virtual dog was astonishingly believable. Unfortunately, he didn't publish a formal model on nonverbal behavior patterns. It is also unclear if the model can be generalized for human nonverbal behavior.

Conclusions and Open Problems

Developing believable characters has been a major concern of several fields, including animation, computer graphics, and artificial intelligence [78]. It is astonishing that there have been no comprehensive models that formalize nonverbal behavior patterns and their link to character attributes and that can be used for implementing believable characters. This chapter discussed the background theory for creating believable characters, specifically looking into psychology, animation, communication, and acting to create a repository of models that can be used to towards a comprehensive nonverbal behavior model and formulate its link to character attributes.

As the discussion above shows, there is a range of research work that has tackled different aspects of the problem. Personality research has explored the development of character attribute models. We have presented research from the fields of psychology, sociology, communication, acting, kinesiology, and ergonomics, which have all offered formalizations and explanations of nonverbal behavior. However, there are still several important open problems that need to be resolved to create adaptive believable characters.

One open problem is the development of a verified and validated model for patterns of nonverbal behavior and what these patterns mean. Another is in understanding how animators compose personality through intricate nonverbal behavior patterns, having significant impact on how character is read by the audience. A bigger goal would be to understand the link between nonverbal behavior patterns and character personality, or what nonverbal behavior patterns we tend to associate with various character types. Yet another important direction is the development of tools that encode such patterns and their link to personality, thus allowing artists to be more creative with these personalities at a much higher level, rather than struggle with low-level design of personality and their link to nonverbal behaviors.

Aside from computer science, interactive entertainment, or serious games, the development of research projects that tackle these goals will have broad contributions to different communities. Deepening our understanding of nonverbal behavior through these application areas is in itself a contribution to our understanding of human behavior.

References

1. E. S. Association, "Essential Facts about the Computer and Video Game Industry," 2008.
2. E. S. Association, "Video Games and Families," 2008.
3. C. Hyderabad, FXLabs, Eros, "International Launch of 3D Game on Ghanjini," in *Business Standard*, 2008.
4. W. Swartout, R. W. J. Hill, J. Gratch, L. W. Johnson, C. Kyriakakis, C. LaBore, R. Lindheim, S. Marsella, D. Miraglia, B. Moore, J. F. Morie, J. Rickel, M. Thiébaux, L. Tuch, and R. Whitney, "Toward Holodeck: Integrating Graphics, Sounds, Character, and Story," in *Proceedings of 5th International Conference on Autonomous Agents*, 2001.
5. M. Seif El-Nasr and B. Smith, "Learning through Game Modding," in *Games, Learning, and Society*, Wisconsin, 2005.
6. Wired, "Military Training is Just a Game," in *Wired*, 2003.
7. D. G. Walshe, E. J. Lewis, S. I. Kim, K. O'Sullivan, and B. k. Wiederhold, "Exploring the Use of Computer Games and Virtual Reality in Exposure Therapy for Fear of Driving Following a Motor Vehicle Accident," *CyberPsychology and Behavior*, vol. 6, pp. 329–334, 2003.
8. D. Sieberg, "War Games: Military Training Goes High-Tech," in *CNN Sci-Tech*, November 23, 2001.
9. C. S. Green and D. Bavelier, "Action Video Game Modifies Visual Selective Attention," *Nature*, vol. 423, pp. 534–537, 2003.
10. a. G. Marsella, "Modeling Coping Behavior in Virtual Humans: Don't worry, Be Happy," in *2nd International Join Conference on Autonomous Agents and Multiagent Systems*, Australia, 2003.
11. J. Marsella, and Labore, "Interactive Pedagpgocal Drama," in *4th International Conference on Autonomous Agents*, 2000.
12. M. Mateas and A. Stern, "Towards Integrating Plot and Character for Interactive Drama," in *Socially Intelligent Agents: The Human in the Loop AAAI Fall Symposium 2000*, 2000.
13. F. Thomas and O. Johnston, *The Illusions of Life: Disney Animation*. New York: Abbeville Press Publishers, 1981.
14. L. Bishko, "The Animation Bible: A Practical Guide to the Art of Animating from Flipbooks to Flash," M. Furniss, Ed.: Abrams, 2008.
15. E. Hooks, *Acting for Animators*: Heinemann, 2003.
16. J. S. Wiggins, "The Five-Factor Model of Personalty: Theoretical Perspectives," New York: Guilford Press, 1996.
17. R. R. McCrae and J. Allik, *The Five-Factor Model of Personality Across Cultures*: Springer, 2002.
18. P. Ekman and W. V. Friesen, "The repertoire of nonverbal behavior: categories, origins, usage, and coding," *Semiotica*, vol. 1, pp. 49–98, 1969.
19. J. Hodgson, *Mastering Movement: the life and work of Rudolf Laban*: Routledge, 2001.

20. L. Zhao, "Synthesis and acquisition of Laban movement analysis qualitative parameters for communicative gestures," in *Computer and Information Science* Philidelphia: University of Pennsylvania, 2000.
21. K. Johnstone, *Impro for Storytellers*: Theatre Arts Books, 1999.
22. K. Johnstone, *Impro: Improvisation and the Theatre*: Theatre Art Books, 1987.
23. L. R. Aiken, *Personality: Theories, Research, and Applications*: Prentice Hall, 1993.
24. I. B. Weiner and R. L. Geene, *Handbook of Personality Assessment*: Wiley, 2007.
25. G. Lombroso, *criminal Man, According to the Classification of Cesare Lombroso*. Montclair, N. J.: Patterson Smith, 1972.
26. E. Kretschmer, *Psysique and Character: an investigation of the nature of consitution and of the theory of temperament*. New York: Cooper Square Publishers, 1970.
27. W. H. Sheldon, C. W. Dupertuis, and E. McDermott, *Atlas of men: a guide for somatotyping the adult male at all ages*. New York: Harper, 1954.
28. S. Freud, *The Ego and the Id*. New York:: Norton, 1989.
29. C. F. J. W. Monte, *Beneath the Mask*. Hoboken, N.J: John Wiley, 2003.
30. M. V. Franz and J. Hillman, *Lectures on Jung's Typology: The Inferior Function*. Irving, Texas: Spring Publications, 1979.
31. C. G. Jung, *The Psychology of Individuation*. London: Routledge & K. Paul, 1964.
32. C. E. Watkins and V. L. Campbell, *Testing and Assessment in Counseling Practice*. Mahwah, N.J: L. Erlbaum Associates, 2000.
33. R. B. Ewen, *An Introduction to Theories of Personality*: Lawrence Erlbaum, 2003.
34. P. T. J. Costa and R. R. McCrae, *NEO PI-R Professional Manual* Odessa, FL: Psychological Assessment Resources, 1992.
35. I. B. Weiner and R. L. Geene, "Handbook of Personality Assessment," 2007.
36. Stanislavski, *An Actor Prepares*. New York: Theatre Arts Books, 1936.
37. Stanislavski, *Building a Character*. New York: Theatre Arts Books, 1949.
38. E. Andre, M. Klesen, Gebhard, S. Allen, and T. Rist, "Integrating models of personality and emotions into lifelike characters," in *Affective interactions:towards a new generation of computer interefaces* New York: Springer-Verlag 2000, pp. 150–165.
39. L. Chittaro and M. Serra, "Behavioral programming of autonomous characters based on probabilistic automata and personality," *Journal of Computer Animation and Virtual Worlds*, vol. 15, pp. 319–326, 2004.
40. A. M. C. Campos, E. B. Santos, A. M. P. Canuto, R. G. Soares, and J. C. Alchieri, "A flexible framework for representing personality in agents.," in *In Proceedings of the fifth international joint conference on Autonomous agents and multiagent systems* Hakodate, Japan, 2006.
41. E. H. Vick, "Designing Intentional, Emotional Characters Personality and Personality Dynamics in Video Games," *Journal of Game Development*, vol. 2, pp. 53–61, 2007.
42. B. Harger, "Entertaining AI: Using Rules from Improvisational Acting to Create Unscripted Emotional Impact," in *Game Developers Conference*, 2008.
43. B. Harger, "Workshop on Improvisational Acting," in *AAAI Symposium on Intelligent Narrative Technologies*, 2007.
44. M. Saltzman, "Game Design: Secrets of the Sages - Creating Characters, Storyboarding, and Design Documents," in *Gamasutra*. vol. March 15, 2002.
45. S. Genevieve, *Delsarte System of expression*: Dance Horizons, 1977.
46. T. Shawn, *Every Little Movement*: Ted Shawn, 1974.
47. C. L. Moore, *Movement and Making Decisions: the body-mind connection in the workplace*. New York: Dance Movement Press, 2005.
48. R. G. Harper, A. B. Weins, and J. D. Matarazzo, *Nonverbal Communication: The State of the art*. New York: John Wiley and Sons, 1978.
49. A. T. Dittman, "The Body Relationship-Speech Rhythm Relationship as a cue to Speech Encoding," in *Nonverbal Communication - Readings with comentary*, S. Weitz, Ed. New York: Oxford University Press, 1972.
50. R. L. Birdwhistell, *Introduction to Kinesics: An annotation system for analysis of body motion and gesture*. Louisville, KY: University of Louisville, 1952.

51. J. Spiegel and P. Machotka, *Messages of the body*. New York: Free Press, 1974.
52. A. Scheflen, *Body Language and Social Order*. New Jersey: Prentice-Hall, Inc., 1972.
53. D. McNeill, *Hand and Mind: what gestures reveal about thought*. Chicago: University of Chicago Press, 1995.
54. J. Cassell, "A framework for gesture generation and interpretation," in *Computer Vision in Human-Machine Interaction*, A. Pentland and R. Cipolla, Eds. New York: Cambridge University Press, 1998.
55. J. Cassell, C. Pelachaud, N. Badler, M. Steedman, B. Achorn, T. Becket, B. Douville, S. Prevost, and M. Stone, "Animation conversation: rule-based generation of facial expression gesture and spoken intonation for multile conversational agents," in *SIGGRAPH Computer Graphics Proceedings* 1994.
56. S. Marsella, S. Carnicke, J. Gratch, A. Okhmatovskaia, and A. Rizzo, "An exploration of Delsarte's structural acting system," in *6th International Conference on Intelligent Virtual Agents*, 2006.
57. P. Hackney, *Making Connections: Total Body Integration Through Bartenieff Fundamentals*: Routledge, 2000.
58. C. L. Moore, *Beyond Words*: Gordon and Breach, 1988.
59. Kestenberg, "The Kestenberg Movement Profile".
60. H. G. Wallbott and K. R. Scherer, "Cues and Channels in emotion recognition," *Journal of Personality and Social Psychology*, vol. 51, pp. 690–699, 1986.
61. J. Tracy and R. W. Robins, "The prototypical pride expression: Development of a nonverbal behavior coding system," *Emotion*, vol. 7, pp. 789–801, 2007.
62. K. Amaya, A. Bruderlin, and T. Calvert, "Emotion From Motion," in *Proceedings of the conference on Graphics interface*, 1996.
63. M. Seif El-Nasr, "Exploring Non-Verbal Behaviors Using Acting Methods," in *International Conference on Interactive Storytelling*, 2008.
64. M. Seif El-Nasr and H. Wei, "Exploring Non-Verbal Behavior Models for Believable Characters," in *1st Joint International Conference on Interactive Digital Storytelling*, Erfurt, Germany, 2008.
65. J. Cassell, "More than just another pretty face: Embodied conversational interface agents," *Commucations of ACM*, vol. 43, pp. 70–78, 2000.
66. H. Vilhjalmsson and J. Cassell, "BodyChat: autonomous communicative human figure animation," in *2nd International conference on Autonomous Agents*, 1998, pp. 269–277.
67. J. Bates, Loyall, B., and Reilly, S., "An Architecture for Action, Emotion, and Social Integrating Reactivity, Goals and Emotion in a Broad Agent," Carnegie Mellon University, Pittsburgh CMU-CS-92-142, 1992.
68. B. Loyall, "Believable Agents," in *Computer Science Department* Pittsburgh: Carnegie Mellon University, 1997.
69. M. Mateas and A. Stern, "Interactive Drama," Carnegie Mellon University, Pittsburgh 2001.
70. V. Kerlow, *The Art of 3D Computer Animation and Effects*, 3rd ed.: Wiley, 2004.
71. M. Comet. http://www.comet-cartoons.com/3ddocs/charanim, accessed 2009.
72. K. Perlin, and Goldberg, A., "Improv: A system for Scripting Interactive Actors in Virtual Worlds," *Computer Graphics*, vol. 29, 1995.
73. K. Perlin, "Real-time Responsive Animation with Personality," *IEEE Transactions on Visualization and Computer Graphics*, vol. 1, 1995.
74. J. Allbeck and N. Badler, "Representing and Paramaterizing Behaviors," in *Life-Like Characters: Tools, Affective Functions and Applications*, H. P. a. M. Ishizuka, Ed.: Springer, 2003.
75. K. Perlin, "Building Virtual Actors Who Can Really Act," in *International Confernece on Virtual Storytelling*, 2003.
76. K. Perlin, "Better acting in computer games: the use of procedural methods," *Computers and Graphics*, vol. 26, 2002.
77. B. Blumberg, "Anticipatory AI and compelling characters," in *Gamasutra*, 2006.
78. J. Gratch, J. Rickel, E. André, J. Cassell, E. Petajan, and N. Badler, "Creating Interactive Virtual Humans: Some Assembly Required," *IEEE Intelligent Systems*, vol. 17, 2002.

Chapter 23
Computer Graphics Using Raytracing

Graham Sellers and Rastislav Lukac

Introduction

In the field of computer graphics, almost any technique for generating an output image can be viewed as a data transformation. The output image is a function of some input data set and the rendering algorithms used to generate that image are mapping functions. The source of the data set may be explicit, such as models and structures produced by an artist or designer, or be implicit, such as the result of a physical simulation or the surface of a fractal.

There are many methods for transforming the input visual scene description into the target image. Rasterization, the process of converting an image described in vector for into a raster image [Foley 90] is a popular technique, particularly useful in modern, hardware accelerated systems. However, it tends to break down, losing its efficiency and attractiveness when scene complexity increases and geometric primitives shrink in size. Furthermore, since rasterization methods are often tuned to render simple geometry such as triangles, direct rasterization of implicit surfaces such as quadrics is not straight forward. In offline systems, a commonly used algorithm for the rendering of very fine geometry and implicit surfaces is the Reyes algorithm [Cook 87]. The Reyes algorithm, developed in the mid 1980s by a group that was to become Pixar, renders implicit geometry and smooth surfaces by recursively subdividing it into polygons until each facet becomes smaller than a single pixel. Each polygon is then rendered as a flat, single colored primitive.

Fortunately, as computing power available to software developers has been increasing and graphics hardware has been becoming more and more flexible and programmable, sophisticated rendering methods become implementable in real-time computer graphics systems. This chapter focuses on raytracing, the process

G. Sellers
Advanced Micro Devices, Inc., Orlando, FL, USA
e-mail: Graham.Sellers@amd.com

R. Lukac (✉)
Epson Edge, Epson Canada Ltd., Toronto, ON, Canada
e-mail: lukacr@colorimageprocessing.com

B. Furht (ed.), *Handbook of Multimedia for Digital Entertainment and Arts*,
DOI 10.1007/978-0-387-89024-1_23, © Springer Science+Business Media, LLC 2009

of generating an image by tracing the path of light through pixels in an image plane [Whitted 80], which is one of such advanced computer graphics methods. Raytracing is a well studied subject and entire volumes could be (and have been) written on the subject. It is our intention to provide the reader with a basic understanding of the subject. Namely, the next section presents a brief historical overview of raytracing. The core of this chapter lies in the few next sections which describe the raytracing fundamentals, including the raycasting algorithm, ray intersection tests, shading and lighting effect calculations, and secondary ray generation. This part of the chapter also surveys raytracing from the visual scene complexity, image quality and computational complexity perspectives. Finally, this chapter concludes with a summary of the main raytracing ideas.

The Origins of Raytracing

Raytracing was first introduced to the computer graphics community by Arthur Appel in 1968 as a method known as raycasting [Appel 68]. In fact, raycasting was previously used in physical simulations of optical lenses, radio wave propagation and other sources of radiation. Although raycasting and raytracing are technically different, the concepts are similar and the terms have been used interchangeably in the past. Recent literature has begun to use the terminology more accurately to distinguish algorithms based in classical raycasting from those implementing true raytracing.

Appel's algorithms described methods for casting rays from an observer into a scene and testing for intersections of that ray with the geometry. For each pixel, a ray is sent into the scene and is tested against every element of geometry for an intersection. As intersections are found, the closest contact point is recorded. Once the entire scene has been traversed for every pixel, an image may be generated using the color of the objects at each intersection point. In its simplest implementation, each object has a single, solid color which is copied into the final pixel. This alone is sufficient to produce an image. Also, as a depth calculation is necessary to determine the closest object to the viewer, this data may be recorded, essentially producing a depth buffer for free.

Appel, however, took the algorithm further. By considering the material properties of the object under the current pixel, and by taking into account the effect of the lights in the environment, an approximation of the shading of the object may be generated. The advantage of Appel's raycasting method over the older scanline and rasterization based methods is that complex, implicit surfaces could be modeled and rendered more accurately. Previously, an implicit surface had to be broken into smaller, simpler geometric primitives, such as triangles, and rendered as a piecewise approximation Using the raycasting approach meant that any surface for which an intersection test could be derived could be rendered with great accuracy.

In 1979, Turner Whitted built upon the work of Appel by extending the raycasting algorithm to handle reflections and refractions [Whitted 80]. Rather than simply considering the shading of the surface at the point of intersection, Whitted's new algorithm generated up to three new rays known as secondary rays, as opposed to the so-called primary rays, which are shot from the observer into the scene. The three secondary rays are known as the shadow ray, the reflection ray, and the refraction ray because they allow, respectively, the accurate simulation of shadows, reflections and refraction in transparent objects. Each secondary ray is treated much like the primary rays, and as they intersect objects in the scene, they may generate secondary rays of their own.

Since the algorithm had now become a recursive one, its computational complexity grows in an exponential manner when many reflective objects and lights are present in the scene. Several advanced techniques have been developed to simulate the scattering of rays through materials and wavelength dependent effects such as those produced by prisms. Examples of these advanced techniques can be found in [Hanrahan 93] and [Weidlich 08]. Also, much work has been done on improving the speed of the tracing algorithms using compact data structures [Houston 06] or more efficient ray-geometry intersection functions [Henning 04]. However, Whitted's trace, reflect, refract, recurse method is the one used by the vast majority of raytracing software available today.

Raytracing

Raytracing is the term used to describe the recursive algorithm first described in [Whitted 80]. Whitted built upon the previous work of Arthur Appel [Appel 68] by adding the generation of secondary rays. Appel's original algorithm, known as raycasting, included only first hit tests and shadow rays. However, with the addition of basic shading, this was sufficient to generate rudimentary images.

The Raycasting Algorithm

As its name suggests, the raycasting algorithm operates by casting rays from a viewer into a scene. Each ray is tested against objects in the scene for intersections in order to calculate the observed color of the objects' surface. This is opposite to the physical phenomena understood to occur in nature, where photons are emitted by light sources, bounce from object to object and eventually reach an observer. Algorithms to simulate the behavior of photons emitted by light sources and detected by an observer have been studied; this research area is known as photon mapping [Jensen 96].

Although similar to raytracing in many ways, photon mapping is often much more computationally expensive due to the low likelihood that a photon emitted

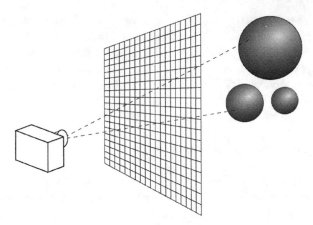

Fig. 1 Schematic representation of the scene

in a random direction from a light source will actually reach the observer. Therefore, much of the research conducted in the area of photon mapping is directed towards methods for reducing the computational burden of calculation through approximation, caching and other optimizations. For example, see the methods presented in [Jarosz 08]. For detailed treatment of the photon mapping topic refer to [Jensen 01].

As already mentioned in the previous section, raycasting is based on primary and secondary rays. A ray is represented by its origin and direction in a vector space. Primary rays originate at the viewer and are directed into the scene. Figure 1 shows a schematic representation of the scene. The screen is represented as a plane in three-dimensional (3D) space between the observer and the scene geometry. This virtual plane represents the output image. For each pixel on the screen, a ray is generated with its origin at the observer, as depicted in Figure 1 by dotted lines. The direction of the ray is calculated such that it passes through the current pixel center. Generally, the pinhole camera model is used to project the grid structure of the pixels on the screen in a regular manner onto the viewing plane to produce an undistorted image [Glassner 89]. However, nonlinear mappings such as those described in [Glaeser 99] may also be used to produce fisheye effects and other projections of the scene. Once the ray's origin and direction are known, the ray is projected into the scene and an intersection test is performed against all items of scene geometry, here represented by spheres.

The form of the intersection test depends on the geometry being tested. A basic raytracer will include a suite of geometric primitives such as spheres, planes, and quadrics. However, any geometry may be rendered using a raytracer as long as a suitable intersection test may be derived. The concept of raytracing, demonstrated through the determination of the intersection between a ray and a surface of the object, is presented below.

Ray Intersection Tests

Operating in a 3D vector space, for a ray originating at the observer $\mathbf{o} = [o_1, o_2, o_3]$ and directed towards a pixel centered at $\mathbf{p} = [p_1, p_2, p_3]$, the corresponding direction $\mathbf{d}$ is given by

$$\mathbf{d} = \frac{\mathbf{p} - \mathbf{o}}{\|\mathbf{p} - \mathbf{o}\|} \tag{1}$$

where $\|\cdot\|$ denotes the Euclidean norm of its vector argument. Thus, any point $\mathbf{x} = [x_1, x_2, x_3]$ along the ray may be expressed as

$$\mathbf{x} = \mathbf{o} + t\mathbf{d} \tag{2}$$

The goal of the intersection function is to find the value of a scaling parameter t.

Figure 1 shows the modeling scenario where the ray intersects a sphere. This scenario allows a relatively simple derivation of the intersection function. Considering a sphere with center $\mathbf{c} = [c_1, c_2, c_3]$ and radius r and a point $\mathbf{x}$, on this sphere, the following can be written:

$$\|\mathbf{x} - \mathbf{c}\|^2 = r^2 \tag{3}$$

Substituting Equation (3) into Equation (2) gives

$$\|\mathbf{o} + t\mathbf{d} - \mathbf{c}\|^2 = r^2 \tag{4}$$

To simplify this expression, a vector $\mathbf{v}$ defined as

$$\mathbf{v} = \mathbf{o} - \mathbf{c} \tag{5}$$

can be substituted into Equation (4), resulting in the following:

$$
\begin{aligned}
\|\mathbf{v} + t\mathbf{d}\|^2 &= r^2 \\
\mathbf{v}^2 + t^2\mathbf{d}^2 + 2\mathbf{v} \bullet t\mathbf{d} &= r^2 \\
\mathbf{d}^2 t^2 + 2\mathbf{v} \bullet \mathbf{d}t + \mathbf{v}^2 - r^2 &= 0
\end{aligned}
\tag{6}
$$

where $\bullet$ denotes the dot product of two vectors.

Because $\mathbf{d}$ is a unit vector, Equation (6) can be further simplified as follows:

$$t^2 + 2\mathbf{v} \bullet \mathbf{d}t + \mathbf{v}^2 - r^2 = 0 \tag{7}$$

which is a quadratic equation with the solutions

$$
\begin{aligned}
t &= \frac{-2\mathbf{v} \bullet \mathbf{d} \pm \sqrt{(2\mathbf{v} \bullet \mathbf{d})^2 - 4(\mathbf{v}^2 - r^2)}}{2} \\
&= -\mathbf{v} \bullet \mathbf{d} \pm \sqrt{(\mathbf{v} \bullet \mathbf{d})^2 - (\mathbf{v}^2 - r^2)}
\end{aligned}
\tag{8}
$$

The value of the scaling parameter t cannot be obtained in situations when the ray does not intersect with the sphere. Since such situations correspond to negative values of the term inside the square root, a fast test for the presence of an intersection may be written as follows:

$$(\mathbf{v} \bullet \mathbf{d})^2 - (\mathbf{v}^2 - r^2) \geq 0 \qquad (9)$$

Equation (7) has only one solution if the ray grazes the sphere. In the case where a ray originates within the sphere, which may happen, for example, if a sphere is used as the bounding volume for the scene, one of two calculated values of t will be negative. If t is zero, the ray has originated on the surface of the sphere. Finally, Equation (7) has two solutions if the ray passes directly through the sphere. In this case, one solution corresponds to the entry into the sphere whereas other is for the exit. Once the value of t is known, coordinates of the intersection point are obtainable by substituting t back into Equation (1).

Performing Surface Shading

The determination of the intersection of the primary ray with the scene geometry allows surface shading to be performed at the intersection point. Many shading models have been devised [Blinn 77], [Cook 82], [Oren 95], and one or more may be used in combination to produce a variety of realistic and abstract effects. Shading models may take into account both the effect of lights in the scene on the point under consideration and the effect of any light emitted by the surface at that point.

Ambient lighting is used as a rather crude approximation to global illumination. Under the ambient model, each surface has an ambient color, which is the color that the surface is displayed at in the absence of any other lighting information. The use of an ambient term simply allows objects to be displayed without needing to perform any lighting or shading calculation. Using only ambient lighting will produce a very flat image, with entire surfaces displayed as a single color.

More visually appealing lighting effects may be simulated using different lighting models such as those suggested by Blinn, Cook, Oren and others. The lighting model includes an approximation of the reflectance of the surface, and a model of the light in question. Models of lights include point lights, which are the simplest type of light, spot lights, directional lights, and area lights. These models commonly require the normal of the surface at the point under consideration [Kajiya 86].

Calculation of Surface Normals

Methods used to calculate surface normals vary in complexity and depend on the properties of the surface to be modeled. The normal of a flat surface is constant across the surface plane and therefore may be precalculated and stored with the geometry to avoid calculating it as part of the shading process. As a plane may be defined by a point and a normal vector, this may be a suitable representation of flat geometry. However, modeling software often stores geometry in the form of meshes of polygons, generally triangles or quadrilaterals [Reddy 97]. In these cases, the content creation software may store the normal of the surface with each polygon. If the normal information is not available in the original data file, the normal of each facet in the model may be calculated by taking the cross product of any two vectors on the plane. To approximate smooth surfaces, a normal for each vertex of the model is usually calculated by taking a weighted average of the normals of the polygons sharing that vertex [Woo 02]. The normal vectors may then be interpolated across the polygon. This is the basis for Phong shading [Phong 73], which is described below.

The surface normals of other geometric primitives may be calculated at the intersection point. The normal at the surface of a sphere, for example, is simply the direction vector from the center of the sphere to the intersection point. For higher order primitives such as quadrics, the calculation becomes more complex, but is still tractable [Woo 02].

There are surfaces, however, where the normal varies either in an unpredictable way or in a manner too complex to be analytically calculated at every intersection point. In these cases other methods of generating surface normals are usually employed. For instance, structured, parametric noise can be used to provide consistent results. A popular example of such a noise function, implemented in many graphics software packages over the years, is Perlin noise [Perlin 01], proposed by Ken Perlin in 1985.

Other functions [Peachy 85], [Marschner 05], usually pseudo-random in their nature, have been devised to simulate naturally occurring materials such as marble, concrete, brushed metal and wood. Using such pseudo-random functions allows the simulation of rough or bumpy surfaces. Repeatable and consistent results are of particular importance in computer animation, as variations in surface appearance from frame to frame can be visually distracting. Finally, if no approximation to the perturbations in surface normal can be found, a normal map may be used. This map is a data set that is precomputed, measured or even manually created in order to be used as a lookup table [Blinn 78]. Given intersection coordinates as input, usually in the object-local reference frame, the table returns a value to be used to modify the normal of the underlying geometry. The normal map method can be used to model or measure any surface. It may, however, require large amounts of storage space. Moreover, since normal maps have limited resolution, the method often produces blurred or inconsistent results at high magnification.

Calculation of Lighting Effects

The first step in the calculation of the effect of a light on a surface is to determine if there is a line-of-sight from the point under consideration to the light [Appel 68]. This determination is what produces shadows, and is generated by tracing a virtual ray, known as a shadow ray, through the scene geometry to the light. The ray is traced in the same manner as any other ray in the system. It has its origin at the point to be lit and is traced in the direction towards the light. If any geometry lies between the ray's origin and the light, then the point is in shadow. Unfortunately, this causes that transparent objects cast shadows. In order to simulate light passing through transparent objects, special cases must be built into the lighting calculation. For point and spot lights, this line-of-sight test is sufficient to produce shadows of scene geometry. The next step is to determine the amount of light transported from the light to the viewer by the point under consideration.

Point and spot lights are two models that may be used in computer graphics applications [Woo 02]. Point lights are assumed to emit an equal amount of light in all directions. Spot lights, on the other hand, follow a slightly different model which includes a directional component in the amount of light that they emit. The direction of the ray traced from the surface intersection may be represented in spherical coordinates as a two dimensional vector representing azimuth and elevation. This direction is used as an input parameter to a model of the spot light. The spot light model produces varying amount of light as the light vector changes direction. For a simple, circular spot light, a radial falloff is implemented to produce the round spot effect. For more complex light shapes, such as rectangles or other silhouettes, it is possible to create more advanced models.

Once the amount of light reaching a surface has been calculated, it is used in various lighting models to produce an approximate shading of the surface. The diffuse reflection model generates the appearance of a rough or matte surface. A common model of diffuse reflection used in raytracing is the Lambertian reflection model, which is named for Johann Lambert as it is an interpretation of Labert's Cosine Law [Lambert 1760]. As the equations used do not include a term describing the viewing angle, it makes the assumption that the amount of light reflected is by a surface is approximately the same in all directions. According to this model, the intensity of the diffusely reflected light can be determined as follows:

$$I_d = \mathbf{L} \bullet \mathbf{N} \tag{10}$$

where $\mathbf{N}$ and $\mathbf{L}$ denote, respectively, the normal vector of the surface and the vector pointing towards the light (which is the same as the shadow ray's direction vector calculated earlier).

Because the dot product of two vectors is greatest when they are collinear, it becomes apparent that the intensity of the diffusely reflected light is greatest when the normal of the surface points directly towards the light. The intensity of the diffuse reflection is scaled by the intensity of the light source, I_l, and the light's color, C, which are often premultiplied, yielding the following:

$$I_d = I_l C(\mathbf{L} \bullet \mathbf{N}) \tag{11}$$

Glossy and other mirrored surfaces exhibit specular highlights and are shaded using a specular reflection model such as that used in [Phong 73]. A perfectly specular surface will reflect all light that hits it. However, as in computer graphics, specularity is only a model of a lighting effect, it will not produce a reflection of other scene geometry. Specular lighting models include the view direction as part of the reflectance equation. For example, the specular distribution described in the Phong illumination model is expressed as follows:

$$I_s = (\mathbf{R} \bullet \mathbf{V})^\alpha \tag{12}$$

where I_s is the intensity of the specular highlight, $\mathbf{V}$ is the vector from the viewer to the point to be lit, $\mathbf{R}$ is the vector to the light reflected through the plane of the surface, and α is a shininess constant for the material under consideration.

The computed diffuse and specular components of the lighting model are weighted and summed according to the parameters of the surface under consideration. Each parameter of the surface, that is, ambient, diffuse and specular components, is expressed as a color. This color is multiplied by the color of the light to produce an output color, as contributed by the light in question. Figure 2 (a), (b), and (c) show the effect of the ambient, diffuse, and specular contributions of a point light on a simple sphere. The weighted sum of each of the contributions is shown in Figure 2(d).

As light is additive, all lights are considered in turn and their effects summed to produce a final output color. This may be implemented either by calculating the effect of each light on the scene in turn and accumulating the results, or by summing the effects of each light at each point to be shaded.

Generation of Secondary Rays

The combination of procedures for determining a primary ray intersection, shading and output color used in the image constitutes the system known as a raycaster. As proposed by Whitted [Whitted 80], to simulate effects such as reflection and refraction, secondary rays are generated. When a primary ray-geometry intersection is detected, this may generate one or more secondary rays. According to Whitted, secondary rays may be classified into two types; reflected rays and transmitted rays. Additionally, the shadow ray discussed above is technically a secondary ray. For each of the secondary rays, a new path is traced through the scene geometry and intersection tests are performed as they would be for primary rays.

The reflected ray is that light that bounces from the surface and does not enter it. The angle between the surface normal and direction from which a ray contacts a surface, is known as the angle of incidence. The reflected portion of the light generates a new ray leaving the surface of the geometry at the angle of reflection, which is the same as the angle of incidence. This ray is projected into the scene and tested against the scene geometry for intersections. As intersections are found, shading calculations are performed in a similar manner to those of the primary rays. The result is a light intensity value which is scaled by the parameters describing the shininess of the surface.

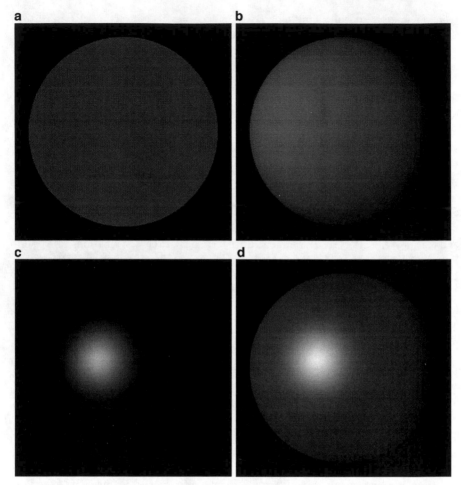

Fig. 2 Lighting effect simulation on a simple sphere using: (**a**) ambient, (**b**) diffuse, (**c**) specular and (**d**) combined contributions of three previous models

A transmitted ray is generally the result of refraction, where a portion of the light energy from the primary ray enters the medium. In order to calculate the direction of the transmitted ray, the indices of refraction of the medium on either side of the boundary must be known. Given this information and the angle of incidence, the angle of refraction can be calculated using Snell's law, which states the following:

$$\frac{\sin \theta_1}{\sin \theta_1} = \frac{n_1}{n_2} \tag{13}$$

where θ_1 and θ_2 are the angles of incidence and refraction, respectively, and n_1 and n_2 are the indices of refraction of the two mediums. By rewriting the above equation in a vector form, the directions of the reflected and refracted rays can be determined as follows:

$$\cos \theta_1 = \mathbf{N} \bullet (-\mathbf{L})$$

$$\cos \theta_2 = \sqrt{1 - (n_1/n_2)^2 - (1 - (\cos \theta_1)^2)}$$

$$\mathbf{V}_{reflect} = 1 + 2\mathbf{N} \cos \theta_1 \qquad (14)$$

$$\mathbf{V}_{refract} = \frac{n_1}{n_2}\mathbf{L} + \left(\frac{n_1}{n_2}\cos \theta_1 - \cos \theta_2\right)\mathbf{N}$$

As an optimization that may be made in the implementation of a raytracer, the medium in the absence of geometry may be assumed to have an index of refraction of one. Therefore, as n_2 is now one, the index of refraction for each piece of geometry becomes equal to the ratio of the indices of refraction of the medium to that of its surroundings, simplifying (14) to

$$\mathbf{V}_{refract} = \mathbf{L} + (\cos \theta_1 - \cos \theta_2)\mathbf{N} \qquad (15)$$

Controlling Scene Complexity

Because each intersection of a ray with scene geometry may generate additional rays, the number of rays to be traced through the scene grows geometrically with the number of ray-geometry intersections, and therefore with scene complexity. In extreme cases, the number of rays traced and therefore the number of intersection tests performed can reach infinity. Fortunately, very few surfaces are perfectly reflective or transparent and absorb some of the light energy falling on them. For this reason, the total light energy represented by the secondary rays diminishes with each intersection and the effect of the secondary rays on the output image is less significant with each bound. Note that once a ray escapes the volume enclosing the scene geometry, it can no longer generate any ray-geometry intersections and it will not contribute further to the output image.

To reduce computational complexity and therefore calculation time required to generate the output image using the raytracing algorithm, various methods are usually employed to limit the number of recursions which may be generated by a single primary ray. In its simplest form, this can be achieved by placing an upper limit on the number of bounces allowed [Shirley 05]. In a more sophisticated system, the projected effect of the ray on the output image may be estimated after each intersection [Hall 83]. If the expected contribution of either a reflected or transmitted ray falls below a particular threshold, the new ray is not traced. By altering this threshold, a rough approximation to a final image may be generated quickly for preview purposes, or a more refined, final output.

Figure 3 shows examples of an output image generated using primary and shadow rays only for recursion depths of zero to five. In Figure 3(a), no reflection is seen because the reflection rays are not generated at the primary ray intersection point. This causes the spheres to appear flat and dull. Figure 3(b) depicts reflections

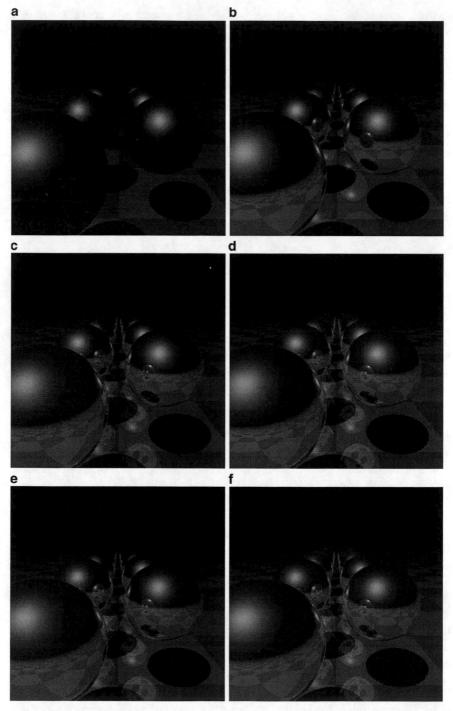

Fig. 3 An image generated using primary and secondary rays for (**a**) zero, (**b**) one, (**c**) two, (**d**) three, (**e**) four and (**f**) five bounces

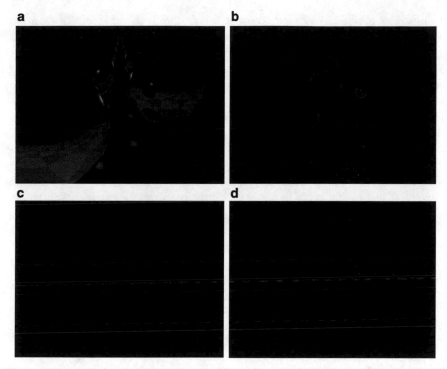

Fig. 4 Difference images between each successive bounce: (**a**) first, (**b**) second, (**c**) third and (**d**) fourth bounce

of the other spheres in the scene due to a first bounce. However, in the reflections of the spheres on the floor they still have a dull and flat appearance. By adding successively more bounces, enhanced detail in the reflections can be seen, as demonstrated in Figure 3(c) to Figure 3(f), and the differences between each successive recursion of the ray tracing algorithm becomes harder and harder to distinguish. Namely, as shown in Figure 4, very little additional information is added past the third bounce. Therefore, the raytracing process can be stopped in this case after three or four bounces.

Image Quality Issues

The primary image quality concern with ray traced images is aliasing artifacts [Cook 86]. As ray tracing is a point-sampling technique, it is subject to spatial aliasing when it reaches or exceeds the sampling limit. This limit is described by the Nyquist theorem [Nyquist 28], which states that the maximum frequency of a signal that may be represented by a point-sampled data set is half of the sampling frequency of that set. Any content of a signal beyond this limit will manifest as an aliased signal at a lower frequency. It follows from this theorem that, in the two-dimensional output image, the sampling rate of the image is determined by the spacing of the pixels, in other words, the image resolution. However, the input signal is essentially the scene geometry, which may contain very fine details. Aliasing can appear in a number of ways. The most obvious effect is jagged edges of objects in the output image. Another serious artifact is the disappearance of fine details, including very small objects. Because objects in a ray-traced scene may be represented analytically, it is possible for a small object to fall between primary rays. In this case, no intersection will be detected; the small object will not have any effect on the output image and will therefore not be visible. In an animation where the small object moves between frames, in some frames the object will generate an intersection and in others it will not. It will therefore seem to appear and disappear as it moves.

Figure 5 shows an image with the checkered texture generated procedurally; it has infinite detail and the smallest squares seen in the distance cover an area significantly smaller than a pixel. As can be seen, the image rendered with no antialiasing (Figure 5a) has noticeably lower quality compared to the image rendered with a moderate level of antialiasing (Figure 5b).

To compensate for aliasing artifacts, various antialiasing techniques have been devised. Most methods for reducing aliasing artifacts are based on the concept of super-sampling, which refers to the computation of samples at a higher frequency than the output resolution [Dobkin 96]. A simple approach to super-sampling consists of taking multiple samples for each pixel in the output image, and using the averaged value of these samples as the output value. This is equivalent to generating a higher resolution output image and then down-sampling it to the desired output resolution. Namely, each pixel is subdivided into several subpixels; for example,

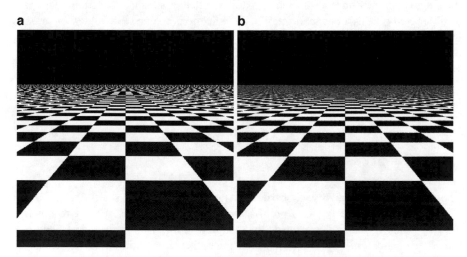

Fig. 5 An infinite checkered plane rendered (**a**) without antialiasing and (**b**) with modest antialiasing

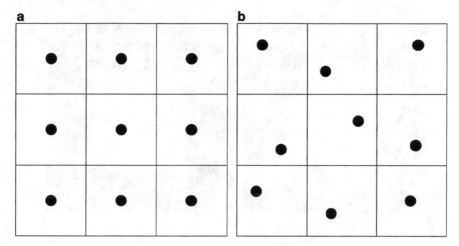

Fig. 6 Grid sampling: (**a**) regular pattern and (**b**) pseudorandom pattern

into a three by three grid, producing nine subpixels per output pixel. A primary ray is then generated passing through each of the subpixels. If the center of each subpixel is used as the target for the primary ray then aliasing artifacts can still be seen, albeit at higher frequencies. This is because the sampling pattern is still regular, and there may still be scene content that would generate image data beyond the new, higher sampling frequency. To compensate for this, more sample points can be added, thus dividing each output pixel into more and more subpixels. Alternatively, an irregular sampling pattern can be created by moving the sample positions within the subpixels.

This is known as jittered grid super-sampling. Figure 6(a) shows the spacing of the three by three subpixels of the regular grid. The randomized positions used in a jittered grid are shown in Figure 6(b). The advantage of arranging the subsample positions on a pseudorandom grid is that not only are the effects of aliasing reduced, but straight lines at all angles are equally well represented, which is not the case when a regular grid pattern is used.

Figure 7 shows the same image rendered with a regular sampling grid in Figure 7(a) and with a jittered grid in Figure 7(b). Inset at the top of each image is a magnified section of the upper edge of each square. As it can be seen, the appearance of jagged hard edges in the rendered image reduces with the increased number of shades used to represent the edge.

There are a large number of other methods of implementing antialiasing. Many of these methods are adaptive [Painter 89], [Mitchell 90], allowing higher levels of antialiasing to be applied at edges, or other areas with high frequency content. However, an in-depth analysis is beyond the scope of this article and we will not discuss the topic further here.

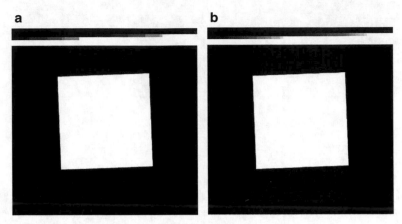

Fig. 7 Image rendered (**a**) with a regular smapling grid and (**b**) with a jittered grid

Acceleration of Raytracing

As already discussed, the computations involved in raytracing can quickly become extremely complex. To generate a high-resolution output with acceptable levels of antialiasing and detailed scene geometry, billions of calculations may need to be performed. Possibly the largest bottleneck in any raytracer is the intersection calculations. Turner Whitted estimated that for reasonably complex scenes, almost 95% of the computation time is spent performing intersection tests [Whitted 80]. As primary rays enter the scene, they must be tested for intersection with all elements of the scene geometry. The performance of a raytracer is thus heavily influenced by its ability to coarsely discard large parts of the scene from the set of geometry that must be tested for intersection against a given primary ray [Clark 76]. Furthermore, any secondary rays generated as a result of theses intersections must also be tested against the scene geometry, potentially generating millions of additional intersection tests.

There has been a large amount of work performed in the area of acceleration and optimization of raytracing algorithms [Weghorst 84], [Kay 86]. Whilst optimizing the intersection test itself can produce reasonable results, it is important to try to minimize the number of tests that are performed. This is usually achieved by employing hierarchical methods for culling; mostly those based on bounding volumes and space partitioning tree structures [Arvo 89].

Bounding Volumes

When using a bounding hierarchy approach to coarsely culling geometry, a tree is constructed with each node containing the bounding volumes of finer and finer pieces of the scene geometry [Rusinkiewicz 00]. At each of the leaf nodes of the tree, individual geometry elements of the scene are contained in a form that is directly tested for intersection with the ray being traced. Two important considerations must be made when choosing a structure for the tree representing the bounding hierarchy. First, the geometric primitive representing the bounding volume must be one that is simple to test for the presence of an intersection with a line segment in a three-dimensional space. All that is important for a quick determination whether there is an intersection with the bounding volume or not. If it can be determined that no intersection is made with the bounding volume, all of the geometry contained within that volume may be discarded from the potential set of geometry that may be intersected by the ray. As all that is desired is to know whether a ray may intersect geometry within the volume, the exact location of the intersection of the ray and the geometric primitive is not important; it is sufficient to know only whether there is an intersection with the primitive. Second, as the use of bounding volumes for culling geometry is an optimization strategy, the time taken to generate the bounding volumes should be less than the time saved by using them during the raytracing process. If it were not, then the total time required to generate the bounding hierarchy and then use it to render the image would be greater than the time required to render the image without the acceleration structure.

For these reasons, spheres are often used as the geometric primitive representing bounding volumes [Thomas 01]. Unlike finding a sphere that encloses a set of geometry reasonably tightly, finding the smallest enclosing sphere for a set of geometry is a rather complex task. Although the bounding sphere does not necessarily represent the smallest possible bounding volume for a specific set of geometry, it is relatively trivial to test against for the presence or absence of an intersection. The lack of an intersection between the ray and the bounding volume allows the volume to be skipped in the tree, but the presence of an intersection with a bounding volume does not necessarily indicate the existence of an intersection with part of the geometry contained within it. Therefore, if an intersection with part of the bounding hierarchy is detected, then the volumes and geometry within that bounding volume must also be tested. It is possible that a ray may intersect part of the bounding hierarchy yet not intersect any geometry within it.

Space Partitioning Tree Structures

Popular examples of space partitioning data structures are binary space partitioning trees [Fuchs 80], octrees and kd-trees [Bentley 75]. These tree structures recursively subdivide volumes into smaller and smaller parts.

The binary space partitioning tree was originally described by Henry Fuchs in 1980 [Fuchs 80]. In this method, a binary tree is constructed by recursively subdividing the three-dimensional space of the scene by planes. At each node, a new plane is constructed with geometry that falls on one side of the plane in one child branch of the tree and geometry falling on the other side of the plane placed in the other. Eventually, each child node of the binary tree will contain a minimal number of geometric primitives, or it will no longer be possible to further subdivide the space without intersecting scene geometry. In the latter case, a decision must be made as to whether to include the geometry in both children of the subdivision plane or to cease the subdivision process.

The octree is a space partitioning tree structure that operates on volumes of three-dimensional space. The entirety of the scene geometry is enclosed in an axis aligned bounding box. At each node, the space is subdivided in half in each axis, giving node eight child nodes. Any geometry that straddles more than one of the children is placed within the current node. That geometry that is not cut by the subdivision is carried further down the recursion until it too is cut. The recursion stops either when no geometry is left to carry to the next smaller level, or after some predefined number of steps to limit the recursion depth. Each node maintains a list of the geometry that falls within it. As rays are cast through the scene, a list of octree nodes through which the ray will pass is generated, and only the geometry contained within those nodes need be tested against for intersections. This has the potential to greatly accelerate the tracing process, especially in cases where the scene is made up of a large amount of very fine geometry.

Hardware Accelerated Raytracing

Recently, interest has been shown in using hardware to accelerate ray tracing operations, particularly within the context of real-time raytracing. In some instances, standard PC hardware has been shown to have become fast enough to produce high quality raytraced images at interactive and real-time rates. For example, Intel has shown a demonstration of the popular video game Enemy Territory: Quake Wars rendered using raytracing [Phol 09]. In this project, the team was able to achieve frame rates of between 20 and 35 frames per second using four 2.66GHz Intel Dunnington processors. While not technically hardware acceleration, this demonstrates what is currently possible using very high-end hardware. Furthermore, Intel's upcoming Larrabee product is expected to be well suited to raytracing [Seiler 08].

Moving further along the spectrum of hardware acceleration, the Graphics Processing Unit (GPU) has been used for raytracing. At first, it was necessary to map the raytracing problem to existing graphics application programming interfaces, such as Open Graphics Library (OpenGL) as in [Purcell 02]. More recently, the GPU has been used as a more general purpose processor and applications such as raytracing have become more efficient on such systems. For example, NVidia presented an implementation of a real-time raytracing algorithm using their Cuda platform [Luebke 08].

Dedicated hardware has also been investigated as a means to achieve high performance in ray tracing applications. An example of such work can be found in [Schmittler 04], where a dedicated raytracing engine was prototyped using a field-programmable gate array (FPGA). The same team has continued to work on the system [Woop 05] and has achieved impressive results using only modest hardware resources. The outcome has been a device designed to accelerate the scene traversal and ray-geometry intersection tests. Using a 66MHz FPGA, the project has shown raytraced scenes at more than 20 frames per second. It can be expected that should such a device scale to the multi-gigahertz range that is seen in modern CPU implementations, significantly higher performance could be achieved.

Summary

This chapter presented the fundamentals of raytracing which is an advanced computer graphics methods used to render an image by tracing the path of light through pixels in an image plane. Raytracing is not a new field; however, there is still currently a large amount of active research being conducted on the subject as well as in the related field of photon mapping. Probably the main boosting factor behind these interests is that direct rendering techniques such as rasterization start to break down as the size of geometry used by artists becomes finer and more detailed, and polygons begin to cover screen areas smaller than a single pixel. Therefore, more sophisticated computer graphics solutions are called for. Microfacet-based techniques, such as the well-known Reyes algorithm, constitute such a modern solution. Although these techniques have been used for some time to render extremely fine geometry and implicit surfaces in offline systems such as those used for movies, raytracing is believed to become a computer graphics method for tomorrow. With the continued increase in computing power available to consumers, it is quite possible that interactive and real-time raytracing could become a commonly used technique in video games, digital content creation, computer-aided design, and other consumer applications.

References

[Appel 68] Appel, A. (1968), Some Techniques for Shading Machine Renderings of Solids. In Proceedings of the Spring Joint Computer Conference, Volume 32, 37–49.

[Whitted 80] Whitted, T. (1980), An Improved Illumination Model for Shaded Display. In Communications of the ACM, Volume 26, Number 6. 343–349.

[Phong 73] Bui, T. P. (1973), Illumination of Computer Generated Images, Department of Computer Science, University of Utah, July 1973.

[Perlin 01] Perlin, K. (2001), Improving Noise, In Computer Graphics, Vol. 35, No. 3

[Jensen 96] Jensen, H. W. (1996), Global Illumination using Photon Maps, In Rendering Techniques '96, Springer Wien, X. Peuvo and Schr"oder, Eds., 21–30.

[Phol 09] Phol, D. (2009), Light It Up! Quake Wars Gets Ray Traced, In Intel Visual Adrenalin Magazine, Issue 2, 2009.

[Purcell 02] Percell, T., Buck, I., Mark W. R., and Hanrahan, P. (2002), Raytracing on Programmable Graphics Hardware, In ACM Transaction on Graphics. 21 (3), pp. 703–712, (Proceedings of SIGGRAPH 2002).

[Luebke 08] Luebke, D. and Parker, S. (2008), Interactive Raytracing with CUDA, Presentation, NVidia Sponsored Session, SIGGRAPH 2008.

[Seiler 08] Seiler, L. et al. (2008), Larrabee: A Many-Core x86 Architecture for Visual Computing, In ACM Transactions on Graphics. 27 (3), Article 18.

[Schmittler 04] Schmittler, J., Woop, S., Wagner, D., Paul, W., and Slusallek, P. (2004), Realtime Raytracing of Dynamic Scenes on an FPGA Chip, In Proceedings of Graphics Hardware 2004, Grenoble, France, August 28th–29th, 2004.

[Woop 05] Woop, S., Schmittler, J., and Slusallek, P. (2005), RPU: A Programmable Ray Processing Unit for Realtime Raytracing, In ACM Transactions on Graphics 24 (3), pp. 434–444, (Proceedings of SIGGRAPH 2005).

[Jarosz 08] Jarosz, W., Jensen, H. W., and Donner, C. (2008), Advanced Global Illumination using Photon Mapping, SIGGRAPH 2008, ACM SIGGRAPH 2008 Classes.

[Nyquist 28] Nyquist, H. (1928), Certain Topics in Telegraph Transmission Theory, in Transactions of the AIEE, Volume 47, pp. 617–644. (Reprinted in Proceedings of the IEEE, Volume 90 (2), 2002).

[Fuchs 80] Fuchs, H., Kedem, M., and Naylor, B. F. (1980), On Visible Surface Generation by A Priori Tree Structures, in Proceedings of the 7th Annual Conference on Computer Graphics and Interactive Techniques, pp. 124–133.

[Cook 87] Cook, R. L., Carpenter, L., and Catmull, E., The Reyes Rendering Architecture, In Proceedings of SIGGRAPH '87, pp. 95–102.

[Foley 90] Foley, J. D., van Dam, A., Feiner, S. K., and Hughes, J. F. (1990), Computer Graphics: Principles and Practice, 2nd Ed.

[Hanrahan 93] Hanrahan, P. and Krueger, W. (1993), Reflection rrom Layered Surfaces due to Subsurface Scattering, in Proceedings of SIGGRAPH 1993, pp. 165–174.

[Weidlich 08] Weidlich, A. and Wilkie, A. (2008), Realistic Rendering of Birefringency in Uniaxial Crystals, in ACM Transactions on Graphics 27 (1), pp. 1–12.

[Henning 04] Henning, C. and Stephenson, P. (2004), Accellerating the Ray Tracing of Height Fields, in Proceedings of the 2nd International Conference on Computer Graphics and Interactive Techniques in Australasia and South East Asia, pp. 254–258.

[Houston 06] Houston, B., Nielson, M. B., Batty, C., and Museth, K. (2006), Hierarchical RLE Level Set: A Compact and Versatile Deformable Surface Representation, in ACM Transactions on Graphics, Volume 25 (1), pp. 151–175.

[Jensen 01] Jensen, H. W., Realistic Image Synthesis Using Photon Mapping (2001), AK Peters, Ltd. ISBN 978-1568811475.

[Glaeser 99] Glaeser, G. and Gröller, E. (1999), Fast Generation of Curved Perspectives for Ultrawide-angle Lenses in VR Applications, in The Visual Computer, Volume 15 (7–8), pp. 365–376.

[Glassner 89] Glassner, A. S. (1989), An Introduction to Ray Tracing, Morgan Kaufmann, ISBN 978-0122861604.

[Blinn 77] Blinn, J. F. (1977), Models of Light Reflection for Computer Synthesized Models, in Proceedings of the 4th Annual Conference on Computer Graphics and Interactive Techniques, pp. 192–198.

[Cook 82] Cook, R. L. and Torrance, K. E. (1982), A Reflectance Model for Computer Graphics, in ACM Transactions on Graphics, Volume 1 (1), pp. 7–24.

[Oren 95] Oren, M. and Nayar, S. K. (1995), Generalization of the Lambertian Model and Implications for Computer Vision, International Journal of Computer Vision, Volume 14 (3), pp. 227–251.

[Kajiya 86] Kajiya, J. T. (1986), The Rendering Equation, Computer Graphics, Volume 20 (4), pp. 143–150, Proceedings of SIGGRAPH'89.

[Reddy 97] Reddy, M. (1997), The Graphics File Formats Page, http://www.martinreddy.net/gfx/3d-hi.html, Updated June 1997, Retrieved February 8, 2009.

[Woo 02] Woo, M., Neider, J. L., Davis, T. R. and Shreiner, D. R. (2002), OpenGL Programming Guide, Third Edition, Addison Wesley, ISBN 0-201-60458-02, p. 667.

[Peachy 85] Peachy, D. (1985) Solid Texturing of Complex Surfaces, in Proceedings of the 12ᵗʰ Annual Conference on Computer Graphics and Interactive Techniques, pp. 279–286.

[Marschner 05] Marschner, S. R., Westlin, S. H., Arbree, A. and Moon, J. T. (2005), Measuring and Modeling the Appearance of Finished Wood, in ACM Transactions on Graphics, Volume 24 (3), pp. 727–734.

[Blinn 78] Blinn, J. F. (1978) Simulation of Wrinkled Surfaces, in Proceedings of the 5ᵗʰ Annual Conference on Computer Graphics and Interactive Techniques, pp. 286–292.

[Lambert 1760] Lambert, J. H. (1760), Photometria sive de mensura et gradibus luminis, colorum et umbrae.

[Bentley 75] Bentley, J. L. (1975), Multi Dimensional Binary Search Trees Used for Associative Searching, in Communications of the ACM, Volume 18 (9), pp. 509–517.

[Cook 86] Cook, R. L. (1986), Stochastic sampling in computer graphics, in ACM Transactions in Graphics, Volume 5 (1), pp. 51–72.

[Dobkin 96] Dobkin, D. P., Eppstein, D. and Mitchell, D. P. (1996), Computing the Discrepancy with Applications to Supersampling Patterns, in ACM Transactions on Graphics, Volume 15 (4), pp. 345–376.

[Clark 76] Clark, J. H. (1976), Hierarchical Geometric Models for Visible Surface Algorithms, in Communications of the ACM, Volume 19 (10), pp. 547–554.

[Weghorst 84] Weghorst, H., Hooper, G., and Greenberg, D.P. (1974), Improved Computational Methods for Ray Tracing, in ACM Transactions on Graphics, Volume 3 (1), pp. 52–69

[Kay 86] Kay, T. L. and Kajiya, J. T. (1986), Ray Tracing Complex Scenes, in Computer Graphics, Volume 20 (4), pp. 269–278

[Arvo 89] Arvo, J. and Kirk, D. (1989), A Survey of Ray Tracing Techniques, in An Introduction to Raytracing, Academic Press Ltd. (publishers), ISBN 0-12-286160-4, pp. 201–262.

[Rusinkiewicz 00] Rusinkiewicz, S. and Levoy, M. (2000), QSplat: A Multiresolution Point Rendering System for Large Meshes, in Proceedings of the 27ᵗʰ Annual Conference on Computer Graphics and Interactive Techniques, pp. 343–352.

[Thomas 01] Thomas, F. and Torras, C. (2001), 3D Collision Detection, A Survey, in Computers and Graphics, Volume 25, pp. 269–285.

[Painter 89] Painter, J. and Sloan, K. (1989), Antialiased ray tracing by adaptive progressive refinement, in Proceedings of the 1989 SIGGRAPH Conference, pp. 281–288.

[Mitchell 90] Mitchell, D. P. (1990) The Antialiasing Problem in Ray Tracing, SIGGRAPH 1990 Course Notes.

[Shirley 05] Shirley, P., Ashikhmin, M., Gleicher, M., Marschner S., Reinhard E., Sung K., Thompson W., Willemsen P. (2005), Fundamentals of Computer Graphics, 2ⁿᵈ Ed., pp. 201–237. A.K. Peters Ltd., ISBN 978-1568812694.

[Hall 83] Hall, R. A. and Greenberg, D. P. (1983), Ray Tracing Complex Scenes, in Computer Graphics, Volume 20 (4), pp. 269–278.

Chapter 24
The 3D Human Motion Control Through Refined Video Gesture Annotation

Yohan Jin, Myunghoon Suk, and B. Prabhakaran

Introduction

In the beginning of computer and video game industry, simple game controllers consisting of buttons and joysticks were employed, but recently game consoles are replacing joystick buttons with novel interfaces such as the remote controllers with motion sensing technology on the Nintendo Wii [1] Especially video-based human computer interaction (HCI) technique has been applied to games, and the representative game is 'Eyetoy' on the Sony PlayStation 2. Video-based HCI technique has great benefit to release players from the intractable game controller. Moreover, in order to communicate between humans and computers, video-based HCI is very crucial since it is intuitive, easy to get, and inexpensive.

On the one hand, extracting semantic low-level features from video human motion data is still a major challenge. The level of accuracy is really dependent on each subject's characteristic and environmental noises. Of late, people have been using 3D motion-capture data for visualizing real human motions in 3D space (e.g, 'Tiger Woods' in EA Sports, 'Angelina Jolie' in Bear-Wolf movie) and analyzing motions for specific performance (e.g, 'golf swing' and 'walking'). 3D motion-capture system ('VICON') generates a matrix for each motion clip. Here, a column is corresponding to a human's sub-body part and row represents time frames of data capture. Thus, we can extract sub-body part's motion only by selecting specific columns. Different from low-level feature values of video human motion, 3D human motion-capture data matrix are not pixel values, but is closer to human level of semantics.

The motivation of this paper starts from the following observations. Video based human motion data is essential for human computer interaction, but there is a semantic gap between human perceptions and the low-level feature values of video human motions. It might be partially covered by some good machine learning algorithm,

Y. Jin, M. Suk, and B. Prabhakaran (✉)
MySpace (Fox Interactive Media) 407 N. Maple Dr. Beverly Hills, CA. 90210
Department of Computer Science, University of Texas at Dallas, TX, USA
e-mail: ychin@myspace.com; mhs071000@utdallas.edu; praba@utdallas.edu

B. Furht (ed.), *Handbook of Multimedia for Digital Entertainment and Arts*,   551
DOI 10.1007/978-0-387-89024-1_24, © Springer Science+Business Media, LLC 2009

but it is quite susceptible to variations in subjects and environments. Thus, we need to refine video human motion's low-level features by using more semantically well represented data, such as motion-capture data in this case. We show how we can use 3D motion-capture data as Knowledge-Base for understanding video human motion classes. For achieving this goal, there is a barrier. Two motion examples belonging to one class (e.g, 'backhand' motion) of video and 3D motion-capture data are visually similar to human. But based on the under-lying data representation, video and 3D motion-capture motion data are heterogeneous in nature. Video low-level features are extracted from pixel's intensity values and 3D motion-capture matrix is translational and rotational DOF values of human motions.

To refine video low-level feature data, we mix human video low-level features and semantic 3D motion-capture features and use it as the "hidden" states in the Hidden-Markov Model (HMM). HMM already has been used widely for speech recognition and human gesture recognition as well. In this paper, we show that HMM can combine the two heterogeneous data and merge the 'knowledge-based' semantic 3D motion capture data as the hidden state. We show this 3D motion capture assisted HMM model can significantly improve video human motion recognition rate.

The player's motions on the 3D game are recognized as input through the camera, the video-base human motions are estimated from the HMM. The 3D game can be controlled with the estimated results. To synthesize the human motion on the game, we prepare several atomic motion clips. For a video motion sequence, the same motion clip as the motion estimated from the HMM is selected as output. The gap between several different motion clips can be smoothly interpolated.

Related Work

Video based human gesture problem have attracted great interest in computer vision, machine learning and vision-based computer graphics area. Human action recognition problem can be separated into several different approaches. First, in a gait tracking based method, Yacoob et al. [22] tracked legs and got the parameterized values for matching in the Eigenspace. Second, in a motion feature values based approach, Huang et al. [21] computed the principle component analysis with feature values of human silhouette. Using these reduced dimensional motion feature values, they tackled the gait-analysis problem. Masoud et al. [4] also used motion extracted directly from images. They represent motion feature as a feature image. Subsequently feature images were mapped to lower-dimensional manifold that is matched with the most like human action class. Third, some approaches require some devices for taking refined level human actions. Li et al. [23] used data-globe for capturing American Sign Languages and get feature values using SVD.

Hidden Markov Model [20] is really powerful and useful modeling for recognizing speech and video human gestures. Yamato et al. [15] first applied HMM model for recognizing video human tennis gesture categories and pointed out when training and testing data from different subjects, the accuracy dropped. Yang et al. [16] showed how vector quantization can be applied with feature values with HMM and applied with isolated and continuous gesture recognition as well. Eickeler et al. [19] rejected unknown gestures with HMM model by learning undefined action classes. They also demonstrated HMM can deal with recognizing very subtle gestures, such as "hand waving", "spin", "head moving" and showed HMM can reduce significant error much better than Neural Networks [18]. There are approaches which try to merge some "knowledge" into HMM model for performance enhancement. Yoshio et al. [3] combined HMM with automation process by using one to one gesture recognition results. It is a very local knowledge and delays the decision process. Recently, Neil et al. [1] used domain knowledge for improving the maximum likelihood estimates. Some "rules" defined by domain expert can smoothen human tennis action commentary.

Vision-based human motion input is the most convenient and real-life applicable way for capturing human actions. From this characteristic, there are many graphic applications which accept vision input and use its low-dimensional values as the control signals [5] [6] [7] [8]. Park et al. [5] synthesized 3D human motion which follows 2D video human action's trajectories in the soccer video clips. Jinxiang et al. generated new 3D character motions based on video human actor's poses [6] and synthesize facial expressions followed by vision face expression through parameterized PCA comparison [7]. 2D video sequences give high-level information from sequences of images [8] to animation and the motion capture data which embedded the refined knowledge for high-quality expression [7]. On the other hand, 3D motion capture data can help video based human motion recognition problem with the semantic characteristics. Hodgins et al. [10] segmented motion capture data into distinct behaviors in unsupervised way very accurately and it is much simpler than video segmentation [2]. Li et al. [23] achieved very high performance ratio for segmenting and classifying human motion capture data in real-time. Tian et al. [24] classified hands signal using 3D motion capture data by minimizing the back projection error between each frame of video and 3D motion sequence using Dynamic Time Warping technique. It has similar intuition to this paper. Here, we apply 3D motion-capture data examples for recognizing human whole body motion and demonstrate how we can mix the heterogeneous data (video and 3D motion-capture) and embed into hidden markov model. Thus, we can show how much 3D motion capture assisted methodology can help quantitatively with the traditional HMM model approach.

Proposed Approach

In this work, we propose a way of using 3D motion-capture data streams to recognize video human motion data. Here, we consider 3D motion capture data as the knowledgebase since there exits human efforts and knowledge while we are taking 3D human motion capture data. A subject wears reflective markers [13] which are corresponding to body joint segments (e.g., 'lower back', 'upper back', 'thorax' -these belong to 'Torso'). Each joint's degree of freedom is the column vector value and rows are the time frames in the 3D motion capture matrix. Thus, we can select specific body segment in which we are interested. Degree of freedom values are also close to human semantic representation. First, to make a correspondence between video and 3D motion capture data, 3D motion capture data must be down-sampled since its frame rate (120 fps) is 4 times faster than video motion's frame rate (30fps) -see Figure 1. After down sampling, we can have the 3D motion capture frames $(3df_1, 3df_5, 3df_9, \ldots 3df_m)$ corresponding to the video frames $(vf_1, vf_2, vf_3, \ldots, vf_n)$ where down sampling ratio is $m = 4(n-1) + 1$.

Second, we extract the representative features and combine into a single matrix. The feature vector of a video frame (vf_i) has 10-dimensional values

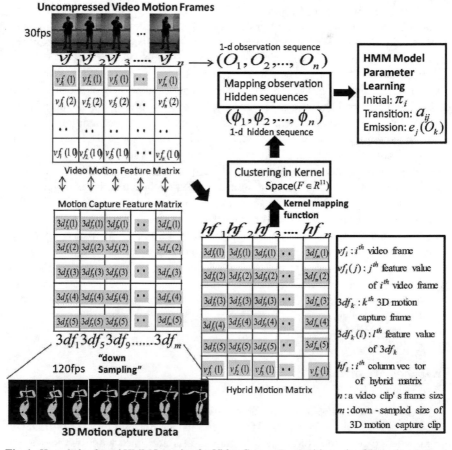

Fig. 1 Knowledge-based HMM Learning for Video Gesture Recognition using 3D motion-capture Data Stream

$(vf_i(1), vf_i(2), \ldots, vf_i(10))$ based on human motion shape descriptor, which is the column vector in the video motion feature matrix in Figure 1. We spatially reduce a motion capture frame $(3df_i)$ to 5-dimensional values. We will explain the detail of extracting low-level feature from uncompressed video frames in Section "3D Human Motion Capture Data" and get semantically reduced low dimensional representation from 3D motion capture matrix in Section. To mix these two heterogeneous data type, we build 6-dimensional hybrid matrix hf_i and put them into higher dimensional kernel space $(F \in R^{11})$.

Thus, we can translate the hybrid data matrix into a 1-dimensional sequence, which is the "hidden" state transition sequence. Corresponding to this "hidden" state sequence, there is a 1-dimensional sequence of size n by clustering the 10 dimensional video streams. Based on this one to one mapping between observation sequences $(O_1, O_2, \ldots O_n)$ and hidden states $(\phi_1, \phi_2, \ldots \phi_n)$, we can get parameters $(\lambda = \pi_i$ (Initial Parameter), a_{ij} (Transition Parameter), $e_j(O_k)$ (Emission Parameter)) of the current HMM model I by using all the video human motion clips $i \in I$ in the training set.

This proposed approach enables us to directly compute parameters of HMM model from 3D motion-capture data as the "hidden" states. Thus, we don't need to go through the learning process of HMM (such as 'Baum-Welch' algorithm), which is computationally expensive and suffers from "bad" local maxima from time to time. In the experiment part, we show that our proposed method (knowledge-based parameter learning) outperforms the traditional 'Baum-Welch' algorithm.

Human Motion Analysis & Comparison

Video Human Motion Feature Extraction

We use the Motion History Image (MHI) [11] for computing how motion images are moving. MHI sets the temporal window size ($=c$) as the 'motion history' (-we use 4 frames as the size of τ). It recursively calculates a pixel's motion intensity value ($= H_\tau(x,y,t)$) based on the motion image $M(x,y,t)$. Motion image $M(x, y, t)$ is a binary image which contains "1" for all active pixels and "0" for all others (see Figure 2). For computing motion history intensity $H_\tau(x, y, t)$, all pixels (x, y) whose motion image value $M(x, y, t)$ is equal to "1" contains τ ($H_\tau(x, y, t) = \tau$) and other pixels contain max $(0, H_\tau(x, y, t - 1) - 1)$ as their motion history intensity values. In the sub-image (I_{sub}^t) at time t (Figure 2), a pixel 'A' has τ as the pixel value in the motion history image since the motion image value of a pixel A is '1'. On the other hand, the motion image value of a pixel 'B' is '0'. Thus, $H_\tau(B_x, B_y, t)$ value ($\tau - 2$) is decided by choosing the maximum value between 0 and $H_\tau(B_x, B_y, t - 1) - 1$. MHI shows recently moving image pixels brighter. In this work, we need the representative values for each motion image, "low-level feature" values. To get such low-level feature values, we compute

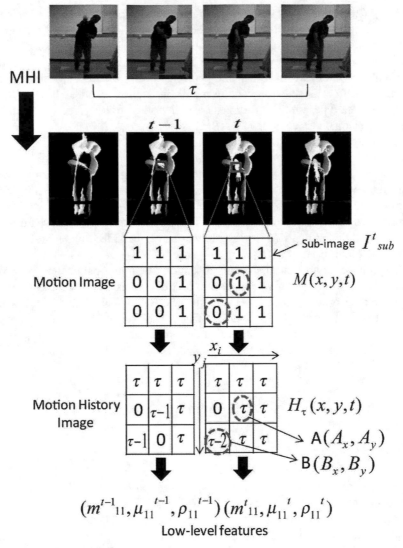

Fig. 2 Motion History Image based Video Human Motion Low-level feature Extraction

scale and rotational invariant shape moment variables by using motion history scalar values as the pixel's intensity values ($\sigma(x, y)$)

$$\sigma(x, y) \Leftarrow H_\tau(x, y, t) \tag{1}$$

For explanation about the way of extracting low-level features from the motion history image result matrix, we choose sub-image (I_{sub}^t). To compute the spatial moments values from this sub-image (=size is 3×3 pixels, where x_j, y_j is an origin pixel of sub-image),

$$m_{11} = \sum_{x=x_i}^{x_i+2} \sum_{y=y_j}^{y_j+2} H_\tau(x,y,t)xy \tag{2}$$

$$\begin{aligned}m_{11} = \;& \tau(x_iy_j) + \tau(x_i+1)y_j + \tau(x_i+2)y_j + \tau(x_i+1)(y_j+1)\\ &+\tau(x_i+1)(y_j+2) + (\tau-2)(x_i)(y_j+2) + \tau(x_i+1)(y_j+2)\\ &+\tau(x_i+2)(y_j+2)\end{aligned} \tag{3}$$

If only a τ window parameter has been chosen, then we can easily compute the spatial moment value by multiplying with pixel's coordinate. This value is variant to geometric transformation. So, centralized moments value is also extracted by adjusting with x and y coordinates of the mass center.

$$\mu_{11} = \sum_{x=x_i}^{x_i+2} \sum_{y=y_j}^{y_j+2} H_\tau(x,y,t)\left(x - \frac{m_{10}}{m_{00}}\right)\left(y - \frac{m_{01}}{m_{00}}\right) \tag{4}$$

Additionally, normalized central moment value $\left(\rho_{11} = \frac{\mu_{11}}{m_{00}^2}\right)$ is another representative value. When we extract low-level feature of an image (uncompressed one), we compute three moments values $(m_{11}, \mu_{11}, \rho_{11})$ for the whole image ($x_i = 0$ to width, $y_j = 0$ to height in Eq. 2, 4). Next, video human motion data is variant with each subject's shape and movement characteristics. So, we construct a total of 10-dimensional video human motion low-level feature data matrix by adding 7 Hu moments [9][14] variables, which is invariant to rotational, scale and reflection.

3D Human Motion Capture Data

We consider one human motion is characterized by different combination of three main body parts: torso, arms and legs. Each body parts include several segments. For example, we divide 29 segments of human body into three sets, namely "torso," "arms," and "legs." The torso consists of 7 segments (with degree of freedom in parenthesis), namely root (6), lower back(3), upper back(3), thorax(3), lower neck(3), upper neck(3), and head(3) segments. The arms consists of 7 pairs of segments including left and right side, namely clavicle(2), humerus(3), radius(1), wrist(1), hand(2), fingers(1), and thumb(2). And, finally, legs consists of 4 pairs of segments including left and right side, namely femur(3), tibia(1), foot(2), and toes(1). For extracting spatial relationships and reducing dimensions (from 62 to 3 dimensions) among the 3 different body components, we separate a motion data matrix ($M_{f \times m}$) into three sub matrices ($M^\alpha = M_{f \times k}, M^\beta = M_{f \times j}, M^\gamma = M_{f \times r}$, where $m = k + j + r$) belonging to torso, arms and legs part respectively. From three sub matrices, SVD decomposes "singular" values (see Figure 3).

$$M^i = U\Sigma V^T, M^i v_1 = \sigma^i v_1, i \in \{\alpha, \beta, \gamma\} \tag{5}$$

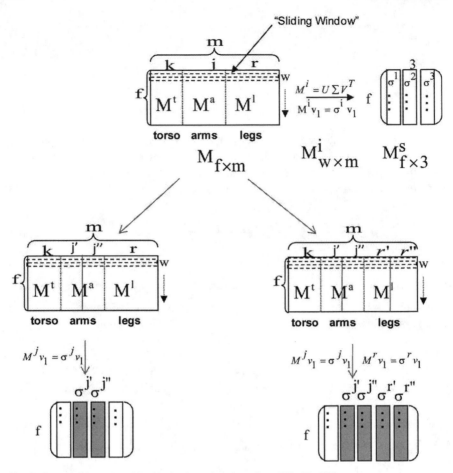

Fig. 3 Spatial Dimensional Reduction into singular values (3D, 4D, 5D)

Three "singular" values $(\sigma^\alpha, \sigma^\beta, \sigma^\gamma)$ which represent torso, arms and legs parts are the coefficient of each frame as the spatial feature, then we have a reduced matrix $M_{f \times 3}$ for a single human motion clip. Singular values represent the periodic and continuous characteristics of human's motion. Increasing singular value of one body part indicates that part is used more intensively than other parts for a particular motion (see Figure 4).

3-dimensionally segmented human motion segments (M^t, M^a, M^l) can be divided further for describing more detailed human motions (see Figure 3). For getting 4D spatial motion representation, we can divide M^a into $M^{j'}$ (Right Arms), $M^{j''}$ (Left Arms) two column-based sub matrix. Likewise, we can also break up one M^l (Legs) into two $M^{r'}$ (Right Legs), $M^{r''}$ (Left Legs) sub matrix, thus it can be 5 dimensional spatial representation (Torso, RA (Right Arms), LA (Left Arms), RL (Right Legs), LL(Left Legs)). We can see the effect of separating into different number of human body segments and how spatially reduced compact representation can keep the semantic meaning of human motion in Figure 5.

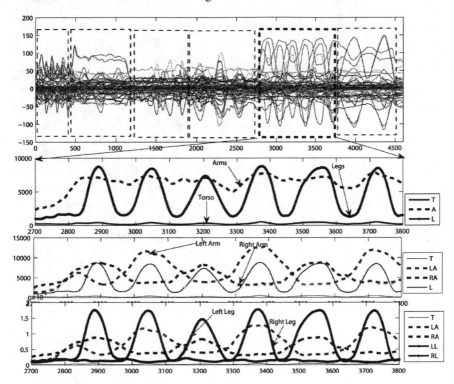

Fig. 4 SVD Spatial Feature Dimension Reduction Comparison with "knee-elbow twisting" motion example (x-axis: time-frame, y-axis: svd values)

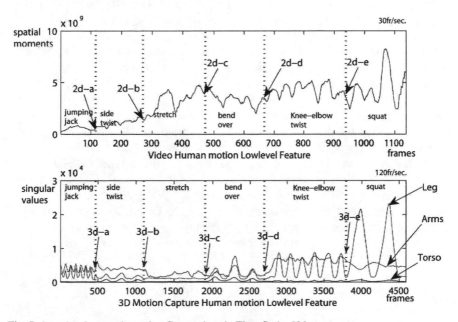

Fig. 5 Low-level extraction value Comparison in Time Series Value

We demonstrate a motion clip of "side-twisting" (5 times repeated action). From top to bottom, 3D, 4D and 5D represent "side-twisting" action respectively. At the moment that a subject twists mostly with shrinking body and attaching knee-elbow, we can observe that Legs and Arms singular value reach the peak at each period. In 4D spatial representation, RA (Right Arms), LA (Left Arms) reach the top in alternative way since "side-twisting" action consist of changing each arm periodically. We can get more detailed description than previous representation in 5D spatial reduction values. Not only RA, LA appears alternatively, RL (Right Legs), LL (Left Legs) also show the highest singular values by turns. This is exactly same as human motion description about "side-twisting": "a subject twists his or her body alternatively using left arms, right legs and vice versa". Up to now, we have demonstrated that we can spatially reduce human motion capture data dimensions while keeping the semantic meaning of motions. Next, we would like to represent human motion more compactly from 3, 4, 5 dimensional matrix to quantization value by extracting temporal relations. To achieve this, we utilize the Gaussian Mixture modeling in the following section.

Motion Feature Value Comparison between 3D Motion Capture and Video Human Motion

For the low-level feature comparison between video and 3D motion-capture human motions, we use the same motion examples. This example includes 6 different continuous motion classes ('jumping jack', 'side twist', 'stretch', 'bend over', 'and knee-elbow twist ',' squat'). In Figure 5, we map the low-level features of different motions into time-series order. At the motion changing time frames (2d-a, 2d-b, 2d-c, and so on), spatial moment feature values do not change apparently. On the other hand, the motion changing times (3d-a, 3d-b, 3d-c ...) is easy to detect. More than this, as we described in the previous section, the spatially extracted SVD representation values are according to human's semantic perception about the motion class. For example, 'squat' motion clip parts consists of two times periodic 'squat' motion. When the actor is doing 'squat' action, the actor uses extensively legs and less intensively arms without changing torso much. This description about the 'squat' motion clip is explicitly represented in the SVD representation values of 3D motion-captured 'squat' motion. We can see the semantic characteristics of 3D motion-capture low-level features in other motion classes (e.g., 'jumping jack' - frequently using legs and arms, 'knee-elbow twists'- six periodic legs and arms combinations) -see Figure 5.

Controlling 3D Human Motion using Video Human Motion Annotation

Based on the previous observation about the semantic characteristic of 3D motion capture data, we proposed the KBH (Knowledge-Based Hybrid)-HMM model in section 24 In this section, we show the application of 3D assisted video human motion recognition for synthesizing virtual human motion. (see Figure 6) Arikan et al. [25] have presented a framework to synthesize new human motions. If user paints annotations (e.g, walk, run or jump) on a timeline, the system assembles a new motion from a motion database annotated with an appropriate set of vocabulary. As the point that the system provides the user with intuitive controls to generate the specified motion, the proposed framework retrieves and visualizes 3D human motion corresponding to 2D video human motion used as user input With the training dataset, we learned the parameters for HMM model of each motion class. Thus, given a video motion sequence O_i, our framework computes the most probable HMM model by $\max_i P(O_i|\lambda_i)$. Then, it calls the recognized small motion clip (e.g., 'backhand', 'left-kick' in Figure 7). To make the final output smooth, it interpolated between two different motions clips belong to different motion clips. This framework can reduce the computation time for visualizing 3D human motion

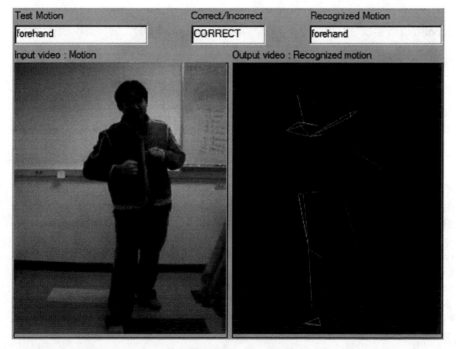

Fig. 6 Demo program showing the result (right window) corresponding to forehand motion of a subject (left window)

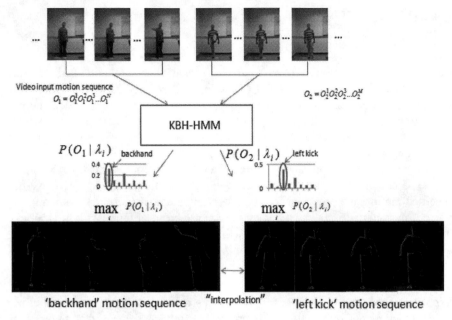

Fig. 7 Framework for synthesizing virtual motions corresponding to video human motion sequence recognition based on KBH (Knowledge-Based Hybrid) Hidden Markov Modeling

capture data in real-time since we already learned the KBH-HMM model parameters during training session and a single periodic motion unit process is faster than frame by frame process.

Conclusion

We present a framework which can be applied to vision-based 3D game by controlling 3D human motion from 2D video recognition. Extracting semantic low-level features from video human motion data is still a major challenge because it is dependent on each subject's characteristic and environmental noises. On the other hand, 3D motion capture data is clean and semantic. Therefore, 3D motion capture data is very useful to recognize video human motion if it is combined with low-level features extracted from the video human motion data. We propose the KBH-HMM model in which 3D motion capture data is clustered with low-level features and merged into the Hidden Markov Model as the hidden state. The video human motion recognition rate is significantly improved by 3D motion capture assisted HMM model. For a video motion sequence, the motion recognized by the KBH-HMM model calls the atomic motion clip corresponding to the video human motion.

References

1. D. Marshall, T. Ward, and S. McLoone. From Chasing Dots to Reading Minds: The Past, Present, and Future of Video Game Interaction. ACM Crossroads, 13(2), Fall 2006.
2. Neil Robertson and Ian Reid, "A general method for human activity recognition in video", Comput. Vis. Image Underst., 104(2), 2006, 232–248.
3. Zelnik-Manor, L. Irani, M., "Event-based analysis of video", Computer Vision and Pattern Recognition, 2001. CVPR.
4. Iwai, Y. Shimizu, H. Yachida, M., "A Method for Human Action Recognition", Image and Vision Computing, 21, 2003, 729–743.
5. MinJe Park, Min Gyu Choi, Yoshiisa Shinagawa and Sung Yong Shi, "Video-Guided Motion Synthesis Using Example Motions", ACM Transactions on Graphics (TOG), 25(4), 2006, 1327–1359.
6. Jinxiang Chai and Jessica K. Hodgins, "Performance Animation from Low-dimensional Control Signals", ACM Transactions on Graphics (TOG), 24(3), 2005, 686–696.
7. Jin-xiang Chai and Jing Xiao and Jessica Hodgins, "Vision-based Control of 3D Facial Animation", SCA '03: Proceedings of the 2003 ACM SIGGRAPH/Eurographics symposium on Computer animation, 2003, 193–196.
8. David P. Gibson and Neill W. Campbell and Colin J. Dalton and Barry T. Thomas, "Extraction of Motion Data from Image Sequences to Assist Animators", Proceedings of the British Machine Vision Conference 2000, 302–311.
9. MK Hu, "Visual pattern recognition by moment invariants", IRE Trans. Information Theory, vol. 8, no. 2, pp.179–187, 1962.
10. J. Barbic and A. Safonova and J. Pan and C. Faloutsos and J. Hodgins and N. Pollard, "Segmenting Motion Capture Data into Distinct Behaviors", In Proceedings of Graphics Interface (GI'04), 2004.
11. Aaron F. Bobick, James W. Davis, "The Recognition of Human Movement Using Temporal Templates", IEEE Transactions on Pattern Analysis and Machine Intelligence, 23(3), 2001, 257–267.
12. CMU Motion Capture Database, http://mocap.cs.cmu.edu
13. UTD Motion Data Online Repository, http://multimedia.utdallas.edu/MDB/search.jsp
14. Intel Open Source Computer Vision Library, http://www.intel.com/technology/computing/opencv/
15. Yamato, J. Ohya, J. and Ishii, K. "Recognizing Human Action in Time-Sequential Images using Hidden Markov Model", Computer Vision and Pattern Recognition, 1992. Proceedings CVPR '92, 379–385.
16. J. Yang and Y. Xu, "Hidden Markov Model for Gesture Recognition", Atech. report CMU-RI-TR-94-10, Robotics Institute, Carnegie Mellon University, May, 1994.
17. Yohan Jin, B. Prabhakaran, "Semantic Quantization of 3D Human Motion Data Through Spatial-Temporal Feature Extraction", Proc. of 14th International Conference on Multimedia Modeling (MMM2008), Kyoto, Japan, Jan 9–11, 2008.
18. Gerhard Rigoll and Andreas Kosmala and Stefan Eickeler, "High Performance Real-Time Gesture Recognition Using Hidden Markvo Models", Lecture Notes in Computer Science, 1998.
19. Stefan Eickeler and Andreas Kosmala and Gerhard Rigoll, "Hidden Markov Model Based Continuous Online Gesture Recognition", Int. Conference on Pattern Recognition (ICPR), 1206–1208, 1998.
20. Lawrence R. Rabiner, "A tutorial on Hidden Markov Models and Seleted Applications in Speech Recognition", Readings in speech recognition, 1990, 267–296, Morgan Kaufmann Publishers Inc.
21. P.S. Huang, C.J. Harris, M.S. Nixon, "Human gait recognition in canonical space using temporal template", IEEE Proceedings of VISP 14(2), 1999.
22. Y. Yacoob, M.J. Black, "Parameterized modeling and recognition of activities", Computer Vision and Image Understanding, 73(2), 1999, 232–247.

23. Chuanjun Li, S. Q. Zheng and B. Prabhakaran, "Segmentation and Recognition of Motion Streams by Similarity Search", The ACM Transactions on Multimedia Computing, Communications and Applications (ACM TOMCCAP), Vol. 3(3), August 2007.
24. Tai-Peng Tian and Stan Sclaroff, "Handsignals Recognition From Video Using 3D Motion Capture Data", Proceedings of the IEEE Workshop on Motion and Video Computing, 2005.
25. Arikan, O., Forsyth, D. A., and O'Brien, J. 2003. Motion synthesis from annotations. ACM Transactions on Graphics 22, 3, 402–408.

Chapter 25
Information Technology and Art: Concepts and State of the Practice

Salah Uddin Ahmed, Cristoforo Camerano, Luigi Fortuna, Mattia Frasca, and Letizia Jaccheri

Introduction

The interaction between information technology (IT) and art is an increasing trend. Science, art and technology have been connected since the 60's, when scientists, artists, and inventors started to cooperate and use electronic instruments to create art. In 1960 Marshall McLuhan predicted the idea that the era of "machine-age" technology was next to close, and the electronic media were creating a new way to perform art [1].

The literature is full with examples of artists applying mathematics, robotic technology, and computing to the creation of art. The work in [2] is a good introduction to the merge of IT and art and introduces genetic art, algorithmic art, applications of complex systems and artificial intelligence. The intersection is drawing attention of people from diverse background and it is growing in size and scope. For these reasons, it is beneficiary for people interested in art and technology to know each other's background and interests well. In a multidisciplinary collaboration, the success depends on how well the different actors in the project collaborate and understand each other. See [3] for an introduction about multidisciplinary issues. Meyer and others in [4] explains the collaboration process between artists and technologists.

The definitions of visual art have extended far beyond the canvas since the beginning of the twentieth century. The increased availability of computers has caused a burgeoning of computer based visual art, also known as digital art. This has developed into a broad range of computer graphics, animation, cybernetic sculptures, laser shows and Internet-gaming. While the aesthetic experience has always

S.U. Ahmed and L. Jaccheri (✉)
Norwegian University of Science and Technology, Norway
e-mail: {salah, letizia}@idi.ntnu.no

C. Camerano, L. Fortuna, and M. Frasca
Engineering Faculty, Dipartimento di Ingegneria Elettrica, Elettronica e dei Sistemi (DIEES), University of Catania, Italy
e-mail: {cristoforo.camerano, lfortuna, mfrasca}@diees.unict.it

B. Furht (ed.), *Handbook of Multimedia for Digital Entertainment and Arts*, DOI 10.1007/978-0-387-89024-1_25, © Springer Science+Business Media, LLC 2009

meant some interaction among the creator (artist), the creation (artwork), the viewer (spectator), the current "electronic age" allows a truly two-way involvement, with the possibility of input from both the creator and the viewer altering the creation.

The "new media art" is an umbrella term, which generically describes artwork that incorporates an element of new media technology. New media technologies are defined as technologies that were invented, or began integration into society from the mid 20th century. The most significant new technology, which has affected visual art is computer software, which enables individuals to digitally manipulate images. Traditional visual art is enriched through new way of expression: another art form, which has become prevalent in the digital age is "interactive art". In this genre, the aim of the artist is to stimulate a two-way interaction between his works and the spectator. This process has become increasingly possible via new media technologies. It implicates creative activity in a context which now not only includes professionals such as graphic artists and composers, but the wider public as well. Spectators are no longer situated within a pure passive role: spectators today play an interactive role within the artist to create new media art.

The relationship between technology and visual art is well explained in [5] and [6]. In these works F. Popper introduces the concept of "synaesthesia" between art, human emotion and technology. The emphasis is on the visual aspects and their strict connection to emotions. Popper in his work "Art-Action and Participation" examines the interplay of art, craft, and technology in five major categories: laser and holographic art, video art, computer art, communication art, and installation demonstration and performance art [7]. At a time in which simulation and reality become interchangeable and humans and machines are intellectually connected, Popper began to study the new way of conceiving the visual arts through the experiences of other artists. Popper also looks at the social and political impact of the rapid communication of ideas, experience, and images. Popper in his works shows how the kinetics art influences all contemporary art expressions.

Cultural and social transformation from this age to nowadays elaborates a new method to reflect on art and technology. Nowadays, the number of artists participating in multimedia software games, interactive robotics and new electronic applications is continuously increasing in art projects like interactive art installations. As this intersection of art and technology grows, it involves people from different disciplines with different interests creating a milieu of interdisciplinary collaborations. At the Engineering Faculty of University of Catania and the Norwegian University of Science and Technology we explore the intersection of information technology and art to understand different entities that are involved in the intersection. In the general context of the intersection between IT and art we focus on three subsets of IT, which are software, electronics, and robotics. This choice is dictated by the nature of research and art projects we are working on.

The objective of this chapter is to provide a framework of the intersection between IT and art based on our theoretical (literature review) and practical work (participation to IT intensive art projects). We have explored the intersection between technology and art through a deep investigation based on papers, articles and books, conferences, art projects, festivals and art centres, practical examples of interaction between information technology and art carried out in university of all over the world and in laboratories and research centres. We have explored this intersection through a detailed and systematic study of literature and we have also presented the criteria used to select the articles in order that the readers get an overview of the scope and the focus of the literature review. In [8] we have also identified the search strategies, including a list of searchable electronic database of scientific publications and a starting list of keywords. Relevant publications are those that address artist attitude towards technology, engineer attitude towards art, influence and usage of IT in art or of art in computing, and features of artistic software.

The Conceptual Framework

The conceptual framework described in [8] is our attempt to clarify the intersection of IT and art by identifying the involved actors, their interests, place of interaction, and reasons behind collaboration. In this section we will present the conceptual framework. The study and our literature review is described by several entities such as "who", "where", "why" and "what" which stand, respectively, short for "who" are people involved, "where" the intersection take place, "why" the people are interested to the intersection and "what" tools or electronics or software are used in this intersection between IT and art.

Who

In the intersection between art and IT we find artists like cyber-artists, designers, software engineers [9, 10], researchers, electronic and robotic engineers, theorists and critics [11] engineers and researchers [12,13,14]. The roles of artists, researchers, engineers and critics are neither exhaustive nor mutually exclusive. These roles have different backgrounds and viewpoints. One person can have many roles at the same time, for example, when the interactive filmmaker Florian Thalhofer creates the interactive documentary software Korsakov; he is both an artist and a software developer [15]. Technologists include people like software engineers and hardware engineers. But if we take the wider intersection of technology and art, technologists will include engineers from different disciplines like, mechanical, robotics and electrical engineers, just to cite some examples. In the following we will tend to refer to engineers and artists without trying to classify, each time, which kind of engineer and artist we are referring to.

Nowadays software, electronics, mathematics, robotic technology, genetic art, algorithmic art, led installations and artificial intelligence in union with music, dance, sculpture and painting expression are used to involve the audience as part of an interactive dialog with technology. Ref. [16] provides a good example of explanation about how these different technologies can be used to involve audience and create interactive dialog processes.

The role of software developer is explained for example by Machin in [17]. In order to build software tools for artists, pragmatics analysis of context and behaviour is crucial because art is heavily immersed in practice and action, and because art is valued on its ability to communicate [18].

At the same time other artists, such as Marco Cardini in his cyber art installation, want to create an immersive atmosphere in which the artist set an interactive dialog with audience involved [19]. In [20, 21, 22] a new way to create visual art is explored, through the research of strange attractors, patterns and shapes, through kinematics ad robotics. The importance of aesthetics in engineering is another topic discussed several times by various authors such as for example Adams [23].

Where

The dimension of the framework 'where' refers to the places or the context where IT and art meets each other. It is common that the intersection happens in the context of some institutional support. In the framework presented in [8], the following contexts are mentioned: educational institutes such as Art schools, computing schools, software industry, research institutes, art projects and art centres and festivals.

Another place of intersection between technology and art is Internet: in the recent years more and more artists are exploring the Internet as a medium to reach their audience and spectators [24], so Internet has became a new dimension where people can create different kind of web-art through special tool for artist [25, 26, 27, 28].

In art schools and computing schools interdisciplinary courses are conducted which include students from both art, computing discipline, robotic course, complex systems course [29]. Besides these interdisciplinary courses, there are also cases where the need of computing education is realized in the art discipline, and the need of art education in the computing discipline.

In addition to IT and entertainment industry, art and computing schools, there are research institutes where a research setting is intentionally created for artists and technologists to work closely together. These research institutes may be a part of a university or an industry. Often, this kind of collaboration is done through "Artist-in-residence" programs, for example, the Xerox PARC artist-in-residence program [30], COSTART project [31], "Robot Artist in Resident Project" [32]. The objectives of these programs are fostering of innovation and creativity. In an art project, the objective is to realize an artwork, whose main mission is to convey the artistic message that the artist wants to express.

Why

The 'Why' dimension refers to the reasons why artists and technologists want to interact. One of the main reasons artists seek help from the technologists is to get support with the tools that they need for the realizations of their artwork [33].

We make an attempt to classify the reasons for cooperation into six categories:

- **Learning about interdisciplinary cooperation.** The potential reciprocal interaction between artists and technologists is challenged by the demands of the user (artists). These demands stimulate engineers and researchers to extend technology with possibilities that go beyond its intended use [33].
- **Innovation of products and interfaces.** As an example we look into Human-Robot-Interaction (HRI), which aims at developing principles and algorithms to allow more natural and effective communication and interaction between humans and robots. Research ranges from how humans will work with remote, tele-operated unmanned vehicles to peer-to-peer collaboration with anthropomorphic robots. Many researchers in the field of HRI study how humans collaborate and interact and use those studies to motivate how robots should interact with humans 34.
- **Aesthetics in computing.** In [35] Fishwick reports the result of a survey on the usefulness of aesthetic methods on several areas of computer science. The result shows that data structure, algorithms, digital logic, computer architecture was chosen by the respondents as some of the fields where aesthetic computing can be used. Information visualization and software visualization are other fields that can contribute to bringing art/aesthetics inside of computing [36]. Paul Fishwick has coined the term "Aesthetic Computing" to refer to a new area of study, which is concerned with the impact and effects of aesthetics on the field of computing. As an example, the discrete models found in computing can be transformed into visual and interactive models, which might increase the understanding of the students. Fishwick represents a method for customizing discrete structures found in mathematics, programming and computer simulation. In [35] discrete models are transformed to geometric models. Moreover, Adams addresses the importance of teaching aesthetics in engineering education and the role of aesthetics in engineering [37].
- **Develop and exhibit IT based Artworks.** One main motivation for the cooperation between artists and engineers is that large artistic projects must rely on IT knowledge to be successful. For example, in [17] Machin underlines the importance of mature requirement elicitation techniques, which enable the capture of the artist's ideas without inhibiting the artistic process. Researchers are interested in comparing the software development methods in art projects and analyze which ones suit better an art project in a certain context. In [13] Candy and Edmonds investigate the most appropriate evaluation methods in software intensive art projects and if the evaluation should be done by artists or it should include software engineers as well. Where the artworks are implemented in limited time and budget and where artists lead the project, the maintenance and upgrading

issues are often overlooked. Thus the maintenance and upgrade of these kinds of software supported artworks become one of the prime sectors where art projects need engineering help.

- **Reflection on society through art.** Erkki Huhtamo, Mathew Fuller, Florian Cramer, Jeffery Cox, Lev Manovich fall in this category. The people in this category are often called theorist or art critics whose main role is to besides other criticize artworks and social and cultural affects of art in our society. Many of the people mentioned here have several roles, varying from artist, teacher, theorist and programmer. For example Erkki Huhatamo is a lecturer, researcher, writer and curator all by the same time. Manovich is a lecturer and writer of many articles and books. His book, "The Language of New Media" is considered by many reviewers to be the first rigorous theorization of the subject. Even though there might not be a person who can be termed as only theorist, we mention them as a separate category here as we find a significant portion of research articles that we have reviewed are contributed by these theorists and art critics.

- **Dissemination of research results.** In recent years emergent scientists create interactive installations that allow for immersive relationships to develop between the spectator and the artwork. For examples one of the five presented projects in the Section "Description of the Projects" is "Chaotic Robots for Art": the realization of this, takes inspiration from the theory of strange attractors of Chua's circuit [38] and from the innovative conception of visual art developed by Frank Popper. The gallery of strange attractors of the Chua's circuit [39, 40] is widely known in the literature. The wide variety of patterns based on strange attractors achieved an aesthetic level such that more people worked in order to emphasize in art the impressive features of strange attractors considering chaos as bridge between Art and Science. Many engineers such as Moura L., and Reichardt J., also start in their work a new way to create cyber paint through robotics [41, 42]. The role played by simple mechanical systems that generates complex strange attractors has been remarked in different works and with different strategy, and the emergence concepts in generating new patterns has been emphasized in researches with the final objective to demonstrate the new paradigm of shapes and complexity [43, 44]. There is a growing tendency to develop new kind of robots for art [45] and the research of new modelling methods with a biological approach applied to entertainment robotics and bio-robotics [46]. In this sense for example bio-robotics for art is ever closer to the mechanism that ensure that a robot can have a brain similar to the man's brain. For example a new class of visual-motor neurons, recently discovered in the monke's brain, the so called "Mirror neurons" are used in robotics and they represent today the key element in the understanding of phenomena like imitation, evolution of language, autism, knowledge of the behaviour of others [47]. In [48] Wolpert studied practical examples and models for the motor commands inside the brain through the concepts of mirror neurons and with the background of the Simulation theory of Mind-Reading of Gallese and Goldman, [49]. All the concepts and the theories studied by Wolpert and Gallese are often used in robotics because of the increasing trend to combine art and bio-inspired robotics.

Table 1 Who, where, and why dimension of the intersection of software and art

Who Where	Artists	IT Engineers	Researchers	Theorists
Education Institutes	Learning, Develop	Learning	Learning, Innovation	
Research Institutes	Innovation, Disseminate	Innovation, Aesthetics, Disseminate	Learning, Innovation, Disseminate	
IT Industry	Innovation	Innovation	Innovation	
Public Art projects	Develop	Develop, Innovation	Learning	Reflection
Festivals	Learning, Develop	Innovation, Learning	Disseminate	Reflection

In Table 1 we give a visual representation of the where, who, and why dimension.

What

The 'what' dimension of the framework refers to the tools and technologies used in the intersection of art and IT. After identifying people (who), reasons behind their interest at the intersection (why) and the places/sectors (where) art intersects with software, here we present some practical examples of what (tools and technologies) binds the relationship between software and art. In the framework presented in [8] different categories of tools and software are identified, for example, graphics manipulation software, multimedia authoring, 3D graphics manipulation software, sound manipulation software, video manipulation software, and other applications.

Here we take a wider perspective by looking at kinetic art in addition to software art. The term kinetic art refers to a particular class of artistic sculpture made primarily at the end of years 1950s. Kinetics art contains moving parts or depends on motion for its effect: for example wind, a motor, or the observer generally powers the moving parts.

Jean Tinguely is another artist that with his works realises an infinity of constructivist images by means of constructions whose elements rotate with different, incommensurable speeds. The Meta Matics of Tinguely at CAMeC (Centro Arte Moderna e Contemporanea at La Spezia) are machines, which automatically create infinite sequences of drawings. The principle of these machines is that of Lissajous figures, i.e: the superposition of different harmonic oscillations [50]. Carried out in a precise way, such movements result in stark geometric images with pretty Moiré-pattern-effects: this is what we see in many early computer-generated graphics. But the mechanical imperfections of Tinguely's machines create an abundance of irregularities, deviations and interruptions, which result in a suggestion of expressive human gesture. The Meta Matics presented a pastiche of the abstract-expressive painting of the 1950's. Their position in art history may be compared with Jackson Pollock's all-over's.

Pontus Hultèn organized a futuristic exhibition on art and mechanical technology at the Museum of Modern Art in New York (MOMA) in 1968 with the title "The Machine: As Seen at the End of the Mechanical Age". Today this art sculpture of P. Hulten is shown at MOMA gallery of New York [51]. Pontus Hultèn understood such transformation to make an impact on the audience visually, but often on the exhibition space as well via sound, smell, taste, image and light effects.

For visual artists the computer is a design tool. Utilising the available techniques of pasting, erasing, displacement, and multiplication, artists are able to develop their own 'electronic palette' to assist them with their creations. Researchers, like Oates, look at computer art as an information system and propose to extend IS research agenda to include computer art [52].

The technologies used for creating visual art can enable collaboration, lending themselves to sharing and augmenting by creative effort similar to the open source movement, in which users can collaborate to create unique pieces of art.

Artists tend to use software for different purposes. Quite often they use commercial software; often they are interested in open source software as a cheap alternative. In few cases, artists develop their own software. Most of the time they use the software as it was intended to be used by the creator of the software but sometimes they can be creative and use it in a different way which was not intended. For example the artist Jen Grey used the proprietary software Surface Drawing in a unique way to draw live models, a purpose which was not intended [53]. Some software is used as a tool to develop artwork; some as a media to support artists' activities indirectly (for example collaboration) while others are general purpose programming languages used to build applications. Besides these, there is also customized software i.e., software that is built for a specific artistic purpose. Several papers mention this kind of software which was developed by either artists alone, or with the help of programmers as part of an art project. These tools provide the reader an overview of what type of software and tools are used or required by the artists.

Artwork support tools, i.e. tools used to develop artworks, are mainly special purpose artistic software which specializes on some tasks such as visualization, sound manipulation or animation.

Apart from the artwork support tools there are other tools and software that artists use for supporting other activities such as communication, publicity, sharing works, ideas etc. Internet and Web tools have become not only a medium for the artist to publish and present their work and activities, but also a medium for communicating and collaborating with other artists. "The digital arts site Rhizome is recognized for the crucial role it plays enabling exchange and collaboration among artists through the network" states Walden in his review on the book Net_Condition: Art and Global Media [54]. The other purposes of website include, publishing artworks, selling art products, virtual tour of museums and creating online communities, discussion groups or forums, and blogging.

Domain specific programming language are preferred by artists compared to the general purpose programming languages unless the artist does not aspire to be a professional programmer. This is because general languages can be daunting due to the steep learning curve associated with learning programming. Besides, artists often prefer to work with intermediate tools where the need for programming is reduced. But that does not make any limitation for artists to learn the general purpose programming languages. Some of the papers that we have reviewed mention a number of general purpose languages which were used to realize artworks or some artistic software, for example, C++, ActionScript, UML, 2D OpenGL.

Moreover the role of open source software has to be mentioned as an important factor for making artists more interested to software. Artists tend to move towards using open source technology not only because they are cheap, even free of charge, but also because many artists believe in the open source ideology. In [55] Halonen mentions that new media art is based on cooperation to a greater degree than many art forms that can be created alone. He identified four groups with diverse motives: i) using open source network as an important reference for professional image, ii) using open source projects as a platform for learning, iii) an opportunity to seek jobs and iv) enrich professional networks. From our project experience, we identified that some artists want to have open source projects so that they can build an interested community around the project which might assist in the further development, upgrade and maintenance of the project at a low cost. Open source and free software usage in artists community is also encouraged by different art festivals such as piksel (http://www.piksel.org), makeart (http://makeart.goto10.org/). The interest is also visible by the activities of different art organizations/institutes such as APO33 (http://apo33.org) ap/xxxxx (http://1010.co.uk/) Piet Zwart Institute (http://pzwart.wdka.hro.nl/).

Description of the Projects

In this section we use the framework introduced to present five of our projects. Each project is described by a short introduction, followed by the who (and when), where, why, and what perspectives. In the introduction we try to reconstruct the artistic idea or the research motivation for the artwork. This partly overlaps with the why dimension.

Flyndre

Flyndre [56] is an interactive art installation (see Fig. 1). It has an interactive sound system that has the artistic goal to reflect the nature around the sculpture. To implement this goal the produced sound changes depending on parameters like the local time, light level, temperature, water level, etc. Flyndre relies on Improsculpt, a software tool for live sampling and manipulation, algorithmic composition and improvised audio manipulation in real time.

Fig. 1 Flyndre

Who

The sculpture was built by Nils Aas. Then work of adding sound features was initiated in 2003 by composer, musician and programmer Øyvind Brandtsegg. Brandtsegg used a customized version of his music composition tool Improsculpt. Brandsegg had started the development of Improsculpt in 2000 and the first version of the software was completed in 2001. Brandtsegg collaborated with engineers regarding the development, testing and deployment of the sound system. A group of software engineering students and researchers at NTNU has re-factored the software modular architecture.

The first version of the software was a single script file that was hard to modify, maintain and upgrade. Students from NTNU were involved to develop and improve aspects of Improsculpt from the software engineering point of view. The software architecture has been re-designed to make it modular, easy to extend and modify. Another group of students with multidisciplinary background has improved the Internet based communication between the sculpture and the servers at NTNU that process sounds. The students developed the technical framework for the networking and the sensors systems (i.e. for capturing parameters by the sensors and for transferring them via the Internet to the sound processing station). A third group has developed an open source version of Improscuplt and published it as open source by uploading a project in Sourceforge. Besides, utilization of wiki and Concurrent Versioning System (CVS) introduced by the software engineers was found to be very useful by the artist. A summary of these activities is published in [56].

Where

The intersection between IT and art in this case is in the context of a real life art project. It is a public art project meaning that the artwork is placed in a public place. According to the presented framework, it falls in the category of public art. The student work falls in the category of educational institutes. The sculpture is located in Inderøy, Norway. Visitors can walk around the sculpture or sit nearby to watch it and listen to its music.

Why

In case of Flyndre the collaboration is between artists, IT engineers, and researchers. The project involves many students as mentioned in the 'who' part of the description. The main reason behind the intersection is technological help to the artist who wants to develop and exhibit an IT based artwork. The artist needed technological support to improve the architecture of Improsculpt. For installing the sound on Flyndre, the artist collaborated with the sound engineers. From the artist point of view cooperation is motivated by his desire to use technology in the artwork and learn about tools and technology. Researchers and engineers were motivated by learning goals.

What

The sound installation Flyndre makes use of a loudspeaker technique in which the sound is transferred to the metal in the sculpture. The music is influenced by parameters such as high tide and low tide, the time of year, light and temperature, and thus reflects the nature around the sculpture. The computer that calculates the sound from the sensor data using the Improsculpt software is located in Trondheim. The sensor data and the sound signals are streamed via the Internet between Inderøy and Trondheim.

There is a website of the project which provides a live streaming of the sound that is played by the sculpture. The web site includes on-the-fly animated Flash application that displays the current parameters of the environment and the current music played by the sculpture. The archive of the previously played music by the sculpture is also accessible through the web site. At the controlling core of the sound installation there is a custom version of the software Improsculpt. It is software for live sampling and manipulation, algorithmic composition and improvised audio manipulation in real time. The main tools and technologies used in the project are Csound, Python, Wiki, Sourceforge, and CVS.

Sonic Onyx

Sonic Onyx is an interactive sculpture that enables people to send files and plays them back (see Fig. 2). Anyone located inside the space of the sculpture can send text, image or sound files from Bluetooth enabled handheld devices such as mobile phones or laptops. The received files are converted into sound and mixed with other sound files. The converted sound file is then played back by the sculpture. The project is an example of artists, engineers, and researchers working together. There are many actors involved in the project making it a multidisciplinary project and collaboration.

Fig. 2 Sonic Onyx

Who

The actors involved in the project come from different backgrounds. The project includes the people involved from the development phase of the project to the users of the artwork. The actors of the project are namely the artist, software engineers, and researchers. Besides these actors there are the users which include students and teachers of the school. Samir M'Kadmi is the artist of the project. There are five software engineering students and their supervisor, two IT consultants, three researchers (from NTNU). The physical structure was build by a mechanical company. The users, or visitors of the sculpture are mainly students and teachers of the school but anyone can visit the sculpture.

Why

The artist needed help from the software engineers and developers to develop the artwork. Technology consultants had an important role here as software developers were still students and had lack of experience. Researchers were interested to observe and analyze different characteristics of the project. For the students (developers of the project), it is also a reason to learn to work in a multidisciplinary project apart from the main objective of realizing the artwork and providing technology and tools support for the project. The technology consultant worked also in providing technology and tool support both to the artists and software developers.

Where

According to the framework the intersection of art and technology comes here in the form of an art project. The final objective of the project has been to create a piece of artwork which will is open for public and mounted in a public space. It falls in the category of public art and art project.

What

The software tools and technologies that are used in the project are mainly open source. Linux has been used as the operating system of the server. Pure Data has been used for sound processing and Python has been used for the application.

The Open Wall

The Open Wall is a 80×30 pixels resolution 201 inch LED screen. The Open Wall is a wall-mounted LED installation (see Fig. 3). One goal of the Open Wall project is

Fig. 3 The Open Wall

to inspire reflection about Information and Communication Technology with focus on openness, copyrights, and authorship [57].

Who

In 2005 architect Åsmund Gamlesæter initiates this project as he wanted to build a LED facade for an experimental house. The house was built by a group of students and was supposed to stay for one year. The architect asked CIS (Computer and Information Science) department for help and cooperation. Hardware design was the most important task when the installation was built for the first time.

When the experimental house was removed, the boards were taken over by CIS. In 2007, as a result of a master thesis, the Open Wall software goes open source with BSD license. In January 2008 three groups of students re-build the installation during a three weeks intensive course. The students reuse the existent hardware and software and develop the missing pieces of the software and the content.

Why

The projects has many actors, each having different point of views. Engineers and researchers see the cooperation with artists as a source of inspiration and a possibility to reflect about technology and find inspiration for innovations. In particular, the SArt perspective is to inspire reflection about Information and Communication Technology with focus on openness, copyrights, and authorship. Artists want to engage in projects like this to explore the possibility of technology and interaction with technical people and researchers. Students choose this project as part of their curriculum because they like to co-operate with other students with different background. Technology gets old quickly. Technologists experience this inevitable assumption as a source of both frustration and motivation to learn all the time about new technology. An important lesson we learn in this project is that visitors criticize our work as the technology, which was developed 3 years ago (at time of writing this paper). An important question that arise is therefore: "how important is the type and novelty of technology in a cooperation project between artists and technologists?".

Where

The installation is first installed on the façade of an experimental house in the town of Trondheim. A sister installation is build and installed in a discothèque in town. The current Open Wall is in a meeting room at the Department of CIS. The installation is available through a WEB interface, which allows its users to both upload and see pictures on the Open Wall. The software of the installation is available at sourceforge.net.

What

The Open Wall is a wall mounted LED piece consisting of 96 circuits boards (16×6 boards) containing 2400 orange LED lights with 5 cm distance in all directions to the next light. The wall is 480 cm long and 180 cm high. Each board has 25 LED lights on its surface, emitting light with 99 possible intensities. Each board has its own microprocessor, power connection, and Ethernet. Connection to the main controller device is established through a set of switches or hubs. In short, this is a massive parallel network of boards. The software governing the installation is written in Java and available at http://sart.svn.sourceforge.net. In the context of a multidisciplinary project work, three groups have developed 3 projects based on The Open Wall, and one of the groups, inspired by living art which would 'die' if nobody cares about it, presents a bunny that changes its state (i.e. sleep, awake, excited) according to activities in the room. The second group brings the discussion to political and social themes by reflecting about the wall and its open source and creative possibilities. They use the wall to display texts from "Steal This Book" by Hoffman '70. The idea of the third group is to display an ECG wave propagating along the wall screen as on an ECG monitor. All three groups discuss the possibilities to include interactivity through sensors (e.g. movement in "Lux Vitae", people position "Bull devil 7", sound level in "Heart and software"). With the installation in place, the employees of CIS start to play with it and develop a web based interface which enables users to upload and see the content of the wall with an Internet browser.

Fig. 4 The four Chaotic Robots for Art

Chaotic Robots For Art (Fig. 4)

This research begins from the study of the cooperative behaviour of inspection robots by combining the concept of art and complex systems. The role of chaotic synchronization in the generation of the kinematic trajectory shows the discovering of new aesthetic features of the motion in mechanical control systems.

The target of the project is to show emergent spatial attractors generated by clusters of robots called "Chaotic Robots for Art". The project idea takes inspiration from our studies on groups of robots to working together, with different skills. We use dynamical chaos instead of classical random algorithms to drive robots in a given arena, and we use typical chaotic laws to drive our robots. The use in engineering-entertainment area of interactive technologies suggests the idea to establish new ways and new methods to create art with the intent to satisfy an increasing need to bring new technologies to users.

Who

The actors involved in the project are three engineers (two electronic engineers and one software engineer) that take inspiration from different artists, researchers and robotic engineers, cyber-artist, theorists and critics.

From the late of 2005 at laboratories of University of Catania Luigi Fortuna, Mattia Frasca and Cristoforo Camerano began to apply on entertainment robotics their previous results of nonlinear dynamics theory for the generation of patterns and strange attractors [20].

These three artists engineers try to create an immersive relationships between the spectator and the artwork: these relationships are controlled by complex sensor-triggered interfaces which incorporate movement, speech, touch and light information on entertainment robotics.

Where

The final objective of this art project is to create a piece of artwork mounted in a public space like museums, art schools and researcher centres. Up to now people can manage the "Chaotic Robots" to create art at the DIEES laboratories of the Engineering Faculty at the University of Catania.

Why

This research and art project includes cooperative robots, strange attractors synchronization, and led trajectories analysis. It is inspired by the Popper theories [6], and aims at integrating robots in virtual arts. The key element is the spectator interaction and participation. The reflection in a 3D space of the shapes and patterns of cooperative robots generate the artwork.

Another important key-element in the background of the presented research is the idea to find similarities through a real dancer and a dancer robot.

For this reason in the middle part of our experiments, we tried to compare the trajectories of our chaotic dancer robot with the trajectories of a real dancer that plays in the same room in the given arena. The research revealed the discovery of a class of strange trajectories and patterns that are shown in Fig. 5.

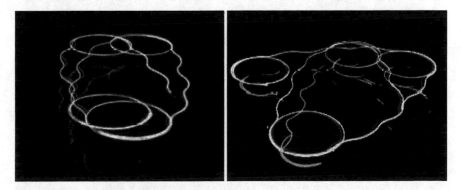

Fig. 5 The robots perform typical Chaotic Attractors

The hypothesis is that the possibilities to reveal the beauty and the charm of typical chaotic forms of strange attractors can suggest a possible interesting alternative for future development of entertainment robots applications for art and this new way of establishing interactive dialogs between audience and the used technology can became a new way to create immersive Cybernetic-Painting-Art.

What

HRI (introduce in the framework in the previous section) is implemented through a SCADA-System (Supervisory Control And Data Acquisition-System) that is a simple GUI (Graphical User Interface) that is able to control the chaotic robots. The target of the project is to show emergent spatial attractors for art generated by clusters of robots. The research revealed the generation of emerging sets of strange attractors, spatially distributed, and the generation of a gallery of strange attractors in a 3D space. We realized mobile robots by using different kinematic structures and the Lego Mindstorms system allowed us to easily implement them.

The task of each robot in the cluster is to provide specific functions and to explore the environment in different points in order to get complete specific information.

The scenario where the measurements must be taken is a three-dimensional space with spatial coordinates (x; y; z) where equipments must be dynamically located in order to perform different types of investigations and where the kinematism assures the realization of a congruent set of detections. Randomized trajectories are generated for each robot and a random search algorithm is used to improve the detection performance of the clusters. In particular, instead of using randomized positions a strategy based on chaotic trajectories has been conceived. In this way, even if a randomized motion is performed, the robots in the cluster can be synchronized each other to coordinate their behaviour.

The use of synchronized clusters of robots is adopted in this work in order to implement coordination of robot trajectories both inside each cluster and among the various clusters and at the same time this mechanism of synchronization should be adopted in order to have symmetries in the trajectories.

The trajectories that are shown in the Fig. 5 represent a strange attractor gallery of experimental routes generated by using mechanical device synchronization. In particular, the control strategy adopted consists in emphasizing the cooperation and the randomized motion avoiding collisions among robots. In order to trace the trajectories, the robots were equipped with markers (different led were equipped on each robot) and the whole environment was totally obscured. Then, photos with long exposure times or videos of the robot motions were taken. In the latter case the video is then post-processed in order to have the complete trajectory of the robot. In all experiments shown the size of the arena was fixed to 3, 5m × 4m and the height of the arena walls was 40cm. The control laws used for all robots is a typical logistic function or other chaotic laws. Actually, in spite of each robot being fed with the same set of rules, its detailed behaviour over time is unpredictable, and each instance of the outcome produced under similar conditions is always a singular event, dissimilar from any other.

The robots controlled by chaotic laws perform interesting chaotic dynamics such as "Multi Scroll" Attractor.

By analysing the above described course of action of the set of four robots, we note that from initial random steps of the procedure, a progressive arrangement of patterns emerges, covering the shown trajectories. These autocatalytic patterns are definitely non-random structures that are mainly composed of clusters of ink traces and patches: this shows the artistic emergence of complexity in real time and space.

Interactive Bubble Robots For Art

This project takes inspiration from the study of the interactive processes between human and robot defined as HRI and from the study of Mirror Neurons to study elements of imitation and learning of the movement sequences.

The target of the project is to show artistic emergent spatial patterns that reflect the processes of learning through imitation and the processes of understanding the behaviour of others. The study reveals the opportunity to implement through two identical Bubble Robots the concepts of the "Mirror Neurons" to study the applications in art of the 3D spatial shapes described by the trajectories of the robots (see Fig. 6).

Who

HRI is a multidisciplinary field with contributions from the fields of human-computer interaction, artificial intelligence, robotics, robotics art, bio-robotics, natural language understanding and social science. In this context, DIEES researchers are currently exploring different applications areas for HRI systems.

Fig. 6 The two Interactive Bubble Robots for Art

Application-oriented research is used to help bring current robotics technologies to bear against problems that exist in today society.

Where

Public space like museums, art schools and research centres can benefit from this research art project. This art project has the final scope to create a piece of artwork opened to the public. At moment people can work with the "Interactive Bubble Robots for Art" to create art at DIEES laboratories at the University of Catania.

Why

The mechanism of Mirror Neurons in the brain of the macaque is able to show the congruence between the observed action and the executed action. The Simulation theory of Mind-Reading (Gallese and Goldman, 1998) requires two different kinds of simulation: "Predictive" simulation that, under the hypothesis that the observer has the same final goal of the observed one, after the simulation process results in an action, and a "Retrodictive" simulation that represents a "Postdictive" simulation that produces the same observed action by predicting it.

Motor control theory, studied by Wolpert [48], requires two different kinds of motor commands. The "Action-to-Goal" model receives information about an action and then makes a goal for it, while in the "Goal-to-Action" model one system generates a specific action for the goal that is shown as input. At the same time, the "Forward Model" (still proposed by Wolpert) represents a "predictor" receiving a replica of the motor command and generating the expected action for it. On the contrary, the "Inverse Model" represents a "controller" and produces motor commands that are specific to realize a desired final goal. Researchers used this biology models to perform a simulation model for Art applications through two identical rolling robots that implemented the mechanism of mirror neurons.

What

The two rolling robots are equipped with special sensors to detect light and sound. In the upper side of robot structure there are 21 leds used for the implementation of the mechanism of imitation of mirror neurons. The sphere that surrounds the robot is in plastic, and consists of two matching halves. The first Bubble Robot performs his chaotic trajectory in the given arena according to a chaotic control law based on logistic map. The second Bubble Robot has a special control unit that contains the Mirror Neurons "neural net" software implementing the imitation mechanism. With this procedure, the two Bubble Robots can be distinguished as an "Observer Robot" and an "Observed Robot".

When one robot moves in the arena, the trajectories are mapped through the flash lights of the leds. The "Observer Robot" is able to understand and learn through imitation. In fact the led system of the first robot activates the mirror neurons of the second robot. In our model, the vision (visual neuron) is represented by the sensors of the "Observer Robot" which detect variation of the light emitted by the first robot. The "Observer" Bubble Robot reacts as a monkey when it sees another monkey that performs a behavior similar to its personal behaviour and initiates to imitate the first monkey.

Through the described research, a model of the mirror neurons system has been applied to robotics. The model implements at each stage an unsupervised learning mechanism, and the experiment seems to confirm that the model applied to the Chaotic Bubble Robots provides a direct support for the simulation theories of Mind-Reading and the interpretation of the inverse model of the control loop [48, 49].

The robots are able to understand and learn through imitation: a robot comes in harmony with each other through these neurons. A robot can create art and the other is able to imitate his gesture of art.

Discussion and Conclusion

In this chapter we have given an introduction to the multidisciplinary field of IT and art by giving some hints of the historical perspective (in the introduction) and by providing four categories (who, where, why, what) that can be used to reflect about existing literature. We have used these four viewpoints to describe five projects we currently work with. Our literature classification is unavoidably incomplete. First, even if we have used a systematic review to collect papers at the intersection of IT and art, we are aware that we have covered a limited part of the extensive literature in the field. This depends from the fact that all the authors have a background as IT researchers. This happens even if, as shown by the description of our projects, we are used to work with artists and to listen to their perspective. In the future we have to continue and intensify this cooperation with artists. Moreover we aim at working together with art theorists to enrich our horizon concerning literature sources.

As shown in Table 2, the framework makes possible the comparison of different art projects. We have used the framework to compare three Norwegian projects with two Italian projects and we claim that the framework enables us to understand the similarities and to reflect over the differences. On the "who" dimension we notice that all the five projects encompass researchers. Concerning the "why" dimension, our framework focus on the motivation of the cooperation. At the same time an artwork is always driven by an artistic idea and the cooperation between the actors aiming at realizing the artwork is strongly related to the artistic idea even if it does not necessarily coincide with it.

From the five projects we can observe few trends. In project "Sonic Onyx" and "Flyndre", the artists are the driving force and they first came up with the ideas to create artworks using technology. In these two projects, artists came into contacts

Table 2 Summary of the five projects according to the framework

Project	Who	Where	Why	What
Flyndre	Programming artist & researchers & engineers	Public (sculpture park) and Internet (flyndresang.no)	Develop & Learning co	Sound Python C-Sound Improsculpt Flash
Sonic Onyx	Artist & researchers & engineers	Public (school)	Develop & Learning	Sound & Light Linux Pure Data Python
The Open Wall	Architect & researchers (hw and sw)	1. Public (house facade) 2. Research (meeting room) & Internet (theopenwall.no)	1. Develop 2. Learning & Aestetics & reflection & Disseminate	Led Art Linux Java Wiki
Chaotic Robots for Art	Researchers & artists (dancers)	Research	Develop & Learning & Aestetics & Disseminate	Kinematics, Chaos Theory, C-language, Trajectories Led Art
Interactive Bubble Robots for Art	Researchers	Research	Aestetics & Disseminate	Kinematics, Java, Mirror Neurons, Trajectories Led Art

with the technologists to seek help for the development of the artworks. In projects "Chaotic Robots for Art" and "Interactive Bubble Robots for Art", technologists developed ideas to create artwork using robotics. The resulted works represents the urge/desire of technologists to create artistic or aesthetic applications using technology. In the project "Chaotic Robots for Art" the technologists collaborated with artists to explore the artistic possibilities of application of chaotic laws into robotics. In the project "The Open Wall" the initiation in the project and the collaboration between artists and technologists is multifaceted. An architect initiated the project. The artistic possibilities are kept open and addressed by both technologists and artists who challenge the technical limitations of the wall to express novel applications as well as enhancing the capabilities of "The Open Wall".

In the projects "Chaotic Robots for Art" and "Interactive Bubble Robots for Art", kinematics is an important tool to create three-dimensional artwork: this connects IT based art with kinetic art. The kinematics aspects of Chaotic Robots and Bubble Robots give inspiration to two dimensional artworks, like "The Open Wall" and open up for possibilities of transforming static two dimensional led systems as the Open Wall into tree-dimensional artworks.

Presenting the projects over the framework shows us that the "who, why, where, what" characteristics can be matched properly with framework. The concepts of the framework are present in our projects.

On the "what" column, devoted to tools and techniques, we give the main functionalities of the artworks, being sound for "Flyndre", sound and light for "Sonic Onyx", led art for "The Open Wall", and Kinematics and led art for the two projects "Chaotic Robots for Art" and "Interactive Bubble Robots for Art".

The framework allows us to reflect about art projects and to pose questions that can generate research questions and inspiration for further work. We conclude our work with a set of questions that are important for us. Here we list the questions that we have developed by looking at the combination of the theoretical framework and our practical projects and that will drive our work in the future years.

- **Who:** Given an artwork. Who is the author? Who is the responsible? Which roles are driving the project? Why do we miss one role, like for example theorists in our five projects?
- **Where:** Which effect has the "where" dimension on an artwork? If we look at the Open Wall, taking the installation from the public space into a meeting room in a University department has consequences in this respect. If the installation could be regarded as a piece of art when it was the public space, it has become a technological prototype or tool when taken into a private space in a University. Which is the role of the web interface with respect to the artwork?
- **Why:** How can we attract and facilitate multidisciplinary participation in the development of projects like this? How can we convince Industry and Public Funding Agencies to found these projects?
- **What:** Which are the tools that make each project successful and which are those that hinder the success of our project? Can we facilitate good software evolution by publishing it as Open Source? Which software license should an artwork that is published as open source should have? Which is the role of the source code? Is this product, like for example "The Open Wall", a piece of art or is it a tool for artist expression? How can theories from fields such as kinematics, dynamical nonlinear systems, neurobiology, and chaotic trajectories challenge the now main stream computer based digital art?

References

1. E. A. Shanken., "Art in the Information Age: Technology and Conceptual Art", LEONARDO, Vol. 35, No. 4, 2002, pp. 433–438.
2. R. Ascott, "Behaviourist Art and the Cybernetic Vision in Cybernetica": Journal of the International Association for Cybernetics (Namur), 1964.
3. J. Meyer, L. Staples, et al., "Artists and Technologists working together (panel)". Proceedings of the 11th annual ACM symposium on User interface software and Technology, San Francisco, California, United States, ACM Press, 1998.

4. A. Trifonova, S. U. Ahmed, L. Jaccheri, "SArt: Towards Innovation at the intersection of Software engineering and art." 16th International Conference on Information Systems Development. Galway, Ireland, Springer, 2007.

5. F. Popper, "Art of the Electronic Age", New York: Harry N. Abrams, Inc, 1993.

6. F. Popper, "From Technological to Visual Art", The MIT Press, 2007.

7. F. Popper, "Art: Action and Participation", New York University Press, 1975.

8. S.U. Ahmed., L. Jaccheri, A. Trifonova, G. Sindre, "Conceptual framework for the Intersection of Software and Art". Handbook of Research on Computational Arts and Creative Informatics – A book edited by James Braman, Towson University, Towson, MD, USA, Giovanni Vincenti, Gruppo Vincenti, S.r.l., Rome, Italy, 2008.

9. T. Bollinger, "The interplay of Art and Science in Software." Computer 30(10), 1997, pp.128, 125–127.

10. G. Bond, "Software as Art." Communications of the ACM 48(8), 2005, pp. 118–124.

11. F. Cramer, U. Gabriel, "Software Art and Writing." American Book Review Vol. 22(6), 2001.

12. O. Bertelsen, S. Pold, "Criticism as an Approach to Interface Aesthetics. Proceedings of the third Nordic conference on Human-computer interaction, Tampere, Finland, ACM Press, 2004.

13. E. Edmonds, G. Turner, L. Candy, "Approaches to interactive art systems". Proceedings of the 2nd international conference on Computer graphics and interactive techniques in Australasia and South East Asia. New York, NY. USA, ACM Press, 2004, pp. 113–117

14. L. O. Chua, "CNN: A vision of complexity," Int. J. Bifurcation and Chaos Vol. 7(12), 1997, pp. 2219–2426.

15. M. Blassnigg, "Documentary Film at the Junction between Art and Digital Media Technologies." Convergence-The International journal of New Media Technologies 11(3), 2005, pp. 104–110

16. "Ars Electronica Symposium", Ars Electronica in Linz, Austria, 1979.

17. C. Machin, "Digital artworks: bridging the Technology Gap". Proceedings of the 20th Eurographics UK Conference, IEEE Computer Society, 2002.

18. J. B. Gross, "Programming for Artists: a Visual Language for Expressive Lighting Design". IEEE Symposium on Visual Languages and Human-Centric Computing, IEEE Computer Society, 2005.

19. M. Cardini, "Arcus Pulcher Aetheri", progetto sinfonico 'Pittura Cibernetica e Musica', musica di Heinrich Unterhofer, orchestra Haydn di Bolzano, Auditorium di Bolzano, Trento e del MART di Rovereto, 2004.

20. L. Fortuna, M. Frasca, C. Camerano., "Strange Attractors, kinematic Trajectories and Synchronization". International Journal Bifurcations and Chaos, Dec 2008.

21. A. Buscarino, L. Fortuna, M. Frasca, G. Muscato., "Chaos does help motion control", Int. J. Bifurcation and Chaos, Vol. 17, No. 10, 2007, pp. 3577–3581.

22. M. Bucolo, L. Fortuna, M. Frasca, S. Giudice., "From Local Activity Lemma Beyond the Wave Computation Reaction Diffusion CNN based Networks", International Journal of Bifurcations and Chaos, Vol. 16, No. 2, 2006, pp. 411–418.

23. C. Adams, "Technological allusivity: appreciating and teaching the role of aesthetics in engineering design". Proceedings of the Frontiers in Education Conference, Atlanta, GA, IEEE Computer Society, 1995.

24. G. Nalder, "Art in the Informational Mode". Proceedings of the Seventh International Conference on Information Visualization, IEEE Computer Society, 2003.

25. http://www.javamuseum.org/blog/

26. http://webcanvas.com/#-875,-1520,1

27. http://www.nga.gov/kids/zone/zone.htm

28. http://www.waitarttool.com/home.cfm?content=aboutwait

29. G.Garvey, "Retrofitting fine Art and Design Education in the Age of Computer Technology". ACM SIGGRAPH Computer Graphics, 31(3), 1997, pp. 29–32.

30. C. Harris, "Art and Innovation: the Xerox PARC Artist-in-Residence program". Cambridge, Massachusetts, MIT Press, 1999.

31. L. Candy, "COSTART Project Artists Survey Report: Preliminary Results", Loughborough University, 1999.
32. L. Moura, "Robot Artist in Resident Project" 2006, http://www.leonelmoura.com
33. S. Jones, "A Cultural Systems Approach to Collaboration in Art & Technology". In Proceedings of the 5th conference on Creativity & cognition, New York, NY, USA: ACM Press. 2005, pp. 76–85.
34. E. Meisner, V. Isler, J. Trinkle, "Controller Design for Human-Robot Interaction", Department of Computer Science Rensselaer Polytechnic Institute, NY, 2007.
35. P. Fishwick, T. Davis, J. Douglas, "Model representation with Aesthetic Computing: Method and Empirical study." ACM Trans. Model. Comput. Simul., 15(3), 2005, pp. 254–279.
36. P. Fishwick, "Aesthetic Computing: A Brief Tutorial. In F. Ferri (Ed.), Visual Languages for Interactive Computing: Definitions and Formalizations", Idea Group Inc, 2007.
37. C. Adams, "Technological Allusivity: Appreciating and Teaching the role of Aesthetics in Engineering Design". Proceedings of the Frontiers in Education Conference, 1995., Atlanta, GA, IEEE Computer Society, 1995.
38. L. O. Chua, "The genesis of Chuas Circuit", Arch. fur Elektron. Ubertragungstechnik, vol. 46, 1992, pp. 250–257.
39. M. Bucolo, A. Buscarino, L. Fortuna, M. Frasca, "From Dynamical Emerging Patterns to Patterns in Visual Art", International Journal of Bifurcation and Chaos, Vol. 18, No. 1, 2007, pp. 51–81
40. P. Arena, S. Baglio, L. Fortuna, G. Manganaro, "Generation of n-double scrolls via Cellular Neural Networks". IEEE CAS Vol. 24, 1996, pp. 241–252.
41. L. Moura, H. Pereira, "Man+Robots Symbiotic Art". Villeurbanne: Institut d'Art Contemporain, 2004, pp. 111.
42. J. Reichardt "Cybernetic Serendipity", London, 1968, http://www.medienkunstnetz.de /exhibitions/serendipity/images/3/
43. P. Arena, M. Bucolo, S. Fazzino, L. Fortuna, M. Frasca, "The CNN paradigm: Shapes and Complexity". Int. J. Bif. Chaos, 15, 2005, pp. 2063–2090.
44. A. Buscarino, L. Fortuna, M. Frasca, A. Rizzo., "Dynamical network Interactions in distributed Control of Robots", Chaos, Vol. 16, No. 1, 015116-1-10, 2006.
45. S. Halme, T. Schnberg, Y. Wang, "Motion Control of a spherical Mobile Robot". Proc. Int. Workshop on Advanced Motion Control, 1996.
46. G. Metta, G. Sandini, L. Natale, L. Craighero, L. Fadiga, "Understanding Mirror Neurons: A bio-robotic Approach". LIRA-lab DIST, University of Genova, and University of Ferrara, 2002.
47. N. Ramnani, R. Miall, "A System in the Human Brain for Predicting the Actions of others". Nature Neurosci., 7, 2004, pp. 85–90.
48. D. Wolpert, Z. Ghahramani, J. Flanagan, "Perspectives and Problems in Motor learning". Trends Cogn. Sci., 5, 2001, pp. 487–494.
49. V. Gallese, A. Goldman, "Mirror Neurons and the Simulation Theory of Mind-reading". Trends Cogn. Sci., 2, 1998, pp. 493–501.
50. CAMeC (Centro Arte Moderna e Contemporanea della Spezia); http://camec. spezianet.it/opere_azione/tinguely.html
51. Museum of Modern Art (MOMA COLLECTION/P.HULTEN); http://www.moma.org/ collection/browse_results.php?object_id=81631
52. B. Oates, "New frontiers for Information Systems Research: Computer Art as an Information System." European Journal of Information Systems 15(6), 2006, pp. 617–626.
53. J. Grey, "Human-computer Interaction in Life Drawing, a fine artist's Perspective". In Sixth International Conference on Information Visualisation (IV'02). Los Alamitos, CA, USA: IEEE Computer Society, 2002, pp. 761–770.
54. K. Walden, "Reviews : Peter Weibel and Timothy Druekrey (eds), Net_Condition: Art and Global Media". Convergence The International journal of New Media Technologies, 8(1), 2002, pp. 114–116.

55. K. Halonen, "Open Source and New Media Artists. Human Technology", An Interdisciplinary Journal on Humans in ICT environments, 3(1), 2007, pp. 98–114.
56. A. Trifonova, O. Brandtsegg, L. Jaccheri, "Software engineering for and with Artists: a case study", 3rd International Conference on Digital Interactive Media in Entertainment and Arts (DIMEA 2008), Athens, Greece, 2008.
57. L. Jaccheri, A. Trifonova, G. Tufte, E. Gangvik, "The Open Wall", The 3rd International Conference on Digital Live Art (re)Actor3, Liverpool, UK, 2–3 September 2008.

Chapter 26
Augmented Reality and Mobile Art

Ian Gwilt

Introduction

The combined notions of augmented-reality (AR) and mobile art are based on the amalgamation of a number of enabling technologies including computer imaging, emergent display and tracking systems and the increased computing-power in hand-held devices such as Tablet PCs, smart phones, or personal digital assistants (PDAs) which have been utilized in the making of works of art. There is much published research on the technical aspects of AR and the ongoing work being undertaken in the development of faster more efficient AR systems [1] [2]. In this text I intend to concentrate on how AR and its associated typologies can be applied in the context of new media art practices, with particular reference to its application on hand-held or mobile devices.

Overview of AR

Unlike the experience of virtual reality (VR), where we are expected to locate ourselves in an alternative disembodied computer generated space, the notion of AR or mixed-reality (MR), implies that we can retain a much stronger sense of our physical presence and location, while interacting with a digitally mediated environment.[1]

---

[1] The terms MR and AR are commonly interchanged to describe a variety of technologically facilitated environments. However, within this text I have used the term AR in relation to a particular technological model of MR. The term AR is used to refer to the use of computer image-processing, tracking and rendering techniques which are displayed through the use of mobile videophones, PDAs, or as initially used in Head Mounted Display (HMD) technologies. The term MR refers to a more general interpretation of the technologically facilitated mixing of digital and material spaces

I. Gwilt (✉)
Faculty of Design Architecture and Building, University of Technology, Sydney
e-mail: Ian.gwilt@uts.edu.au

B. Furht (ed.), *Handbook of Multimedia for Digital Entertainment and Arts*,
DOI 10.1007/978-0-387-89024-1_26, © Springer Science+Business Media, LLC 2009

Fig. 1 Virtual-reality model

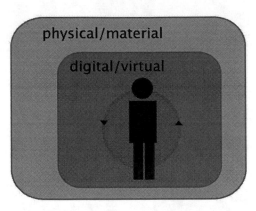

Steve Benford, from Nottingham University's Mixed Reality Lab defines AR as the following:

> Whereas virtual reality involves cutting yourself off from the real world - in order to immerse yourself in a computer generated - virtual world, augmented reality involves overlaying a virtual world onto your view of the real world, so that you can experience both at the same time. The computer might label physical objects with instructions, guidance and directions, or the everyday physical world might become populated with virtual characters and objects. [3]

Moreover, from a technical perspective the basic premise for VR is that the user is immersed in the digital/virtual and excluded from the physical/material (see Fig. 1). Whereas, in the case of AR/MR the user interacts with the computer environment (digital/virtual), while still being located in the physical space (physical/material) (see Fig. 2). Furthermore, there is ongoing input/output, influential, and implicit activity between the two environments. The defining quality of AR/MR is framed around the interplay between physical space and digital mediated spaces (both perceptually and formally), and this tenet is at the centre of the effective use of AR as an artistic tool.

AR Mobile Art

AR technologies allow an artist to mix digital content with the video processed image of a physical object or environment, together on the screen of a mobile device. In media terms, this digital content can take a variety of forms including three-dimensional computer models, animations, digital images, video clips, audio files and so on. By using AR technologies it is possible to augment the video image of real objects and spaces with computer-generated material to build relational narra-

---

using a variety of techniques to overlay, and create multi-faceted environments through the use of sensors, video projections, interactive artifacts and so on.

Fig. 2 Mixed-reality model
*(Diagram concepts courtesy
of Mark Billinghurst from The
Human Interface Technology
Laboratory New Zealand -
HIT Lab NZ).*

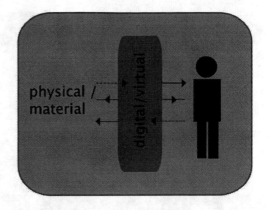

tives and to add real-time layers of contextualised information and content. Another
key quality of AR is the ability to co-locate the physical object or space, with the
overlaid digital content through the use of image tracking techniques [4] [5], to
create a spatial relationship between object and digital content. This technique is
commonly exploited in the creation of AR mobile artworks.

Although originally developed to be used with head-mounted video glasses similar to the type used in VR (a preceding technology to AR), there is a strong move
towards the operating of AR software on mobile devices such video phones and
PDAs [6]. This shift crucially does two things; firstly, it moves the technology and
access to the technology into an increasingly accessible public platform, which is
widely distributed and can be applied in diverse cultural contexts. Secondly, the
move from HMDs (which place the video image directly in front of the users eye-
sight) to handheld devices, which do not restrict the users awareness of physical
space, creates a fundamental paradigm shift from the immersive notions of VR, into
the realm of mixed-reality. This enables relationships between computer-generated
content and physical environments to be explored; in fact, according to Anders [7]
the key to successful AR constructs depends on establishing a cognitive and spatial relationship between physical and digital environments. Moreover, this can be
achieved by expanding the potentials of augmenting spaces, artifacts and people [8].
A number of works which attempt to apply AR technologies in the context of art
practice have been created [9], and in the following section I will describe a piece
of my own work, *save_as* (2007) which combines a physical artifact together with
computer/mobile technologies to enable an augmented relationship between a physical object and digital information.

Case Study: AR Mobile Art

The AR mobile artwork entitled *save_as* utilizes the video capabilities of a hand-
held PDA, together with image recognition and image tracking computer code, to
place digital content in direct relation to a physical artifact. In this case the physical

Fig. 3 *Save_as* (2007) installation view. Augmented sculpture, acrylic, 220 mm × 180 mm × 90 mm, wall mounted, PDA, camera, computer software. Image Gwilt 2007

artifact is an acrylic model of a computer desktop folder. Partially opened, the folder can be observed attached upside-down to a gallery wall, at about 1.5 meters off the ground (see Fig. 3). Visitors are free to walk up to and examine the three-dimensional folder, which is an enlarged sculptural representation of the typical computer folder icon. On entering the exhibition space a PDA with video camera attachment is supplied to the visitor. The visitor is encouraged to view the physical folder with the aid of the PDA camera, and the PDA display screen. Observing the wall mounted folder through the PDA, the user is able to see digital content superimposed over the image of the physical object. In this case the physical folder is overlaid with virtual texts that appear in front of the folder. The artwork is programmed in such a way that when the PDA camera recognizes the folder on the wall it places a two-word text combination on the camera screen in front of the object (in an analogy of the naming conventions we see associated to computer desktop folders and files). These dual word combinations are drawn from two lists; one list is comprised of common software command texts such as 'save', 'cut', 'paste' and 'delete'; the other list is made up of personal pronouns, including, 'him', 'her', 'them', 'our' etc. The randomly selected word combinations combine to create statements such as 'save me', 'cut him' and 'delete her'. There is a new word combination displayed every 6 seconds (see Fig. 4). By combining pronouns, with terminology drawn from generic computer interface actions the intention of the artwork is to establish a relationship between people and technology, analogue and digital. Moreover, these word combinations of personal pronouns and common computer commands seek to question our relationship and engagement with the domestic computer through this creative arrangement.

Fig. 4 *Save_as* (2007) screen detail. Image Gwilt 2007

In common with the broader notions of mixed-reality art, this AR mobile art-work is grounded in both digital and material cultures. The model of the physical folder is combined with the digital possibilities of computer-based modeling, image processing, tracking and display technologies. Furthermore, the temporal animation dynamics of the digital are combined with material fabrication and spatial consider-ations to form a hybrid artifact that employs media-making techniques and concepts from both digital and material art practices. Through the notion of mixed-reality art a fluid interplay between digital and material practices takes place, breaking down the perceived binary opposition between the real artifact on the gallery wall and the augmented digital render on the mobile device.

The artwork was realized with the support of technologists from The Human Interface Technology Laboratory New Zealand (HIT Lab NZ). Through this engage-ment propriety image recognition software was developed that allowed the PDA device to recognize the physical folder. The use of the actual form of the physical folder to trigger the display of the computer-generated augmented content created a significant point of difference between this artwork and a number of other AR based artworks. Traditionally, AR utilizes a marker based tracking system (simple black and white squares and graphics) to identify the position between the camera and a physical object or surface [10]. Following in the trend to produce less visu-ally obtrusive tracking devices [11] this artwork uses the actual form of the physical model to trigger and locate the digital content in the work. This technique of 'mark-erless AR tracking' is described by the author of the computer code, Sun-Kyoo Hwang as follows:

A key part of this installation is using object based/markerless tracking to find the 3D cam-era pose from an input video image. The most important challenge is to develop efficient algorithms that can work on a low computing-power device such as a PDA. Our approach is to find four significant corner points of the folder object and compute the 3D camera pose by homography. [12]

Conclusion

From a creative point of view the potentials of AR mobile art are extremely broad, when we consider the potential to add digital content to a physical environment or space. The move towards the use of markerless tracking systems [1] [11] is also interesting, in that as the technological interaction becomes more transparent there is potentially less conflict between creative content and the requirements of the technology. Moreover, the shift from the use of AR through HMDs to mobile devices opens up further opportunities wherein the peripatetic interaction with AR through the use of mobile devices means that artworks can be created for increasingly varied locations and circumstances. Shifting the digital interface into the public arena through the use of mobile devices also highlights the gestural interactions that accompany these technologies. The physical action of holding up a mobile phone to observe an augmented artwork establishes a connection between digital techno-science and cultural engagement through the creative potentials and social interaction of AR facilitated artworks [13].

The hybrid potentials of AR mobile art establishes a scenario where we can begin to observe how the imposition of one space onto the other, (digital / physical) begins to have an influence on how we think about each space, leading to changes in both technological and perceptual readings through unusual creative interplays. By considering these conjunctions and their associated traits, both material and digital, we can begin to reflect on the attempt in AR to operate in tandem the real-world and computer elements of the works. From a conceptual perspective AR works are not an attempt at a mimetic replacements of one space with the other. But rely on an additive experience enhanced by the potentials of each space (digital / physical), realized through the combined engagement with both. Moreover, interaction within these types of constructs draws attention to the differences and similarities between a predominately physical experience and a predominately digital experience. The success of an AR mobile artwork therefore, is contingent on an understanding of the relational complexity of this hybrid experiential mix. This can be achieved by successfully manipulating the facilitating technologies, both digital and material, to weave the desired type of interplay between two sets of typologies.

References

1. F. Zhou, H. B-L. Duh, M. Billinghurst, "Trends in augmented reality tracking, interaction and display: A review of ten years of ISMAR," Mixed and Augmented Reality, ISMAR 2008. 7th IEEE/ACM International Symposium, 15–18 Sept. 2008, pp.193–202
2. O. Bimber and R. Raskar, "Spatial Augmented Reality: Merging Real and Virtual Worlds" Wellesley MA, A K Peters Ltd, 2005
3. S. Benford, "BBC - ARTS - Blast Theory MLR" interview with Professor Steve Benford, principle investigator at Nottingham University's Mixed Reality Lab. 2002, retrieved Jan 31st 2009 from http://www.bbc.co.uk/arts/shootinglive/2002/blasttheory/mrl.shtml
4. D. Koller, G. Klinker, E. Rose, D. Breen, R. Whitaker, "Real-time Vision-Based Camera Tracking for Augmented Reality Applications", in Proceedings of the Symposium on Virtual Reality Software and Technology (VRST-97), Lausanne, Switzerland, September 15–17, 1997, pp. 87–94
5. A. J. Davison, "Real-Time Simultaneous Localisation and Mapping with a Single Camera," Proceedings of the 9th IEEE International Conference on Computer Vision (ICCV'03) - Volume 2, 2003, pp.1403
6. D. Wagner and D. Schmalstieg, "First Steps Towards Handheld Augmented Reality", proceedings of the 7th IEEE International Symposium on Wearable Computers 2003, pp. 127
7. P. Anders, "Envisioning Cyberspace", New York, McGraw-Hill, 1998, pp. 171
8. K. H. Veltman, "Understanding new media: augmented knowledge and culture", Calgary, University of Calgary Press, 2006, pp. 308
9. R. Grasset, E. Woods, M. Billinghurst, "Art and Mixed Reality: New Technology for Seamless Merging Between Virtual and Real" IMedia-Space Journal. Issue 1-2008
10. H. Kato and M. Billinghurst, "Marker Tracking and HMD Calibration for a Video-Based Augmented Reality Conferencing System," (iwar '99), proceedings of the 2nd IEEE and ACM International Workshop on Augmented Reality, 1999, pp. 85
11. D. Wagner, T. Langlotz, D. Schmalstieg, "Robust and unobtrusive marker tracking on mobile phones", proceedings of ISMAR2008, 7th IEEE/ACM International Symposium on Mixed and Augmented Reality, Cambridge, 15–18 Sept., 2008, pp. 121–124
12. S.-K. Hwang, I. Gwilt, M. Billinghurst, "Markerless AR Tracking on a Mobile Device for Digital Art", 4th International Workshop on the Tangible Space Initiative, Nov. proceedings of the Sixth IEEE and ACM International Symposium on Mixed and Augmented Reality (ISMAR), Nara, Japan, 2007
13. H. Fischer, "Digital shock: confronting the new reality", Montreal, McGill-Queen's 2006, pp. 23

Chapter 27
The Creation Process in Digital Art

Adérito Fernandes Marcos, Pedro Sérgio Branco, and Nelson Troca Zagalo

Introduction

The process behind the act of the art creation or the creation process has been the subject of much debate and research during the last fifty years at least, even thinking art and beauty has been a subject of analysis already by the ancient Greeks such were Plato or Aristotle. Even though intuitively it is a simple phenomenon, creativity or the human ability to generate innovation (new ideas, concepts, etc.) is in fact quite complex. It has been studied from the perspectives of behavioral and social psychology, cognitive science, artificial intelligence, philosophy, history, design research, digital art, and computational aesthetics, among others. In spite of many years of discussion and research there is no single, authoritative perspective or definition of creativity, i.e., there is no standardized measurement technique. Regarding the development process that supports the intellectual act of creation it is usually described as a procedure where the artist experiments the medium, explores it with one or more techniques, changing shapes, forms, appearances, where beyond time and space, he/she seeks his/her way out to a clearing, i.e., envisages a path from intention to realization. Duchamp in his lecture "The Creative Act" states the artist is never alone with his/her artwork; there is always the spectator that later on will react critically to the work of art. If the artist succeeds in transmitting his/her intentions in terms of a message, emotion or feeling to the spectator then a form of aesthetic osmosis actually takes place through the inert matter (the medium) that

A.F. Marcos (✉)
ENGAGE Lab, Dept. of Information Systems, University of Minho, Guimarães, Portugal
Computer Graphics Center, Guimarães, Portugal
e-mail: marcos@dsi.uminho.pt; marcos@ccg.pt

P.S. Branco
ENGAGE Lab, Dept. of Information Systems, University of Minho, Guimarães, Portugal
e-mail: pbranco@dsi.uminho.pt

N.T. Zagalo
ENGAGE Lab, Dept. of Communication Science, University of Minho, Braga, Portugal
e-mail: nzagalo@ics.uminho.pt

B. Furht (ed.), *Handbook of Multimedia for Digital Entertainment and Arts*,
DOI 10.1007/978-0-387-89024-1_27, © Springer Science+Business Media, LLC 2009

enabled this communication or interaction phenomenon to occur. The role of the spectator may become gradually more active by interacting with the artwork itself possibly changing or becoming a part of it [2][4].

When we focus our analysis on the creation process in digital art we easily conclude it is intrinsically linked with the design and development of computer-based artworks. By exploring computer technologies digital art opens to new type of tools, materials and artworks as also establishes new relationships among creators, artworks and spectators or observers, largely not comparable to previous approaches.

Indeed we can describe art objects as simple symbolic objects that aim at stimulating emotions. They are created to reach us through our senses (visual, auditory, tactile, or other), being displayed by means of physical material (stone, paper, wood, etc.) while combining some perceptive patterns to produce an aesthetic composition. Digital art objects differ from conventional art pieces by the use of computers and computer-based artifacts that manipulate digitally coded information and digital technologies, i.e., they explore intensively the *computer medium*, what opens unlimited possibilities in interaction, virtualization and manipulation of information. These digital art objects or artifacts, where some are possibly non-tangible, constitute, in fact, the resulting product from the artistic creation process that together establishes a common communicational and informational space. Information or information content, meaning the intended message of each artifact, is a central constituent of this common communicational and informational space. Accordingly, artistic artifacts, may these be of digital or physical nature can be defined as informational objects. The computer medium is defined here as the set of digital technologies ranging from digital information formats, infrastructures to processing tools that together can be observed as a continuum art medium used by artists to produce digital artifacts [9][10] (see Fig. 1).

When we consider the creation process itself, we can establish its beginnings when the creator gets an hold of the first concept or idea resulting from his/her subjective vision, gradually modeled into a form of (un)tangible artifact. It constitutes the message, this *about* something, the artist wants to transmit to the world. When

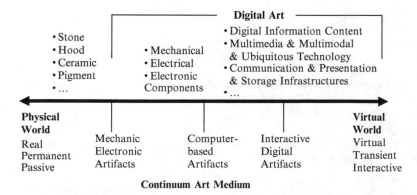

Fig. 1 The Continuum Art Medium

digital content is used in this process, it can be both the means and the end product. On one hand, the digital content can be explored as the means to create non-digital artifacts, as for instance, digitally altered paper-based photography, and, on the other hand, be the end-result intended as it is the case in animated comics.

In fact, digital art applies the computer medium both as raw material (e.g. the digitally coded information content) and as a tool of enhancing creativity. The reader shall become aware of the fact that raw material is related here to unprocessed (or in minimally processed state) material that can be acted by the human labor to create some product. Similarly, digitally coded information content can be manipulated by digital artists to create artistic objects. When in the creation process, digital artists apply information content along with technologies from multimedia, virtual reality, computer vision, digital music and sound, etc. as also the information and communication infrastructure available such are the internet, presentation devices, and storage arrays, among others, to create interactive installations and generate digital artifacts. Therefore, the computer medium traverses effectively all the stages of the creation process, from concept drawing until the final artifact production and exhibition. Today's powerful editing and programming tools make it possible to an artist to modify, correct, change and integrate information content as valuable raw material in the creation process, that may be presented in several digital formats such are text, image, video, sound, 3D objects, animation, or even haptic objects.

We are here interested in the creation process of the artifact per si, following a model based in what Routio, in his works on arteology (the science that studies the artifacts), labels as *project-specific artistic development* that purports to assist the creation of a single artifact (or a series of them) by defining its goals and providing the conceptual model on which the work of art shall be based [12]. Thus and because it deals intensively with the computer medium, in digital art this creation process inherits aspects from computer systems development (even hardware/software engineering) and design process. The artifact's message, narrative and end-shape design is pivotal as also its technological implementation and final deployment within a exhibition space [7][8].

Moreover, artistic communities need to have access to common technological infrastructures that facilitate collaboration (collaborative editing, annotating, etc.), communication and sharing of work experiences, of materials, being these, unprocessed digital content or final artifacts, activities that are essential for a soft progress from the starting concept to the final artwork. We argue here that as in other human activities, artistic creation benefits from the collaboration within a community of equals while having access to materials and tools. Such common information space is in effect a creative design space; thought design (in the sense of shaping) is the fundamental activity in the creation process of digital art.

In this chapter we propose to analyze and discuss the main concepts and definitions behind digital art while proposing a model for the creation process in digital art. It allows for a smooth progress from the concept/idea until the final product (artwork) while exploring the computer medium to its maximum potential. The chapter is divided in the following sections: first we give an overview of the background of digital art in terms of its fundamental concepts and developing vectors.

Next we describe the creation process for digital art, embracing the creative design space architecture while presenting concrete examples. Finally we draw out some conclusion.

Digital Art Fundamentals

Digital art has its roots within the first decades of the twentieth century with isolated experiments created by a few visionaries whose results were mostly exhibited in art fairs, conferences, festivals and symposia devoted to technology or electronic media. These first artworks have been mostly classified as marginal to the mainstream art world. Alike in the Dadaist art movement some of these artworks were seen as a form of *anti-art*.

The development of science and technology has been the principal engine of the evolution of digital art. But, what we know today as digital art has been strongly influenced by several art movements such were, among others, Fluxus, Dada, and Conceptual Art. These movements brought into digital art the emphasis on formal instructions, the focus on concept, on the event *per se*, and also, the emphasis on the viewer's participation, contrasting to the art based on unified static material objects. From the Dadaism specifically, digital art inherited the concept of creating art by using precise predefined rules, i.e., a finite set of instructions generates the final artwork (a poem, a painting). The rule' or algorithm' instruction was adopted as the conceptual central element in the creation process. *Instruction-based* art is a fertile soil of today's digital art. Similarly, the Fluxus art movement has also extensively explored the idea of instruction-based generated art along with the immersion of the audience in the event, forcing an *interaction* between the spectator and the artworks. Influences from the Conceptual art, a movement emerged in the 1960s, came from its central statement "the idea or concept is the most important aspect of the work". This is still a way of thinking and practice common to many digital artists in all over the world. The concept or idea is the leitmotif for the shaping of the digital artifact. It means that "all of the planning and decisions are made beforehand and the execution is a perfunctory affair, i.e., the idea becomes a machine that makes the art", by artist Sol LeWitt (1967).

Digital art, as it is known nowadays, entered the world art in the late 1990s when museums and art galleries started increasingly to incorporate digital art installations in their exhibitions. The Intercommunication Center (ICC) in Tokyo, Japan; the Center for Culture and Media in Karlsruhe, Germany; the Ars Electronica Festival in Linz, Austria; the EMAF - European Media Arts Festival, Osnabrück, Germany; the VIPER (Switzerland); the International Art Biennale of Cerveira, Portugal; and the DEAF - Dutch Electronic Arts Festival are examples of initiatives that have supported and initiated digital art consistently all over the last two decades. Digital art is today a proper branch of contemporary art [10][11].

Today's digital artifacts range from virtual life as it is the case of *A-Volve* (1994) from Christa Sommerer and Laurent Mignonneau, a virtual environment where

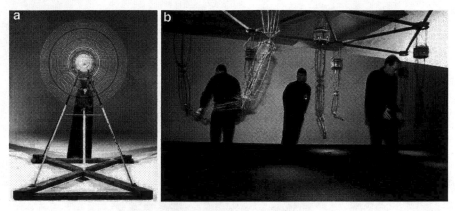

Fig. 2 In the left: *Rotary Glass Plates (Precision Optics [in motion])*, 1920, by Marcel Duchamp. In the right: *Autopoiesis*, 2000, by Kenneth Rinaldo (courtesy of the author)

aesthetic creatures try to survive; to artificial life robotics installation such is *Autopoiesis* (2000), by Kenneth Rinaldo that presents sculptures with sensors that react to the visitor by moving their arms towards the person provoking attraction or repulsion (see Fig. 2). Virtual Characters (usually called Avatars), Internet art and Cyborgs are topics where digital artists are active nowadays. A more comprehensive overview of the today's aesthetic digital artifacts can be obtained from Paul Greene [11].

Definitions

Digital art is in fact a recent term that became a general designation for several forms of computer-supported art, from *computer art* (since 1970s), *multimedia art*, *interactive art*, *electronic art* and more recently, *new media art*. Under the definition of digital art there are several art branches commonly connected to the specific media or technology they are based on.

We define *digital art* as *art that explores computers (tools, technologies and digitally coded information content) as a tool and material for creation*.

In the course of this definition digital art has to incorporate the computer medium in its creation process, even if the final artifact does not visibly integrate computer or digital elements.

In Fig. 3 we present an overview of the different artistic areas related to digital art. As we can observe, digital art embraces, by definition, all type of computer-supported art.

Digital art is mainly based on three grounding concepts: *controlled **randomness** access*; *presentational **virtuality*** and ***interactivity*** that have been behind emergent

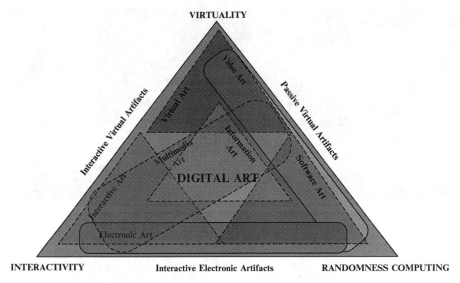

Fig. 3 A general categorization of digital art

artwork from the 1960s to today's digital art installations. They can be described as follows:

- *Randomness Access*: (pseudo) non-deterministic instruction-based algorithms open the possibility of instant access to media elements that can be reshuffled in seemingly infinite combinations;
- *Virtuality*: the physical object is migrated into a *virtual* or *conceptual object*. The *concept* itself becomes perceptible through its virtualization;
- *Interactivity*: the viewer may assume an active role in influencing and changing the artwork itself.

The artwork is often transformed into an open structure in process that relies on a constant flux of information and engages the participant in the way a performance might do. The audience becomes a participant in the work, resembling the components of the project that may display information of a specific perceptive nature (visual, auditory, tactile, or other). The artist plays usually the role of facilitator for the participant's interaction.

Creation Process

The creation process in digital art relies often on collaborations between an artist and a team of programmers, technicians, engineers, scientists and designers, among others. This collaboration implies a multidisciplinary work involving art, science, technology, design, psychology, etc., that form a common communicational and informational space. Due to the widespread of the digitally coded information content that is increasingly available in high expressive multimedia formats, the creation process is becoming more and more based on the manipulation and integration of digital content for creation of artworks.

Accordingly, we need a common creative design space where digital artists can smoothly progress from the concept/idea until the final product (artwork) while exploring the computer medium to its maximum potential. This common creative design space incorporates necessarily a communicational and informational space beneath, where digitally coded information content of different nature and level of processing is available for the artists' use. Furthermore, tools for editing, design or for any specific processing and composing have to be offered along with facilities for communication and collaboration among the community members. The creative design space shall also provide tools to support all the activities at all phases of the creative design process, ranging from the drafting phase, passing through the artifact's implementation phase until the artifacts exhibition preparation (exhibition space design) as also the access to physical and/or digital exhibition space. This way, the creative design space will facilitate the establishment of communities of interests in art, where people from different backgrounds share materials (raw material), and digital collections while collaborating throughout common goals.

The meaning of design in this context, appoints to a conscious effort to create something that is both functional and aesthetically pleasing. Design is here taken from both the perspective of design in engineering and from a more inventive view as it is the case in applied arts.

As Löwgren and Stolterman [8] state design is always carried out in a context (p. 45). In digital art, design of digital artifacts is mainly based on the conceptualism's aphorism where the initial "idea or concept becomes a machine that makes the art" (Sol LeWitt, 1967). However, unlike in the pure design process, where the problem-solving guides de action of the designer, in digital art such systematic manner appears not primarily to solve a problem but to enhance the intention to the realization, i.e., the final artifact. Generally, artists follow an alike process in developing their creative ideas, though they may be less conscious of the process they are following. Initially the artist will tend to experiment in a rather random manner, collecting ideas and skills through reading or experimentation. Gradually a particular issue or question will become the focus of the experimentation and concrete implementation, formulating alternative ways, trying them, in order to adopt a refined one that will be pursued through repeated experimentation [7]. Thus the design process itself evolves from a vision or idea (even if it is not aware for the creator) until the final digital artifact is released. The message the spectator can obtain from the artifact in terms of a personal or group experience is the central issue the digital artifact holds.

From this point of view the digital artifact is nothing but a designed thing built around a core of digital technology. In digital art context, the artifact is an object embracing information content displayed by means of digital media or a combination of digital and physical components. The artifact acts as a materialization of a message, a piece of information, throughout the presentation of information content intended to stimulate emotions, perceptive experiences on side of the user. Thus, artistic digital artifacts, being these of pure digital or a combination with physical constituents are more adequately defined as *informational objects*.

Digital content is defined as informative material of digital nature that holds the ability to be acted to transmit a message. Some authors, as for instance Robert Musil in his unfinished novel *"The Man without Qualities"*, refer to digital technology and by legacy, digitally coded information content, as the material without qualities due to its pervasive characteristics and constantly development. These are, however, characteristics that open, almost on a daily basis, new challenges and possibilities for aesthetical experiments since the computer medium can constantly wear new presentational facets.

The Process

The creation process in digital art is mainly based on the design of the artifact's message and its development. The computer medium in the form of editing, communication and collaboration tools as well as digitally coded information content is likely to be always present and traversing the overall creation process.

As depicted in Fig. 4 the creative design process is launched when the artist gets hold with an initial idea/concept. Then, the artist starts to design the concept, entering a process that will lead into the final artifact. This process is not a linear process, on the contrary, artists may go back and further in the activity sequence, skipping one or focusing the work in another. The process is usually highly dynamic, yet, the artist's vision is always present. The creation process involves the following phases:

Message Design phase:

- Concept Design: in this activity the artist gets involved in converting his/her idea/concept or vision into a set of sketches, informal drawings, i.e., the abstraction is concretized in a perceptive structure. The artist does exploratory drawings that are not intended as a finished work. The outcomes of this activity are, thus, sketches, drawings that allow the artist to try out different ideas and establish a first attempt for a more complex composition.
- Narrative Design: here the artist takes the drawings resulting from the concept design activity and designs a composition, a construct of a sequence of events that set up the message that will allow the users/viewers an emotional connection which grants memories and recounting of the artwork. The narrative of the message behind the initial concept is designed taking into consideration aspects such as the structure of its constituent parts and their function(s) and relationships. The narrative assumes the form of a chronological sequence of themes, motives and plot lines. The outcome of this activity can be resumed as the design of the message as a story.
- Experience Design: this activity embraces the process of designing the message, taking into account its related concept and narrative, to design and conceptualize specific characteristics of each narrative event from the point of view of the

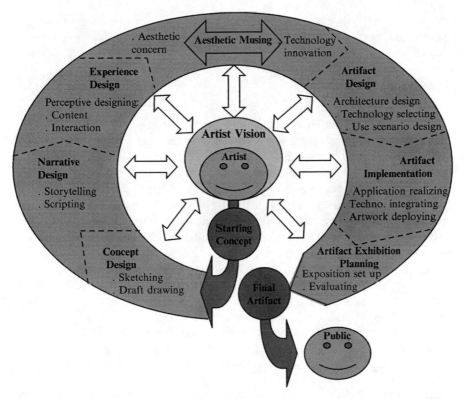

Fig. 4 Overview of the Creative Design Process phases

human experience it shall provide. This design or planning of the human experience is made based on the consideration of an individual's or group's needs, desires, beliefs, knowledge, skills, experiences, and perceptions. The experience design attempts to draw from many sources including cognitive and perceptual psychology, cognitive science, environmental design, haptics, information content design, interaction design, heuristics, and design thinking, among others.

Aesthetic Musing: this is a central activity in the creative design process, it represents the moments of contemplation where the artist revise his/her vision against the decisions made (to be done) during the design and development of the artifact. We identify two guiding vectors in aesthetic musing of artifacts:

- Aesthetic concern: process of integrating characteristics in the artifact that eventually provide a perceptual experience of pleasure, meaning or satisfaction, arising specifically here from sensory manifestations of the artifact such are shape, color, immersion, sound, texture, design or rhythm, among others. Beauty here relates almost exclusively to the aesthetic dimension of the perceptive nature of the artifact components.
- Technology innovation: process of integrating novelty in the reshape, use, combination and exploitation of digital technology. This appoints to the computer medium dimension of the beauty creation, i.e., the technology is a driven force to

set up new aesthetic dialogues. Taken the fact of the digital technology is under accelerated development; integration of high levels of technology innovation in digital art is commonly desired.

Artifact Development phase:

- Artifact Design: this activity relates to all aspects concerned with the design of the computer system or application that will support the final artifact. This includes the design of the system architecture, interface and interaction, as well as the selection of technology to implement them. Since the artifact is to be acted usually by an audience of viewers, we have also considered in this activity the design of the use scenario from the technological point of view. Design adopts here a hybrid perspective mixing aspects from applied arts and engineering. It applies principles from a more rigorous design based on exploitation of technology, science and even mathematical knowledge along with the aesthetical concerns.
- Artifact Implementation: in this activity the artist proceeds to the implementation of the artifact itself. This incorporates tasks as programming, testing and debugging, as well as, technology integration and the final artifact deployment. This demands from the artist to hold programming and technological skills if he/she wants to have a more direct control over the implementation process. The artist can even be assisted by a team of programmers and technologists; however, to be in command of the artwork, the artist has to be skilled in technology to a certain level.
- Artifact Exhibition Planning: this activity joins together all aspects related with the setting up of the artifact exhibition. This represents the final stage of the overall creative design process, where the artifact is brought into the world, i.e., the art object meets the audience. The success of this meeting will depend increasingly on the attractiveness of the artifact, the way the exhibition space is organized, how the logistic of its different components are managed and supported and also on the contextualization of the artifact in the overall exhibition. Notice this activity will be based on the decisions made before in terms of the message design, the artifact implementation, and above all, on the use scenario configuration. Artifacts may be presented in museums, art halls, art clubs or private art galleries, or at some virtual place such is the Internet.

The Creative Design Space Architecture

The creative design space is the local, physical and virtual, where the creative design process is realized. As previously defined, a creative design space is a digital communicational and informational space that enables the generation of artistic content, the storage, transmission and exchange of digital data while providing the exhibition and presentation space for access to information and content by both specialists and the public.

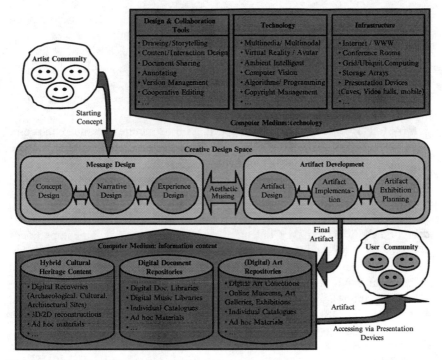

Fig. 5 The Creative Design Space Architecture

The creative design space aims at supporting an artistic community by enabling all the main activities of the creative design process by providing tools for design, shaping, planning, collaboration, communication and sharing of information as well as giving access to digitally coded information content of diverse nature. Usually, such a space has also to provide exhibiting facilities for presentation of final artifacts to the audience.

As a whole, the creative design space as depicted in Fig. 5 is not entirely affected either by technological advances or the needs of users and creators. The flow of work from one activity to another remains conceptually the same.

As previously noticed, the computer medium is likely to traverse all the stages of the creative design process, from concept drawing until the final artifact production and exhibition. As we can observe in the figure 5 the computer medium can be divided in two main lines of contributions, namely:

- **Computer medium** as technology: we identify here three principal types of tools:

  - Design & Collaboration Tools: they include all type of tools and applications that support activities related with design, drawing, planning, etc. as well as those allowing the collaboration among groups of artists to happen throughout communication, sharing of files, joint editing and annotating, etc.

- Technology: we consider here all the computer technologies that are offered not only as tools or applications but principally as technological areas whose knowledge, procedures and techniques can be exploited in benefit of the creative design process. Programming languages, toolkits, specific algorithms, concepts and architectures, scripting techniques or procedures in areas such are virtual reality, computer vision or ambient intelligent are good examples of the technology mentioned here.
- Infrastructure: this relates to all supporting infrastructures that make the computer medium to happen, in terms of communication, conferencing, storage facilities, computing capacity, presentation devices, etc.

- **Computer medium** as digitally coded information content: we identify here three principal types of information content:

- Hybrid Cultural Heritage Content: this relates to all kind of content, partial or full digital, collected from different cultural heritage sources such are archeological sites, museum, 2D and 3D digital recoveries of architectural and historical findings, etc. Cultural heritage content has been serving as raw material for the shaping of digital artifacts that aim at transmit specific cultural messages. For instance, digitally altered photography is exploiting to a great extend digital photographs of famous paintings.
- Digital Document Repositories: these relate to the more formal document repositories ranging from text and image documents, digital music databases, from institutional or personal catalogues and collections. This type of information content is adequate, for instance, to be applied in artifacts that explore more official information sources, as for instance, the ones based on narratives referring to historic, real-life elements (dates, names, events).
- Digital Art Repositories: these relate to digital-born art objects, media, documents, etc. owned by art galleries, museums, festivals, art houses, individual or ad hoc collections that are accessible online. Under this classification we consider also all the artifacts generated within the creative design space that can be digitally stored.

Artists enter the creative design process by providing a starting concept. Then, all along the message design and artifact development phases, the artist may bring into play several types of tools, by a single manner or collaborating with colleagues, while using digitally coded information content. Incorporated in this information content we might have also parts of or complete artifacts. They can be, possibly, reused as simple musing objects or be even transformed into new forms. Thus, the management of copy rights in the accessing and re-use of digital content is a mandatory requirement for a successful development of the community of interest over the common creative design space.

Notice that the final artifact is released into the digital repositories and not directly to the audience. This is because the access to the digital artifacts has to be done by presentation devices within an exhibition space, being this physical such is a museum room or virtual like the Internet.

Discussion

We are aware of the risks behind the proposal of a creative development process model, when the phenomenon of artistic creation or creativity is still not explained at all. However, digital art is an art branch that relies intensively on the computer medium.

Digital art brought the *interaction* and *virtuality* (in the sense of the immaterial) in art, as artists explore new forms of involving the spectator in the artwork and enhancing the shift from object to *concept* in the form of the "virtual object". This virtual object is usually seen as a structure in the process, sometimes dynamic and volatile, that creates expressive effects, stimulates emotions and perhaps feeling on the part of the spectator, who might become an active player when *interacting* with the artwork itself and changing it in unforeseen new shapes.

Furthermore digital artists often explore the concept of *combinatorial* and *strict rule-based* process inherited from the Dadaism poetry, as well as, *controlled randomness* to generate and activate instructions for information access and processing. This leads to the materialization of artworks resulting from pure instruction-based procedures as was the work of the American composer John Cage, whose work carried out in the 1950s and 1960s, explored extensively these concepts. Cage described music as a structure divisible into successive parts that could be filled by means of automatically controlled randomness and instruction-based algorithms. This open an infinite set of possibilities for creation.

On the other hand, the intensive development of the information society has implications in the widespread of huge volumes of rich multimedia content and their usage in shaping digital artifacts. One way or other, our civilization' heritage is turning into digital format and, to a great extent, available for free. Design and processing tools are become common place and increasingly trouble-free thought they will integrate artificial intelligence in order to facilitate the creation process. Art shall become, in short time, a prerogative of everybody, granted the access to the computer medium. Therefore, the emergence of collaborating artists' communities sharing a common informational and communicational space increases the need for concrete implementations of the creation process where people may work alone but also act in group by sharing ideas and content with colleagues linked over a common creative design space.

We have observed that regardless of the specific digital medium employed, the creation process is essentially the same. People start with a first idea or concept and go along all or some of the different creation process phases. Important differences between artists in their methods of realizing an artifact can generally be ascribed to the differing technical requirements of the digital medium. These differences are superficial and mainly related to the technical understanding of the specific digital medium and the related computer-based technologies.

In fact the most important aspect in the digital art outcome is the concept embedded in. The concept is what the artist wants to show to the audience, .i.e., it is this "about something". The specific digital medium is the mode of expression or communication used by the artist to convey the concept at hand. It may be concrete, as in the case of an interactive installation, or ephemeral, as in the case of a sound recording or motion picture. Although copies of these latter works exist in physical form, they are not meant to be appreciated for their physical manifestation. Digital art may embrace ephemeral artworks that are meant to be appreciated in the dimension of time rather than all at once in space.

Thus, we can summarize the creation process in digital art as the application of an individual's concept to a specific digital medium or groups of media, by exploring the potentialities of the computer technologies and infra-structures along a set of phases that start in the design of the message and ends in the deploying of the final artifact.

We are aware of the complexities behind objectives to achieve normalization of art-based processes. Art is still dominated by subjectivity, creativity and non-quantifiable outcomes that are opposed to science objectivity and methodological replication goals. However, digital art is an art branch that relies intensively on the computer medium, thus the computing science. Consequently deconstructing the design process behind digital artifacts must open new avenues for the digital art analysis but even more important enhance community knowledge about replicable methods usable in the design and creation of new digital artifacts.

Conclusions and Future Work

In this chapter we have analyze and discussed ground concepts and definitions behind digital art, emphasizing how the computer medium is itself the tool and the raw material in its creation. We have presented a model for digital art creation that consists of a creative design process implemented by means of a common design space where digital artists can smoothly progress from the concept until the final artifact while exploring the computer medium to its maximum potential.

We have seen the creation process in digital art is essentially about design of the message and experience the artifact will transmit and allow, as also its implementation as a computational system or application.

The computer medium affects here the role as the tool to enhance the creation process; as also as the raw material when the digitally coded information content and computer components are primarily explored in the shaping of the artifact. We have also stated the activity of digital art creation is mostly about collaboration among a multidisciplinary team. It requires a common communicational and informational space where the different activities of the creation process can be realized along with communication and collaboration facilities, as also, the access to digital information content and exhibition spaces have to be provided.

References

1. Beveridge, W.E.B. (1957). *The Art of Scientific Investigation*, (New York; Vintage Books).
2. Duchamp, M. (1959). *The Creative Act*. Lecture at the Museum of Modern Art, New York, October 19, 1961. Published in Art and Artists, 1, 4 (July 1966).

3. Eco, U. (1962). *The Open Work*. Harvard University Press, (1989).
4. Eliot, T.S. (1920). *Tradition and Individual Talent in The sacred wood; essays on poetry and criticism*. London: Methune, [1920]. ISBN:1-58734-011-9.
5. Grau, O. (2003). *Virtual Art – From Illusion to Immersion*. Cambridge, Massachusetts: The MIT Press.
6. Greene R. (2005). *Internet Art*. London: Thames & Hudson Ltd.
7. Laurel, B. (ed), (2003). *Design Research: Methods and Perspectives*. The MIT Press.
8. Löwgren, J., & Stolterman, E. (2007). *Thoughtful interaction design – a design perspective on information technology*. Cambridge, Massachusetts: The MIT Press.
9. Marcos, A. (2007). Digital Art: When artistic and cultural muse and computer technology merge. *IEEE Computer Graphics and Applications, 5(27)*, 98–103.
10. Marcos, A., Branco, P., Carvalho, J. (2009). *The computer medium in digital art's creative development process*. In James Braman & Giovanni Vincenti (Eds.), *Handbook of Research on Computational Arts and Creative Informatics*: IGI Publishing.
11. Paul, Ch. (2005). *Digital Art*. London: Thames & Hudson Ltd.
12. Routio, P. (2007). *Arteology, the Science of artifacts*. University of Arts and Design Helsinki (UIAH). Printed from the Internet at: http://www2.uiah.fi /projects/metodi/108.htm (visited at 01.02.2009)
13. Wilson, S. (2002). *Information Arts: Intersections of Art, Science, and Technology*. Cambridge, Massachusetts: The MIT Press.

Chapter 28
Graphical User Interface in Art

Ian Gwilt

Introduction

This essay discusses the use of the Graphical User Interface (GUI) as a site of creative practice. By creatively repositioning the GUI as a work of art it is possible to challenge our understanding and expectations of the conventional computer interface wherein the icons and navigational architecture of the GUI no longer function as a technological tool. These artistic recontextualizations are often used to question our engagement with technology and to highlight the pivotal place that the domestic computer has taken in our everyday social, cultural and (increasingly), creative domains. Through these works the media specificity of the screen-based GUI can broken by dramatic changes in scale, form and configuration. This can be seen through the work of new media artists who have re-imagined the GUI in a number of creative forms both, within the digital, as image, animation, net and interactive art, and in the analogue, as print, painting, sculpture, installation and performative event. Furthermore as a creative work, the GUI can also be utilized as a visual way-finder to explore the relationship between the dynamic potentials of the digital and the concretized qualities of the material artifact.

As the image, functionality and modality of the GUI is moved across, and between media types (recontextualized as a form of art), it can also act as a syncretic agent in the establishing of hybrid mixed-reality forms and readings. Unlike the VR experience, where we are expected to locate ourselves in an alternative disembodied computer space, the concept of mixed-reality implies that we can retain a much stronger sense of our physical presence and location, while interacting with a digitally mediated environment. The notion of mixed-reality art is framed both perceptually and formally around the interplay between physical and digitally mediated spaces. Mixed-reality art allows for the formulation of multi-modal combinations of environments referencing the qualities we assign to the digital - dynamism, complexity, interconnectivity, mutability and so on, to work in tandem with the material

I. Gwilt (✉)
Faculty of Design Architecture and Building, University of Technology, Sydney
e-mail: Ian.gwilt@uts.edu.au

B. Furht (ed.), *Handbook of Multimedia for Digital Entertainment and Arts*,
DOI 10.1007/978-0-387-89024-1_28, © Springer Science+Business Media, LLC 2009

culture of physical art forms, objects and spaces and the qualities we assign to these, such as - value, originality, weight and stability. The desktop metaphor of the GUI can be read as a dual metaphor, which recalls actions and qualities from both digital and material cultures. Through the premise of mixed-reality the GUI interface resonates in both digital and physical environments, where the mutability of its devices and metaphors can be used to contest the usual technological and cultural significances assigned to them.

Strategies for the Re-contextualization of the GUI in Art Practice

As a technological tool the GUI acts as a human computer interface where familiarity with the desktop metaphor is intended to give the user a sense of immediacy, enabling the user to look past the medium of the computer altogether in an attempt to make the technology transparent and to establish a sense of the empirical experience. However, at the same time the notion of hypermediacy [1] suggests that the user is constantly presented with the interface through the interplay and arrangement of complex digital media.[1] This dual tendency situates the GUI at the centre of our contemporary relationship with computer technologies, to the extent that our quasi-ritualistic interactions with the GUI can be used and indeed have been used to initiate a number of digitally informed creative practices. These appropriations are commonly realized in three main ways: firstly, by the utilization of the established aesthetic of the computer interface; secondly, by producing unexpected media interpretations of GUI iconography; and thirdly, through the concepts of mixed-reality art in multimodal reframings of the GUI. In many cases the digital/material dialectic has been problematized through the types of strategies which we associate with Conceptual art movements of the 60s and 70s. This includes the use of the creative tactics of interventions, readymades and documentation processes.[2]

---

[1] Bolter and Grusin discuss the idea of the transference of image from one media to another and the associated cultural and semantic implications associated with this activity [1]. They argue that the remediated experience (throughout media both old and new) is made up of the contradictory duality of immediacy and hypermediacy. The concept of immediacy refers to the notion of a 'live point of view', present in digital media. Immediacy suggests a transparent experience where the nature of the delivery medium disappears and the content / experience becomes the main focus. Conversely, the idea of hypermediacy implies that this primary experience is always intrinsically linked to the nuances of the delivery medium, from the texture of paint on canvas, to split-screen television news interviews and the screen architecture of web browser navigation devices. Hypermediacy suggests that the affect of the media is always present in the content delivery.

[2] Conceptual art represented a dematerialization of the art object and a questioning of art's medium specificity. Moreover, it was interested in the redefining of the spaces in which we might encounter art. Tony Godfrey defines the works, concepts and actions of Conceptual art into four main categories. Firstly: readymades, wherein the artist recontextualizes existing material to comment on meaning or significance, (as exemplified through the work of Duchamp), secondly; interventions, the placing of an element in a different or unexpected context, thirdly; documentation, of social, cultural, or scientific phenomena or systems, and fourthly; words and the use of the written texts or trysts as artistic commentary, information, instruction or criticism [4].

The Visual and Conceptual Configuration of the GUI

The history of digital computing is a relatively short one, which has already been extensively documented [2]. However, it is important here to locate the role of GUI in relation to the computer's expedient growth into everyday use, as it can be attributed with playing a major part in the rapid dissemination of domestic computer-based technologies. It is a commonly held belief that important cultural shifts are based around enabling technologies [3][4], and that these shifts are frequently aligned with an associated visual aesthetic. I would argue that the GUI is the associated visual aesthetic of domestic digital computing (enabled through the underlying technologies of computer programming and microchip advancements). The GUI has become a techno-cultural phenomenon, creating a cultural shift through which easy access to digital content is achieved by the manipulation of a series of visual icons, menu systems, mouse, keyboard and cursor [6]. The GUI is literally an interface between the numeric languages of computer code, the semantic particulars of command-line interfaces, and an adaptable series of user outcomes, which can be understood and applied by the populace. The success of the GUI as a visual signifier for computer technologies is grounded in this wide spread popularity as an interface between human and machine. Moreover, the prevailing use of icon based visual architecture and the desktop metaphor means that the GUI has gained sufficient cultural recognition that it can now be seen as a technological referent for artistic commentary.

Just as the work of Andy Warhol in the 1960s drew on a culture of commodity consumption and mass production in the economic boom of industrial America, the computer interface as a communal artifact and point of social convergence has also begun to inform a sector of contemporary art practice in the era of the digital economy. As Pop art elevated the images of material consumption to art status, the aesthetics of computer information technology - in both hardware and software - have become the image of digitization in the early part of the twenty first century. The material canonization of the GUI aesthetic can be compared to the Pop art tropes of the 1960s, which had the ability to elevate the mundane content of commercial consumption to cult status. Commenting on this relationship between the interface and material form in art, Louise Poissant states that 'the renewal of art forms has materialized through a series of iconoclastic gestures, which has introduced new materials that were first borrowed from the industrial world or from everyday life and progressively from the domain of communications and technology' [7]. Moreover, the hybrid nature of mixed-reality art has the potential to recreate the sensibilities of the digital aesthetic in a variety of cultural environments and media forms, through the weaving together of both interface and material culture. These new laminates can be seen as a contributing agent in this acceptance of the digital form. As Lev Manovich states 'Content and interface merge into one entity and no longer can be taken apart.' [6].

The GUI as an Environment for Art Practice

In previous texts I have extensively discussed the work of a number of artists who have been creatively repositioning the GUI as image and artifact since the mid 1990s.[3] In the following section I would like to describe the work of two contemporary artists who are continuing in this tradition. As the GUI evolves through new three-dimensional interfaces, complex data retrieval/visualization possibilities and Web 2.0 initiatives, new possibilities for re-imagining the GUI in a creative context are established. As we consider these artworks we should keep in mind the digital/physical lineage of these artifacts. The GUI recontextualized as art gives us the opportunity to look critically at the evolution of the computer desktop metaphor and its appropriation back into object based artifacts. As Melinda Rackham comments:

> Most people today are aware that the GUI has influenced print design and commercial media, but are unaware to the extent that internet works and desktop icons are being made in traditional art forms like painting, sculpture, drawing, engraving, and even needlepoint. [8]

Moreover, the transformation from digital to material artifact sets up the potential for these representations of computing technology to be accepted as precious, rarified artworks, which command value and prestige. Again in the words of Melinda Rackham, 'unlike the more ephemeral and distributed net art, these works often have a ready made object based art market willing to purchase them.' [8].

A rapidly developing digital paradigm, in which we are seeing the increased public engagement with geographical and other space-based rich data retrieval, and visualization possibilities is also being referenced in art practice. Enabled through the uptake of in-car way-finding systems, Google Earth and Google maps software etc., these tools have their own set of visual icons and GUI devices. A work entitled *Map* (2006) by Aram Bartholl, humorously comments on this cultural shift. In this work the red place marker icon used in the Google map software is materialized as if it were seen in the actual physical location that has been identified by an online Google map search (Fig. 1). Made from wood and fabric, the physical marker corresponds proportionally to the scale that it is seen at on the map in the Web browser (when viewed at maximum zoom) [9]. This creative intervention elicits a response from passers-by when placed in a public space, and indicates how the referencing of the GUI is continuing to evolve artistically through new applications of technology, and continuing to bleed into physical spaces through these art practices.

In another GUI based work, the artist Ben Fino-Radin makes reference to the notion of sharing and communities. In the sculptural pieces of *Hyperlink* (2006), Fino-Radin weaves together the visual symbol for connectivity from the Internet

---

[3] For further information on artistic references to the GUI see the following texts: From Digital Interface To Material Artifact, Proceedings of ISEA 2008 The 14th International Symposium on Electronic Art, Pages: 202–203, Year of Publication: 2008, ISBN: 978-981-08-0768-9 A Brief History of the Graphical User Interface in Contemporary Art Practice, 1994–2004, Proceedings of the Ninth International Conference on Information, Pages: 931–936, Year of Publication: 2005, ISBN ~ ISSN:1550-6037, 0-7695-2397-8

Fig. 1 Aram Bartholl *Map* (2006) installation view. Image Aram Bartholl

Fig. 2 Ben Fino-Radin *Hyperlink* (2006) plastic needlepoint canvas and yarn. Image Ben Fino-Radin

(the pointing finger cursor) with the real-world arts and crafts notions of social circles and communities, typically associated with needlepoint and embroidery practices (see Fig. 2). As Fino-Radin explains about his own work, 'the environments I create with these objects are a space for the vernacular of two seemingly different cultures (crafts and computers) to rub up against each other and create a new culture/tribe with psychedelic/spiritual depth.' [10].

Conclusion

Despite critics, the desktop interface has proved to be an enduring and practical interface between user and computer, and the recent iterations of the GUI are still very much grounded in the paradigms of the original desktop and windows metaphors. These visual icons and navigation systems have stood the test of time, surviving a period of highly dynamic and volatile technological growth in the rise of consumer computing. However, the current trend towards the realist representation of desktop icons, facilitated by increasing computer-processing power, may eventually complete the visual transition between the notion of a 'traditional' digital GUI aesthetic - one of limited colour and simple geometric forms - to one comprised of photo-realistic imagery. This visual synthesis, from symbol to image, may not inherently change the functionality of the desktop interface (although it may contribute to the notions of transparency as discussed above). Nevertheless, it may lead to a weakening in the flexible interpretation of the desktop interface metaphor, which through the use of a graphic language, signals that it is an agent of mediation. Whereas, the user expectations of a photo-realistic icon may well have a more strongly correlated expectation of functionality in relation to the behaviors of its real-world counterpart. The continuation in this trend towards a photo-realistic interface potentially assigns the GUI (as a distinguishable visual form) to history. New technological developments including dynamic information systems, increasingly efficient voice recognition, biometric sensing devices and perceptual computing techniques (where the computer responds directly to physiological input signals), all point to the possible end of the dominance of the desktop metaphor and the GUI as the widespread domestic computer interface. The question is - will these shifts in the form of the GUI negatively impact on its use as an artistic social cultural referent, or continue to offer new and different creative opportunities.

References

1. J. D. Bolter, and R. Grusin, "Remediation: understanding new media", MIT Press, 1999.
2. P. E. Ceruzzi, "A history of modern computing", MIT Press, 1998.
3. P. Hayward, "Culture, technology and creativity in the late twentieth century", John Libbey, 1990.
4. R. Pepperell, and M. Punt, "The Postdigital Membrane: Imagination, Technology and Desire", Intellect Books, 2000.
5. T. Godfrey, "Conceptual art", Phaidon, 1998, pp. 7.
6. L. Manovich, "The Language of New Media", MIT Press, 2001, pp. 88, pp. 67.
7. L. Poissant, "The Passage from Material to Interface", "Media Art Histories", O. Grau. The MIT Press 2007, pp. 229.
8. M. Rackham, "arteface", unpublished text taken from introductory section for gallery show proposal, curated by Melinda Rackham and Ian Gwilt. For details of the proposal contact Melinda@anat.com.au, 2005.
9. A. Bartholl, "Net Data vs. Every Day Life", Retrieved Jan 24th 2009, from http://www. datenform.de/mapeng.html 2006.
10. B. Fino-Radin, (2006). "Ben Fino-Radin – Hyperlink" Retrieved Jan 31st 2009 from http://www.benfinoradin.info/hyperlink.htm 2006.

Chapter 29
Storytelling on the Web 2.0 as a New Means of Creating Arts

Ralf Klamma, Yiwei Cao, and Matthias Jarke

Introduction

Both non-digital and digital stories draw attentions of the audience and make people remember stories for a longer period of time due to interesting plots, involved emotions and strong expressiveness of narrations. The essence of stories has not been changed for thousands of years in spite of the emergence of digital media. Stories are one of the most important arts collected or created by human beings. Stories are embedded in fine arts, e.g. the impressionist artwork *Dance at Le Moulin de la Galette* by Auguste Renoir tells one of the most vivid stories quietly. Stories create arts as well, e.g. George Lucas' *Star Wars* episodes have a significant impact on culture and society and perform exact the roles of art pieces.

Various multimedia content including videos, music, images, podcasts, digital maps, 3D models, and games etc. has emerged on the Web 2.0. Arts are collective human intelligence and survive over centuries, while the terminologies like digital media, storytelling, or Web 2.0 are associated with a rather "short" transition period of time. This contrast raises new challenges how Web 2.0 based storytelling contributes to arts for communities or even for society.

Multimedia content has been widely employed in the computer gaming branch, such as the quite mature video game market, as well as the emergent educational gaming and serious games. Video games attract a large number of players, because it stimulates the competition and cooperation of players on the one hand. On the other hand, the stories supporting video games play an important role. How can we organize a collection of diverse media from the multimedia forest full of "chaos"? One approach is to make that media tell stories which involve personal experiences and emotions. The storytelling process could be a process of creating arts in an unconscious way. Meanwhile, storytelling is an effective approach to sharing experiences and knowledge among user communities of common interest

R. Klamma, Y. Cao (✉), and M. Jarke
Informatik 5 (Information Systems), RWTH Aachen University Ahornstr. 55, D-52056, Aachen, Germany
e-mail: {klamma, cao, jarke}@dbis.rwth-aachen.de

B. Furht (ed.), *Handbook of Multimedia for Digital Entertainment and Arts*, DOI 10.1007/978-0-387-89024-1_29, © Springer Science+Business Media, LLC 2009

[1, 11, 26]. Nonetheless, much social networking sites use the term "share a story". New information and communication technologies as well as Web 2.0 support story-telling with seamless integration of various multimedia content. Besides books and paper based documents, stories have been told in films, TVs, and nowadays widely in the Internet. Hence, how stories are told with the Web 2.0 technologies such as weblogs, videos, and images becomes a potential and interesting research field.

There is no doubt that only a few stories could become arts. Arts are created and deposited as a tedious knowledge process across a wide range of communities and over a long period of time. Information increases rapidly on the Web 2.0 while the number as well as the knowledge of experts does not. It is hard to judge the correctness of online information. Links can be distinguished between authority and hub. Is a story told online trustworthy? Experts and their knowledge have been cultivated in communities of practice [29], in which people are motivated to practice together and learn among themselves due to common interests. Expertise knowledge is accordingly collected and experts arise. Hence, experts have their own particular knowledge domain and are not universal on Web 2.0 (cf. Figure 1). Accordingly, arts can be created through storytelling in communities of practice.

The motivations of storytelling could be concluded as knowledge creation and sharing for arts concisely. Stories are told both for fun and for learning across user communities. However, the real and hidden motivations of storytelling on the Web 2.0 can help developers design and develop advanced multimedia information systems to meet requirements of user communities. Web 2.0 enables every Internet users to tell stories easily just with a mouse click, which lowers the barriers of media or art access and control greatly. It is also instructive to observe how the major role

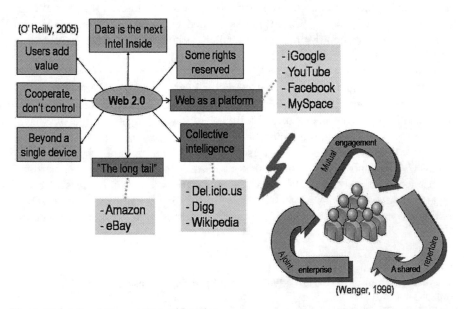

Fig. 1 Web 2.0 and Communities of Practice

has been exchanged from experts to amateurs or wide crowds. Here, experts refer to those who use traditional media such as films and TVs, while amateurs and wide crowds are emergent super stars or invisible hero or heroins on Web 2.0.

In fact, with the same multimedia content a story can be told in a totally different way. First, sequences of the multimedia content can be organized in diverse ways. Second, the same multimedia content can be shared by or be used to compose different stories. However, the currently prevailing Web 2.0 platforms or social networking sites lack approaches to flexible authoring of multimedia content. The existing technologies produce a great amount of user-generated content, of which no certain purpose is connected with multimedia content. Storytelling is an effective and entertaining approach to pass and embed certain meaning and certain purposes to multimedia content. It expresses that media has its semantics only if it is used in a context.

On the one hand, storytelling focuses on the research of contextualizing and re-contextualizing multimedia content with Web 2.0 approaches such as content tagging, rating with feedback. On the other hand, the roles of communities of practice, the intertwining roles of amateurs and experts on the Web with user generated multimedia stories help the storytelling approach create artworks.

Furthermore, the mobility and mobile multimedia information systems are realized by diverse service development, which is in line with the *Service Oriented Architecture* and the *Software as a Service* paradigms. Storytelling platform realization is also discussed in this chapter. For example, the Web 2.0 based *YouTell* is a storytelling Web site for personalized storytelling and expert-finding. Besides the storytelling board, an additional user model is conceptualized to assign different media operation rights to users with different roles. The Web 2.0 features such as tagging and ranking stories are also employed. Story search algorithms are developed including a profile-based algorithm. In addition, experts with certain knowledge can be identified in communities of practice. The storytelling process is intertwined with a set of Web 2.0 approaches and expert finding. The art value of multimedia stories is enhanced accordingly.

Use Scenarios

As a case study, we make storytelling available in the Bamiyan Development Community (www.bamiyan-development.org) within the Virtual Campfire project [4]. The joint aims of the community is the preservation and development of the Bamiyan Valley in Afghanistan. The cooperation work is carried out by different communities including architects, cultural scientists, computer scientists, web designers etc. The valley, in the heart of the Hindu Kush Mountains, is perhaps best known for the tragic demolition of the two Buddha statues which are listed among UNESCOs World Heritage Sites. This part of Afghanistans cultural heritage, and its preservation, can have a major impact on sustainable tourism and economic development for the whole region.

Scientists and professionals who fled from the oncoming war took part of the then paper-based archives with them, scattering those archives all over the world. The generation of scientists and professionals trained and working before the war is now reaching retirement age. Afghan scientists, and professionals trained in other countries, are coming to Afghanistan to help rebuild scientific infrastructures and management of the cultural heritage. While the older scientists and professionals have at least some archived knowledge about the status quo of Afghan sites and monuments before the war, young scientists and professionals use modern information technology and new scientific methods to actualize the knowledge about the sites and the monuments. In order to bring both together, they need a channel to communicate and cooperate among them. Thus, an international and intergenerational cooperation was initiated, because no cultural heritage management work was done over two decades on site in Afghanistan during the civil war.

Web 2.0 based storytelling is an effective and useful tool for the communities working on cultural heritage conservation in Afghanistan. Professional communities start to make extensive use of Web 2.0 tools and platforms to enhance their knowledge work. But, with the Web 2.0 and the new computing capabilities in the mobile ubiquitous Internet, the relationship between professionals in their closed communities and amateurs in the Web 2.0 is debated again.

Researchers, engineers and other professionals document the status of the niches of the Bamiyan Buddha in the Bamiyan Valley during a campaign. They make use of special measurement equipment for 3D-stereometry and widely available devices such as Global Positioning System (GPS) enabled camera systems. All resulting materials, e.g. digital images with additional stored GPS coordinates, will be requested by a mobile multimedia database on a laptop of a researcher. The international community can immediately access the materials by the community information system. They can tag the multimedia and they can relate it in other media. Moreover, professional communities can create a multimedia story which can be used to train the local staff in Afghanistan [24] (cf. Figure 2). So the local communities can gain knowledge to head for professional communities.

Related Work

This section pertains to the concepts and practices of Web 2.0, Community of Practice,and storytelling. Several existing storytelling platforms are also surveyed then. Above all, the main difference between Web 2.0 and Web 1.0 is the idea that computers are more media than tools. The term "Social Software" characterizes this very concisely. Social Software is well known by examples like the digital image sharing platform Flickr (http://www.flickr.com), the digital video sharing platform YouTube (http://www.youtube.com) or the social bookmarking platform del.icio.us (http:// del.icio.us) and can be broadly defined as environments that support activities in digital social networks [12]. Digital social networks are a connected social graph of human and non-human (media) actor representations mainly realized by

Fig. 2 Professional communities build-up with educational gaming

means of computer-mediated communication. Because of Social Software, professionals or knowledge workers [7] face dramatic changes in the way they work. Knowledge work can be defined as using your intellectual and social capital to create new knowledge on some media. Knowledge work is not performed in isolation but in communities where knowledge workers create, share, and deploy embedded in a social context.

Community of Practice and Web 2.0

Wenger et al. [30] defines: "Communities of Practice are groups of people who share a concern, a set of problems, or a passion about a topic, and who deepen their knowledge and expertise in this area by interacting on an ongoing basis". The current state of Social Software and its use for knowledge work is at a very early stage. While it is quite obvious to most observers that as mainstream knowledge work uses Social Software, the consequences of using Social Software in professional communities has also impacted on the relationships between amateurs and experts. A second observation is that Social Software is becoming mobile. Major research and development initiatives are realizing mobile broadband access to the Internet, strengthening this significant trend. Mobile Social Software will be a major topic for the near future. Knowledge work supported by Social Software has not only to be designed for well equipped office workers but also for road warriors, trippers, the new mobile "Digital Bohemia" and for knowledge workers like our colleague who are trying to preserve our cultural heritage in Afghanistan.

Knowledge Work and Web 2.0

According to the McKinsey Global Survey of how businesses are using Web 2.0 [2] 75 % of the executives in companies believe that Web 2.0 technologies and business processes [17] help to manage collaboration internally in the two equal areas of product development and knowledge management. After many years of experience with successful and less successful organizational knowledge management projects most experts are sure that knowledge management failed not because of technology but because of the top down and mistrust based management approaches of higher management [6]. Why should the situation be radically different in the Web 2.0? In the debate on Web 2.0 most people agree that the technology behind Web 2.0 is neither new nor very advanced. It is claimed that the mindset of people has changed. We would argue that it is not the mindset which has changed but the majority of the Web 2.0 users are very different from the users of the Internet 10 years ago. Due to the massive availability of broadband connections millions of new users are using the Web 2.0 in a very different way to users of the Web 1.0. One of the main drivers is Social Software which allows users to do things online (like sharing digital

Table 1 Impact of Web 2.0 on knowledge work and knowledge management

Cultural and Technological Shift by Social Software		Impact on Knowledge Work	Impact on Professional Communities
Web 1.0	Web 2.0		
Personal website and content management	Blogging and wikis, User generated content, Participation	Microcontent, Providing commentary, Personal knowledge publishing, Establishing personal networks, Testing ideas	Social learning, Identifying competences, Emergent collaboration, Trust & social capital
Directories (taxonomy) and stickiness	Tagging ("folk-sonomy") and syndication	Ranking, Sense-making, Re-mixing, Aggregation, Embedding	Emergent Metadata, Collective intelligence, Wisdom of the crowd, Collaborative Filtering, Visualizing knowledge networks

images or digital videos) in a very convenient way. Among these new users are also professionals who are changing their work styles to use the new possibilities. Here, we want to summarize the impact of some Social Software attributes on knowledge workers and on professional communities in general (cf. Table 1).

Projects like Wikipedia create knowledge prosumers, who play a role of both producer and consumer, and participation become essential by replacing old-fashioned content management systems with wikis and blogs in organizations. Users play a significant role besides merely providing content in Web 2.0 and we have to identify their new competences. Especially, through new media like blogs and wikis, emergent collaboration of knowledge workers could be encouraged with new functions like the creation and testing of not worked out ideas in personal knowledge networks.

Maintenance of knowledge directories and taxonomies is now replaced by tagging mechanisms creating so-called "folksonomies". Interoperability between content and services is realized by syndications tools (RSS) solving the old problem of "sticky" data, that cannot be taken from one application to another. But does Web 2.0 provide an effective approach to knowledge management among individuals, organizations and communities? Many knowledge management initiatives at the moment merely transfer Web 2.0 into existing knowledge management strategies. Even worse, technically overambitious approaches which led to many failures in the first wave of knowledge management of the 90s return in the guise of the new king "Social Software". Why not discover the power of multimedia story-telling for the Web 2.0? Why not combine the powerful concepts like communities of practice and emergent metadata?

In addition, experts are seen as an important role in storytelling processes. The reasons are that experts have personal reputation in online communities, which is considered as an important motivational factor to participate in topic-centered communication spaces, and topic-centered materials are key content in recommender systems [16].

Storytelling on Web 2.0

Some multimedia sharing social network sites like Flickr and YouTube are popular for sharing stories. Users can specify tags and give feedback to the multimedia content. Even more metadata is extracted automatically for images than for videos. The popularity of multimedia can be measured by the viewing times which are recorded by the system. With the wide spreading of those stories, a lot of civil journalists [19] and Web idols especially in the adolescence communities are emerging. In the Web 2.0 world, users are enabled to integrate as well as combine several multimedia content according to their preferences by means of creating playlists or collections. Unfortunately, more interaction is not supported.

Digital storytelling combines narrative with digital content such as photos, streaming videos and recorded sounds and produces digital stories usually in the form of a movie. Due to its great expressiveness and its capability to be effectively applied to nearly any topic, digital storytelling has been proposed for educational and learning purposes, such as a pedagogic technique [20], as a tour guide, even as an entertainment means. Although the basic elements of a digital story are narrative along with multimedia data, the generated story could be either linear, or non-linear. Linearity in a story would mean that the flow of the story follows simple rules and it has a certain beginning and a certain end. However, non-linearity is introduced in order to tell more complex stories. Different points of view could affect the normal flow of a story or conflicts interests could alternate parts of a story having as a result stories with nonlinear characteristics. The way, which non-linearity is expressed, varies depending the goal and the medium. For instance in movies flashbacks are the most usual means of non-linearity, while in case of digital stories, as a possible way of expressing non-linearity is the proposed Movement Oriented Design (MOD) [21] technique.

Another popular approach for digital storytelling is the interactive storytelling. At the interactive storytelling scenario, the user not only creates a story but he/she is also the protagonist of the story. Dynamic narratives are created with which the user can interact. User's decisions have an impact on story plot development, and the outcome is more personalized than the conventional linear storytelling, while different stories beginnings and ends might happen. Interactive storytelling is mostly used at interactive fiction games, while the story flow could follow a linear or a non-linear way of narration. The need for more personalized storytelling has led to the suggestion of many adaptive storytelling techniques. The level of adaptation is depending on the goals and results of each proposed technique. Interactive storytelling provides adaptation on user's interests and stimulation in a highly rich multimedia environment. Other level adaptation are proposed based on social filters, such as the

Table 2 Storytelling for knowledge management

Knowledge-intensive processes	Storytelling approaches	Examples
Transaction model	single images, audio slides or videos	TV, films
Integration model	social tagging for multimedia	Flickr, YouTube, EduTech [8], MIST [26]
Collaboration model	collaborative multimedia authoring	Storytelling Alice [11], YouTell
Expert model	role models, expert finding	YouTell

community interests which a user belongs [3], or even location aware adaptation taking into advantage the mobility status of users.

Moreover, tagging is explained as an activity across three established fields: information architecture, social software and personal information management [22]. Tagging stories can help users to search and find proper stories efficiently. Social tagging can even make good use of collective wisdom [15]. From the literature survey, few research results show that Web 2.0 approaches are applied in storytelling platforms.

Collaborative story creation is considered as an important approach to be applied in many e-learning systems for children and adolescence [1, 11]. It is useful for knowledge management. Davenport distinguishes knowledge-intensive processes in four models according to level of interdependence and the complexity of work. He sets the former between individual actors and collaborative groups, while he specifies the latter between routine work and interpretation judgment [5]. Table 2 interprets the knowledge models related to different storytelling approaches and platforms in summary.

Above all, storytelling platforms are a kind of recommender systems to deliver proper multimedia content on a certain topic. Besides positive roles like experts in storytelling systems, there might be some negative roles too. Some patterns or roles like spammers or trolls in communities are analyzed and specified in our previous research [13].

Existing Storytelling Platforms

Dramatica (www.dramatica.com) is a comprehensive framework for creating multimedia stories. However, it does not allow any kind of non-linearity. In Dramatica i it is left to the creativity of the authors to express their episodic knowledge as a linear story so that dedicated aspects of the story are filled with content. Dramatica is also capable supporting semantic knowledge.

MovieLens (http://movielens.umn.edu) is a personalized movie recommendation system developed by the GroupLens Research Group of the University of Minnesota. MovieLens uses collaborative filtering to generate movie recommendations. It clusters users with similar opinions about movies. Each member of the system has a "neighborhood" of other like-minded users. Ratings from these neighbors are used to create personalized recommendations for the target user. The system runs in a Web browser. It does not support non-linearity, also multimedia capabilities are very restricted.

INSCAPE (www.inscapers.com) is designed to support the author along the whole story creation process. There are a variety of formats, such as theater, movies, cartoons, puppet shows, video games, interactive manuals, training simulators, etc. Idea in this system is that even people with average computer skills to be able to complete interactive stories and create simulations [9]. This environment covers the authoring tasks through five dedicated modules as shown in the image below: Plan and sketch stories, import and manage assets, control story flow and transitions, add interactive actions and events, edit and preview stories in real-time. This product is designed to work in Windows OS, consume lot of resources like CPU, RAM and space. This system is oriented for business customers.

BBC TELLING LIVES of your digital stories (www.bbc.co.uk/tellinglives) launched by British television channel BBC has to provide opportunity for users living in England to make own stories. The form was introduced to the UK by Daniel Meadows of the Cardiff University School of Journalism. Technology allows anyone to tell stories in their own way. Digital stories, which are allowed to create, are short films made by people using computers and personal photographs. There is no need of high computer skills. But restriction to living place or to length of the movies makes this site inconvenient for good storytelling.

TechLens (http://techlens.cs.umn.edu/cgi-bin/tl3/anCMS.cgi) is developed by the GroupLens Research Group at the University of Minnesota. The aim of the system is to learn users' research interests from their profiles, and to use collaborative filtering algorithms to produce relevant results. TechLens also allows users to maintain individual preferences about their searches. Users can save their searches, along with the reviewed items from that result set. Users can revisit these saved searches at any time for further review, or include them in any of their portfolios. TechLens can recommend research papers for an individual user, or collectively for a group of users - team.

Art-SCENE (www-hcid.soi.city.ac.uk/research/Artsceneindex.html) stands for Analyzing Requirements Trade-offs: Scenario Evaluations developed by City University of London [32]. It is an interactive tool for discovering, acquiring and describing requirements for new systems using scenarios. It has two main parts: 1. A scenario generation tool that automatically generates scenario normal and alternative courses from a use case specification; 2. A walk through tool for systematically discovering and documenting requirements from the scenarios. It comes in three forms to support: Web-enabled scenario walk-throughs for multi-site projects; Web-enabled walk-throughs in the work place on PDAs; and local scenario walk-throughs using a Microsoft Excel version.

SofiaTraffic (http://sofiatraffic.info) system is designed for mobile users. The purpose of the system is to make users familiar with the traffic condition in city of Sofia (Capital of Bulgaria). On the site is city map and mobile users can point the jammed street and intersections. It is also possible to vote the some street is no more problem

	Easy to access (price, other restrictions)	Community support	Interactive	Collaborative	Using different medias	Platform independent	Support non-linearity	Using storytelling templates	Story validation, story comparison, Similarity search-conflicts
Dramatica	-	+	++	-	+	--	--	--	--
Movielens	++	+	++	++	--	++	+	--	--
INSCAPE	--	++	++	-	++	--	++	--	+
BBC TELLING LIVES your digital stories	-	+	+	-	+	++	+	--	-
TechLens	++	++	++	++	--	++	+	--	--
ART-SCENE	++	+	+	+	+	+	+	--	--
SofiaTraffic	+	++	++	++	-	-	+	--	--

Fig. 3 A comparison of the existing storytelling platforms

to drive on it. The system can be interpreted as community of practice (drivers who have access to the Internet via mobile phones or PDA's) and collaborative, since it is very important to get real time feedback from the users.

Figure 3 presents a summary of all systems presented. Features presented in the table are very important for one storytelling system nowadays to meet all the requirements of the users.

YouTell: A Web 2.0 Service for Community Based Storytelling

How to apply storytelling for professional communities can be enabled by Web 2.0 and Social Software. We have designed and developed youTell using Web 2.0 service for community based storytelling. It is based on a social software architecture called *Virtual Campfire*.

Virtual Campfire

In order to make knowledge sharing a success for any kind of professional community, independent of size or domain of interest, a generic community engine for Social Software is needed. After some years of experience, with the support of professional communities two different products emerged: a new reflective research methodology called ATLAS (Architecture for Transcription, Localization, and Addressing Systems) [10] and a community engine called LAS (Lightweight Application Server) [23]. The research challenge in ATLAS was to incorporate the community members as stakeholders in the requirements and software engineering process as much as possible. In the end, all community design and engineering activities should be carried out by the community members themselves, regardless of their technical knowledge. While this ultimate goal of taking software engineers out of the loop is rather illusionary in the moment, we have targeted realizing a generic architecture based on the research methodology. It allows community members to understand their mediated actions in community information systems. In its reflective conception the community information systems based on ATLAS are tightly interwoven with a set of media-centric self monitoring tools for the communities. Hence, communities can constantly measure, analyze and simulate their ongoing activities. Consequently, communities can better access and understand their community need. This leads to a tighter collaboration between multimedia community information systems designers and communities. Within UMIC we have developed this complex scenario of a mobile community based on our real Bamiyan Development community, and the ATLAS/LAS approach. Virtual Campfire is an advanced scenario to create, search, and share multimedia artifacts with context awareness across communities. Hosted on the basic component the Community Engine, Virtual Campfire provides communities with a set of Context-Aware Services and Multimedia Processor Components to connect to heterogeneous data sources. Through standard protocols a large variety of (mobile) interfaces facilitate a rapid design and prototyping of context-aware multimedia community information systems. The successful realization of a couple of (mobile) applications listed as follows has proved the concept and demonstrated Virtual Campfire in practices: MIST as a multimedia based non-linear digital storytelling system; NMV as a MPEG-7 standard based multimedia tagging system; (Mobile) ACIS as a Geographic Information System (GIS) enabled multimedia information system hosting diverse user communities for the cultural heritage management in Afghanistan; and finally CAAS as a mobile application for context-aware search and retrieval of multimedia and community members based on a comprehensive context ontology modeling spatial, temporal, device and community contexts. All these applications employ the community engine and MPEG-7 Services within the Virtual Campfire framework. Other services and (mobile) interfaces are applied according to different communities requirements. Virtual Campfire is running on Wireless Mesh Networks to apply high and stable network data transfer capability, and low cost, in developing countries.

In order to use Web 2.0 feature, related community concepts for storytelling, a prototype called YouTell has been developed within the Virtual Campfire scenario. Figure 4 gives an overview of this new web service. Additionally to storytelling functionality an expert-finding service is integrated. Web 2.0 techniques as tagging and giving feedback contribute to a comprehensive role model for storytelling too. Tags can be analyzed for a dynamic classification of experts. This role model is also used to represent the behavior and influence of every user.

In our previous research, we have focused on how to generate stories by applying the Movement Oriented Design (MOD) paradigm, which divides stories into *Begin*,

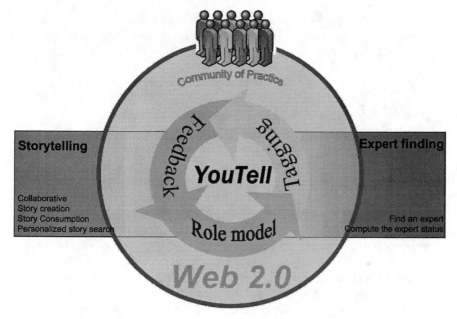

Fig. 4 An overview on the YouTell concepts

Middle, and *End* parts [21]. We have designed and deployed a so-called Multimedia Integrated Story-Telling system (MIST) to create, display, and export non-linear multimedia stories [26]. MIST proves to be applied in domains of cultural heritage management well, in order to organize a great amount of multimedia content related to a monument or a historical site. MIST can also be used as an e-learning application to manage multimedia learning stuff or as an e-tourism support system to generate personalized tour guide.

Drawbacks or missing features are also exposed during the deployment. First of all, MIST lacks the mechanism to support users' collaborative storytelling explicitly. That means, more than one users are able to work on the same story together, while their activities are not recorded for each user respectively but mixed. Second, MIST can be used to create and view stories. But users can not give any personal comments to the stories. Third, it is almost impossible to search stories in the large story repositories, since these multimedia stories do not possess proper metadata to describe it content. Finally, MIST lacks authority, if a story has a serious usage e.g. learning knowledge in a certain area. The question arises, who are the experts in the storytelling communities and have more potentials to create arts?

YouTell enables communities to have joint enterprises (i.e. story creation), to build a shared repertoire (i.e. stories) and to engage mutually (i.e. expert contacts). Therefore, YouTell build a platform for a community-of-practice with a number of *experts* [29]. YouTell has also employed the most highlighted Web 2.0 features like tagging and feedback from *amateur*. Hence, the conflict between *experts* and *amateur* is dealt wish in YouTell.

The main design concepts as well as algorithms of the YouTell system are an appropriate role model as well as user model for storytelling, Web 2.0 tagging features, the profile-based story search algorithm, and expert finding mechanism.

The Role Model

All roles which should be taken into account for storytelling is specified in YouTell (cf. Figure 5). A new YouTell user *John Doe* gets necessary rights to execute basic features like tagging, viewing, rating and searching for a story.

Experts are users which have the knowledge to help the others. There exist three different sub roles. A *YouTell technician* can aid users with administrative questions. A *Storyteller* knows how to tell a thrilling story. And finally a *Maven* is characterized as possessing good expertise. A user has to give a minimum number of good advices to the communities in order to be upgraded to an expert.

Administrators have extended rights which are necessary for maintenance issues. The *system admin* is allowed to change system and configuration properties. *Story sheriffs* can delete stories and media. Additionally, there exists the *user admin*. He manages YouTell users and is allowed to lock or delete them.

A *producer* create, edit and manage stories. The producer role is divided into the *production leader* who is responsible for the story project, the *author* who is responsible for the story content, the *media producer* who is responsible for used media, the *director* who is responsible for the story, and finally the *handyman* who is a helper for the story project.

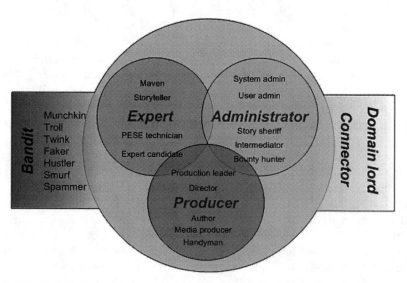

Fig. 5 The YouTell role model

The role called *Bandits* classifies users which want to damage the system. According to their different behavior, they can be a *troll*, a *smurf*, a *hustler* or a *munchkin*.

In contrast to *bandits* there exist two prestige roles: the *connector* and the *domain lord*. Whereas the *connector* knows many people and has a big contact network, the *domain lord* both has a great expertise and, at the same time, is an excellent storyteller.

Web 2.0 for Storytelling: Tagging and Rating

If a YouTell user wants to create a story, he first has to create a story project. With regard to his wishes he can invite other YouTell members to join his project. Every team member is assigned to at least one producer role. Every YouTell user can tag stories to describe the related content. Because the widely-in-use plain tagging approach has several disadvantages [14], a semantic tagging approach is used, too. Besides, users' rating and viewing activities on stories are also recorded. As depicted in Figure 6, A YouTell story are described with tags, rated by users. The popularity is also reflected by the viewing times.

Profile-based Story Searching

In comparison to MIST, YouTell has enhanced the story searching feature greatly. Additionally to a content based search by title or tags, a profile based search is offered to users. Figure 7 shows how the profile based story search works.

In the following the corresponding algorithm is explained in detail. The set of all stories, which haven't been seen and created by the user is described trough $S = \{S_1, ..., S_n\}$. The function $\mu : S \longmapsto WL$ assigns a set of tags to a story, R is the set of all ratings, R_{S_i} is set set of ratings of story S_i, $S_i \in S$.

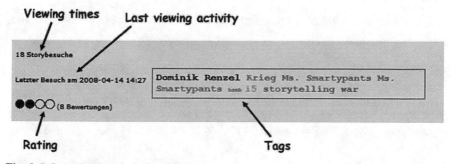

Fig. 6 Information board of a YouTell story

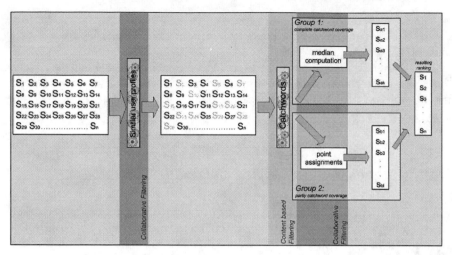

Fig. 7 Profile based story search algorithm

Input of the algorithm is a user made tag list $W = \{sw_1, \ldots sw_k\}$. Additionally further information are necessary: the maximal result length n and the set of story ratings B of user with a similar profile. For computation of these users the Pearson r algorithm is taken(cf. [28]).

Considered are user with similar or opposite ratings. If the ratings are similar the Pearson value is near to 1, if they are opposite the value is sear to -1. In the first case stories with similar ratings, in the second case stories with opposite ratings are recommended. The value has to be in a threshold L to be suitable. The Pearson value is computed with the following formula:

$$w_{a,b} = \frac{\sum_{i=1}^{m}(r_{a,i} - \overline{r_a}) \cdot (r_{b,i} - \overline{r_b})}{\sqrt{\sum_{i=1}^{m}(r_{a,i} - \overline{r_a})^2 \sum_{i=1}^{m}(r_{b,i} - \overline{r_b})^2}}$$

The Pearson value between user profile a and compared profile b is represented through $w_{a,b}$. The variable m corresponds to the story count, i is a particular story and r its rating. The average ratings of profile a is displayed through $\overline{r_a}$.

It holds $B = \{B_{S_1}, \cdots, B_{S_k}\}$ with $S_i \in S, 1 \leq i \leq k$. Furthermore B_{S_i} corresponds to the set of story ratings of user with a similar profile for story S_i and finally it holds $\lambda(R_{S_i}) = B_{S_i}$.

1. step:

Group the stories: The first group G_1 corresponds to the story set $S_1, \cdots, S_m$, $S_i \in S$ with $W \subseteq \mu(S_i)$ and $\lambda(R_{S_i}) \in B$. The second group G_2 contains the stories $S_1, \cdots, S_l, S_j \in S$ with $\mu(S_j) \cap W \neq \emptyset, W \not\subseteq \mu(S_j)$ and $\lambda(R_{S_i}) \in B$.

2. step:

1. Take group $G_1 = \{S_1, \cdots, S_m\}$.

   a. Compute the story ratings median B_{S_i} for every story S_i.
   b. Build a ranking corresponding to the medians

2. If $|G_1| < n$, take group $G_2 = \{S_1, \cdots, S_l\}$.

   a. Be $P : S \longmapsto \mathbb{R}$ a function, which assigns a number of points to every story.
   b. For every $j, 1 \le j \le l$ it holds $P(S_j) = 0$
   c. For every tag sw_i

         For every story S_j

               If $sw_i \in \mu(S_j)$:

                   Compute the median m_j of ratings B_{S_j}

                   Map the result to the range [1,5]: $m'_j = m_j + 3$

                   $P(S_j) + = m'_j$

   d. Sort the stories by their score.

3. Build an overall ranking with the rankings from group 1 and group 2. This ranking is the output of the algorithm.

Expert Finding System

Users who have questions can contact an expert. A special algorithm and useful user data are necessary to determine the users knowledge, in order for the users to find the best fitting expert.

For every user there exists a user profile which contains the following information:
Story data are generated when a user visits or edits a story.
Expert data are created with given/ received expert advices
Personal data represent the user knowledge the user has acquired in the real world. These data are typed in by the user itself.

With these information three tag vectors are created. They will be weighted summed up and normalized. Such a vector has the following form:

$$\begin{bmatrix} taga\ valuea \\ tagb\ valueb \\ tagc\ valuec \\ \cdots \quad \cdots \end{bmatrix}$$

The final value of each tag represents the users knowledge assigned to the related tag. A value near to zero implies that the user only knows few, where as a value near 1 implies expertise at this topic.

Now it will be described how the data vector is composed. First the story data vector will be created. For every story a user has visited and for every story for which the user is one of the producer, the corresponding story/media tags will be stored in a vector. The respective value is computed with the formula $value = AV \cdot DV \cdot BF$ and

- $AV \, \hat{=}$ count of appearances of a tag
- $DF \, \hat{=}$ date factor: The older a date, the more knowledge is lost. The value lies between 0 and 1. A 1 stands for an actual date, a zero for a very old one. Four weeks correspond to a knowledge deficit of 5 percent. It holds: $DF = 1 - (\lfloor \frac{\#weeks}{4} \rfloor \cdot 0.05)$.
- $BF \, \hat{=}$ rating factor: This value is computed by the explicit and implicit feedback which has been given.

Then the story data vector d is computed:

$$d = \text{Story visit vector} \cdot 0.35 + \text{Story edit vector} \cdot 0.65.$$

After that a normalization to the range $[0, 1]$ will be done: Let $S = \{s_1, ..., s_n\}$ be the set of all tags, which occur within the set of data vectors and let $v(s)$ be the corresponding value.

$$\forall s \in S \, v(s)_{\text{norm}} = \frac{v(s) - v_{min}}{v_{max} - v_{min}}$$

and $v_{min} = \min\{v(s_1), ..., v(s_n)\}, v_{max} = \max\{v(s_1), ..., v(s_n)\}$.

In a second step the expert data vector is computed. For every expert advice a user has given/ obtained the corresponding tags are stored in a vector. The respective value will be calculated analogously to the above computation and it holds:

$$\text{expert data vector} = advice_{\text{given}} \cdot 0.8 + advice_{\text{obtained}} \cdot 0.2.$$

Third the personal data vector is computed. With the information the system got from the user tags and its corresponding values will be obtained. These will be taken for this vector.

In a last step the final vector will be computed:

$$\text{data vector} = 0.4 \cdot \text{expert data vector} + 0.4 \cdot \text{story data vector}$$

$$+0.2 \cdot \text{personal data vector.}$$

To find an expert first a vector $v = \{s_1, w_1, ..., s_m, w_m\}$ will be created with the tags the user has specified. Then this vector will be compared with all existing data vectors $w_1, \cdots, w_n$. The user with the best fitting vector will be the recommended expert.

The vectors have the following form:

$$z = (s_1, w_1, s_2, w_2, \cdots, s_m, w_m),$$ whereas s_i is the i-th tag and w_i the corresponding value.

1. Repeat for every vector $w_j, 1 \leq j \leq n$
2. $\text{diff}_j = 0$

3.   Repeat for every tag s_i, $1 \leq i \leq m$ of vector v
4.   If $s_i = s_{j_k}$, $s_{j_k} \in w_j$: $\text{diff}_j = \text{diff}_j + (w_i - w_{j_k})$
5.   else $\text{diff}_j = \text{diff}_j + 1$

Output of this algorithm is the user for which data vector u holds: $u = w_j$ mit $\text{diff}_j = \min\{\text{diff}_1, \cdots, \text{diff}_n\}$.

Web 2.0 for the Expert-finding Algorithm

How does Web 2.0 features like tagging and esp. feedback influence on expert-finding? Users can give feedback to stories and for expert advices. Feedback is very important for YouTell, because it delivers fundamental knowledge for executing the profile based search and defining the user's expert status. Furthermore the visualization of feedback results (i.e. average ratings, tag clouds) help user to get an impression of the experts/story's quality.

Explicit and implicit feedback techniques are used. After visiting a story respectively getting an expert advice the user has the possibility to fill out a questionnaire. This explicit form of giving feedback is fundamental for YouTell. But not every user likes filling out questionnaires [31]. Therefore, also implicit feedback is employed. Although this is not as accurate as explicit feedback, it can be an effective substitute [31]. In YouTell the following user behavior will be considered: The more one user visits one story the more interesting it is. The more a story is visited by all users, the more popular it is.

In addition, the integrated mailbox service offers the possibility to handle all necessary user interaction of the YouTell community. Users need to send messages when they want to ask an expert, give an expert advice, invite a new team member, etc.

Implementation of the YouTell Prototype

An overall architecture of YouTell is illustrated in Figure 8. YouTell is realized as client/server system and is integrated in the LAS system [25] implemented in Java. The client, implemented as a web service, communicates via the HTTP protocol with the las server by invoking service methods. The LAS server handles the user management and all database interactions. New services like the expert, mailbox, YouTell user and storytelling service extend the basic LAS features and fulfill all functionality needed by YouTell.

The story service extends already existing MIST features and includes methods for the management of story projects and searching for stories. The expert service contains functions for computation and management of the expert data vectors. The mailbox service manages the mailbox system. The YouTell user service extends the LAS user service and offers the possibility to add and edit user specific data.

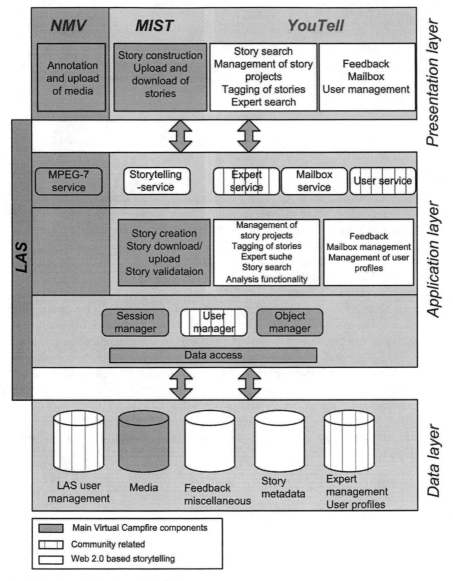

Fig. 8 System architecture of YouTell

In addition, YouTell needs several different servers to work properly. The client system communicates via the HTTP protocol with an Apache tomcat server. Their Servlets and JSPs are executed for the user interface of YouTell (cf. Figure 9). In YouTell the storytelling board is integrated with Java applets which run on the client. All media of the YouTell community are stored on a FTP server. The communication with the used databases (eXist and DB2) is realized by the LAS server.

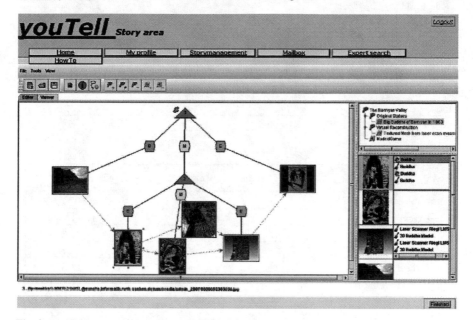

Fig. 9 YouTell screenshots and functionality description

YouTell Evaluation

The evaluation of YouTell consists of three parts. First users had the possibility to test the YouTell prototype. The results are described in Sub Section. After that the algorithms for profile based search (Sub Section 29) and for expert finding (section 29) are evaluated. The algorithms need a great amount of data to work properly. Because the available data were not sufficient, test data had to be generated for a convincing system evaluation result.

Prototype Testing

The YouTell prototype has been published on a web server and was available for all interested user. The users were requested to test YouTell for one month. At the end of that period they were asked to fill out a questionnaire. In parallel statistical data about the YouTell usage where collected by MobSOS. It is a mobile multimedia testbed and is able to test, evaluate and analyze web services [18].

Figure 10 shows how often LAS services have been called. From the statistics, it shows that the story service has been used most frequently and expert service calls took the longest time.

	Average call duration (seconds)	Duration sum of all calls (minutes)	Call count
expert service	31,24	342,8	544
mailbox service	1,89	13,2	285
story service	1,37	386,56	10128
user service	10,79	39,15	1301
total	4,71	781,71	12258

Fig. 10 Calling statistics

Rating	Count	Minimum	Maximum	Average	Standard deviation
Usability					
Expert search	8	1	5	2,88	1,246
Mailbox area	7	1	5	2,71	1,380
My profile	10	1	5	2,30	1,160
Project creation	7	1	6	2,86	1,952
Project editing	7	1	6	2,57	1,813
Story editing	4	2	4	2,75	0,957
Story search	7	2	5	2,57	1,134
Story consumption	7	2	5	2,86	1,215
YouTell	10	2	6	3,10	1,449
Load time	9	4	6	4,67	0,707
Stability	10	1	5	3,40	1,075
YouTell sum-up	10	1	4	2,10	0,876

Fig. 11 Questionnaire results

The questionnaire has been completed by 10 persons within a test session. Figure 11 shows some results. The worst rating was given for the loading times. Additionally, YouTell is not user friendly enough. YouTell as a whole has been rated with an average score of 2.1 and corresponds to the German school grade "good". To sum up the results, YouTell has been accepted by the test user but has to be improved.

Profile Based Story Search

To evaluate the profile based story search an approach analogously to the proceeding of Shardanand and Maes ([28]) has been performed.

1. Delete 20 percent of story visits of an arbitrary chosen user U
2. Run profile based story search without specifying tags. Compare results and removed stories. Store percentage of coverage.

Table 3 Evaluation result: achieved hit rate (in pro cent)

	Minimum	Maximum	Mean	Standard variance
Profile based search with keywords	60	100	97.11	8.237
Profile based search without keywords	60	100	92.69	12.445

3. Run profile based story search with specifying tags that where assigned to the deleted story set. Compare results and removed stories. Store percentage of coverage.

The evaluation results are shown in Table 3. The average hit rate of 97,11 indicates that not all removed stories are found. There exists a simple reason for this. Only stories visited by similar users can occur in the result set. Because all removed stories haven't been visited by similar users, the algorithm delivers the exactly right results.

Also in step 3 of the evaluation proceeding not all stories are found. But this was expected and the hit rate corresponds to the analysis results of Shardarnand and Maes [28].

Expert Finding Algorithm

The expert finding algorithm delivers user/tag pairs with an expert value lying between one and zero. To evaluate the algorithm the value distribution has been analyzed.

In Figure 12 the distribution of the expert values is depicted. For every number on the x- axis the frequency of user/tag pairs with an appropriate expert value is denoted. Figure 13 shows the same values separated by the singular tags.

So both figures show that the expert knowledge distribution is approximately normally distributed. Because the test data were predominantly normally distributed this result was expected. In Figure 12 the expert value 1 has a peak which seems to be unusual at first glance. This can be explained by the used normalization: After computing the data vectors they will be normalized in the range from 0 to 1 separated by the tags. Therefore, for every tag exists a user/tag pair with the value 1 resp. 0. This approach establishes the possibility to represent the knowledge assigned to particular a tag within the YouTell community. Figure 13 shows that the distinct knowledge function differ. This implies that the knowledge about particular topics is differently pronounced within the YouTell test community.

In addition to classification of the users' knowledge, the expert finding algorithm delivers a measurement for analyzing the community knowledge.

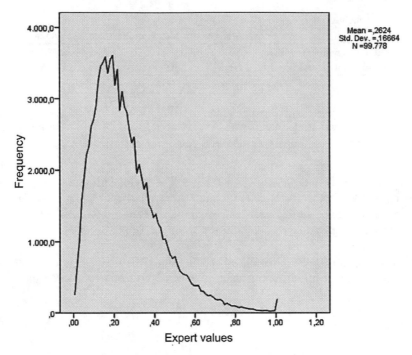

Fig. 12 Distribution of expert knowledge

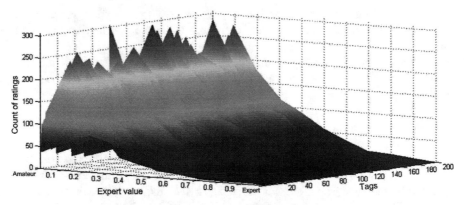

Fig. 13 Distribution of expert knowledge according to keywords

Summary

In this chapter, storytelling is discussed as a new means of creating arts based on Web 2.0 features and communities of practice. We illustrate a use scenario to demonstrate why and how storytelling is useful. The related work about the tagging approach and storytelling platforms etc. is discussed in Section 29. Section 29 pertains to the design and main features of the community-based storytelling system

YouTell. Section 29 introduces the implementation of prototype YouTell. Evaluation results based on hands-on experiences from the user communities are presented in Section.

In summary, we combine Web 2.0 and communities of practice with expert finding in a storytelling platform YouTell to create arts. YouTell is featured with a role model for storytelling system, the tagging concepts, the profile based story search approach, and the expert finding mechanism. The YouTell architecture is discussed together with the prototype implementation issues. The prototype evaluation results show that the usefulness and performance in profile based story search as well as expert finding mechanism. Generated stories have been further applied to create educational games in order to train the professional communities [24]. Besides conceptual approaches and technical realization, the First International Workshop on Story-Telling and Educational Games (STEG'08) has been organized as an annual event to bring researcher communities on storytelling together.

In the ongoing future research, new questions arise. How can diverse user communities work together seamlessly to create art through Web 2.0 based storytelling approach? How can amateur be upgraded into experts? The process of the idea sharing can also be carried out in YouTell. More application case studies can be explored. How can various Web 2.0 media organized via the YouTell storytelling platform? We can imagine that a number of Weblog entries or even bookmarks can be organized in a user generated sequence for the storytelling purpose. Stories will be exploited for entertainment with some speech bubbles, so that the expressiveness of the story narration could be enhanced or some art comments can also be given on the bubbles (see Fig. 14).

Fig. 14 Narrating a story with speech bubbles

Besides the use scenario for professional communities who are working on cultural heritage management conservation in Afghanistan. Another scenario is developed to create stories for promotion and enrichment of the museum archives. We seek to share knowledge and train new researchers by research on advanced storytelling platforms and services for the Battleship "G. Averof" [27]. It provides communities more opportunities to create, access, share, and even reuse the large valuable multimedia collection about the Battleship "G. Averof" with the Web 2.0 storytelling technologies. Artworks can be shared in a better way across a larger community. Story templates will be also systematically surveyed. A story template engine and the corresponding story template editor will be provided to YouTell to enable user communities mash-up stories. Web 2.0 based storytelling contributes to advanced research on social software, storytelling, multimedia metadata, GIS, and information technologies for arts, museums, architecture, cultural heritage management.

References

1. S. Benford, B. B. Bederson, K.-P. Akesson, V. Bayon, A. Druin, P. Hansson, J. P. Hourcade, R. Ingram, H. Neale, C. O'Malley, K. T. Simsarian, D. Stanton, Y. Sundblad, and G. Taxén. Designing storytelling technologies to encouraging collaboration between young children. In *CHI '00: Proceedings of the SIGCHI conference on Human factors in computing systems*, pages 556–563, New York, NY, USA, 2000. ACM.
2. J. Bughin and J. Manyika. How businesses are using web 2.0: A mckinsey global survey. Internet, http://www.mckinseyquarterly.com/article_page.aspx?ar=1913&L2=13&L3=11 &srid =9&gp=1, 2007, [Last Access: April 2007].
3. Y. Cao, R. Klamma, and A. Martini. Collaborative storytelling in the web 2.0. In R. Klamma, N. Sharda, B. Fernández-Manjón, H. Kosch, and M. Spaniol, editors, *Proceedings of the First International Workshop on Story-Telling and Educational Games (STEG'08) at EC-TEL 08, Sep. 16, 2008, Maastricht, the Netherlands.*
4. Y. Cao, M. Spaniol, R. Klamma, and D. Renzel. Virtual Campfire – A Mobile Social Software for Cross-Media Communities. pages 192–195, 2007.
5. T. H. Davenport. *Thinking for a Living: How to Get Better Performance and Results from Knowledge Workers*. Harvard Business School Press, 2005.
6. T. H. Davenport and L. Prusak. *Working Knowledge: How Organizations manage what they know*. Boston Business School Press, Boston, MA, 1998.
7. P. F. Drucker. Knowledge work productivity: The biggest challenge. *California Management Review*, 1(2):79–94, 1999.
8. P. EduTeCH. Internet, http://bsgconsulting.org/ini/edu_par_ger.html, 2008 [Letzer Zugriff am 01.05.2008].
9. S. Göbel, F. Becker, and A. Feix. Inscape: Storymodels for interactive storytelling and edutainment applications. In *International Conference on Virtual Storytelling*, pages 168–171, 2005.
10. M. Jarke and R. Klamma. Reflective community information systems. In Y. M. et al., editor, *Proceedings of the International Conference on Enterprise Information Systems (ICEIS 2006)*, LNBIP, pages 17–28, 2008.
11. C. Kelleher, R. Pausch, and S. Kiesler. Storytelling alice motivates middle school girls to learn computer programming. In *CHI '07: Proceedings of the SIGCHI conference on Human factors in computing systems*, pages 1455–1464, New York, NY, USA, 2007. ACM.

12. R. Klamma, M. Spaniol, Y. Cao, and M. Jarke. Pattern-based cross media social network analysis for technology enhanced learning in europe. In W. Nejdl and K. Tochtermann, editors, *Proceedings of the First European Conference on Technology Enhanced Learning, Crete, Greece, October 3-5*, volume 4227 of *LNCS*, pages 242–256, Berlin Heidelberg, 2006. Springer-Verlag.
13. R. Klamma, M. Spaniol, and D. Denev. Paladin: A pattern based approach to knowledge discovery in digital social networks. In K. Tochtermann and H. Maurer, editors, *Proceedings of I-KNOW '06, 6th International Conference on Knowledge Management, Graz, Austria, September 6 - 8,2006, J.UCS (Journal of Universal Computer Science) Proceedings*, pages 457–464. Springer, 2006.
14. R. Klamma, M. Spaniol, and D. Renzel. Community-Aware Semantic Multimedia Tagging - From Folksonomies to Commsonomies. In K. Tochtermann, H. Maurer, F. Kappe, and A. Scharl, editors, *Proceedings of I-Media '07, International Conference on New Media Technology and Semantic Systems, Graz, Austria, September 5 - 7*, J.UCS (Journal of Universal Computer Science) Proceedings, pages 163–171, 2007.
15. C. Marlow, M. Naaman, D. Boyd, and M. Davis. Ht06, tagging paper, taxonomy, flickr, academic article, to read. In *Proceedings of the seventeenth conference on Hypertext and hypermedia (HT'06), August 22-25, 2006*, pages 31–39. ACM, 2006.
16. T. Reichling, M. Veith, and V. Wulf. Expert recommender: Designing for a network organization. *Journal of Computer Supported Cooperative Work (JCSCW)*, 16(4 5):431–465, 2007.
17. T. O. Reilly. What is Web 2.0? Internet, http://www.oreillynet.com/pub/a/oreilly/tim/news/2005/09/30/what-is-web-20.html, 2005 [Letzer Zugriff am 01.05.2008].
18. D. Renzel, R. Klamma, and M. Spaniol. MobSOS - A Testbed for Mobile Multimedia Community Services. In *Proceedings of the Workshop on Image Analysis for Multimedia Interactive Services 2008 (WIAMIS 2008)*, page tba., Klagenfurt, Austria, May 2008. IEEE Computer Society.
19. H. Rheingold. *Smart Mobs: The next social revolution*. Perseus Books, 2002.
20. B. R. Robin. Educational uses of digital storytelling. Internet,http://www.coe.uh.edu/digital-storytelling/evaluation.htm, 2008 [Letzer Zugriff am 01.05.2008]. Instructional Technology Program, College of Education,University of Houston.
21. N. Sharda. Movement Oriented Design: A New Paradigm for Multimedia Design. *International Journal of Lateral Computing (IJLC)*, 1(1):7–14, 2005.
22. G. Smith. *Tagging - People-Powered Metadata for the Social web*. New Riders, Berkeley, CA, USA, 2008.
23. M. Spaniol, Y. Cao, and R. Klamma. A Media Theoretical Approach to Technology Enhanced Learning in Non-technical Disciplines. In M. W. E. Duval, R. Klamma, editor, *Creating New Learning Experiences on a Global Scale, Proceedings of Second European Conference on Technology Enhanced Learning, EC-TEL 2007, Crete, Greece, September 2007, LNCS 4753*, pages 307–321. Springer-Verlag, 2007.
24. M. Spaniol, Y. Cao, R. Klamma, P. Moreno-Ger, B. F. Manjón, J. L. Sierra, and G. Toubekis. From story-telling to educational gaming: The Bamiyan valley case, 2008.
25. M. Spaniol, R. Klamma, H. Janßen, and D. Renzel. LAS: A Lightweight Application Server for MPEG-7 Services in Community Engines. In K. Tochtermann and H. Maurer, editors, *Proceedings of I-KNOW '06, 6th International Conference on Knowledge Management, Graz, Austria, September 6 - 8*, J.UCS (Journal of Universal Computer Science) Proceedings, pages 592–599. Springer-Verlag, 2006.
26. M. Spaniol, R. Klamma, N. Sharda, and M. Jarke. Web-based Learning with Non-Linear Multimedia Stories. In W. Liu, Q. Li, and R. W. H. Lau, editors, *Advances in Web-Based Learning, Proceedings of ICWL 2006, Penang, Malaysia, July 19-21*, volume 4181 of *LNCS*, pages 249–263. Springer-Verlag, 2006.
27. E. Stefanakis and G. Kritikos. The battleship "G. Averof" promotion and enrichment of the museum archives. In *Proceedings of the XXI ISPRS Congress, Commission IV, WG IV/1, Beijing, China, July, 2008*, 2008.

28. P. M. Uprenda Shardanand. Social Information Filtering: Algorithms for automating word of mouth. *CHI 95 Proceedings*, pages 210–217, 1995.
29. E. Wenger. *Communities of Practice: Learning, Meaning, and Identity*. Cambridge University Press, Cambridge, UK, 1998.
30. E. Wenger, R. McDermott, and W. M. Snyder. *Cultivating Communities of Practice*. Harvard University Press, Boston, MA, 2002.
31. R. W. White. Implicit feedback for interactive information retrieval. *SIGIR Forum*, 39(1): 70–70, 2005.
32. K. Zachos and N. Maiden. Art-scene: enhancing scenario walkthroughs with multi-media scenarios. *Requirements Engineering Conference, 2004. Proceedings. 12th IEEE International*, pages 360–361, Sept. 2004.

## Part V

CULTURE OF NEW MEDIA

Chapter 30
A Study of Interactive Narrative
from User's Perspective

David Milam, Magy Seif El-Nasr, and Ron Wakkary

Introduction

The topic of interactive narrative has been under debate for several years. What does it mean to be engulfed in an interactive narrative? Can users engage in a meaningful interactive narrative experience? Who tells the story, the designer or the player? While answers to these questions have not been formulated, the community is split. Some regard the question of interactive narrative as an oxymoron, philosophically regarding narrative and play as two separate entities [1, 2]. Others regard narrative as an integral aspect of any interactive or media production [3], [4].

A reasonable approach to this dilemma is to explore these questions through the design, development, and evaluation of interactive narrative experiences. Many researchers have explored the design of interactive narratives integrating believable agents [15], drama managers [6], user modeling [7], [8], [9], and planning systems [10]. In our view, the design of a good interactive narrative requires the understanding of the participants and their experience. Even though research is ongoing in the development of interactive narratives, there is very little research exploring how users view their interactive narrative experience. This chapter focuses on a research study that attempts to understand the interactive narrative experience through the voices of the participants themselves, using a phenomenological method.

For the study, we chose to use *Façade* as an interactive narrative experience; *Façade* was developed by Mateas and Stern and released to the public in 2005 [11]. While some may argue that video and computer games are rich with examples of interactive narrative, we believe *Façade* is a better choice to explore. Most video and computer games use puzzles, quests, destruction, or collection as their core mechanics, where narrative is often used for motivation or game aesthetics. *Façade* focuses on social relationships, conflict, and drama as its core mechanics.

In this paper, we report results from a qualitative study exploring the questions: how do participants define interactive narrative before playing *Façade*

D. Milam, M.S. El-Nasr (✉), and R. Wakkary
School of Ineractive Arts and Technology, Simon Fraser University, Surrey, BC, Canada
e-mail: {dma35, magy, rwakkary}@sfu.ca

B. Furht (ed.), *Handbook of Multimedia for Digital Entertainment and Arts*,
DOI 10.1007/978-0-387-89024-1_30, © Springer Science+Business Media, LLC 2009

and what are their impressions and experiences after playing *Façade*? Husserl's phenomenological philosophy [12] best suit our research question since it seeks a descriptive analysis of several individuals understanding of a phenomenon. Historically, the evaluation of computational artifacts do not employ phenomenological methods, but instead use empirical methods, such as human factors, HCI, and usability. However since interactive narrative in video games incorporates the player's social and psychological participation, using a phenomenological approach is best as it gives us an eye on the players' lived experience to better understand the enjoyable qualities of this medium. For our purposes, we attempt to suspend judgment in order to articulate the essence of interactive narrative from the participants' in depth perceptions of their interactions. We use a phenomenological method of data analysis to interpret the participants' experience based on the works of Moustakas [13] and Colaizzi [14].

The primary contribution of this work is in presenting results exploring the experience of *Façade*. We describe the study we conducted looking at participants' views and thoughts about interactive narrative before and after playing *Façade*. We analyze the participants' responses and organize them into themes centered upon two lenses: *System Constraints* and *Role Playing*. In addition, we reflect on the relationship between these lenses and participants' background, previous play experiences, and culture as well as discuss implications for future interactive narrative designs.

Previous Research

Interactive Narrative Architectures

During the past few years there has been much research that explored the design of interactive narratives. Many research projects are within the Artificial Intelligence field. The Oz project is presented as one of the earliest works in this area, where researchers concentrated on developing an interactive drama architecture composed of believable agents [5] with emotional responses [10], [15], and a drama manager that guides the drama as it unfolds [6]. One of the OZ project's visual prototypes entitled *The Woggles* consisted of a goal directed reactive agent architecture that adapted virtual character behaviors' to characters' personality and emotional states. Inspired by *Disney's Illusion of Life* [16] this introduced a new visual form of interactive entertainment as part of interactive story systems for the participant. The authoring environment also allowed characters to behave and act based on the enactment of goals. The Oz architecture comprised of a simulated physical environment which contained the automated agents, a user interface, and planner. Following their work, Mateas and Stern developed ABL (A Behavior Language), which allowed designers to author character behaviors with joint goals. This language is used to author behaviors for *Façade* [11], [17]. Since we are using *Façade* for our study, we will describe it in more depth in section "Façade".

Stanford University's Virtual Theater project is similar to the OZ project. They also developed intelligent, automated characters that acted in an improvisational environment. The synthetic actors contained a social-psychological [18] model to bring "life-like" qualities to their performances. The project aimed to provide a multimedia environment in which users played different roles in an improvisational theater company. Intelligent agents filled in the roles that were not assumed by the user. They improvised, and collaborated with the user in the creative process.

There are several research projects that explored different types of interactive narrative experiences, such as emergent narrative and third-person interaction models [19, 20]. FearNot!, Fun with Empathic Agents Reaching Novel Outcomes in Teaching, is a virtual drama for children developed with the goal of addressing the bullying problem in schools. The interactional structure of FearNot! was inspired by the political improvisational theatre developed by Brazilian dramatist Augusto Boal [21]. In his improvisational games, he divides the audience into groups; each group takes responsibility of one character within the improvisation; they elect one actor who performs the role of the character. They then meet with the actor and negotiate with him/her what he/she should do at the moment. The actor then takes the advice and improvises with the other characters within the scenario. The scenario is then stopped; each actor goes to their teams and discusses strategies to do next, and so on. FearNot!'s appraisal-driven agent architecture replicated this technique as a mechanism for generating an emergent narrative. It divides the narrative into several pieces; for each piece, the scenario is shown and then the user interacts with the character by selecting a coping strategy and reasoning with the character as to why such strategy will work. The resolution of the narrative happens in the last narrative piece and is dependent on user's suggestions and advice.

Cavazza's group has offered additional insight into a third-person interaction models for multi-agent interactive narratives. Using his plan-based hierarchical task network controlling characters' potential behavior, he created a familiar situation comedy as a prototype to explore this model further to affect stories. For this example, he addressed how a player's direct physical interaction with virtual objects could change or mislead an unfolding story. In the prototype, the player acts as an invisible actor, or in "god" view, and can change the story world to foil plans or coach players into achieving their goals.

In addition, researchers recognize the utility of user modeling on drama management as a facilitator of conflict and drama [7], [22], [23]. Szilas discusses a simulated model of the user that gathers data specific to the story told so far. This assessment is based on a model of how the user perceives the possible action presented. He used scores calculated based on this assessment to derive narrative effects which helps the intelligent narrator predict the impact of each event.

Seif El-Nasr draws from well established theories in theater, performance arts, film, and animation to enrich the user's dramatic experience in interactive narrative [22]. The prototype developed, called *Mirage*, is similar to Mateas and Stern's beat system, but incorporates user modeling techniques to predict the users' character. Based on this model, the system chooses story beats and character behaviors as well as adapts visual scene elements, such as camera movement, character staging, character movement, and lighting color/angle/position. These adaptations were made to stimulate self-growth, self-reflection, empathy, and anticipation.

Evaluating the User's Experience within Interactive Narrative

The research works discussed above have a strong design and computational focus. Very few researchers focused on empirically evaluating the interactive narrative experience. From these few empirical studies, there are some who adopted a quantitative method evaluating their interactive narrative experience through likert scale questionnaires gauging specific areas of interest [19], [23]. Quantitative methods have several disadvantages, however, including constraining participants' responses to the questions posed. Alternatively, other researchers explored using qualitative methods to understand participants' experiences. We discuss phenomenological methods in more detail in section "Method".

Our study is similar to the phenomenological approach taken by Mallon and Webb [24] discussion of player engagement in commercial adventure role playing games. They too focus on illuminating the player experience in terms of player motivations, strategies, and game play-patterns to strengthen the narrative potential of the game mechanics. Many of our lessons in the reflection section are consistent with their observations specifically in regard to player-game character interplay and balancing the player's freedom and control of the narrative. Their findings differ as they chose a comparative analysis of eight commercially available adventure role playing games that emphasize different core game mechanics such as examining and collecting artifacts, navigating within a larger game world in pursuit of goals, and fighting to ward off enemies.

Two research projects have previously evaluated the experience of *Façade*. One study focused on evaluating the conversation interaction identifying participants' interpretation of conversation breakdown and character responses. They used qualitative analysis based on grounded theory where they triangulated data in the form of: observation notes, participants' interpretations of their actions after showing them the video of their interaction with *Façade*, and system tracing revealing the systems' inner interpretations of participants' utterances [26]. Some of their findings were similar to what we found in our study, as discussed later. The second study focused on evaluating participants' experiences across three different versions of *Façade*: two virtual desktop versions: in one version users' type in their utterances and the in the other users speak their dialog; the third version is an Augmented Reality version where Trip and Grace are projected into the participants' physical space through an HMD (Head Mounted Display). They used qualitative analysis based on grounded theory to gauge the participants' sense of presence vs. engagement. Their results indicate that even though participants were more present in the AR *Façade* they were not as engaged as within the virtual desktop interface [27]. While these studies are closer to what we are exploring here, there are several differences. First, we present a phenomenology study of the users' experience of an interactive narrative. Thus,

Fig. 1 Screenshot of Trip and Grace with the participant interaction

while we touch on many aspects of conversation (as discussed later), this is only one of the many elements we examine. Second, our subject pool is very different due to a different geographic location, culture, and school philosophy. Third, the study procedure and design presented is purely phenomenological in nature.

Façade

The story of *Façade* [28] introduces the player as a long time friend of Trip and Grace, two Non-Player characters, who have invited the player for an evening get together at their apartment. The participant takes on a first person perspective and the player uses the keyboard to interact with Trip and Grace through natural language (as shown in Figure 1). The player is also free to move about the apartment, manipulate objects, and perform simple social gestures, such as kiss or hug. The game begins inside the hallway outside Trip and Grace's apartment, where they can be overheard arguing. Once inside the apartment, the player gets caught between Trip and Grace's arguments, as the drama unfolds. It is up to the player to resolve the course of the drama. While typing responses, Trip and Grace respond verbally. Once the story concludes, a script is generated showing all the dialogue that occurred. Figure 2 shows an excerpt.

Method

Our study uses a qualitative phenomenological methodology to understand the user's in depth experience. A phenomenological philosophical approach is chosen in our study because we believe current user models employed in interactive narrative can improve through an understanding of the player's lived experience. A robust user model is strengthened by how it engages player behavior and is therefore much more than a mechanism to assign player actions into lists of variables and predicted outcomes.

...

ED: did you cheat on him grace?

GRACE: Ah!

TRIP: Heh, hey... heh heh heh, hey, no no no, don't -- don't try to... don't -- don't try

to accuse me of -- of -- of anything with Maria...

GRACE: Oh God...

TRIP: No -- no, no, Grace, don't, don't even about think that --look, look --

TRIP: look, our -- our 'friend' has just gone too far this time, that's all that's

happening here...!

ED: so you did trip?

TRIP: No no, there's nothing to... uhh...

GRACE: No, of course, Trip, there's nothing, there's nothing... -- (interrupted)

ED: that is low

GRACE: No?

ED: grace you should leave...

...

Fig. 2 Dialog excerpt of Trip and Grace's conversation with the participant playing Ed (Participant ID: 8)

Founded by Husserl at the turn of the twentieth century to understand the meaning for several individuals lived experience, phenomenological methods are commonly used today in the social sciences such as psychology, sociology, and education. Husserl's reflective examination of the structures of lived experience criticized a positivist and empiricist conception of the world as an objective universe of facts. There are many branches of phenomenology by disciples of Husserl and for this study we focus on transcendental phenomenology by Moustakas [13] which contains four basic assumptions [25].

(1) Knowledge begins with a description of the experience returning the traditional task of philosophy as a search for wisdom.
(2) Phenomenology involves an attempt to suspend all judgments about what is real until they are based in more certainty.
(3) The intentionality of consciousness posits that the reality of an object is intimately linked to one's consciousness of it and the meaning if found within.
(4) Phenomenology calls for the refusal of subject-object dichotomy. Reality is only in the meaning of the experience of the individual. According to Moustakas, the goal of phenomenological research is to provide the reader with an accurate understanding of the essential, invariant structure (or essence) of an experience.

Mallon and Webb used a focus group approach for data collection that ranged from 2–4 participants in each group. The first group comprised of 11 subjects that played four adventure role playing games to form preliminary findings. The second group comprised of 13 different subjects that evaluated four different adventure role playing games. The second group was also presented with debate topics informed by the first group preliminary findings. Participants played the games for several hours before discussion as this was necessary to become familiar with them. Their methods differed from ours in duration of play, the number of games studied, and the double focus group structure. For our study we conducted sessions individually to minimize influence by other participants. This was also the case because *Façade* is designed for single player interactions.

Study Design

Participants

We recruited eleven participants from the School of Interactive Arts and Technology (SIAT) at Simon Fraser University (SFU). To minimize influence of previous knowledge, we asked for participants who never played *Façade* before, but who have a new media understanding. All eleven participants were undergraduates at SIAT enrolled in the Foundations of Game Design course–a course within the media arts stream within SIAT, which indicates that these participants had a variety of artistic and design interests.

Four female and seven male students participated in this study. The average age was 24 years with a varied cultural backgrounds, including six Canadians, two Canadian with Chinese decent, one Canadian with Japanese decent, one Iranian, and one Turkish (refer to Table 1).

Table 1 Participant Profiles

ID	Sex	Age	Cultural background	Gamer type	Development Background
01	F	27	Canadian/Japanese	role-play	artist/designer
02	F	28	Canadian	prefers old games	artist/designer
03	M	23	Turkey	action/FPS/RPG	artist/designer
04	F	20	Canadian/Chinese	RPG/Action/ Mobile	artist
05	M	22	Canadian/Chinese	MMORPG/WOW	designer
06	F	22	Iranian	action	artist/designer
07	M	29	Canadian	FPS	designer
08	M	21	Canadian	Action/adventure	artist
09	M	29	Canadian	action/RPG/ MMORPG/Mobile	designer
10	M	21	Canadian	action/RPG	programmer
11	M	22	Canadian	action/FPS	artist/designer

Even though all participants were recruited from the Game Design course, which suggests interest in interactive entertainment, our interview questions regarding the games they enjoy playing revealed a variety of tastes and interests. Table 1 shows the breakdown of participants by age, gender, cultural background, game genre they enjoy, and their academic background. As can be seen from the table, participants have very different tastes, some enjoy action and shooter games, others enjoy role-playing games which includes story and character development, some enjoy short casual games such as mobile games, others enjoy adventure style games that focus on characters, story, and puzzles quoting some Chinese and Japanese games. It is important to note that three out of the eleven participants took a course on interactive narrative, where they experienced new research-based projects experimenting with interactivity and narrative.

Procedure

The study was divided into four phases. All phases occurred in a one-on-one session format taking place in a computer lab, lasting approximately one-hour. Phase I lasted approximately 10 minutes, starting with an ice-breaker conversation, where the participant was asked to discuss his interests. He was then cued to talk about games he enjoyed playing, his cultural background, as well as his view of interactive narrative.

In phase II, the researcher asked the participant to read a description of *Façade* [www.interactivestory.net/#Façade] and watch a YouTube clip [youtube.com/watch? v=GmuLV9eMTkg]. The researcher then conducted a one-on-one interview exploring the participant's view on interactive narrative. This phase lasted around 10 minutes.

The researcher then proceeded to set up *Façade* for the participant to play for phase III. During this phase, the researcher refrained from speaking and instead took notes of noticeable actions the participant took and any other interesting observations (which were then noted as discussion points for phase IV). During play, participants were encouraged to speak about their experience, if they were comfortable to do so. Afterwards, we saved the recorded the session script of their interaction. This phase lasted around 20 minutes.

Phase IV involved a *Façade* post-play interview which varied in duration per participant but overall lasted 20 minutes. The interview questions were devised based on what the participants remembered from their play session along with their reflections. For example, the researcher asked a participant "what stuck out in your memory", "elaborate on their non-verbal behavior such as laughing or hand-tossing", or perhaps "what they thought about their story ending?" These questions became catalysts to discuss other aspects of participants' play experience. We address all four phases in our analysis organized by shared patterns of experiences across phases.

Many perspectives exist regarding validation of qualitative research data. We address this issue by: (1) including an internal and external reviewer who over-saw the analysis process and (2) reporting on results of member checking, where the analysis is sent to participants for validation. To date, we have received positive responses from eight out of the eleven participants; they all agreed with the analysis made and meanings formulated.

Analysis

We employed Colaizzi's method [14] for analyzing the participants' transcripts. Written transcripts were read several times to obtain an overall feeling for them. From each transcript, significant statements that pertain directly to their lived experi-ence were identified. We looked for explicit or implicit value judgments in regards to what the participant seemed to either criticize or desire. Significant statements from each participant were extracted into *meaning units* and correlated with similar state-ments made by other participants. The formulated meanings were then clustered into *themes* to provide a structural description of "how" the experience happened the way it did. In this section, we present the findings as a composite description that incorporates both the direct statement and the structural description that is the "essence" of the phenomenon.

We found a total of 289 significant statements in the phase I, II, and IV tran-scribed interviews (each statement averaged 3–4 sentences long) extracted from approximately 930 statements. Using this method, we identified eleven themes that occurred in phase I, twelve themes that occurred in phase II, and sixteen themes that occurred in phase IV. Since phase III is the game play phase, we will not report on it in this chapter.

Theoretical Lenses for Discussing Participants' Experience

Informed by game design as seen through play testing [4, 29] procedures and payer *agency* [30] which is the ability for players to take meaningful actions within a narrative and to see the results of their choices, we developed two lenses: *System Constraints* and *Role Play*. We use these lenses to distill the rich participant re-sponses to better understand the pleasures unique to interactive storytelling. These lenses touch upon several theoretical perspectives on how to enhance the partici-pant experience and suggest future research directions. We chose these two lenses because it was the best possible way to articulate the participant experience using current game play research and theory. The first lens frames the participant's views in terms of game mechanics, boundaries governed by rules, and outcomes tied to goals. The second lens focuses on the participants themselves: how they prepared for role play and the process by which they interacted in the narrative. The Role Play lens operates independently from rule-based constructs.

The *System Constraints* lens encompasses four concepts: **boundaries, freedom, goals, and control**. These constructs are emphasized as important concepts within the interactive media literature. First by defining boundaries while preserving freedoms, player agency is enhanced. Second, the implementation of system architectures to facilitate agency through adaptable goals linked to changing outcomes is in itself a technical challenge. There are numerous examples, such as *Mimesis*, which dynamically generated coherent action sequences to achieve a specific set of in-game goals [31] and *GADIN* which used a dilemma based choices to create dramatic tension [32]. When these constraints are balanced, we argue the participant experience is enhanced.

As participants assume and embark on a play or interactive experience, he also takes on a theatrical role [33]. This concept is not limited to role play games; we broaden the term to include taking a role within any interactive experience. This lens describes role play in terms of two perspectives informed by creative drama [34]: preparation for role play and process of role play, both following a dramatic structure.

These lenses are important to consider as complementary when exploring the quality of an interactive narrative. While *System Constraints* defines a structure of participant interaction within a story there will inevitably be usability and HCI challenges to address. These challenges are dependent on the individual participant characteristics and interpersonal differences in their understanding of *Role Play*.

Summary of Participants' Statements

We plotted the participants' statements collected across each phase and graphed them to see how many statements participants devoted to particular lens within each phase. Figure 3 shows the number of statements given each lens within each phase. As shown, we see each lens received increasing numbers of statements as the session progressed and that the *role play* lens most sharply increased. Because this increase is most prominent in the last phase, this indicates participants associated role play as a fundamental component of interactive narrative only *after playing*.

Figure 4 shows the participant's statements per lens organized individually. As shown, the number of participant statements varied by individual although their responses tended to emphasize the role play lens. Each lens received comments from all participants.

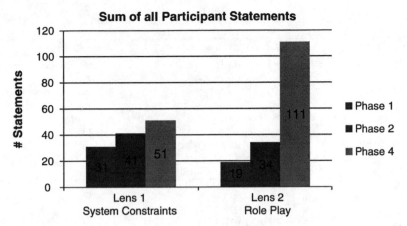

Fig. 3 Sum of all participant statements organized by shared experience

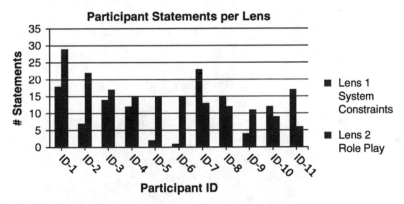

Fig. 4 Participant statements per lens organized individually

Results

Lens 1: System Constraints (Informed by Boundaries, Freedom, Goals, and Control)

As shown in figure 3, the cumulative statements of all phases associated with this lens accounted for 42% of the total statements. It is interesting to note from this figure each phase received proportionally increasing comments. Specifically phase I and II received approximately equal responses when compared to lens 2: Role play, which indicates that both lenses are fundamental in the initial and pre-play conceptions of interactive narrative. Table 2 introduces the coded themes we used to describe each phase that relates to lens 1: *System Constraints*. In Figure 5, the total number of statements associated with this lens is broken down into a per-participant representation. Some themes are clearly consistent across all phases like clear goals,

Table 2 Themes associated with the *System Constraints* lens (freedom, goals, and control) in interactive narrative

Phase I Themes	Phase II Themes	Phase IV Themes
• Clear Goals	• Clear Goals	• Clear Goals (narrative vs.
• Feeling Lost	• Variable Outcomes or Too Many	Puzzle)
• System Design: Outcomes,	Outcomes	• Unsure of Control
Character Attributes, and	• Freedom and Control	(narrative vs. Puzzle)
Selective Perspective	• System Mechanics: NL Text	• Loss of Control – No
• Being Influenced	Interaction Model	Ownership
• Temporal Effects	• Variability/Boundary	
	• System Mechanics: Technical	
	language confusing or unclear	

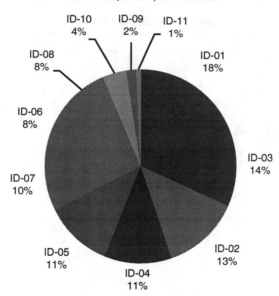

Participant Representation
Freedom, Goals, and Control

Fig. 5 The *System Constraints* lens is comprised of 125 statements centred upon freedom, goals, and control

even though the reference changed from games the participant enjoyed, to *Façade's* description, to their own post play interpretations. The rest of the themes are informed by rules that define boundaries for play, the extents players are in control, and how these facilitate the sense of freedom.

Phase I: Initial Conceptions of IN Pertaining to System Constrains Lens

Participants have all played different kinds of computer games (refer to table 1), and thus their responses to our questions about interactive narratives drew upon the games they played and enjoyed. During the first phase, three clear themes emerged from their interviews that relate to lens 1. These themes support the player sense of freedom by incorporating variability and meaningful choices to shape the story. Furthermore, players understand *their* purpose in participating and retain a sense of control even as their goals are influenced.

Freedom and variable outcomes allowed by system design were noted as important factors of interactive narrative by seven participants. For example, two participants defined interactive narrative as a story that a player takes an active role in terms of unfolding it" and that it allows "flexibility" for the users to "experience what is the story." The rest of the participants expressed variable outcomes as a main feature of interactive narrative discussing how the system can let the player change the narrative path through "choice points", "triggers", "finding story pieces", or through replay to achieve different endings or plots. Three participants recalled a graduate student interactive film project [35] where the viewer perspective on the narrative could be switched from the viewpoint of many characters thereby altering the story telling.

The importance of *clear goals and purpose* was strongly expressed by three participants. One described the collection of important items (referring to *Prince of Persia*) as one way to clearly communicate goals, saying "there are certain things that I have to get...If I don't get it 'this happens' if I get it 'that happens'. When goals were not clear in games, this participant felt lost. He discussed this issue in particular saying, "I wouldn't know what to do, would I? ... How would I know how to finish the game?"

Some participants discussed how the system *influences them or nudges* them towards successful paths to achieve their goals while retaining *players' sense of control*. In particular, three participants recalled being influenced by games to make choices to fulfill their goals in accordance with the story while "making you feel like you're in control." One participant relied on "useful" information from the game as a guide especially "if you think you are stuck in one part, they will be helping you for that part."

Phase II: Pre Play Conceptions of IN from the *Façade* Description Pertaining to System Constrains Lens

When participants learned about *Façade* as a new kind of interactive narrative they were confronted with a description of an unfamiliar experience. Although showing a YouTube video revealed a taste of the moment to moment game play, the larger story goals and varied story outcomes were not clearly conveyed which led to a variety of responses. Specifically, we identified six themes that emerged from interviews within phase II pertaining to the lens of *System Constraints*.

Participants within this phase used their previous game experiences to relate to *Façade*. Five participants in particular tried to associate the concept of *clear goals and boundaries* that they often experience in games to *Façade*. Some were confused as they could not find a clear goal or boundaries from *Façade's* description; others embraced this lack of clear goals as a new type of game allowing participants the freedom to explore whatever they like. One said "it's not making enough sense," when she tried to establish a goal for playing *Façade* as trying to get the characters out of trouble. Another simply described himself as a goal oriented-type and disassociated himself from *Façade* given its uncertain goals. Two participants felt a little confused not knowing how to win. Three participants expressed concern regarding the variety established with the story with no clear boundaries or goals. In addition, another participant felt there were more possibilities and that "anything could happen."

Freedom, agency, and control were themes that emerged through the interviews with at least six of the participants. Agency is defined as the satisfying power to take meaningful action and see the results of our decisions and choices [30]. Because some participants became excited and felt a strong sense of freedom, some prematurely assumed a high degree of player agency, as one explained "I'm creating my own story." Another participant enjoyed the idea of pushing the NPC's in any direction he wants. However, some participants viewed this freedom with skepticism because the authors' defined choices are not provided which made them feel a little nervous. This view relates back to the lack to boundaries or clear goals discussed above. Some were excited about the sense of freedom given by the interface; they believed anything could be typed which encouraged them to think that they can play any role such as a detective or comedian.

Related to the freedom afforded by the interface – *the ability to type anything*, nine participants discussed this feature. All nine participants were interested in the ability to "talk to someone" and be free to "type whatever you want." Some, however, were more excited than others. Some participants had negative previous experiences with dialogue in video games, which led to a more aversive reaction. Four already familiar with branching narrative in games wanted to know more about how the system analyzed syntax and keywords and felt concerned "they [Trip and Grace] won't understand what I say" or slang expressions since predefined "clicking and choosing choices" is not an option.

Phase IV: *Façade* Post-play Interview Pertaining to System Constrains Lens

The themes discussed in the phases I and II were amplified through the post *Façade* interviews. The post-play discussion predominantly centered upon control issues and loss of story ownership. Analysis of the interviews conducted during phase IV revealed four themes pertaining to the *system constraints* lens.

In particular, five participants addressed *clear, discernable goals* as a strategy for success in the unfolding narrative. These participants associated a certain function to their role in an effort to figure out a winning strategy or to solve an abstract puzzle. One participant discussed clear goals as a method of measuring rewards or punishments, and found the interactive experience disengaging due to its lack of such elements which are most common in games. Without clear goals, another participant said, "I didn't know exactly what I should be doing. ... You're trying to get involved in it or step away from it and they keep either pushing or pulling independent of what's going on and you don't really know where you might go with it."

Seven Participants were *confused as they could not identify the method of narrative control*. For example, one participant commented, "I was just typing and I don't know how exactly it worked, whether it will just hear what I said to one or the other or if it just kind of analyzes what I said and make something happen. Yeah, I just didn't know." Another participant commented on the mechanic of picking up the wine bottle; he said, "...the fact that you could pick it up makes you think you could do something with it" such as offer the characters more to drink.

Ten participants felt *loss of control and loss of ownership*. They commented that their interaction had little or no effect on the story. One felt "it wasn't my story at all, and it was like I had no part in it. It wasn't about me and it wasn't about anything I would know." One participant said, "I haven't done anything, I was just there." Another participant said, "I wasn't even part of the conversation anymore [...] but I don't want to be bzzzzz, bzzzzz each time;" another said "I could not break this conversation if my life depended on it." One participant commented that using text conversations was "like I have a weapon, but I don't know how to use it."

Four participants focused on the *conversation pacing*. Their comments were similar to results discussed in the previous study on *Façade* conversations [19]. In particular, one commented that the pace was "really fast" and that the story wouldn't "stall for you [...] because too many things happened while typing." Three participants elaborated upon their experience in other turn-based games where "if you stall the game stalls," or "my action should trigger the next interaction." Some commented that they didn't have enough "space to say my things;" they were contently "being cut-off", as it takes them time to type or they lost the opportunity due to pacing.

Lens 2: Role Play

As shown in figure 3, the cumulative statements of all phases associated with this lens accounted for 56% of the total statements. As discussed above, we define role play in terms of two perspectives: psychological and social preparation to play a role and the process of role playing.

Although each phase received increasing comments (similar to the *System Constraints* lens) this trend is skewed in that phase I and II received around 11% and 20.5%, respectively, while phase IV received 65% of the statements associated with this lens. This shows that participants had more to say about the intricacies of role

Table 3 The Role Play lens is comprised of statements centred upon Preparation for Role Play and Interaction while Role Playing across three phases

	Phase I Themes	Phase II Themes	Phase IV Themes
Preparation for Role Play	• Back-story • Learning • Interactive Narrative in Previous Media • Disassociation of Interactive Narrative as a Game • Being influenced • Performance	• Cogitative Energy • Real life vs Games • Chat Previous Experience • Role Play • Player Centric Narrative • System Mechanics: Naturalness and Story Flow • Social Situation	• Back-Story • Story Priming and Misalignment • Interactive Narrative is Not a Game • Interactive Fiction: Reading & Conversation • Participant Performance & Participant Interaction • Story Interaction • Replay Thoughts • Character Believability (Action, Language and Comprehension) • Previous Lived Experience • Cultural Influences • Social Participation (seeking to disengage) • On Awkwardness • Testing the Boundaries
Interaction while Role Playing			

play after the experience of playing *Façade* than before. This suggests that role-play in the context of an interactive narrative was specifically brought on by the *Façade* experience.

Participants' approaches to role play were informed by themes outlined in table 3. In Figure 6, the total number of statements associated with the *Role Play* lens is broken down into a per-participant representation. In each phase, we discuss the themes through two different perspectives: preparation for role play and the process of role playing. These perspectives are informed by previous work in creative drama [34]. Creative drama is the process of storytelling through story dramatization techniques involving players, students and a teacher who takes the role of a coach. The story dramatization techniques include the use of several tools, including song, props, games, and rituals, and is guided by a six step process, which they call the Six 'P's of story dramatization:

(1) Pique, where the teacher arouses the curiosity of the students. They suggest several strategies including song, props, games, rituals, etc.

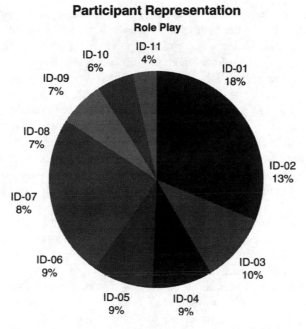

Fig. 6 The Role Play lens is comprised of 164 total statements and is divided into preparation and process perspectives

(2) Present, where the teacher takes the role of the storyteller and presents the story.
(3) Plan, at this stage the teacher transitions and prepares students to start playing and learn by doing.
(4) Play, this part is when students play. This takes in various forms from theatre games, to acting out a story, to telling each other stories, with the teacher as a side coach.
(5) Ponder, after the playing activity comes reflection on the play activity. Reflection is an important aspect of this process as it allows students to share each other's experiences and start reflecting on what they learned through the process. It can also takes on a critical form. Cooper and Collins suggest using several structured forms of reflection, such as critique sheets, questions such as 'what worked?', 'what did we learn in this process?', 'how can we make it better?'
(6) Punctuate, in this step the teacher brings the activity to a closure. Teachers use many strategies to close an activity; these strategies vary from rituals, song, story, or a game.

We used of creative drama as a lens to explain role play within the context of this study and looked at *Pique*, *Present*, *Plan* and *Play* from the participant's perspective. Specifically, for our study *Pique* helped in the preparation for role play, where we focused on the arousal of player curiosity through back-story and mindset on interactive narrative informed by games they enjoy. Mindset is described as a habitual way of thinking that influences a set of beliefs, behavior, or outlook. Several factors influenced mindset including graphics, previous experience with narrative in games, and previous usage of chat interfaces. *Present* also aides in the preparation of role play as is seen through the discussion of back-story in previous games participants played and in *Façade* in terms of developing relationship with characters.

The process for role play perspective addresses themes in relationship to *plan and play* dramatization techniques in creative drama. Themes related to *plan* addressed how participants discussed player-centric vs. performer-centric strategies as a method of role play. *Play* is described in terms of satisfying & cohesive interaction with believable characters in an adaptable story. Satisfying and cohesive interaction is also addressed in relationship to the socially awkward situation and breaking implicit social boundaries.

Many themes were repeated across phases even though the reference changed from games the participant enjoyed, to *Façade's* description, to their own post play interpretations. For example, role play preparation was consistently informed by the back-story and influences of chat interfaces on the mindset that either motivated or discouraged play. In addition, the process of role play was informed by multiple distinctions between players vs. performer interactions and the specification of character and story properties necessary for satisfying interaction. The rest of the themes discussed elaborate on these repeated trends.

Phase I: Initial Conceptions of IN Pertaining to Role Play Lens

In phase I the discussions focused on the preparation for role play in terms of back-story and the participant mindset.

Preparation for Role Play

As participants described the interactive narrative experiences they enjoyed, they discussed back-story as an integral part that allowed them to role play. **Back-story** is defined as the background story behind the characters or setting involved in the narrative, scene, or artwork participants are about to experience; this includes character goals, motivations, history, and relationships with other characters including the user character (in case of an interactive media production).

During the interviews in phase I, three out of eleven participants discussed the role of back-story in preparing them to interact within an interactive experience. Three participants were able to plan and refine their goals using the back-story. They described it as "something [that] explain[s] the situation" or a method that allows "you [to] get to know someone."

In addition, back-story was also described as a method of exposition, by which storytellers reveal virtual characters' motivations and story events as they occur. One participant discussed how he relied on cut-scenes or other "subtle hints" to relate "mysterious" story events to explain why something happens within the storyline.

In addition to back-story, mind set is also a concept that came up in five participant interviews. Mindset was regarded as an important factor that influenced that participant's motivation. For example, one participant was quick to *dissociate interactive narrative as a game* altogether. This player was not drawn to "story games," because it required active thinking "I can't remember story games as much as action games."

The Process of Role Playing

There is no single process of role play. In our description we used creative drama as a theoretical basis that looked at the process of role play that involved elements of *pique* and *present* (from the description above). In *plan* and *play*, we made a distinction between the act of *playing* a role and *performing* a role [36]. When *playing a role* the ludic pleasure of winning or losing prevailed, while when *performing a role* the player assumed some character traits that defined his or her identity within the interactive experience; his engagement while *performing* is in acting "in character" while maintaining story constraints.

The *performative* aspect of "playing in character" was discussed by one participant in this phase. His comments support the difference between play-centric vs. performative-centric role play and cited multiplayer online role playing games (MMORPG) such as *World of Warcraft* and *Final Fantasy XI* as examples. In performative-centric role play several people opt to perform within a group either through designated servers or through role play guilds geared toward player development. Each member takes on a role of a character and performs through the interface provided. In such a case, he would play true to his game character for example "conduct the battle in character" and swap his character stories in the virtual tavern, although this would make typing more laborious.

This participant also discussed play-centric role play. Such a role is distinguished from performance centric role play, as the participant discussed, players would say distinctly out of character statements, such as complaints about laggy server speeds or even unrelated comments, such as "I've got my buddy over and we're having a beer."

Phase II: Pre Play Conceptions of IN from the *Façade* Description Pertaining to Role Play Lens

Participants continued to discuss back-story and mindset that can motivate or discourage participants from role playing. We found familiarity using a text interface also played a role in shaping mindset.

Preparation for Role Play

The *Façade* introduction informed nine participant's mindset and their plan to interact as it showed the *Façade* conversation-based interface and graphics used. All nine participants were excited regarding their ability to "talk to someone", flirt, and otherwise be free to "type whatever you want" which made the situation appear very "lifelike". Two participants stated they avoid conversation and dialog-based video games explaining that they avoid reading-heavy games altogether due to the high cognitive load. They also commented that they "skip right through [conversations or text]."

Familiarity using a text interface in games also influenced nine participant's mindset and ability to role play. Four, already familiar with (branching) narratives, wanted to know more about how the system analyzed syntax and keywords. They were concerned with the system's ability to understand their words or phrases, saying the system "won't understand what I say," noting certain phrases and slang expressions. One participant wondered if the system would allow him to use emoticons (non-verbal textual communication) within the chat conversations such method is considered standard in text based chats and is a very effective way of conveying feelings.

The influence of graphics was also noted. One participant commented on the cartoon-like graphics that were "not completely realistic" which led her to think about her role in terms of a role playing simulation rather than a realistic scenario. This participant then diverted towards a play centric rather than a performance centric role play due to the influence of graphics.

The Process of Role Playing

Eight Participants had questions concerning how to effectively enact their role. They discussed the two perspectives of performance centered vs. player centered approach to role play. The performance centric approach was concerned with how participants perform a character within the story, while the player centric approach concentrated on role play with the goal to broadly influence the story resolution. The play centric approach was discussed from several perspectives as well. From a character based approach, participants discussed being informed by the character's frame of reference and participating in the *Façade* story. Conversely, some participants saw their role more as an author to shape the story and thought of it more as a story simulation. These different perspectives required different understanding of *Façade's* affordances for participants to plan their role play.

Eight participants had questions concerning their *character traits and role*. At a basic level, two participants misunderstood their role (and were corrected by the observer). One said, "I don't know which character I could be" and another wanted to play the role of Trip. The rest were concerned about the means by which their characters can effectively shape the story. One participant understood her role to "solve their marriage problem through interactions", but questioned the influence of gender or sincerity of her character on the story outcome. Similarly, another participant wanted to know more about his own characteristics (classes, skills, abilities) in order to perform his role within the story. Three participants were interested in understanding how the NPC characters react in different situations. One participant, in particular, did not see the function of conversation within interactive narrative, such as *Façade*. He saw chat interfaces as purely conversational and devoid of narrative or dramatic structure.

Three participants discussed the role of *story mechanics*, which included their avatar actions and behaviors, in providing a means to play within the interactive narrative. Prior to playing *Façade*, these participants were excited to "alter the story" through "pushing characters to do specific actions", and then watch them "adapt." One was interested in "creating and following [his] own story."

Phase IV: *Façade* Post-play Interview Pertaining to Role Play Lens

This phase included an explosion of statements and discussions concerning both preparation for role play and the process of role play. As shown in Figure 3, these topics received much more attention during this phase then before.

Preparation for Role Play

Back-story and mindset continued to be discussed as factors that helped prepare participants for role play. Five participants discussed *back-story* as a factor that influenced how they learned about and developed relationships with characters. These participants wanted to know the characters' personalities and the "inside story" from one "point of view" or another. They discussed how such knowledge would help them "choose proper words", facilitate a "more of an immersive" one-on-one dialogue, and plan "different ways of [role] playing". In addition, three participants were especially interested to know or learn more about their own back-story "who's friend I was", which one is "more closer", and "what kind of friends am I to them?. . .I don't know how deep my relationship is to them?" They discussed how such knowledge could more clearly define social "boundaries" in the social situation. This came up as a significant factor as one participant tried to understand the reason he was kicked out of the apartment after confronting Trip about his marriage problem. Confused, he stated, ". . .they first want me to be involved in the conversation, but now they don't want me to?"

Four participants expected a different story outcome from the one presented. This expectation was formed based on their previous experiences. This unmet expectation negatively impacted these participants' experiences with *Façade*. For example, one participant didn't see how going back to an old college friend could lead to "this story that you wouldn't expect." This participant had fundamental problems with the back-story. She wanted to go back in time and have Trip explain how she had in fact introduced the couple 10 years ago "so he could tell me what happened." This participant felt frustrated that this particular approach was not recognized and chose not to play again. Another participant mentioned being "biased" in his comedic approach to role-play. He saw *Façade* as a platform for humorous text-based conversation, which clearly did not match the author's intentions. Another participant said, "you are getting different experiences, but it is not the experience I thought it would be."

The participant's ***previous gaming experience*** affected the mindset of five participants as they identified that their *Façade* experience was unlike the games they frequently play. Two participants described it as a "new form of entertainment" and "a story with game attributes." One participant was drawn to the "real life situation," while another found "no clear path" interesting to "puzzle it out." Another felt the interaction with the characters was "less pleasing," because she didn't feel they were even "half real."

These differences also centered upon their observations using the ***real time chat interface.*** Two participants tried to understand the role of conversation in *Façade* through their own experience with popular games, such as *King's Quest* and *Princess Maker*. One found typing in commands was similar to King's Quest although in *Façade*, he was unclear about the mechanics or character actions that he can type. Another participant talked about Princess Maker, a relationship development game, where you "feel you're reading the story," because you can "pull out the menu and see the conversations that happened before." In *Façade* rather, she felt "through the conversation you pick up pieces from here and there," with no coherent stream or documentation to go back to.

One participant, using *World of Warcraft* as a reference, discussed negative aspects of using chats. He specifically discussed system lags which caused him to stop playing. He explained, "if there's something the matter with the way I can chat, then I give up. . .I can't continue to play because that is my voice."

The Process of Role Playing

Participants again commented on their role play effectiveness from a character and story simulation viewpoint, but this time with finer granularity. Several themes surfaced as participants started to role play, including believability of characters, the awkwardness of the situation, influence of real life relationships, and story cohesion through interaction.

Four participants discussed ***Grace and Trip's performance and believability*** in terms of actions, language usage, and language comprehension. One found their acting was "pretty good," while another found Trip's character to be "God awful" and "completely whiney." One said, ". . .they make you feel like you're talking to a person," but they were really "not listening." Two felt they were "not reacting as people really would in a conversation" or "not listening," because they "didn't need me and didn't answer me back half the time." One exclaimed "are you reading what I'm writing!?" Another said, "I was like sit down, calm down, you know listen; you're not listening, listen to me, can I ask you a question all that just to be, you know (laugh)." Another participant was expecting a "better" reaction after repeatedly kissing the characters, which got him kicked out.

Five participants discussed the topic of *Façade's awkward situation*. Participants described example awkward moments for them, including the phone call, "being trapped between arguments", "two people yelling at each other", and "bickering" which made them feel "confused", like "I don't want to be here", and "I don't see where you were going with this." One participant wanted to leave as soon as it became awkward because "in real life, I probably will not let myself get into that situation."

Five participants discuss the influence of their *own experiences and relationships*. Three participants discussed "already knowing" your friends' personality prior to a similar argumentative experience. Such a priori knowledge is important as it guides the "choice of words" and actions. One said, in regard to her experience with her parents, "I find the best strategy is to console them separately." In *Façade*, participants expressed their ignorance of the characters, which led to failure to identify with them. For example, one participant said her friends are "not like those people" and wanted to quit playing as soon as the situation became awkward.

There were also unexpected *cultural implications involving character interactions*. This specifically surfaced for two participants, while Canadians one was of Japanese decent and the other was of Chinese decent. Regarding politeness, one said "I don't think I should go around touching things," which limited her environmental and character interactions. This participant felt she was unable to "touch" Trip and Grace even though this was one of the interaction features. This participant also preferred to remain quiet (not interrupt), and wait for the conversation to naturally end which rarely happened in the argument. She also wanted to make some hot tea with Grace in the kitchen as a means to separate Grace from Trip. This strategy was not understood by the system. Similarly, another participant wanted to take off his shoes upon entering the apartment. He said afterwards, "it sets a barrier to tell me what is not provided."

Five participants discussed the *cohesiveness of story interaction*. One participant found *Façade's* conversation-based interaction "great" and more interesting than the marital subject matter of story itself. This participant, however, changed her affinity frequently as the story progressed, which made the story less cohesive as she was "especially confused at the last part," when Grace asks, "is what you've said tonight supposed to add up somehow, to something?" Three participants mentioned general difficulties and uncertainty with this model of interaction as it continuously asked them to split their attention between following the story and taking the time to type responses. One was so consumed by the conversations between the two characters that he missed many opportunities to interact. Another said, "I wasn't sure if I should talk or what was supposed to happen because it was like tension building so I'm thinking do I break it or do they break it themselves."

Three participants emphasized more "meaningful" and "productive" interaction opportunities as part of *satisfying interaction*. For example, when "they [Trip and Grace] would ask me a question and, well clearly, I'm going to interact" but this would only serve to "piss the other one off" and seemed counter-productive.

Another two participants thought the story tension could be relieved if they were able to cooperatively share activities, such as painting pictures together or rearranging the furniture since these are contested conversation topics. Since many participants' responses were ineffective in stopping or changing the overall attitude of the argument, two participants acquiesced to their role by following the natural flow of the escalating story argument. These participants were not initially inclined to role-play in this manner; one reverted to this approach after he was kicked out of the apartment the first time, while the other felt more immersed when he "just accepted it."

The dramatic climate of *Façade's* social situation discouraged six participants from fully engaging in or seeking to change the narrative. One was "really sensitive about negative energy." Three were not motivated in the story; they made comments, such as "why should I even care about fixing a relationship?", "I just wanted to let them figure it out", and "I'm going to remove myself from the equation" to let them "work it out," which still caused a "disturbing emotional effect." Two participants were disengaged enough to want to "give up" and "get out" of the situation. One succinctly stated "I just don't care" while another said "I felt like, I don't know, like a poor friend who doesn't know anything who doesn't know how to help because she doesn't know."

Two participant's viewed their play experience as a form of **breaking implicit social boundaries** or "not playing by the rules." After he was disengaged by his initial interaction, one continued playing *Façade* with the mindset that it is a "social experiment". The other treated it as a "comedy" by default saying maybe on his "fourth or fifth try" would he try to help the characters and "play it the proper way".

Finally, those who viewed the **performative** aspect of their role commented on their ability to shape the story through direct involvement with the characters. Four players commented on their constrained ability to "start some topic", "change the subject", "lead the conversation", or "alternate the argument into something else." One player acted with a purpose to "egg them on," because she "had things to say. . .I had things to say to both of them. . .", "I could be all nice-nice", or "I could work Trip a little bit". All four, however, expressed their frustrations by saying, "I just wanted to get in [the conversation]", "you can't really find a hole to go into", "trying to somehow insert myself in there," and "you realize you're the 3rd party in the room."

Reflections on Interactive Narrative

This phenomenological analysis resulted in an exhaustive description of the player narrative interaction in the *System Constraints* and *Role Play* lens above. In this section we aim to discuss how these lenses can influence future designs of interactive narrative, specifically through dependencies of game mechanics, player-character relationship, game character(s) and the interactive story design. Our lessons are also consistent with many of Mallon's [24] observations in relationship to commercial adventure role playing games. From these dependencies there are possibly infinite permutations to the design of interactive narrative. Each configuration may preference one participant profile over another in order to constrain interactions while preserving the sense of agency. These design choices will affect the resulting experience of these interactions. Identifying a desired user experience and benchmarking this experience with actual participant comments is key to the success of future designs of interactive narrative.

The presentation of constraints informed mindset (role play preparation) well before actual play occurred. Participants formulated impressions about their role playing ability based upon system constraints. This idea has been shown in psychology literature that impression formation plays an important role on judgment and perception [24]. The sense of freedom and variable outcomes suggested by the *Façade* web introduction led many to believe that they were free to write or do anything at any point in time. This made it difficult to predict the players' intentions as a method of role play had not been defined or conveyed to the user. Furthermore some were misled as if they were participating in a real-time chat conversation. Both of these factors led to an aversion reaction while playing. It also resulted in losing a sense of control.

Lesson#1: *designers need to address the participants' mindset early during their interaction by balancing the presented freedoms with the system constraints.*

Constraints were also set up through one's understanding of back-story to inform interaction. This interaction is informed through an initial understanding of the character's stories, personality traits, feelings, emotions, motivations, and goals. This particular pattern also surfaced in the role play lens where participants indicated how knowing characters' back-story could facilitate their performance through informed interaction.

Lesson# 2: *designers need to cue and prepare participants for action through the back-story.*

In terms of **role identification**, many participants felt no ownership and a loss of control while playing because they had difficulty identifying with their role. Participants identified with their role through conversation and their ability to pursue discernable goals. Conversation had become the source of many frustrations as well because many of their choices were not interpreted within the context of *Façade's* interactive narrative. For example, they commented on the lack of strategies to corner one character which was also discussed in the *Façade's* study reported in [19]. In addition several participants experienced problems with the conversation pacing and interaction using natural language: when they should type, when they should listen, how fast they should type before the characters move on to the next beat. A few participants also discussed the loss of control due to not knowing what words would affect the interaction which undermined their ability to effectively role play. These circumstances led them to conclude that characters were not listening to them.

Lesson# 3: *designers need to introduce means of interaction through using a tool or interface that can promote user's to effectively perform or play their role*

Participants also identified with their role through the pursuit of discernable goals in the narrative. To many this was a new form of interactive 'puzzle' that they couldn't map to their previous gaming experiences. Some have tried to map *Façade's* play experience to other games, such as King's Quest and Princess Maker. These mappings created false expectations of clear goals and a puzzle with some "positive outcome", which caused the experience of loss of control to be more pronounced. As one participant said, it is like having a weapon that you cannot use.

Lesson# 4: *designers need to understand participant's past experience and introduce their interactive models based on the participant's previous learned patterns or present a learning method for preparing participants to interact*

Maintaining a cohesive story became a struggle for many because their attention was split between following the story and typing to change it somehow. The novel encoding and management of a dramatic arc [6] indeed had elements of tension in what was "about to happen" for some participants although this was also frequently viewed as counter-productive in that the player was not involved enough into the action or plot. After multiple play attempts some had found the experience frustrating as they were inclined to manipulate the story against the primary story arc. This course of action made it difficult to identify intriguing characteristics of the main characters and social dynamics that would invite them to replay.

Lesson# 5: *designers need to demystify the process of cohesive story interactions with a desired user experience in mind*

As noted in our previous study [37], it is important to consider the players background, previous experiences, and mindset in the future designs of interactive narrative. We noticed the player's mindset was influenced by the perceived usage of a real time chat interface as a method to keep track of conversation or as a "voice". This changed the emphasis placed upon their avatar as merely an interface to choose amongst story choices or as an active character in the story. The ***player-character relationship*** also influenced the process by which participant's behaved. Player-centric vs. performer –centric role play changed the expectation of system constraints dependent on whether participants "role-played" respective of previous action/RPG games or "played in character" [36] with an entirely different understanding of dramatic conventions frequently found in MMORPG's. This depended on whether they viewed their character's play in relationship to a game or a performance in a story. For example, one participant commented on the cartoon-like graphics that were "not completely realistic" which made her view her role as playing a game. Similarly, one participant cared little for the dramatic coherence and logical sequencing of events; instead he saw his role as a performer. Another recalled improvisational theater and was very clear how the player-character methods differ.

Lesson# 6: *designers need to acknowledge that different styles of play exist and encourage them through previously learned patterns*

The participant's individual differences such as prior experiences with family and friends and cultural inconsistencies also played a role in this assessment. They described several inconsistencies between their previous experiences with such situations and their experience in *Façade*. For example, one participant noted that in their real-life experience, they would know their friends and thus would know how to interact with them. Others said in real-life they would just avoid such friends. These previous experiences shaped their understanding and their engagement with an experience such as *Façade*. Cultural inconsistencies that involved character interaction made some participants susceptible to miss-assess the social situation as well. For examples, subtle queues for interaction were missed for one participant due to her inability to interrupt other characters as interruption is considered impolite in her culture. These are examples of cultural norms that were expected within the minds of the participants as part of the social interaction norms, but were not facilitated within *Façade*. Believability is also informed by the interactions between characters as participants also commented on the awkward situation created.

Lesson# 7: *designers need to design for participant inconsistencies and different cultural experiences taking into account their target market*

The process of satisfying and cohesive story interaction is informed by the participant's motivation to alter its course, ability to follow the story, and the desire to adhere to implicit (social) boundaries for the sake of the dramatic or rewarding plot. This affected how participants evaluated the story which informed how they interacted and engaged with the experience. Many found conversing on the topic of a doomed relationship or being stuck in an awkward situation unappealing for instance two participants desired to "give up" and "get out" of the situation. Additionally, many participants were not able to follow the story coherency, for example after getting kicked out of the apartment in an attempt to assist the situation. Another was confused why the characters couldn't discuss their memories when the marriage conflict began. Lacking social appeal led some participants to test the boundaries of the system rather than genuinely interact with the story. Playing a social situation is almost non-existent in previous forms or interactive models. This, thus, has caused much confusion and left many players feeling awkward and removed from participating.

Lesson# 8: *designers need to identify a process of story interactions with a desired user experience in mind*

Conclusion

In this chapter, we focus on exploring the meaning of interactive narrative from the users' perspective. We presented data and analysis of eleven participants' interviews. For our analysis, we used phenomenology, because we are interested in hearing participant's voices of their own experience and we believe that an understanding of the player's lived experience can improve interactive narrative experiences. Transcriptions of the interviews as well as all analysis phases were member checked by the participants themselves as well as reviewed by an external reviewer to establish validity. The contribution of this study is in the data presented as well as the methods used. We hope this data and our reflections can be used to influence future interactive narratives' design in relationship to the participant experience.

To summarize our contributions, we will iterate the main points we discussed in the chapter, we found that users' statements fall into two lenses: System Constraints and Role Play. The System Constraints lens is concerned with player agency through perceived boundaries while preserving freedoms and ability to define goals for their experience. The Role play lens is concerned with two perspectives. The first is the participants' preparation for role play influenced through participant's previous experiences and mindset as well as the experience design in terms of back-story, graphics, and how it prepares the user for interaction. The second is the process of role play which is informed by multiple distinctions between players vs. performer interactions and the specification of character and story properties necessary for satisfying and cohesive interaction. Through statements from participants we outline eight lessons showing how these lenses can influence future designs of interactive narrative, specifically through dependencies of game mechanics, player-character relationship, game character(s) and the interactive story design.

References

1. E. Adams, "Three Problems for Interactive Storytellers," *Gamasutra*, 1999.
2. M. Eskelinen, "The Gaming Situation," *Game Studies, The International Journal of Computer Game Research*, vol. 1, 2001.
3. H. Jenkins, "Game Design as Narrative Architecture," in *The Game Design Reader*, K. S. a. E. Zimmerman, Ed. Boston: MIT Press, 2006.
4. E. Zimmerman, "Narrative, Interactivity, Play, and Games," in *First Person, New Media as Story, Performance, and Game*, N. a. H. Wardrip-Fruin, Pat, Ed. Cambridge, MA: MIT Press, 2004.
5. B. A. Loyall, "Believable Agents: Building Interactive Personalities," in *Computer Science Department*, vol. PhD. Pittsburg: Carnegie Mellon University, 1997, pp. 222.
6. P. Weyhrauch, "Guiding Interactive Drama," in *School of Computer Science*, vol. PhD. Pittsburgh, PA: Carnegie Mellon University, 1997.
7. N. Szilas, "A Computational Model of an Intelligent Narrator for Interactive Narrative," *Applied Artificial Intelligence*, vol. 21, pp. 753–801, 2007.
8. M. Seif El-Nasr, "Interaction, Narrative, and Drama Creating an Adaptive Interactive Narrative using Performance Arts Theories," 2007.
9. D. Thue, V. Bulitko, and M. Spetch, "Making Stories Player-Specific: Delayed Authoring in Interactive Storytelling," presented at The First Joint International Conference on Interactive Digital Storytelling (ICIDS), Erfurt, Germany, 2008.
10. J. Bates, B. Loyall, and S. Reilly, "An Architecture for Action, Emotion, and Social Behavior," *Computer Science*, pp. 14, 1992.
11. M. Mateas and A. Stern, "*Façade*: An Experiment in Building a Fully-Realized Interactive Drama," presented at Game Developers Conference, San Jose, CA, 2003.

12. Husserl, *Ideas: General introduction to pure phenomenology*. Evanston, IL: Northwestern University Press, 1931.
13. C. Moustakas, *Phenomenological Research Methods*. Thousand Oaks, CA, 1994.
14. P. F. Colaizzi, *Psychological research as the phenomenologist views it*. New York: Oxford University Press, 1978.
15. S. Reilly, "Believable Social and Emotional Agents," in *Computer Science*, vol. PhD. Pittsburg: Carnagie Mellon University, 1996.
16. O. Johnston and F. Thomas, *The Illusion of Life: Disney Animation*. New York: Disney Editions, 1981.
17. M. Mateas and A. Stearn, "Procedural Authorship: A Case-Study Of the Interactive Drama *Façade*," presented at Digital Arts and Culture (DAC), Copenhagen, 2005.
18. D. Rousseau and B. Hayes-Roth, "A Social-Psychological Model for Synthetic Actors," presented at Second international conference on Autonomous agents, Minneapolis, USA, 1998.
19. R. Aylett, S. Louchart, J. Dias, A. Paiva, and E. Vala, FearNot*! - An experiment in emergent narrative*, 2005.
20. D. Pizzi and M. Cavazza, "Affective Storytelling based on Characters' Feelings," University of Teesside, 2007.
21. A. Boal, *Theater of the oppressed*. New York: Urizen Books, 1979.
22. M. Seif El-Nasr, "An Interactive Narrative Architecture based on Filmmaking Theory," 2004.
23. D. Thue, V. Bulitko, M. Spetch, and E. Wasylishen, "Learning Player Preferences to Inform Delayed Authoring," presented at AAAI Fall Symposium on Intelligent Narrative Technologies, Arlington, VA, 2007.
24. B. Mallon and B. Webb, "Stand up and take your place: identifying narrative elements in narrative adventure and role-play games," *Computers in Entertainment (CIE)*, vol. 3, pp. 6, 2005.
25. J. W. Creswell, *Qualitative Inquiry and Research Design: Choosing Among Five Approaches (Paperback)*. Thousand Oaks, CA: Sage Publications, 2006.
26. M. Mehta, S. Dow, M. Mateas, and B. MacIntyre, "Evaluating a Conversation-centered Interactive Drama," presented at In Conference on Autonomous Agents and Multi-Agent Systems (AAMAS'07), 2007.
27. S. M. Dow, M.; Lausier, A.; MacIntyre, B.; Mateas, M., "Initial Lessons from AR *Façade*, An Interactive Augmented Reality Drama.," presented at ACM SIGCHI Conference on Advances in Computer Entertainment (ACE'06), Los Angeles, 2006.
28. M. M. A. Stern, "Architecture, Authorial Idioms and Early Observations of the Interactive Drama *Façade*," 2002.
29. T. Fullerton, C. Swain, and S. Hoffman, *Game Design Workshop, designing, prototyping, and playtesting games*: CMP Books, 2004.
30. J. Murray, *Hamlet on the Holodeck, The Future of Narrative in Cyberspace*. MIT Press, 1997.
31. R. Young, M. Riedl, M. Branly, A. Jhala, R. Martin, and C. Saretto, "An architecture for integrating plan-based behavior generation with interactive game environments," *Journal of Game Development*, vol. 1, 2006.
32. H. Barber and D. Kudenko, "Generation of dilemma-based interactive narratives with a changeable story goal," presented at Proceedings of the 2nd international conference on INtelligent TEchnologies for interactive enterTAINment, Cancun, Mexico, 2008.
33. B. Laurel, *Computers as Theatre*. Reading, MA: Addison-Wesley, 1991.
34. P. Cooper and R. Collins, *Look What Happened to Frog: Storytelling in Education*. Scottsdale, Arizona: Gorsuch Scarisbrick, 1992.
35. K. Johnson, "Lost Cause: An Interactive Movie Project," in *School of Interactive Arts and Technology*, vol. Master of Arts. Surrey: Simon Fraser University, 2008.
36. J. Tanenbaum and K. Tanenbaum, "Improvisation and Performance as Models for Interacting with Stories," presented at First Joint International Conference on Interactive Digital Storytelling (ICIDS), Erfurt, Germany, 2008.
37. D. Milam, M. Seif El-Nasr, and R. Wakkary, "Looking at the Interactive Narrative Experience through the Eyes of the Participants," presented at First Joint International Conference on Interactive Digital Storytelling, Erfurt, Germany, 2008.

Chapter 31
SoundScapes/Artabilitation – Evolution of a Hybrid Human Performance Concept, Method & Apparatus Where Digital Interactive Media, The Arts, & Entertainment are Combined

A.L. Brooks

Introduction

'SoundScapes' is a body of empirical research that for almost two decades has focused upon investigating noninvasive gesture control of multi-sensory stimuli and potential uses in therapy and the arts. In this context noninvasive gesture refers to motion in invisible activity zones of a system input device utilizing technology outside of human vision. Especially targeted are disabled people of all ages, and special focus has been on the profoundly impaired who especially have limited opportunities for creative self-articulation and playful interaction. The concept has been explored in various situations including: - live stage performances; interactive room installations for museums, workshops, and festivals; and in health-care sessions at hospitals, institutes and special schools. Multifaceted aspects continuously cross-inform in a systemic manner, and each situation where the motion-sensitive environment is applied is considered as a hybrid system. Whilst simplistic in concept, i.e. learning by playful and creative doings, inherent are complexities of optimizing the interactive system to user-experience and evaluation of same. This chapter presents the system in context to its conceived-for-target community; it also presents the parallel practice-led investigations in performance art. Reciprocal design and reflective cross-analysis of the activities has resulted such that performance informs design and strategies of intervention and evaluation with impaired users, and vice versa.

The background and motivation behind the research is presented and followed by a section over viewing the applied work within the community of disabled users. Parallel inquiries within performance art utilizing the same technological apparatus and concept of gesture control follows. Conclusions reflect on the evolution of the work and how serendipitous moments inductively informed development of concept, apparatus and method, such that my research was responsible for an

A.L. Brooks (✉)
Department of Medialogy, Aalborg, University Esbjerg, Denmark
e-mail: tonybrooks@aaue.dk

B. Furht (ed.), *Handbook of Multimedia for Digital Entertainment and Arts*, 683
DOI 10.1007/978-0-387-89024-1_31, © Springer Science+Business Media, LLC 2009

international patent (US 6893407). Final outcomes point to the future need for augmented inter/multi-disciplinary research collaborations upon which to explore both the technological and humanistic sides of interactive systems and the potentials. In this way a body of research questioning technology for the marginalized is envisaged to inform and benefit at a societal level including offering new opportunities for education and practice.

Background

Two decades of exploratory practice-led research of digital interactive media, entertainment, and the arts is presented as a hybrid entity that synthesizes physical rehabilitation therapy training for people with physical impairment and contemporary performance art. A background with family members having profound disability, an education as an engineer, and a vocation in performance art resulted in conceiving the concept. Development was practice-led by me in various institutes in Scandinavia. Expert input informed the inquiries.

Evident from self-funded preliminary research that began in 1987 was the common desire of people with profound disability to be able to create and play in a similar way as peers without disability. The problem was that interface design at the time did not address physical dysfunction, and thus access was severely curtailed. A need was for a flexible interactive system that could be mix'n'matched so that components could be selected, adapted and personalized to a personal profile where physical ability – no matter how small or restricted – could manipulate digital responsive stimulus. Targeted were user-experiences of FUN and achievements guided by a facilitator whose mindset supported the non-formal situation. In this way a supplemental new tool for therapists was conceptualized.

Early explorations included testing a biosignal device called Waverider that was manufactured by a California company called MindPeak. The system worked via sensors attached to the forehead in order to detect neural activity. Brain activity generates electric fields that can be recorded with electrodes (Misulis 1997). The data is then mapped as MIDI signal protocol to auditory or other feedback stimulus. Stage performances have been presented with such systems (e.g., Lucier 1976) and also in therapy and gameplay (Warner n.d.). However, tests were unsatisfactory as users were not enthusiastic about the attachments due to preparation time, where gels are required for optimal sensor signal capture; the wires were encumbering and the elastic headband uncomfortable. The desired immediacy of control was not usable for the concept goals of direct and immediate response with minimum latency.

From the preliminary research I created a prototype noninvasive infrared-sensor-based apparatus to source human motion within a volumetric invisible active zone. Multiple sensors could run adjacent or cross-hatch without corruption of data (Figure 1). The protocol was MIDI which meant it could easily communicate with various existing equipment such as samplers, synthesizers and other performance gear to manipulate auditory stimulus. Participants could make music by controlling

Fig. 1 Prototype SoundScapes sensor device

digital keyboards and related gear through motion in the invisible infrared sensor space. A commercial infrared sensor device called the Dimension Beam was later found to offer improved sensing capabilities and these were used in many of the studies.

Subsequent investigations of the field of noninvasive input devices resulted in exploratory testing of other interface technologies. Two technologies that offered a similarly invisible but different capture profile than my prototype were ultrasound and camera. The profile of the ultrasound sensor is linear, i.e. a line in space along which ranging echoes are transmitted and received by the sensor head – this, when mapped to suitable music equipment, enables a 'keyboard in space' effect. Interference of the ranging beam results in a shorter time between transmitted and received signals and this defines MIDI pitch or control outputs. The device tested was the Soundbeam[1] that was originally manufactured in UK for dancers to control their own accompanying music. This device had inbuilt MIDI scales that simplified setup compared to my original infrared prototype, e.g., for a therapist who was possibly technophobic. However, scales can get tedious and computer mapping software adds functionality. Camera sensors were tested with various software including the Eyesweb and Cycling74 MAX add-on Jitter. In the case of cameras the sensing is perpendicular to the field of view – planar.

Both ultrasound and camera devices required a compromise as silent data capture from intuitive natural 3D gesture was a goal in sessions where focus was on the feedback in minimal lighting conditions to optimize user immersion in the experience.

---

[1] http://www.soundbeam.co.uk

The ultrasound device emitted a disturbing ticking sound – it also required extended set up time as it was echo-sensitive to hard surfaces in the surrounding environment such that false triggering and corrupt data resulted. Also multiple arrays could not be used as each sensor responded to another's echo. In my research three headed sensor arrays are often used to control Red, Green and Blue filters of an animation, this was impossible at the time with the ultrasound devices.

The camera device was also problematic as it required stable and sufficient lighting to see the input gesture; this was often above desired level required for immersion (unpublished). Variable light on the subject corrupted when interactive visuals were used. Additionally, at that time, the planar field of view could not be segmented into active and non-active areas.

Improvements over time in both these technologies included that the linear sensor became quieter and less sensitive to hard surfaces and I began to use infrared filters with the camera that enabled use in minimal/variable lighting conditions. Advances in computer vision also enabled segmentation of the camera field of view so that assignments could be mapped in various ways (e. g., figure 17). These improvements resulted in all three technologies being used in my research as selectable input devices according to a therapist's motion training goal for participant, i.e. linear, planar or 3D. Variation motivated users as similar outcomes resulted from different forms of motion.

The infrared sensors also had issues to be aware of according to desired output as the volumetric data was formed as invisible concentric rings that needed to be traversed to reach other targeted data. Thus programming of the volumetric data to MIDI output was needed if specific outcomes of data generation were required. Weaknesses in each technology as an interface was thus apparent.

When MIDI mapping beyond simple triggering or controlling of auditory feedback was desired the modular graphical development environment software MAX was commonly used. Via MAX various alterations could be achieved such as scaling small range of input data to large output, or sequencing of input to play melodies so that phrasing exercises were implemented. Compositions could be recorded and gifted as archived achievements from training. Vibro-acoustic chambers were later introduced as tactile output medium generators resulting from the manipulated audio. In these cases the participant was lying or sitting on the vibration chamber and the sensor device positioned to motivate motion in the active zone – with the reward being the tactile and auditory stimuli. Users responded favorably to the stimulus (Brooks et al. 2002).

Around 1993 the Danish disco and architectural lighting company Martin sponsored five different motorized mirror lighting units; these were extremely effective at engaging the participant who, through a system translation of MIDI to DMX (light communication protocol), could control the lights. Later, in 1999 in support of my Cultural Olympic installation in Sydney, five 'intelligent robotic devices' with moving heads were sponsored. Physical synchronization of human head to moving robotic head was with participants who were profoundly disabled but still able to control their head. Magical results of empowerment were evident as the children 'toyed' with the robotic devices and often expressed with huge smiles and exclamations (e.g., Brooks 2004; Petersson and Brooks 2007). Similar results were from empowering control of visual stimulus in the form of animation coloring, virtual reality artifacts/environment navigation, and abstract painting with dynamic body/limb gesture (Brooks et al. 2002). The robotic devices were also successfully used with acquired brain injured (Brooks 2004) and excluded children (Brooks and Petersson 2005).

A conclusion to system output mediums was that similar positive responses were evident from the various stimuli i.e. auditory, visual, or tactile, as well as synchronous physical control of a robotic device. With system input device also being selectable a flexible system evolved to best-fit users and to be adaptable and personalized. Immersion, engagement and optimal user-experience were targeted by the delivery of output audiovisuals being via a large screen and multiple speakers system. Standard desktop monitors were less effective in achieving desired user-experience. Figure 2 illustrates a session with auditory, vibroacoustic, and visual stimulus together.

The next section briefly illustrates how digital empowerment can make a difference in the communities of people with disability.

Painting for Life

Recognized as a 'quality of life' activity, traditional painting is used at many establishments for people with disability. Consequences from such endeavors can be

Fig. 2 Multi-sensory session set up at a special needs school in Sweden 1999

mess-making that necessitates preparations that can diminish the experience for all, e.g., plastic covers around the space, plastic protective body attire, clean up tasks for staff. Frustration has also been observed due to impairment being emphasized through the tools/interfaces, environment and situation. It is also expensive to purchase canvas, paintbrushes, and paints, and often staffing levels cannot address needs in a satisfactory manner. These problems can lead to such life quality activities being reduced or even eliminated from care programs.

Digital empowerment of painting was found to offer a non-messy, non-frustrating situation where the tool/interface could be easily adapted and personalized for optimal interaction and material costs after the initial system setup were negligible; a user just moved and painted. There was no need of protection for the participant or the environment. If desired the painting could be printed out as a tangible achievement to show friends, family and therapist. Figure 3 illustrates how traditional aids are used, figures 4–6 illustrate digital painting by gesture algorithm and with any limb (e.g., hand – left image), or alternative means (e.g., tongue and head – center image), or with another person such as a parent, facilitator/therapist or helper (Brooks 2004).

Strategies of Use

Named as the SoundScapes system, (from its auditory and visual components), it evolved to include empowered gesture control of digital video games and Vir-

Fig. 3 Painting with canvas, brush and paint (photo - Vitor Pi - LIGA Foundation)

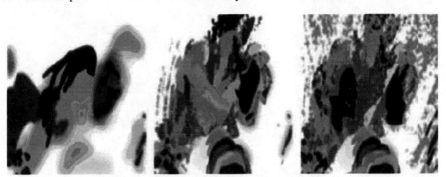

Figs. 4-6 Digital painting by gesture, alone by hand, head/tongue, or together

tual Reality as early as 1998. Investigations of games and virtual reality involved acquired brain injured patients at a Danish government training clinic in Copenhagen as well as with more profoundly disabled at various special needs establishments throughout Scandinavia. Evaluations of system use across the range of impairments were of indicated positive response where creative expression and play were evident. These user-experiences were exhibited at The Scandinavian Rehabilitation Messe and gratis copies of the games made available to interested parties to disseminate the work. Questionable was level of game comprehension vs. long-term benefit for profoundly disabled. Also, a reluctance of higher functioning to be able to escape the 'therapy mind-set' was evident.

Interface programmability for resolution and size of active zone (Virtual Interactive Space – VIS) gives options to a facilitator according to a user profile and goal of session. As well as active zones it was found important to offer zones where motion would not generate data. Figure 7 (above), and 8–7 (above), and 8 illustrate with active zones of the infrared volumetric sensor as dark gray ovals either side of a head, around a torso, and purposefully occluded by torso.

Figure 7 (above), and 8 illustrates how two volumetric infrared sensors were set up either side of a participant's head. In between is non-active. This was often used by users as a pause zone or a place to rest and communicate a change was needed (most could not talk), or they desired an end to the session. Similar use was within the performance art activities where the nil-activity afforded by the stillness zones, became significant performance tools, e.g., silence in music-making and no color/white or black in visual-manipulations. Figure 7 (above), and 8 shows two ways of working with the system enhancement. On the left is shown how active zones can be positioned anywhere around the body (even cross-hatched) without corruption to signal. On the right is shown how occlusion is used to generate data by enabling ir light to be generated through movement, e. g., dance, or in therapy with balance training, or rotation exercise (Brooks 2004, Brooks and Petersson 2007).

A goal from interaction was user afferent-efferent neural loop closure via pleasurable experiences resulting in fun where the 'digital mirroring' of body function acted as a reflective self-motivating inspiration for participation in training sessions (Figure 9).

Fig. 7 (above), and 8   Invisible interface active zones for sourcing motion data

Fig. 9   Simple digital mirroring technique (picture Hasselblad)

Such self-motivation was evident even in those with profound disabilities as was exemplified during evaluation consultations when I visited the 1999 commissioned SoundScapes facility to discus experiences with staff I had trained to use the system.

One report indicating the potentials of the system as a self-training home device informed of an occasion when two helpers accompanied two users with profound disabilities. Staff and users were from one of the partnering neighboring institutes that commissioned the multi-sensory facility. As usual, following arrival, a one-to-one session was set up with the other one-to-one partnership waiting their turn next door in the cafeteria. On this occasion, which was a first session with this user using the system, there was not much activity after the initial introduction and guidance. Knowing that on occasions this can happen the helper went to get a coffee and left the user alone to explore. The coffee break turned into a lengthy dialogue with her colleague and some time later when she was walking back down the corridor to return to the SoundScapes room she heard lots of music coming from behind the door. Listening for a while she believed that another member of staff had entered and was playing with the system. However, on entering she was surprised to see the user alone. When he recognized that she had returned she said that he looked across at her, smiled, and signified that now he was ready to play. This desire for a private space influenced my design of a workshop I hosted in April 2007, at the fabulous Casa da Musica, in Porto, Portugal. This is introduced later in this article.

Similar achievements were evident in other instances from self-determined exploration without guidance. It's timely to mention that over-zealous guidance has been observed as having a detrimental effect as often the user needs time to achieve a sense of self-identity and confidence before committing to the session. Thus training of interactive systems in this context is not only about how to utilize the system but also in how to facilitate with the user.

All-inclusive Inquiry

The goal of my research evolved to explore how to create a system that would offer potential access to creative and playful pleasurable experiences for all despite age, ability or social standing. Consultations, training workshops and designing commissioned sites for the SoundScapes system installation led to many shared experiences from users and staff. These informed ongoing system, method, and apparatus refinements. A need was evident for an integrated means to evaluate user-experiences relative to the system use along with means to monitor session-to-session user progress. Sourced human signals offered such means as being the same data that controlled the responsive virtual content as it could be archived as meaningfully representational of participant input. Correlated to session videos circular causality patterning of interactions could be determined. Evaluations inform refinements and thus the system evolves with the profiled person (also vice-versa). But a satisfactory systematic effect analysis model has yet to be defined. In line with Marston's (1928) water analogy (p. 79) I consider another effect analysis model yet to be defined is when a reactive participant and a responsive multimedia system are optimally combined such as in SoundScapes, the interactive entity - 'inbetweenness' - questions investigation beyond, and of, constituents, i. e. natural and created (Eaglestone and

Bamidis 2008). I refer to this as Virtual Interactive Space (VIS) (e.g., Brooks 1995, 1999, and 2000) and this is my evolving inquiry vehicle of choice.

System Actability, Usability, Usefulness and Affordability

The actability of the system is defined as the metric of an information system that questions its ability to perform actions, and to permit, promote, and facilitate the performance of actions by users, both through the system and based on information from the system (Goldkuhl and Ågerfalk 2000). Whilst used mostly within a business context I believe that it applies to the goals of SoundScapes and as Ågerfalk and Cronholm (2001) state it depends on the social structures surrounding it and thus I abridge to the context of my research where action is defined from its physical implication of motivated human activity, goal, and operation related to learning (Leont'ev 1981).

Actability relates to usability which is defined as the extent to which a product can be used by specified users to achieve specified goals with effectiveness, efficiency and satisfaction in a specified context of use (ISO 9241-11, 1998). To be implemented the system had to be useful and meaningful – it also needed to be affordable as these communities are often not funded for research or health-care due to the inherent diversity and complex idiosyncratic issues (Davies 2005, p. 285).

Untraditional Therapeutic Practice

Gesture-control of video games (e.g., Figure 10–12) has been included in Sound-Scapes since 1998 as a form of "serious play" where the gameplay goal was for functional training of the user/player. This evolution of the work preempted more recent activities with commercial noninvasive sensors such as the Sony EyeToy® and Nintendo Wii® that have elements that target such training and exercise. Brooks and Petersson (2005) explored a commercial game device by questioning computer-aided evaluation via a secondary multiple camera analysis system (MCA – see Brooks et al. 2002) with twenty two high-functioning children at day-care hospital wards in Denmark and Sweden. Typical responses are shown by the child in Fig. 11. Opencv patch sources data in Fig. 12.

My research found that game play was not optimal for those whose comprehension was limited such that they could not understand a rule-based play situation. Boredom was evident after early tests – suggested due to the limited progress available to users - and a loss of engagement, interest, and motivated participation. Thus, despite a motion-controlled game play commercial product being realized because of the research subsequent research has focused on more abstract 'artistic' content feedback content that is not rule-based. In this way, art, in the form of music-making and painting via the digital tools available from the digital interactive media

Figs. 10–12   Gesture-control of video games (pictures Bruno Herbelin, SensoramaLab)

system has been found effective to achieve the desired user-experience. Such a focus is in line with Hummels, Djajadiningrat, and Overbeeke (2001) who refer to designing a 'context for experience' rather than object-oriented entities, and Buxton (2007) who discus user-experience from a design perspective. The afferent-efferent neural feedback loop closure that has been assessed of SoundScapes optimal sessions is seemingly more prevalent when inquiring user aesthetic resonance (Ellis 1996, 2004; Brooks et al. 2002) by abstract 'artistic' content feedback as opposed to video games. In this respect my research speculates on participant brain/CNS activity in regards mirror neuron simulation which occurs from action-hearing and action-seeing in sessions where action is self-executed.

Self-determined action (rather than game-determined) is motivated where technology mediates pleasing/fun feedback stimuli that is directly and immediately associated to the action sequence which is responding to the self. In this way inter-subjective stimulus evolves intra-subjective consequences. Consequences associate to the stimuli affordances, participant's perception and sequential executed action, and sense of awareness of the linkage chain. Self-agency is promoted and the inner empowerment is symbolized by observed representation that is referred to as aesthetic resonance (e.g., Brooks et al. 2002, Ellis 1996, 2004). Judgment of aesthetic resonance is associated to the assessors' first hand experience and is thus a relative to the acquaintance principle (Wollheim 1980).

This untraditional therapeutic practice was focused on motion in invisible space where a tailored virtual environment was controlled. A non-therapeutic mindset was targeted and training intervention was not focused on the physical limb but rather on the VE content feedback and interaction. In other words training intervention instruction was directed as being product focused rather than process so as to influence user mindset, i.e. "in order to make the ball go to the right you need to move the right arm", rather than, "you need to move your right arm to make the ball go to the right" which directs the focus onto limiting impairment. Such inflections were found important so that the user had a focus on the game or art creation rather than on the body part employed in the training.

Adapted and personalized to each individual user the system gave positive indications across a range of disabilities. From the most marginalized such as those with profound multiple disabilities, intellectually challenged, down syndrome, autism, and others who had been born with impairments and where augmenting life quality was targeted, to other groups such as acquired brain injured, mostly stroke or car accident victims, who had been born without disability.

The human performance application for those with impairment was design-influenced by my performance art whereby, on stage I used my body as the medium, and in MoMA commissions, I designed/refined from observing experiences of visitors. My knowledge gain carried across to the research within the community of disabled people.

This approach is in line with Robert E. Parks, the American urban sociologist, who was one of the main founders of the original Chicago School of sociology. His concept of 'real research meaning getting ones pants dirty' analogizes to my work where I believe that insight gained from my domestic experiences with disabled people and my active exploration of the same apparatus in performance art as used in the special needs sector resulted in tacit knowledge (Polanyi 2002 [1958]) that can be called upon 'in-action' as a facilitator as well as for 'on-action' evaluations. Evaluations are thus validated under the 'acquaintance principle' (Wollheim 1980, p. 233) from aesthetic theory, which relates to how first hand experience is required before validating judgment and sharing understanding. Pollini (2008, p. 37–38) details the facilitator role being reflective of experience and knowledge.

Transcending to and from Entertainment and the Arts

The first part of this chapter has introduced how digital interactive media has been used in an untraditional way in health-care practices to motivate participation in rehabilitation training. The human performance aspects of users with disability in the created interactive spaces/environments relates to my own art and how I perceive it to be creating for another's creativity with success represented by aesthetic resonance. This aesthetic is an inner resonance recognized from achieved user-experience. Having experienced a vocation as a stage performer I relate to emotions achieved through a satisfying entertainment of an audience. Thus, in the therapy the user entertains him or her-self through the mediating interactive digital media system. This can be from controlling a game or creating art, i.e. music making or painting via digital tools, and is evident as FUN resulting from the created situations. Facilitator knowledge of the potentials of the digital media is essential to user-experience, successful guidance (targeted as via mediating technology), and user self-determined entertainment.

The same system that was created specific for the rehabilitation training was used by me to perform abstract expressionistic stage art and interactive installations at various large exhibitions. These include ongoing tours in Museums of Modern Art as well as at International-National Cultural events (e. g., Danish NeWave, New York 1999; Cultural Olympiad 1996, 2000; and European Cultural Capital events 1996, 2000). Underground events were as informative to the concept as the larger venues (see next section). Insight was gained from these situations. By combining self-reflection with collaborative inter-/multi-disciplinary reflective analysis of the human performance situations a significant input to designing the system, facilitating sessions, and evaluating outcomes evolved.

Underground Non-formal Learning

An example of how learning was apparent from the entertainment and arts is where I directed, produced and performed in a one-man-show realized as the inaugural Aarhus Festival Fringe ('Festuge'). This 1999 event took place in an emptied storage rooms that were adjacent to my sizable interactive room installation titled Circle of Interactive Light (COIL), hosted by the Radisson SAS Scandinavia Hotel, Aarhus, Denmark. The Festival committee had declined my proposal to bring together East and West German artists to feature alongside North and South Korean artists as too politically sensitive. The festival theme was 'THE WALL, Ten Years After' – and my proposal involved artists of distinction from both sides of the Berlin Wall and the DMZ to discus and showcase how political issues affect art and artists lives. Understandable that the committee declined!

The eventual "FESTUGE FRINGE" protest performance featured my digital interactive media in the form of the motion sensitive system utilized in various ways with projections inside and outside the human body. The final section of the performance was where I used fourteen infrared sensors to control one sound and a library of image manipulations. The purpose was to explore non-control and subliminal performance by enabling the feedback to control me and this was done by mapping the data to maximum parameter control of a specific aspect of the sound envelope. In four of the twelve performances I achieved what I refer to as non-control with subliminal interaction. This was where I, as performer, experienced being as one with the feedback stimuli. If conscious intent or query was involved, the experience

and higher-state of interaction (or inbetweenness – see Kidd) was lost. I relate this
targeted non-control and interaction to the therapy work with profoundly disabled
where often the user's abilities are of a non-controlled state so my learning experiences as performer/user assist by informing my role as facilitator.

Following the performances the wall would open to exhibit the technology used,
and then audience walked through the wall into the COIL exhibition space where
they could experience the virtual interactive spaces and debate over a drink in the
café I had built for the occasion. The piece titled "Behind the Wall" targeted beyond
Berlin and DMZ issues as it reflected on human barriers across ages and cultures –
and especially committees.

The next section introduces the ArtAbilitation[2] workshops from 2007 and 2008.
The ArtAbilitation movement has evolved from the SoundScapes work. It is where
digital interactive media is used to create an entertaining user-experience.

ArtAbilitation Workshops, Casa da Musica, Porto, Portugal

The "Ao Alcance de Todos - Within Everyone's Reach" festival was hosted at Casa
da Música (Figure 13), Porto, Portugal in April 2008. Eight one hour workshops
were held with 144 disabled children and adults attending with caregivers. The
workshops were created in a room 238 square meters floor area and approximately
20 meters high. Additionally, a symposium for professionals was hosted immediately following the workshops for 35 professionals (international, national, regional,
and local // social workers, psychologists, researchers, teachers, and students ...)
- many of whom had attended the workshops. This event was a continuation of
the previous year's inaugural event where the theme was 'Music, Technology and
Disability', and where six workshops were attended by 91 attendees including 61
from special care institutes, of which 39 had profound disability. 30 student music
teachers also attended. A local crew assists in the realization of the workshops (see
Petersson and Brooks 2007; Brooks 2008).

This section does not detail the workshops but rather it exemplifies the design
issues where digital interactive media, entertainment and the arts are combined to
result in various user-experiences that inform the ongoing research and refinement
of the acknowledged international ArtAbilitation movement (Wiederhold 2007).

I begin by giving an overview of commonalities in designing both workshops.
The 2007 workshop is then detailed in more depth followed by the 2008 workshop.
Both workshop designs targeted participant learning from interactive experiences
where active participation formed a context for meaning. Offered were opportunities for augmenting learning and awareness. Observations were of self-determined
active participation that established goals that in turn engaged interest, curiosity
and play. In this way, motivation to achieve goals is considered intrinsic rather than
extrinsic, which can result from an activity, task or goal introduced by someone else,

[2] http://www.ArtAbilitation.net

Fig. 13 Casa da Musica, Porto, Portugal (photo with permission Casa da Musica)

and or with possibly over zealous guidance/facilitation. Contextual design thus became a way to configure learning resources and interaction (Kress & van Leeuwen,
2001). Exploration, play and transformation were also targeted in both events such
that each participant had an 'action-stillness' profile that evolved through interactions. Each cycle of activity was considered a new creation that contributed to
form patterning of actions resulting from the activity. Each activity was designed
to increment challenges of confrontation. The resultant 'play' and created 'creativity' scenarios involved manipulation of provided tools. The manipulation required
a degree of competence that was learnt through exploration of the tool's traits
(Bruner 1972).

Absence of negative consequences seemingly encouraged participant free expressive explorations, which in turn, can over time result in development of un-
employed skill (Beach, 1942). Such development is significant even if it is at a
micro scale, i.e. micro-development (Yan and Fischer 2002). Responsive environment composition and learning process/outcome evolve as the assessment focus
instrument of observers. Realized was new learning spaces and approaches to learning and rehabilitation through emphasizing user's creation of meaning via serious
play. The approach is that no aspect of the learning process and outcome is taken for
granted. Rather it is formulated into play and creative activities that are inherent to
e.g., games and art making. The activities of play and creativity conceal the embedded learning and training involved for the user. An emphasis is on a supplementing
tool for traditional practices rather than a replacement. In this sense, learning is at a
'subliminal' level for the user as he or she engages in the responsive environment.
Thus, motivation is optimized through action and stillness cycles where the user

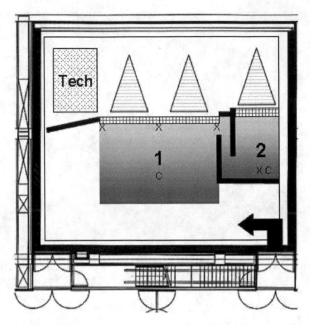

Fig. 14 Sala de Ensaio 1, Casa da Música, Oporto, Portugal (C = camera) – (Brooks 2008)

iteratively explores and transforms the feedback media. This process contains choices and decisions that indicate learning, e.g. in the form of increased repertoire of expressions, changes of skills, and new patterns of social interaction (Brooks 2008).

In the 2007 workshop a private (2) and a public (1) area were designed – see Sala de Ensaio diagram (Figure 14). This was inspired from the evaluation consultations mentioned earlier in this chapter where a caregiver experienced that a private space, without any intervention, was desired before a user felt comfortable enough to express through the SoundScapes system. My previous research (Brooks et al. 2002) presented how certain individuals prefer to explore, play and create without any others being present (Figures 15–16). Exemplifying the SoundScapes open system and concept a digital video camera was used to create a feedback loop play-space where participant gesture distorted image silhouette and color change to a RGB lighting system that reacted to voice input. Interactions in the private space were video taped and analyzed as achieving a positive flow state (Csikszentmihályi 1996). It was observed in the private space that the chain of exploration-play-creation began with a curiosity that evolved out of the isolation and initial stillness that was first encountered within the created environment. Thereby, stillness became part of the action and vice versa. Indications pointed to how interactive play and creativity that offered choices between interaction and rest in a silent space enhanced the sense of control.

A created public space (Figures 17–18) questioned participant perception and awareness where peer-support and scaffolding of exploration was evident. Overhead infrared camera tracking was mapped to auditory music making (Figure 17)

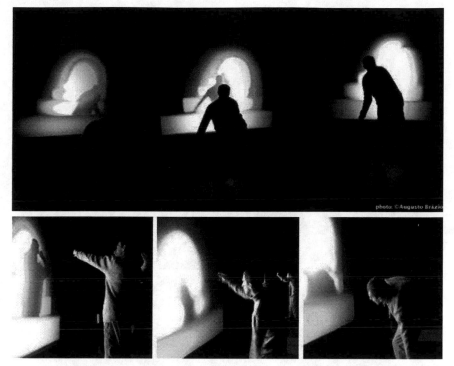

Figs. 15-16 Private space images of total engagement from ArtAbilitation 2007, (photo credit Augusto Brazio, Casa da Musica)

and image effects (Figure 18). Many results occurred from this space. One memorable instance was when a woman who was profoundly physically disabled insisted in exploring the interactive space out of her wheelchair – evident was that crawling around required immense effort (Figure 18). Her motions were tracked to open up a digital mask that concealed an image of a famous Portuguese footballer. Her disabled colleagues were supporting by shouting instructions. Motivation was staggering to achieve the whole erosion of the mask. Another instance was where an autistic group was in the workshop and one of them began to move and open up the same mask. The first exposed facial element of the footballer was the chin and immediately another autistic male shouted out the name of the recognized footballer. In both instances (and others) the public virtual interactive space empowered immediate learning to be exhibited (Petersson and Brooks 2007).

Five physical 'VIS rooms' were created in the 2008 workshop. Each was designed to offer differing experiences of empowerment through motion creating images and auditory feedback. Large sub-woofer speakers positioned on the wooden floor gave tactile stimulation which was especially important for the attending class of young deaf children. Findings were that the interactive spaces offered a place where comprehension of tasks could be shared from the strong to the weak in each group. Again wheelchairs were discarded to explore by crawling around the spaces.

Figs. 17-18 Public interactive space: two designs utilizing overhead camera tracking

Targeted tangible outcome was that each participant received a painting that they created through gesture. Reports of how many showed these paintings to family, friends and non-attending staff stated to the powerful effect.

Both workshops exhibited action-stillness cycles, which consisted of iterative loops of exploring and transforming, constitute one part of a theoretical map for the purposes of analyzing critical incidents in a non-formal learning process. These cycles are related to the user's learning experience. The other part of the theoretical map concerns design issues in the form of use qualities relative to the user's interactive experience; transparency, social-action space, user control/autonomy, pliability, playability and seductivity (Löwgren and Stolterman 2005). During a whole session cycle of action and stillness, facilitators have the possibility to reflect upon the indications of learning that occur during the process. The user profile influences the facilitator's decisions on how to set up the attributes of the responsive environments relative to the desired learning process and the expected outcome of that process. Once these prerequisites are set, the user is expected to 'experience from the interaction and learn from the experience'.

Hence, the aim of the workshop events was to investigate the user's performance in using responsive environments designed to engage participants in experience-learning through action and stillness cycles. A sub-question concerns the ability of perception and the associated learning curve of the attendees with cognitive disabilities to be able to easily correlate across dimensions of scale and plane – a matter which influences the participant's interactive as well as learning experience.

The final reported event is one that was built upon previous work where third party performance gesture created visuals to complement classical music situations.

Visualizing classical music

The previous sections present the motion-sensitive environment and its use as a rehabilitation training supplement within the community of people with a disability, both profound from birth, and acquired. The use of the created interactive system is presented in intimate institute settings for individuals and a later section shares two examples of larger workshop situations where groups attended. This section exemplifies how a similar concept and technique of using digital interactive media was implemented to elicit dynamic performance data from a situation that featured the 'Orquestra Nacional do Porto' - regarded by many as The Portuguese National Orchestra. This was again in Casa da Musica, Porto, Portugal but this time in the main 1200 seat state-of-the-art auditorium. See publication Interpretation[3] (Brooks 2008).

A goal of the exploratory study was to dynamically complement the music by offering an experience of inter/multi-sensory stimulation for both audience and performers. This built upon my earlier work in Auckland, New Zealand, and Aarhus, Denmark where the different situations, one with orchestra and one with choir, both had a similar stimulation goal. An aim of this work is to offer inclusive access so that even people who are deaf may have an opportunity to appreciate classical music. Important to mention is how in the choir study three sensors mapped to RGB enabled the conductor to paint the choir backdrop through his gestured interactions with the singers. The session was in the Danish Radio TV studio and six 'takes' were recorded. It was evident that his gestures were expanding as he became used to the interaction and – in his own words - "how it felt that the air around my body was activated". This expansion of gesture relates to the work in the disability sector where targeted in subliminal motivated augmented motion.

The following Figs. 19–26 illustrate the result from the visualization experiment. Overhead cameras and stage sensors sourced the performance data and this was

---

[3] http://www.icdvrat.reading.ac.uk/2008/interpretations.htm

Fig. 19 Data from stage performance – conductor gesture, section/musician expressiveness, lights and music - sourced to dynamically affect the synchronized visuals for environment change in real-time (photo credit João Messias, Casa da Musica)

Fig. 20 Sourced stage data mixed and matched to digitally mirror performance in abstract – here camera and music stand lights - creating and effecting projected visuals (photo credit João Messias, Casa da Musica)

Fig. 21 Projected moving image dynamically matched to digitally mirror performance (photo credit João Messias, Casa da Musica)

mapped by created algorithms to effect the environment variables in real-time to complement the music. A technical deficit proved the biggest hurdle and results were unsatisfactory as image mixing was via switching instead of faders on a mixer. Thus, nuance of performance was unable to be matched as I desired. However, as an experiment to explore the concept it did build my knowledge of the concept. The work is planned to evolve further locally for the next phase of experiments due to the problems of accessing the specialized equipment required for technical setup. The work has been accepted for the Cultural Olympiad 2012 London.

Fig. 22 Projected image (center of screen) shows data capture from camera overhead (photo credit João Messias, Casa da Musica)

Conclusions and Future Directions

This article informs of digital interactive media sculpted into a responsive gesture driven environment that is used within rehabilitation training. Entertainment achieved through a user creating and playing acts as a stimulant towards augmenting life quality and motivating participation in training that otherwise is boring, tedious and mundane – often for both patient and therapist/facilitator. Artistic composition in the form of music-making and digital painting is empowered through an interface and multi-sensory virtual environment content that is adaptive and flexible enough to address idiosyncratic needs. However, whilst I create for another's creativity, my

Fig. 23 Musicians can observe effect of their own performance (photo credit João Messias, Casa da Musica)

art is not the 'product' of the users' interaction, i.e. the music or painting, as many judge, but rather it is the aesthetic resonance that is achieved in and of the user. Ellis (1996, 2004) describes aesthetic resonance achieved within his 'Sound Therapy' body of research. This was extemporized in a 2002 article (Brooks et al. 2002) following findings that explored interactive visuals in the form of animations, virtual reality, and robotic lighting devices with colored and patterned gobos. This aesthetic is a representation of a system where affordances were perceived and the targeted action achieved. Resultant sense of self-agency and inner empowerment is realized cumulating to signify a state of flow that is identified by the facilitator. Investigation is of how to optimize user experience toward self-determined development via the virtual interactive space (VIS) that is created between the user and the system.

706 A.L. Brooks

Fig. 24 Conductor engaged in role as he manipulates responsive image artifacts (photo credit João Messias, Casa da Musica)

Fig. 25 Selective use of dynamic shadow effects are merged into environment (photo credit João Messias, Casa da Musica)

Potential micro-development (Yan and Fischer 2002) is a suggested potential even for those who are profoundly impaired. Problematic on the other hand is where a user is fixated on formal therapeutic conditioning and gets tied up in the 'cor-

Fig. 26 View from behind the control station where author interacts (photo credit Paul Sharkey)

rect way of doing' instead of 'just doing' with a focus on the mediating feedback content rather than on the impaired feed-forward function. User achievements are commonplace.

The activities of exploring interactive systems in the field of disability are seemingly growing. In Denmark commercial suppliers that sell targeted games for this market attempt a monopoly with substandard goods and services that tend to diminish opportunities for end users rather than increase. After two decades of research it is clear that open flexible and affordable systems that have selectable libraries of input device as well as selectable libraries of content stimuli are optimal. Systems that can be adapted, and personalized within customized environments tailored to an individual profile offer maximum opportunities and benefit. That benefit is not restricted to those with impairment as fun social interactions can motivate in playing games or making art.

Interface technologies have improved and motion detection devices such as the Nintendo Wii offer a data device that permits access to data and thus can advance the field in an affordable flexible package – either as a controller for games or music/art making. An approach I made to Sony Computer Entertainment Europe (SCEE), London, after the launch of the EyeToy asking such access to interface data was rejected. Their representatives stated discriminatingly that they did not wish to be seen exploiting disabled people. With such technology available it is a shame that such a commercial profile prevents opportunity inquiry. However, computer vision and graphical card advances makes affordable non-commercial sensor, single or multiple camera systems, a reality and our students in MEDIALOGY[4] in Esbjerg are active exploring both user-centered games and art as controlled mediums in the SensoramaLab VR complex.

Such diversity in the SoundScapes concept is recognized by Eaglestone & Bamidis (2008) as elements of a hybrid system consisting of networks of complex inter-connected subsystems comprising 'created technical systems' and 'natural human systems'. The MAX software has also undergone huge improvements since I first used it as version 2.5 in the early 1990s. Integrated capability to manipulate digital audio signals in real-time from a computer became a reality via the MSP (Max Signal Processing) add-on, thus there was no longer a requirement for external audio hardware. Subsequently another package developed and released for the MAX software environment in 2003 was Jitter, which enabled control of real-time video, 3D and matrix processing. Latest MAX activities is a partnering with a loop-based sequencer software named Ableton Live that offers intuitive live performance capabilities where MIDI manipulations can slot into a playing song such that it remains 'musical'. Whilst developed for DJs and VJs the potentials in my research for such a tool is acknowledged and this is a future direction when the packages are released. Other explored software includes Touch Designer by Derivative, and Syntetik's awesome Studio Artist interfaced with a Wacom Cintiq tablet.

In this sense a tool to supplement traditional training becomes available if the community of therapists and medical staff are prepared to accept an alternative approach in the form of a hybrid non-formal learning apparatus and method. If they do and are prepared to collaborate in evolving the concept with other interested researchers from the related disciplines then the next-generation of therapists may well be teamed with digital artists, computer scientists, and fMRI neurologists in creating, facilitating, and evaluating the human in new ways, with new methods, and with new apparatus, where FUN is the targeted user-experience and human benefit the ultimate goal. New virtual interactive spaces for learning are exhibited in this work that combines digital interactive media with entertainment and the arts.

---

[4] http://www.medialogy.eu

References

1. K. E. Misulis. "Essentials of Clinical Neurophysiology." Butterworth-Heinemann, 1997.
2. A. Lucier. "Statement On:luciermisulis Music for Solo Performer." In: D. Rosenboom (Ed.), Biofeedback and the Arts, Results of Early Experiments. Aesthetic Research Center of Canada Publications, 1976.
3. D. Warner. "Rock 'n roll Science:warner Playing the Body Electric" [online] Available from http://www.virtualgalen.com/virtualhealing/dr-dave.htm.
4. A. L. Brooks, A. Camurri, N. Canagarajah and S. Hasselblad. "Interaction with shapes and sounds as a therapy for special needs and rehabilitation." In:brooks International Conference on Disability, Virtual Reality and Associated Technologies (4th). Veszprém, Hungary, 18–20 September. P. Sharkey, C. S. Lányi, and P. Standen, (Eds.). Reading: University of Reading, pp. 205–212, 2002.
5. A. L. Brooks. Robotic Synchronized to Human Gesture as a Virtual Coach in (Re)habilitation Therapy. In: 3rd International Workshop on Virtual Rehabilitation (IWVR2004), VRlab, EPFL, Lausanne, Switzerland, pp. 17–16, 2004.
6. E. Petersson and A. Brooks. Non-formal therapy and learning potentials through human gesture synchronized to robotic gesture. International Journal Universal Access in the Information Society. Springer 6(2), pp. 167–177, 2007.
7. W. M. Marston. Emotions of Normal People, Routledge, 1928.
8. A. L. Brooks. SoundScapes: A concept of Virtual Interactive Space (V.I.S.) [unpublished]. World Summit for Social Development/NGO Forum 6–12 March, Holmen, Copenhagen, 1995.
9. A. L. Brooks. Virtual interactive space (V.I.S.) as a movement capture interface tool giving multimedia feedback for treatment and analysis. In: "Bridging Cultures" – program of The 13th International Congress of the World Confederation for Physical Therapy, Yokohama Japan, May 23–28, Science Links Japan: http://sciencelinks.jp/jeast/article/200110/000020011001A0418015.php, 1999.
10. A. L. Brooks. Virtual interactive space (V.I.S.). In: 'Pushing the limits: optimising potential through science and technology', Congress Program and Abstract Book, 5th Scientific Congress, Sydney 2000 Paralympic Games, Oct. 11–13, Convention Centre, Darling Harbor, Sydney, Australia, 2000.
11. A. L. Brooks. HUMANICS 1 – a feasibility study to create a home internet based telehealth product to supplement acquired brain injury therapy. In: International Conference on Disability, Virtual Reality and Associated Technologies (5th). Oxford University, UK, 20–22 September 2004. Sharkey, P., McCrindle, R. and Brown, D. (eds.) Reading: University of Reading, pp. 43–50, 2004.
12. A. L. Brooks and E. Petersson. Recursive reflection and learning in raw data video analysis of interactive 'play' environments for special needs health care. In: Proceedings of 7th International Workshop on Enterprise networking and Computing in Healthcare Industry, Korea HEALTHCOM 2005, IEEE Signal Processing Society, USA, pp. 83–87, 2005.
13. A. L. Brooks and S. Hasselblad. Creating aesthetically resonant environments for the handicapped, elderly and rehabilitation: Sweden. Proceedings of 6th International Conference on Disability, Virtual Reality and Associated Technologies (ICDVRAT), Esbjerg, Denmark, 18th–20th September, pp. 191–198, 2004.
14. A. L. Brooks. Enhanced Gesture Capture in Virtual Interactive Space. Computers in Art, Design, and Education (CADE), 29 June–01 July, Copenhagen Business School, Denmark and Malmö University, Sweden, 2004.
15. A. L. Brooks and E. Petersson. Stillness design attributes in non-formal rehabilitation: CADE2007 - Computers in Art Design and Education. Perth, Curtin University of Technology, pp. 36–44, 2007.

16. G. Goldkuhl and P. J. Ågerfalk. "Actability: A way to understand information systems pragmatics." CMTO Research papers No. 2000:13, Linköping University. Presented at the 3rd International Workshop on Organisational Semiotics, 4 July 2000, Stafford, UK, 2000.

17. P. J. Ågerfalk and S. Cronholm. "Usability versus Actability: A Conceptual Comparative Analysis." Presented at the HCI International conference New Orleans, USA, Lawrence Erlbaum and Associates, pp. 235–237, 2001.

18. A. N. Leont'ev. "Activity, consciousness and personality." NJ: Prentice-Hall, Englewood Cliffs, 1981.

19. R. Davies. "Commentary on P. J. Standen and D. J. Brown – Virtual Reality in Rehabilitation of People with Intellectual Disabilities: Review." CyberPsychology and Behavior, 8(3), 2005.

20. A. L. Brooks and E. Petersson. "Play Therapy Utilizing the Sony EyeToy®." In: Annual International Workshop on Presence (8th), London, 21–23 September 2005. Slater, M. (ed.) London: University College London, pp. 303–314, 2005.

21. C. Hummels, T. Djajadiningrapt, and K. Overbeeke. "Knowing, doing and feeling: Communicating with your digital products. Interdisziplinäres Kolleg Kognitions und Neurowissenschaften, Günne am Möhnesee, March 2–9, pp. 289–308, 2001.

22. B. Buxton. "Sketching User Experiences: getting the design right and the right design," Elsevier, 2007.

23. M. Polanyi. "Personal Knowledge: Towards a Post-Critical Philosophy," Routledge, 2002 [1958].

24. R. Wollheim. "Art and Its Objects," 2nd ed., Cambridge University press, 1980.

25. P. Ellis. "Layered analysis: A video-based qualitative research tool to support the development of a new approach for children with special needs." The Bulletin for the Council for Research in Music Education. University of Illinois at Urbana-Champaign, USA, 130, pp.65–74, 1996.

26. P. Ellis. "Caress – 'an endearing touch'." In: J. Siraj-Blatchford (ed.) Developing New Technologies for Young Children. London: Trentham Books, pp. 113–137, 2004.

27. A. Pollini, Experimenting with an Ubiquitous Computing Open Architecture, [PhD Thesis] http://www.ist-palcom.org/publications/files/PhD-Thesis-Pollini.pdf, 2008

28. E. Petersson and A. L. Brooks. ArtAbilitation®: An Interactive Installation for the Study of Action and Stillness Cycles in Responsive Environments. Computers in Art, Design, and Education (CADE 2007) http://cedar.humanities.curtin.edu.au/conferences/cade/pdf/CADE2007Conferenc eprogram&abstracts.pdf, 2007.

38. A. L. Brooks. Towards a platform of alternative and adaptive interactive systems for idiosyncratic special needs, Proc. 7th Intl Conf. on Disability, Virtual Reality and Assoc. Technologies with ArtAbilitation, pp 319–326, Maia, Portugal, 8–11 Sept. 2008.

30. B. K. Wiederhold. Virtual Healers, International Association for CyberTherapy & Rehabilitation, 2007.

31. G. Kress and T. van Leeuwen. "Reading Images. The Grammar of Visual Design." London, Routledge, 1996.

32. J. S. Bruner. "Nature and Uses of Immaturity." In: J. S. Bruner, A. Jolly and K. Sylva (eds.), Play – Its Role in Development and Evolution. Basic Books, 1976

33. F. A. Beach. "Comparison of Copulatory Behavior of Male Rats Raised in Isolation, Cohabitation, and Segregation." Journal of Genetic Psychology, 60, pp. 121–136, 1942.

34. Z. Yan and K. Fischer. "Always Under Construction: Dynamic variations in adult cognitive development," Human Development, 45, pp. 141–160, 2002.

35. M. Csikszentmihályi. Creativity: Flow and the Psychology of Discovery and Invention. New York: Harper Perennial, 1996.

36. J. Löwgren and E. Stolterman. Thoughtful Interaction Design, Boston, MIT, 2005.

37. B. Eaglestone and P. D. Bamidis. "Music composition for the multi-disabled: A systems perspective." Disability Human Development, 7(1), pp. 19–24, 2008.

38. A. L. Brooks. Interpretations: inter-sensory stimulation concept targeting inclusive access of-fering appreciation of classical music for all ages, standing, & disability, Proc. 7th Intl Conf. on Disability, Virtual Reality and Assoc. Technologies with ArtAbilitation, pp 15–22, Maia & Porto, Portugal, 8–11 Sept. 2008.

Images are marked with credit to photographer or permitting body. Otherwise copyright is with the author.

Additional images are viewed at the author's online gallery - http://gallery.mac.com/anthony.lewis.brooks

Chapter 32
Natural Interaction in Intelligent Spaces: Designing for Architecture and Entertainment

Flavia Sparacino

Introduction

Designing responsive environments for various venues has become trendy today. Museums wish to create attractive "hands-on" exhibits that can engage and interest their visitors. Several research groups are building an "aware home" that can assist elderly people or chronic patients to have an autonomous life, while still calling for or providing immediate assistance when needed.

The design of these smart spaces needs to respond to several criteria. Their main feature is to allow people to freely move in them. Whether they are navigating a 3D world or demanding assistance, we can't strap users with encumbering sensors and limiting tethers to make them interact with the space. Natural interaction, based on people's spontaneous gestures, movements and behaviors is an essential requirement of intelligent spaces. Capturing the user's natural input and triggering a corresponding action is however, in many cases, not sufficient to ensure the appropriate response by the system. We need to be able to interpret the users' actions in context and communicate to people information that is relevant to them, appropriate to the situation, and adequately articulated (simple or complex) at the right time.

On the basis of my work and research I will argue that intelligent spaces need to be supported by three forms of intelligence: *perceptual intelligence*, which captures people's presence and movement in the space in a natural and non-encumbering way; *interpretive intelligence*, which "understands" people's actions and is capable of making informed guesses about their behavior; and *narrative intelligence*, which presents us with information, articulated stories, images, and animations, in the right place, at the right time, all tailored to our needs and preferences.

All three forms of intelligence need to co-exist and co-operate for an Intelligent Space to be effective. Narrative intelligence is important so that the space provides us with relevant information that matches our interests and needs. We need systems able to select how much information to give, with what detail and composition, and

F. Sparacino (✉)
Sensing Places and MIT, Santa Monica, CA, USA
e-mail: flavia@sensingplaces.com

B. Furht (ed.), *Handbook of Multimedia for Digital Entertainment and Arts*,
DOI 10.1007/978-0-387-89024-1_32, © Springer Science+Business Media, LLC 2009

how to sequence and articulate various fragments. A lack of interpretive intelligence will produce applications that are unable to determine the appropriate time to get our attention on a specific matter or story, and which nag the user about whether he or she wants this or that. Context modeling and behavior modeling are ways of approaching interpretive intelligence, the first one from the situation's perspective and the second one from the user's perspective. Perceptual Intelligence is about endowing spaces with eyes, ears, and sensors that allow them to capture how they are being used by people. This is, in its full complexity, still an open field of research: scene interpretation and object recognition are today active and open territories for scientific investigation.

Augmenting a space with all three forms of intelligence can be seen as endowing the space with a mind of its own, which transforms it from a simple container of people and things to an active participant and cooperating agent of our lives. Perceptual intelligence represents the bottom layer of this virtual brain, and processes sensorial inputs. Interpretive Intelligence is the middle layer whose role is to "make sense" of the input data: it identifies situations and people's behaviors. Narrative Intelligence is the upper layer, a bit like the brain cortex, and it regulates the output and communication between the intelligent space and us (Fig. 1).

The above description of space intelligence has provided a high level framework for the author's research. In the following sections of this paper I will first illustrate

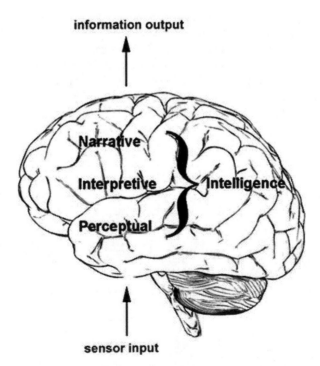

Fig. 1 Layered intelligence model for interactive spaces

in more detail the three forms of space intelligence. I will then describe incremental contributions to intelligence modeling for spaces I developed in the past years with a focus on applications for architecture and entertainment. The main contribution of this paper is to show that Bayesian networks are an ideal modeling tool for all three forms of space intelligence and to provide a unifying mathematical description for robust sensing, user and context modeling, and articulated information delivery (storytelling).

Related Work

The work here presented is highly interdisciplinary and it draws from various disciplines.

Smart Spaces

The author began research in Smart Spaces and Natural Interfaces in collaboration with Alex Pentland at MIT [29, 41, 44, 45]. A variety of research groups today have taken this field of investigation further, with a main focus on assisted living and on creating spaces that are useful for ordinary everyday activities. Georgia Tech has developed the Aware Home, a place embedded with technology that enables older adults to age in place, and which helps people communicate with distant relatives and friends [22]. Microsoft's Easy. Living is an intelligent environment that contains myriad devices that work together to provide users access to information and services [7]. These devices may be stationary, as with acoustic speakers or ceiling lights, or they may be mobile, as with laptop computers or mobile telephones. Microsoft's goal is to allow typical PC-focused activities to move off of a fixed desktop and into the environment [24]. The Stanford Interactive Workspaces project is exploring new possibilities for people to work together in technology-rich spaces with computing and interaction devices on many different scales [19]. Their work aims at augmenting a dedicated meeting space with large displays, wireless/multimodal I/O devices, and seamless integration of mobile and wireless appliances including handheld PCs. Rather than seeing the space as a pro-active facilitator Stanford's room is a reconfigurable platform for running a variety of applications. MIT's Intelligent Room is a highly interactive environment that uses embedded computation to observe and participate in normal, everyday events. Microphone and camera arrays enable it to listen to people and observe what they do. People can speak with, gesture to, and interact with it in several ways [6, 9]. A robust agent-based software infrastructure supports the operation of these tools. The room's intelligence is modeled by a multi-agent society that builds a higher level and context based representation of the user's activity. Each activity has an associated software agent, called behavior agent, which responds to the user's actions and performs the corresponding appropriate reaction [12]. The room detects and reacts to activities such as watching a movie, meetings, entering the room. When new sensors are added to the space, the behavior rules need to be manually modified to take advantage of the new input information. The space intelligence model proposed in this paper uses instead a unified mathematical framework, Bayesian networks, both for perceptual intelligence and user modeling. Thanks to the properties of Bayesian networks, context or user behavior is modeled not as a set of fixed high level rules, but it is grounded on data observation, and therefore it can adapt or fine tune the room's response to the actual behavior of people in it, both instantly and through time. Additionally the Bayesian network architecture makes it easy to add new sensors or new responses to the room without having to re-program the entire system to take new elements into account. As the applications of interest to the author are geared towards entertainment and to support new forms of interactive architecture, this paper also highlights the importance of and describes narrative intelligence, which allows the intelligent space to use its resources to articulate an audiovisual narration as a function of the user's estimated interests and behaviors in the space.

In a recent paper Emiliani and Stephanidis have examined the requirements that spaces with ambient-intelligence technologies need to have to support elderly people and people with disabilities. According to their work, the main high-level design features of a system with ambient intelligence are that it be unobtrusive (i.e., many distributed devices are embedded in the environment, not intruding upon our consciousness unless we need them), personalized (i.e., it can recognize the user, and its behavior can be tailored to the user's needs), adaptive (i.e., its behavior can change in response to a person's actions and environment), and anticipatory (i.e., it anticipates a person's desires and environment as much as possible without mediation) [11]. The work presented in this paper uses similar requirements for an entertainment space (i.e. a museum) and it offers a layered model of intelligence with a unified mathematical representation which also includes narrative intelligence. Early work by the author on space intelligence applied some of the ideas discussed in this paper towards the design of an interactive museum exhibit [36].

Perceptual Intelligence and Natural Interaction

Pavlovic [27] and Wu [47] have explored use of hand gestures in human computer interaction, with an emphasis on 3D tracking and multi-modal approaches for gesture recognition. Starner [42] has shown one of the first examples of effective gesture recognition using HMMs. Brand, Oliver, and Pentland [5] have demonstrated the higher performance of coupled HMMs for tasks which require gesturing with both hands at the same time. Campbell and others [8] have studied the effects of the appropriate feature choice for a gesture recognition task, using stereo vision.

The author has developed a variety of natural interfaces for art and entertainment Installations [33, 37]. The work on natural interfaces has grown from a monocular real time body tracking technique, called Pfinder (person finder), and the real time blob tracking approach associated with it and described in section 32 [46]. Stereo tracking of pointing and command gestures, and HMM based gesture recognition is discussed in [40]. Jojic, Brumitt, and Meyers [20] also use stereo cameras to detect people pointing and estimate the direction of their pointing. As opposed to the blob tracking approach developed by the author, they use disparity maps which are less sensitive to lighting changes. In the blob-based approach, light invariance can be achieved using adaptation, or implementing color invariant classification [4].

Bayesian Networks for User Modeling and Interactive Narrative

The work of Pearl [28] is fundamental to the field of Bayesian networks. Jordan's book [21] had the merit of grouping together some of the major advancements since Pearl's 1988 book. Jensen [17, 18] has written two thorough introductory books that provide a very good tutorial, or first reading, in the field. Bayesian networks have gained popularity in the early nineties, when they were successfully applied to medical diagnosis [13].

Albrecht et al [1], have been among the first to model the behavior of a participant in a computer game using Bayesian networks. They use several network structures to predict the user's current goal, next action, and next location in a multi-user Dungeon adventure game. With respect to their work, the system here presented performs not just user state estimation, which can also be used to predict the next action that the user will do, but it also adds a probabilistic mechanism for content selection. The focus of the narrative intelligence model here presented is to function as a sensor-driven computational system that uses the same unifying mathematical framework (Bayesian Networks) for sensor modeling (tracking, gesture recognition), user estimation, and content selection. Jebara [16], uses CHMMS, which are a particular case of Dynamic Bayesian Networks, to perform, first analysis, and then synthesis, of a player's behavior in a game. Conati et al. [10] have built an intelligent tutoring system able to perform knowledge assessment, plan recognition and prediction of students' actions during problem solving using Bayesian networks. Jameson [15], provides a useful overview of student modeling techniques, and compares the Bayesian network approach with other popular modeling techniques.

The narrative intelligence model here presented is inspired by work in probabilistic knowledge representation. Koller and Pfeffer have used probabilistic inference techniques that allow most frame bases knowledge representation systems to annotate their knowledge bases with probabilistic information, and to use that information to answer probabilistic queries. Their work is relevant to describe and organize content in any database system so that it can later be selected either by a typed probabilistic query or by a sensor driven query [23]. Using a content database, annotated probabilistically, the sto(ry)chastics system selects the most appropriate content segment at each time step, and it delivers, interactively in time and space, an audiovisual narration to the museum visitor as a function of the estimated visitor type.

Criteria for Intelligent Space Design

Perceptual Intelligence

To transform a space in a computer and sensor-driven narrative space we need to be able to interact with the digital content on display in ways that are not as limiting as when we interact with the familiar keyboard and mouse. Furthermore, it is unrealistic to encumber participants with gloves, cables, or heavy virtual reality glasses: these fail to fully engage people as the technology dominates over the experience. Touch-based screens or hardware-based sensors tend to wear and break after use by hundreds of people and therefore require frequent replacement and a high maintenance load. Ideally we want to endow our interactive spaces with eyes, ears and perceptual intelligence so that they can interpret people's natural movement, gestures, and voice. Our spaces should be aware of visitors approaching an object of interest, of how they approach it, (speed, direction, pauses): they should be able to understand pointing gestures as commands, as well as occasionally understand more sophisticated gestures (zoom-in, zoom-out, rotate, move up, move down, me, you, etc.) and voice commands. Unencumbering computer vision interfaces or other wireless sensors, such as infrared sensors, electric field sensors, civil use sonars and radars, are the ideal input device or communication interface with the space.

The robustness and reliability of a natural interface is also very important. If the interface breaks often or does not work consistently, the "magic" of involvement and immersion in the interactive experience vanishes. Therefore ideally more than one sensor should be used to capture the participant's input. Cooperation of sensor modalities which have various degrees of redundancy and complementarity can guarantee robust, accurate perception. We can use the redundancy of the sensors to register the data they provide with one another. We then use the complementarity of the sensors to resolve ambiguity or to reduce errors when an environmental perturbation affects the system.

Interpretive Intelligence

To make good use of reliable measurements about the user, we need to be able to interpret our measurements in the context of what the user is trying to do with the digital media, or what we, as designers, want people to do, so that they get the most out of the experiences we wish to offer. The same or similar gesture of the public can have different meanings according to the context and history of interaction. For example, the same pointing gesture of the hand can be interpreted either as a zoom-in command gesture, or more simply, as a selection gesture. In a similar way, the system needs to develop expectations on the likelihood of the user's responses based on the specific context of interaction and content shown. These expectations influence in turn the interpretation of sensory data. Following on the previous example, rather than teaching both the user and the system to perform or recognize two slightly different gestures, one for zoom-in and one for selecting, we can simply teach the system how to correctly interpret slightly similar gestures, based on the context and history of interaction, by developing expectations on the probability of the follow-on gesture. In summary, our systems need to have a user model which characterizes the behavior and the likelihood of responses of the public. This model also needs to be flexible and should be adaptively revised by learning the user's interaction profile. Together with a user model, the system should build a model of the "situation" in which the user is involved while interacting with digital media (context modeling).

Narrative Intelligence

In order to turn computers into articulated storytellers that respond to people's natural gestures and voice, we cannot simply model interaction as a list of coupled inputs and outputs. This simply defines a map of causes and effects that associates an action of the user to a response produced by the interactive space. Systems authored with this method tend to produce applications that are repetitive and shallow. We need instead narrative machines that are able to orchestrate stories whose composition and length can vary as a function of the publics' interests. Just as a museum guide adapts his/her explanation of the artwork on display according to the visitors' base knowledge and curiosity, our narrative engines should be able to take into account and adapt to the publics' needs. To accomplish this goal we need to model the story we wish to narrate so that it takes into account and encompasses the user's intentions and the context of interaction. Consequently the story should develop on the basis of the system's constant evaluation of how the user's actions match the system's expectations about those actions, and the system's goals.

Intelligence Modeling

Over the last decade, a method of reasoning using probabilities, variously called belief networks, Bayesian networks, probabilistic causal networks, influence diagrams, knowledge maps, etc., has become popular within the AI community, and the machine learning, and pattern recognition communities. (Dynamic) Bayesian networks have been successfully applied to a variety of perceptual modeling tasks such as multimodal sensing for gesture recognition and sensor fusion [27], speech recognition [25], and body motion understanding [26]. Research in user and context modeling applies Bayesian networks to identify the behavior of a participant in a computer game [1], to interpret a car driver behavior [30], to understand the needs of a student. More recently the author has investigated Bayesian networks for story modeling and content selection in sensor-driven interactive narrative spaces [35]. In this paper I will argue that Bayesian networks are an ideal intelligence modeling tool as they can be used effectively to model respectively perceptual, interpretive, and narrative intelligence for interactive spaces.

Applications

This section describes three examples of spaces, or space-components, the author developed which each contribute, piece-wise, to the construction of intelligent environments. In some cases the system only has perceptual intelligence, whereas in others, the interpretive and narrative intelligence modeling is the focus of the contribution. Since the aim of this paper is to provide a unified view of space modeling techniques, the following sections will summarize the approach and results obtained. The reader will find a more accurate description of the implementation details in the included bibliography.

Perceptual Intelligence: Navigating the Internet City

This section presents a natural interface to navigate inside a 3D Internet city, using body gestures. This work uses a combination of computer vision and pattern recognition techniques to capture people's interaction in a natural way. A wide-baseline stereo pair of cameras is used to obtain 3D body models of the user's hands and head. The interface feeds this information to an Hidden Markov Model (HMM) gesture classifier to reliably recognize the user's browsing commands. With regard to the intelligence modeling framework here described, Smyth [32] demonstrated that HMMs are equivalent to dynamic Bayesian networks. To illustrate the features of this interface I describe its application to a custom built 3D Internet browser which facilitates the recollection of information by organizing and embedding it inside a virtual city through which the user navigates [35].

Natural Interfaces: Motivation

Recent technological progress today allows most home users to be able to afford powerful graphics hardware and computer processors. With this equipment people can navigate in sophisticated 3D graphical environments and play engaging computer games in highly realistic and fascinating 3D landscapes. Such progress has not been paralleled by equivalent advances in man-machine interfaces to facilitate access and displacement in virtual worlds. People still use quite primitive and limiting interfaces: the joystick, button-activated game consoles, or the computer keyboard itself. Full immersion and skillful exploration of 3D graphical environments are limited by the user's ability to use these interfaces, and repetitive use often involves undesired and painful medical consequences to the user's wrists, fingers, arms, or shoulders. New, more natural interfaces are needed to navigate inside virtual worlds.

On the other hand, people today spend an increasingly large amount of time exploring the Internet: a bi-dimensional environment, which is quite unsophisticated and simple compared to the previously mentioned popular computer games. While the Internet allows designers to author and display animated web pages, with moving text and images, the browsers we have available today are still quite primitive. Internet browsers are flat: they are based on the old multimedia metaphor of the book, with 2D pages filled with links to other pages, and bookmarks as a memory aid, to represent and organize the information available on the net. The only advantage of such information-interface is its non-linearity and rapid, visible access to interconnected data. The main disadvantage is that it is easy to get disoriented while navigating the Internet, as we rapidly lose track of what we've seen before the current page, and do not have perspective of what is accessible from the current location. The Internet could benefit from the same 3D graphical progress which has determined the surge of the computer games industry, and provide the public with 3D graphical browsers to help us better visualize, organize, and remember information [39].

This section presents two connected contributions: an Internet 3D web browser and a natural interface to browse it. Our browser is based on the architectural metaphor of the city and organizes information by embedding it inside a virtual urban space. Providing a natural interface to navigate in our 3D web browser is similar to designing a new interface for a 3D computer game. The author envisions that, in a not so distant future, we will have a large flat panel display in our home which is like windows to the internet city. We will navigate through this world with natural gestures, and eventually also voice commands, in ways similar to the ones described in this document.

City of news: an Internet City in 3D

City of News is an immersive, interactive web browser that makes use of people's strength at remembering the surrounding 3D spatial layout. For instance, everyone can easily remember where most of the hundreds of objects in their house are located. We are also able to mentally reconstruct familiar places by use of landmarks, paths, and schematic overview mental maps. In comparison to our spatial memory, our ability to remember other sorts of information is greatly impoverished. City of News capitalizes on this ability by mapping the contents of URLs into a 3D graphical world projected on a large screen. This gives a sense of the URLs existing in a surrounding 3D environment and helps the user remember the previous exploration path leveraging off his/her spatial memory. The URLs are displayed so as to form an urban landscape of text and images through which people can navigate (Figs. 2 and 3). The 3D web landscape is a city. Known cities' layout, architecture, and landmarks are input to the program and are used as orientation cues and organizing geometry. This virtual internet world grows dynamically as new information is

Fig. 2 Aerial view of City of News

Fig. 3 City of News after exploration

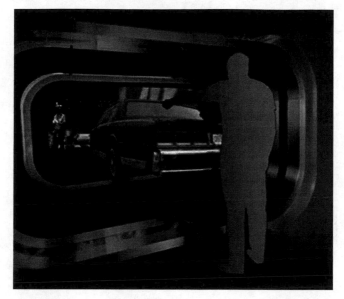

Fig. 4 User standing at the interactive setup

loaded, and anchors our perceptual flow of data to a cognitive map of the virtual internet city. Following a link causes a new building to be raised in the district to which it belongs, conceptually, by the content it carries, and content to be attached onto its "façade". By mapping information to familiar places, which are virtually recreated, City of News stimulates in its users association of content to geography. The spatial, urban-like distribution of information facilitates navigation of large information databases, like the Internet, by providing the user with a cognitive spatial map of data distribution.

To navigate this 3D environment, people sit or stand in front of a large screen (Figs. 4 and 5) and use hand gestures to explore or load new data. Side-pointing gestures allow users to navigate along an information path. Holding both arms up drives the virtual camera above the City and give an overall color-coded view of the urban information distribution. When a new building is raised and the corresponding content is loaded, the virtual camera will automatically move to a new position which corresponds to an ideal viewpoint for the information landscape. All the virtual camera movements are smooth interpolations between "camera anchors" that are invisibly dynamically loaded in the space as it grows. These anchors are like rail tracks which provide optimal viewpoints and constrain navigation so that the user is never lost in the virtual world.

2D Blob Tracking

Real-time 3D tracking is a method for estimation of 3D geometry from blob features. The notion of "blobs" as a representation for image features has a long history

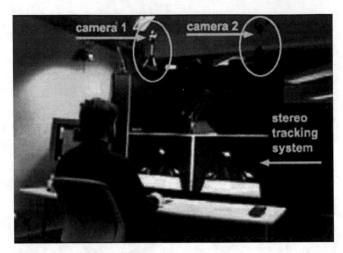

Fig. 5 User sitting at the interactive setup

in computer vision. The term "blob" is somewhat self-explanatory ("something of vague or indefinite form"), but a useful definition from a computational point of view is that a blob is defined by some visual property that is shared by all the pixels contained in the blob and is not shared by surrounding pixels. This property could be color, texture, brightness, motion, shading, a combination of these, or any other salient spatio-temporal property derived from the signal (the image sequence). Blobs are usually thought of as regions with dimensions that are roughly the same order-of-magnitude, in part because we have special terms for other features, e.g., "contours", "lines", or "points". But these other features can also be viewed as degenerate cases of blobs, and, in fact, straight contours and points are perfectly well represented by the blob model.

Blobs can be reliably tracked even in complex, dynamic scenes, and can be extracted in real-time without the need for special purpose hardware. These properties are particularly important in applications that require tracking people, and for this reason they have been used for real-time whole-body human interfaces [46] and for real-time recognition of American Sign Language hand gestures [42]. In the City of News setup, in which the upper body is used as the navigating interface to the Internet browser, it is important to have a more exact knowledge of body-parts position. A monocular system would not be able to accurately recover the location pointed at by the user in the 3D landscape. A projection error onto the 3D landscape would cause the user to navigate to a completely different location than what he/she intended. Not having such precision available would be equivalent to having a mouse with a coarse resolution which can cause a user to click and launch undesired applications, or involuntarily click on a different link than the desired one. A stereo tracking system, with the ability to recover the 3D geometry of the user's input features—hands and head—is an important step towards precise and reliable man-machine interfaces to explore 3D data.

For both 2D and 3D blobs, there is a useful physical interpretation of the blob parameters. The mean represents the geometric center of the blob area (2D) or volume (3D). The covariance, being symmetric, can be diagonalized via an eigenvalue decomposition to yield a rotation matrix and a diagonal size matrix. The diagonal size matrix represents the size of the blob along independent orthogonal object-centered axes and the rotation matrix brings this object-centered basis in alignment with the world coordinate basis. This decomposition and physical interpretation is important for estimation, because the shape is constant (or slowly varying) while the rotation is dynamic.

Person Tracking and Shape Recovery

The useful 3D geometry of the human body is estimated from blob correspondences in displaced cameras. The relevant unknown 3D geometry includes the shapes and motion of 3D objects, and optionally the relative orientation of the cameras and the internal camera geometries. The goal is to recover the 3D shape from the 2D shapes (Fig. 6).

The system first uses a color classifier to identify pixels with a skin color by log likelihood calculation in the MAP sense, as described in [47]. It then determines all connected skin-colored regions in the image with the k-means algorithm. It finally discards the smaller blobs until three blobs are found: left hand, right hand, and head. Simple heuristics allow the program to easily assign which blobs correspond to which body part: the head is usually on top and in the center, and at start, the right hand is usually on the right-hand side of the head. When a person first enters the space, the stereo calibration is obtained recursively by incorporating the three blob correspondences (face, left hand, right hand) into a EKF/LM estimator [2, 3]. The calibration parameters converge typically in the first 20 to 40 frames (roughly 2 to 4 s), if there is enough motion; longer if there is little motion. To evaluate the calibration quantitatively, the right hand acts as a 3D pointer and traces the 3D shape of known objects. The error of reconstruction of a hand position is on the order of 2 to 3 cm when the user is up to 4 meters away from the screen. This error is due both to estimation error and the crudeness of using the hand position to represent a point in space.

Fig. 6 3D tracking of user's hands and head, view from the left and right camera

Gesture Recognition

A gesture-based interface mapping interposes a layer of pattern recognition between the input features and the application control. When an application has a
discrete control space, this mapping allows patterns in feature space, better known
as gestures, to be mapped to the discrete inputs. The set of patterns form a gesture-
language that the user must learn. To navigate through the Internet 3D city the user
stands in front of the screen and uses hand gestures. All gestures start from a rest position given by the two hands on the table in front of the body. Recognized command
gestures are (Figs. 7 and 8):

- "follow link" → "point-at-correspondent-location-on-screen"
- "go to previous location" → "point left"
- "go to next location" → "point right"

Fig. 7 Navigating gestures in City of News (user sitting)

Fig. 8 Navigating gestures in City of News at SIGGRAPH 2003 (user standing)

Fig. 9 Four state HMM used
for Gesture Recognition

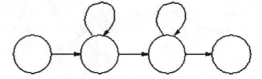

- "navigate up" → "move one hand up"
- "navigate down" → "move hands toward body"
- "show aerial view" → "move both hands up"

Gesture recognition is accomplished by HMM modeling of the navigating gestures [31] (Fig. 9). The feature vector includes velocity and position of hands and head, and blobs' shape and orientation. We use four states HMMs with two intermediate states plus the initial and final states. Entropic's Hidden Markov Model Toolkit (HTK: http://htk.eng.cam.ac.uk/) is used for training [48]. For recognition we use a real-time C++ Viterbi recognizer.

Comments

I described an example of a space which could be in a section of the living room in our home, or in the lobby of a museum, in which perceptual intelligence, modeled by computer vision and Hidden Markov Models— a particular case of a Bayesian Networks— provides the means for people to interact with a 3D world in a natural way. This is only a first step towards intelligence modeling. Typically an intelligent space would have a variety of sensors to perceive our actions in it: visual, auditory, temperature, distance range, etc. Multimodal interaction and sensor fusion will be addressed in future developments of this work.

Interpretive Intelligence: Modeling User Preferences in The Museum Space

This section addresses interpretive intelligence modeling from the user's perspective. The chosen setting is the museum space, and the goal is to identify people's interests based on how they behave in the space.

User Modeling: Motivation

In the last decade museums have been drawn into the orbit of the leisure industry and compete with other popular entertainment venues, such as cinemas or the theater, to attract families, tourists, children, students, specialists, or passersby in search of alternative and instructive entertaining experiences. Some people may go to the museum for mere curiosity, whereas others may be driven by the desire of a cultural experience. The museum visit can be an occasion for a social outing, or become an opportunity to meet new friends. While it is not possible to design an exhibit for all these categories of visitors, it is desirable for museums to attract as many people as possible. Technology today can offer exhibit designers and curators new ways to communicate more efficiently with their public, and to personalize the visit according to people's desires and expectations [38].

When walking through a museum there are so many different stories we could be told. Some of these are biographical about the author of an artwork, some are historical and allow us to comprehend the style or origin of the work, and some are specific about the artwork itself, in relationship with other artistic movements. Museums usually have large web sites with multiple links to text, photographs, and movie clips to describe their exhibits. Yet it would take hours for a visitor to explore all the information in a kiosk, to view the VHS cassette tape associated to the exhibit and read the accompanying catalogue. Most people do not have the time to devote or motivation to assimilate this type of information, therefore the visit to a museum is often remembered as a collage of first impressions produced by the prominent features of the exhibits, and the learning opportunity is missed. How can we tailor content to the visitor in a museum so as to enrich both his learning and entertaining experience? We want a system which can be personalized to be able to dynamically create and update paths through a large database of content and deliver to the user in real time during the visit all the information he/she desires. If the visitor spends a lot of time looking at a Monet, the system needs to infer that the user likes Monet and should update the narrative to take that into account. This research proposes a user modeling method and a device called the 'museum wearable' to turn this scenario into reality.

The Museum Wearable

Wearable computers have been raised to the attention of technological and scientific investigation [43] and offer an opportunity to "augment" the visitor and his perception/memory/experience of the exhibit in a personalized way. The museum wearable is a wearable computer which orchestrates an audiovisual narration as a function of the visitor's interests gathered from his/her physical path in the museum and length of stops. It offers a new type of entertaining and informative museum experience, more similar to mobile immersive cinema than to the traditional museum experience (Fig. 10).

The museum wearable [34] is made by a lightweight CPU hosted inside a small shoulder pack and a small, lightweight private-eye display. The display is a commercial monocular, VGA-resolution, color, clip-on screen attached to a pair of sturdy headphones. When wearing the display, after a few seconds of adaptation, the user's brain assembles the real world's image, seen by the unencumbered eye, with the display's image seen by the other eye, into a fused augmented reality image.

Fig. 10 The museum wearable used by museum visitors

The wearable relies on a custom-designed long-range infrared location-identification sensor to gather information on where and how long the visitor stops in the museum galleries. A custom system had to be built for this project to overcome limitations of commercially available infrared location identification systems such as short range and narrow cone of emission. The location system is made by a network of small infrared devices, which transmit a location identification code to the receiver worn by the user and attached to the display glasses [34].

The museum wearable plays out an interactive audiovisual documentary about the displayed artwork on the private-eye display. Each mini-documentary is made by small segments which vary in size from 20 seconds to one and a half minute. A video server, written in C++ and DirectX, plays these assembled clips and receives TCP/IP messages from another program containing the information measured by the location ID sensors. This server-client architecture allows the programmer to easily add other client programs to the application, such as electronic sensors or cameras placed along the museum aisles. The client program reads IR data from the serial port, and the server program does inference, content selection, and content display (Fig. 11).

The ongoing robotics exhibit at the MIT Museum provided an excellent platform for experimentation and testing with the museum wearable (Fig. 12). This exhibit, called Robots and Beyond, and curated by Janis Sacco and Beryl Rosenthal, features landmarks of MIT's contribution to the field of robotics and Artificial Intelligence. The exhibit is organized in five sections: Introduction, Sensing, Moving, Socializing, and Reasoning and Learning, each including robots, a video station, and posters with text and photographs which narrate the history of robotics at MIT. There is also a large general purpose video station with large benches for people to have a seated stop and watch a PBS documentary featuring robotics research from various academic institutions in the country.

Sensor-Driven Understanding of Visitors' Interests with Bayesian Networks

In order to deliver a dynamically changing and personalized content presentation with the museum wearable a new content authoring technique had to be designed and implemented. This called for an alternative method than the traditional com-

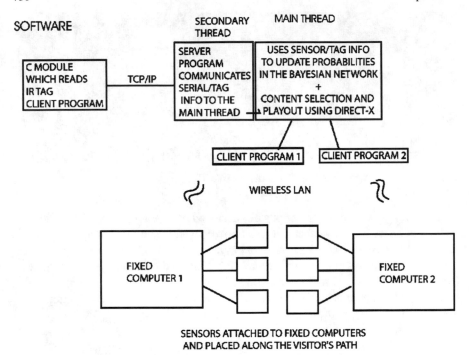

Fig. 11 Software architecture of the museum wearable

plex centralized interactive entertainment systems which simply read sensor inputs and map them to actions on the screen. Interactive storytelling with such one-to-one mappings leads to complicated control programs which have to do an accounting of all the available content, where it is located on the display, and what needs to happen when/if/unless. These systems rigidly define the interaction modality with the public, as a consequence of their internal architecture, and lead to presentations which have shallow depth of content, are hard to modify, and prone to error. The main problem with such content authoring approaches is that they acquire high complexity when drawing content from a large database, and once built, they are hard to modify or to expand upon. In addition, when they are sensor-driven they become depended on the noisy sensor measurements, which can lead to errors and misinterpretation of the user input. Rather than directly mapping inputs to outputs, the system should be able to "understand the user" and to produce an output based on the interpretation of the user's intention in context.

In accordance with the simplified museum visitor typology discussed in [34] the museum wearable identifies three main visitor types: the busy, selective, and greedy visitor type. The greedy type, wants to know and see as much as possible, and does not have a time constraint; the busy type just wants to get an overview of the principal items in the exhibit, and see little of everything; and the selective type, wants to see and know in depth only about a few preferred items. The identification of other visitor types or subtypes has been postponed to future improvements and de-

Fig. 12 The MIT robotics exhibit

velopments of this research. The visitor type estimation is obtained probabilistically with a Bayesian network using as input the information provided by the location identification sensors on where and how long the visitor stops, as if the system was an invisible storyteller following the visitor in the galleries and trying to guess his preferences based on the observation of his/her external behavior.

The system uses a Bayesian network to estimate the user's preferences taking the location identification sensor data as the input or observations of the network.

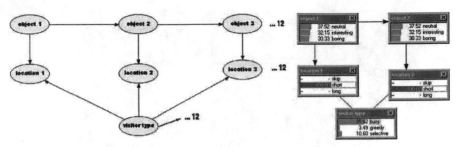

Fig. 13 Chosen Bayesian Network model to estimate the visitor type

The user model is progressively refined as the visitor progresses along the museum galleries: the model is more accurate as it gathers more observations about the user. Figure 13 shows the Bayesian network for visitor estimation, limited to three museum objects (so that the figure can fit in the document), selected from a variety of possible models designed and evaluated for this research.

Model Description, Learning and Validation

In order to set the initial values of the parameters of the Bayesian network, experimental data was gathered on the visitors' behavior at the Robots and Beyond exhibit. According to the VSA (Visitor Studies Association, http://museum.cl.msu.edu/vsa), timing and tracking observations of visitors are often used to provide an objective and quantitative account of how visitors behave and react to exhibition components. This type of observational data suggests the range of visitor behaviors occurring in an exhibition, and indicates which components attract, as well as hold, visitors' attention (in the case of a complete exhibit evaluation this data is usually accompanied by interviews with visitors, before and after the visit). During the course of several days a team of collaborators tracked and make annotations about the visitors at the MIT Museum. Each member of the tracking team had a map and a stop watch. Their task was to draw on the map the path of individual visitors, and annotate the locations at which visitors stopped, the object they were observing, and how long they would stop for. In addition to the tracking information, the team of evaluators was asked to assign a label to the overall behavior of the visitor, according to the three visitor categories earlier described: "busy", "greedy", and "selective" (Fig. 13).

A subset of 12 representative objects of the Robots and Beyond exhibit, were selected to evaluate this research, to shorten editing time (Fig. 14). The geography of the exhibit needs to be reflected into the topology of the network, as shown in Fig. 15. Additional objects/nodes of the modeling network can be added later for an actual large scale installation and further revisions of this research.

The visitor tracking data is used to learn the parameters of the Bayesian network. The model can later be refined, that is, the parameters can be fine tuned as more visitors experience the exhibit with the museum wearable. The network has been tested and validated on this observed visitor tracking data by parameter learning

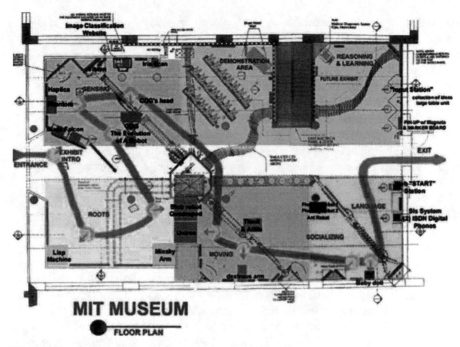

Fig. 14 Chosen Bayesian Network model to estimate the visitor type

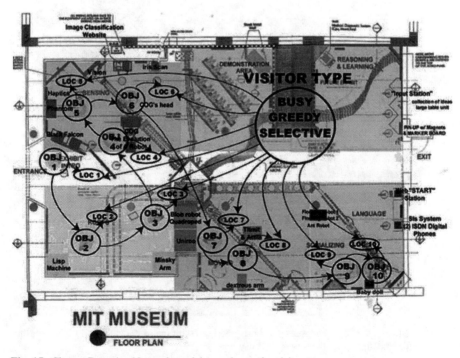

Fig. 15 Chosen Bayesian Network model to estimate the visitor type

using the Expectation Maximization (EM) algorithm, and by performance analysis of the model with the learned parameters, with a recognition rate of 0.987. More detail can be found in: Sparacino, 2003.

Figures 16, 17 and 18 show state values for the network after two time steps. To test the model, I introduced evidence on the duration nodes, thereby simulating its functioning during the museum visit. The reader can verify that the system gives plausible estimates of the visitor type, based on the evidence introduced in the system. The posterior probabilities in this and the subsequent models are calculated using Hugin, (www.hugin.com) which implements the Distribute Evidence and Collect Evidence message passing algorithms on the junction tree.

Comments

Identifying people's preferences and typologies is relevant not only for museums but also in other domains such as remote healthcare, new entertainment venues, or surveillance. Various approaches to user modeling have been proposed in the literature. The advantage of the Bayesian network modeling here described is that it can be easily integrated in a multilayer framework of space intelligence in which both the bottom perceptive layer and the top narrative layer are also modeled with the same technique. Therefore, as described above, both sensing and user typology identification can be grounded on data and can easily adapt to the behavior of people

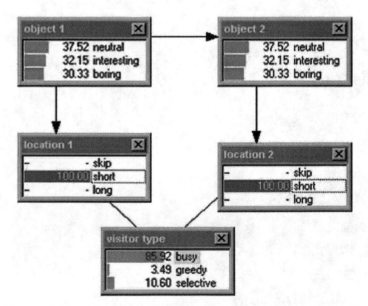

Fig. 16 Test case 1. The visitor spends a short time both with the first and second object –> the network gives the highest probability to the busy type (0.8592)

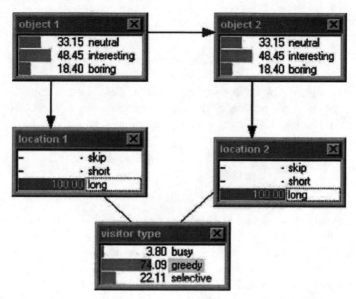

Fig. 17 Test case 2. The visitor spends a long time both with the first and second object –> the network gives the highest probability to the greedy type (0.7409)

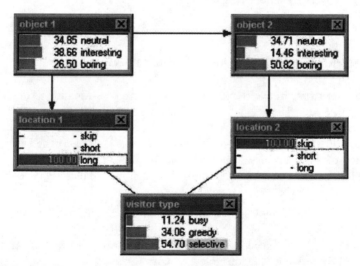

Fig. 18 Test case 3. The visitor spends a long time with the first object and skips the second object –> the network gives the highest probability to the selective type (0.5470)

in the space. This work does not explicitly address situation modeling, which is an important element of interpretive intelligence, and which is the objective of future developments of this research.

Narrative Intelligence: Sto(ry)chastics

This section presents sto(ry)chastics, a user-centered approach for computational storytelling for real-time sensor-driven multimedia audiovisual stories, such as those that are triggered by the body in motion in a sensor-instrumented interactive narrative space. With sto(ry)chastics the coarse and noisy sensor inputs are coupled to digital media outputs via a user model (see previous section), which is estimated probabilistically by a Bayesian network [35].

Narrative Intelligence: Motivation

Sto(ry)chastics, is a first step in the direction of having suitable authoring techniques for sensor-driven interactive narrative spaces. It allows the interactive experience designer to have flexible story models, decomposed in atomic or elementary units, which can be recombined into meaningful sequences at need in the course of interaction. It models both the noise intrinsic in interpreting the user's intentions as well as the noise intrinsic in telling a story. We as humans do not tell the same story in the same way all the time, and we naturally tend to adapt and modify our stories to the age/interest/role of the listener. This research also shows that Bayesian networks are a powerful mathematical tool to model noisy sensors, noisy interpretation of intention, and noisy stories.

Editing Stories for Different Visitor Types and Profiles

Sto(ry)chastics works in two steps. The first is user type estimation as described in the previous section. The next step is to assemble a mini-story for the visitor, relative to the object he/she is next to. Most of the audio-visual material available for art and science documentaries tends to fall under a set of characterizing topics. After an overview of the audio-visual material available at MIT's Robots and Beyond exhibit, the following content labels, or bins were identified to classify the component video clips:

- Description of the artwork: what it is, when it was created (answers: when, where, what)
- Biography of author: anecdotes, important people in artist's life (answers: who)
- History of the artwork: previous relevant work of the artist
- Context: historical, what is happening in the world at the time of creation
- Process: particular techniques used or invented to create the artwork (answers: how)
- Principle: philosophy or school of thought the author believes in when creating the artwork (answers: why)
- Form and Function: relevant style, form and function which contribute to explain the artwork.

– Relationships: how is the artwork related to other artwork on display
– Impact: the critics' and the public's reaction to the artwork

This project required a great amount of editing to be done by hand (non automatically) in order to segment the 2 h of video material available for the exhibit in the smallest possible complete segments. After this phase, all the component video clips were given a name, their length in seconds was recorded into the system, and they were also classified according to the list of bins described above. The classification was done probabilistically, that is each clip has been assigned a probability (a value between zero and one) of belonging to a story category. The sum of such probabilities for each clip needs to be one. The result of the clip classification procedure, for a subset of available clips, is shown in Table 1.

To perform content selection, conditioned on the knowledge of the visitor type, the system needs to be given a list of available clips, and the criteria for selection. There are two competing criteria: one is given by the total length of the edited story for each object, and the other is given by the ordering of the selected clips. The order of story segments guarantees that the curator's message is correctly passed on to the visitor, and that the story is a "good story", in that it respects basic cause-effect relationships and makes sense to humans. Therefore the Bayesian network described earlier needs to be extended with additional nodes for content selection (Figs. 19 and 20). The additional "good story" node, encodes, as prior probabilities, the curator's preferences about how the story for each object should be told. To reflect these observations the Bayesian network is extended to be an influence diagram [14]: it will include decision nodes, and utility nodes which guide decisions. The decision node contains a list of all available content (movie clips) for each object. The utility nodes encode the two selection criteria: length and order. The utility node which describes length, contains the actual length in seconds for each clip. The length is transcribed in the network as a positive number, when conditioned on a preference for long clips (greedy and selective types). It is instead a negative length if conditioned on a preference for short content segments (busy type). This is because a utility node will always try to maximize the utility, and therefore length is penalizing in the case of a preference for short content segments. The utility node which describes order, contains the profiling of each clip into the story bins described earlier, times a multiplication constant used to establish a balance of power between "length" and "order". Basically order here means a ranking of clips based on how closely they match the curator's preferences expressed in the "good story" node. By means of probability update, the Bayesian network comes up with a "compromise" between length and order and provides a final ranking of the available content segments in the order in which they should be played.

Sto(ry)chastics is adaptive in two ways: it adapts both to individual users and to the ensemble of visitors of a particular exhibit. For individuals, even if the visitor exhibits an initial "greedy" behavior, it can later adapt to the visitor's change of behavior. It is important to notice that, reasonably and appropriately, the system "changes its mind" about the user type with some inertia: i.e. it will initially lower the probability for a greedy type until other types gain probability. Sto(ry)chastics can also adapt to the collective body of its users. If a count of busy/greedy/selective

Table 1 Video segments from the documentation available for the MIT Museum's Robots and Beyond Exhibit

Categories/ Titles	Bit inside	Bit intro	Cogdrum	Cogfuture	Coghistory	Cogintro	Dex design	Dex intention	Dex intro	Dex stiffness
Length in seconds	021	090	083	043	051	041	114	034	072	096
Description, DSC	0.7	0.2	0.3	0	0	0.8	0.1	0.3	0.5	0.4
History, HST	0.1	0	0	0	0.5	0	0	0	0	0
Context, CTX	0	0	0	0	0	0	0	0	0.2	0
Biography, BIO	0.1	0.2	0	0	0.1	0	0.2	0	0	0
Process, PRC	0	0	0.6	0	0	0.2	0.3	0	0	0.2
Principle, PNC	0	0.4	0.1	1	0.2	0	0	0.2	0.1	0.4
Form and Function, FAF	0	0.2	0	0	0.2	0	0.4	0.5	0	0
Relationships, REL	0.1	0	0	0	0	0	0	0	0	0
Impact, IMP	0	0	0	0	0	0	0	0	0.2	0
Total P	1	1	1	1	1	1	1	1	1	1

All video clips have been assigned a set of probabilities which express their relevance with respect to nine selected story themes or categories

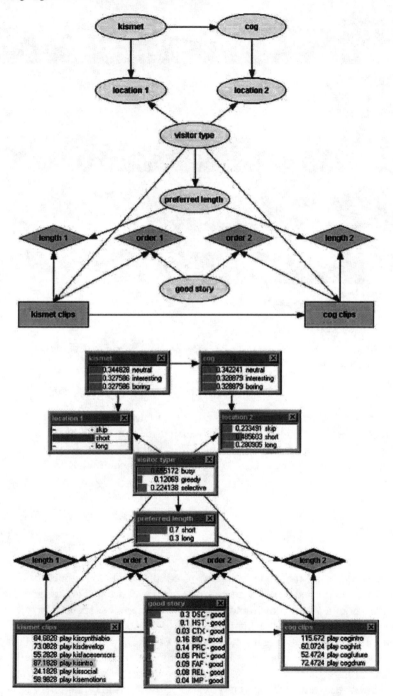

Fig. 19 Extension of the sto(ry) chastics Bayesian network to perform content selection

Cog - Greedy Type

Cog- Busy Type

It- Greedy Type

It - Busy Type

Kismet: Selective Type

Kismet: Busy Type

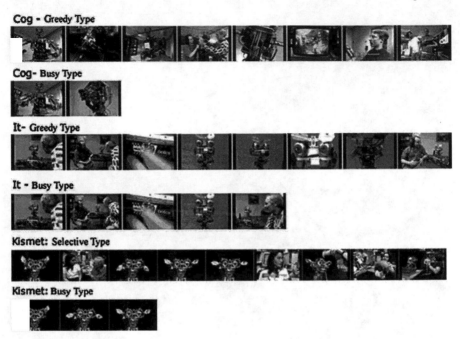

Fig. 20 Storyboards from various video clips shown on the museum wearable's display at MIT Museum's Robots and Beyond Exhibit

visitors is kept for the exhibit, these numbers can later become priors of the corresponding nodes of the network, thereby causing the entire exhibit to adapt to the collective body of its users through time. This feature can be seen as "collective intelligence" for a space which can adapt not just to the individual visitors but also to the set of its visitors.

Comments

The main contribution of this section is to show that (dynamic) Bayesian networks are a powerful modeling technique to couple inputs to outputs for real time sensor-driven multimedia audiovisual stories, such as those that are triggered by the body in motion in a sensor-instrumented interactive narrative space. Sto(ry)chastics has implications both for the human author (designer/curator) which is given a flexible modeling tool to organize, select, and deliver the story material, as well as the audience, that receives personalized content only when and where it is appropriate. Sto(ry)chastics proposes an alternative to complex centralized interactive entertainment programs which simply read sensor inputs and map them to actions on the screen. These systems rigidly define the interaction modality with the public, as a consequence of their internal architecture. Sto(ry)chastics delivers an audiovisual narration to the visitor as a function of the estimated type, interactively in time and space. The model has been tested and validated on observed visitor tracking data using the EM algorithm. The interpretation of sensor data is robust in the sense that it is probabilistically weighted by the history of interaction of the participant as well as the nodes which represent context. Therefore noisy sensor data, triggered for example by external or unpredictable sources, is not likely to cause the system to produce a response which does not "make sense" to the user.

Discussion and Conclusions

This paper presented a layered architecture of space intelligence, which the author believes is necessary to design body-driven interactive narrative spaces with robust sensing, tailored to the users' needs, able to understand context and to communicate effectively. The author proposes Bayesian Networks as a unifying framework to model perceptual intelligence, interpretive intelligence (user and context modeling), and narrative intelligence. Three applications have been presented to illustrate space intelligence: browsing a 3D virtual world with natural gestures in City of News; identifying visitors' preferences and types for museum visits assisted by mobile storytelling devices; and sto(ry)chastics a real-time content selection and delivery technique which takes into account the user profile, and measurements about his behavior in the space.

The applications here described represent incremental steps towards a full implementation of space intelligence. The work carried out so far highlighted and confirmed several advantages of the proposed Bayesian modeling technique. It is:

1. Robust: Probabilistic modeling allows the system to achieve robustness with respect to the coarse and noisy sensor data.
2. Flexible: it is possible to easily test many different scenarios by simply changing the parameters of the system.
3. Reconfigurable: it is easy to add or remove nodes and/or edges from the network without having to "start all over again" and specify all the parameters of the network from scratch. This is a considerable and important advantage with respect to hard coded or heuristic approaches to user modeling and content selection. Only the parameters of the new nodes and the nodes corresponding to the new links need to be given. The system is extensible story-wise and sensor-wise. These two properties: flexibility and ease of model reconfiguration allow for example: the system engineer, the content designer, and the exhibit curator to work together and easily and cheaply try out various solutions and possibilities until they converge to a model which satisfies all the requirements and constraints for their project. A network can also rapidly be reconfigured for other purposes.
4. Readable: Bayesian networks encode qualitative influences between variables in addition to the numerical parameters of the probability distribution. As such they provide an ideal form for combining prior knowledge and data. By using graphs, it not only becomes easy to encode the probability independence relations

amongst variables of the network, but it is also easy to communicate and explain what the network attempts to model. Graphs are easy for humans to read, and they help focus attention, especially when a group of people with different backgrounds works together to build a new system. In this context for example, this allows the digital architect, or the engineer, to communicate on the same ground (the graph of the model) with the museum exhibit curator and therefore to be able to encapsulate the curator's domain knowledge in the network, together with the sensor data.

Future work will conduct further testing of the proposed intelligence model in a more complex space that requires the use of multiple sensors and sensor modalities to observe the behavior of people in it.

References

1. Albrecht DW, Zukerman I, Nicholson AE, Bud A (1997) Towards a bayesian model for keyhole plan recognition in large domains. In: Jameson A, Paris C, Tasso C (eds) Proceedings of the Sixth International Conference on User Modeling (UM '97). Springer, pp 365–376
2. Azarbayejani A, Pentland A (1996) Real-time self-calibrating stereo person tracking using 3-D shape estimation from blob features. In: Proceedings of the 13th ICPR. Vienna, Austria
3. Azarbayejani A, Wren C, Pentland A (1996) Real-Time 3-D Tracking of the Human Body. In: Proceedings of IMAGE'COM 96, Bordeaux, France, May
4. Brainard DH, Freeman WT (1997) Bayesian color constancy. J Opt Soc Am, A 14(7): 1393–1411 July
5. Brand M, Oliver N, Pentland A (1997) Coupled hidden Markov models for complex action recognition. In: Proceedings of IEEE Conference on Computer Vision and Pattern Recognition (CVPR). Puerto Rico, pp 994–999
6. Brooks RA, Coen M, Dang D, DeBonet J, Kramer J, Lozano-Perez T, Mellor J, Pook P, Stauffer C, Stein L, Torrance M, Wessler M (1997) The intelligent room project. In: Proceedings of the Second International Cognitive Technology Conference (CT'97). Aizu, Japan, pp 271–279
7. Brumitt B, Meyers B, Krumm J, Kern A, Shafer S (2000) EasyLiving: Technologies for intelligent environments. In: Proceedings of Second International Symposium on Handheld and Ubiquitous Computing (HUC 2000), September
8. Campbell LW, Becker DA, Azarbayejani A, Bobick A, Pentland A (1996) Invariant features for 3-D gesture recognition. In: Proceedings of IEEE International Conference on Automatic Face and Gesture Recognition, Killington, Vermont, USA
9. Cohen M (1998) Design principles for intelligent environments. In: Proceedings of the Fifteenth National Conference on Artificial Intelligence (AAAI'98), Madison, WI
10. Conati C, Gertner A, VanLehn K, Druzdzel M (1997) On-line student modeling for coached problem solving using Bayesian networks. In: Proceedings of 6th International Conference on User Modeling (UM97), 1997. Chia Laguna, Sardinia, Italy
11. Emiliani PL, Stephanidis C (2005) Universal access to ambient intelligence environments: opportunities and challenges for people with disabilities. IBM Syst J 44(3):605–619
12. Hanssens N, Kulkarni A, Tuchinda R, Horton T (2005) Building agent-based intelligent workspaces. In: Proceedings of the 3rd International Conference on Internet Computing, pp 675–681
13. Heckerman D (1990) Probabilistic similarity networks. Technical Report, STAN-CS-1316, Depts. of Computer Science and Medicine, Stanford University

14. Howard RA, Matheson JE (1981) Influence diagrams. In: Howard RA, Matheson JE (eds) Applications of decision analysis, volume 2. pp 721–762
15. Jameson A (1996) Numerical uncertainty management in user and student modeling: an overview of systems and issues. User Model User-Adapt Interact 5:193–251
16. Jebara T, Pentland A (1998) Action reaction learning: analysis and synthesis of human behaviour. IEEE Workshop on The Interpretation of Visual Motion at the Conference on Computer Vision and Pattern Recognition, CVPR, June
17. Jensen FV (1996) An Introduction to Bayesian Networks. UCL Press
18. Jensen FV (2001) Bayesian networks and decision graphs. Springer-Verlag, New York
19. Johanson B, Fox A, Winograd T (2002) The interactive workspaces project: experiences with ubiquitous computing rooms. IEEE Perv Comput Mag 1(2), April-June
20. Jojic N, Brumitt B, Meyers B, et al (2000) Detection and estimation of pointing gestures in dense disparity maps. In: Proceedings of Fourth IEEE International Conference on Automatic Face and Gesture Recognition
21. Jordan MI (1999) (ed) Learning in graphical models. The MIT Press
22. Kidd C (1999) The aware home: a living laboratory for ubiquitous computing research. In: Proceedings of the Second International Workshop on Cooperative Buildings – CoBuild'99, October
23. Koller D, Pfeffer A (1998) Probabilistic frame-based systems. In: Proceedings of the Fifteenth National Conference on Artificial Intelligence, Madison, Wisconsin, July
24. Krumm J, Shafer S, Wilson A (2001) How a smart environment can use perception. In: Workshop on Sensing and Perception for Ubiquitous Computing (part of UbiComp 2001), September
25. Nefian A, Liang L, Pi X, Liu X, Murphy K (2002) Dynamic Bayesian networks for audio-visual speech recognition. EURASIP, J Appl Signal Process 11:1–15
26. Pavlovic V, Rehg J, Cham TJ, Murphy K (1999) A dynamic Bayesian network approach to figure tracking using learned dynamic models. In: Proceedings of Int'l Conf. on Computer Vision (ICCV)
27. Pavlovic VI, Sharma R, Huang TS (1997) Visual interpretation of hand gestures for human-computer interaction: a review. IEEE Trans Pattern Anal Mach Intell, PAMI 19(7):677–695
28. Pearl J (1988) Probabilistic reasoning in intelligent systems: networks of plausible inference. Morgan Kaufmann, San Mateo, CA
29. Pentland A (1998) Smart room, smart clothes. In: Proceedings of the Fourteenth International Conference On Pattern Recognition, ICPR'98, Brisbane, Australia, August 16–20
30. Pynadath DV, Wellman MP (1995) Accounting for context in plan recognition, with application to traffic monitoring. In: Proceedings of the Eleventh Conference on Uncertainty in Artificial Intelligence, UAI, Morgan Kaufmann, San Francisco, 1995, pp 472–481
31. Rabiner LR, Juang BH (1986) An introduction to hidden Markov Models. IEEE ASSP Mag pp 4–15, January
32. Smyth P (1998) Belief networks, hidden Markov models, and Markov random fields: a unifying view. Pattern Recogn Lett
33. Sparacino F (2001) (Some) computer vision based interfaces for interactive art and entertainment installations. In: INTER_FACE Body Boundaries, issue editor: Emanuele Quinz, Anomalie n. 2, Paris, France, Anomos
34. Sparacino F (2002a) The Museum Wearable: real-time sensor-driven understanding of visitors' interests for personalized visually-augmented museum experiences. In: Proceedings of Museums and the Web (MW2002), April 17–20, Boston
35. Sparacino F (2003) Sto(ry)chastics: a Bayesian Network Architecture for User Modeling and Computational Storytelling for Interactive Spaces. In: Proceedings of Ubicomp, The Fifth International Conference on Ubiquitous Computing, Seattle, WA, USA
36. Sparacino F (2004) Museum Intelligence: Using Interactive Technologies For Effective Communication And Storytelling In The Puccini Set Designer Exhibit." In: Proceedings of ICHIM 2004, Berlin, Germany, August 31-September 2nd

37. Sparacino F, Davenport G, Pentland A (2000) Media in performance: Interactive spaces for dance, theater, circus, and museum exhibits. IBM Syst J 39(3 & 4):479–510 Issue Order No. G321-0139
38. Sparacino F, Larson K, MacNeil R, Davenport G, Pentland A (1999) Technologies and methods for interactive exhibit design: from wireless object and body tracking to wearable computers. In: Proceedings of International Conference on Hypertext and Interactive Museums, ICHIM 99. Washington, DC, Sept. 22–26
39. Sparacino F, Pentland A, Davenport G, Hlavac M, Obelnicki M (1997) City of news. Proceedings of the: Ars Electronica Festival, Linz, Austria, 8–13 September
40. Sparacino F, Wren C, Azarbayejani A, Pentland A (2002b) Browsing 3-D spaces with 3-D vision: body-driven navigation through the Internet city. In: Proceedings of 3DPVT: 1st International Symposium on 3D Data Processing Visualization and Transmission, Padova, Italy, June 19–21
41. Sparacino F, Wren CR, Pentland A, Davenport G (1995) HyperPlex: a World of 3D interactive digital movies. In: IJCAI'95 Workshop on Entertainment and AI/Alife, Montreal, August
42. Starner T, Pentland A (1995) Visual Recognition of American Sign Language Using Hidden Markov Models. In: Proc. of International Workshop on Automatic Face and Gesture Recognition (IWAFGR 95). Zurich, Switzerland
43. Starner T, Mann S, Rhodes B, Levine J, Healey J, Kirsch D, Picard R, Pentland A (1997) Augmented reality through wearable computing. Presence 6(4):386–398 August
44. Wren C, Basu S, Sparacino F, Pentland A (1999) Combining audio and video in perceptive spaces. In: Managing Interactions in Smart Environments (MANSE 99), Trinity College Dublin, Ireland, December 13–14
45. Wren CR, Sparacino F et al (1996) Perceptive spaces for performance and entertainment: untethered interaction using computer vision and audition. Appl Artif Intell (AAI) J, June
46. Wren C, Azarbayejani A, Darrell T, Pentland A (1997) Pfinder: real-time tracking of the human body. IEEE Trans Pattern Anal Mach Intell PAMI 19(7):780–785
47. Wu Y, Huang TS (2001) Human hand modeling, analysis and animation in the context of human computer interaction. In: IEEE Signal Processing Magazine, Special Issue on Immersive Interactive Technology, May
48. Young SJ, Woodland PC, Byme WJ (1993) HTK: Hidden Markov model toolkit. V1.5. Entropic Research Laboratories Inc

Chapter 33
Mass Personalization: Social and Interactive Applications Using Sound-Track Identification

Michael Fink, Michele Covell, and Shumeet Baluja

Introduction

Mass media *is the term used to denote, as a class, that section of the media specifically conceived and designed to reach a very large audience... forming a mass society with special characteristics, notably atomization or lack of social connections* (en. wikipedia.org).

These characteristics of mass media contrast sharply with the World Wide Web. Mass-media channels typically provide limited content to many people; the Web provides vast amounts of information, most of interest to few. Mass-media channels are typically consumed in a largely anonymous, passive manner, while the Web provides many interactive opportunities like chatting, emailing and trading. Our goal is to combine the best of both worlds: integrating the relaxing and effortless experience of mass-media content with the interactive and personalized potential of the Web, providing *mass personalization*.

Upon request, our system tests whether the user's ambient audio matches a known mass-media channel. If a match is found the user is provided with services and related content originating from the Web. As shown in Fig. 1, our system consists of three distinct components: a client-side interface, an audio-database server (with mass-media audio statistics), and a social-application web server. The client-side interface samples and *irreversibly* compresses the viewer's ambient audio to summary statistics. These statistics are streamed from the viewer's personal computer to the audio-database server for identification of the background audio (e.g., 'Seinfeld' episode 6,101, minute 3:03). The audio database transmits this

M. Fink (✉)
Center for Neural Computation, The Hebrew University of Jerusalem, Jerusalem 91904, Israel
e-mail: fink@cs.huji.ac.il

M. Covell and S. Baluja
Google Research, Google Inc., 1600 Amphitheatre Parkway, Mountain View, CA 94043, USA
e-mail: covell@google.com; shumeet@google.com

B. Furht (ed.), *Handbook of Multimedia for Digital Entertainment and Arts*,
DOI 10.1007/978-0-387-89024-1_33, © Springer Science+Business Media, LLC 2009

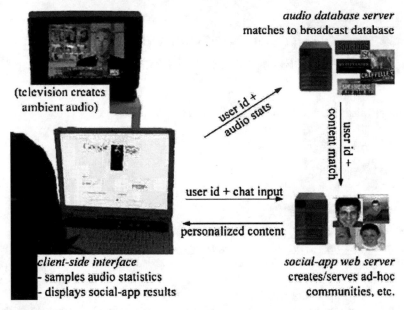

Fig. 1 Flow chart of the mass-personalization applications

information to the social-application server, which provides personalized and interactive content back to the viewer. Continuing with the previous example, if friends
of the viewer were watching the same episode of 'Seinfeld' at the same time, the
social-application server could automatically create an on-line ad hoc community
of these "buddies". This community allows members to comment on the broadcast
material in real time.

Although we apply our techniques to television, we do not use the visual channel as our data source. Instead, we use audio for three pragmatic reasons. First,
with visual data, the viewer must either have a TV-tuner card installed in her laptop
(which is rare), or have a camera pointed towards the TV screen (which is cumbersome). In contrast, non-directional microphones are built into most laptops and
shipped with most desktops. Second, audio recording does not require the careful
normalization and calibration needed for video sources (camera alignment, image
registration, *etc.*). Third, processing audio is less computational demanding than
processing video, due to lower input-data rates. This is especially important since
we process the raw data on the client's machine (for privacy reasons), and attempt
to keep computation requirements at a minimum.

Personalizing Broadcast Content: Four Applications

In this section, we describe four applications to make television more personalized, interactive and social. These applications are: personalized information layers, ad hoc social peer communities, real-time popularity ratings, and TV-based bookmarks.

Personalized Information Layers

The first application provides information that is complementary to the mass-media channel (e.g., television or radio) in an effortless manner. As with proactive software agents [11], we provide additional layers of related information, such as fashion, politics, business, health, or traveling. For example, while watching a news segment on Tom Cruise, a fashion layer might provide information on what designer clothes and accessories the presented celebrities are wearing (see "wH@T's Layers" in Figs. 2 and 3).

The feasibility of providing the complementary layers of information is related to the cost of annotating the database of mass-media content and the number of times any given piece of content is retransmitted. We evaluated how often content is retransmitted for the ground-truth data used in Section "Evaluation of System Performance" and found that up to 50% (for CNN Headlines) of the content was retransmitted within 4 days, with higher rates expected for longer time windows. Thus, if 'Seinfeld' is annotated once, years of reruns would benefit from relevant information layers. Interestingly, a channel like MTV (VH-1), where content is often repeated, has internally introduced the concept of pop-ups that accompany music clips and provide additional entertaining information. The concept of complementary information has passed the feasibility test, at least in the music–video domain.

In textual searches, complementary information providing relevant products and services is often associated via a bidding process (e.g., sponsored links on Web search sites such as Google.com). A similar procedure could be adapted to mass-personalization applications. Thus, content providers or advertisers might bid for specific television segments. For example, local theaters or DVD rental stores might bid on audio from a movie trailer (see "Sponsored Links" in the center right panels of Figs. 2 and 3).

In many mass-media channels, textual information (closed captioning) accompanies the audio stream. In these cases, the closed captions provide keywords useful for searching for related material. The search results can be combined with a viewer's personal profile and preferences (ZIP code and 'fashion') in order to display a web-page with content automatically obtained from web-pages or advertisement repositories using the extracted keywords. A method for implementing this process was described by Henzinger et al. [5].

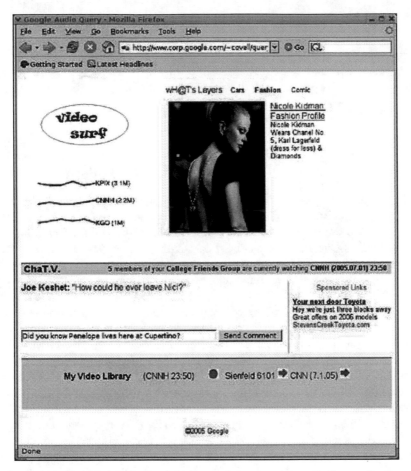

Fig. 2 An interface showing the dynamic output of the mass-personalization applications during a CNN documentary on actor Tom Cruise. Personalized information layers are shown as "wh@t's h@t Layers" (*top*) and as sponsored links (*right-side middle*). Ad-hoc chat is shown under "ChaT.V." (*left-side middle*). Real-time popularity ratings are presented as *line graphs* (*left top*) and Video bookmarks are under "My Video Library" (*bottom*). The material that is presented to the viewer is driven both by the broadcast program to which she is listening (as determined by the ambient audio identification) and by an interest profile she might provide

In the output of our prototype system, shown in the top right panels of Figs. 2 and 3, we hand labeled the content indices corresponding to an hour of footage that was taped and replayed. This annotation provided short summaries and associated URLs for the fashion preferences of celebrities appearing on the TV screen during each 5-s segment. While we did this summarization manually within our experiment, automatic summarization technologies [8] could be used to facilitate this process and bidding techniques could be used in a production system to provide related ads.

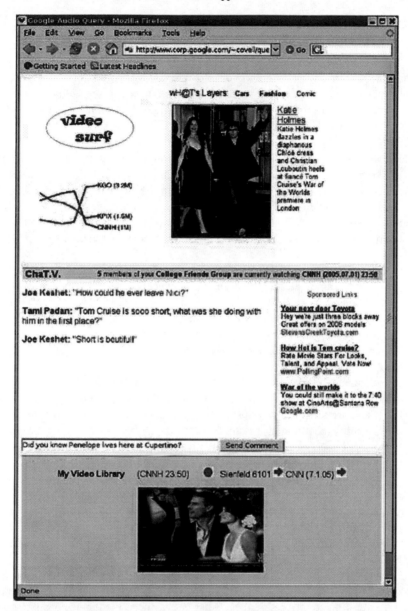

Fig. 3 As the documentary progresses, the information on the dynamic webpage is automatically updated. The Personalized information layers and the sponsored links now show new custom tailored content. Additional chat comments are delivered in real time and the current show's popularity ratings are continuously revised

Ad-hoc Peer Communities

As evidenced by the popularity of message boards relating to TV shows and current events, people often want to comment on the content of mass-media broadcasts. However, it is difficult to know with whom to chat *during* the actual broadcast. The second application provides a real time venue for commentary, an ad hoc social community.

This ad hoc community includes viewers watching the same show on TV. We create this community from the set of viewers whose audio statistics matched the same content in our audio database. These viewers are automatically linked by the social-application server. Thus, a viewer who is watching the latest CNN headlines can chat, comment on, or read other people's responses to the ongoing broadcast. The group members can be further constrained to contain only people in the viewer's social network (i.e., on-line friend community) or to contain established experts on the topic.

Importantly, as the viewer's television context changes (by changing channels) a resampling of the ambient audio can guarantee that the relevant community is automatically updated as well. The viewer need never indicate what program is being watched; this is particularly helpful for the viewer who changes channels often, and is not aware of which show or channel she is currently watching.

This service provides a *commenting medium* (chat room, message board, wiki page or video link) where responses of other viewers that are currently watching the same channel can be shared (see "ChaT.V." in the center left panels of Figs. 2 and 3). While the Personalized Information Layers allow only limited response from the viewer and are effectively scripted prior to broadcast according to annotations or auction results, the content presented within the peer community application is created by ongoing collaborative (or combative) community responses.

As an extension, these chat sessions also have an interesting intersection with Personalized Information Layers. Program-specific chat sessions can be replayed synchronously with the program during reruns of that content, giving the viewer of this later showing access to the comments of previous viewers, *with the correct timing* relative to the program content. Additionally, these chat sessions are automatically synchronized even when the viewer pauses, rewinds or fast-forwards the program.

To enable this application, the social-application server simply maintains a list of viewers currently 'listening to' similar audio, with further restrictions as indicated by the viewer's personal preferences. Alternately, these personalized chat rooms can self assemble by matching viewers with shared historical viewing preferences (e.g., daily viewings of 'Star Trek'), as is commonly done in "collaborative filtering" applications [10].

Real-time Popularity Ratings

Popularity ratings of broadcasting events are of interest to viewers, broadcasters, and advertisers. These needs are partially filled by measurement systems like the Nielsen ratings. However, these ratings require dedicated hardware installation and tedious cooperation from the participating individuals. The third application is aimed at providing ratings information (similar to Nielsen's systems) but with low latency, easy adoption, and for presentation to the viewers as well as the content providers. For example, a viewer can instantaneously be provided with a real time popularity rating of which channels are being watched by her social network or alternatively by people with similar demographics (see ratings graphs in top left panels of Figs. 2 and 3).

Given the matching system described to this point, the popularity ratings are easily derived by simply maintaining counters on each of the shows being monitored. The counters can be intersected with demographic group data or geographic group data.

Having real-time, fine-grain ratings is often more valuable than ratings achieved by the Nielsen system. Real-time ratings can be used by viewers to "see what's hot" while it is still ongoing (for example, by noticing an increased rating during the 2004 Super Bowl half-time). They can be used by advertisers and content providers to *dynamically* adjust what material is being shown to respond to drops in viewership. This is especially true for ads: the unit length is short and unpopular ads are easily replaced by other versions from the same campaign, in response to viewer rating levels [3].

Video "Bookmarks"

Television broadcasters, such as CBS and NBC, are starting to allow content to be (re-) viewed on demand, for a fee, over other channels (e.g., iPoD video downloads or video streaming), allowing viewers to create personalized libraries of their favorite broadcast content [9]. The fourth application provides a low-effort way to create these video libraries.

When a viewer sees a segment of interest on TV, she simply presses a button on her client machine, to "bookmark" that point in that broadcast. The program identity and temporal index into that content can be saved using Synchronized Multimedia Integration Language (SMIL) [1]. Using the SMIL format has the advantage of being standardized across many platforms, allowing for freer distribution without compromising the rights of the copyright owners.

The program identity can be indicated using a pointer to the redistribution service the content owner requests. Alternatively, due to its compact representation, the actual identifying fingerprint could be written directly into the SMIL file. This SMIL-encoded bookmark can either be used to retrieve the entire program, a segment of the program as determined by the content owner (for example from the beginning of a scene or news-story), or simply the exact portion of the program from which the fingerprint was created. As with other bookmarks, the reference can then easily be shared with friends or saved for future personal retrieval.

Figure 2 shows an example of the selection interface under "My Video Library" at the bottom of the second screen shot. The red "record" button adds the current program episode to her favorites-library. Two video bookmarks are shown as green "play" buttons, with the program name and record date attached.

As an added benefit, the start time for the bookmarked data can be adjusted to allow for the delay inherent in the viewer's reaction time. If the "record" button was pressed a minute or so after the start of a new segment, the content owner can provide index for the start of the segment as the "in" edit point saved in the SMIL file, with the exact time at which the viewer pressed the record button being saved as the first "seek point" (in case that really was the time she wanted).

The program material associated with the bookmarks can be viewed-on-demand through a Web-based streaming application, among other access methods, according to the policies set by the content owner. Depending on these policies, the streaming service can provide free single-viewing playback, collect payments as the agent for the content owners, or insert advertisements that would provide payment to the content owners.

Supporting Infrastructure

The four applications described in the previous section share the same client-side and audio-database components and differ only in what information is collected and presented by the social-application server. We describe these common components in this section. We also provide a brief description of how these were implemented in our test setup.

Client-Interface Setup

The client-side setup uses a laptop (or desktop) to (1) sample the ambient audio, (2) irreversibly convert short segments of that audio into distinctive and robust summary statistics, and (3) transmit these summary statistics in real-time to the audio database server.

We used a version of the audio-fingerprinting software created by Ke et al. [7] to provide these conversions. The transmitted audio statistics also include a unique identifier for the client machine to ensure that the correct content-to-client mapping is made by the social-application server. The client software continually records 5-s audio segments and converts each snippet to 415 frames of 32-bit descriptors, according to the method described in Section "Audio Fingerprinting". The descriptors, not the audio itself, are sent to the audio server. By sending only summary statistics, the viewer's acoustic privacy is maintained, since the highly compressive many-to-one mapping from audio to statistics is not invertible.

Although a variety of setups are possible, for our experiments, we used an Apple iBook laptop as the client computer and its built-in microphone for sampling the viewer's ambient audio.

Audio-Database Server Setup

The audio-database server accepts audio statistics (associated with the client id) and compares those received "fingerprints" to its database of recent broadcast media. It then sends the best-match information, along with a match confidence and the client id, to the social-application server.

In order to perform its function, the audio-database server must have access to a database of broadcast audio data. However, the actual audio stream does not need to be stored. Instead, only the compressed representations (32-bit descriptors) are saved. This allows as much as a year of broadcast fingerprints to be stored in 11 GB of memory, uncompressed, or (due to the redundant temporal structure) in about 1 GB of memory with compression.

The audio database was implemented on a single-processor, 3.4 GHz Pentium 4 workstation, with 3 GB of memory. The audio-database server received a query from the viewer every 5 s. As will be described in Section "Audio Fingerprinting", each 5-s query was independently matched against the database.

Social-Application Server Setup

The final component is the social-application server. The social-application server accepts web-browser connections (associated with client computers). Using the content-match results provided by the audio-database server, the social-application server collects personalized content for each viewer and presents that content using an open web browser on the client machine. This personalized content can include the material presented earlier: ads, information layers, popularity information, video "book marking" capabilities, and links to broadcast-related chat rooms and ad-hoc social communities.

For simplicity, in our experiments, the social-application server was set up on the same workstation as the audio-database server. The social-application server receives the viewer/content-index matching information, with the confidence score, originating from the audio-database server. The social-application server also maintains client-session-specific state information, such as:

1. The current and previous match values and their confidence
2. A viewer preference profile (if available)
3. Recently presented chat messages (to provide conversational context)
4. Previously viewed content (to avoid repetition)

With this information, it dynamically creates web pages for each client session, which include the personalized information derived from the viewer profile and her audio-match content.

Audio Fingerprinting

The main challenge for our system is to accurately match an audio query to a large database of audio snippets, in real-time and with low latency. High accuracy requires discriminative audio representations that are resistant to the distortions introduced by compression, broadcasting and client recording. This paper adapts the music-identification system proposed by Ke et al. [7] to handle TV audio data and queries. Other audio identification systems are also applicable (e.g., [13]) but the system by Ke et al. [7] has the advantage of being compact, efficient, and non-proprietary (allowing reproduction of results).

The audio-identification system starts by decomposing each query snippet (e.g., 5-s of recorded audio) into overlapping frames spaced roughly 12 ms apart. Each frame is converted into a highly discriminative 32-bit descriptor, specifically trained to overcome typical audio noise and distortion. These identifying statistics are sent to a server, where they are matched to a database of statistics taken from mass-media clips. The returned hits define the candidate list from the database. These candidates are evaluated using a first-order hidden Markov model, which provides high scores to candidate sequences that are temporally consistent with the query snippet. If the consistency score is sufficiently high, the database snippet is returned as a match. The next two subsections provide a description of the main components of the method.

Hashing Descriptors

Ke et al. [7] used a powerful machine learning technique, called *boosting*, to find highly discriminative, compact statistics for audio. Their procedure trained on la-beled pairs of positive examples (where q and x are noisy versions of the same audio) and negative examples (q and x are from different audio). During this train-ing phase, boosting uses the labeled pairs to select a combination of 32 filters and thresholds that jointly create a highly discriminative statistic. The filters localize changes in the spectrogram magnitude, using first- and second-order differences across time and frequency (see Fig. 4). One benefit of using these simple difference filters is that they can be calculated efficiently using the integral image technique suggested by Viola and Jones [14].

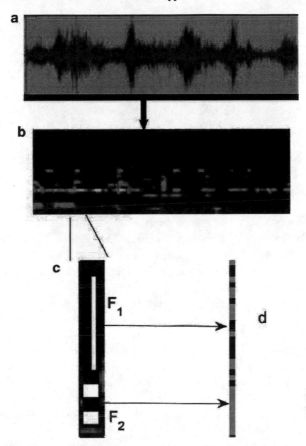

Fig. 4 Audio (**a**) is converted into a spectrogram (**b**). The spectrogram frames (**c**) are processed by 32 contrast filters and thresholded to produce a 32-bit descriptor (**d**). Contrast filters subtract neighboring rectangular spectrogram regions (*whiteregions – blackregions*), and can be calculated using the integral-image technique. Also see Ke et al.: http://www.cs.cmu.edu/~yke/musicretrieval

   The outputs of these filters are thresholded, giving *a single bit per filter* at each audio frame. These 32 threshold results form the only transmitted description of that frame of audio. This sparseness in encoding ensures the privacy of the viewer to unauthorized eavesdropping.

   The 32-bit descriptor itself is then used as a key for direct hashing. The boosting procedure generates a descriptor that is a well-balanced hash function. Retrieval rates are further improved by querying not only the query descriptor itself, but also a small set of similar descriptors (up to a hamming distance of two). Since the 32-bit output statistics are robust to the audio distortions in the training data, positive examples (matching frames) have small hamming distances (distance measuring differing number of bits) and negative examples (mismatched frames) have large hamming distances.

Within-Query Consistency

Once the query frames are individually matched to the audio database, using the efficient hashing procedure, the potential matches are validated. Simply counting the number of frame matches is inadequate, since a database snippet might have many frames matched to the query snippet but with completely wrong temporal structure.

To insure temporal consistency, each hit is viewed as support for a match at a specific query-to-database offset. For example, if the eighth descriptor (q_8) in the 5-s, 415-frame-long 'Seinfeld' query snippet, q, hits the 1,008th database descriptor ($x_{1,008}$), this supports a candidate match between the 5-s query and frames 1,001 through 1,415 in the database. Other matches mapping q_n to $x_{1,000+n}$ ($1 \leq n \leq 415$) would support this same candidate match.

In addition to temporal consistency, we need to account for frames when conversations temporarily drown out the ambient audio. We use the model of interference from [7]: that is, as an exclusive switch between ambient audio and interfering sounds. For each query frame i, there is a hidden variable, y_i: if $y_i = 0$, the ith frame of the query is modeled as interference only; if $y_i = 1$, the ith frame is modeled as from clean ambient audio. Taking this extreme view (pure ambient or pure interference) is justified by the extremely low precision with which each audio frame is represented (32 bits) and is softened by providing additional bit-flip probabilities for each of the 32 positions of the frame vector under each of the two hypotheses ($y_i = 0$ and $y_i = 1$). Finally, the frame transitions between ambient-only and interference-only states are treated as a hidden first-order Markov process, with transition probabilities derived from training data. We re-used the 66-parameter probability model given by Ke et al. [7].

In summary, the final model of the match probability between a query vector, q, and an ambient-database vector with an offset of N frames, x^N, is:

$$P\left(q \mid x^N\right) = \prod_{n=1}^{415} P\left(\langle q_n, x_{N+n} \rangle \mid y_n\right) P\left(y_n \mid y_{n-1}\right),$$

where $< q_n, x_m >$ denotes the bit differences between the two 32-bit frame vectors q_n and x_m. This model incorporates both the temporal consistency constraint and the ambient/interference hidden Markov model.

Post-Match Consistency Filtering

People often talk with others while watching television, resulting in sporadic yet strong acoustic interference, especially when using laptop-based microphones for sampling the ambient audio. Given that most conversational utterances are 2–3 s in duration [2], a simple exchange might render a 5-s query unrecognizable.

To handle these intermittent low-confidence mismatches, we use post-match filtering. We use a continuous-time hidden Markov model of channel switching with an expected dwell time (i.e. time between channel changes) of L seconds. The social-application server indicates the highest-confidence match within the recent past (along with its "discounted" confidence) as part of the state information associated with each client session. Using this information, the server selects either the content-index match from the recent past or the current index match, based on whichever has the higher confidence.

We use M_h and C_h to refer to the best match for the previous time step (5 s ago) and its respective log-likelihood confidence score. If we simply apply the Markov model to this previous best match, without taking another observation, then our *expectation* is that the best match for the current time is that same program sequence, just 5 s further along, and our confidence in this expectation is $C_h - l/L$ where $l = 5$ s is the query time step. This discount of l/L in the log likelihood corresponds to the Markov model probability, $e^{-l/L}$, of not switching channels during the l-length time step.

An alternative hypothesis is generated by the audio match for the *current* query. We use M_0 to refer to the best match for the current audio snippet: that is, the match that is generated by the audio fingerprinting software. C_0 is the log-likelihood confidence score given by the audio fingerprinting process.

If these two matches (the updated historical expectation and the current snippet observation) give different matches, we select the hypothesis with the higher confidence score:

$$\{M_0, C_0\} = \begin{cases} \{M_h, C_h - l/L\} & \text{if } C_h - l/L > C_0 \\ \{M_0, C_0\} & \text{otherwise} \end{cases}$$

where M_0 is the match that is used by the social-application server for selecting related content and M_0 and C_0 are carried forward on to the next time step as M_h and C_h.

Evaluation of System Performance

In this section, we provide a quantitative evaluation of the ambient-audio identification system. The first set of experiments provides in-depth results with our matching system. The second set of results provides an overview of the performance of an integrated system running in a live environment.

Empirical Evaluation

Here, we examine the performance of our audio-matching system in detail. We ran a series of experiments using 4 days of video footage. The footage was captured from 3 days of one broadcast station and 1 day from a different station. We jack-knifed this data to provide disjoint query/database sets: whenever we used a query to probe the database, we removed the minute that contained that query audio from consideration. In this way, we were able to test 4 days of queries against 4 days (minus 1 min) of data.

We hand labeled the 4 days of video, marking the repeated material. This included most advertisements (1,348 min worth), but omitted the 12.5% of the advertisements that were aired only once during this four-day sample. The marked material also included repeated programs (487 min worth), such as repeated news programs or repeated segments within a program (e.g., repeated showings of the same footage on a home-video rating program). We also marked as repeats those segments within a single program (e.g., the movie "Treasure Island") where the only sounds were theme music and the repetitions were indistinguishable to a human listener, even if the visual track was distinct. This typically occurred during the start and end credits of movies or series programs and during news programs which replayed sound bites with different graphics.

We did *not* label as repeats: similar sounding music that occurred in different programs (e.g., the suspense music during "Harry Potter" and random soap operas) or silence periods (e.g., between segments, within some suspenseful scenes).

Table 1 shows our results from this experiment, under "clean" acoustic conditions, using 5- and 10-s query snippets. Under these "clean" conditions, we jack-knifed the captured broadcast audio without added interference. We found that most of the false positive results on the 5-s snippets were during silence periods, during suspense-setting music (which tended to have sustained minor cords and little other structure).

To examine the performance under noisy conditions, we compare these results to those obtained from audio that includes a competing conversation. We used a 4.5-s dialog, taken from Kaplan's TOEFL material [12].[1] We scaled this dialog and mixed it into each query snippet. This resulted in 1/2 and 51/2 s of each 5- and

Table 1 Performance results of 5- and 10-s queries operating against 4 days of mass media

| | Query quality/length | | | |
| | Clean | | Noisy | |
	5 s	10 s	5 s	10 s
False-positive rate	6.4%	4.7%	1.1%	2.7%
False-negative rate	6.3%	6.0%	83%	10%
Precision	87%	90%	88%	94%
Recall	94%	94%	17%	90%

False-positive rate=FP/(TN+FP); False-negative rate=FN/(TP+FN); Precision=TP/(TP+FP);
Recall=TP/(TP+FN)

---

[1] The dialog was: *(woman's voice)* "Do you think I could borrow ten dollars until Thursday?," *(man's voice)* "Why not, it's no big deal."

10-s query being *uncorrupted* by competing noise. The perceived sound level of the interference was roughly matched to that of the broadcast audio, giving an interference-peak-amplitude four times larger than the peak amplitude of the broadcast audio, due to the richer acoustic structure of the broadcast audio.

The results reported in Table 1 under "noisy" show similar performance levels to those observed in our experiments reported in Subsection "In-Living-Room" Experiments. The improvement in precision (that is, the drop in false positive rate from that seen under "clean" conditions) is a result of the interfering sounds preventing incorrect matches between silent portions of the broadcast audio.

Due to the manner in which we constructed these examples, longer query lengths correspond to more sporadic discussion, since the competing discussion is active about half the time, with short bursts corresponding to each conversational exchange. It is this type of sporadic discussion that we actually observed in our "in-living-room" experiments (described in the next section). Using these longer query lengths, our recall rate returns to near the rate seen for the interference-free version.

"In-Living-Room" Experiments

Television viewing generally occurs in one of three distinct physical configurations: remote viewing, solo seated viewing, and partnered seated viewing. We used the system described in Section "Supporting Infrastructure" in a complete end-to-end matching system within a "real" living-space environment, using a partnered seated configuration. We chose this configuration since it is the most challenging, acoustically.

Remote viewing generally occurs from a distance (e.g., from the other side of a kitchen counter), while completing other tasks. In these cases, we expect the ambient audio to be sampled by a desktop computer placed somewhere in the same room as the television. The viewer is away from the microphone, making the noise she generates less problematic for the audio identification system. She is distracted (e.g., by preparing dinner), making errors in matching less problematic. Finally, she is less likely to be actively channel surfing, making historical matches more likely to be valid.

In contrast with remote viewing, during seated viewing, we expect the ambient audio to be sampled by a laptop held in the viewer's lap. Further, during partnered, seated viewing, the viewer is likely to talk with her viewing partner, very close to the sampling microphone. Nearby, structured interference (e.g., voices) is more difficult to overcome than remote spectrally flat interference (e.g., oven–fan noise). This makes the partnered seated viewing, with sampling done by laptop, the most acoustically challenging and, therefore, the configuration that we chose for our tests.

To allow repeated testing of the system, we recorded approximately 1 h of broadcast footage onto VHS tape prior to running the experiment. This tape was then replayed and the resulting ambient audio was sampled by a client machine (the Apple iBook laptop mentioned in Subsection "Client-Interface Setup").

The processed data was then sent to our audio server for matching. For the test described in this section, the audio-server was loaded with the descriptors from 24 h of broadcast footage, including the 1 h recorded to VCR tape. With this size audio database, the matching of each 5-s query snippet took consistently less than 1/4 s, even without the RANSAC sampling [4] used by Ke et al. [7].

During this experiment, the laptop was held on the lap of one of the viewers. We ran five tests of 5 min each, one for each of 2-foot increase in distance from the television set, from 2- to 10-feet. During these tests, the viewer holding the iBook laptop and a nearby viewer conversed sporadically. In all cases, these conversations started 1/2–1 min after the start of the test. The laptop–television distance and the sporadic conversation resulted in recordings with acoustic interference louder than the television audio whenever either viewer spoke.

The interference created by the competing conversation, resulted in incorrect best matches with low confidence scores for up to 80% of the matches, depending on the conversational pattern. However, we avoided presenting the unrelated content that would have been selected by these random associations, by using the simple model of channel watching/surfing behavior described in Subsection "Within-Query Consistency" with an expected dwell time (time between channel changes) of 2 s. This consistent improvement was due to correct and strong matches, made before the start of the conversation: these matches correctly carried forward through the remainder of the 5 min experiment. No incorrect information or chat associations were visible to the viewer: our presentation was 100% correct.

We informally compared the viewer experience using the post-match filtering corresponding to the channel-surfing model to that of longer (10-s) query lengths, which did not require the post-match filtering. The channel-surfing model gave the more consistent performance, avoiding the occasional "flashing" between contexts that was sometimes seen with the unfiltered, longer-query lengths.

To further test the post-match surfing model, we took a single recording of 30 min at a distance of 8 ft, using the same physical and conversational set-up as described above. On this experiment, 80% of the direct matching scores were incorrect, prior to post-match filtering. Table 2 shows the results of varying the expected dwell time within the channel surfing model on this data. The results are non-monotonic in the dwell time due to the non-linearity in the filtering process. For example, between $L = 1.0$ and $L = 0.75$, an incorrect match overshadows a later, weaker correct match, making for a long incorrect run of labels but, at $L = 0.5$, the range of

Table 2 Match results on 30 min of in-living room data after filtering using the channel surfing model

Surf dwell time (s)	Correct labels
1.25	100%
1.00	78%
0.75	78%
0.50	86%
0.25	88%

[a]The correct label rate before filtering was only 20%

influence of that incorrect match is reduced and the later, weaker correct match shortens the incorrect run length.

These very low values for the expected dwell times were possible in part because of the energy distribution within conversational speech. Most conversations include lulls and these lulls are naturally lengthened when the conversation is driven by an external presentation (such as the broadcast itself or the related material that is being presented on the laptop). Furthermore, in English, the overall energy envelope is significantly lower at the end of simple statements than at the start and, English vowel–consonant structure gives an additional drop in energy about 4 times per second. These effects result in clean audio about once each 1/4 s (due to syllable structure) and mostly clean audio capture about once per minute (due to sentence-induced energy variations). Finally, we saw very clean audio with longer durations but less predictable, typically during the distinctive portions of the broadcast audio presentation (due to conversational lulls while attending to the presentation). Conversations during silent or otherwise non-distinctive portions of the broadcast actually help our matching performance by partially randomizing the incorrect matches that we would otherwise have seen.

Post-match filtering introduces 1–5 s of latency in the reaction time to channel changes during casual conversation. However, the effects of this latency are usually mitigated because a viewer's attention typically is not directed at the web-server-provided information during channel changes; rather, it is typically focused on the newly selected TV channel, making these delays largely transparent to the viewer.

These experiments validate the use of the audio fingerprinting method developed by Ke et al. [7] for audio associated with television. The precision levels are lower than in the music retrieval application that they have described, since broadcast television is not providing the type of distinctive sound experience that most music strives for. Nevertheless, the channel surfing model ensures that the recall characteristic is sufficient for using this method in a living room environment.

Discussion

The proposed applications rely on personalizing the mass-media experience by matching ambient-audio statistics. The applications provide the viewer with personalized layers of information, new avenues for social interaction, real time indications on show popularity and the ability to maintain a library of the favorite content through a virtual recording service.

These applications are provided while addressing five factors, we believe are imperative to any mass personalization endeavor:

1. Guaranteed privacy
2. Minimized installation barriers
3. Integrity of mass media content
4. Accessibility of personalized content
5. Relevance of personalized content

We now discuss how these five factors are addressed within our mass-personalization framework.

The viewer's privacy must be guaranteed. We meet this challenge in the acoustic domain by our irreversible mapping from audio to summary statistics. No one receiving (or intercepting) these statistics is able to eavesdrop on background conversations, since the original audio never leaves the viewer's computer and the summary statistics are insufficient for reconstruction. Thus, unlike the speech-enabled proactive agent by [6], our approach cannot "overhear" conversations. Furthermore, the system can be used in a non-continuous mode such that the user must explicitly indicate (through a button press) that they wish a recording of the ambient sounds. Finally, even in the continuous-case, an explicit 'mute' button provides the viewer with the degree of privacy she feels comfortable with.

Another level of privacy concerns surround the collection of "traces" of what each individual watches on television. As with web browsing caches, the viewer can obviate these concerns in different ways: first and foremost by simply not turning on logging; by explicitly purging the cache of what program material the viewer has watched (so that the past record of her broadcast-viewing behavior is no longer available in either server or client history); by watching program material without starting the mass-personalization application (so that no record is ever made of this portion of her broadcast-viewing behavior); by "muting" the transmission of audio statistics (so that the application simply uses her previously known broadcast station to predict what she is watching).

The second factor is the minimization of installation barriers, both in terms of simplicity and proliferation of installation. Many of the interactive television systems that have been proposed in the past, relied on dedicated hardware and on the accessibility to broadcast-side information (like a teletext stream). However, except for the limited interactive scope of pay-per-view applications, these systems have not achieved significant penetration rates. Even if the penetration of teletext-enabled personal video recorders (PVRs) increases, it is unlikely to equal the penetration levels of laptop computers in the near future. Our system takes advantage of the increasing prevalence of personal computers equipped with standard microphone units. By doing so, our proposed system circumvents the need for installing dedicated hardware and the need to rely on a side information channel. The proposed framework relies on the accessibility and simplicity of a standard software installation.

The third factor in successful personalization of mass-media content is maintaining the integrity of the broadcast content. This factor emerges both from viewers who are concerned about disturbing their viewing experience and from content owners who are concerned about modified presentations of their copyrighted material. For example, in a previously published attempt to associate interactive quizzes and contests with movie content, the copyright owners prevented them from superimposing these quizzes on the television screen during the movie broadcast. Instead, the cable company had to leave a gap of at least 5 min between their interactive quizzes and the movie presentation [15]. Our proposed application presents the viewer with personalized information through a separate screen, such as a laptop or handheld device. This independence guarantees the integrity of the mass media channel. It also allows the viewer to experience the original broadcast without modification, if so desired, by simply ignoring the laptop screen.

Maintaining the simplicity of accessing the mass personalization content is the fourth challenge. The proposed system continuously caches information that is likely to be considered relevant by the user. However, this constant stream is passively stored and not imposed on the viewer in any way. The system is designed so that the personalized material can be examined by the viewer in her own pace or alternatively, to simply store the personalized material for later reference.

Finally, the most important factor is the relevance of the personalized content. We believe that the proposed four applications demonstrate some of the potential of personalizing the mass-media experience. Our system allows content producers to provide augmented experiences, a non-interactive part for the main broadcast screen (the traditional television, in our descriptions) and an interactive or personalized part for the secondary screen. Our system potentially provides a broad range of information to the viewer, in much the same flavor as the text-based web search results. By allowing other voices to be heard, mass personalization can have increased relevance and informational as well as entertainment value to the end user. Like the web, it can broaden access to communities that are otherwise poorly addressed by most distribution channels. By associating with a mass-media broadcast, it can leverage popular content to raise the awareness of a broad cross section of the population to some of these alternative views.

The paper emphasizes two contributions. The first is that audio fingerprinting can provide a feasible method for identifying which mass-media content is experienced by viewers. Several audio fingerprinting techniques might be used for achieving this goal. Once the link between the viewer and the mass-media content is made, the second contribution follows, by completing the mass media experience with personalized Web content and communities. These two contributions work jointly in providing both simplicity and personalization in the proposed applications.

The proposed applications were described using a setup of ambient audio originating from a TV set and encoded by a nearby personal computer. However, the mass-media content can originate from other sources like radio, movies or in scenarios where viewers share a location with a common auditory background (e.g., an airport terminal, lecture, or music concert). In addition, as computational capacities proliferate to portable appliances, like cell phones and PDAs, the fingerprinting process could naturally be carried out on such platforms. For example, SMS responses of a cell phone based community watching the same show can be one such implementation. Thus, it seems that the full potential of mass-personalization will gradually unravel itself in the coming years.

Acknowledgements The authors would like to gratefully acknowledge Y. Ke, D. Hoiem, and R. Sukthankar for providing an audio fingerprinting system to begin our explorations. Their audio-fingerprinting system and their results may be found at: http://www.cs.cmu.edu/~yke/musicretrieval.

References

1. Bulterman DCA (2001) SMIL 2.0: overview, concepts, and structure. IEEE Multimed 8(4): 82–88
2. Buttery P, Korhonen A (2005) Large-scale analysis of verb subcategorization differences between child directed speech and adult speech. In: Proceedings of the workshop on identification and representation of verb features and verb classes
3. Covell M, Baluja S, Fink M (2006) Advertisement replacement using acoustic and visual repetition. In: Proceedings of IEEE multimedia signal processing
4. Fischler M, Bolles R (1981) Random sample consensus: a paradigm for model fitting with applications to image analysis and automated cartography. Commun ACM 24(6):381–395
5. Henzinger M, Chang B, Milch B, Brin S (2003) Query-free news search. In: Proceedings of the international WWW conference.
6. Hong J, Landay J (2001) A context/communication information agent. Personal and Ubiquitous Computing 5(1):78–81
7. Ke Y, Hoiem D, Sukthankar R (2005) Computer vision for music identification. In: Proceedings of computer vision and pattern recognition
8. Kupiec J, Pedersen J, Chen F (1995) A trainable document summarizer. In: Proceedings of ACM SIG information retrieval, pp 68–73
9. Mann J (2005) CBS, NBC to offer replay episodes for 99 cents. http://www.techspot.com/news/
10. Pennock D, Horvitz E, Lawrence S, Giles CL (2000) Collaborative filtering by personality diagnosis: a hybrid memory- and model-based approach. In: Proceedings of uncertainty in artificial intelligence, pp 473–480
11. Rhodes B, Maes P (2003) Just-in-time information retrieval agents. IBM Syst J 39(4):685–704
12. Rymniak M (1997) The essential review: test of English as a foreign language. Kaplan Educational Centers, New York
13. Shazam Entertainment, Inc. (2005) http://www.shazamentertainment.com/
14. Viola P, Jones M (2002) Robust real-time object detection. Int J Comput Vis
15. Xinaris T, Kolouas A (2006) PVR: one more step from passive viewing. Euro ITV (invited presentation)

Index